W9-BYU-744

THE BIOGRAPHICAL HISTORY OF BASKETBALL

THE
BIOGRAPHICAL
HISTORY OF
BASKETBALL

*More than 500 Portraits of the Most Significant On- and Off-Court
Personalities of the Game's Past and Present*

PETER C. BJARKMAN

MASTERS PRESS

NTC/*Contemporary Publishing Group*

WINGATE UNIVERSITY LIBRARY

Library of Congress Cataloging-in-Publication Data

Bjarkman, Peter C.
  The biographical history of basketball : more than 500 portraits of the most significant on-
and off-court personalities of the game's past and present / by Peter C. Bjarkman.
      p.   cm.
    ISBN 1-57028-134-3
    1. Basketball players—United States—Biography.   2. Basketball coaches—United States—
Biography.   3. Basketball—United States–History.   I. Title.
  GV884.A1B52   1998
  796.323'092'273
  [B]—dc21   97-49369
                                                                                                    CIP

This book is for Tom Bast,
one of the publishing industry's
most significant players.

Interior design by Kim Heusel
Cover design by Nick Panos
Cover artwork from PicturesNow.com, San Rafael, California

Published by Masters Press
A division of NTC/Contemporary Publishing Group, Inc.
4255 West Touhy Avenue, Lincolnwood (Chicago), Illinois 60646-1975 U.S.A.
© 2000 Peter C. Bjarkman
All rights reserved. No part of this book may be reproduced, stored in a retrieval
system, or transmitted in any form or by any means, electronic, mechanical, photocopying,
recording, or otherwise, without the prior written permission of
NTC/Contemporary Publishing Group, Inc.
Printed in the United States of America
International Standard Book Number: 1-57028-134-3

00 01 02 03 04 CU 18 17 16 15 14 13 12 11 10 9 8 7 6 5 4 3 2 1

Contents

Introduction

America's
One-on-One Game

There is no longer much debate that basketball—especially the professional variety, with its larger-than-life celebrity superstars named Air Jordan, Bird, Shaq, and Magic—today reigns as America's favored arena and video sport. Basketball, with its soaring slams and racehorse action, unarguably provides the premier sporting entertainment spectacle of the century's final decade. Michael Jordan has long since overhauled even Babe Ruth and Joe DiMaggio as the country's largest-ever sports icon; Dennis Rodman looms unrivalled as the nation's most flamboyant media bad guy; Shaquille O'Neal rules the airwaves as both a living and breathing cartoon superhero and a multifaceted music-video superstar who can command even larger audiences as product pitchman, movie idol, and rap artist than he does as elite pro hoops all-star. In the popular imagination, in television ratings, and in the merchandise marketplace, the modern-era version of basketball has now far outdistanced in popular appeal both baseball, with its main currency of nostalgia and myth, and football, with its transparent corporate structure and its rampant warfare imagery.

What remains debatable is only the issue of why basketball has so rapidly swung to the top of America's fan preference polls. Elements of the answer likely lie in astute marketing strategies employed by corporate peddlers of athletic shoes, soft drinks, and other symbols of conspicuous consumption, as well as in the relentless video-oriented salesmanship of the NBA's skilled promotional wizards. Another clue follows from the inherent structure of James Naismith's indoor game itself—the thrill-a-minute athleticism and high-scoring action that distinguishes the "cage game" from slower-paced baseball, more rigidly structured football, and low-scoring hockey and soccer. Part of basketball's extensive appeal also likely lies in the dribble-and-shoot sport's near-perfect reflection of a surrounding late-20th-century national urban landscape. Basketball is the appropriate mirror image of a frantically paced, highly impersonalized, and risk-laden inner-city scene that has in large part become our 1990s American self-image.

Basketball's most undeniable appeal, however, seems to reside in the game's supersized superstars and in the indelible star quality of the roundball indoor sport itself. Naismith's ball and basket game is in reality the ultimate star-oriented type of athletic contest. A single headlining basketballer can (and usually will) remain in the spotlight almost constantly during the entire course of any single game. A baseball slugger like Ken Griffey Jr. or Mark McGwire earns his turn at bat only four or five times in most games; a spectacular fielder may (and often does) stand around for innings without any ball being hit in his direction; a top pitcher goes to work on the field only every fourth or fifth day that the team plays. A front-line running back or crack quarterback may tote or heave the pigskin during 20 percent or less of the gridiron action with lengthy stretches in between. Yet basketball's Michael Jordan will likely have the ball in his hands almost every 10 or 15 seconds and thus flashes his brilliance during as much as 30 or 40 percent of any given Chicago Bulls game (perhaps 80 percent when an important game inevitably reaches "crunch time" during the final quarter). In terms of pure exposure, baseball or football heroes hardly stand a fighting chance when compared with their basketball rivals.

Just as basketball with its urban flavor and space-age veneer has coincided fortuitously with end-of-the-century American values, so has the sport's inherent preference for individual star quality merged with our contemporary culture of unending celebrity worship. Basketball is the ultimate "star game," and modern-day Americans of all ages and outlooks seem altogether obsessed with idolizing celebrity status. It matters little that our celebrities may disappoint us or even shock us with their boorish and often scandalous behavior; this will only add to their personal luster and the magnetism of their images. O. J. Simpson emerged as even more of an object of fascination for the American public as an accused murderer than he had once been as star running back or as Hollywood cinema performer; Princess Diana was never so popular for Americans as when she died violently in a headline-grabbing event tinged with the trappings of scandal and soap opera. Sports fans bemoan the escalating salaries of pro athletes (most recently basketball's Kevin Garnett, who averages less than 20 points per game but pockets more than $30 million for his services) and profess longing for an era in which the pros at least seemingly played more for love of the game than love of the lucre. Yet when faced with loss of the most recognizable names and faces on the field of play—as when replacement baseball players oozing with "love of the game" took up roster spots during the strike-decimated 1994 spring training season—the same rooters depart in droves and shun games not populated with their overpaid celebrity heroes.

Basketball indeed has a long history of single-star emphasis. Its history is also replete with a larger-than-expected impact of the individual athletic talent and the lasting marks of the individual innovative off-court genius. This is the only sport, for starters, which traces its roots back directly to a single and identifiable inventor. Abner Doubleday assuredly did not dream up baseball as entrenched legend would have us believe, but James Naismith did concoct dribbling and shooting at overhead baskets (or passing and shooting at overhead baskets, since Naismith's original rules didn't yet allow for the practice of dribbling). Basketball's numerous major rule changes also all have individual names attached

Transcendental Graphics

Basketball turned a corner in its evolution when jump-shooters arrived in the shadows of World War II to tilt the balance away from intimidating giants like George Mikan and Bob Kurland. As the sport's first agile seven-footer, Oklahoma A&M star Kurland guarded the hoop at the defensive end with discouraging effectiveness in the mid-1940s.

to them. Some landmark changes resulted from seemingly unfair domination of play by single titans like George Mikan and Bob Kurland (who together motivated the legislations which widened free-throw lanes and outlawed defensive goaltending as a viable strategy), or like Wilt Chamberlain who provoked an offensive goaltending rule and Kareem Abdul-Jabbar (nee Lew Alcindor) who stimulated a decade-long ban on slam dunking. And playing styles as well can be attached to the personalities of distinct coaches and athletes with names like Walter Meanwell, Phil Woolpert, Doc Carlson, Hank Luisetti, Bob Cousy, Bob Davies, and (in the modern era) Red Auerbach. Other adjustments were born of the personal insight of individual sideline observers, like NBA executive Danny Biasone who dreamed up the 24-second shot clock to kill stalling and discourage brutal fouling, or coaches Ward Lambert and Bill Reinhart who drew the first blueprints for a revolutionary fast-break offense.

Baseball, just like basketball, has always had its huge heroes and oversized icons to bolster its fan appeal. Since baseball long occupied the more prominent spot on the American sporting scene, it is the baseball icons who remained most visible and were most firmly entrenched in the national consciousness. But diamond celebrities pale in their individual impacts and central positions when compared to parallel models from basketball. Babe Ruth did in large part cause a batting revolution with his longball swings in the early 1920s; yet Ruth's slugging was nowhere near as individual in its impact on baseball as was Luisetti's one-hand shooting or Mikan's goaltending defense on the game of basketball. Ruth indeed had his legions of immediate imitators, but he caused no one to drastically rewrite the rule book or seriously reassess the very essence of the game.

Authors Donald Dewey and Nicholas Acocella, writing a parallel volume to this present one treating the most influential and memorable personages in the diamond sport, faced a more arduous task in convincing readers that many individuals have indeed made single-handed innovations that substantially changed baseball's evolutionary course. It is the main contention of Dewey and Acocella's tome, *The Biographical History of Baseball*, that we would today be watching an entirely different game—or perhaps not watching at all—if not for the individual impacts of the hundreds of baseballers (players, owners, commentators, and fans) covered in their treatise. Yet even with the most major figures—say, names like McGraw, Cobb, Ruth, Joe Jackson, DiMaggio, Stengel, Mays, or Aaron—it stretches credibility to assert that the sport would not largely have its modern-day appearance and flavor if one or more had never donned a uniform or entered a big-league stadium. By stark contrast, eliminate Luisetti's one-handed shooting, Mikan's box office appeal, Biasone's ingenious shot clock, Chamberlain's herculean scoring, or Jordan's airborne intensity—any one of the lot—and basketball today would indeed look remarkably different, if indeed the game held our attention at all. Strike Doubleday from the history books and one changes only the apocryphal legend. Eliminate Naismith from the pages of history and risk a major void in the inventory of American sporting spectacles.

While Stanford University's Hank Luisetti did not invent one-handed shooting, basketball's first national star in the late '30s was unquestionably its pioneering and eye-catching champion.

In short, the sport attributed to Cooperstown and Doubleday "evolved" slowly and was not invented instantly; the curveball, forkball, spitball, emery ball, or "whatever ball"—despite several popular legends about miraculous appearances—cannot be traced to any single innovator, if indeed there ever was one. Babe Ruth perhaps came the closest to being an essential and irreplaceable landmark in baseball's evolution, with his seemingly single-handed invention of home run slugging. But in the end, even Babe Ruth was more of a popularizer than an innovator. Changes in the conditions of baseball play wrought by the rule requiring a fresh ball always in play (one that was white and visible instead of tobacco-stained and invisible) did as much for souped-up offense as did the lumber-happy Ruth. The new era of slugging, which Babe Ruth represented, can thus be attributed as much to the introduction of the clean ball and the outlawing of the spitter as a legal pitch after 1920, as it can to Ruth's remarkable innovations in hitting style.

Bold pioneering on the part of individual tinkerers is not at all a stretch when it comes to accounting for most of basketball's sudden departures in rules and playing styles. Today it is the on-court icons who are the game's biggest magnets. If there are Chicago Bulls fans on every playground, street corner, and bar stool, this is largely because Michael Jordan (with a huge boost from relentless television marketing) has enlisted their idolization and their subsequent loyalty, just as Magic attracted Lakers fans in the '80s and Bird was a magnet for boosters of Celtic green. With baseball, by stark contrast, the real pull and the real affiliations are with teams and not with individual stars. With baseball these team affiliations are set in stone for most fans by generational ties; we root for the teams of our fathers and uncles or the one in the city or region in which we grew up. The coming and going of stars—even of a DiMaggio, Mantle, Ruth, Banks, Mays, or Aaron—is largely secondary to such loyalties. A Detroit Tigers fan does not trade in his stripes if Al Kaline or Norm Cash or Harvey Kuenn is unexpectedly traded or retired. This is part and parcel of the game's generation-to-generation ebb and flow.

Basketball's one-man invention is, of course, unique in the field of sports history. At least this is true for those team games from any corner of the globe that have captured and sustained huge participant and spectator appeal. The game Naismith envisioned for his physical education classes at Springfield was not at all the game we ended up with over the long haul. The bulk of the original 13 rules posted on the gymnasium wall in December 1891 by Naismith are still largely intact (if somewhat modified) in today's version. Yet, basketball for Naismith was more like volleyball with peach baskets. Nonstop scoring, dunking, dribbling, and most of the grace and glamour of the modern racehorse game had no place in Naismith's imagination. But one man did, nonetheless, give birth to the idea that underpins the entire institution we now know as basketball.

While basketball commenced with an inspired and identifiable creator, all of its important departures and evolutions also bear the boldly outlined fingerprints of individual innovators. Collegiate coaches first imposed their distinctive styles and patterns of play once paid mentors became a necessary feature of the game. Indeed, the obvious need for merging controlled team patterns with individual athleticism (i.e., a single player's one-on-one "moves") makes basketball uniquely dependent on the intervention of sideline coaching. Coaches first drew the patterns of play that, on the one hand, served to identify regional styles and, on the other, soon worked as well to immortalize the more ingenious among individual innovators. In the East, the early preference was for two-handed shooting, dribbling, and freelance individual moves; the Midwest was noted for more long passing and early experiments with one-handed shooting (especially from the pivot); the Western colleges built a reputation in early decades for a fast-breaking style with all five men running at the same time. Against this backdrop, coaching legends like Walter Meanwell at Wisconsin and Henry Carlson at Pittsburgh earned lasting reputations with set patterns of offensive movement, while George Keogan (Notre Dame), Cam Henderson (Marshall), and John Lawther (Penn State) carved niches with their pioneering defensive schemes. But basketball didn't really gain wide appeal until individual players themselves became the innovators. As long as basketball was a game of tightly controlled weaves and patterns on offense and innovative zone alignments on defense, the sport had limited mass appeal among legions of spectators. It was the jump shots, the one-on-one breaks to the basket, and the soaring dunks of the playground freelance style that captivated mass audiences throughout all regions.

Basketball's first half-century was admittedly played out largely in deep shadows. College stars existed (like Steinmetz in Wisconsin or Page and Schommer at Chicago), but their appeal was strictly local in nature and usually spread no further than the circulation of the local town newspaper. Innovations took place for the most part out of the limelight, and what was eye-catching in one sector of the country often remained totally unknown in most others. And while barnstorming pros had some small impact on collegians in their immediate area, against whom they often played and whose playing styles they dramatically influenced, the basketball professionals for many decades remained quite as obscure and off the beaten track as did baseball's Blackball stars, who were likewise relegated to the shadowy Negro leagues and thus performed out of the daily view of a mainstream sporting press. Where there was lasting influence, it came largely through ex-pros bringing their proven styles into the college ranks as coaches. New York City's Joe Lapchick and Nat Holman (both stars with the Original Celtics of '20s and '30s fame) were two prime examples. Brothers Lew Wachter (Dartmouth) and Ed Wachter (pro star with the barnstorming Troy Trojans and later a longtime coach at RPI, Williams, Harvard, and Lafayette colleges) were two others.

The college version of the game gained its first firm toehold with the ticket-buying public as a direct result of one of the most dramatic examples of individual innovation found anywhere in American sports history. More than any other factor, it was the college doubleheaders staged in New York's Madison Square Garden in the '30s and '40s that first fostered intersectional battles and thus sparked widespread fan interest. The pioneering extravaganza drew 16,000 in the wake of the Great Depression (January 1931) for a *tripleheader* (featuring the famed St. John's "Wonder Five") promoted by Mayor Jimmie Walker to benefit the city's unemployed. Another landmark event was the December 1934 twin bill matching again St. John's versus powerhouse Westminster (Pennsylvania) and NYU versus top drawing card Notre Dame. Such venues were the brainchild of a single sportswriter-turned-promoter blessed with unequaled foresight and tenacious marketing skills. New York's Edward "Ned" Irish more than any other individual put college basketball squarely on the nation's sports calendar. And Irish's promotional gambles were, in turn, given an important jump start by the December 1936 Garden appearance of Stanford star Hank Luisetti and his pioneering one-handed shooting style. Irish had created a new Gotham-based audience for big-time basketball and Luisetti soon enough gave that audience a full-blown excuse to begin flooding numerous other East Coast, Midwest, and West Coast arenas.

The popularity of the pro game can equally be traced largely to the influence of a single pioneer with remarkable box-office appeal. It was George Mikan—among the ballplayers themselves—whose solo act seemingly overnight made the play-for-pay game popular with fans long addicted to college venues; Mikan's impact came first during the height of the war years as a college headliner (three-time national scoring leader) at Chicago's DePaul University, and then in postwar seasons as the first professional superstar with teams in Chicago (for but one season in the struggling NBL) and Minneapolis (for the next seven seasons in the NBL, BAA, and NBA). While Luisetti over in the collegiate ranks needed Ned Irish to offer him and his contemporary cagers an adequate public stage, likewise, Mikan needed a Maurice Podoloff. Lacking even the slightest previous familiarity with Naismith's game, corporate lawyer Maurice Podoloff had, nonetheless, been handpicked by Eastern hockey arena owners to administer their new gamble known as the Basketball Association of America, based on an assumption that proven skills as president of the American Hockey League might have at least some small carryover effect. Without Podoloff's no-nonsense business approach and cutthroat merger tactics (forcing the NBL into complete merger with the BAA in 1949), even Mikan's immense fan magnetism would never have been quite enough to wrench the professional game out of its lackluster barnstorming past and launch it into a modern pro-oriented future.

While Mikan brought the first significant audiences to pro basketball, behind the scenes it was thus another identifiable pioneer who made the administrative moves guaranteed to salvage the sport's future. Podoloff, more than anyone else, guided pro basketball's first successful and lasting "national" league through its leanest initial seasons. He did so primarily by initiating a draft of college players in 1947, and then by enticing the player-rich Minneapolis, Rochester, and Syracuse franchises to jump the older NBL and join forces with his own fledgling East Coast circuit. In 1954, the man who would serve the newly formed NBA as president for 17 years also launched a third important departure when he secured the league's first television contract for $3,000 per game. A most amazing aspect of the pro game's pioneering leadership was perhaps the fact that Russian-born and Connecticut-raised Podoloff had never even seen a basketball game at the time he took over the infant league's management. It was all strictly a matter of business, and Podoloff knew business tactics well, even if he didn't know much about the American indoor sport, which after only a few short winters under his guidance would at long last rival his own Canadian-flavored game of hockey.

Three events hold primary responsibility for basketball's eventual emergence by midcentury as a major sport on equal footing with football and baseball. The first was the elimination of the center jump after each and every made basket. With this major innovation at the end of the '30s (1937–38) the sport was ready to up its tempo a full notch or two and become for the first time a true "racehorse style" game. Pioneering of the jump shot and of one-handed shooting was the second major leap toward basketball's future. One-handed shooting—especially one-handers heaved on the run—further freed court action from the plodding style of play that had dominated since the nailing up of the first peach baskets. For nearly half a century, play was organized by a strategy of passing repeatedly in set patterns and weaves until a man broke open inside for an uncontested layup, or perhaps was freed momentarily on the outside for a long-range stationary two-handed bomb. Finally, on the heals of one-handed jumpers, would come the evolution of the playground one-on-one style, pioneered primarily by the inner-city black athlete of the postwar era. Although the radical shift to sky-walking and slam-dunking forwards and to big mobile guards would not reach its pinnacle of impact until the birth of the rival ABA pro league in the mid-1960s, the first great playground showmen had already emerged in colleges and in the NBA with the likes of Elgin Baylor, Maurice Stokes, and Oscar Robertson and dozens of their lesser imitators during the mid-1950s.

It was the jump shot first and foremost that liberated cage play from the pitfalls of plodding pace and brutal hacking-and-shoving under-the-hoop free-for-alls. And like so many tentative steps in the game's history, this one also came onto the scene as a result of individual innovators. Hank Luisetti was the first, and while Luisetti did not invent one-handed shooting, he certainly was its pioneering, eye-catching champion. In Luisetti's shadow soon came Ken Sailors of Wyoming in the early '40s. Sailors like Luisetti developed his skills out West yet made his national reputation only when given a center stage at basketball's true mecca in Madison Square Garden. That defining moment for Sailors came with a brilliant shooting and dribbling performance that earned "outstanding player" honors in the 1943 NCAA title game between victorious Wyoming and runner-up Georgetown University. But the most important and influential innovator was perhaps Jumpin' Joe Fulks of the Philadelphia Warriors who took the fledgling BAA pro league by storm with his unorthodox yet deadly "behind-the-ear" heaves in the first seasons after World War II. The BAA's first scoring champ, Fulks shocked the nation's still small army of pro hoops fans with a dazzling 63-point performance against Indianapolis in February 1949, upping the single-game league record by an unthinkable 33 percent. And Paul Arizin was soon teaming with Fulks in the Philadelphia Warriors lineup to cement the new jump shot as the undisputed court weapon of choice.

Individual shooting prowess was soon matched by individual ballhandling skills. While Fulks and Sailors and Arizin let fly with their unstoppable one-handed bombs, Bob Cousy and Bob Davies in the same decade invented the first prototypes of the modern point guard. Cousy's behind-the-back blind passes became the new goal of every schoolyard fantasy. Davies—"The Harrisburg Houdini"—earned lasting credit for the earliest behind-the-back dribbles, but also utilized a full arsenal of passing, shooting, and dribbling tricks to lift both Seton Hall University (winner of 43 straight with Davies at the controls) and later the NBL–BAA–NBA Rochester Royals to championship status. With such ballhandling wizards on the scene, the sport now took on a new dimension of scintillating entertainment. Slick ballhandling prowess became equally as much an on-court sideshow spectacle as it was a most effective offensive weapon. It was, of course, in the end, something of both.

Evolution of the modern game now lacked only the emergence of the individual defensive star and the dominating rebounder who would serve as catalyst for the fast-breaking style that had become the sport's new mainstay strategy. The prototype was the model fine-tuned in the pro ranks by Red Auerbach's Boston Celtics and their superstar center Bill Russell. If jump shooters had tilted the balance away from big men like Bob Kurland and George Mikan who had dominated the '40s, Russell, and soon also Wilt Chamberlain, reasserted the reign of the intimidating shot blocker and board sweeper.

A final stage in basketball's evolution as exciting entertainment spectacle came with the arrival of the scintillating black playground stars of the '50s and

'60s. First the college game was drastically transformed in the early '50s by a new generation of daring leapers and shooters, the largest portion of them black and many from the inner-city playgrounds of New York, Philadelphia, Chicago, and Los Angeles. "Black hoops" grew out of freelance playing styles native to the urban schoolyards and the inner-city playgrounds. It was a survivors' game of improvised feints and fakes, thundering self-expressive acrobatic dunks, and intimidating one-on-one personal "moves" toward the hoop. With these weapons, inner-city youngsters battled for personal "reps" and for rare momentary feelings of individual freedom which came from soaring above or slipping around a face-to-face adversary. In this new style of playground basketball, "deception" thus became a vital key to success; for youngsters battling for daily survival on ghetto streets, basketball was, in fact, a unique escapist world in which the weapon of deception was for the first time a legitimate accepted strategy and not a guaranteed source of further trouble. Basketball—playground style—was, thus, also a game that was far more instinctual than it was scientific.

None among these earliest black stars were any more influential than Elgin Baylor, pioneer of the game's third dimension of flight, and Oscar Robertson, the first-ever truly complete offensive machine. Baylor was the original prototype of the shake-and-bake skywalker, a true avatar of athletic aviators who would point the way toward the marvelous balletlike spectacle which a previously earthbound sport might now become. Oscar was basketball's original (and also its best) complete offensive intimidator, a smooth-as-silk basket-producing machine who scored at will from any spot on the floor and against any defender, and, when double- and triple-teamed, also passed the ball to open teammates every bit as effectively as he shot it. With these eye-poppingly athletic ebony heroes, basketball finally became, in the popular imagination, an exquisitely entertaining one-on-one contest between a limitlessly creative dribbler-shooter and a most-often hopelessly outclassed solo defender.

With the emergence of the playground game, basketball had reached its full potential as a sport of highly stylized individual "moves" through which each player indelibly asserts his own distinctive and defining personal style. Basketball as played in the college and pro arenas and on city playgrounds everywhere was indeed by the mid-'50s what Pete Axthelm has defined as the true "city game"— the defining sport of the inner-city ghetto playground and, as such, a huge piece of the fabric of inner-city life itself. Axthelm's definition of basketball's rare appeal to the urban schoolyard athlete has yet to be topped: "The game is simple, an act of one man challenging another, twisting, feinting, then perhaps breaking free to leap upward, directing a ball toward a target, a metal hoop 10 feet above the ground. And a one-on-one challenge takes on wider meaning, defining identity and manhood in an urban society that breeds invisibility." (*The City Game*, 1970)

Basketball as we have known it over the past half-century is thus truly a "one-on-one" game, equally as much so in the professional arena as it is on the neighborhood playground. Here is the only sport where it takes no more than two individuals to launch a competitive contest that has all the trappings of the formal five-on-five affair. This is also the one team sport where the individual player can profitably practice alone for limitless stretches, perfecting the game's essential skills with little more than a backyard goal and a ball. The sport's literature and lore is full of accounts of young hopefuls named Robertson, Bradley, West, Mount, or Maravich spending countless hours in inner-city schoolyards or rural barnyards, honing their future skills by throwing a threadbare ball at a netless hoop. Basketball is not only possible as a solo game, but it is also endless fun.

Since basketball, more than other major team sports, has always focused primarily on the solo performer, it seems natural enough for a formal history of the game's great moments and defining events to be shaped in terms of the significant contributions and personal careers of its most memorable or influential personalities. Here are the capsule stories of the sport's most important 500-plus on-court and off-court personalities drawn from the full century separating James Naismith from Michael Jordan and peach baskets hung on musty gym walls from state-of-the-art space-age NBA arenas. College competition receives equal billing with the Johnny-Come-Lately professional game; and coaches and game officials are recognized to only slightly lesser degree than the ballplayers themselves. Even the century-old but only recently widely popular women's version of the sport finds its place here within the unfolding accounts of the game's ongoing evolution.

The bulk of this book consists of three long chapters reviewing basketball's most central players, coaches, and contributors over three historical epochs that constitute the game's first century. The first of these epochs (Chapter 5) comprises the first half of the present century, a five-decade span in which basketball spread like wildfire to all corners of the nation's map and all segments of its population, and evolved in the process into something very different from the recreational free-for-all contest that young Jim Naismith had originally envisioned for his classes of YMCA trainees. Rule changes, strategy-shaping coaches, and a handful of innovative players predominate in this opening chapter of the game's history. A second epoch (Chapter 6) stretches from the upheaval following the second great war to the rebirth of the game as television entertainment spectacle at the dawn of the century's final two decades. This is basketball's coming-of-age period in which a strategic and often stodgy game of set-shooting and strong-armed physical tactics is swept aside by the run-and-gun whirlwind spectacle of jump shooting, slam-dunking, and thrill-a-minute fast-break actions. Its landmark events are the birth of the jump shot, the arrival of stylish inner-city black ballplayers (proponents of "urban street cool"), and the resulting evolution of one-on-one freelance styles of play. The final epoch (Chapter 7) is that of the 1980s and 1990s when the NBA becomes basketball's main showcase and when the sport itself finally overhauls baseball and football as the nation's spectator game of choice. Basketball's place of eminence at century's end has as much to do with a shifting set of values in the surrounding culture as it does with clever marketing and the emergence of the game's most talented athletes ever.

In order to place the hundreds of brief biographical and career sketches presented in a proper context, the present volume also provides capsule histories of the century-old collegiate game (Chapter 1) and half-century-old professional game (Chapter 2), histories which focus as much upon vital innovations, drastic shifts in both rules and playing styles, and dominating personalities of the game's different eras, as upon yearly championship victories or capsule accounts of landmark games. While unorganized (or loosely organized) professional play dates back almost as far as the collegiate competitions, a stable and visible national pro

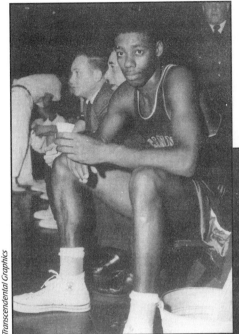

Transcendental Graphics

Oscar Robertson, left, was basketball's original all-around offensive intimidator. At the University of Cincinnati "The Big O" became the nation's first three-time collegiate scoring champion, and with the NBA franchise located in the same city, Oscar posted a near triple-double average across his first five full pro seasons.

Elgin Baylor of Seattle University and the Los Angeles Lakers was an original prototype for the shake-and-bake skywalker and the primary exemplar of an unfettered black playground style of one-on-one offensive play.

Transcendental Graphics

league as we now know it has only recently celebrated its Golden Anniversary season (1996) amidst a good deal of hoopla and nostalgic reminiscence. While the college game boasts much deeper roots that cover nearly twice the territory, nonetheless both versions of the sport find their true launching pad embedded in the dozen or so years surrounding the nation's second world war. This book's opening two chapters search out those roots as vital backdrop to the careers and contributions of individual players, coaches, officials, and administrators capsulized throughout the main text.

Two final sections of this book provide a needed touchstone Time Line for the sport's defining events along with a suggested reading list of supplemental sources. The former provides a year-by-year summary of important off-court decisions and on-court actions that have been the landmarks of the game's evolving history. The latter provides an essential library—divided into useful categories such as team histories, coffee table pictorials, pro and college histories, autobiographies, and statistical analyses—which should point a useful direction for anyone desiring to delve at much greater depth into basketball's full century of unsurpassed lore and legend.

One comment about methodology seems in order here. The "biographies" included throughout these pages are, in reality, brief (and in some cases not-so-brief) portraits of the basketball lives of their subjects. Unlike many standard biographical encyclopedias, this one does not provide the reader with data concerning dates or places of birth and death, family members, schooling (aside from collegiate basketball careers), or other details of the subjects' lives away from the sport of basketball. Such information, where of interest, is readily available from other sources, such as the second and fourth volumes of David Porter's *Biographical Dictionary of American Sports* (Greenwood Press, 1988–89). My interest here has been strictly in demonstrating those defining accomplishments and events from the lives of basketball's most noteworthy figures that have contributed directly and in the manner outlined by these portraits to the evolution of America's foremost national sport.

In subsequent pages the reader will find a unique approach to the history of America's most native and most popular spectator game. From James Naismith on to Hank Luisetti, and from Phog Allen down to Ned Irish, and then on to Dr. J, Larry Bird, and Air Jordan, here are all the major contributors, strategy innovators, rule makers and breakers, idle tinkerers and bold experimenters, risk-prone entrepreneurs, and—above all—athletes of both star quality and journeyman status, who after one fashion or another, blazed new trails with their record-setting achievements and their innovative playing styles. In some cases, they are the sport's most widely celebrated figures, and in other cases, they are the lost pioneers who have remained largely hidden behind the progress of basketball history. But in each and every case they are the men and also the women who have, by their presence, sustained and often even altered the always fascinating and highly competitive game that has remained an important cornerstone of America's booming sports and entertainment culture.

Chapter One

March Toward Madness

College Basketball's First Century

College basketball has enjoyed several defining moments that have drastically reshaped future directions for the sport. None of these crossroads was more vital than the pair that occurred almost simultaneously near the end of the 1930s (during the 1937 and 1938 seasons), on the very eve of the hardwood sport's half-century anniversary. First came a revolutionary rule change canceling the center jump after each and every made basket. By eliminating both the stoppage of action and the repetitive marches to center court after each score, for the first time college games could now truly become the action-filled, high-scoring spectacles we celebrate today. A second defining event was the establishment of postseason national tournament competitions to provide the winter-long season with meaningful direction and also a climactic purpose. Both landmark events together contributed heavily to a burgeoning new audience for college basketball, one that has continued to surge nonstop across the more than half-century which has followed.

Basketball's first five-plus decades were not without their own brand of raw excitement, a bevy of attractive campus stars, and an ever-expanding and sometimes even quite rabid fan following. But the decades before Luisetti at Stanford or Rupp at Kentucky witnessed largely an era of narrow regional interests, an epoch of domineering coaches (Meanwell in Wisconsin, Lambert at Purdue, Carlson at Pittsburgh, Notre Dame's George Keogan, and above all, "Phoghorn" Allen in Kansas), who always held a far bigger piece of the spotlight than did their constantly changing players, and also an era of constant rules-shifting, which chipped away at the stability and thus the broad appeal of the sport. College basketball was indeed nearly as popular as its fall gridiron rival in some corners of the land—especially in the isolated heartland sectors of Kentucky, Kansas, and Indiana, in the big-city mecca of New York where Ned Irish was already ballyhooing intersectional matches between popular local teams and attractive clubs from the provinces as early as 1931, and in certain isolated pockets of basketball fanaticism far out on the Pacific Coast.

In brief, the flavor of the sport was largely provincial in nature. If Buck Freeman's "Wonder Five" outfit at St. John's was the rage of New York City at the close of the Roaring '20s, it was certainly never winter-season front-page news anywhere else across the land. Baron Rupp would not become a household name for sports fans in most quarters of the nation until well after World War II, despite his 80 percent winning ratio throughout the decade of the '30s. Small campus arenas and cramped gymnasiums in most parts of the country meant that the biggest college cage stars—Paul Endacott of Kansas or Vic Hanson with Syracuse or Johnny Wooden at Purdue—performed their nightly magic in relative obscurity. While professional baseball heroes like Babe Ruth and collegiate footballers like Red Grange achieved substantial and even reverential attention in the sporting press (Ruth logged more ink than any of the nation's presidents during his heyday), few newspapers outside of those located in the campus towns themselves covered basketball action on any kind of semiregular basis.

While numerous rule changes and constant shifting of regional styles of play worked against an identifiable spectacle with which basketball fans could readily relate, some of the changes during the '30s were, nonetheless, moving the game rapidly toward a more fan-friendly spectacle. Basketball in the teens, '20s, and early '30s (even the more popular collegiate variety) was a slow-paced game with little sustained action and painfully little scoring. Dominant teams, like the St. John's Wonder Five ball club of the 1929–30–31 seasons often achieved their successes largely because of their deadly strategies (deadly for both fans and the opposition) of stalling on offense, holding the ball at the far end of the court (there was no backcourt rule to prevent it), and deftly passing back and forth for long stretches of time until the perfect uncontested set shot or layup eventually became available.

Fans who witnessed a landmark January 1931 benefit tripleheader in Madison Square Garden were thus "entertained" by scores of 21–18 (Columbia surprising Fordham), 16–14 (Manhattan edging NYU), and 17–9 (the latter score resulting from St. John's painstaking slowdown tactics against CCNY which brought a game-long cascade of resounding boos and catcalls from the 16,000 fans). Realizing the game needed a drastic overhaul in order to retain existing audiences and attract new ones, the lords of the college sport reacted in 1932 with a center line painted at midcourt and a rule requiring the ball to be moved into the frontcourt within 10 seconds. Three seasons later (in 1935) a three-second rule banning offensive players from camping under the basket was also belatedly adopted.

But it was not until the eve of the 1937–38 college season that the biggest obstacle to offense-oriented basketball was finally removed. This came with the liberating deletion of the constantly repeated center jump. Since the game clock continued to run throughout such pauses after each field goal, as much as 12 minutes of playing time was being lost from each game. Once the new rule was in effect, offenses immediately opened up their attacks, and literally overnight, game scores more than doubled almost everywhere. Basketball was finally ready to greet its modern epoch, and it was the collegiate players, coaches, and game officials who would lead the way headlong into the thrill-packed future.

2

The center jump rule adjustment immediately had a most far-reaching effect on the pace and thus the nature of modern basketball play. Even before Stanford's Hank Luisetti broke loose with an incredible 50-point outburst in Cleveland (versus Duquesne) little more than a month into the new season, St. John's and Illinois had already availed themselves of the streamlined game with a record-setting scoring performance of their own during the first Madison Square Garden doubleheader of the winter. Illinois won that contest 60–45 behind a hot-handed guard named Lou Boudreau, an eventual baseball Hall of Famer. Such lofty scoring had previously been ruled out by dead time alone—time wasted while players walked repeatedly back and forth between center jumps with the scoreboard clock eating up potential minutes of play. Now the sport could leap forward from the slow-paced game of crosscourt passing and offensive positioning envisioned by Dr. Naismith himself (Naismith had ruled out "running" and didn't conceive of dribbling) to the spontaneous action-packed freelance type of run-and-gun action we have come to expect (and usually relish) today.

The college version of Naismith's sport is, of course, nearly as old as the indoor cage game itself. The first reported intercollegiate contests were played by both men and women in the very shadows of Naismith's first trial run at the Springfield YMCA. While a rough-and-tumble men's version may have been what Naismith had intended to design, women (especially women college students) overnight found the new sport's appeal equally alluring. Some of the earliest organized college competitions, in fact, are reported to have been held among all-female teams. And within a year of Dr. Naismith's invention, a Springfield neighbor—Lithuanian-born physical education instructor Senda Berenson—was both organizing women's games at nearby Smith College in Holyoke and also publishing the first set of *Spalding Guidebook* rules for inspired female competitors.

Women had thus enthusiastically adopted Naismith's invention literally within weeks of its original 1891 debut. Not only did instructor Naismith invite female students to join games at the Springfield YMCA that very first winter, but one of those pioneering women participants (Maude Sherman) soon became his wife. Full-fledged collegiate women's games also date back to the selfsame year or two when male college play was first launched, and coeds at Stanford and Cal-Berkeley are alleged to have staged a primitive contest (complete with bloomers and long black hose for uniforms) as early as the winter of 1896. The earliest documented women's matches may thus actually predate (or at least approximate) the very first male campus contests.

It would be Berenson's early rules, of course, that would send the women's version in quite a different direction from the game that men were playing. Berenson gained much of the credit for such segregational tactics by adapting Naismith's rules to fit Victorian notions of female daintiness—players were to stand demurely in one of three fixed regions of the court and were barred from snatching the ball from opponents. Other versions of "women's rules" also appeared in places like nearby Mount Holyoke College (also in Holyoke) and far away Sophie Newcomb College (located in New Orleans and later a part of Tulane University). One far-reaching rule change for women competitors was actually the result of a blind mistake in interpreting a set of explanations provided by Naismith himself. Requesting a written set of rules from the game's originator,

Newcomb College instructor Clara Baer misread an accompanying diagram enclosed by Naismith that merely suggested zones on the floor where players might stand to commence play. Designing her own version called "basquette," Baer incorporated the long-standing and much-rued legislation that echoed Berenson's Smith College guidelines and prevented frontcourt and backcourt players from stepping out of their fixed zones. By thus restricting running and barring roughhousing, these adopted standards for girls basketball included all the era's popular assumptions about the fragility of women. The inevitable result was, not surprisingly, a static version of women's "basquette" that would prevail for almost three-quarters of the coming century.

Naismith's original notion of basketball play was itself a far cry from the rapid-action, star-oriented, and highly competitive entertainment spectacle we embrace today. Naismith, in fact, had a very different notion in mind when he invented the game for the sole purpose of entertaining and exercising his group of bored and often rowdy future YMCA secretaries (that is, instructors and administrators). The 13 rules with which he started are still to no small degree present in basketball's modern versions. The ball is to be moved around the court by passing and not by carrying or kicking; running (traveling) with the sphere is illegal, and so are tackling, swatting, or otherwise assaulting the player who possesses it. The entire contest turns on throwing the ball into the raised basket, and the elevation of the goal prevents defenders from easily blocking the goal with their bodies (Naismith didn't, of course, envision today's seven-footers or rubber-legged leapers). But the intention of play was far different in Naismith's mind than it is in the minds of today's players, coaches, and enthusiastic spectators. Winning a contest was an afterthought, much subordinated to more important altruistic notions of camaraderie, healthful competition and physical exercise, and good clean fun for all participants. Any notion of a spectator spectacle was completely foreign and even something of an anathema to the game's founding father.

Today college basketball sits near the pinnacle of the American sporting scene. No event—not even the heavily hyped Super Bowl of January nor the nostalgically revered World Series of October—captures as large or as intense an audience as the postseason NCAA tournament that is now known in every corner of America simply as March Madness. Despite setbacks over the years—most especially a devastating game-fixing scandal at midcentury that nearly compromised altogether the sport's integrity—the game has lurched steadily forward and has even been a rapid-growth industry ever since its miraculous recovery from the near-death experience of those betting scandals of the early '50s. Along the way have also arisen some of the greatest legends and most intriguing personalities of American sports history.

Immaculate Conception and Miraculous Reception

Basketball, quite unlike all other spectator sports, can precisely pinpoint its moment of origin. The bare facts of Naismith's single-handed invention of the sport remain an often retold staple of American sports history. But the origin of college competitions is not quite as clear-cut, and this is especially true when it comes to documenting the very first legitimate collegiate game.

There are indeed several candidates for what might have been the earliest college game. The best cases perhaps can be made for the Iowa versus Chicago and Yale versus Penn contests of 1896 and 1897. Each of these pioneering games has its own special claims for pioneering bragging rights. Yet each also owns a feature or two that would convince many to set it aside as a mere historical curiosity and not the sought-after landmark event. On January 16 of 1896, Naismith's Springfield colleague Alonzo Stagg (later of football fame and already coaching an undergraduate cage team he had patched together) brought his Chicago University squad to Iowa City for its first contest against outside competition. Stagg's boys prevailed 15–12, yet in true Naismith spirit, the contingent of Iowa athletes (all enrolled at the state university in that city) were official representatives of the Iowa City YMCA and not of the University of Iowa. This was likely the first five-on-five contest—even the true beginnings of five-man basketball—but arguably must be dismissed as representing a genuine "intercollegiate" competition. While the Yale-Penn match of March 1897 lags behind the Iowa City game by more than a full year, it nonetheless also boasts the distinction of being a five-versus-five affair, with Yale breezing to victory by a slightly more modern-looking tally of 32–10.

Eleven months earlier (on February 9, 1895), Hamline College of Minnesota fell to the Minnesota State School of Agriculture by a yawn-producing 9–3 score. The teams were clearly comprised of collegians this time around, but the squads in this case were also nine-man units. A similar nine-versus-nine affair also transpired on March 23, 1895, in Pennsylvania, with Haverford besting Temple 6–4. Both losing outfits were, by coincidence, also organized and coached by original Naismith students (Ray Kaighn at Haverford and Charles Williams at Temple), who had together participated in the famed first Springfield YMCA exhibition back in 1891.

There were other sporadic starts and these included both men's and women's competitions. There had been games reported as early as 1893 involving college contingents in Iowa and Minnesota and all again involving Naismith's own Springfield disciples. Women's teams representing Stanford and California reputedly met sometime in the winter of 1896, as reportedly did squads from Smith and Vasser. And the crack Yale University team accomplished the first extended barnstorming excursion during the winter of 1899–1900, trekking to Chicago and back during the Christmas holidays, winning several games en route, but having a handful of others wiped out by last-minute cancellations. It is Yale, then, which stakes the ablest claims for pioneering in the college sport. In addition to their landmark contest with Penn and their partially aborted Midwestern junket (both inaugural events), the Eli position as pacesetter is also backed by bold experimentations with a new method of offensive attack known as the dribble.

Serious college rivalries took shape, however, only with the first organized conference competitions. The Ivy League (nee Eastern League) and Big Ten Conference (nee Western Conference) progenitors were among the bold pioneers. The first winter season of a new century witnessed vanguard primitive attempts at such leagues, all clustered in the nation's northeastern sector. Connecticut's "big three" of Yale, Trinity, and Wesleyan formed the first formalized circuit that would loosely be called the Triangle League. Later that same winter the New England League took shape with Dartmouth, Holy Cross, Amherst College, Williams College, and

Trinity College joining forces; and the Eastern League, comprised initially of Columbia, Cornell, Harvard, Princeton, and Yale, was soon to follow.

Identification with one confederation obviously did not preclude affiliation with still another as the dual memberships of Trinity and Yale vividly attest. Yale would claim the first title in what would eventually call itself the Ivy League. The Western Conference, in turn, had been formed for football competitions back in 1895, but the future "Big Ten" also took up basketball play in 1905 with the seven gridiron schools (Minnesota, the first year's winner, plus Wisconsin, Indiana, Chicago, Illinois, Purdue, and Iowa) competing in the initial winter's round-robin for cage play.

Basketball's opening decades also boast some oversized heroes who have today been largely and unjustifiably forgotten by roundball history. H. O. "Pat" Page (an innovative pioneer of guard play) and John Schommer (the first prototype center) provided backbone for Joseph Raycroft–coached University of Chicago teams that proved nearly invincible at the end of the century's first decade. The speedy Page was twice an All-American, later a coaching legend himself for both his alma mater and Butler University of Indianapolis, and a clear choice as 1910 national Player of the Year. Schommer earned his lasting fame as inventor of the modern-style backboard but earlier preceded Page by precisely one season as the nation's top player while also averaging 10 points per game, enough to pace Western Conference athletes in scoring three winters running. Vic Hanson authored a legend at Syracuse while pacing the Orangemen to a 48–7 three-year mark and a consensus 1926 national championship; Hanson's play a decade and a half after Page and Schommer was remarkable enough to earn a spot on sportswriter Grantland Rice's mythical midcentury All-Time All-American squad. Christian Steinmetz of Wisconsin was a still earlier nonpareil who accomplished rare offensive feats with the game's first 1,000-point career total (1903–05) and a then-remarkable single-game outburst of 44 points versus outmanned Beloit. And a Clemson player named J. O. Erwin outdid even Steinmetz with a still more remarkable one-night scoring explosion (58 points), which incredibly has lasted unscathed to the present day as a school mark, and it occurred strangely enough in Clemson's first-ever varsity intercollegiate game.

The distinctive flavor of college play across the first five decades was largely one of stark regionalism. The game evolved somewhat differently in different parts of the land, and rarely did teams from different regions collide to test different coaching styles and different strategies for offensive and defensive play. One such landmark collision came when Adolph Rupp and his emerging Kentucky University team first ventured into New York City in 1935 to meet Howard Cann–coached NYU (18–1 that season) at Madison Square Garden. Local-leaning officials blithely allowed NYU frontcourt brutes King Kong Klein and Slim Terjesen to shove and batter Wildcats center LeRoy "Cowboy" Edwards under the home-team bucket while Rupp's men were repeatedly whistled for blocking fouls at the other end. The results (NYU 23, Kentucky 22) and Rupp's accompanying outrage were typical of such rare, and almost always one-sided, intersectional collisions.

As the game evolved in fits and starts, its seminal figures were almost exclusively innovative coaches like Rupp and Cann who shaped the nature of playing tactics both with their own teams and throughout their own regions. Most fell into two camps—one favoring plodding and more scientific play while both shooting and defending the ball, and the other advocating a much more wide-open racehorse style of offensive game. Despite regional leanings there were proponents of both styles spread out widely across all sectors of the country.

Joseph Raycroft was one farsighted mentor who exercised an early and major influence in the Midwest and also pioneered by drawing a regular salary for his services. Raycroft's talented and impeccably trained University of Chicago teams won 78 of 90 matches during the new century's first decade, peaking with a 21–2 record that earned a "mythical" national championship during the 1908 season. That title came via a first-ever national playoff held between consensus East and West regional champions. The East Coast selection fell easily to Pennsylvania with its all-star forward Charles Keinath (a renowned fancy dribbler); after losing their first three matches, the Quakers won a string of 22, which included eight Eastern League games. Chicago earned a spot in the best-of-three against Penn by capturing a playoff with Western Conference cochampion Wisconsin. The final tally was 18–16 when Pat Page hit a last-minute shot while surrounded by three defenders. Page was again the hero of the national series, making a shot from under his legs to seal a 21–18 win on the home floor and also pacing a 16–15 victory in Philadelphia. There were three unbeatable elements behind the powerhouse Chicago Maroons team of the century's first decade. The school owned the deadly combination of a paid coach (Raycroft), a quick ballhandling guard (All-American Page), and a lanky and athletic center (All-American Schommer).

A decade later, Walter "Doc" Meanwell was developing a popular and successful style of play up the road from Chicago at the University of Wisconsin. Meanwell thundered onto the scene in the Western Conference with two unbeaten campaigns (1912, 1914) and an overall 44–1 ledger during his first three seasons on the job. Unlike many of his colleagues in the young coaching profession, Meanwell himself had never played the still relatively novel game of basketball. But that shortcoming was seemingly no obstacle to his emerging as one of the game's most innovative first-generation mentors. Meanwell despised the dribble, advocated tight man-on-man defense, and taught an offensive system based on short-pass patterns and patient selection of unmolested shots. Another "Doc" who nursed the game in new directions earned an actual medical degree at Pittsburgh in 1920, yet found his true calling only when he took over the school's basketball program two years later. Henry Carlson earned his own special niche with his invention of the "Figure 8" offensive weave pattern (he called it a "continuity attack") and with the two "mythical" national championships which this playing style eventually bought for his team in 1928 and 1930. But he is perhaps best remembered for his early experiments with fundamentals of the offensive stall; Doc Carlson could not tolerate zone defenses, and on several occasions had his team hold the ball for much of the game in order to counter such "tactless" zone play.

Carlson was also as much a showman as he was a chalkboard innovator, and his colorful sideline displays would often bring memorable responses from opposition arena crowds witnessing his team on the road. He was known to throw peanuts into the stands to hostile road crowds while his visiting Panthers slowed down their offense against hated zone defenses. On one occasion, he was struck on the head with an umbrella wielded by a matronly patron at Washington and Jefferson, and on still another, he had a bucket of ice water poured on his head from the stands behind the Pittsburgh bench by enraged West Virginia partisans (he had been shouting, "This burns me up," at the game officials just before his unexpected shower).

While Raycroft and Chicago grabbed headlines in the '00s, Meanwell at Wisconsin established trends in the '10s, and Carlson of Pittsburgh demanded attention throughout the '20s, other regions were soon equal hotbeds of experimentation and landmark innovation. New York City was another such early cradle, and its most influential coach—despite Holman at CCNY, Ed Kelleher at Fordham, and Howard Cann at NYU—was James "Buck" Freeman with his "Wonder Five" four-year team at St. John's. The Wonder Five first emerged on the scene in 1928, and their debut constituted the arrival of the first among many subsequent legendary New York City collegiate clubs. It was Freeman's team more than any other that truly put New York (and thus East Coast) cage play back on the map at the close of the '20s and dawn of the '30s. With its four Jewish starters (Jack "Rip" Gerson, Max Posnack, Allie Schuckman, and Mac Kinsbrunner) and fifth teammate (Matty Begovich), the Roman Catholic college would make plenty of news on the hardwoods over the next several seasons.

As unseasoned freshmen, they upset CCNY, captured 18 of 22, and averaged better than 36 points a game while holding opponents to less than 10 per contest. With a 23–2 ledger as sophomores, their nearly error-free ball-control game had already become a marvel of the region. The 10-point margin of victory maintained through the 1928–29 season was truly marvelous for an era when most teams only scored around 30 in a contest. As juniors the unbreakable pattern continued—domination of the New York scene, patient offense, and air-tight defense both based on a strategy of keeping the ball away from the opponents, and a 24–1 ledger at season's end. The senior year would prove even better as Freeman's outfit would pile up 21 more victories against stiffer opposition, run its winning streak to 27 before being tripped for the only time all winter by NYU, and set new standards for defensive stinginess. In the end the four-year record stood at 86–8; but there were greater legacies than the mere tally of victories and losses. One was the new popularity for the cage sport, which would make huge crowds at Madison Square Garden for college games a staple of the coming decade. A second was the introduction of the 10-second backcourt rule preventing excessive stalling, a legislation made necessary by the action-killing, ball-holding techniques that Freeman's teams had built into an all too effective and indefensible art form.

Doc Meanwell's arch Midwestern rival in both Western Conference (Big Ten) competitions and theoretical approaches to basketball strategy was Ward "Piggy" Lambert, head man at Purdue from the opening storm clouds of World War I (1916) through the closing salvos of World War II (1946). Lambert advocated a more wide-open racehorse style of play that was the antithesis of Meanwell's dribble-free and painfully patient passing offenses. While his 371 career wins would not be surpassed until 1997 (by Gene Keady), Lambert's Purdue teams already reached their peak in the early '30s with a lineup that featured home-grown three-time All-American John Wooden in the backcourt and towering Charles "Stretch" Murphy under the basket. Murphy established an important prototype, the sure-handed rebounder who could clear defensive boards and fire the necessary outlet passes to fuel Lambert's fast-breaking attack. But perhaps the ultimate credit for a modern fast-break-style game goes not so much to Lambert as to a pair of even more "run-and-gun" crazy proponents at Rhode Island State and George Washington University almost a full decade later. It is Red Auerbach's earliest mentor, Bill Reinhart, who perhaps deserves chief kudos for fostering racehorse basketball in its present form. With only moderately talented George Washington teams in the late '30s, Reinhart nonetheless fashioned the classic attack (three players charging down the lanes at full speed) that provided the modern blueprint. And somewhat earlier, colorful Frank Keaney already had his Rhode Island State teams utilizing the same strategy to balloon their scoring average above a point per minute by 1927, 1,000 points for the season in 1937, 70 points per game by 1939, and 2,000 total points with the 1945 campaign.

All these innovations and pioneers aside, across the first half-century of basketball play, nowhere was the game any more deeply entrenched or more carefully nurtured than on the plains of Kansas under the legendary Forrest "Phog" Allen, disciple and colleague of the game's transplanted inventor. Allen had taken over at Kansas for Naismith himself, who had arrived at Lawrence in 1899, introduced his game there, and then served for a handful of winters (1899 through 1909) as the first varsity coach. And for years Allen continued to have the game's father (who remained a professor of physical education until his retirement in 1937) residing in his own backyard. But Allen envisioned and soon developed a very different game from the one Naismith had imagined. When chided by his mentor that basketball was not an activity one coached, a young Allen countered that at least you could teach the boys "to pass at angles and run in curves." He taught much more, lessons that almost immediately lifted Kansas to its first lofty heights in only his third and fourth seasons on the job. Allen's 1922 and 1923 squads posted a first-ever undefeated Missouri Valley Conference record and a pair of consensus national championships and featured All-American guard Paul Endacott, a 5'10" firebrand who controlled center jumps and shone as a defensive specialist.

Ironically, one of Phog Allen's greatest legacies would turn out to be not Endacott, but rather another less-heralded player from his 1923 championship team. Adolph Rupp played only sparingly for Allen but emerged in Kentucky in 1930 as an unknown replacement for John Maurer and was soon building a legend of his own that would first rival and then surpass even that of his master. His very first club went 15–3 to match the career .825 winning percentage he would post over the following four-plus decades. Rupp had memorable teams even in his first decade, such as the one starring Cowboy Edwards that went to New York in 1935 and established the attractiveness (and often blatant unfairness and one-sidedness) of intersectional competitions.

While Allen and Rupp were building their great teams in the hinterlands in the '20s and '30s, the first large crowds were being drawn to the game's meccas on the East Coast. The first inkling of the sport's robust appeal came in 1920 when 10,000 packed New York's 168th Street Regimental Armory to see the year's best attractions—NYU at 11–1 and featuring future coach Howard Cann as its star player and City University at 13–2—lock horns in an exciting 39–21 match that fell to the NYU Violet. Big arenas and field houses were springing up elsewhere as well, especially in the Midwest in places such as Iowa City where the state university had constructed a 16,000-seat arena in the mid-'20s. The Palestra opened in Philadelphia on January 1, 1927 (it was built for the then-lofty price tag of $750,000), and only weeks later drew 10,000 to watch Penn battle Princeton. Such crowds soon meant more visibility and renown for the game's recognizable stars—Endacott at Kansas, Hanson for three seasons of the mid-'20s in Syracuse, Purdue's Stretch Murphy, Indiana's Branch McCracken, Wisconsin's Harold "Bud" Foster, and Montana State's John "Cat" Thompson.

Before it could truly enter its modern age, basketball had to shape, hone, and regularize its rules. A telling moment came in 1929 with what would later be referred to as "The Last Great Dribble Debate" and would feature some of the game's largest personalities of the time. Controversy surrounding the act of dribbling was nothing new to the sport. The strategy had almost immediately entered the game as part and parcel of efforts during the first few winters to relax Naismith's original strictures against running with the ball. Pivoting (moving one foot) was first ruled not to be a traveling violation, but soon it was discovered that action picked up if a man with the ball being tightly guarded could be allowed to escape by tossing the ball into the air and recapturing it (the "air dribble"). Yale's team reportedly expanded the strategy as a serious weapon by also bouncing the sphere while moving toward the goal. Such methods of escaping the defense seemed to many to be a vast improvement, yet soon the early basketball establishment was radically divided over both the advisability and appropriateness of dribbling the ball. Several new dribbling legislations would go in and out of favor during the next several decades (one of them being that the dribbler could not also shoot the ball at the basket).

So heated was the battle that the National Association of Basketball Coaches was finally created specifically to protect the sport against the encroachments of the anti-dribbling forces. There is a most delightful story surrounding the meeting of coaches to resolve the dribbling issue one last time in the late '20s. Wisconsin's Doc Meanwell had led a final onslaught by conservatives in 1929 to kill the dribble by limiting players to a single legal bounce. Meanwell, who believed that the pro-style game of continuous passing made dribbles unnecessary and even unaesthetic, would present one side to the annual NABC meeting and receive a 9–8 vote in his favor. The coaches' group then adjourned to watch a pro game featuring Cleveland's Rosenblums and the Original Celtics, a match which seemed to argue for Meanwell's version of the game that might be played with passing and shooting exclusively. Then Nat Holman, who was already coaching the CCNY team while still himself playing for these same Celtics, asked for a reconvening of the group. In an impassioned speech he pointed out that college youngsters were not prepared to play like pros and needed the dribble as a strategy. The vote was retaken, and this time the forces loyal to Holman and other dribble supporters finally held sway.

Basketball's newfound audience—spawned by the rule modifications and strategy innovations of the decades between the two world wars—would be first fully exploited in New York City. What had become widely known as "The City Game" was booming by the time the '20s flip-flopped into the '30s. Howard Cann rebuilt sagging fortunes at NYU and peaked with his 1934 victory over Holman's CCNY club in a clash of unbeatens. Freeman's Wonder Five captured

Important Rule Changes in Basketball's First Half-Century

1893—Pivot play (shifting one foot while anchoring the other) is ruled not to constitute a "traveling" violation.

1895—Backboards introduced to eliminate crowd interference (from balcony) with shots at the goal. Free-throw line moved in from 20 feet to 15 feet.

1896—Field-goal value is changed from three to two points and free throws from three points to one point.

1897—Yale University team introduces "dribbling" as offensive strategy since there is no rule to ban such a maneuver. Number of players fixed at five on a side (previously seven-man and nine-woman teams were commonplace).

1898—Overhead dribble and double dribble are banned.

1901—Dribbler not allowed to shoot ball at basket or score points (rule remained in effect until 1915).

1910—Glass backboards introduced as improvements on metal screens and wooden backboards.

1914—Rough scrambles for out-of-bounds balls eliminated by new rule awarding ball to team opposite the one that last touched the ball inbounds.

1916—Glass backboards temporarily banned by requirement of white paint for all backboards.

1924—Free throws no longer awarded for non-contact violations like traveling (those violations which are not personal fouls).

1929—Collegiate Joint Rules Committee outlaws dribbling (under the influence of Wisconsin's Walter Meanwell), then immediately reverses its decision (under the influence of CCNY's Nat Holman).

1930—Five-second backcourt held-ball rule adopted to discourage stalling on offense.

1933—Ten-second backcourt violation also adopted to prevent stalling on offense.

1936—Three-second lane violation established (offensive player cannot remain within foul lanes for more than three seconds at a time).

1937—Center jump eliminated after made free throws.

1938—Center jump eliminated after made field goals.

Source: *Hoopla: A Century of College Basketball, 1896–1996*, by Peter C. Bjarkman (Masters Press, 1996)

the public's imagination as well as most of the games played during the same epoch. Clair Bee was already building relentless winners at LIU with 26–1, 24–2, and 25–0 ledgers in 1934, 1935, and 1936. And Nat Holman had taken over on a part-time basis for CCNY while continuing his professional barnstorming career (mostly with the Original Celtics and Brooklyn, Syracuse, and Chicago ABL clubs) as a sidelight, thus transferring his own polished pro style of play to his well-schooled college charges. The "Holman Wheel" was a patient offensive scheme in which all five players cut and swerved through endless loops around the basket until the uncontested shot could be found. Holman's teams only thrice lost as many as six games in a single season throughout the entire span between 1920 and 1940; more important, the Holman trademark offensive strategy was soon a much-imitated favorite everywhere throughout the northeast quadrant of the country. It was Holman's system if not Holman's teams that soon ruled the New York roundball scene.

It took an innovative genius of another sort, however, to exploit fully this great new surge of basketball interest. He would arrive in the form of a farsighted dreamer named Edward "Ned" Irish, a budding sports journalist who was at first merely enamored with covering the cage sport, but who soon became obsessed with the notion of being college basketball's original promoter *par excellence*. Legend is mixed with fact when it comes to Irish's first insights into the marketing potential of the college hoops sport. It is widely reported that he initially stumbled upon the idea for larger venues when he tore his own trousers while trying to crawl through a window and into a stuffy Manhattan College gymnasium so that he could cover a sold-out city series game. The tale may indeed be entirely apocryphal, yet the details of his subsequent steps are very much a matter of record. Soon Irish was taking time off from sportswriting to schedule and promote doubleheaders matching local schools with showcase teams from other regions. His first triumph arrived with a $20,000 gate and 16,188 head count for a twin bill featuring a stellar card that included St. John's versus Pennsylvania's Westminster College and NYU facing Notre Dame. The landmark date was December 29, 1934. Earlier, Irish had also assisted *New York World Telegram* sportswriter Dan Daniel in staging an all-local January 1931 triple bill that featured Columbia, Fordham, Manhattan, NYU, St. John's, and CCNY.

Ned Irish had flung open doors for the college game (even if he once had to crawl through windows himself) with his innovative doubleheaders and tripleheaders in Madison Square Garden. It was with Irish and these Garden bills of fare that basketball went big time and that New York City suddenly became a center-stage venue for the increasingly popular sport. The twin bills ballooned to eight per year over the next several seasons and brought to town such novel acts from the provinces as Kentucky with Cowboy Edwards and Stanford with Hank Luisetti, along with other marquee intersectional attractions like the teams from Colorado, Oklahoma A&M, Notre Dame, Loyola-Chicago, and Bradley. They also brought a steady stream of overflow crowds to witness the action. With a handful of big-ticket events, a minor sport was transformed almost overnight into a five-star spectacle.

The new Garden attractions were, from the start, an exciting venue for pitched battles between the city's top teams and the best that the rest of the nation had to offer. It was these clashes between regions with distinct playing styles, played out on New York's grandest stage, that would first break down the game's stark regionalisms and bring basketball—especially among the collegians—into its modern era on the eve of the second great world war. One such entrenched regionalism about to evaporate was West Coast one-handed gunning versus East Coast two-handed set-shooting. The moment for dramatic confrontation came in late December of 1936 with one of the most memorable single games of the sport's history—certainly "the" most important single game in the first half-century of college competitions. Clair Bee's long-unbeaten LIU Blackbirds (with their invincible lineup of Ben Kramer, Art Hillhouse, Jules Bender, and Leo Merson) would be forced to stake their reputation and test their merit against a touring Stanford ball club and Hank Luisetti's notorious one-handed push shot. With a 43-game victory streak squarely on the line, LIU was paralyzed by Luisetti and the freelancing Stanford attack designed by Johnny Bunn. The West Coast star turned 18,000 heads in the grandstands and dozens more on press row with his 15 points (the final score was only 45–31), which came on a volley of unstoppable running one-handers. In a single evening Stanford earned a No. 1 ranking, Luisetti created a New York fan and media frenzy, and the college cage game was changed forever.

Hank Luisetti was the game's first true matinee idol—darkly handsome, unassuming although charismatic, entirely unselfish on the basketball court, and loaded with supreme athletic talent. He excelled in every phase of the game—rebounding, passing, dribbling, defending, running the floor, and shooting on the dead run. He was also a remarkable team player and an innovator touched by the unpredictable winds of rare good fortune, much of the latter provided by his perfectly timed East Coast visits. While he certainly didn't invent the one-handed toss, he nonetheless gave it full legitimacy and currency. Luisetti enjoyed his defining moment when he gunned down Clair Bee's team in the Garden and took the New York media by storm in the process. Shortly thereafter he would increase the legend with an eye-opening 50-point game in Cleveland Arena versus overwhelmed Duquesne, on a night when his teammates returned every pass and forced him to shoot often. The outburst against Duquesne was truly remarkable, coming in the low-scoring era it did. And it was achieved by a reluctant star who would have much preferred sharing the offensive burden with his overly cooperative teammates.

Luisetti's lasting influence on the East Coast version of the game was soon almost everywhere evident. Even entrenched conservatives like Nat Holman soon gave in to the winds of change, and coaches who had earlier sworn like Holman that they would never allow one-handed shooting on their teams were exploiting the new style and stuffing their lineups with players enamored of the new offensive maneuver. A dozen seasons later Holman would be caught boasting that with Tony Lavelli's hook shots for Yale, Paul Arizin's jumpers for Villanova, and the running push shot of his own star Irwin Dambrot, the East could hold its own with any sector when it came to sharp one-handed shooters.

Luisetti's shooting opened one door for the college game. A second door was cracked with the significant rule changes of 1937 and 1938 involving the archaic center jump. The game was still slow (by modern standards), low-scoring, and dominated by two-handed set shooting. But the main fetters had already been removed once continuous action and shooting on the run were encouraged. And most significant of all, a considerable amount of playing time had now been put back on the scoreboard clock. This was the clock time earlier lost while players and officials trudged back to center court for new jump-ups after each and every score, all with the game clock relentlessly ticking away.

Another spin-off of Irish's suddenly popular Madison Square Garden extravaganzas was the annual postseason tournament. It was an idea that seemed to be long overdue when it first arrived with the six-team affair sponsored by the Metropolitan Basketball Writers and staged at Madison Square Garden to cap the 1938 season. The inaugural National Invitation Tournament reflected its organizers' desire for a strong East-West flavor with Colorado, Oklahoma A&M, Temple, and Bradley joining the host schools from LIU and NYU; it also succeeded wildly both at the gate and on the playing floor. But the idea for such tournaments was not new and indeed stretched back as far as 1904, when Hiram College, Wheaton College, and Latter

Transcendental Graphics

Villanova's Paul Arizin (with ball) led the nation in scoring in 1950 before taking his high-scoring act to the NBA's Philadelphia Warriors.

Day Saints University (today Brigham Young) met at the St. Louis World's Fair for what was ambitiously billed as an Olympic World's College Basket Ball Championship. Other attempts had been made by the college coaches to institute a year-end championship, and the first truly national tournament was the NAIA event which originated in Kansas City in 1937 as replacement for a national AAU playoff which had been relocated to Detroit. The showcase small school affair, which preceded the NIT by a full year, offered a field of 32 teams and a full week of nearly round-the-clock playoff showdowns.

By the close of the 1930s, with war clouds looming everywhere on the near horizon, college basketball had finally come of age. The game had been modernized both by modifications to the playing structure and bold innovations among the crack athletes themselves. For the first time there was a distinctly national flavor to the sport, with teams from East and West and North and South now frequently meeting head-on to test regional supremacies. Large audiences flocked into packed venues (especially those in New York or Philadelphia and in the large field houses on many Midwestern campuses) and the game was welcoming its first nationally recognized stars with names like Luisetti of Stanford, Wintermute of Oregon, Jaworski of Rhode Island, Torgoff of Long Island, and Nowak of Notre

Dame. Unrestrained optimism was felt everywhere in the air, and basketball's long-anticipated moment in the sun now seemed also to sit visibly on the next horizon.

Enter the Giants and the Jumping Jacks

World War II brought some significant unanticipated interruptions and adjustments to the sport. Numerous top players were lost to the full-scale war effort; others were shuffled between campuses as a result of the military's hastily instituted special training programs. Future NBA stalwart Dick McGuire, for one, debuted in December with St. John's (earning rare distinction during the 1944 season as the first freshman ever to capture the annual award given by the New York Basketball Writers Association to the outstanding player in the metropolitan area); but McGuire finished the season with Dartmouth College (where he was sent abruptly in late winter for Navy wartime training under the V-12 program) and thus miraculously appeared with the Big Green in the NCAA title game versus Utah. Another outcome of such shuffling found many schools playing reduced schedules or laboring under reduced circumstances (NCAA champion Utah played only on the road when its field house became a military armory), while still others of necessity competed against a makeshift hodgepodge schedule of occasional collegiate teams and more frequent military base training outfits.

One of the most dramatic interruptions of the status quo was found in the plight of the crack 1943 University of Illinois team. The seasoned powerhouse outfit of the Midwest, Illinois owned the Big Ten competition that year at 12–0 (17–1 overall with only a meaningless early-season loss to a Camp Grant military ball club when coach Doug Mills chose to play a lineup comprised of his reserves). But the Illinois "Whiz Kids" team passed on postseason competition when the outfit voluntarily broke up on March 1 so that its stellar lineup of Andy Phillip (a future NBA star), Ken Menke, Art Mathisen, Jack Smiley, and Gene Vance could jointly enlist for the then-raging war effort. Illinois's departure from the field left the path to a national championship wide open for a Wyoming team featuring jump-shooting pioneer Ken Sailors. It also sabotaged, in the process, what might have been an inevitable Madison Square Garden showdown for the NCAA title between Sailors (the country's best player) and the Big Ten team that was truly the best the East or West had to offer.

Wartime restrictions wrought another type of major influence as well—the widespread influence of freshmen. McGuire starred for eventual 1944 NIT champion St. John's at the beginning of the season and was an impact player for NCAA finalist Dartmouth when tournament time rolled around that same year. Arnie Ferrin with Utah was the NCAA tournament MVP while another first-year man at St. John's—Bill Kotsores—paralleled the achievement as MVP of the still more prestigious NIT. And Utah captured the NCAA shootout over Iowa State, Ohio State, and Dartmouth with an entire lineup of novice freshmen, doing so a full half-century before Michigan's headline-grabbing Fab Five freshman quintet of NCAA finalists.

But despite noxious wartime interferences, the popularity of the new postseason tournaments nonetheless blossomed. Both events were now centered in

Transcendental Graphics

With a 17–1 record, the "Whiz Kids" of Illinois may have been the nation's top outfit in 1943, yet elected to bypass the wartime NCAA tournament to enlist in the armed forces. From left are coach Doug Mills, Art Mathisen, Jack Smiley, Gene Vance, Ken Menke, and future NBA star Andy Phillip.

New York City where basketball continued to find its largest and most enthusiastic audiences. The NIT had been strictly a Madison Square Garden event from the opening bell. And between 1943 (the fifth year of the event) and 1950 (after a single 1949 title game in Seattle) the NCAA group also scheduled its championship contest into the same arena approximately two weeks after the NIT curtain closer. Both tournaments were also initially restricted to small and highly select fields of invited competitors. The NIT at first admitted six schools to its opening rounds (two with byes) while the NCAA selected only eight (four for the West Regional and four in the East). By 1951 the NIT had jumped to a dozen participants, while the NCAA had swelled to 16. And often both affairs shared some of the very same teams making twin appearances in the season's year-end playoff derby. Colorado and Duquesne were the first to attempt such double dips in 1940; Utah's all-freshman club captured the 1944 NCAAs only after bowing out in the first round of the NIT to Kentucky; Rupp's Kentucky "Fabulous Five" repeated an NCAA championship in 1949 after tumbling to Loyola-Chicago in the NIT quarterfinal (a game later tainted by point-shaving revelations); CCNY walked off with both titles in 1950; and Dayton, North Carolina State, and St. John's made their last joint appearances during the early '50s.

The first major invitational tournament to arrive on the scene was the aptly named National Invitation Tournament, another invention of Ned Irish and his New York backers at the tail end of the '30s. Irish had long dreamed of such an affair that might serve to decide a national collegiate champion and stuff the local coffers at the same time. Now with the Metropolitan Basketball Writers Association acting as a formal sponsor of an event that Irish could promote as the "Rose Bowl of Basketball," the wily promoter again sprang into action.

The debut NIT event provided a rousing lidlifter for the new concept at the end of the 1937–38 campaign. The entertainment-packed spectacle opened on a high note when NYU and LIU squared off for the first time ever, and Howard Cann's NYU team gained local bragging rights with a 39–37 squeaker. Ultimate bragging privileges eventually fell to the team out of Philadelphia, however, as Temple's Owls made easy work of Colorado and its football All-American Whizzer White in the one-sided finals, pulling away down the stretch to a 60–36 laugher. But the second postseason belonged to a local favorite in the guise of Clair Bee's powerhouse LIU club. Bee's team held off Chicago's Loyola College when Mike Sewitch, despite his broken arm, put a tight blanket over the Ramblers' 6'8" scoring star Mike Novak and held him without a single bucket during the 12-point LIU victory. Ironically, the second NIT event would be something of a landmark affair, providing the first and, surprisingly, the last time that two undefeated clubs would square off at season's end with a national title at stake.

Collegiate coaches and athletic administrators could not fail to see the cash-cow potential in the new postseason event, and the NCAA organization would not tarry long before climbing onto the bandwagon. Why let all the promotion and thus all the profits of the colleges' athletic labors fall into the hands of Irish and a small group of New York entrepreneurs? With the newspaper writers' New York City example squarely before them, the coaches now quickly moved for their own event. Only a single season after the NIT lidlifter, the college administrations from around the rest of the country had hastily arranged a regional playoff system, one planned out and administrated largely by Ohio State head coach Harold Olsen. The NCAA inaugural was slightly more complex in design even if it featured a more modest venue for its action—four teams from each section would meet in semifinals and finals at two regional sites, followed by a title match at a neutral Midwest location that would cut travel expenses. The first title game was thus played on the Northwestern University campus in Evanston, Illinois, and all too fittingly featured Olsen's own Ohio State ball club. Oregon's "Tall Timbers" defeated Olsen's Buckeyes 46–33 in a game that gave only small signal of the marvelous tradition it was launching. The NCAA lidlifter event was nonetheless a modest success, since 6,000 turned out for the Western playoffs in San Francisco and 3,500 (one-third capacity) entered the Philadelphia Palestra for two nights of action in the East. This meant a net loss of only about $2,500 for the collective NCAA coffers.

In the shadows of the war the college game turned another dramatic corner with the arrival of the first two seven-foot stars. Actually neither was seven feet tall (Kurland was a mere fraction under, and Mikan measured out at 6'10"), nor

Ohio State (white uniforms) and an Oregon player battle for a rebound during the finals of the first-ever NCAA tournament in 1939 in Evanston, Illinois.

Transcendental Graphics

were they the first towering goons to see hardwood action. Phog Allen once had a true seven-footer enrolled in Kansas (Harry Kersenbrock, who was scheduled to suit up for the 1928–29 season) but he had drowned in a boating accident before ever playing a game. Harry Boykoff (St. John's), John Mahnken (Georgetown), Mike Novak (Loyola), and Don Otten (Bowling Green) were some other war-era giants who proved demon goaltenders. But Kurland and Mikan unquestionably redefined the role of the towering big man from that of curious goon to that of potent offensive and defensive force. For the first time a single player could dominate a game merely by setting up under the basket and guarding the goal against enemy shots at one end of the floor while stuffing it full of easy two-pointers at the other end. And the entire sport would inevitably change quite radically with the concept.

Kurland enjoyed the greatest successes on the college level. He would be the first to lead his school to consecutive national titles in the NCAA tournament. In the process he would also be the first to earn back-to-back trophies as NCAA Final Four Most Outstanding Performer. While he trailed Mikan (the nation's leader) in scoring average during their senior season (1946), his 643 total points (Mikan had only 555) was nonetheless a new national record. And his NCAA tournament scoring average was nearly seven points better than Mikan's. Mikan could, in the end, boast more total points and also one prestigious NIT team title, and the two split up the five games in which they faced each other head-to-head (Mikan 3–2). Kurland, for his own part, however, was a rare physical specimen and a multitalented all-around player who brought a towering new dimension to the evolving cage game.

Mikan was always seemingly a step behind, yet he hardly played entirely in Kurland's shadow. There would be no national title (NCAA variety) for Mikan and his DePaul team, but there would be numerous moments of sustained glory. One of those moments came in the NIT of 1945, when champion DePaul made a shambles of the record book with 10 new team scoring records. Mikan himself accounted for 10 individual marks, including 120 points over three games and a Garden record 53 in the semifinals blowout, which equaled the entire team total for embarrassed opponent Rhode Island State. Perhaps the most memorable single image of collegiate basketball action at the height of the war years was drawn from a pair of titanic postseason collisions between Mikan and Kurland. The highlight moment of the Kurland-Mikan rivalry came when they squared off in the American Red Cross War Fund Benefit Game of 1945, matching Mikan's NIT champions against Kurland's NCAA winners. The game was somewhat disappointing in its eventual outcome, with Mikan fouling out after 14 minutes with but 9 points and Kurland collecting only 14 despite playing unmolested by Mikan during the entire second half. The first matchup between the pair during the 1944 NIT semifinals (which DePaul won 41–38) also found neither behemoth measuring up to his season's scoring average. Both fouled out and Mikan was again held under double figures. But these battles of genuine titans, for all their letdowns, also provided a rare glimpse of the future of college basketball as it would soon be played between hulking gladiators of enormous athletic talent.

While Kurland and Mikan were redefining the post-position play of the big man and requiring the rule books to be rewritten (the goaltending rule was enacted on their account in 1944), there were two further developments altering the game during the early and mid-'40s. First, Bob Davies at Seton Hall (author of behind-the-back dribbles) and then Bob Cousy at Holy Cross (practitioner of behind-the-back passing) brought to Eastern arenas a new style of flashy backcourt play. With them and their imitators was thus born the prototype of the modern "point guard" as well as the prototype of the showboating basketball entertainer. And Luisetti's one-handed shooting style had also now witnessed dramatic further evolution. While Joe Fulks today receives most of the credit from NBA historians for developing the jump shot on the professional level, Wyoming's Ken Sailors was also, earlier in the decade, fine-tuning the experiment in college arenas. Sailors put on a memorable one-man show in Madison Square Garden during the championship evening of the 1943 NCAA tourney. A swarming defender as well as a crack long-range shooter, the 5'11" forward threw in 16 (the only man in double figures) and put on what the New York press labeled "a dazzling exhibition of dribbling and shooting" in his team's romp over Georgetown. When Sailors also paced the Cowboys to an overtime defeat of NIT winner St. John's two nights later on the same floor (Red Cross Benefit), it also represented a huge step forward for the still second-fiddle NCAA tournament.

While the postwar economic boom of the late '40s launched the infant pro game, it also first put even stronger props under college play. Both tournaments seemed to thrive, as did popular regular-season doubleheaders, in Eastern arenas and heated conference competitions in the South, Midwest, and Pacific Coast regions. There were some early warning signals that all was not well with the obvious popularity of open wagering (especially in New York) and even several loud hints of scandal. There had been reports, and even confessions, of an attempt to fix a 1945 game between Akron and Brooklyn College for the benefit of gamblers. Star players at George Washington University and Manhattan College reported receiving bribe offers. And Phog Allen in Kansas made more enemies than friends when he repeatedly spoke out about perceived dangers involving rampant wagering on college contests. But no one paid much serious attention.

If one team dominated the late 1940s, it was the Wildcats juggernaut that Adolph Rupp launched annually out of Lexington, Kentucky. With a stable of war veterans on hand in time for the 1946 and 1947 seasons, Rupp enjoyed remarkable depth of talent unparalleled on any other campus. He also had built the game to unrivaled heights of popularity in his adopted Bluegrass state. So many top-notch players reported to Rupp for fall practice in the first postwar season that they had to be divided into an "A squad" (the varsity coached by Rupp with 19 members) and "B squad" (a practice unit coached by assistant Harry Lancaster). The biggest and best of the recruits was Ohio native Alex Groza, a 6'7" giant who appeared on campus for brief service at the start of the 1944–45 season before taking a year-and-a-half sabbatical for military duty. One breakthrough for Kentucky's program came during Groza's absence with a dramatic NIT championship victory over Rhode Island State in March 1946. It was one of the most thrilling postseason games ever, matching the 27–2 Ruppmen fueled by freshman hotshot Ralph Beard against the vaunted Frank Keaney running attack with All-American Ernie Calverley at the controls. Calverley had put Rhode Island State into the title round with a remarkable 58-foot shot against Bowling Green. But Beard would shut down the Rhodey ace during the championship affair, limiting the Rams' top weapon to only eight points. When Calverley fouled Beard in the closing seconds, the cool freshman dropped in the game-deciding free throw.

Rupp's first truly great contingent was his "Fabulous Five" outfit featuring guard Beard and center Groza and including Ken Rollins, Cliff Barker, and Wah Wah Jones. This group followed the 1946 NIT triumph with three of the best sustained seasons in NCAA history. There were three 30-win outings (34–3, 36–3, 32–2), two national titles, three straight appearances in a postseason championship game, a remarkable .927 winning percentage, and an 8–2 postseason ledger. It began with a near miss in defending the NIT crown when Utah's deliberate style calmed Kentucky's whirlwind attack 49–45 in the 1947 NIT finale. Next, Groza, Beard, and Jones keyed a three-pronged offense that brought the SEC school its first NCAA crown in a season that also featured a fifth consecutive Southeastern Conference championship. The Ruppmen nearly pulled off an unprecedented double victory a season ahead of Holman's CCNY crew during the final weeks of the 1949 campaign. The NCAA banner was won handily over Oklahoma A&M with Groza collecting more than half the points, but unheralded Loyola pulled off a huge upset that ruined NIT plans. Rupp's starting five were so good it was a wonder that they were ever beaten in a clutch game. It would later turn out, of course, that they had only been beaten—when they were—largely by their own mischievous hand.

What Rupp and Kentucky failed to accomplish in the postseason of 1949 was surprisingly done only a year later by Nat Holman and his CCNY team. The Beavers' double victory in the NIT and NCAA was indeed shocking in light of the team's rather lackluster performances during late stages of the campaign. The tourney victory streak came on the heels of a very average late-season finish in which the Beavers posted three surprise losses to upstate opponents and some less-than-spectacular victories over mediocre city rivals. Given renewed life with a pair of postseason bids (there was no other New York team that merited consideration), CCNY would ironically beat the same team in the finals of both tournaments. Bradley was defeated first in the NIT, 69–61 (with Dambrot, Ed Warner, and Ed Roman sharing the scoring burden), and then again in the NCAA, 71–68 (on a last-minute feed from Dambrot to top reserve Norm Mager). Bradley, under coach Forddy Anderson, stood atop the year's AP poll despite its double loss and seemingly had the finest club of the era next to Kentucky and CCNY. Gene Melchiorre (5'8" guard and budding 1951 All-American) and Paul Unruh (6'4" forward and sensational 1950 All-American) were legitimate stars and also a potent offensive tandem averaging nearly 25 per game between them. It would soon turn out that these three glamour teams—Rupp's, Holman's, and Anderson's—were in reality, however, the three most infamous combos in all of college basketball history.

College basketball's world suddenly unraveled during the 1950–51 season just as major-league baseball's bubble had been rudely burst in 1920 in the wake of the ugly Black Sox World Series affair. Earlier hints of scandal had, as mentioned, long been ignored. But the suspicion of new wrongdoing, which focused on seven colleges (CCNY, LIU, NYU, Manhattan, Kentucky, Bradley, Toledo) and implicated 32 players, burst the game wide open in late-season 1951. Soon there was a nationwide witch-hunt under way, and eventually charges that as many as 86 games had been fixed in 23 cities and 17 states between 1947 and 1950, with scores being manipulated to assure big payoffs for professional gamblers who had rigged the results.

Even Kentucky and the sanctimonious Rupp were caught in the tangled web despite the Baron's confident pronouncement that, "They couldn't touch our boys with a 10-foot pole." As one wag would soon put it, someone had obviously found an 11-foot pole. Rupp himself would surprisingly escape largely unscathed despite a notorious whipping in the New York press and in the courtroom where Judge Saul Streit concluded that Kentucky athletics was "the acme of commercialism and overemphasis" and that coach Rupp "must share the full responsibility" for the plight of former players now facing ruined careers as a result of their foolhardy and illegal actions. Careers of budding stars such as Beard, Groza, Bradley's Melchiorre, and LIU's Sherman White were entirely ruined by lifetime bans from the professional ranks. The NBA, by acting quickly against the college offenders and also dumping Columbia's Jack Molinas from the Fort Wayne roster (where as a promising rookie in 1953 he admitted wagering on his own team's games), came out smelling like a fresh rose and suddenly offered a squeaky-clean alternative to the legions of disenchanted college roundball fans.

The biggest losers were thus the participants in college basketball itself and especially those filling the venues in New York City. What Ned Irish had unleashed in the early '30s, the point-shaving scandals had nearly killed off in the early 1950s. The NCAA quickly moved its tournament onto the road, not to return to the scene of the crime for more than four decades. And the NIT also began its downward slide (contributed to in no small part by a ruling in the mid-'50s that any conference winners had to attend the NCAA playoffs), which in another dozen years would make it largely a laughingstock rival to the NCAA postseason sideshow.

Just as baseball is far too good a game to be ruined even by scandal (viz., the 1919 Black Sox) or self-aggrandizement (viz., the 1994 players' strike), so too was college basketball (especially during the giddy optimistic postwar "boom" era) an addictive spectacle that could not easily be killed off with a single scandal or even with numerous scandals. And just as an unprecedented explosion of slugging offense and irrepressible personality in the gigantic form of Babe Ruth wrenched baseball from its 1920 doldrums, so too did brilliant displays of outlandish offense and bright new stars quickly reinvigorate the college cage game.

It was remarkable—even Bunyanesque—individual scoring displays that first fired the public imagination. On his way to the first 40-plus season's average ever posted, Furman's Frank Selvy logged a seemingly incredible 100 points in a single outing versus Newberry College, shattering the existing record of 73 posted by Temple's Bill "The Owl Without a Vowel" Mlkvy three seasons earlier. (Another Philadelphia gunner, Villanova's Paul Arizin, canned 85 in a 1950 contest with the Philadelphia Air Materials Center, neither a four-year college nor a degree-issuing institution.) The 6'3" guard with a trunkload of unguardable shots had also crossed the 50-point plateau on four other occasions earlier in the campaign, broke the existing one-year marks for average (41.7) and total points (1,209), and ended his senior season with a new career points mark (2,538 points, 32.5 points per game) to add a series of explanation points to his headline-grabbing offensive displays. But Selvy's splash on the sports pages was hardly grander than that of a gangly 6'9" folk hero in southeastern Ohio who, one season earlier, drilled 116 against Ashland Junior College and followed with 113 against Michigan's Hillsdale College only 11 days before Selvy's explosion. Clarence "Bevo" Francis averaged 50.1 as a freshman and an equally mind-stretching 46.5 as a sophomore before leaving school to tour with a pro outfit that played nightly against the Harlem Globetrotters. But since most of his 1953 games were played against non-four-year schools, most of his headline performances were expunged from the record books by high-minded NCAA officials.

Roundball resurrection thus began with the remarkable scoring outbursts of Selvy at Furman and Francis at tiny Rio Grande College in Ohio. It was also soon solidified with the considerable romance surrounding four remarkable new black

Transcendental Graphics

Clarence "Bevo" Francis of Rio Grande College became an instant folk hero in 1953–54 when his awesome scoring displays impacted a scandal-plagued college basketball world much like the 1920s-era home run displays of baseball's Babe Ruth.

stars—the game's first of what would soon become a reigning prototype—Bill Russell at San Francisco, Wilt Chamberlain of Kansas, Elgin Baylor of Seattle, and Oscar Robertson with Cincinnati. Russell paced the first-ever undefeated NCAA tournament champions and anchored a team that set lofty new landmarks for uninterrupted winning. Chamberlain never completely fulfilled his awesome potential by delivering an expected national championship for the Jayhawks, or by producing the assumed deluge of new record-book entries, yet Wilt was nonetheless the biggest sports-page story of the two years immediately following USF's Bill Russell. While Russell provided the defensive paragon the sport had so far lacked (and was not yet quite certain how to accommodate), Wilt promised (even if he didn't completely deliver in college arenas) the unparalleled offensive force fans (and coaches) had always craved. Baylor, for his part, invented hang-time moves and balletlike sorties to the basket two decades before Julius Erving. And Oscar Robertson was simply the greatest all-around offensive intimidator the sport had (or still has) ever witnessed. To-gether they sent college recruiters everywhere looking in a new direction—to the inner-city ghetto playgrounds—for new hordes of undiscovered talent.

If college play had been nearly sabotaged by gambling scandals in New York City in the early '50s, it nonetheless continued to thrive unfettered down the road in Philadelphia. Great rivalries had developed among that city's schools (La Salle, Penn, St. Joseph's, Temple, Villanova) in the '30s and '40s just as they had in New York (NYU, CCNY, LIU, Manhattan, Fordham). The Philadelphia Palestra (official home to Penn, but site for most of the city's frontline college action) had been the near-equivalent of the Garden since its 1927 opening and was arguably a more inti-mate basketball environment and the "most storied gym" in the country. And now in the late '40s and early '50s there were also great teams with incomparable stars. First came the remarkable scoring feats of Paul Arizin at Villanova (national scoring leader in 1950 and owner of one of the most uncanny early jump-shooting styles) and Bill Mlkvy at Temple (1951 scoring champ and rebounding runner-up, and the game's biggest point-maker before Frank Selvy). There was the all-around play of Ernie Beck (the first NCAA rebounding champion when "official" statistics debuted in 1951). There were budding coaching legends to boot in Penn's Howie Dallmar (1949–1954), Temple's Harry Litwack (1953–1973), Villanova's Al Severance (1937–1961), and La Salle's Ken Loeffler (1950–1955). And last and best of all, by the mid-'50s there was also the incomparable Tom Gola at tiny La Salle College, perhaps the most phenomenal all-around talent ever to play the college game.

For one isolated year Temple may have possessed the best backcourt tandem ever seen in the college ranks. It was the one that featured diminutive Guy Rodgers and tiny sensation Hal Lear, one a marvelous ball handler and the other an explosive big-game scorer. Lear's scoring feats were indeed one of the briefest yet most memorable chapters in Philadelphia cage history. He had been the Owls' leading scorer (24.0) throughout his senior season, with Rodgers (18.5) a shade behind. Yet his greatest scoring feats would all be bunched tightly together at the very end of his collegiate career, and thus his national fame would rest on his single unaccountable explosion during five NCAA tourney games. That incredible stretch would find Lear first erupting for 40 points (61.5 percent of the total Temple offense) during a 65–59 East Regional semifinal victory over Connecticut (a game in which Temple's Fred Cohen would also establish a postseason mark by corralling 34 rebounds). Across five tournament games Lear would log 160 points, in the process smashing a previous tourney record of 141 owned by Clyde Lovellette of Kansas. And in the 90–81 Temple consolation game victory over SMU, Lear would grab another postseason mark when he logged a sensational 48-point effort, enough to obliterate the 45-point record of Washington's Bob Houbregs set back in 1953.

For his remarkable efforts Hal Lear would walk off with the tournament MVP trophy after clearly overshadowing outstanding Final Four players such as Bill Russell of San Francisco and SMU's outstanding junior center, Jim Krebs. Most amazing of all, however, was the fact that the Temple sharpshooter's five-game NCAA scoring average (32.0) was a full 25 percent higher than his season-long mark. Few players have ever stepped up quite as big under the pressures of March Madness competition as did Temple's Hal Lear during the memorable postseason of 1956.

But the biggest Philadelphia-area star was the one toiling with Herculean efforts for tiny La Salle. Gola would write one of the most amazing chapters of college basketball history, carrying an unknown Jesuit school to not one but three national championship games (1952 NIT, 1954 and 1955 NCAAs) without benefit of anything that even resembled a supporting cast. His career is indeed a storybook tale from the very outset, beginning with his decision to reject scholarships from North Carolina State and three dozen other big-name institutions to play on the same campus and in the same gym where he had performed as a schoolboy for La Salle High School (and where he was a high school All-American and recorded another 2,222 career points). And his imposing statistics remain largely unchallenged almost a half-century later. Gola is still the all-time leading rebounder with 2,201; another four-year varsity player, Joe Holup of George Washington (1953–56), remains the only other collegian to amass 2,000. And no player to date has yet combined more points and rebounds (2,462 and 2,201 for a total of 4,663), though four decades have passed and names like Chamberlain, Robertson, Maravich, Ewing, Jordan, Rick Barry, David Robertson, and Shaquille O'Neal have repeatedly assaulted the NCAA hardwoods and record books.

For all the number stacking, Gola was, above all else, an unrivaled winner. He was a player who literally could do it all at the college level, and better than

© La Salle University

La Salle star Tom Gola still holds the career record for combined points scored and rebounds gathered.

anyone else, at least until Oscar Robertson arrived in Cincinnati at the end of the same decade. First Gola led La Salle to the top of the NIT heap as a freshman whirlwind who averaged 17-plus in both scoring and rebounding. Surprising postseason victories over Eastern powers Seton Hall (with seven-footer Walter Dukes), St. John's (upset winner over both No. 1 Kentucky and No. 2 Illinois earlier in the season), and Duquesne (the AP's fourth-ranked team) put the Explorers into the title game opposite Dayton (also a top 20 outfit); Gola and teammate Norm Grekin (tourney co-MVPs) inspired a 75–64 La Salle victory. Next, Gola took the Ken Loeffler–coached Explorers all the way to a title victory in the NCAAs as a junior, a feat tarnished only by the fact that unbeaten and top-ranked Kentucky declined a bid when its own top stars (Frank Ramsey and Cliff Hagan) were ruled ineligible for postseason play. Gola's performance also made him the first (and still only) individual to be named both NCAA Final Four Most Outstanding Player and NIT Most Valuable Player.

Gola would likely have boasted two championships to crown his Cinderella story if it had not been for the equal rags-to-riches rise simultaneously unfolding at another tiny Catholic college on the opposite coast. The San Francisco University Dons had made some earlier noise with coach Pete Newell and star Don Lofgran during the 1949 NIT by edging Loyola-Chicago in the title-round shootout. Now coached by Phil Woolpert, the same Dons had found an unlikely new hero in gangly Bill Russell, a skinny 130-pounder at Oakland McClymonds High School, who emerged as a 6'9" 200-pounder by the night of his sophomore-season college debut. Russell, like Gola, was one of the most unpredictable recruits in college basketball annals. He had been an uncoordinated benchwarmer in high school and only an accidental find for San Francisco when Woolpert made an unenthusiastic scholarship offer. But once Woolpert (and assistant Ron Guidice, who painstakingly developed Russell's close-range hook shot) learned how to exploit

College Basketball's Postseason Team National Champions

Year	NCAA Championship	NIT Championship (New York)
1938	None	Temple 60, Colorado 36
1939	Oregon (Howard Hobson) 46, Ohio State 33	LIU 44, Loyola-Chicago 32
1940	Indiana (Branch McCracken) 60, Kansas 42	Colorado 51, Duquesne 40
1941	Wisconsin (Harold Foster) 39, Wash. State 34	LIU 56, Ohio University 42
1942	Stanford (Everett Dean) 53, Dartmouth 38	W. Virginia 47, Western Kentucky 45
1943	Wyoming (Everett Shelton) 46, Georgetown 43	St. John's 48, Toledo 27
1944	Utah (Vadal Peterson) 42, Dartmouth 40 (OT)	St. John's 47, DePaul 39
1945	Oklahoma A&M (Henry Iba) 49, NYU 45	DePaul 71, Bowling Green 54
1946	Oklahoma A&M (Henry Iba) 43, N. Carolina 40	Kentucky 46, Rhode Island State 45
1947	Holy Cross (Alvin Julian) 58, Oklahoma 47	Utah 49, Kentucky 45
1948	Kentucky (Adolph Rupp) 58, Baylor 42	St. Louis University 65, NYU 52
1949	Kentucky (Adolph Rupp) 46, Oklahoma A&M 36	San Francisco 48, Loyola-Chicago 47
1950	CCNY (Nat Holman) 71, Bradley 68	CCNY 69, Bradley 61
1951	Kentucky (Adolph Rupp) 68, Kansas State 58	Brigham Young 62, Dayton 43
1952	Kansas (Phog Allen) 80, St. John's 63	La Salle 75, Dayton 64
1953	Indiana (Branch McCracken) 69, Kansas 68	Seton Hall 58, St. John's 46
1954	La Salle (Ken Loeffler) 92, Bradley 76	Holy Cross 71, Duquesne 62
1955	San Francisco (Phil Woolpert) 77, La Salle 63	Duquesne 70, Dayton 58
1956	San Francisco (Phil Woolpert), 83, Iowa 71	Louisville 93, Dayton 80
1957	N. Carolina (Frank McGuire) 54, Kansas 53 (3OT)	Bradley 84, Memphis State 83
1958	Kentucky (Adolph Rupp) 84, Seattle 72	Xavier-Ohio 78, Dayton 74
1959	California (Pete Newell) 71, West Virginia 70	St. John's 76, Bradley 71 (OT)
1960	Ohio State (Fred Taylor) 75, California 55	Bradley 88, Providence 72
1961	Cincinnati (Ed Jucker) 70, Ohio State 65 (OT)	Providence 62, St. Louis University 59
1962	Cincinnati (Ed Jucker) 71, Ohio State 59	Dayton 73, St. John's 67
1963	Loyola-Chi. (George Ireland) 60, Cincinnati 58 (OT)	Providence 81, Canisius 66
1964	UCLA (John Wooden) 98, Duke 83	Bradley 86, New Mexico 54
1965	UCLA (John Wooden) 91, Michigan 80	St. John's 55, Villanova 51
1966	Texas Western (Don Haskins) 72, Kentucky 65	Brigham Young University 97, NYU 84
1967	UCLA (John Wooden) 79, Dayton 64	Southern Illinois 71, Marquette 56
1968	UCLA (John Wooden) 78, North Carolina 55	Dayton 61, Kansas 48
1969	UCLA (John Wooden) 92, Purdue 72	Temple 89, Boston College 76
1970	UCLA (John Wooden) 80, Jacksonville 69	Marquette 65, St. John's 53
1971	UCLA (John Wooden) 68, Villanova 62	North Carolina 84, Georgia Tech 66
1972	UCLA (John Wooden) 81, Florida State 76	Maryland 100, Niagara 69
1973	UCLA (John Wooden) 87, Memphis State 56	Virginia Tech 92, Notre Dame 91
1974	N. Carolina State (Norm Sloan) 76, Marquette 64	Purdue 87, Utah 81
1975	UCLA (John Wooden) 92, Kentucky 85	Princeton 80, Providence 69
1976	Indiana (Bobby Knight) 86, Michigan 68	Kentucky 81, UNC-Charlotte 76
1977	Marquette (Al McGuire) 67, North Carolina 59	St. Bonaventure 94, Houston 91
1978	Kentucky (Joe Hall) 94, Duke 88	Texas 101, North Carolina State 93
1979	Mich. State (Jud Heathcote) 75, Indiana St. 64	Indiana 53, Purdue 52
1980	Louisville (Denny Crum) 59, UCLA 54	Virginia 58, Minnesota 55
1981	Indiana (Bobby Knight) 63, North Carolina 50	Tulsa 86, Syracuse 84 (OT)
1982	North Carolina (Dean Smith) 63, Georgetown 62	Bradley 67, Purdue 58
1983	N. Carolina State (Jim Valvano) 54, Houston 52	Fresno State 69, DePaul 60
1984	Georgetown (John Thompson) 84, Houston 75	Michigan 83, Notre Dame 63
1985	Villanova (Rollie Massimino) 66, Georgetown 64	UCLA 65, Indiana 62
1986	Louisville (Denny Crum) 72, Duke 69	Ohio State 73, Wyoming 63
1987	Indiana (Bobby Knight) 74, Syracuse 73	Southern Mississippi 84, La Salle 80
1988	Kansas (Larry Brown) 83, Oklahoma 79	Connecticut 72, Ohio State 67
1989	Michigan (Steve Fisher) 80, Seton Hall 79 (OT)	St. John's 73, St. Louis University 65
1990	UNLV (Jerry Tarkanian) 103, Duke 73	Vanderbilt 74, St. Louis University 72
1991	Duke (Mike Krzyzewski) 72, Kansas 65	Stanford 78, Oklahoma 72
1992	Duke (Mike Krzyzewski) 71, Michigan 51	Virginia 81, Notre Dame 76
1993	North Carolina (Dean Smith) 77, Michigan 71	Minnesota 62, Georgetown 61
1994	Arkansas (Nolan Richardson) 76, Duke 72	Villanova 80, Vanderbilt 73
1995	UCLA (Jim Harrick) 89, Arkansas 78	Virginia Tech 65, Marquette 64 (OT)
1996	Kentucky (Rick Pitino) 76, Syracuse 67	Nebraska 60, St. Joseph's 56
1997	Arizona (Lute Olson) 84, Kentucky 79 (OT)	Michigan 82, Florida State 73
1998	Kentucky (Tubby Smith) 79, Utah 69	Minnesota 79, Penn State 66

Bill Russell of San Francisco demonstrates his inside dominance as teammate Carl Boldt (19) and La Salle's Bob Maples (14) watch during the 1955 NCAA championship game.

Transcendental Graphics

Russell's unorthodox shot-blocking defensive talents, USF had the makings of a truly invincible team.

Behind the dexterous Russell USF unleashed a remarkable winning skein (26 straight) in 1954–55, which would culminate with a showdown in Kansas City against Gola. The battle of imposing titans would surprisingly hinge not so much on Russell's unparalleled shot-stopping or Gola's unrivaled shot-making, but rather on a remarkable performance by Russell's teammate (and future fellow Boston Celtics star), K. C. Jones. Gola (with only 16 points) was neutralized in the championship game by Jones and his harassing defense, and USF walked off with a 77–63 victory and a national banner of its own. Russell and USF would return for a second championship party and extend their consecutive-games winning streak to 55 in the process, but they did so in the end without K. C. Jones. Jones had used up his college eligibility by the time the second postseason invitation rolled around. But it hardly made any difference to Woolpert's talent-rich team; Russell was still there, and even Russell by himself could be quite enough. This time the final victim would be Iowa from the Big Ten Conference. This was the Bucky O'Connor–coached Iowa outfit that provided college hoops with its second "Fab Five" squad, following Rupp's Kentucky group by a half dozen seasons and preceding Michigan's version by nearly four decades. But this Iowa five featuring a balanced scoring attack of Bill Logan, Carl Cain, Bill Seaberg, Bill Schoof, and Sharm Scheuerman was not quite as fabulous in the end as the single towering USF star who plugged up the foul lanes, shut off the enemy basket, and controlled just about every college game he played in with his one-man-gang shot-rejecting defensive tactics.

The early '50s witnessed an off-court event that would prove in later years to have lasting significance. The venerable Southern Conference (an unwieldy circuit which had some years contained as many as two dozen teams) broke apart and was replaced by the upstart Atlantic Coast Conference in time for the 1954 season. The ACC would immediately transform itself into a prime fixture of the college basketball wars. Several decades down the road the Carolina-Maryland-Virginia–based confederation could even stake legitimate claim as the best college hoops circuit around, and by almost any available standard for measurement. The conference, which didn't earn its first Final Four entrant until 1957 (with undefeated champion North Carolina), today outdistances the entire NCAA tournament field with most conference victories, best conference-winning percentage, and most NCAA title-game appearances.

While Russell had brought unprecedented defense to the game, another trio of black stars would soon upgrade offensive performance. Heading the list was the oversized Chamberlain, who came to Kansas as the final act of Phog Allen's reign, and also amid loud rumors of impropriety. Chamberlain was widely suspected of being subsidized to play even when he was a schoolboy at Philadelphia's Overbrook High. Allen, for his part, considered Wilt his greatest recruiting coup, even though he had long railed against "goons" taking over the sport. He had, admittedly, finally won a national title early in the decade with 6'9" Clyde Lovellette carrying the load. Lovellette had carved his own piece of history as the only national scoring leader to win an NCAA team championship as the result of his offensive prowess. Now Allen was forced to retire even before Wilt could suit up with the varsity, but his replacement (and former player) Dick Harp would—thanks to Phog—be inheriting a true big man for all ages, one who promised even more firepower than Lovellette.

Chamberlain's career never seemed to reach cruising altitude, especially after Allen's boasts that his arrival meant guaranteed championships for the loaded Jayhawks. Two Kansas seasons were something of a foreshadowing of future disappointments based largely on overzealous expectations that would also haunt "The Big Dipper" for a decade and a half at the professional level. Chamberlain was unparalleled among giants for strength, coordination, and speed; he was also triple-teamed with exotic defensive schemes and abused with roughhouse tactics from his first to last games in Lawrence. Yet he still scored (he was fourth in the

Wilt Chamberlain came to the University of Kansas in 1956 carrying the most impossible set of expectations ever attached to a raw recruit.

Transcendental Graphics

nation as a sophomore and third behind Robertson and Baylor as a junior) and still transformed his team into a regular winner (24–3 in 1957 and 18–5 in 1958). And he also hoisted his team—scoring 40 percent of the Kansas points—into the most remarkable NCAA title game ever.

Chamberlain aside, the big story throughout much of the 1956–57 season would involve the first truly notable team from the new ACC Tobacco Road lineup, one coached by veteran mentor Frank McGuire. The upstart league had opened its doors in 1954 with memorable scoring stars like Dickie Hemric at Wake Forest and Buzz Wilkinson at Virginia. Now it could boast a yearlong unbeaten club that seemed ready to duplicate USF's feat of running through an entire regular and postseason schedule unblemished. But waiting in the wings, of course, was Chamberlain and upset-minded Kansas. The expected year-end title matchup featuring 31–0 North

At 5'7", North Carolina backcourt ace Tommy Kearns was a most surprising selection to jump center against Wilt Chamberlain in the 1957 triple-overtime NCAA championship game.

© University of North Carolina

Carolina versus Chamberlain-led Kansas and stretching for three overtimes may well have been the single greatest college game ever staged. From the opening tap it was a supreme strategic battle that began with a moment of unexpected humor and ended with a handful of most surprising heroes.

Comic relief was provided in the opening seconds when 5'7" Tommy Kearns faced Wilt for the opening tip (one of the masterful psychological weapons McGuire employed during his battle with Goliath). But as the game unfolded, there was little respite from the mounting tension; the teams pounded each other into near exhaustion, Carolina star Lennie Rosenbluth fouled out before the end of regulation, and a pressure-packed foul shot by Kearns sent the game into its first extra session. Finally the tide turned slowly in Carolina's direction during a third overtime session with center Joe Quigg ultimately collecting the game-winning free throws. McGuire's Tar Heels had survived two straight triple-overtime games in the Final Four to win the title, a most improbable occurrence and one likely never to be repeated. In the end the 1957 matchup had also been a game that seemed to capsulize Chamberlain's all-too-brief collegiate career. Wilt was a touring force as the game's leading scorer (23) and rebounder (14), yet was not superior to a better-balanced team and the swarming defenses it stacked against him. The plight only worsened in 1958 with the Jayhawks slipping out of the Big 8 Conference top slot and sitting home during postseason play. And after another season of constant on-court harassment, Chamberlain would decide that college basketball wasn't much fun and would opt to play instead with the Globetrotters until he was eligible to take his act over to the NBA.

Wilt was soon gone but Seattle University's Elgin Baylor was now also on the scene. Baylor's college career was also an abbreviated one, consisting of only two seasons played in the national limelight after transferring to the larger West Coast school following one season with NAIA College of Idaho. But his impact was every bit as huge as Chamberlain's, both as a team leader and as a fixture among the nation's top handful of scorers (third as a sophomore and second behind Oscar a season later). Baylor also would lose a disappointing bid for a championship, when his own solo act, like Wilt's, was not quite enough to overcome five talented opponents. Seattle surprised the nation behind Baylor's 32.5 season-long average in 1958 and rode a series of upsets over San Francisco, California, and Kansas State into an NCAA showdown match with Rupp's final championship team at Kentucky. Plagued by foul trouble, an injured rib cage, and a swarming Wildcats defense, Baylor still mustered 25 points and 19 rebounds. But it was not quite sufficient to neutralize Kentucky's overall superior team strength.

Postseason disappointments for Chamberlain and Baylor seem less biting when compared with those suffered by the fourth black superstar of the '50s, Oscar Robertson. At least Kansas and Seattle tasted the NCAA title round. Robertson arrived with the Bearcats as the most complete first-year player ever and would soon be the most complete second- and third-year specimen as well. Oscar was first to top the nation in scoring as a sophomore and first to string together three scoring titles, as well as first to garner three Player of the Year trophies. He was an unstoppable force one-on-one, he scored more points than anyone ever had (2,973), posted the highest average ever (33.8), and pocketed 14 University Division individual records before graduation. But the Big O's headline presence actually detracted from a truly balanced Cincinnati team, or one that was designed to get over the final hurdle and win a coveted NCAA crown. With Robertson constantly drawing the ball and thus also all the defensive attention, the Cincinnati ball club twice visited the Final Four and for three winters posted remarkable season-long winning proficiency. The Bearcats' ledger for the period was 79–9; they never lost a home game in those three seasons. But the George Smith–coached Missouri Valley Conference champions could never climb all the way into a national title game. The primary reason was a single University of California squad coached by Pete Newell that twice blocked the entrance to college basketball's Valhalla with its exceptional defensive strategies. Against the Golden Bears in back-to-back national semifinals, Robertson was twice held to only slightly more than half his average (18 and 19), and both times the Bearcats were edged by less than double digits.

There were two further postseason frustrations for Oscar and the Cincinnati faithful. One was the fact that Oscar's lone rival as the nation's best player, Jerry West at West Virginia, did manage to climb into the 1959 national championship game while Robertson was being left on the sidelines as bridesmaid. And a second, more painful still, was that upstate rival Ohio State with Jerry Lucas and John Havlicek also reached the season's spotlight game in the very senior season that should have been Oscar's own final showcase. West would also taste bitter disappointment in his own personal quest for a team title when the same Newell-coached Golden Bears edged his Mountaineers by a single point despite Jerry's own 28 points, 11 rebounds, and Final Four outstanding player honors. Lucas and Havlicek

Fabulous Oscar "The Big O" Robertson of Cincinnati became the first sophomore ever to win a national scoring title and be named National Player of the Year. Robertson was also the first three-time owner of both prestigious distinctions.

Transcendental Graphics

were more charmed and would win it all as sophomores before themselves bombing during Final Four rematches as both juniors and seniors.

But if Oscar left the Bearcats program personally frustrated, Cincinnati fans would soon have the final and loudest laugh. It was without Oscar that the Bearcats ironically reached their several zenith seasons. Before the next recruiting class was done, the half dozen seasons between 1958 and 1963 would be marked forever as the Cincinnati era of college basketball history. Oscar's presence had meant great recruiting (Ron Bonham, Tom Thacker, Tony Yates, Larry Shingleton, George Wilson) even if it hadn't meant any additions (outside of three new Missouri Valley plaques) to the trophy case. A new coach—George Smith's assistant Ed Jucker—also brought a drastically revised style of play. And for the next three seasons, Cincinnati without Oscar was surprisingly lodged in the championship game. When Ohio State, still boasting Lucas, and Cincinnati, now without Robertson, faced off in the national title game in 1961, it marked the first time that a pair of in-state rivals had met for the ultimate national bragging rights. Now it would be Lucas and company who would experience the full frustration of losing in the year's most important game, and theirs would be a lingering frustration that would be played out over two seasons and not merely one.

Cincinnati had come on strong under its new coach and new stars after an expected early-season period of adjustment and an embarrassing loss to a Seton Hall team, which Oscar by himself had outscored three seasons earlier. By tournament time Jucker's Bearcats were on a sustained roll that had seen them win 20 straight after adopting the rookie coach's disciplined patterned offense. The defending champions on their side of the ledger had been quite lucky to get past an early-round match with Louisville, but this did not overshadow the fact that, with 27 straight wins and a No. 1 AP ranking, Ohio State seemed even better than a year earlier. Cincinnati benefited from the psychological edge drawn from a feeling it had been snubbed by a Buckeyes program that had long refused to play it; but the revamped Bearcats were no slouches, either, with a 26–3 ledger, the No. 2 national ranking, and a balanced attack keyed by 6'9" junior center Paul Hogue.

Once the two Ohio powers finally collided, the match was everything that pregame hype had built it up to be. For only the third time, the national championship tussle would need overtime to be decided, the defending champions staying alive in regulation play when future coaching legend Bob Knight hit his only basket of the game to pull the Buckeyes even at 61 just before the final buzzer. The Bearcats then pulled away in the opening minutes of an extra session and desperately held on as the clock finally expired. Despite a gambling offense and pressure defense, Cincinnati was nearly perfect all night, committing only three turnovers and three second-half fouls during the thrilling 70–65 upset of the defending champion Buckeyes.

If there was a question whether or not the 1961 title game had been a fluke, that question was answered unequivocally a year later. Again the in-state rivals survived the long season to lock horns in the title showdown that just about everyone expected. And again it was the Bearcats who emerged victorious, though this time around they enjoyed a significant assist from Lady Luck, since Lucas had been injured in the semifinal match with Wake Forest. It was a strained kneecap suffered while rebounding, and it rendered the Buckeyes' biggest weapon ineffective for the revenge game against the Bearcats. Lucas started against Cincinnati but was no longer mobile enough to keep pace with Paul Hogue in the battle to control the boards. Ohio State fell 71–59 in a one-sided affair nowhere near as tight as the score indicated. Lucas, Havlicek, and an assortment of teammates had wrapped up their three dream seasons at 78–6 and owned the distinction of being the first team ever to reach the NCAA title game three times without interruption. But such is the stigma placed on losing that they would more likely be remembered as first to fall twice running in the NCAA title game. Cincinnati (twice with Robertson and twice without) had earned its own niche as first to reach the national semifinals four straight times. One minidynasty had now fallen and another had seemingly been born.

Wooden of Westwood

Chamberlain, Baylor, Russell, and Robertson had underscored a new black presence rampant throughout the sport by the end of the '50s. But two landmark NCAA title games of the early and mid-'60s soon clinched the issue. The first came in 1963 in Louisville when Cincinnati closed in on a third straight championship against a Chicago-based and history-bound Loyola team making its very first NCAA postseason appearance after three earlier visits to the NIT. The second memorable shootout transpired only three seasons later in College Park,

Maryland, when one of Rupp's finest Kentucky title pretenders met an upstart team from Texas Western guided by a future coaching legend named Don Haskins.

Many longtime NCAA watchers still consider the 1963 NCAA title face-off between Cincinnati and Loyola College of Chicago to be the most gripping season-ending game ever played. The setting for the second straight year was Louisville's Freedom Hall, and the storybook matchup was created when Jucker's defending champions breezed by Texas, Colorado, and Oregon State, while George Ireland's unheralded Ramblers surprised Illinois in the Regionals, then shot down Duke, the nation's second-ranked team, despite an MVP performance by Art Heyman.

Loyola carried a racial banner throughout the 1962–63 season with four black starters—senior Jerry Harkness and juniors Les Hunter, Vic Rouse, and Ron Miller. In the Mideast Regional finals in East Lansing, they had faced and defeated an SEC championship team from Mississippi State that only one season earlier had boycotted postseason play rather than face integrated competition. Despite losing Paul Hogue to graduation, the Cincinnati Bearcats had dropped only one game all season and had given every indication of being primed to pull off the first three-peat in national titles. As a result, few championship matchups have ever carried a more memorable story line than the one now on tap. Loyola under coach George Ireland was a most unusual NCAA title team in still another respect. Ireland would disdain using any of his seldom-seen bench players and instead gut out the entire 45-minute overtime contest with his five tireless starters. The game itself was exciting enough to diminish all the hype surrounding Cincinnati's quest for three trophies and Loyola's mission for racial respect. For the second time in three seasons the Bearcats were forced into overtime when a last-second toss by Harkness left the issue unresolved until a final dramatic extra session.

The overtime was as gripping as any in a quarter-century of tournament annals. The teams traded two baskets apiece, which left the count at 58–58 with Loyola again playing for a final game-deciding shot. Another desperate attempt at a game-winner by Harkness was partially blocked by Ron Bonham, but the embattled Loyola forward retained control of the ball and then somehow found Les Hunter for a second desperation jumper from the far corner. The errant shot would carom directly to the 6'6" Vic Rouse stationed on the right side of the hoop and unaccountably left unguarded by the scrambling Bearcats defenders. Rouse simply laid the ball back into the hoop as time expired and the Cinderella miracle was complete. For the first and only time, a 100–1 long shot had walked off with a national title.

Three seasons later the contest for a national basketball championship was once again drawn along racial lines and embedded in the press with unavoidable racial overtones. This was, after all, the tenor of the times in mid-'60s America. Victory by Texas Western over the 1966 Kentucky team was, in the end, perhaps even more dramatic and certainly far more significant in its blatant symbolism. It was also one of the most surprising matchups in NCAA history. Junior college transfer Bobby Joe Hill turned the tide against Kentucky in the first half at ancient Cole Field House. The lightning-quick 5'10" playmaker worked his magic with consecutive steals off befuddled Wildcats guards Tommy Kron and Louie Dampier, and the resulting easy layups sent the Ruppmen into a tailspin from which they never fully recovered. Texas Western surprised the national television audience as it shot holes in the prevailing prejudices of the day (as well as in the Kentucky defense) while unveiling a disciplined team game down the stretch and holding on for a thrilling 72–65 upset victory.

The storied matchup between Texas Western and Kentucky at the height of the turbulent '60s was thus a landmark moment in college basketball history and American sports history as a whole. This was the first time that an all-black team (comprised of Hill, Nevil Shed, Dave Lattin, Orsten Artis, and Harry Flournoy) had started the NCAA tourney's prestigious final game. The significance of the moment was underscored by two intertwined factors: Kentucky's opposing five were all white, and the nation at the time was embroiled in a sea of long-latent racial tensions. And there was also fallout from the Texas Western victory that, in the long run, was most distasteful on an entirely different front. It would soon become public knowledge that while blazing important athletic and social trails in one direction, Haskins and his El Paso program had also been in the forefront of another not-so-admirable trend regarding black athletic recruitment. Haskins's players had landed a priceless basketball championship for their school (certainly the prestigious title meant, at the very least, expanded profits from alumni contributions and future game ticket sales), but they themselves would never receive either college degrees or any other obvious career-life compensation for their valiant and valuable efforts.

Between these two triumphs for basketball integration were sandwiched a pair of NCAA titles for a John Wooden–coached UCLA team that was poised to launch the biggest sports story of the entire decade. Wooden had made plenty of noise for a decade or more with his balanced teams out on the West Coast that had previously posted a couple of top 10 rankings and four Pacific-8 championships. And then in 1962 there was a near miss at a potential national title when only a buzzer-beating basket by Tom Thacker had allowed defending champion Cincinnati to escape against the Bruins during a Final Four semifinal thriller. The team that would finally put Wooden and the Bruins on the map was the one that found two missing elements just in time for a final season with star guard Walt Hazzard at the team's controls. This was a ball club that was relatively small in physical stature and lacked a single imposing physical presence. But it was also a perfectly drilled team and one that could win games in countless ways.

One of the newfound ingredients was a zone press installed by Wooden to dictate the pacing of games in his own team's favor. The second was a perfect sixth man named Kenny Washington. The 6'3" sophomore out of South Carolina filled in all over the court and was equally adaptable at the guard and forward slots; he was also a spark plug of the late-game pressing surges that often put his team over the top. The regular winning thus began in the winter of 1963–64, the junior campaign for Gail Goodrich and the senior season for Fred Slaughter and Jack Hirsch, as well as for Walt Hazzard. It included a 30–0 1964 campaign in which the NCAA title was captured against Duke on the strength of a combined 53-point outburst by Goodrich and Washington. And it peaked with an equally impressive 28–2 encore and a repeated championship victory against Michigan in which Goodrich closed his brilliant career with a 42-point explosion that buried the Wolverines and their All-American star Cazzie Russell.

Wooden's back-to-back triumphs in the middle '60s might have been land-mark enough, even if they had been the end-all and be-all of the UCLA domination and not merely a preface to the incredible run that was about to unfold. In the broader scope, Wooden's reign breaks neatly into two remarkable three-year teams anchored by two of the greatest post-position players in the sport's history. Around these twin peaks is neatly packaged the two-year preliminary reign with the 1964 and 1965 squads, a transition pair of seasons in the early '70s when even the loss of Alcindor was not enough to disarm the mighty Bruin juggernaut, and one final swan-song season with perhaps the Westwood Wizard's most unaccountably underrated team. Together this series of lofty peaks makes up the most remarkable chain of events in college cage history.

John Wooden had enjoyed a respectable college hoops career even before he reached his pinnacle in Los Angeles in the late '60s. The key to Wooden's decade-plus span of success was his clear-cut genius for flexibility. It was his ability, year after year, to adapt and integrate into his predefined system the diverse talents of those immensely productive players he had continually recruited. New superstar playing skills would demand redesigned offensive and defensive schemes; shifting social and political attitudes among his players would require equally large adjust-ments in tolerance. Methods to battle newly designed offensive and defensive schemes by the opposition were constantly called for, and so was a considerable raising of the coach's social and political consciousness. A pro-establishment men-tor, who at first could not tolerate even displays of shaggy facial hair among his troops, was eventually accommodating both Alcindor's darkest moods and Walton's left-wing activism.

When it comes to selecting the single greatest team in college history, few can disagree with the Alcindor-led Bruins. They lost but twice in three full seasons and, furthermore, avoided losing in an environment where every fan and pundit and second-guesser in the land had burdened them with an impossible and damning label of invincibility. And if the late '60s Bruins are the best-ever team, the choice for the greatest-ever impact player is equally clear-cut. Lew Alcindor has almost all the arguments stacked in his favor. Here was not only the most heavily recruited high school talent ever, at least outside of Wilt Chamberlain, but the one schoolboy star who entered the big-time college scene and continued to achieve every lofty goal placed in his path. All three varsity years he led his team all the way to the promised land, pacing an undefeated squad his first season and then losing only a single game in each of his final two campaigns. A player with awesome physical tools, who could undoubtedly have scored almost at will and racked up astounding numbers for points and rebounds, also turned out to be the perfect team player, willing to subordinate every personal achievement and personal record to the needs of team domination. No other college cage star—again outside of Chamberlain— was ever so universally expected never to lose even a single game. And none ever came so perfectly close to accomplishing exactly that unreasonable expectation.

This does not mean that the "Alcindor Years" in Westwood were nothing but a joyride for the coach who was blessed with so much talent. Wooden was never entirely comfortable with the team he had now successfully recruited. Alcindor was unquestionably destined to be the greatest player ever when he arrived in Westwood, and he was also likely to be the biggest challenge that this or any coach would ever face. For Alcindor carried along with his dunking and shot blocking and board sweeping his own set of monumental problems. His distinctive Afro hairstyle and his fiercely independent spirit themselves were a new and daunting challenge for a dogmatic coach who demanded absolute conformity from his tightly controlled team.

Yet if the pressure of simply playing not to lose was always there, it was a pressure that was handled admirably. Alcindor's final record against the best the nation had to offer would stand at a most incredible 88–2. His triple crown of NCAA titles and also of Final Four MVPs were the first in history. And the string of NCAA titles, which ran the UCLA count to five in six years, allowed Wooden to overtake Adolph Rupp as the most successful coach in NCAA tournament annals.

Through three seasons the Bruins built nearly unblemished records, romped in three title games, and featured a player who single-handedly owned the NCAA Final Four weekend in each of his three varsity seasons. A couple of key players were lost for Alcindor's senior season (Mike Warren graduated and Lucius Allen succumbed to academic difficulties), yet the impact was largely insignificant in the long run. There were also a couple of earthshaking upset losses along the way. One was to Houston in the middle of Alcindor's junior season and was largely the result of an eye injury suffered by "The Big A" a week earlier. The other during Alcindor's final regular-season game resulted from carelessness against league rival Southern California and was the first-ever loss for UCLA at Pauley Pavilion. There were also a number of dangerously close calls in early-season matches with pesky Purdue and archrival Notre Dame. But in the true pressure games—with the single exception of the Houston debacle in the Astrodome—the Bruins and Alcindor always won, whatever the challenge they faced.

If there was any single campaign during the dozen seasons that Wooden and his teams owned the college scene in which the Bruins by all rights should have been knocked off their lofty perch, it was the 1969–70 season, the very first in the wake of Alcindor. The big man was now gone and the coach faced not only the awesome task of filling this huge void, he would also now again have to readjust his complete game plan to fit his altered circumstances. But any momentary dip in the Bruins' talent level was falsely anticipated and perhaps only a product of wishful thinking almost everywhere outside of Westwood.

It was great guard play that always made the Wooden machine run smoothly, and this was demonstrated beyond any doubt over the next two seasons while Bill Walton waited patiently in the wings. When the '70s first unfolded and Alcindor took his towering act off to the NBA, Wooden may well have lost the true envy of every coaching staff in the land. But the coffers were hardly now empty, and the Wizard was, in fact, left with nothing short of one of his most balanced and talented squads ever. Jacksonville and Villanova were the championship game fodder during the next two seasons of Final Four return trips, while the latest Bruins stars were a frontcourt tandem of Sidney Wicks (1971 National Player of the Year) and Curtis Rowe, and a backcourt contingent comprised of Henry Bibby alongside John Vallely one season and Bibby teamed with Terry Scofield the other.

With Bill Walton moving up to the varsity in the fall of 1971, it looked for all the world as if the rest of the collegiate field was again staring at three years of chasing after an invincible Wooden team built upon the same model as the one featuring Alcindor. The Walton-led team was perhaps even stronger than the Alcindor squad. Walton's low-post play was complemented by a perfect high-post player in Keith Wilkes and also by a pair of capable team players and experienced outside shooters in Larry Farmer and Henry Bibby. Walton for his own part—as impossible as this might seem—appeared to have even more natural tools than Alcindor. Wooden himself was quoted upon occasion as saying precisely this much. If the new star recruit's political activism left the coach quietly grumbling, his game-time performances certainly never did. "If you were grading a player for every fundamental skill," observed the Wizard, "Walton would rank the highest of any center who ever played." Postseason play that year only seemed to add an exclamation point to Wooden's lofty assessment. While Florida State managed to hold the first edition of "The Walton Gang" to its smallest victory margin of the year (81–76), Hugh Durham's Seminoles could do little more than previous challengers to prevent a sixth straight UCLA national championship.

The highlight of the 1973 season, Walton's junior campaign, was the eventual overhauling of Bill Russell and company's untouched streak of 60 straight victories. It was one important remaining milestone that the Alcindor group had never been able to reach. It was perhaps indeed the only important milestone left that Wooden's Bruins didn't already own. But the record win streak, in the end, took a backseat to still another title and also to one single incredible solo Bill Walton performance, which must rank among the most memorable moments of postseason lore. Walton had saved his own grandest moment of the year for the biggest stage and largest prime-time national television audience. The flamboyant redhead sank 21 of 22 shots from the floor (mostly of the layup variety) and rang up 44 points in the one-sided 87–66 victory over Memphis State. It was a standard to which Walton would unfortunately never again quite measure up. And in its wake the UCLA ledger now stood at 7 straight championships, 9 out of the past 10. The Bruins had also hammered out another distinction for relentless winning, becoming the first major college team to post back-to-back perfect seasons in the modern era of postseason tournament play.

The peak had now been reached, and the denouement would now begin, gradual as it might prove to be. The story of the 1974 season would thus be largely the story of the ending of two incredible victory strings—the three-year unbeaten mark, which closed against Notre Dame in South Bend at 88 straight, and then finally the seven-year hold on the national title, which had already become perhaps the most untouchable record in all of American sports. But even before those record strings would come to an end there would also be some early-season fireworks. The first palm-wringing moment came in a clash with Maryland at Pauley Pavilion. Len Elmore battled Walton even on the boards from start to finish, yet the scoreboard read 65–64 in favor of the home team at the buzzer, when Maryland's crack guard John Lucas could not get off a potential game-winning shot as time expired. The narrow escape from the onslaught of one ACC powerhouse was followed by a ballyhooed challenge from another—N.C. State and skywalking David Thompson. The N.C. State game on a neutral floor in St. Louis proved far more one-sided than had been expected. Even though Walton rode the bench for better than half the game in serious foul trouble, new seven-foot understudy Ralph Drolinger filled in competently and State could never take full advantage in the 16-point UCLA victory.

The greatest thorn in the side of Wooden's second-greatest team was yet to be provided by State and the incomparable Thompson. By all rights the showdown between Thompson and company and Walton's Gang should have come about a full season earlier than it actually did. Yet when time for year-end championships had come around in March 1973, Thompson and his 27–0 Wolfpack were forced to sit helplessly on the sidelines and wait their turn for a meaningful crack at the seemingly invincible Bruins. The ACC front-runners had been placed on probation by the NCAA and were ineligible for tournament participation. A year later the Bruins would not so easily escape the wrath of the hungry Wolfpack, a team out to prove that, despite its December thrashing by the defending champions, it was nonetheless the best outfit in the land. In the end it can be said that the Walton Gang finally achieved something during the 1974 national semifinals that Wooden-coached teams had almost never done over the previous dozen or so years: They simply beat themselves. Of course, N.C. State and its star David Thompson seemed to own something of an emotional advantage going into the pressure-packed rematch with Wooden's upset-ripe defending champions. The game was played in State's backyard in Greensboro. But it was a series of overtime turnovers—so uncharacteristic for a Wooden-coached team—and clutch foul shots in the closing seconds by Thompson and Monte Towe that allowed N.C. State to nurse an 80–77 victory to the wire.

There was still a last brief gasp of life left in a remarkable Wooden program that had made such a habit of spawning championship-caliber teams. There would thus be one final hurrah for Wooden in the shadows of his second great team, and it would come one season later with a mad dash to a 10th NCAA championship, which featured a hair-raising semifinal overtime victory against Louisville and a draining shootout with Kentucky. Wooden had already proved he could win with well-balanced teams before the arrival of his two giants, Alcindor and Walton, and he would now prove it yet one final time. Sophomore Richard Washington now provided the heavy firepower with 54 points during two Final Four victories; but Marques Johnson, Dave Meyers, Pete Trgovich, Andre McCarter, and seven-footer Ralph Drolinger equalized the workload night in and night out throughout a 28–3 season.

In retrospect there are few useful yardsticks against which John Wooden's incredible dozen years at the top of the college basketball world can be fairly measured or even entirely grasped. His lead over all other challengers is so wide as to defy any such meaningful comparison. Not only had he taken his team to the Final Four in 12 of 14 seasons; not only had he at one point won 28 straight games in the single-elimination postseason Big Dance; not only did his record for the dozen years stand at 47 victories in 52 NCAA tournament outings. But in 10 trips to the national championship game he had come away with 10 championships. It had not been a dynasty run without its special trials and tribulations. Nonetheless, college basketball had never seen anything like it before. And more than likely it will never see anything quite like it again.

March Madness

The single interruptions to Wooden's dozen-year reign had been the Texas Western miracle of 1966 and the marvelous North Carolina State team that featured David Thompson. Thompson arguably stands alongside Robertson, Gola, Russell,

Maravich, Baylor, and Bill Bradley as the greatest college players of all time. College basketball's original skywalker was an avatar of human flight who simply had to be seen in person to be fully appreciated. A full decade before Michael Jordan recast the notion of superstar in the NBA, David Thompson seemed to be the first coming of Jordan at the collegiate level. Imagine the marvelous high-flying and slam-dunking MJ in a '90s Bulls uniform and you have a fairly accurate portrait of Thompson with the Wolfpack in 1974. Thompson was every bit as flashy, every bit as lethal (he averaged 27 points per game for three years), and every bit as important to his team's ability to win against all comers and against all odds—even eventually against Wooden's Bill Walton–led Bruins.

If Thompson was the showcase individual player of the '70s, Pete Maravich holds that distinction for the '60s. Maravich actually bridged the two decades by debuting in fall 1967 and graduating to the NBA in summer 1970. In between he dismantled just about every NCAA record for offensive performance. And he did so with a style that has never quite been matched in college play or even in the professional arenas. Even Jordan did not have quite the individual flair: Pistol Pete was more of a crowd-pleasing dribbler, showboat passer, and long-range bomber than MJ. And there was never anyone before or since who owned anything like the numbers Maravich posted. As the only gunner besides Oscar to pace the nation's scorers in all three of his varsity seasons, Pete established point-making records that will likely never be matched or even roughly approximated—3,667 career points, 1,381 in a season, more than 44 points per game for an entire career, 28 career games scoring more than 50, ten 50-point games in a single winter. He was perhaps the closest thing to a pure legend that college basketball has ever known. It would almost take a separate chapter in the NCAA record book to house all of Pistol Pete's milestones (he still holds 15 individual NCAA marks) by the time he was done drilling nets and burning opponents.

Maravich was more than the most prolific scorer ever, and his reputation was equally large as college basketball's supreme ballhandling sideshow. The single downside was that Pete usually played over his teammates' heads, bounced spectacular passes off their legs and shoulders, gambled and freelanced himself on defense, and soloed in search of big scoring nights rather than hard-earned team victories. It was a style that would eventually earn a seven-figure pro contract at the end of the line but contribute to few team victories along the way. LSU, with the sport's greatest showman, posted two .500 campaigns before finally going 22–10 in 1970 and enjoying a third-place NIT finish. Maravich never saw the inside of the NCAA postseason tournament.

The only individual rivals to Maravich in the '60s were perhaps Alcindor and Princeton's Bill Bradley. But one played on a team that was far too good as a unit ever to allow him quite his own individual due. And the other suffered an opposite fate of playing on a team too weak to vault him all the way to the game's summit. Alcindor was twice Player of the Year and thrice Final Four MVP, yet despite a 26-plus scoring average, the "Big A" never rewrote any individual entries in the NCAA record book; Bradley also garnered distinction as the nation's top performer (1965) and owned the third-highest career average (30.2) when he graduated, yet only once could he lift his Princeton Tigers higher than the NCAA regional semifinals. Bradley's unparalleled value was best indicated by the little-cited fact that only

High-scoring "Pistol Pete" Maravich of LSU was the talk of the basketball world at the end of the 1960s.

Transcendental Graphics

Maravich (48.2 percent) and Chamberlain (41 percent) logged a higher career percentage of his team's total points.

There were also small-college stars in the '60s and '70s who impacted mightily on the game from their backwater venues. Earl Monroe, for one, racked up incredible scoring totals at Division III Winston-Salem College in North Carolina. The future NBA "Pearl" in 1966–67 unleashed what remains unquestionably the greatest one-man single-season performance of collegiate history (with 1,329 points,

In his final college game, Princeton's Bill Bradley provided the greatest curtain-closer ever, a tournament-record 58 points against Wichita State in the NCAA tournament consolation game.

Transcendental Graphics

a 41.5 average, and almost unimaginable 60 percent field-goal accuracy). Rangy 6'8" Travis Grant at Kentucky State paced his team to three straight NAIA titles, hammered home 75 in a single game as a sophomore, and, over a four-year career (1969–72), built a 33.4 average and amassed 4,045 points (still Division II records after a full quarter-century). Niagara's Calvin Murphy was yet another small-school titan who turned heads and rewrote record books with his offensive wizardry. And Julius Erving at Massachusetts performed in the Yankee Conference shadows for two brief seasons while giving plenty of signals of the overall skills, if not of the full flashiness, of the pro star about to emerge. The junior Dr. J joined a unique circle of four forerunners (Walter Dukes, Bill Russell, Elgin Baylor, Paul Silas) with 20-plus career scoring and rebounding averages. But like Maravich, neither Monroe nor Erving played in the NCAA tourney and neither had a grand stage to strut the otherworldly skills that would soon explode upon the ABA-NBA scene.

Calvin Murphy was perhaps the most remarkable small man ever to play the game of college basketball. Murphy was every bit as phenomenal as Maravich, especially if one considers his diminutive physical stature. Here was the player everyone judged too small to play successfully in the big-time college game. Here was also a 5'9" relentless shooting machine who was as talented a pure scorer as anyone who ever rattled the rafters of a local college gym or lit up a local playground scene. Like Maravich, Murphy entertained fans with lightning-quick change-of-direction dribbles, uncanny blind passes, and an array of off-balance bombs from anywhere within sight of the basket. At the same time, he also devastated enemy defenses with bushels of points, including 68 against Syracuse during his junior season. He averaged 38.2 as a sophomore (second to Maravich) and 33.1 for his full career at Niagara University. In his later pro career with the Houston Rockets, the pint-sized hotshot would set new standards for free-throw shooting accuracy (95 percent for a single season and above 90 percent in five others) that long remained untouched by other marksmen. Murphy's lifetime 89.2 percent from the charity stripe in NBA action trails only the 89.3 percent of Rick Barry.

The tradition of Maravich and Murphy at the end of the '60s was carried on by a few additional peerless practitioners of one-on-one play in the first few seasons of the '70s. Austin Carr carved out a lasting legend at Notre Dame that would be highlighted by a 41.3 scoring average in seven NCAA tourney games between 1969 and 1971. Even more brilliant in postseason play than during the rest of his remarkable record-laced career, Carr still holds NCAA tournament scoring standards for career average, single-tournament average (52.7 in three games in 1970), and single-game points (61 versus Ohio University in 1970). And for one winter there was also Johnny Neumann at SEC also-ran Mississippi. A 6'6" guard-forward from Memphis, the tireless Ole Miss gunner would debut with a lofty 40.1 average to pace the country in scoring during the first campaign after Maravich's departure from LSU. Neumann would immediately forego the remainder of his college eligibility to ink a contract with the hometown ABA Memphis Pros. A singular spectacular sophomore season and a quick departure for a disappointing pro career (he averaged 14.9 in five ABA seasons and 5.6 in two NBA campaigns) would leave Johnny Neumann on a pedestal with Maravich himself as the only other career 40-point scorer in NCAA annals.

And coach Wooden also produced his own considerable stable of stars beyond Alcindor and Walton, led by names like Sidney Wicks, Curtis Rowe, Richard Washington, Henry Bibby, Keith Wilkes, and Marques Johnson. Wicks (21.8 points per game, 12.8 rebounds per game) shared National Player of the Year accolades with Notre Dame's Carr in 1971, the former picking up the U.S. Basketball Writers Association plaque while the latter garnered the AP, UPI, and Naismith trophies. And later in the decade a similar honor for Marques Johnson (who swept all the major awards in 1977) left Wooden with seven winners of that prestigious designation in the 11 seasons between 1967 and 1977.

Wooden's reign, if not his legend, finally ended with retirement in 1975, but the coach who followed the Wizard to the championship throne would soon be building some substantial legacies of his own. Bob Knight, of course, had himself played on an NCAA title winner with Fred Taylor's Ohio State Buckeyes 15 seasons earlier. He would thus join Dean Smith, Vic Bubas, Bones McKinney,

College Basketball's 15 All-Time Greatest Players

Tom Gola (La Salle, 1952–55, Center-Guard)—His career record total of 2,201 rebounds has never been matched, nor has his combined career points-rebounds total (4,663). He single-handedly led tiny La Salle College to back-to-back NCAA title games (1954, 1955) and was arguably the most versatile collegiate player of all time (splitting playing time between the center and guard positions).

Lew Alcindor (UCLA, 1967–69, Center)—He was the biggest impact player in college history on the most dominant three-year team ever (88–2, three NCAA titles). He was twice named National Player of the Year and to date he is the only three-time NCAA Tournament Final Four Most Outstanding Player. He was the most heavily recruited high school athlete ever (surpassing Wilt Chamberlain in this regard).

Bill Russell (USF, 1954–56, Center)—He was one of seven players to average 20 points and 20 rebounds for an entire career and one of only four to accomplish this feat over three full seasons. He anchored the first undefeated NCAA national champion (29–0 in 1956), and he is the only player to collect 50-plus rebounds in a single Final Four (1956). He also paced a then-record 60-game winning streak.

Oscar Robertson (Cincinnati, 1958–60, Forward)—He was the first-ever sophomore national scoring champion, the first player to lead the nation in scoring for three full seasons, and the first three-time NCAA National Player of the Year. With only sparse teammate support, Robertson took Cincinnati to back-to-back NCAA national semifinal games. He was the prototype for the all-around offensive intimidator and the pioneer of black playground "one-on-one" playing style.

Hank Luisetti (Stanford, 1936–38, Forward)—He pioneered one-handed shooting and, in the process, introduced a modern style of offensive play. Luisetti was the first national superstar and was twice the national scoring leader (1936 and 1937). He scored 50 points in a single game during an era when entire teams rarely matched that lofty point total.

Elgin Baylor (College of Idaho, Seattle, 1955, 1957–58, Center-Forward)—He was one of seven players to average 20 points and 20 rebounds for a career and the only member of that group with a career scoring average above 30 points per game. Baylor was the national rebounds leader while also averaging 29.7 points per game (1957). He was the 1958 NCAA Final Four Most Outstanding Player and the pioneer of "hang time" airborne moves and the prototype for the black freelancing playground style of play.

Bill Walton (UCLA, 1972–74, Center)—He was the second-biggest impact player in collegiate history (behind Alcindor) on the second-most dominant three-year team ever (86–4, two NCAA titles, three Final Four appearances). Walton paced a still-record 88 straight victories and also produced the most dominant NCAA championship game one-man performance on record. He was a three-time National Player of the Year (1972, 1973, 1974).

and Dick Harp on the short list of men who had both coached and performed in Final Four action. The self-styled "General" would also eventually boast impressive credentials as the only man among seven coaches to reach the Final Four at least five times to also put at least five teams into the NIT semifinal round. And his résumé was destined to be rounded out with yet another rare distinction, as one of three mentors (alongside Pete Newell and Dean Smith) to capture basketball's championship Triple Crown—the NCAA, NIT, and Summer Olympics. When coach Knight walked off with his first NCAA banner in 1976 he would do so with one of the most potent two-season teams ever assembled. A season earlier Indiana had run through its rugged schedule with 31 straight victories before a heartrending single-bucket loss to Kentucky in the regional finals had ended championship dreams. All-American Scott May had returned to the General's lineup in time for the Kentucky showdown—after missing several postseason

Pete Maravich (LSU, 1968–70, Guard)—Maravich established unapproachable scoring records with three seasons averaging more than 40 points per game and a record 3,667 career points. The three-time national scoring leader was also the 1970 NCAA National Player of the Year. He has been tabbed as one of the all-time greatest pure shooters, passers, ball handlers, and unbridled showmen.

Bill Bradley (Princeton, 1963–65, Forward)—Bill Bradley stands with Gola and perhaps also Baylor as the most-skilled all-around player. A National Player of the Year and NCAA Final Four Most Outstanding Player (1965), he is the career NCAA tournament record holder for highest free-throw percentage and also record holder for most individual points in an NCAA Final Four game (58 against Wichita State in the 1965 third-place consolation game).

Ralph Sampson (Virginia, 1980–83, Center)—A three-time NCAA National Player of the Year (1981, 1982, 1983), Ralph Sampson also was the NIT Final Four Most Outstanding Player as a freshman (1980). He paced Virginia to an overall 88–13 four-season record, three ACC titles, NIT, and NCAA Final Four appearances. He was the second-most heavily recruited high school star ever, after Lew Alcindor.

Jerry Lucas (Ohio State, 1960–62, Center)—Jerry Lucas was the leader of an OSU team that made three straight NCAA Championship Game appearances. He was twice tabbed National Player of the Year (1961, 1962), and he was a three-time national leader in field-goal percentage, two-time national pacesetter in rebounding (1961, 1962), and was twice named the Final Four Most Outstanding Player (1960, 1961).

Elvin Hayes (Houston, 1966–68, Center)—Elvin Hayes was named NCAA National Player of the Year in 1968 over Lew Alcindor. He had career averages above 30 in scoring (31.0 points per game) and near 20 in rebounding (17.2). He averaged 36.8 points per game as a senior but trailed Maravich and Calvin Murphy in the national scoring race. He played in the shadows of both Alcindor and Maravich and, nonetheless, still ranked as one of the most complete big men in college basketball history.

Bob Kurland (Oklahoma A&M, 1943–46, Center)—Bob Kurland, the Helms Foundation National Player of the Year in 1946, was the first athletically talented seven-footer in cage history and the first player to pace his team to repeat NCAA Tournament national titles. He was also the first-ever two-time NCAA Final Four Most Outstanding Player (1945, 1946) and the only player to score more than half of his team's points in NCAA Final Four action.

David Thompson (North Carolina State, 1973–75, Forward)—Acknowledged as perhaps the most acrobatic and most aesthetic player of all time, David Thompson was twice named NCAA National Player of the Year (1974, 1975) and also the NCAA Tournament Final Four Most Outstanding Player (1974). He paced N.C. State's historic 1974 Final Four victory that ended UCLA's record 38-game NCAA tournament victory streak and also stopped the Bruins' string of seven straight national titles.

Larry Bird (Indiana State, 1977–79, Forward)—An unmatchable offensive force who carried his undefeated no-name team to No. 1 national rankings and NCAA title game of 1979, Larry Bird was named NCAA National Player of the Year (1979) as a senior. He finished in the top three in the national scoring race in all three varsity seasons, twice as a near-miss runner-up.

games with a broken arm—but the top Hoosier star was clearly rusty from the layoff and contributed only two points.

But if Knight and his Hoosiers were sabotaged by this late-season injury in '75, they were never slowed by anything fate or top-flight rivals might muster one winter later. Facing one of the most challenging schedules of any eventual NCAA champion, the rock-solid lineup of May, Kent Benson, Quinn Buckner, Bobby Wilkerson, and Ted Abernethy ran roughshod over 32 straight opponents en route to their championship showdown with Big Ten neighbor Michigan. With two conference rivals meeting in the title round for the first time ever, Indiana nearly suffered another postseason disaster when point guard starter Wilkerson was knocked unconscious and out of play by a stray elbow during the game's opening moments. Sophomore reserve Jim Wisman filled in admirably to pilot Knight's offense and Indiana rolled to its undefeated season with an 86–68 romp. But for their bad break at the end of the 1975 season, Knight's Hoosiers might easily have captured a pair of titles and also a pair of unblemished seasons. And had they done so, Bob Knight might well have looked even more like a legitimate successor to the recently deposed Wizard of Westwood.

Knight would return to the championship circle twice more in the '80s. His 1981 team starring sophomore sensation Isiah Thomas captured an NCAA finale (against Dean Smith and North Carolina) played against the eerie backdrop of a failed presidential assassination. After a lengthy delay of the game's tip-off while an anxious nation awaited word on the condition of wounded President Ronald Reagan, NBC finally pushed ahead with the anticlimactic basketball game in which Thomas dominated the action with 23 points and Indiana dominated the scoreboard 63–50. Knight's 1987 squad with hotshot senior Steve Alford, prevailed on the floor of the Louisiana Superdome with one of the best-remembered displays of last-minute heroics. Unsung Keith Smart proved the ultimate hero with 12 of the Hoosiers' final 15 tallies against the Syracuse Orangemen and also hit the game-deciding jumper with five seconds left on the clock.

Indiana's fifth national championship in 1987 also hinged on a new rule, which was itself perhaps the most significant development of that entire season. A three-point field goal was for the first time awarded for all successful goals made from outside an arc measured at 19'9" from the center of the basket. Scoring marks around the country immediately underwent new onslaughts and Indiana was as successful as anyone with the newly legislated "trey" or "home run" shot, hitting more than half (50.8 percent) of its season's long-range attempts. By NCAA tournament time it would be this new offensive weapon, especially in the hands of Indiana's Steve Alford, that would already be playing a significant role in determining the new national champion.

Knight and his front-running Indiana teams, for all their championship successes, never enjoyed a monopoly with the sports-page headlines in the Hoosier state during the late '70s. The limelight always had to be shared with favorite son Larry Bird, one of college hoopdom's most charismatic figures and a player Knight had once recruited but lost before the first drills of fall practice. Bird first signed up with the Hoosiers on the eve of the illustrious 1975 season, but quickly decided he would fit in far better on some less imposing campus. When the French Lick sensation ultimately landed on the Indiana State campus in Terre Haute, then arrived seemingly overnight on the NCAA scene in 1977, he perfectly fit the image of a heartland-born and bred country ballplayer spawned in small-town rural Indiana.

By his junior year, Bird had embellished his own legend (32.8 points per game average as the nation's third-leading scorer) and also lifted Indiana State into national prominence (25–3, 16th in the UPI coaches poll) for the first time in school history. Red Auerbach was the first to jump on the bandwagon when he drafted Bird for the NBA Celtics at the end of his second (junior) season. Since he had already redshirted a year on the heels of his departure from Knight's program, the Sycamores star could indeed have packed it in as a junior for instant riches with the pros. But Bird smelled a national title, and his decision to play at the collegiate level one final season proved in the end a wise one. So, of course, did Auerbach's gamble in drafting a player who would not join his rebuilding NBA team for yet another full year.

When UCLA's Richard Washington joined Indiana's Scott May and Kent Benson in the 1976 NCAA semifinals (shown here), it would be the final time that more than half of the first-team consensus All-Americans would appear together during a Final Four showdown.

Transcendental Graphics

Bird enjoyed a stellar senior campaign (28.6 points per game) as the country's No. 2 scorer. His lofty scoring and all-around play were supplemented by such superb passing ability that he also averaged six assists per game. With Bird carrying almost the entire load, the Sycamores remained unbeaten throughout the regular season (also the number one team in both newspaper polls). There were plenty of skeptics, of course, who claimed that Bird provided little more than a one-man team, that the Missouri Valley ball club had benefited from a soft schedule, and that Indiana State would fold up in March when Bird inevitably faltered against top-notch defenses. A sometimes reluctant press seemed to have little choice, however, but to rank the unbeaten Sycamores atop the wire service polls throughout the entire 15-week season.

While Bird was the prototype farmyard ballplayer, his chief spotlight rival was the perfect prototype of the inner-city playground nonpareil. Earvin "Magic"

College basketball was turned in a bold new direction when Earvin "Magic" Johnson (with ball) of Michigan State and Larry Bird (33) of Indiana State faced off during the dramatic and much-hyped 1979 NCAA championship game.

Transcendental Graphics

Johnson headlined for Everett High in East Lansing, Michigan, then followed hometown friend Jay Vincent to the neighborhood campus at Michigan State. Freshmen were once again eligible for varsity play, and Johnson wasted little time emerging as a bright star during his first campaign in the Big Ten, scoring 17 a game and averaging nearly eight assists and an equal number of rebounds. As a sophomore he was even better as a floor leader, although the numbers he posted remained largely the same. But Magic played on a balanced MSU squad that also featured Greg Kelser as its agile 6'7" scoring forward and high school mate Jay Vincent as the rugged 6'8" post-position fixture.

Bird and Magic would meet face-to-face in a celebrated NCAA title showdown that contributed as much as anything to making college tournament play finally a prime-time "made-for-television" event. The showdown moment culminated a heady season for both of college basketball's newest superstars. But first-year ISU coach Bill Hodges did suffer a serious scare of major proportions when Bird broke the thumb on his nonshooting hand during the closing moments of the Missouri Valley Conference tourney. Even with a subpar Bird at season's end, ISU climbed some major hurdles during early NCAA action. A solid Oklahoma team was bested with ease when the handicapped Bird canned 29 points and claimed 15 rebounds despite his heavily bandaged left hand. Against fifth-ranked Arkansas and All-American Sidney Moncrief, Bird poured in 25 in the first 27 minutes of play and again led all scorers at game's end with 31. And versus DePaul in the national semifinal, Bird made all the key shots down the stretch and enjoyed another typical 16-for-19 shooting night.

But when it came to the championship tussle, Cinderella's chariot was about to turn into a full-fledged pumpkin. And Magic Johnson had much, if not everything, to do with that transformation. In the much-awaited matchup at Salt Lake City's Special Events Center, Johnson would once again rise to new heights while Bird would finally prove altogether human. MSU coach Jud Heathcote schemed a trapping defense that stymied Bird from the start. The critics, at long last, were now proved at least partially right about ISU's shortcomings once Bird himself was effectively contained. In the face of relentless MSU pressure the Sycamores star could make only seven of 21 shots from the floor. By contrast Magic benefited from stellar play by companion Kelser, and the two clicked on numerous fast-breaking outlet plays. Kelser bagged 19 (matching Bird), Johnson would tally 24 points and pull down seven rebounds, and MSU coasted 75–64. When the shouting finally ceased, it was Magic Johnson who walked off with both the tourney MVP trophy and the NCAA championship plaque.

While Larry Bird and Earvin Johnson were stealing the center-stage spotlight of collegiate play at the end of the '70s, there was another development vital to the game's future taking place behind the scenes and outside the limelight during much of the same decade. This was the quiet birth of a new jazzed-up women's college game, which gained momentum with adoption in 1969 of a five-player, full-court version played with a 30-second shot clock and paralleling men's racehorse action. Momentum in women's athletics had resulted directly from the women's liberation movement of the '60s, and a true turning point had arrived with the first national women's basketball championship tournament held in 1972 at West Chester, Pennsylvania, under auspices of the Association of Intercollegiate Athletics for Women (AIAW). Throughout the remainder of the decade there was an ongoing evolution of the women's style of play and a major corner was turned with the advent of scholarships in 1974. Momentum gained throughout the decade would crest with the first nominal enforcements of Title IX legislation (forcing sex equity in education) by the end of the '70s.

If the '70s witnessed the rebirth of the women's hoops sport, the '80s would record its full coming of age. It was a decade that first saw the ever-opportunistic NCAA enter the picture (in 1982) and acknowledge recent growth by taking over sponsorship of a second year-end women's tournament. (The AIAW tourney collapsed after a single season of head-to-head competition with the NCAA-sponsored event.) And it was also a decade that welcomed the first substantial contingent of noteworthy women players. Ann Meyers and Nancy Lieberman (later Lieberman-Cline) had closed out the '70s with their considerable brilliance. Meyers gained West Coast headlines as the first female with a UCLA basketball scholarship; Lieberman—the first "flash-and-dash" style women's star—posted impressive statistics (2,430 points, 18.1 points per game) at Old Dominion University, helped found an experimental women's pro league, became a pioneering spokeswoman for the sport, and penned a best-selling post-career autobiography entitled *Lady Magic*, which lent still further notice to the rapidly emerging women's game she herself enriched.

Lynette Woodard and Cheryl Miller—the game's first black female stars—would open up the '80s with more noticeably athletic play and a resulting slew of new scoring records. Woodard became the all-time point-maker (3,649 points) in her years at Kansas, then blazed new trails as the first female Harlem Globetrotter. USC's Miller, whose brother Reggie was also destined for NBA celebrity, remains, to date, the greatest women's player of all time. Her 3,405 high school career points and 3,018 college tallies would make her one of the most productive offensive weapons in all of cage history. And other super-talented women players also set milestones and attracted increasing audiences. Lusia Harris at Delta State played in an era before female All-Americans or national Player of the Year Awards existed yet carved a large niche as AIAW tourney MVP for three straight seasons. And Carol Blazejowski, as a 5'11" scoring machine at Montclair State, was perhaps the biggest pioneering star of them all. "The Blaze" still holds "unofficial" records for career scoring average (31.7) and season's scoring average (38.6), both set back in 1978 before the onset of NCAA-sanctioned record keeping.

The decade of the '80s on the men's side of the ledger would be most memorable primarily for four consecutive NCAA title games that each earned a special place in cage legend and lore. The '80s would, in fact, launch a two-decade span that might fairly be labeled as a gilded epoch of true competitive balance. Gone was the era of the dominating superstar such as Oscar Robertson or Elgin Baylor, Bill Russell or Tom Gola, Lew Alcindor or Larry Bird—the nonpareil scorer or defender who might single-handedly dominate a season or a league or even a postseason tournament. And it was in the postseason tournament that this balance was now annually most evident.

The 1981–82 season was, for much of the year, distinguished by the clarion arrival of a new powerhouse conference (The Big East, launched in 1980) and its contingent of powerhouse clubs led by Georgetown, Villanova, St. John's, and Syracuse. Georgetown had come roaring out of the Big East pack at the close of the campaign seemingly ready to charge through the 48-team NCAA field as the number one seed of the West Regional. But in the end, the season and the tournament would be stolen by another newcomer who was also about to make his dramatic debut. Georgetown and freshman star Patrick Ewing would face off in the finals with North Carolina and its own freshman standout Michael Jordan. MJ's clutch jumper decided the issue when the perfectly aimed missile found nothing but net with 15 seconds remaining. In a dramatic finish to the title contest Jordan had, for the very first time (but hardly the last), staked a claim on the nation's growing basketball fandom.

Such heroics for the Atlantic Coast Conference were not over with Jordan's amazing clutch shot. A single year later it would be the Tar Heels' arch Tobacco Road rival North Carolina State that would turn up in the NCAA Finals in Albuquerque, matched up against a heavily favored Houston team known for its spectacular above-the-rim style of combat. The result would be still another last-second victory, this time even more dramatic than its predecessor authored by Jordan. Houston, with its upscale Phi Slamma Jamma image and its potent offense built around "Doctors of Dunk" Akeem (Hakeem) Olajuwon, Larry Micheaux, and Clyde Drexler, was the season's yearlong front-runner and the odds-on postseason choice. Jim Valvano's N.C. State ball club had barely played .500 ball in its own conference

Cheryl Miller of Southern Cal was arguably the greatest women's player of all time and the only three-time female National Player of the Year.

© University of Southern California

and then somehow miraculously survived nail-biting single-point or overtime victories during the ACC tournament semifinals (versus Jordan and the Tar Heels) and in three of their five NCAA matches en route to the season's final crucial game. In yet another cardiac championship finish, N.C. State prevailed against Houston's distraught Cougars when Lorenzo Charles corralled and stuffed home teammate Derek Whittenburg's off-target desperation heave mere seconds before the final buzzer had sounded.

If the Big East had risen to sudden prominence with Georgetown's emergence during Ewing's freshman season, it would clinch a spot among the elite conferences during the same big man's final two seasons in the lineup for coach John

Thompson and his reloaded Hoyas. Georgetown battled back into the Final Four in 1984 (Ewing's junior season), and this time around would not be denied in its quest for a first national title. Georgetown's championship-round rivals would be the same Houston Cougars club that had been rudely upset in the championship game by N.C. State the previous March. Guy Lewis's Phi Slamma Jamma Cougars were now back on track hoping for a full crack at redemption. In the expected struggle of titans, Olajuwon would battle Ewing to a complete standstill, outpointing his rival 15 to 10 and deadlocking in the backboard competition with nine caroms apiece. But Georgetown had the better reinforcements with stellar freshmen Michael Graham (6'9") and Reggie Williams (6'7"), and the rookie pair posted 11 of the victors' 15 second-half field goals as the Hoyas prevailed 84–75.

Ewing would have yet a final season to defend the national title for both himself and his teammates. For the third time in four campaigns with Ewing in the lineup, the Hoyas posted 30 or more wins; for the second straight season they stood atop both wire service polls entering postseason action; and for the third time in Ewing's illustrious career, a visit to NCAA warfare would be saddled with bitter disappointment. Yet if Final Four action provided another letdown for John Thompson and Patrick Ewing, it would prove to be anything but disheartening for the young Big East circuit whose banner Georgetown was carrying. With St. John's joining Villanova and Georgetown in the Big Dance, for the first time on record the season's final weekend would witness a national semifinals populated by three teams from the very same conference. A last-second bucket by Memphis State in the Midwest Regional semifinals was all that had prevented Boston College from giving the upstart Big East a clean sweep of the Final Four berths. As it was, one of the charmed three that had made it to Lexington was now destined for an improbable upset role as March basketball's all-time Cinderella champion.

Villanova University had clawed its way to the title match despite a 19–10 pretourney ledger, the worst ever for an eventual NCAA champion. Rollie Massimino's Wildcats were, nonetheless, an inspired team, and their .786 field-goal percentage in the championship game not only toppled records but also turned the tide against a stunned group of Hoyas. With their 66–64 victory that closed the door on Ewing's Hoyas, Villanova had authored one of the most shocking upsets ever witnessed since the inauguration of postseason play to crown a national champion.

There were significant rule changes throughout the '80s and '90s that continually reshaped and refocused the college game. The most immediately visible of these alterations had to do with three-point field goals and also with the adoption of still another distinguishing feature of the professional game—a 45-second shot clock governing offensive performance and speeding up game action. The shot-clock legislation was perhaps the sport's biggest facelift since the elimination of center-court jumps after made baskets, and it came to the college game with the 1985–86 season, more than three decades after the pros had adopted similar game-altering legislation. This was not the first tinkering with a shot-clock notion in the collegiate ranks: at the outset of the '70s women's coaches not only caught up with the present (by adopting men's rules for their version) but peered into the future and instituted a pro-style 30-second shot clock to force the pace of the action. On the men's side the NCAA powers were apparently equally pleased with the up-tempo game and the anti-freeze legislations they had now wrought, and within eight seasons (1993–94) the shot-clock time for men's games was reduced further, to 35 seconds.

It was in the late '80s also that college basketball events began flooding the cable television airwaves as never before. Most of the attention peaked, of course, with the showcase tournament games at season's end. The Duke versus Michigan shootout in the 1992 NCAA tournament final was the most-watched contest in television history. But if this single game had the largest raw audience (an estimated 53 million viewers in homes covered by the Nielsen ratings), it remains only third on the list of highest TV shares (the estimated percentage of home televisions tuned in), trailing the 1979 (Magic Johnson facing Larry Bird) and 1985 (Villanova upsetting Georgetown) college tournament finales. In 1993 expert college basketball analyst Mike Douchant (in his book *Tourney Time*) ranked the 20 highest-rated television games and all were not surprisingly NCAA finals. As with almost all American spectator sports, the marriage with television had meant an exposure explosion that could hardly have been imagined when an estimated audience of approximately 500,000 viewers (almost 100 times smaller than the electronic audience for the Duke-Michigan title match) had tuned in for the 1946 NCAA final, played in Madison Square Garden between Oklahoma A&M and North Carolina and televised locally for the first time by WCBS-TV.

Postseason and regular-season television interest also spelled bigger and bigger contracts for the networks and their advertisers. College basketball's television rights fees jumped above $500,000 in 1969 when NBC first gained an exclusive NCAA contract, then exceeded $1 million for the first time in 1973, when the Thursday-Saturday Final Four arrangement was shifted to Saturday-Monday, thus allowing NBC to feature the championship shootout as prime-time viewing. NBC's contract for NCAA games throughout the decade of the '70s brought to the airwaves the first major network play-by-play voice of college basketball, Curt Gowdy, who once had been a radio broadcaster for the Oklahoma A&M 50-station network at the time of the 1946 NCAA title game and also a featured player on Wyoming's 1941 tournament team. NBC's reign ended after two decades when CBS launched a lucrative seven-year $1 billion contract with the NCAA in 1991, one guaranteeing the network exclusive coverage of all sessions (ESPN had previously featured early-round games) during the showcase tournament.

There were additional spin-offs of the television basketball craze. Ex-coaches (Digger Phelps, Al McGuire, Billy Packer, and Dick Vitale foremost among them) emerged as popular celebrity analysts, and soon these talking heads were nearly as well known—sometimes more so—as the star players and showcase coaches themselves. None of the new breed of flamboyant broadcasters was more notorious nor more successful an ambassador for the college game than ESPN's Dick Vitale. Loud, loquacious, and brashly original, Vitale became a national icon with his endless mantras ("You gotta love it, Baby!" and "It's awesome, Baby" among others), shamelessly plugged his favored players and coaches (especially Indiana's Bob Knight), often exposed the sport's humorous side (with his mythical All-Airport teams, All–Rip Van Winkle teams, All–Thomas Edison teams, and other such entertaining banalities), and created a rich new basketball jargon of his own invention (Surf-and-Turfer for superstar, Windex Man for rebounder, PTPers for prime-time players, and Rolls Roycers for powerhouse conferences). Love him or

Important Rule Changes
in Basketball's Second Half-Century

1944—Defensive goaltending (blocking shots on their downward flight) outlawed (subsequently known as "The Mikan Rule"). Five personal fouls disqualify a player (instead of the four in effect since 1910). One extra foul still allowed during overtime periods.

1948—Glass backboards sanctioned for all games.

1949—Pacific Coast Conference experiments with discouraging deliberate free-throw misses by giving defensive men both inside rebounding positions. Coaches now allowed to talk with their players during time-outs.

1952—Playing time changed from 20-minute halves to 10-minute quarters.

1953—Teams no longer allowed to waive free throws in favor of taking the ball out-of-bounds.

1955—Playing time changed from 10-minute quarters back to 20-minute halves.

1956—Six-foot foul lanes replaced with 12-foot foul lanes.

1958—Offensive goaltending (touching the ball inside the cylinder) outlawed (rule subsequently known as "The Chamberlain Rule").

1968—Dunk shot (plus dunking in pregame warm-ups) is banned (rule subsequently known as "The Alcindor Rule").

1969—Women's games are restructured to include five players on each side, full-court action (players not assigned to offensive and defensive zones), and a 30-second shot clock. Women collegians begin playing by these new "men's" rules.

1977—Dunk shot is once again made legal.

1982—Jump ball now employed only to start games and begin overtime periods. Alternate possession arrow now indicates possessions throughout the game on all previous jump-ball situations.

1983—Jump ball eliminated in five-second "closely guarded" situations. Five-second held ball now a violation and defensive team is awarded possession.

1986—Colleges introduce 45-second shot clock for men's games.

1987—Colleges adopt three-point field goal with line set at 19 feet, 9 inches.

1988—Intentional fouls result in two-shot penalty plus possession of ball.

1994—Shot clock reduced from 45 to 35 seconds for men's NCAA games.

Source: *Hoopla: A Century of College Basketball, 1896–1996*, by Peter C. Bjarkman (Masters Press, 1996)

loathe him, "Dickie V" was not only a shameless self-promoter, but also a tireless and infectious advocate for the raw beauties of college basketball action. He relished and exploited his discovered role as creator of new stars (raving on endlessly about the latest season's flashy slam dunkers, hot-shot shooters, and deft playmakers) and also as symbol for both the overbearing hype and the glamorous "showtime" image that was the new essence of college basketball in the modern video age.

Back on the court, the end of the '80s and dawn of the '90s would also witness a remarkable five-year run by Duke University under its popular mentor Mike Krzyzewski, known universally simply as Coach K. Duke. With stars such as frontcourt ace Christian Laettner and backcourt ace Bobby Hurley, Duke would become a Final Four fixture for five straight seasons, make it into the national title game three times running, and win back-to-back NCAA titles (1991, 1992) for the first time since Wooden's Bruins had rested their laurels two full decades earlier. Over the course of this Duke onslaught, Laettner and Hurley would also set a slew

Lionel Simmons of La Salle University welcomed the 1990s by being named National Player of the Year in 1990. Another La Salle great, Tom Gola, is the only player to top Simmons in NCAA combined scoring and rebounding.

© La Salle University

of individual offensive records. Laettner (a 6'11" forward-center) authored new tournament milestones for career points, career free throws made and attempted, and single-year field-goal percentage, while also becoming the first player ever to visit the Final Four weekend four different times; Hurley, a 6' playmaker, missed duplicating Laettner's four championship-round appearances, yet nevertheless set new standards for tournament three-point field goals and assists. Other glamorous Blue Devil stars would also share the limelight, especially Grant Hill, who was the leading scorer for the 1994 NCAA runner-up squad as well as second-leading rebounder with the 1991 and 1992 national champions. Center Cherokee Parks, forward Antonio Lang, and guard Thomas Hill also played major roles in the Duke tournament onslaught. And coach Mike Krzyzewski—with six Final Four teams in seven seasons and five straight appearances at the Big Dance—would also emerge as the closest thing to John Wooden in a full quarter-century.

The first half of the new decade had no more dramatic story, however, than that attached to the University of Michigan's "Fab Five" team, known ultimately more for its surrounding media hype and its occasional on-court failures than for its slew of triumphs. No five-man recruiting class ever received more advanced press than the one that arrived in Ann Arbor in the fall of 1991 and was expected almost everywhere among the sporting press to instantly vault coach Steve Fisher's program back near the top of the Big Ten Conference pecking order. Jalen Rose and Chris Webber were the front-liners and Juwan Howard, Jimmy King, and Ray Jackson the supporting cast, which seemed to guarantee Michigan supporters an eventual national title. It was inevitably a case of outlandish expectations dimming even the best of triumphs. The Michigan crew would make it to a pair of NCAA title games and actually climb its way to the top even earlier than the most optimistic boosters might have expected. But they would fail in spectacular manner on both occasions, not only losing their two cracks at an NCAA banner, but losing them both in memorable fashion and then disbanding early for the lure of NBA gold. In 1992 the championship loss came in a 20-point blowout at the hands of defending champion Duke, one of the worst pastings in championship history and witnessed by the largest television crowd ever. A year later the title game slipped away when Chris Webber mistakenly called a time-out that the Wolverines no longer had in the closing seconds of a seesaw nail-biter. Webber escaped to the pros before another season could be launched, Howard and Rose bailed out one season later (1994), and only King and Jackson finished out their senior campaign (1995) for the once-sterling quintet.

The middle season of the 1990s would also be noted for the return of long-absent UCLA (now coached by Jim Harrick) to the postseason championship circle. Harrick's outfit, featuring sure-handed 5'10" playmaker Tyus Edney, swift 6'8" All-American Ed O'Bannon, and 6'5" freshman swingman Tobey Bailey, was the first UCLA outfit in that school's impressive history to capture more than 30 games in a campaign (31–2), and the record-breaking victory was a mildly surprising 89–78 title-clincher over defending champion Arkansas. The Bruins' dramatic late-season run at an NCAA title in 1995 (which included playing the championship game without Edney, who was nursing a sprained wrist) represented one of the most storied chapters in UCLA's stellar basketball annals.

Almost as noteworthy by the middle of the '90s was the startling impact made by women's collegiate play. The women's tournament final game had been a television fixture with CBS since 1987, yet hadn't generated more than moderate fan interest for much of its decade in the limelight. But the postseason fare of 1993 and 1995 saw the women's game suddenly turn the corner and garner new booming audiences with its increasingly polished style of play. Sheryl Swoopes of Texas Tech stole the postseason spotlight in 1993 when she set a new record (men's and women's) for individual points in an NCAA title game. Swoopes—the biggest female star since Southern Cal's Cheryl Miller a decade earlier—was relentless from all parts of the floor when she canned 47 while Tech outclassed Ohio State 84–82. Connecticut's Lady Huskies, featuring 6'4" Player of the Year Rebecca Lobo, provided the top thrills in 1995 with the best season-long record (35–0) in either men's or women's cage history. Sandwiched between was a dramatic final-second game-winning shot by Charlotte Smith—a three-point missile launched with 0.7 seconds on the clock—which propelled North Carolina over Louisiana Tech in the 1994 finale. Smith's heart-stopping buzzer-beating heave and Lobo's truly dominant season were sufficient to bring legions of new and appreciative fans to the fast-growing sport of women's college basketball. As the men's game moved more and more toward the NBA style of one-on-one freelance with endless displays of solo dunking, many tradition-minded fans had actually begun to prefer the more fundamentally sound team-style of game featured on the women's circuit.

Another familiar face sat atop the men's collegiate basketball world by the end of the 1996 season. Kentucky returned to the NCAA winner's circle and it was heavily ironic that the first Kentucky triumph since 1978 would coincide with the return of the tournament to New York City for the first time since the early '50s. New York, of course, had been the scene of those early '50s betting scandals that had remained the one black mark on Baron Rupp's glorious career. Now after nearly four decades, Kentucky had seemingly finally found a coach who could fill even Adolph Rupp's championship shoes. Rick Pitino, now in his seventh season in Lexington, would write his own Kentucky legend from one of the most impossible coaching pressure seats found anywhere in the country. Pitino's 1996 Wildcats saw a 27-game win streak shattered in the SEC Tournament Finals, yet regrouped in time to run through San Jose State, Virginia Tech, Utah, Wake Forest, Massachusetts, and finally, Syracuse for the school's sixth NCAA trophy. Four of the six tournament victories were by comfortable margins of 20 or better. Kentucky's quest for a repeat championship would end in failure, however, though the Wildcats nearly reached their improbable goal despite a rash of season-long injuries to top stars and key role players like Derek Anderson, Scott Padgett, Wayne Turner, and Ron Mercer. Riding the scoring and playmaking of a young backcourt tandem, Miles Simon (son of ABA standout Walt Simon) and Mike Bibby (offspring of UCLA great Mike Bibby), Lute Olson's upstart Arizona team halted Kentucky's expected championship drive in a thrill-packed overtime NCAA Final. Upstart Arizona, another team called Wildcats, would be the club to make history this time around by becoming the first ever to upset three number one seeds en route to a postseason title.

The most recent season also witnessed a landmark event of epic proportions when North Carolina's venerable Dean Smith finally overhauled Adolph Rupp's once-unapproachable milestone for career victories. Smith's final North Carolina edition won 28 (enough to boost his career ledger to 879–254) before falling ever so short (by losing to eventual champion Arizona in the NCAA semifinals) of giving Smith a third NCAA banner. Smith was, of course, a direct link back to Rupp, Allen, and Naismith by virtue of his own Kansas connections as a reserve player for Phog Allen's 1952 and 1953 Final Four teams. He was also seemingly one of the most shining examples of all that is still best about the sport—impeccable honesty, charming graciousness, unmovable integrity, and relentless competitiveness mixed with unimpeachable class. Smith would suddenly retire on the eve of a new season, leaving a surprising, yet very deserving, replacement—longtime assistant Bill Guthridge—in his wake. By midseason 1998 Guthridge again had the always-loaded Tar Heels poised at the top of the national polls and prepared for yet another serious postseason championship run.

Fans were increasingly alarmed in the mid-'90s with the growing trend toward early departures of top college stars. Georgetown's Allen Iverson (1997 top NBA rookie with Philadelphia) and Georgia Tech's Stephon Marbury (top draft choice of the Minnesota Timberwolves) were one pair of stellar guards who fled for NBA paychecks after only a single spectacular college season. But each departure only brought new headliners to rapidly fill the void—Raef LaFrentz (Kansas), DeMarco Johnson (UNC-Charlotte), Mike Bibby (Arizona), Antawn Jamison (North Carolina), Ed Cota (North Carolina), and Pat Garrity (Notre Dame) loomed as more-than-adequate 1998 replacements for 1997 All-Americans Ron Mercer (Kentucky), Derek Anderson (Kentucky), Tim Duncan (Wake Forest), Danny Fortson (Cincinnati), and Chauncey Billups (Colorado). If anything, the early departures seemed only to improve the balance in the game, while simultaneously making conferences more competitive top to bottom. It was only a handful of the top schools, after all, which saw their heavily recruited stars make hasty exits for pro dollars and thus leave next year's championship dreams in shambles. More rapid personnel turnover has only worked to restore competitive balance for the Wake Forests, Northwesterns, Purdues, and Arizonas faced with a yearly challenge of competition against the Carolinas, Michigans, Georgetowns, UCLAs, and Kentuckys. Across most of the college landscape, early departures have remained a decided nonissue, and college rivalries continue everywhere as intense as ever.

As college basketball launched its second century with the 1996–97 season, the future appeared bright indeed. The men's springtime NCAA Final Four title chase now stood at the apex of American sporting interests. Widespread fan disillusionment with high salaries in pro sports was now playing in favor of the amateur game. If college basketball itself was not entirely free from rampant commercialism, an occasional taste of competitive dishonesty, and the taint of far too many dollars, nonetheless the warning clarions were no louder than at times in the past. College basketball still seemed to be sitting flush at the center of yet another golden age.*

---

*More comprehensive treatment of college basketball history—from Dr. Naismith in the 1890s to March Madness of the 1990s—is provided by the author's previous book, *Hoopla: A Century of College Basketball, 1896–1996* (Masters Press, 1998).

Chapter Two

Hardwood to Hang Time

Concise History of Professional

Basketball's First Half-Century

What has now become a three-ring entertainment spectacle and lively media circus during the mid-1990s started out as little more than a small-town side-show under the long shadows of World War II. Pro basketball in its infancy— during the unparalleled economic boom era of the late '40s—was hardly more than a third-rate barnstorming affair, which struggled on two separate battlefronts for survival. Early play-for-pay cagers provided their fans with more laughs, lu-nacies, and letdowns than certified athletic legends. There was certainly little enough that was especially glorious about the infant years of the NBA (nee BAA and NBL) and, indeed, much that was downright lamentable. Perhaps the big-gest story surrounding the first few seasons of what is today's most prominent pro sports league was the startling fact that the fledgling operation somehow managed to survive at all. Other earlier attempts had been made to get pro bas-ketball off the ground, and all had ultimately failed. The two late-'40s-era leagues that would eventually constitute the NBA eventually fared a good deal better, but only after a couple of helter-skelter seasons that could hardly be called "big league" by even the loosest of standards.

The confederation of 11 teams that was hastily thrown together by East Coast hockey arena owners in the late summer of 1946 under the name of the Basketball Association of America (BAA) was, by any imaginable assessment, an exasperating bush league, despite the metropolitan associations (New York, Chicago, Philadelphia, Washington, Boston, Cleveland) and large-city arenas into which games were frequently scheduled. And even those arenas were not always the venues of choice for a string of often meaningless games witnessed by preciously few patrons. The New York Knicks only irregularly played in Madi-son Square Garden (their inaugural 1946–47 home schedule featured six games there and the other 24 at a dingy and drafty 69th Regiment Armory), and many of the league's games were set at neutral sites (Hershey, Hartford, Springfield,

Hoboken, and points between), and thus had the strong flavor of earlier-era barn-storming affairs.

The strictly "one-horse-town atmosphere" and often slapstick nature of early BAA action was readily apparent from the very first season and remained in evidence for all three winters of the circuit's infancy. For one thing, the basketball play was unusually dull and uninspiring. Spectacular one-handed shooting on the run, which had increasingly been the rage in college games (ever since Stanford's Hank Luisetti in 1936 and Wyoming's Ken Sailors in 1943 thrilled Madison Square Garden audiences with their unorthodox styles), was still being shunned by old-school pro coaches and their hard-nosed rough-and-tumble players, almost all of whom preferred the stationary two-handed set shot. Fans were few and far between, and desperate owners turned to numerous promotional gimmicks in hopes of attracting audiences to their slow-paced and conservative-style games. There were ladies' nights in Washington, Stan Miasek Night and Bob Dille Night in Detroit (where fans with last names matching those of either star player got in free), and giveaways of almost everything imaginable, from automobiles to cartons of chocolates to $10 clothing certificates. And the players themselves often provided more entertainment for the few on hand with their zany antics than with their stellar athletic performances. Washington's high scorer, Bones McKinney, once turned on a Uline Arena crowd by shooting foul shots with his back to the basket. And McKinney's neophyte coach—Red Auerbach of future Boston fame—enraged, but always entertained, with his stomping the sidelines, baiting of officials, and mocking of patrons behind the team bench. He even spit demonstratively on the floor to rile up opposition hometown crowds.

The first-year BAA played a landmark role tinged with promotional possibilities by introducing the sport's first pair of professional seven-foot behemoths. But like everything else associated with the fledgling circuit, these early gate attractions seemed more like idle curiosities and overblown publicity stunts than anything else. Neither Elmore Morganthaler in Providence nor Ralph Siewert in St. Louis was exceptionally (or even moderately) talented, and neither had even the smallest impact on overall league play. Morganthaler's claim to fame was his handling of a stick of gum, not a basketball. The Providence Steamrollers giant ran up and down the floor with his chewing gum balled behind his ear and would retrieve it from time to time for a refreshing chew. And Siewert—who was appropriately called "Timber" by Bombers fans—was known in his brief stint in the league more for flopping than for leaping. Siewert resembled a felled tree when frequently knocked to the floor by more rugged opponents. Morganthaler (listed as 7'1" in today's *NBA Basketball Encyclopedia*) played two seasons (one with Philadelphia), logged 31 games, and garnered 57 points; that was double the total that "Sky" Siewert tallied in 20 contests split between St. Louis and Toronto. Fortunately for the future status of the big man as gate attraction, and also for the immediate health of the BAA as a league, George Mikan was only one brief season away.

The pioneering players did claim to have more fun than their beneficiaries of following generations. They had to, of course, since salaries were minimal and barnstorming life was arduous. Long hours were spent on cross-country trains (air travel was rare before the early '50s), and marathon card games provided the diversion of choice. A single uniform and a pair of dress shirts (players called them "thousand-miler shirts") had to be worn on the road all season long, and the uniforms often were dirty and salty enough (to say nothing of the odor) to stand upright in the corner of a hotel room by themselves. Players often cut loose on the road, like the time the Boston Celtics were stranded by a blizzard in a Buffalo train station and destroyed a local landmark with their high jinks. Celtics forward Chuck Connors, a 6'6" cutup (later of TV *Rifleman* fame and also briefly a major-league baseball player), was apparently a major instigator when a drunken contingent of bored ballplayers somehow severed the tail of a bronze-coated cement lion.

While many early-day pros probably exaggerated a bit when later claiming they would have played for nothing but mere love of the game, by today's standards they almost did. These were clearly working-class ballplayers and not high-finance capitalists like today's overpriced NBA stars. The entire league revenues for the first BAA season of 1946–47 (net gate receipts were reported at just less than $1.9 million) could barely match the salary of a single NBA benchwarmer today. One enterprising player extended his bankroll by also signing on for extra duties as the team's publicity director. Tom King (5.1 points per game in 51 contests) with the Detroit Falcons earned $8,000 on the court (an exceptionally high salary for those days) and then doubled his take-home pay by carrying his typewriter on road trips and filing game reports and press releases, which were often banged out in the locker room while the player-turned-reporter was still clothed in his dripping uniform.

The rival league, based in the nation's heartland and known as the National Basketball League (NBL), hardly fared much better—at the gate, on the playing floor, or on the nation's sports pages. The Midwest circuit had the better players (in 1947 and 1948 there were names like Mikan and Pollard in Minneapolis; Davies, Risen, and Holzman in Rochester; Zaslofsky with Chicago; Bobby McDermott at Tri-Cities; and Paul Seymour in Syracuse), but could boast little in the way of showcase venues for putting them on display. Most NBL games were played in cramped high school gyms hidden away in backwater towns such as Sheybogan (Wisconsin), Waterloo (Iowa), Moline (Illinois), and Anderson (Indiana). Unlike the BAA, the NBL had been around for a number of winters by the time basketball enjoyed its first promising inroads during the postwar 1940s. The circuit had begun nearly a decade earlier in the late '30s and had limped through the war years with few recognizable names and even fewer stable franchises. The wartime season of 1943–44 had been played with only four clubs (Fort Wayne, Sheboygan, Oshkosh, and Cleveland), and the two surrounding campaigns mustered no more than six (including the racially integrated Chicago Studebakers with three former Harlem Globetrotters on the roster in 1943). But when talented athletes began returning in droves from the war, there was suddenly the promise of new interest in basketball (as well as all manner of other spectacles) throughout the Midwest and elsewhere in the land. Americans everywhere displayed a new spirit, a sudden excess of pocket change, a lust for entertainment bolstered by a new national pride in wartime victories, and an apparent desire to spend, spend, spend. And while East Coast hockey owners thought they had the buildings that could best exploit the sudden demand for sports entertainment, the NBL quickly grabbed up more than its share of available postwar ballplaying talent.

Yet basketball at midcentury was indisputably still a college game, at least in the popular imagination. While men, and even women, had played for pay as early as the first decade after Naismith had invented the sport, these pro hoopsters had always remained lost in the deep shadows of the American sports scene. They had almost no impact on the general public and attracted only tiny circles of dedicated followers. In the '20s and '30s, New York's Original Celtics (with stars such as Dutch Dehnert, Nat Holman, Pete Barry, Johnny Beckman, and Joe Lapchick) and Bob Douglas's popular New York Rens (officially the New York Renaissance Five, after the Renaissance Casino Ballroom in Harlem) drew enthusiastic crowds while on "national tours" and built large legends and lengthy winning streaks against local teams spread across the East and Midwest. But there were no formal leagues of substance to follow daily on the sports pages or to inspire allegiances in other corners of the nation. It was only the unprecedented boom era of postwar America that made the setting finally ripe for a new indoor sport that could rival the college game (and also other pro sports such as football, hockey, and the king of them all, baseball) as entertainment spectacle. What were needed, of course, were stable venues in which teams and leagues and star players hung around in the same locale long enough to earn some notice and spur some sustained fan interest. Unfortunately, the often fitful first efforts to exploit this new burgeoning market of dollar-waving sports fans would result in a decade or more of fumbling and near futility before the enterprise really ever got very far off the ground.

Barnstormers and Dinosaurs

The motives behind founding a new pro circuit known as the BAA reveal much about the lamentable, if nonetheless promising, status of pro basketball in the mid-'40s. Hockey club owners and arena managers wanted to fill their venues on off-nights (when hockey games, circuses, or ice capades were not on the docket) and thus reduce overhead costs on seldom-used buildings. The model had already been provided by one of their number—Ned Irish, the basketball director for Madison Square Garden—who had, during prewar years, amassed his personal fortune by promoting college contests, at the same time also demonstrating beyond question the money-making potential of basketball. With his Garden-based college twin bills, Irish had also stimulated a nationwide interest in the popular campus sport.

Most BAA honchos knew little about basketball, except that it hopefully meant ticket-buying customers. After all, the college teams drew legions of paying fans with bouncing balls and arching set shots. The commissioner they would trust to run their hastily pasted together operation—American Hockey League czar Maurice Podoloff—had himself never even seen a basketball contest before taking over his new administrative assignment. In reality, Podoloff knew almost as little about hockey, but a league president is not hired to coach or to make and interpret playing rules, only to orchestrate business deals, market a product, and adjudicate club owners' petty disputes. Podoloff would soon enough prove a genius at the trade.

The two most important pioneering figures of the fledgling cage circuit would be Boston's Walter Brown (Boston Garden president who would front the Boston Celtics) and New York's Ned Irish (now adding ownership of the BAA Knickerbockers to his other Madison Square Garden basketball duties). Brown—

along with Max Kase, sports editor of New York's *Journal-American*—had been more responsible than anyone for coming up with the original BAA idea. Kase had hoped himself to own the New York entry, but was forced to the sidelines when Irish decided he didn't want any interlopers on his own citywide basketball monopoly. Irish, of course, had already made his lasting mark on the history of the college game in basketball's reigning capital. His tireless promotion of college double- and tripleheaders in the '30s and throughout the war years had put the college sport on firm footing in Gotham. Now, Irish hoped to exercise similar impact in the same building with the newly formed professional league. And Brown, up in Boston, would quickly prove to be pro basketball's biggest and most successful gambler. Over the next half decade his novel experiments with a league all-star contest (first held in Boston Garden in 1951), black ballplayers (launched with the 1950 drafting of Chuck Cooper from Duquesne), and a coach named Auerbach (hired that same season) were all destined to cement the league's bright future.

BAA operations opened for business—of all places—in the hockey hotbed and basketball wasteland of Toronto, Canada. The first official game for the new league—direct ancestor of today's NBA—was staged on November 1, 1946, in Toronto's legendary Maple Leaf Gardens. That landmark contest featured one familiar enough fixture, the New York Knickerbockers, who prevailed by a 68–66 score. Opponents were the short-lived and less memorable Toronto Huskies, a fly-by-night franchise that survived no more than the league's inaugural season. Toronto's captain, Ed Sadowski, was the outstanding individual performer with 18 points.

By modern standards, the official league lidlifter and the entire season that followed were only moderate successes at best. The season's opener was staged before 7,090 somewhat bewildered but highly entertained Canadian fans. A pregame newspaper promotion had promised that any (presumably male) patron would be admitted free if he stood taller than 6'10" Huskies center George Nostrand (Nostrand's actual height was 6'8"), yet there is no record of anyone garnering any free ducats. The bulk of the evening's entertainment was reportedly provided not by the athletes themselves but by colorful whistle-tooter Pat Kennedy, who kept fans in a constant uproar with his dramatic gesturing on each and every foul or violation call. And the most historic moment came at the very outset when former LIU star Ossie Schectman logged the first-ever BAA (and thus also NBA) basket. Knicks center Bud Palmer directed the opening tip-off (won from Nostrand) to New York's high scorer Leo Gottfried. Gottfried, in turn, dribbled partway upcourt and then directed a bullet bounce pass to the driving Schectman, who casually laid in the landmark hoop on the dead run.

It was country boy and self-styled hillbilly Joe Fulks who provided much of the individual fireworks during the league's first season or two. Fulks had made no particular impression as a collegian at Murray State Teachers in Kentucky. Yet with Marine Corps service teams during the war years, he had displayed revolutionary talent (often against former All-Americans with lofty reputations) as an unorthodox jump-shooter and unstoppable scorer. Fulks not only launched his deadly bombs on the run but did so with his unique two-handed over-the-head style that was virtually unblockable. Some called it his "ear shot" since Joe seemed to launch the missiles from behind his right ear. However Fulks's leaping shots might best be described, his huge talent was enough to impress Philadelphia Warriors owner Ed Gottlieb. Gottlieb offered a contract to the skinny 6'5" cornerman (edging out the Chicago Stags for the prize) after hearing about his service ball exploits from Petey Rosenburg, who had himself played for the Philly club owner during earlier barnstorming days (with the SPHAs) and would also be a Warrior recruit for the first BAA season. It would be Gottlieb's Philadelphia team, with Fulks in the fold, that would surprise down the stretch of the inaugural season and emerge as the BAA's first champion.

Fulks bombed home 25 points in the Warriors' debut game against Pittsburgh, and his instant offense from the start made Gottlieb's Warriors a potent club, though not the equal of the more-balanced team in Washington, coached by youthful Red Auerbach and boasting its own stellar lineup of Bones McKinney, John Norlander, and John Mahnken up front and Bob Ferrick and Fred Scolari in the backcourt. Washington won 14 more games than Philadelphia and 10 more than Western Division pacesetter Chicago. Philadelphia's route to the league title was thus a somewhat circuitous one. Schedule-makers had unaccountably decreed that first-place finishers in the two divisions would lock horns in the first postseason round, with runners-up also squaring off. Season-long leader Washington was an immediate victim of the strange arrangement, losing four of six to the upset-minded Chicago Stags. The unusual playoff format left Eastern Division runner-up Philadelphia facing Western Division titlist Chicago for the inaugural bragging rights, and the Warriors, with Fulks, simply had too much firepower for the less offense-minded Stags and their balanced attack of Max Zaslofsky (14.4 points per game), Chuck Halbert (12.7), and Swede Carlson (10.7). Fulks had averaged a then-incredible 23.2 points per game for the full season to far outdistance his nearest competitor, Washington's Ferrick (16.3). George Mikan would soon be the biggest offensive star on the scene, yet Fulks had already revolutionized scoring with his awkward-looking but deadly behind-the-ear jumpers. Two seasons later, Jumpin' Joe would foreshadow the run-and-gun future with an incredible one-game 63-point effort against Indianapolis, which stood for more than a decade as the unassailable league record.

The second season provided one of the sport's most often discredited champions in the guise of the newly arrived Baltimore Bullets. When Detroit, Cleveland, Toronto, and Pittsburgh folded up operations at the end of year one, the Bullets were recruited from the semipro American League to provide a balanced eight-club schedule. Baltimore would not only make the grade but actually claw its way to a postseason crown without big-name stars and on the heels of a strictly average campaign, which saw it tie for second with three of the four Western Division entrants. If the Bullets' six-game victory over Eastern Division pacesetter and defending champion Philadelphia in the finals is sometimes dismissed as the unfortunate product of a hodgepodge playoff arrangement, it should be kept in mind that the Western runner-up did own a better season-long record (28–20) than the Eastern frontrunner (27–21). Buddy Jeannette ran the Baltimore team as both the bench coach and playmaking guard, yet the best overall performance came from 6'2" forward Paul Hoffman, who garnered the league's first-ever Rookie of the Year honors. The season also saw Joe Fulks continue to establish his pioneering influence on the game, again posting the highest scoring average (22.1) although trailing Chicago's Zaslofsky (who played five more games than Fulks) in total points.

George Mikan of the Minneapolis Lakers was pro basketball's first superstar and also the most unstoppable force of the first decade of BAA-NBA history.

Transcendental Graphics

In the end, the real rap on the BAA in 1948 was that its surprise winner in Baltimore was largely a dull team to watch, with no fancy stars or headline names to lace its lineup and with a deliberate style of play inconsistent with the "college-type game" BAA owners were pretending to offer. Out west, the rival NBL boasted a championship Minneapolis Lakers ball club featuring the awesome and charismatic George Mikan plus a flashy leaper named Jim Pollard to spice the mix. And there were other impressive stars in the competing Midwest circuit who excelled at an older "pro-style" game, especially backcourt ace Bob Davies of the Rochester Royals, who dazzled with fancy ballhandling and playmaking despite a knee injury that cost him a dozen games. The BAA may have survived its second season, despite the bailout of a third of its original clubs before the opening tip-off, yet it could hardly boast that its champion or its overall league was the best that pro basketball now had to offer.

The image problem was quickly solved, though more through acts of piracy than any other method. By year number three there was a new kid on the block—planted in Minneapolis—and this new guest would quickly prove to be a full-fledged bully when Mikan and company launched a domination that would last for the next half decade. BAA president Podoloff had pulled off his greatest coup to date when he stole Mikan and both the Minneapolis and Rochester franchises (along with the teams in Fort Wayne and Indianapolis) away from the older league, which had been bolstered, up to then, by the more recognizable star players even if it didn't have the big arenas and the big-city audiences. The two showcase NBL refugees (the one with Mikan and Pollard and the one with Davies and Wanzer) ran away from the rest of the league in regular-season play. The Royals edged the Lakers by a single game in the Western Division standings (where both won a half dozen more than Eastern pacesetter Washington under Auerbach) but lost both matches to Mikan in the short division finals. Minneapolis and Mikan then took their second straight postseason crown in their second league by outlasting befuddled Washington, which could do nothing to slow the 30-plus postseason scoring of the Lakers' unmatchable workhorse. Mikan (28.3) also edged out Fulks (26.0) as the league's new scoring star.

The defection of Mikan and his teammates (and to lesser extent that of Bob Davies and his) sounded a death knell for the NBL. Without it, the scenario of dueling leagues may well have played out in a very different direction. For a dozen seasons the more venerable league struggled to keep its head above water and to compete first with the potent college game and later with the fledgling BAA for the nation's growing basketball audience. In bush-league towns with names like Oshkosh, Anderson, and Sheboygan, the Midwestern circuit failed to win equal recognition, more because of the backwater nature of its playing venues than any shortcomings in player talent or team competitiveness. Its teams were, in fact, a fixture in the championship round during the World Professional Tournament staged in Chicago Stadium each spring between 1939 and 1948; the Oshkosh All-Stars and Chicago Bruins had both been beaten by ace black barnstorming outfits (the Rens in 1939 and the Globetrotters in 1940) before NBL clubs captured all but one of the final eight world titles. League teams appeared in every one of the Chicago finales, and Fred Zollner's Fort Wayne Pistons claimed three straight crowns during the war years. The NBL thus already had several moderately successful years under its belt before the BAA was born, and after 1946 it had undergone a significant upgrading and face-lifting with its commitment to signing up the best among big-name graduating college stars.

The irony here was that the BAA, upon its founding, had determined to provide a product that was a thinly veiled relica of the college sport. Walter Brown, Ned Irish, and others behind the BAA concept had reasoned that fans would flock to see college stars who had used up their eligibility to perform on the NCAA stage long before they had passed their prime years of playing fitness. The BAA game was intended to be different from that provided (in the NBL) by hardened pro stars who played a slower and more brutal version of the sport. It would appeal to fans who liked the college game with its younger athletes, fast-break offenses, and daring one-handed jump-shooting. What had transpired in reality, however, was that the NBL had beaten the BAA to the punch with recruiting of top college talent, especially by grabbing off names like Schayes (NYU), Davies (Seton Hall), Pollard (Stanford), Red Holzman (CCNY), Dick Triptow (DePaul), Alex Hannum (Southern California), George Glamack (North Carolina), Fuzzy Levane (St. John's), Dolly King (LIU)—and, of course, the biggest prize of all in Mikan. At the same time, the BAA in 1948 had been left with a league champion that had won behind a bunch of practitioners (Buddy Jeannette, Chick Reiser, Cleggie Hermsen, Connie Simmons) of the old-style professional game en vogue during the wartime years. It was only Podoloff's strong-arm wholesale raiding of the top NBL franchises (and thus some of its brightest ex-collegians such as Mikan, Davies, and Schayes) that allowed the BAA to tip the balance in its own favor.

If the BAA seemed a shoestring operation, of course, it might have appeared almost first-class by the standards that governed rival NBL operations. Here the players were, on the whole, a notch above, but the arenas were smaller (even in cities like Indianapolis, Syracuse, and Rochester), the travel equally as wretched and grueling, the crowds smaller (except when NBL teams took the Chicago Stadium floor for World Tournament games, which sometimes drew 10,000 or even 15,000), the press coverage at most times nonexistent, and the finances a simple matter of hardscrabble survival. In this league many of the games were even played in high school gyms with but a few hundred seats and baskets crammed against the end walls. The earlier history of the NBL had been largely a forgettable affair, as well, with the players, coaches, schedules, playing rules, arenas, and even the teams themselves changing with alarming regularity. Rock bottom came with the 1943 and 1944 wartime seasons: the first was played with only five entrants, but one (Toledo) completed only four games before disbanding, and the second (Chicago's Studebakers) was torn by racial strife spawned by the league's first and somewhat unsuccessful integration experiment; the second had only four clubs, which all participated in the altogether redundant playoffs. But the NBL had, nonetheless, been holding its annual championships without missing a beat since the final winter of the '30s.

The arenas of the NBL underscored the bush status of pro basketball at the dawn of America's postwar boom era. Even the big-town venues in Rochester and Syracuse provided the stuff of later legends. The oft-times embarrassing signature of the league remained its strange gymnasiums and often bizarre playing circumstances. These were commonplace in the NBL and also extended into early NBA seasons in places like Rochester, Syracuse, and even St. Louis. While dance halls had given way to larger arenas for the league's regular venues, numerous regulation games were still being scheduled for off-the-beaten-path nonleague cities in the search for much-needed attendance (a practice still in effect in the NBA as late as the early '60s). And even the established home courts were prone to some remarkable idiosyncrasies.

Syracuse's State Fair Coliseum was not only musty, dimly lit, and without much ventilation, but also featured basket-supporting guy wires that extended into the grandstands and could be yanked by the crowd to rattle the basket while opposing players were attempting free throws. Edgerton Park Sports Arena in Rochester boasted double doors a few feet behind the basket, and a player charging in for a layup was occasionally known to career through the portals and into a hidden out-side snowbank. Kiel Auditorium in St. Louis featured perhaps the strangest ar-rangement of all. One half of the auditorium was a convention hall featuring the basketball floor and grandstands; the other half was a theater with its stage backed up against the sports arena and separated from the latter by only a thin portable wall. A concert or ballet was often in progress at the same hour as a league game, and if players emerging from the locker room were not careful to enter the correct auditorium door, they could conceivably dribble smack into the midst of an ongo-ing symphony or operatic aria.

There had, of course, been professional basketball long before even the NBL came into existence. The prehistory of professional hoops play is, however, largely a history of helter-skelter barnstorming, especially across the nation's northeast and midwest sectors. Many leagues popped up along the East Coast and across the heart-land during the first four-plus decades of the century, but little permanent structure emerged and no lasting circuits to provide stability of the kind known in profes-sional baseball. Some of these earliest circuits were the original National Basket-ball League (1898 through 1903) restricted to Pennsylvania and New Jersey; the single-season New England and Western Massachusetts leagues of 1903–04; the more healthy Eastern League, which survived from 1910 through 1933 with a de-cade-long hiatus in the '20s; and the New York State League (1912 through 1923) built around the legendary Troy Trojans of Ed Wachter.

The barnstorming era brought several powerful touring clubs that made their bold marks on the sport's evolution. Foremost was the Original Celtics outfit with its Hall of Fame lineup featuring Nat Holman, Joe Lapchick, Dutch Dehnert, and numerous other lesser lights over the years (especially Pete Barry, Johnny Witte, Swede Grimstead, Horse Haggerty, Chris Leonard, Davey Banks, Carl Husta, Nat Hickey, and Johnny Beckman). The Celtics not only won countless games with great efficiency, but also pioneered in the evolution of how basketball was poten-tially played as a team game. The club's first manifestation was founded by Jim Furey in the aftermath of World War I and starred Barry and Witte, who together had performed for a prewar club of the same name (hence "Original Celtics" for Furey's reincarnation). Peak years came in the '20s with Holman, Dehnert, and Lapchick in the lineup, and the team's most profound impact on the sport was its evolution during that era of zone defenses and the famous "pivot" play. The latter was Dehnert's brainchild (legend, however, provides numerous versions of the ex-act circumstances and locale of the invention) and soon became the team's primary marketing and promotional tool.

The Celtics' greatest demonstration of invincibility, however, was ironically to be their final undoing. When banned by the start-up American Basketball League in 1926 from barnstorming against league clubs, the Celtics promptly signed up for the circuit (large crowds and higher paychecks were the incentive), and during two seasons (representing first Brooklyn, then New York), trounced ABL compe-tition so thoroughly that fan interest and ticket sales seriously waned. After New York's 40–9 season of 1928, a cry of "Break Up the Celtics!" became the ABL byword. League founders promptly pulled the plug, and for the 1929 campaign, the invincible five of Barry, Dehnert, Banks, Holman, and Lapchick were scat-tered among the other ABL ball clubs.

Transcendental Graphics

The New York Original Celtics of 1920. Notable members included manager Jim Furey (seated left), captain Johnny Beckman (seated right of ball), Dutch Dehnert (standing second from left), and Pete Barry (standing second from right).

    Another barnstorming-era team of note was the Cleveland Rosenblums (named for the department store magnate who owned them), another fixture in the brief stability of the American Basketball League during the late '20s and early '30s. Cleveland's success arrived only after Max Rosenblum was able to acquire Celtics stars Joe Lapchick, Pete Barry, and Dutch Dehnert. The windfall for Cleveland came on the eve of the 1929 season when the powerful Celtics were disbanded by ABL moguls after back-to-back seasons of total league domination. Rosenblum's restocked club (soon referred to in press accounts as the Rosenblum Celtics) now looked for all the world like a new dynasty on the block, but they (and the ABL as a whole) would, in turn, be scuttled by the 1929 stock market crash and ensuing Great Depression. On the East Coast, the Philadelphia SPHAs had long carved their own niche at the professional level. Eddie Gottlieb's team would dominate the reorganized ABL (reconstructed for the 1934 season and lasting until after World War II) by capturing seven championships across 13 seasons. But the Gottlieb SPHAs already boasted a rich history that stretched back long before its ABL incarnation. Gottlieb himself had helped organize the popular club as early as 1918 with an original sponsorship from the South Philadelphia Hebrew Association (hence the acronymic name). Other early clubs also enjoyed their fleeting reputations and their brief moments in the sun (or more properly the shadows) of barnstorming professional basketball. George Halas sponsored a Chicago Bruins team that had once featured Nat Holman in the lineup while competing in the ABL, then later reappeared for three wartime seasons (1940 through 1942) with the National Basketball League. Another National Football League tycoon, George Preston Marshall, sponsored his own ABL club called the Washington Palace Five, which also enjoyed moderate successes (two second-place finishes) before Marshall sold out in the face of cash-robbing Celtics domination.

And there were also two great black teams on the scene, the Douglas Renaissance Five of New York and the misnamed Harlem Globetrotters spawned by Abe Saperstein in Chicago. The Rens were the better basketball outfit—at least at first—and reached their prime in the early winters of the '30s. Often defeating the best white clubs on their whirlwind tours, the team, originally constructed by Bob Douglas in the mid-'20s, captured wide public notice by splitting a six-game series with the famed Celtics during the 1926–27 winter season. The Rens peaked over the four following winters when a lineup of Bill Yancey, Charles "Tarzan" Cooper (who Lapchick called the best center he ever saw), Clarence "Fat" Jenkins, John Holt, James "Pappy" Ricks, Eyre "Bruiser" Saitch, and 6'5" "Wee Willie" Smith compiled an amazing 473–99 ledger against all comers, which included an unbeaten string of 88 straight.

Abe Saperstein had also put together a traveling roadshow geared to winning games as well as entertaining ticket buyers. The journey of the world-renowned 'Trotters had begun inauspiciously in 1927 (on January 7 in Hinckley, Illinois), established legitimacy throughout the '30s with players like Inman Jackson (pioneer of the comic stunts that became the team's trademark) and Al "Runt" Pullins, then reached high gear in the prewar '40s. Full legitimacy eventually came during the Globetrotters' 13th season on the road. At the 1940 Chicago World Professional Tournament, Saperstein's outfit—sparked by Sonny Boswell's stellar shooting displays—first defeated the renowned New York Rens (still featuring Cooper, Smith, and Saitch in the lineup) in the semifinals and captured a world crown by edging Halas's NBL Chicago Bruins 31–29 in overtime. A half-century later, the modern incarnation of the famed outfit (now known more as basketball clowns than serious cage talents) would reach a milestone with its 20,000th game, by far the most for any professional sports franchise known to exist anywhere in the world.

The only league that enjoyed even a modest stability during all this jumping of cities (by ball clubs) and jumping of ball clubs (by mercenary ballplayers) was the American Basketball League of the late '20s and early '30s. That circuit, in the end, was itself only a short-lived half-dozen year experiment and it unquestionably drew much of its stature from the Original Celtics ball club during their two brief seasons on board. Yet the league also had stars in other quarters such as Benny Borgmann (Fort Wayne), John "Honey" Russell (Cleveland and Chicago), Rusty Saunders (Washington), Nat Hickey (Cleveland), and Carl Husta (also Cleveland) to boost its stock with Midwestern and Eastern fans. Had the external forces of a Great Depression not intervened after only five seasons, the circuit might yet have rolled into the world war years a full decade later, still primed to take full advantage of a new popularity and new economic promise suddenly facing the cage sport. While it didn't, in the end, survive the Celtics debacle and the nationwide economic hard times that soon piled one revenue loss on top of another, nonetheless the ABL had raised basketball consciousness (at least east of the Mississippi) and even provided small hints that a solvent pro circuit might actually someday be possible.

A more stable showcase of the late barnstorming era was the popular World Professional Championship Tournament, launched in Chicago in 1939, and proving a large drawing card for spectators as well as for crack pro teams throughout much of the '40s. It was here that Saperstein's Globetrotters had first made their mark as a serious, competitive, and highly talented basketball force. And it was also here that Mikan and the Chicago American Gears made their first splash in the public arena. Mikan had been signed for an unheard of $60,000 by the hometown Gears as soon as his college eligibility had lapsed with the close of the 1946 DePaul season. It was already too late for NBL competitions that year, but not too late for the most celebrated college star on record to eliminate all doubters with his performance in the world pro tournament. With Mikan scoring an even 100 points in five games, Maurice White's Gears made it into the semifinals before falling to the NBL rival Oshkosh All-Stars with their own more experienced pivotman, Cowboy Edwards. The Gears' season ended abruptly when their rookie pivotman fouled out in the third period. Mikan, nonetheless, won the tournament MVP Award, proved his abilities to dominate in the pros just as he had in college, and stirred a flurry of anticipation everywhere around the NBL for the coming of a new souped-up pro season.

Mikan and his team gave the NBL instant credibility when the established Midwestern pro circuit first faced off against the new Eastern BAA during the winter of 1946–47, but not without first some anxious moments for other NBL club owners when Mikan chose to sit out the opening weeks of the campaign in a contract dispute with owner White. Big George's lucrative five-year deal was reportedly filled with numerous incentives for baskets and free throws made; the new star wanted his money guaranteed and not conditional upon performance. Once it was all worked out (after six Mikan-less weeks for the Gears) and White's franchise player was back in the fold, Chicago finished strong enough to peak for the playoffs and capture a league championship just as expected. The pioneering center, who had revolutionized the college game, now began legitimizing the pro version in the same fashion. Averaging only a fraction above some of the league's other top scorers (16.5 to 14.4 for Rochester's Cervi and 13.2 for Risen of Indianapolis), he nonetheless scored repeatedly on taps and hooks inside, while proving to be the first fully coordinated big man with his crisp passing, tough defense, and aggressive rebounding. The Gears, as a team, did not turn into a winning outfit, however, until Fort Wayne player-coach Bobby McDermott was acquired in a trade and teamed up with Mikan to provide a deadly effective inside-outside combination. In the postseason finals, Rochester held Mikan in check for only one game, the first, before he exploded for 23 and 27 as the Gears coasted during the rest of the five-game series.

Mikan and his teammates enjoyed a gypsy-style existence in the early going, which was enough to prove that pro ball had not yet entirely lost its barnstorming flavor. Without being traded, Mikan would play for two distinct teams that would win titles in three straight seasons, yet also in two different leagues. Chicago's NBL crown of 1947 might easily have hinted of a dynasty in the making, but in reality, it marked only a bittersweet zenith for the Chicago team, which saw its continued championship dreams overnight dismantled by the overzealous plans of the club owner. Maurice White wildly miscalculated the magnitude of the gate attraction represented by Mikan by believing it was enough to support his own entire league. Before a new season opened White had yanked his Gears from the NBL lineup and backed new franchises in outposts such as Atlanta, New Orleans, Denver, and St. Paul. The ill-conceived, ill-fated Professional Basketball League of America failed in a matter of weeks (White losing $600,000 plus his own team), and the American Gears players (including the prime piece of real estate, George Mikan) were hastily reclaimed by NBL officials and assigned to other league clubs. Mikan thus wound up as an unexpected windfall for Max Winter and Ben Berger who had just purchased the moribund Detroit NBL team and taken it up to the Twin Cities for re-christening as the Minneapolis Lakers.

Once relocated in Minneapolis Mikan would pace a new group of teammates to a second NBL title. He would do so by facing off with Rochester's Royals a second straight year for the title showdown, this time wearing a new uniform but packing the same wallop. Once again Mikan won handily, though he received a huge boost in the rematch from added firepower in the form of ex-Stanford All-American Jim Pollard, now also in a Lakers' uniform, and also from a late-season injury to opposing Rochester center Arnie Risen. Risen had been sidelined by a broken jaw, and with him out of the lineup there was no way to slow the Pollard-Mikan onslaught. It was now two titles in a row for the game's biggest star, earned in two different cities and sporting two different uniforms. The vagabond scenario was not over, either, since the often bizarre business alignments that seemed to rule the game would again soon take over Mikan's destiny. For his third pro season George was anchored in the same city, but this time he would be operating in an entirely new league. By late summer 1948 Podoloff's rival BAA had enticed Winter and Berger to combine forces with a big-city circuit that offered far more room for mushrooming profits.

After losing Mikan, the NBL continued to limp along as a much-reduced rival to the BAA. The only thing that seemed to salvage the remnants of the circuit was a surprise deal inked with the entire group of graduating stars from Kentucky's great college team, fresh from scoring an Olympic triumph to add luster to their earlier NCAA and NIT laurels. Before the headlining collegians were added to the fold, the league trudged through one final shambles of a season. There were 10 clubs left, and one of them still had Dolph Schayes, but 4 teams were hastily formed on the eve of the new campaign, and the one in Detroit folded after only 19 games and had to be replaced with still another makeshift outfit in Dayton. Anderson won the final championship in three straight against an Oshkosh All-Stars team that was still featuring an aging LeRoy Edwards, the same Cowboy who had been the league's first showpiece a decade earlier. The few NBL fans still on board must have sensed this final reduced campaign was little more than an afterthought.

If there was a single event or figure that established the pro game in the first half of the '50s, it was George Mikan, basketball's first superstar. Fans came out to see Mikan, first and foremost, and without a player of such magnitude, it is hard to imagine that the new leagues (NBL, BAA, or NBA) would have had much better prospects for survival than any of their forerunners. Mikan was such a drawing card that he quickly became almost bigger than the league itself. This was sufficiently demonstrated when the Lakers paid their first NBA visit to New York in

1950, and the Madison Square Garden marquee simply advertised "Tonight, George Mikan versus the Knicks!"

While Mikan was giving the game flair and box-office appeal on the court, Maurice Podoloff was nailing down its stable future in the commissioner's office. A close examination suggests that Podoloff's invisible role in the league's growing vitality was every bit as major as Mikan's visible and more easily measurable one. First, Podoloff lured into his own league the two best NBL franchises, Minneapolis and Rochester, with the two biggest stars, Mikan and Bob Davies. Next, he orchestrated the anticipated merger of leagues that held a final key to pro basketball's prosperous future. That merger was finally triggered when the NBL showed a last gasp of life by signing up the entire Kentucky starting five (Rupp's famed "Fabulous Five" that had just earned two consecutive NCAA titles) for its new replacement Indianapolis franchise. The Kentucky players were even given full ownership of the expansion ball club, which was a large enough enticement to get them on board with the NBL and not with Podoloff's league. It was also incentive enough for Podoloff, in turn, to invite all the remaining NBL clubs to join hands with his own league. Almost as significant, Podoloff would next exercise a firm (even ruthless) hand when the breaking news of point-shaving scandals threw college basketball into turmoil and threatened for a spell to do the same to the professional version.

The significant turning points came with the 1949–50 and 1950–51 seasons. In the first of these years the BAA merged with the remnants of the NBL, then renamed and restructured itself as the entity evermore known as the National Basketball Association. A first season for the new combined league would still be plagued by a raft of organizational problems. For one thing, the circuit was far too unweildy the first time around, consisting of 17 clubs in three divisions playing an unbalanced schedule that did not provide for equal numbers of games. And the playoff format designed by Podoloff and the club owners left much to be desired also: with three divisional winners, one inevitably enjoyed a bye during the championship semifinals. On the court, however, things were noticeably picking up in quality now that top NBL players were combined with better BAA arenas and bigger BAA audiences. The first-ever game under the new league structure matched the two main drawing cards, Mikan and Fulks. Fulks was no longer a scoring match for Mikan (or even for Groza in Indianapolis or Zaslofsky in Chicago) and would soon have to take a backseat even in Philadelphia to new stars like Arizin (a rookie in 1951) and Neil Johnston (a rookie in 1952). But Mikan and his ball club would again be taking a backseat to no one by year's end. With Mikan averaging more than 30 in the playoffs, Minneapolis ground out an easy title victory over Syracuse in the first championship round-robin played under the NBA designation.

The second NBA season turned even bigger corners, first by honing membership and adjusting divisional alignment (11 teams and two balanced divisions), and second by embracing long overdue racial integration. Chuck Cooper with Boston and Nat "Sweetwater" Clifton with New York pioneered on the latter front, along with Earl Lloyd in Washington. But integration was never quite the front-line story for the NBA that it had been in baseball. Focus was instead on upbeat league action, which witnessed Rochester knock the vaunted Lakers from championship contention early in the postseason (the big factor was a foot injury suffered by Mikan), and which earlier in the year also welcomed the first all-star contest. The latter event was staged in Boston Garden in March and was yet another inspiration of the inventive Walter Brown. Ten thousand turned out to witness a surprising performance by Boston center Ed Macauley, who garnered MVP honors by canning 20 while holding Mikan to just four field goals. Another yearlong attraction was Mikan's head-to-head battle with Indianapolis center Alex Groza for individual honors in both scoring and rebounding. In the final weeks, Rochester rode the momentum of its victory over an injury-slowed Mikan straight to the league championship, climaxed by an exciting showdown with New York. For the first time, the championship series came down to a deciding seventh game and the issue remained in doubt until deciding free throws by Bob Davies in the closing minute of play.

Groza's own promising career would soon come to a crashing halt before it was hardly off the ground. Events unfolding around the Indianapolis Olympians at the outset of the league's third season would provide one of the most bizarre and sad chapters of league history. When news of the 1951 college scandals broke unexpectedly, it was not only the collegians who felt the aftershocks: the careers of two of the pro league's brightest young stars were also left in ruins. On the eve of a new season, Groza and star guard Ralph Beard were taken into custody in Chicago, where they had stopped en route to their team's opener with Tri-Cities to witness the annual college all-star game. Not long afterward both were banned for life by a defensive Maurice Podoloff determined to avoid even the slightest hint of scandal in his own house. The promising Indianapolis franchise was, of course, also ruined beyond repair. The Olympians did increase their victory total by three games in 1951–52—with Leo Barnhorst, Bob Lavoy, and Joe Graboski picking up the scoring load—yet, without Groza and Beard, they were no match for Minneapolis in the opening postseason round. And the club, not surprisingly, survived only one additional season without its two biggest stars to bolster interest at the ticket window.

There has long been much confusion about the integration of pro basketball, and few ever get the story entirely straight. Cooper, Lloyd, and Clifton share the individual honors, yet it is Lloyd who seems to have lost his true place in history. Cooper, of Duquesne, was first plucked in the draft by a bold Walter Brown willing to risk the wrath and raised eyebrows of fans and fellow owners in order to improve the quality of his own club. The Washington Capitols jumped into the fray during the same June 1950 draft session to register their own gamble with Lloyd out of West Virginia State. Sensing where the wind was blowing, the New York Knicks next scrambled to sign up Globetrotters regular Nat Clifton, who had once performed spectacularly for Xavier College in Louisiana. Cooper made the first headlines (second-page as they were) on draft day, Clifton inked the first contract signed by a black, but Lloyd first stepped onto an NBA floor when his own team opened the new season a night before Cooper's Boston club or the Knicks with Clifton.

And even before the NBA season of 1950–51, there had been efforts at token integration in the less visible NBL, though they were hardly recognized as such at the time. Pop Gates had played with a pair of NBL teams—Tri-Cities in 1947 and

Dayton (as player-coach) two years later. The 1943 Chicago Studebakers had pioneered back in the earliest years of the Midwest league with former Globetrotters Roosie Hudson, Sonny Boswell, Tony Peyton, Duke Cumberland, and Bernie Price in their lineup. The Dayton Rens had entered the final NBL season in midstream as an emergency replacement for the folded Detroit franchise and boasted a largely black roster comprised of several New York Rens well beyond their prime (including player-coach Gates, Sonny Wood, Dolly King, and Hank DeZonie) and also featuring future big-league baseball standout George Crowe. The most-overlooked NBL pioneer, however, may have been Dolly King, the former LIU star who had joined the Rochester Royals partway into the 1947 season and performed admirably off the bench for the league's winningest ball club.

Racial integration thus didn't come overnight as it did with baseball. And for the first few years—much like the league itself—it happened far from the limelight. But the door had now been left ajar for the talented ebony players who, by decade's end, would give the pro basketball circuit its first legitimate widespread fan appeal. First came Elgin Baylor—the unprecedented flyer—and Wilt Chamberlain—the greatest-ever scorer—at the tail end of the '50s. Soon Oscar Robertson solidified the new role of black basketball superstar at the outset of the '60s by offering a complete clinic in basketball technique every time he stepped upon the playing floor. These exciting playground stars from the inner cities changed the way the game was played and thus also the way it was watched. They also made the pro game for the first time truly as popular as its collegiate rival. But all that was still a long way off, as there was yet a full decade to traverse between Chuck Cooper in 1950 and Oscar Robertson in 1960. And it was to be the decade in which professional basketball finally became a mainstream American sport.

"Tonight, George Mikan Versus the Knicks"

The first half decade of the enterprise known as the NBA was dominated by the pro game's first dynasty—the Minneapolis Lakers—and its first legitimate superstar—George Mikan. While Mikan had almost single-handedly launched the pro sport in the NBL and BAA at the end of the previous decade, he continued to sustain it in the first half of its first full adolescent decade. There would be better all-around players in the coming years; there would be none who did more to force a total revamping of the game.

With five men (or women) to a team, basketball has always displayed a tendency toward the inordinate influence of the single individual player. The National Basketball Association has seemingly always been dominated by a single superstar—at least in all the epochs when the league has been worth watching. George Mikan, by himself, owned the pioneering era of the late '40s; Russell controlled the first era of true stability, the late '50s; Wilt Chamberlain (shadowed by Oscar Roberston) was the front-page story line throughout the Golden Era '60s; Bird (with a considerable assist from Magic) made possible the resurrection of the '80s; and Air Jordan is synonymous with the celebrity-saturated '90s. While Jordan (or Oscar or Wilt) was arguably the most oversized talent, it was indisputably Mikan who had the biggest impact. If Big George didn't win as many consecutive team titles as Russell or as many scoring crowns as Jordan and Wilt, this was only because his own relentless domination of the opposition had forced the league into making the rule changes (especially the 24-second clock) that made him obsolete. Wilt would have been equally neutralized if the three-second lanes were extended 10 feet; Jordan would have much less luster (and far fewer scoring titles) if traveling were again strictly enforced and slam dunking outlawed.

As the NBA entered its first full decade of play with the onset of the '50s, pro basketball finally seemed an idea that was here to stay. Yet the NBA accent was still clearly on abrupt change, constant flux, and often radical experimentation. Not that such terms could be best used to describe the actual ball-bouncing game being played nightly on the court itself. By today's standards certainly, 1950s professional basketball remained at best a slow, plodding, and often tedious spectacle. It was the league itself, however, that was now a pastiche of constant flow and flux—new cities, new faces, and a parade of new rules aimed at eliminating some already obvious flaws in the game. These rules, of course, were also aimed at neutralizing the dominating force of George Mikan and his Minneapolis Lakers teammates. For the one thing that did not seem to be changing over the first few years of the newly organized professional game was the one-sided nature of league competition. There was little that could be done to maintain competitive balance in the face of the Lakers' seemingly overwhelming edge in raw playing talent.

Actually, the Lakers were not quite the only story in the first official NBA campaign. Another old NBL club, the Syracuse Nationals, had gotten a break from the league's strange schedule and, thus, had run over all opposition for much of the year with the best overall record (51–13, four losses fewer than Minneapolis and Rochester). The Nats were the one old NBL club that, for geographic reasons, had been placed with holdover BAA teams in the new NBA Eastern Division. But since Eastern teams with bigger arenas (like Boston and New York) did not want to travel to small-town Syracuse with its rough crowds and small box-office take, the Nats played the bulk of their games (all but 10) against weaker Western Division rivals, even though their season's record counted in the Eastern Division standings. Syracuse was equally famed for its own rising individual star and also for its rabid fans and opponent-unfriendly arena. NYU great Dolph Schayes might well have played in New York with the hometown Knicks, but Ned Irish had refused to offer the salary he was asking ($1,000 over the BAA salary cap in 1949). When Schayes thus cast his lot with the NBL Nats, the New Yorkers lost not only the potential gate attraction of a popular star who was also Jewish, but also squandered the on-court force that might have put them in a class with any of the league's top dogs for years to come.

In Dolph Schayes the upstate Syracuse club and not the downstate Knicks could boast one of the circuit's biggest fan favorites and (before Pettit at least) the NBA's most promising budding superstar. But in the postseason derby of the league's first go-round, it was not surprisingly Mikan and company who again emerged on the top of the pack. Syracuse had grabbed the home-game advantage in its destined title-round meeting with the Lakers, and Minneapolis would therefore have to capture at least one game in Syracuse (where the Nats were 34–1) to defend their 1949 BAA title. They did so immediately in the opener on a 40-foot game-winner by Bob Harrison, which clinched a pitched battle in which Mikan had scored 37. The defenders then held on with three home-court victories back in Minneapolis and gained the crown in a fight-marred sixth game with Mikan this time garnering 40. Mikan's 31.3 postseason scoring average nearly doubled Schayes's output.

Part of the upsurge of interest in the pro game in the early '50s could be laid to the widespread discrediting of the college version of the sport. The betting scandals that broke as front-page news in 1950 and 1951 had the effect of severely deflating the game in the hotbed that was New York City. And the NBA was quick enough to step directly into the void. To secure its position and keep its own decks spotless, Podoloff's office reacted quickly against Groza and Beard, the two Kentucky stars inplicated in the events of 1948 and 1949. In doing so, the NBA wiped out a potentially strong Indianapolis franchise, yet kept its own house above reproach. It seemed a small price to pay.

There was also the celebrated case of Jack Molinas out in Fort Wayne. And when a second scandal broke in the college game a decade later, the NBA would react once again and even overreact this second time around. The result was the knee-jerk expulsion of potential pro stars Connie Hawkins and Roger Brown, who had been implicated only for casual contacts with men intent on fixing college games. The league remained superficially pure from the outset and thus gained a huge public relations advantage in its battle with the colleges for big-city fans. But there was a price to be paid, especially by Hawkins and Brown.

Minneapolis would win four of the first five NBA titles. Only in 1951 did still another NBL survivor, Rochester's Royals, break the Lakers' title stranglehold. While Minneapolis owned the best team and the best player in the early part of the '50s, there were noteworthy stars emerging elsewhere as well. Philadelphia had two big scorers to rival Mikan in the individual point-making derby and also to bolster the Warriors into legitimate contenders. Fulks had been replaced in Philly by Arizin (a jump-shooter like Fulks himself) and Neil Johnston (owner of a sweeping hook that was more deadly and capable of far greater range than Mikan's). Together they dominated the individual scoring races (Arizin winning one and Johnston three straight) once the shot-clock legislation and wide foul lanes put an end to Mikan. Syracuse, of course, had phenomenal workhorse Dolph Schayes, who was increasingly looking like the league's most admirable if most overlooked and underrated all-around talent. Boston was developing its own niche with Cousy, Sharman, and Macauley. And Fort Wayne had George Yardley and a strong supporting cast that included NBA newcomers Mel Hutchins and Larry Foust, and BAA veterans Andy Phillip and Frankie Brian (once traded from Chicago to Tri-Cities for rookie Bob Cousy).

For the first time in his six-year pro career, Mikan was not the league's scoring champ in 1952, that honor falling (with an assist from a new rule widening the foul lane and thus keeping Mikan farther from the bucket) to deadeye Philadelphia forward Paul Arizin. Thin and frail compared to Mikan or Lovellette, the undersized Philly ace known as "Pitchin' Paul" possessed an awkward arm-flapping style and deadly outside jump shot that would quickly revolutionize the NBA approach to scoring. The game was suddenly shifting toward the perimeter, and only once after 1952 would Mikan average 20 points for a full season's play. And while the league's next three scoring champs—Arizin (6'4"), Neil Johnston (6'8"), and Bob Pettit (6'9")—were all moderate big men, all three also relied on

Fort Wayne's George Yardley (12) battles for the ball with Red Kerr, right, and Bill Kenville, left, of Syracuse in the 1955 NBA Finals. Yardley was the first to score 2,000 points in a single NBA season.

Transcendental Graphics

medium-range jumpers or sweeping hooks rather than short-range layups and tap-ins for the bulk of their offensive arsenal.

If the league was already developing stars, it was certainly not pulling in fans at the rate Podoloff and his aides might have hoped. Indeed, the games seemed to be treading on thin ice. Part of the problem was a holdover from a playing style in vogue for many years in the pro game and supported by numerous NBL veterans such as Al Cervi in Rochester and Buddy Jeannette in Baltimore. And another part of the problem was the dominance of Mikan and the way Minneapolis used the existing rules to its constant advantage. NBA games were turning into brutal and boring slugfests. Several embarrassing games throughout the 1952, 1953, and 1954 seasons (such as the one in which Cousy poured in 50 in the playoffs while camped on the foul line for most of four overtime periods, or the one in which the Pistons held the ball all night against Mikan and won a game with a mere 19 points) were sufficient to emphasize the point that the accent in pro basketball was clearly on brawn and bullyism and not yet on displays of athletic brilliance.

The rules themselves seemed to encourage such roughhouse play. Violent fouling was a standby strategy of the game, for instance, since there was, in the league's earliest years, no limit placed on the number of allowable fouls charged against a team during each quarter of play. When fouls were committed against a player not in the act of shooting, only one free shot was awarded, so that an inevitable basket by a player positioned close to the hoop could be readily taken away by the defense in exchange for only one potential point at the charity line. And the defense could further enhance its advantage by sending bruised and battered opponents to the line, a little worse for wear and in no proper condition to attempt the hard-earned charity shots.

Other rule-governed aspects of the game also encouraged rough-and-tumble as well as slow and dull styles of play. With no requirements on how often or quickly the ball was to be shot at the basket, the leading team found clear advantage in stalling play, often bringing court action to almost a dead standstill down the stretch of a one-sided game. While the leading team stalled, the trailing club hacked away in a desperate attempt to gain ground simply by trading foul shots while the clock remained suspended. Such a tactic of fouling repeatedly on defense also rewarded the trailers, since one foul shot only was awarded, and it was a seemingly wise strategy to trade the one point for a new chance at retrieving the ball and making two.

The Lakers clearly excelled at this style of game. Mikan, or perhaps Jim Pollard, would snare a rebound over the outstretched grasp of shorter opponents. A lob pass to Slater Martin would be followed by a slow dribble into the frontcourt as both offense and defense waited for Mikan to lumber downcourt into the pivot position. Another lob back to the entrenched giant under the opposite-end glass boards would be followed by an easy layup, or perhaps a thundering crash of bodies careening toward a loose rebound.

One popular misconception among NBA followers is that the current 24-second shot clock preventing stalling and slowdown tactics was originally an overnight invention, resulting from some knee-jerk reaction of club officials to a single slowdown game only weeks before the radical rules revision. Yet the one game most responsible for the change actually occurred nearly four seasons before the rule innovation itself—a contest between the Lakers and Pistons played on November 22, 1950. When the Fort Wayne team invaded Minneapolis on that historic evening it was about to face a juggernaut Lakers club that had not dropped a home decision in nearly a year. Certainly drastic strategy was called for, and Pistons coach Murray Mendenhall that night held a surprising and evil trump card up his always tricky sleeve.

To the astonishment and eventual outrage of the partisan crowd, Fort Wayne controlled the opening tip and stationed center Larry Foust at midcourt with the ball tucked under his arm. There Foust stood firm, and the Pistons' novel strategy was very quickly apparent to all in attendance. Occasionally there would be a surprise pass and a flurry of movement, yet Fort Wayne continued the slowdown, leading 8–7 at the end of a single quarter, then trailing but 13–11 at intermission. With the Lakers in the lead during the second half, the Minneapolis players saw little reason to press their stalling opponents. Mendenhall's strategy, however, seemed to be to keep the score tight even when behind. With the Lakers tallying but a single free throw by Pollard in the final period and still leading 18–17 with mere seconds remaining, the Fort Wayne plot suddenly hatched its final bizarre results. Curly Armstrong drove toward the hoop and then fed fast-breaking Larry Foust for a last-second desperation heave that Mikan actually deflected—straight up into the goal. Fort Wayne was the 19–18 winner in the lowest scoring and least savory contest in league history.

Little more than a month later, Indianapolis and Rochester contributed their own reenactment during a contest which ended 73–73 and then dragged on endlessly through five overtime periods and 25 minutes of scoreless standoff. Each frustrating period began with the center-jump winner holding the ball for a single shot only seconds before time expired. When Indianapolis finally converted one of these desperation bombs for a 75–73 road victory, the Rochester fans had already almost all fled the premises in total disgust.

Pro Basketball's Defining Landmark Moments

1946—The modern professional basketball era begins with the founding of the East Coast 11-team Basketball Association of America (BAA) to rival the existing National Basketball League (NBL) operating mainly in the Midwest. The BAA is backed by hockey arena owners who install New Haven–based American Hockey League boss Maurice Podoloff as BAA president.

1948—The Minneapolis Lakers, with George Mikan, switch leagues, abandoning the NBL for the upstart BAA. The Lakers' defection (accompanied by the Rochester and Fort Wayne clubs) places the BAA in a vanguard position by providing the newest circuit with marquee players to go along with its larger arenas and major publicity outlets. The defections of Minneapolis and Rochester also pave the way for imminent merger of the two competing leagues.

1949—First-season BAA scoring leader Joe Fulks of the Philadelphia Warriors foreshadows future prolific point-making with an incredible one-game 63-point outburst versus the Indianapolis Jets. Fulks's one-handed jumpers (plus those of teammate Paul Arizin after 1950) rapidly catch on throughout the league as the popular offensive style of the future.

1949—The merger of the sinking NBL with the more prosperous BAA orchestrated by Podoloff results in a fresh-look unified 17-team circuit now known as the NBA (National Basketball Association). Pro basketball seems to have survived its required handful of seasons on the "critical list," although the league's roster of teams is downsized to 10 clubs during the 1950–51 campaign.

1950—The Boston Celtics make Chuck Cooper of Duquesne the first black player drafted by the league, while the New York Knicks ink Nat "Sweetwater" Clifton from the Harlem Globetrotters as first black signee. The Washington Capitols first break the league's color barrier, however, when West Virginia State's Earl Lloyd debuts against Rochester on opening night of the 1950–51 season.

1954—Syracuse Nationals owner Danny Biasone introduces the concept of the 24-second shot clock as a strategy to overcome deadly offensive slowdowns and ragged play threatening to destroy the league's image. Once adopted, the new rule fuels fan interest and also gives the NBA a distinctive offense-oriented appearance, which distinguishes it from the slower college version of the sport.

1956—The Boston Celtics acquire the top (second overall) college draft pick, Bill Russell, via a trade that sends veteran Ed Macauley and prospect Cliff Hagan to the St. Louis Hawks. With this single move, coach Red Auerbach lays the foundation for the greatest dynasty team in American sports history. Russell overnight revolutionizes team play as the greatest individual defensive force in basketball history.

1962—Wilt Chamberlain, in only his third pro campaign, posts the most phenomenal individual season in pro sports history when he tops the century mark in scoring during a

If historians today find these games intriguing, spectators who witnessed them were far from impressed. Still another painful moment for the league resulted from a 1953 playoff game between Boston and Syracuse that seemed to set new lows for fan boredom. Cousy scored 50 for a new playoff record, but most of Cousy's points were gathered from the foul line (30 made free throws and only 10 baskets) and came during four overtime sessions that were anything but nail-biting. The game seemingly took forever to drag through its final unartistic moments as both teams exploited the system that allowed them to risk one point rather than two by fouling every time opponents inbounded the ball. Before it was over, 107 fouls had been whistled, no player other than Cousy scored more than five baskets during 68 minutes of inaction, and both teams attempted less than 30 field goals while each was awarded more than 60 free throws. Worse still, this game was anything but an exception to the painful rule. During the full total of 23 playoff games that same season, the average was 80 free throws per game.

A year later Cousy and Boston were involved in still another postseason NBA disaster. A bored national television audience tuned in March 1954 to watch the

---

single game, logs 4,000-plus points (40 percent above his closest challenger), and averages better than 50 points per game while playing nearly every minute of every game. Wilt's achievements are never again even approached.

1962—Oscar Robertson nearly duplicates Chamberlain's super-human offensive efforts of the same 1961–62 season, becoming the only player ever to average a "triple-double" with double-figure season averages in scoring (30.8), rebounding (10.4), and assists (11.4). While Wilt provides a one-dimensional inside force, Oscar defines the new prototype for the all-around offensive intimidator.

1967—The ABA experiment begins a nine-year run, which will ultimately collapse, but not before revolutionizing NBA play (with slam dunks, playground freelancing style, and high-scoring forwards) for future decades and introducing some of the game's most colorful new stars (Julius Erving, Connie Hawkins, George Gervin, Spencer Haywood, George McGinnis, Artis Gilmore, Mel Daniels, Dan Issel, Moses Malone) and boldest innovations (multicolored ball, three-point field goals, soaring slam dunks, and equally soaring salaries).

1969—The Celtics' championship streak finally ends at 11 NBA titles in 13 seasons (8 in a row) yet will likely stand forever as the greatest dynasty feat in American sports annals, and also as the true Golden Age of NBA history. Bill Russell's retirement as player-coach finally closes the door on the dozen-year Auerbach–Cousy–Russell era in Boston Garden.

1970—UCLA's Lew Alcindor inspires an unprecedented bidding war before finally signing with NBA (Milwaukee Bucks) and rejecting a bank-breaking ABA offer (New York Nets). The failure to sign Alcindor nearly sinks the ABA's hopes for survival and is a blow from which the struggling junior league never fully recovers. The loss of Alcindor forces the ABA toward eventual absorption by the healthier NBA.

1979—Larry Bird and Magic Johnson arrive on the NBA scene and together pump new life and enthusiasm into a sagging league suffering from dipping TV ratings and ebbing fan support. Bird (Rookie of the Year) and Johnson (ace of the NBA champion Los Angeles Lakers) pave the way for Air Jordan, Shaquille O'Neal, Grant Hill, and the superstar era, which brings the NBA to its zenith during the mid-1990s.

1984—Michael Jordan is selected by the Chicago Bulls after Portland and Houston pass over the North Carolina All-American during the NBA college draft, thus launching the career of the league's biggest superstar and laying the foundation for what becomes the greatest NBA dynasty team since the Celtics of the '60s.

1998—Jordan's Chicago Bulls build the first dynasty championship string since Bill Russell's Boston Celtics with six NBA titles in eight seasons and the two best season-long records ever posted. The emergence of the Bulls dynasty clinches Jordan's rank atop the all-time list of the game's greatest superstars.

Celtics and Knicks plod and punch their way through a marathon parade between the two foul lines as neither team attempted to generate offense, and both settled for slaphappy roughhouse tactics. The few diehards who might have at least maintained enough interest to linger for the final outcome were even deprived of that single consolation, since the three-hour slugfest and free-throw shooting contest overran allotted network time and was abandoned long before it reached its painful 79–78 conclusion in Boston's favor. This time the blow was heavier, since the game happened to be on national television. Cousy's killing of the clock (by dribbling out the game's final minute) and both teams' brutal efforts to kill off any run-and-gun action made it clear, once and for all, that rule changes were now in order if pro basketball were to hang on to current fans and find any new markets for its showcase events like the postseason playoff tournament.

If there is a single moment when pro basketball departed forever from the college game, that moment came in the fall of 1954 with one of the most dramatic rule innovations in American sports history. The genius behind it all was Syracuse owner Danny Biasone, who first articulated for his fellow league bosses the notion that their game could be repaired simply by putting a restriction on how long teams could hold the ball before being forced to fire at the basket. There was no magic behind Biasone's selection of 24 seconds as the appropriate time for an offensive possession. He had simply calculated the approximate time that teams were already taking between shots, easily arrived at by dividing game length (48 minutes) by average shots taken a season earlier. During the season just completed, teams had actually shot about every 18 ticks of the clock, making the proposed limit hardly seem unreasonable. Biasone explained to fellow owners that, since teams seemed to record about 60 shots a game, this averaged out to about one every 24 seconds over the course of normal play. The difference with the new legislation was that such a pace for offense maneuvering would now become mandatory and not be left to mere chance (and thus also susceptible to tampering for strategic benefit). It was a change whose time had clearly come, and a desperate league was clearly ready for some rather dramatic innovations.

And Biasone's rule was not the only change of great impact during the topsyturvy 1954–55 season. A second would be the new dictum that virtually eliminated intentional fouling by limiting each club to five personal fouls per period. Since any more fouling would give added bonus shots (which were regularly converted in a league of so many shooting specialists), this roughhouse tactic of play was curbed almost immediately in the face of the new fouling rule.

No single rule change has ever so drastically transformed an established professional sport as did Danny Biasone's 24-second shot clock. What debuted in the NBA with the opening tap of the 1954–55 season was a vastly different game, one which immediately played to rave reviews and soon generated almost immediate box-office impact. One hundred–point scores now suddenly became commonplace, and the league scoring average soared 14 points above the preceding year. Yet the foremost concern on the sports pages of the day in late autumn of 1954 was precisely how this new up-tempo game would curtail the slow-moving Lakers and cramp the style of an aging George Mikan. For his own part, Mikan had already seen the writing on the wall. Though barely 30, the big guy now realized his day in the sun had passed, and the game he had once dominated was no longer designed to accommodate his limited playing style. Having already earned an off-season law

Bob Cousy was Boston's first superstar and a ballhandling wizard whose moves were copied on every playground in the land.

Transcendental Graphics

degree, Mikan soon made speculation about his effectiveness under the shot clock a moot point by announcing his retirement just three days prior to the opening of Lakers training camp for the new season.

With the new rules had inevitably come a new and more exciting style of play. The legislated shooting time now forced a running game and a hurry-up style of offense, the antithesis of the way Minneapolis had usually played with Mikan plugging the center court. And with the new emphasis on running and gunning, an old dynasty was quickly killed off. Overnight, Mikan was gone, and so were the once-invincible Lakers. Clyde Lovellette could not replace Mikan in 1955. The new big man scored as much as his Hall of Fame predecessor, and the team average (like everyone else's) jumped about 15 points; but the victories dropped by half a dozen, first place was ceded to Fort Wayne in the West, and the Pistons manhandled the Lakers in the division playoff finals. Nor could Elgin Baylor completely reverse the tide, though the flashy new rookie who arrived in 1959 did keep the Minnesota franchise afloat for a couple of final seasons before the bailout to Los Angeles. Baylor did, however, provide the first glimpse of the kind of unparalleled talent that was about to enter the league over the next half dozen seasons. Much of that talent for the very first time would consist of black athletes from the inner-city playgrounds.

If basketball suffered in Minneapolis in Mikan's absence, on a larger league-wide scale the void was quickly enough filled. For several years Red Auerbach and Walter Brown had been fitting together the pieces of a highly competitive team in Boston. Major steps had already been taken with a backcourt consisting of flashy ball handler Bob Cousy and deadeye shooter Bill Sharman that had supplanted Davies and Wanzer in Rochester as the league's best. By 1955 only one piece seemed to be missing from the Boston championship equation. And with one of the most ingenious and fortuitous moves in league history, Auerbach would soon enough find himself that vital missing piece.

Celtics Mystique

The emergence of proficient jump-shooters and the influence of Biasone's shot clock had done much of the work in jazzing up the once stodgy pro game. Freed from brutal fouling and interest-killing stalling, the infant NBA enjoyed an overnight offensive renaissance that attracted thousands of new fans through the turnstiles and in front of the TV screens. The other major elements of basketball's multipronged attraction—disciplined team offensive flow and effective team defense—were now also about to receive a considerable face-lift, thanks to a genius coach in Boston with an eye planted firmly on the future. And once again, it was a single individual who brought about the much-needed revolution. Bill Russell was about to arrive on the NBA scene with an impact nearly equal to that of the recently departed George Mikan.

Russell's arrival with Boston involved almost as many strange twists and fortunate accidents as had Mikan's in Minneapolis a decade earlier. For one thing, it involved one of the most fortuitous if not ingenious front-office decisions of American sports history. Red Auerbach had long known what seemed to be holding back his Boston club from becoming a legitimate championship contender. The Celtics, with Cousy and Sharman in the backcourt and agile Ed Macauley up front, could already score points by the bushels, yet were not very adept at holding down the firepower of opponents. (Under the new 24-second rule, Boston was the first club to average triple figures for a season, yet still give up more than it tallied.) In Bill Russell at San Francisco University Auerbach had glimpsed not only the future of his own club but also the future of the NBA game at large. That future would be a racehorse game that depended not only on fleet ball handlers out on the wings, but also a peerless defender and rebounder plugging the middle and able to launch the running attack with perfectly timed outlet passes. Auerbach thus set into motion in weeks prior to the 1956 college draft, a chain of events (in the form of a risky trade) designed to acquire the key to his own team's rosy future.

Owning the third pick in the upcoming draft, it was no secret that Auerbach coveted Russell as the single component needed to convert his team from an also-ran into a champion. It was also no secret that Rochester, as owner of the top pick, would likely bypass the huge USF center who would demand an unthinkable salary for his services. The Royals, instead, had their sights set on Duquesne's talented guard, Sihugo Green. (Russell was rumored to be considering a deal with the Globetrotters, but insiders knew that the proud athlete would never expose himself

Sihugo Green earned trivial immortality as the player selected ahead of Bill Russell in the history-shaping 1956 NBA college draft.

Transcendental Graphics

to the self-effacing Globetrotters style of court comedy.) St. Louis owner Ben Kerner was apparently willing to deal his No. 2 shot at Russell, though the price would likely be steep. The Hawks' management required Macauley (a local favorite who had starred at Saint Louis University, as well as one of the league's best offensive centers) be included in the deal and promising Cliff Hagan out of Kentucky as well, but it was a price Auerbach didn't flinch at paying. The result would quickly prove to be not only Boston Celtics invincibility, but a new national stature for NBA basketball thrown into the bargain.

The trade that brought Russell from a potential home in St. Louis to Boston was one that, in the long run, benefited both teams. The Hawks acquired from Auerbach two players—Macauley and Hagan—who would be the key to their own winning future. Macauley, once teamed with Pettit, contributed heavily to lifting the Hawks into two straight championship series with Russell and Boston. Retiring to the bench as head coach after the Hawks' championship in 1958, Macauley directed the St. Louis club to two more title showdowns with Boston in 1960 and 1961. With Hagan and Macauley in the fold, Kerner's team had become the equal to any in the league save Boston, and even with the Celtics, the Hawks always held their own. It was also unlikely that Russell could ever have played in St. Louis with its blatantly racist atmosphere. The trade thus seemed a foregone conclusion at the time it was made and one difficult to second-guess from either side once it was executed. Yet it was nonetheless one of the most significant trades to be found anywhere in league history.

Russell immediately provided the missing piece for Auerbach's budding dynasty. With Russell guarding the opposition basket, sweeping rebounds, and dishing outlet passes, the Celtics were ready to unleash a new and deadly version of fine-tuned fast-break basketball. It would be a style and an execution sufficient to dominate the league for more than the next decade. What emerged with the acquisition of Russell and the simultaneous 1956 drafting of Tom Heinsohn out of Holy Cross (a regional pick), was the greatest winning skein in American pro sports history. And what also emerged was consistently the best basketball team over any extended period that had (or still has) ever been pasted together.

Boston's dominance as the sport's greatest dynasty team throughout the late '50s and all of the '60s did not result from any lack of stiff competition. True enough that the champions had to win fewer postseason games than do today's winners—and thus fewer series (two in the early '60s versus four in the early '90s)—to reach the coveted trophy. But the regular NBA season was a far more strenuous haul during the league's formative decades. The argument may well be made that Boston's reign indeed coincided with the league's strongest period ever. Only the NBA of Bird and Magic in the first half of the '80s can rival the quality of a circuit that featured the St. Louis, Boston, Philadelphia, and Los Angeles teams which jockeyed for position in a league filled with stars such as Bob Pettit, Cousy, Russell, Chamberlain, Oscar Robertson, Jerry West, and a dozen or so second-tier titans like Nate Thurmond, Bill Sharman, Jack Twyman, Walt Bellamy, and George Yardley. When Boston reached the NBA Finals or conference finals during the Auerbach era, it was annually faced with battling a Hawks, Warriors, or Lakers lineup that was a virtual all-star roster (say, Pettit, Hagan, Slater Martin, and Ed Macauley for the 1958 Hawks, or Arizin, Chamberlain, Gola, and Guy Rodgers with the 1962 Warriors) by today's expansion-era standards.

What also emerged from the era were not only some of the loftiest stars and teams, but also some of the most intense rivalries of pro basketball history. Fewer teams and a bevy of stars meant powerhouse squads left to battle each other again and again over the course of each season. Chamberlain and Russell would face-off a dozen times a campaign (Jordan locked horns only twice with Karl Malone and John Stockton or Shaquille O'Neal and Kobe Bryant). Rivalries were deep-seated and usually thrilling, and renewable and ongoing because of regular encounters and infrequently shifting rosters over several consecutive seasons. Such heated rivalries between Boston and St. Louis, New York and Minneapolis, Los Angeles and Boston, Boston and Philadelphia, Syracuse and Rochester-Cincinnati, Philadelphia and New York, and St. Louis and Minneapolis were the very essence of pro basketball wars during a Golden Era of the late '50s and early '60s.

The Hope Diamond of these great rivalries was that staged by Boston and St. Louis. During four of five contiguous seasons, the Celtics of Bill Russell and company and the Hawks of Bob Pettit and a cast of dozens ran through a series of winter-long collision courses that wound down with the inevitable April cham-

One of the NBA's greatest rivalries featured the Boston Celtics and St. Louis Hawks in the late '50s. Here, Hawks guard Jack McMahon (15) drives against Boston's Tom Heinsohn, while St. Louis great Bob Pettit and Boston star Bill Sharman look on.

Transcendental Graphics

pionship face-off. And St. Louis, despite giving away Russell (and getting only Hagan and Macauley in return), always held its own with the more balanced and explosive Boston club during several title-round showdowns. Boston survived the first championship clash on Loscutoff's free throw in the final two seconds of a second overtime in Game 7—and then only when Pettit's final heave rolled harmlessly off the rim. St. Louis exploited a Russell injury and an unforgettable 50-point final-game outing by Pettit in the subsequent rematch to gain a sweet revenge. Even after Boston gained its firm foothold on dynasty status, Auerbach's team would still have to climb over the Hawks and Pettit in both 1960 and 1961. It was the exciting postseason events of these two seasons that ultimately established both the true potency of Boston's emerging juggernaut and the true greatness of Bob Pettit as one of the league's most talented unsung heroes. Twice more over the next three campaigns, the archrivals locked horns in a postseason finale, and in the first of these collisions, Boston and Russell didn't display their final dominance until the seesaw tussle again reached the heart-stopping seventh and rubber game. Even in the final matchup of these titans in 1961 (a 4–1 Boston romp), Pettit was still the dominant individual postseason performer (28.6 points per game) even while Boston was now the unquestionably superior total team.

The Boston–St. Louis rivalry at the dawn of the NBA's second full decade would be nearly equalled by the Boston-Lakers and Boston-Philadelphia rivalries that filled out the remainder of that 10-year span. The first pairing of annual head-to-head combatants always seemed, in the end, to play out in Boston's favor, but almost never without last-minute heroics and thus opportunities for plenty of Los Angeles frustration. Wrenching moments of disaster befell L.A., especially on the occasions of the 1962 and 1966 title series. Los Angeles seemed to have the upper hand in '62, when Elgin Baylor exploded for a long-standing postseason record 61 points at Boston Garden during Game 5, putting the Lakers in position to win on their home floor. While the first opportunity to convert a championship was blown back in L.A. with a total team collapse, a second went by the boards as well when Frank Selvy missed a potential game-winning shot with only seconds left on the clock in Game 7. Four seasons later the frustration was reenacted when another Game 7 championship tussle turned Boston's way by the margin of a single two-point basket—this time dropped in by Sam Jones, 25 seconds before the season-ending buzzer.

The Boston-Philadelphia rivalry (launched once Wilt arrived on the scene) focused on in-conference play, but was nonetheless intense when postseason combat rolled around. There were numerous moments of high drama: the first postseason matchup of the giants Russell and Chamberlain with the 1960 Eastern Division Finals in which Boston (4–2 winners) proved basketball was still a team game no matter what awesome individual forces might be unleashed by a towering giant like Wilt; the furious seven-game battle two years later in which teams alternated home-floor wins and the entire issue was decided by a single Sam Jones bucket with two seconds left in the finale; the renewed hostilities of 1965 with Wilt and Philly (now the 76ers) rejoining the Eastern Division and another seven-game cliffhanger transpiring for the conference bragging rights. But no moment was more memorable than the one captured with Johnny Most's classic radio call of John Havlicek's last-second game-winning and series-saving steal—"Havlicek stole the ball! Havlicek stole the ball!" Boston's string of consecutive NBA titles seemed about to collapse at only six in 1965 when Philadelphia owned the ball and a chance at victory in the final seconds of the divisional finals. But Hal Greer's inbounds pass never reached its destination, as Havlicek stepped in front of Chet Walker for the most recounted and replayed defensive move in collective Beantown memory. It was a play and a radio call that immortalized one of the league's most famous broadcasters; it was also a moment that, in the end, seemed to define for eternity Havlicek's brilliant and lengthy Boston career.

As the 1960s opened the league was enjoying an unprecedented boom in raw talent inherited from the college ranks. Elgin Baylor came first as a savior for the rapidly sinking Minneapolis team in 1959, along with Wilt Chamberlain, who shattered all the existing scoring records while still a rookie in 1960. Robertson and West next arrived as the most explosive rookie tandem to date, and the one that would stand as benchmark until Bird and Magic appeared in 1979–80, and Olajuwon, Barkley, and Jordan debuted as the rookie class of 1984–85. Indiana University's phenomenal Walt Bellamy debuted in 1961 with perhaps the most unfairly over-looked rookie season of all time when he averaged better than 30 points and paced the circuit in field-goal percentage while trailing only Chamberlain and Russell in

Pro Basketball Postseason Champions

Year	BAA (1946–49)		NBL (1946–49)
1947	Philadelphia Warriors	def. Chicago Stags (4–1)	Chi. American Gears
1948	Baltimore Bullets	def. Philadelphia Warriors (4–2)	Minneapolis Lakers
1949	Minneapolis Lakers	def. Washington Capitols (4–2)	Anderson Packers
	NBA (1950–98)		
1950	Minneapolis Lakers	def. Syracuse Nationals (4–2)	
1951	Rochester Royals	def. New York Knicks (4–3)	
1952	Minneapolis Lakers	def. New York Knicks (4–3)	
1953	Minneapolis Lakers	def. New York Knicks (4–1)	
1954	Minneapolis Lakers	def. Syracuse Nationals (4–3)	
1955	Syracuse Nationals	def. Fort Wayne Pistons (4–3)	
1956	Philadelphia Warriors	def. Fort Wayne Pistons (4–1)	
1957	Boston Celtics	def. St. Louis Hawks (4–3)	
1958	St. Louis Hawks	def. Boston Celtics (4–2)	
1959	Boston Celtics	def. Minneapolis Lakers (4–0)	
1960	Boston Celtics	def. St. Louis Hawks (4–3)	
1961	Boston Celtics	def. St. Louis Hawks (4–1)	
1962	Boston Celtics	def. Los Angeles Lakers (4–3)	
1963	Boston Celtics	def. Los Angeles Lakers (4–2)	
1964	Boston Celtics	def. San Francisco Warriors (4–1)	
1965	Boston Celtics	def. Los Angeles Lakers (4–1)	
1966	Boston Celtics	def. Los Angeles Lakers (4–3)	
1967	Philadelphia 76ers	def. San Francisco Warriors (4–2)	
			ABA (1968–76)
1968	Boston Celtics	def. Los Angeles Lakers (4–2)	Pittsburgh Pipers
1969	Boston Celtics	def. Los Angeles Lakers (4–3)	Oakland Oaks
1970	New York Knicks	def. Los Angeles Lakers (4–3)	Indiana Pacers
1971	Milwaukee Bucks	def. Baltimore Bullets (4–0)	Utah Stars
1972	Los Angeles Lakers	def. New York Knicks (4–1)	Indiana Pacers
1973	New York Knicks	def. Los Angeles Lakers (4–1)	Indiana Pacers
1974	Boston Celtics	def. Milwaukee Bucks (4–3)	New York Nets
1975	Golden State Warriors	def. Washington Bullets (4–0)	Kentucky Colonels
1976	Boston Celtics	def. Phoenix Suns (4–2)	New York Nets
1977	Portland Trail Blazers	def. Philadelphia 76ers (4–2)	
1978	Washington Bullets	def. Seattle SuperSonics (4–3)	
1979	Seattle SuperSonics	def. Washington Bullets (4–1)	
1980	Los Angeles Lakers	def. Philadelphia Sixers (4–2)	
1981	Boston Celtics	def. Houston Rockets (4–2)	
1982	Los Angeles Lakers	def. Philadelphia Sixers (4–2)	
1983	Philadelphia Sixers	def. Los Angeles Lakers (4–0)	
1984	Boston Celtics	def. Los Angeles Lakers (4–3)	
1985	Los Angeles Lakers	def. Boston Celtics (4–2)	
1986	Boston Celtics	def. Houston Rockets (4–2)	
1987	Los Angeles Lakers	def. Boston Celtics 4–2)	
1988	Los Angeles Lakers	def. Detroit Pistons (4–3)	
1989	Detroit Pistons	def. Los Angeles Lakers (4–0)	
1990	Detroit Pistons	def. Portland Trail Blazers (4–1)	
1991	Chicago Bulls	def. Los Angeles Lakers (4–1)	
1992	Chicago Bulls	def. Portland Trail Blazers (4–2)	
1993	Chicago Bulls	def. Phoenix Suns (4–2)	
1994	Houston Rockets	def. New York Knicks (4–3)	
1995	Houston Rockets	def. Orlando Magic (4–0)	
1996	Chicago Bulls	def. Seattle SuperSonics (4–2)	
1997	Chicago Bulls	def. Utah Jazz (4–2)	
1998	Chicago Bulls	def. Utah Jazz (4–2)	

rebounding for the expansion Chicago Packers. And others were soon on the scene as well: Terry Dischinger in Chicago, Dave DeBusschere in Detroit, Jerry Lucas in Cincinnati, Hal Greer in Syracuse and Philadelphia, Willis Reed in New York, Rick Barry in San Francisco, Earl Monroe in Baltimore, and eventually, Bill Bradley and Cazzie Russell, also in New York.

The decade stretching from the mid-'50s to mid-'60s provided as its showpiece a one-on-one rivalry that would not again be matched until Magic Johnson confronted Larry Bird. Bill Russell versus Wilt Chamberlain resurrected in pro arenas the clash of titans that the college sport had known 10 years before when Oklahoma A&M seven-footer Bob Kurland battled DePaul's George Mikan. But such personalized competition was here intensified by the more frequent head-to-head face-offs offered by the pro schedule with its (then) 70-plus-game schedule and extended playoff format. Wilt was always the unstoppable force when it came to scoring and rebounding, even against the unparalleled defensive genius of Russell. But it was Russell who almost always came out on top in the team aspects of the game.

While Russell and Wilt held center stage, three other stars also proved to be incomparable innovators who also could popularize, enliven, and even reshape the game at every turn. Bob Cousy redefined the small backcourt man as effective playmaker and entertaining showman. Cousy would single-handedly make fancy ballhandling almost as glamorous as point scoring or defensive intimidation. Elgin Baylor in Minneapolis brought the first rare glimpses of an airborne style of play that would capture the imaginations, of not only arena fans, but also a new generation of rural school-yard and ghetto playground dribblers throughout the land. And Oscar Robertson drew up the model of the complete-package all-around offensive intimidator.

Baylor was indeed Dr. J and Air Jordan all wrapped into one explosive package, perhaps missing only the intensive media hype and global television stage that welcomed and underpinned the latter two stars. He personified the shakes and fakes and jazzy feints that marked inner-city black street ball. Oscar, in turn, was debatably the most complete all-around player yet developed and already a legendary total-package offensive star by the time he wrapped up his sophomore season at Cincinnati. Together, the two would implant the image of the black superstar squarely in the public imagination for decades to come. Baylor and Robertson are as responsible as anyone else for redefining basketball in the public eye as largely the urban black man's playground-inspired game.

The early '60s also witnessed the phenomenon of coast-to-coast expansion. This first arrived in autumn 1960 with Bob Short and his wilting Minneapolis Lakers, who sought more lucrative home grounds in the glittering environs (and expanded ticket market) of booming Los Angeles. California venues promised an untapped market only recently opened up to first football (with the transplanted Cleveland Rams and expansion San Francisco 49ers) and then baseball (thanks to O'Malley's Brooklyn Dodgers and Horace Stoneham's New York Giants) on the professional "major-league" level. Eddie Gottlieb's Philadelphia Warriors, with prime drawing card Wilt Chamberlain, soon followed suit when they took their act to San Francisco on the heels of the offense-crazy 1962 season.

The 1961–62 title chase was accompanied by the greatest offensive exposition in NBA history and (along with baseball in 1930) the greatest offensive explosion in American sports history. The entire nine-team league averaged nearly 120 points per club per contest (a level not to be surpassed until 1979) and six players (Chamberlain, Baylor, Bellamy, Robertson, Pettit, and West) averaged above 30 (no other season in league history would have more than three). The trouble was that most fans weren't yet watching—pro basketball was still low man on the Ameri-

Frank Selvy (11) guards Boston's Bob Cousy (14) during one of the famed Lakers-Celtics matchups. Although Selvy once scored 100 points in a single college game, he may best be remembered for the shot he didn't make in the 1962 NBA Finals that could have ended Boston's dynasty halfway through its predestined course.

can sports totem pole—Wilt was in Philadelphia, after all, not New York, and Oscar was buried in Cincinnati, not celebrated in L.A.; and neither spent much time on the front pages of the sports sections no matter how Herculean their nightly efforts. But the year was to prove one of incredible milestones and never-to-be-matched achievements of quite mythic proportions, nonetheless.

Wilt, who had been bending records by frightening margins in his two previous seasons, scored 100 in a single game (yes, 100!) against the Knicks—a feat that may well still be the most miraculous in American sports annals. Fitting for the times, however, the milestone contest was played in Hershey, Pennsylvania, as part of the NBA's traveling road show, and most of the 4,000-odd ticket buyers who had been lured by an opening-game exhibition between squads of NFL players had already departed by the time the NBA teams tipped off. Perhaps 2,000 remained to storm the court when Joe Ruklick fed Wilt with 46 seconds remaining for the thundering dunk that cracked the century mark.

Chamberlain performed more than an adequate encore when he kept his average above 50 for the entire year (topping 60 fifteen times during the winter) and logged 4,000-plus points; only Jordan (and then only once) has climbed over 3,000 (Wilt of course did it twice more himself, during the preceding and following seasons). And Chamberlain wasn't a solo act. Oscar, for his part, enjoyed the greatest all-around numerical season ever witnessed (averaging a triple-double for the entire campaign), and yet such miraculous consistency went virtually unnoticed in light of Chamberlain's humongous scoring. Walt Bellamy in Chicago got into the act with a lofty rookie scoring average (31.6) that was only good enough for third in the league, yet has only ever been bettered by Wilt himself among novices. And Elgin Baylor, restricted to weekend NBA duty by military service, posted another stratospheric scoring average (38.3) that no one but Wilt (not even Jordan) has ever before or since matched. It was indeed an eye-opening tribute to Wilt's unthinkable domination that Baylor averaged more than any other player in history and yet still trailed by a larger margin (a dozen points!) than any league runner-up on record. One can only imagine the deafening media din if Jordan or Shaq or Penny Hardaway in the mid-1990s were ever to average 50 (or even 38 like Baylor), score 100 in one game, or average a season-long (even a monthlong) triple-double. But in 1962 these were only one-column, page-three stories buried inside America's baseball-dominated and football-obsessed sports pages.

The individual 1962 explosions by Wilt, Oscar, and others grabbed hometown back-page headlines smack in the middle of Boston's ongoing reign. But by year's end, the big story was always still Auerbach, Russell, and the Celtics mystique. One Boston Garden era would seemingly end with Cousy's swan-song season in 1963 and a fifth straight banner for the Boston Garden rafters. But the talent was being replenished regularly and relentlessly in Boston, and premature exits by Cousy (1963, age 35), Sharman (1961, age 35), and Heinsohn (1965, age 31) were merely torch-passings and not curtain-lowerings. Frank Ramsey (the original prototype of Auerbach's innovative sixth man), Havlicek (Ramsey's replacement who took sixth-man contributions to even greater heights), and the odd-couple Jones boys along with others (Satch Sanders, Don Nelson, Bailey Howell, Larry Siegfried, Wayne Embry, and Don Chaney) soon followed in precise step with Auerbach's drum. Sam Jones became nearly as pure a shooter as Sharman and an even more productive scorer (25.9 points per game in 1965). K. C. Jones never had Cousy's flash but made it up on defense and still distributed the ball with deadly effectivness from the playmaking slot. With the Joneses now replacing the Cousy-Sharman tandem, there were three more world titles in 1964, 1965, and 1966, all without much serious challenge.

Boston's string would be interrupted in 1967, just long enough for one of the league's strongest one-season teams and also perhaps Wilt's finest moment in the spotlight. There is legitimate argument that the five players put on the floor in Philadelphia for the NBA's 21st campaign were the equal of any five anywhere assembled. A 76ers front line of Wilt Chamberlain, Luke Jackson, and Chet "The Jet" Walker drew immediate comparisons with Mikan, Pollard, and Mikkelsen in Minneapolis 15 years earlier. Hal Greer and Wali Jones in the backcourt and Billy Cunningham off the bench rounded out a group that not only unseated Boston, but did so with a record-breaking winning performance. Philly dominated

Transcendental Graphics

Mastermind Red Auerbach counsels his troops during the 1965 NBA playoffs.

the 81-game season by bumping up the single-season victory record to 68, then ran through the playoffs, losing once to Cincinnati (with Oscar), once to Boston (with Wilt now concentrating on Russell-like defense), and twice to San Francisco (in the Finals, against scoring champion Rick Barry and superlative rebounder Nate Thurmond). After Boston was eliminated in the conference finals, the championship round was almost an afterthought, though every game but two was close and the opener went overtime. Critics were finally muted, if not silenced, when Wilt and not Russell finally wore the championship crown. But Wilt's biggest critics from the past could also now point to the fact that a Chamberlain-led team was only a big winner because the Big Dipper had at long last traded in his awesome scoring (he trailed both Barry and Robertson) for a solid team player's role.

With two years left in the decade, the Celtics were still not quite done, and although Auerbach was now ready to step aside as active coach, Bill Russell would still be there to carry the victory load. Boston reloaded quickly in 1968 and 1969—with Russell doubling as player and coach—and gained another two postseason crowns. Russell's coaching debut was itself an American sports milestone, since he was the first black mentor of a major-sport professional team. It was also a final icing on the Boston dynasty cake. Both championship triumphs came at the expense of a most familiar victim, Jerry West's Los Angeles Lakers. The first time around it was Philly and Chamberlain that offered the bigger hurdle to the Celtics, who had to climb out of a 3–1 deficit in order even to get a crack at West and his teammates. L.A. then retooled for 1969 with none other than Chamberlain, yet was still unable to climb the postseason mountain and get past Russell in the season's final series.

The final two Boston championships indeed clinched the point that it was Bill Russell who was the real glue in the Celtics' winning mixture. Many latter-day analysts have gone as far as claiming that Red Auerbach's impeccable record as the long-reigning leader in lifetime coaching victories is more a tribute to Boston's star center than to any genius in the coach himself. Then again, it cannot be forgotten that it was precisely Auerbach's genius that brought Bill Russell to Boston in the first place. And it was Auerbach who also had the ingenious notion at the time of his retirement that only Bill Russell could successfully coach Bill Russell.

The closing season of the '60s provided one of the more gripping stories of league history. Russell would indeed go out once more a winner during a surprisingly dramatic final two weeks of NBA postseason magic. And Russell's final triumph itself followed one of the most storybook-like scripts that could have been imagined. A Boston team that had been a middle-of-the-pack ball club for much of the year (48–34, fourth place in the East) caught fire at year's end under Russell's savvy inspiration. Big Bill apparently had his club coasting all season and conserving its collective energies for the important April games that truly mattered. It would thus boil down again to a final series with Los Angeles, one this time destined to be the apex of frustration for the ill-starred Lakers and a mountain peak of glory for the pressure-hardened Celtics.

Los Angeles, with Chamberlain now anchoring a lineup that still featured Baylor and West, looked for all the world like a team that would now finally find a way to overwhelm Boston. L.A.'s Dipper had shed his embarrassing loser's tag with the great '67 season in Philly and also seemed still nearer his prime than did the aging Russell. But the deciding game would turn, in the end, on a surprise set of events that forever clinched Russell's real and imagined dominance over his biggest rival. In the closing period of Game 7 Chamberlain removed himself from the fray after injuring his leg with five minutes remaining on the clock. When the game tightened in the closing moments, Wilt signaled his readiness to return to battle; but a miffed coach Butch van Breda Kolff now turned a deaf ear. With Chamberlain sullenly watching from the bench, Russell's crew stormed down the stretch a winner one final time. An off-balance jumper by Don Nelson was the two-point difference. Bill Russell would leave the NBA scene in a remarkable blaze of glory, even if perhaps personally disappointed that Chamberlain's stretch-run absence from the floor stole some of the luster from the moment. Wilt, in turn, suffered his final and most ignoble hour of big-time defeat. Such, in the end, is the magical stuff that NBA legends are made of.

Tall Centers and Short Gates

The decade of the '70s would be one of considerable flux and more than a little back-sliding almost everywhere across the NBA scene. Though it may at first blush seem counterintuitive to claim so, the competitive balance that came with Boston's long-awaited fall from the winner's circle also brought with it an unanticipated letdown—a general nationwide dulling of interest in a professional basketball league. Not only was the juggernaut team suddenly not there any longer—either to love, admire, or even despise—but the popular, and even legendary, stars like Russell, Chamberlain, Robertson, and Jerry West were also now fading from the scene. Exciting new dynasty teams or enticing individual megastars unfortunately did not seem to be emerging anywhere on the horizon to fill the sudden void.

The basketball product had also been diluted by rampant expansion in the late '60s and early '70s and especially by the opening of a new and rival league. When the doors opened on the bold experiment of the American Basketball Association, most agreed that what American sports watchers needed at the time was certainly not another pro hoops circuit. Some of the top college stars were now disappearing to obscure backwater locales like Indianapolis, Anaheim, Dallas, Louisville, and New Orleans where there was no television exposure (and very little press coverage) to trumpet their achievements. And the NBA itself had been stretching its coast-to-coast market (to Seattle, San Diego, Milwaukee, Phoenix, Buffalo, Cleveland, Houston, Portland, and Kansas City–Omaha) during the same decade in an ill-conceived effort to keep pace.

There was a bright start to the decade, which saw an NBA champion finally arrive in the league's biggest marketplace. The New York Knicks emerged not only as champions in 1970 and then again in 1973, but also as one of the most colorful several-season units in league annals. No NBA title run has received more press (at the time or in retrospect) than the one involving the Knicks team starring Walt Frazier, Willis Reed, Dave DeBusschere, Dick Barnett, and Bill Bradley, which gutted out an emotional seven-game title series with Los Angeles in 1970, then returned (fortified by Jerry Lucas and Earl Monroe) to split two more title-round shootouts with the same rivals after a single-season hiatus in which both clubs were upset in their respective conference finals. The highlight came in Game 7 of the 1970 showdown when team captain Willis Reed hobbled onto the Madison Square Garden floor following a Game 5 leg injury and, in the process, provided the spiritual lift necessary for his team to overcome Chamberlain and Jerry West and the rest of the vaunted L.A. scoring machine.

If the league didn't seem to have many five-star attractions left in the wake of Russell and Pettit, and with the rapid aging and inevitable fading of Chamberlain and Robertson, there was, nonetheless, Lew Alcindor with Milwaukee, one of the newest franchise kids on the block, and Dave Cowens in Boston, the league's most venerable address. Alcindor would arrive in expansion Milwaukee in the wake of one of the biggest single recruiting wars to date. Promising the offensive talents of Chamberlain and the defensive prowess of Russell all wrapped into one 7'2" package, the UCLA two-time National Player of the Year was awarded to Milwaukee (winner of a coin flip with Phoenix) in the June NBA draft; but the ABA was in hot pursuit, pooled its leaguewide resources for a major contract offer, and promised Alcindor a spot with his hometown New York Nets. The prize recruit's eventual signing with the NBA (after requesting a single sealed bid from each circuit and accepting the higher offer) was a near-fatal blow for the already struggling lesser league that desperately needed a superstar's glamor and name recognition in order to stay in the hunt for airtime and front-page notice. Cowens, in turn, would resurrect Auerbach's recently sagging club, which was now coached by a most familiar face for Bostonians, that of the rugged and always inventive Tom Heinsohn.

Milwaukee would enjoy an almost overnight rise to the apex with its new franchise-maker safely in the fold with a $1.2 million five-year contract. Indeed, no expansion club had ever risen quite so high quite so quickly, nor would any ever do so again. Alcindor was the indispensable meal ticket, yet the Milwaukee brain trust worked its miracle in part by also attaching its wagon to one of the aging giants of the previous decade. Oscar Robertson was the true catalyst for Milwaukee, and, at long last, one of the game's best-ever performers was able via the trade route finally to enjoy the rare glow of the winner's circle. With Alcindor receiving plenty of help from fellow rookie Bob Dandridge, the Bucks improved by an incredible 29 games over the previous year, yet were still no match for the balanced New York Knicks attack during the postseason's second round. With Robertson added to the mix to run the offense one year later, the Bucks not only established a new record for consecutive wins (20) and ran up the league's best overall record (66–16), but the third-year outfit also posted only the second-ever Championship Finals sweep.

The Celtics and Lakers were also to be heard from yet again as the decade progressed. In Boston, the pilothouse would remain under Auerbach's control with the transfer of leadership from Russell to Heinsohn, and Heinsohn would now write a second legend of his own from the coach's end of the bench. And still another running mate of Russell and Cousy had ironically now taken over as well in Los Angeles, where two-year stints by Butch van Breda Kolff and Joe Mullaney had only extended bridesmaid frustration in the City of Angels. Bill Sharman brought a previously unknown intensity to his job and his team in Los Angeles when he took over the coaching reins from Mullaney on the eve of the 1972 season. And while the Lakers were now adjusting to the retirement loss of an injury-plagued Elgin Baylor, they had already constructed a potent front wall of Jim McMillian, Happy Hairston, and the much-traveled Chamberlain to complement the outside arsenal of Jerry West and the playmaking and all-around offense of Gail Goodrich.

Los Angeles would finally end its lengthy title drought under the newly arrived Sharman in the most spectacular fashion imaginable. Between November 5 and January 9, the strongest lineup in the league didn't suffer a single loss through 33 games, the longest winning skein in major sports history. The L.A. team that was 39–3 at midyear stood 69–13 at the final bell. It was one win more than the standard set by Wilt and his Philadelphia 76ers a half dozen years earlier and a milestone that would stand for the next two decades. If the 1971–72 World Champion Lakers didn't quite equal the 1967 Philadelphia team (a popular choice as the most balanced club ever) on paper, they nonetheless overhauled the Sixers in the record books. And Wilt Chamberlain supporters could now point to the indelible fact that, although Wilt was often accused of lacking Russell's winning attitude, nonetheless, he had anchored perhaps the two greatest one-season teams in basketball annals.

Dave Cowens (plucked with the fourth pick in the 1970 draft behind Bob Lanier, Rudy Tomjanovich, and Pete Maravich) was one of the most unlikely heroes and most unusual combination low-post, high-post players the NBA had ever welcomed. Cowens (at only 6'8"), as much as any big man before or after, truly revolutionized the style of post-position play. The flamboyant and even eccentric redhead played the pivot with a speed and finesse that was heretofore unparalleled in the professional game. And he also proved to be a relentless winner who was the perfect inspirational leader of yet another Boston Celtics championship revival. When he arrived as an unheralded and uncoveted rookie off the campus of Florida State University, he immediately revolutionized inside play by moving the conventional pivot position a full 20 feet from the basket. The strategy soon proved infallible as Cowens utilized his rugged style to transform the Celtics from a dull and lifeless outfit into the familiar fast-breaking thoroughbred of old, a team suddenly capable of seizing two more championships (1974 and 1976) before the decade of the 1970s rolled into its second half.

Boston's return to the top came with Cowens's fourth season yet had already been foreshadowed with a club-record 68 regular-season victories in 1973. It must have seemed an all-too-short period of rebuilding for anyone connected with or pulling for any of the league's 16 other clubs. While Boston now had a new and unconventional bruiser occupying the pivot position, nonetheless, it looked every bit like the finely honed Boston machines of the Auerbach–Russell–Cousy era. Renewed Celtics glory was kindled as much as anything by the emerging stardom of undersized pivotman Dave Cowens, now the league's most tenacious rebounder and also an effective shot-blocker during the first season in which the league had begun tallying statistics for both blocks and steals. Cowens provided the floor leadership as well as the harrassing defense; Havlicek handled the bulk of the scoring (22.8); Paul Silas was a terror on the boards almost the equal of Cowens; Jo Jo White and Don Chaney provided one of the league's best backcourts. Yet even with such balance, the first title under Heinsohn didn't come all that easily. Milwaukee, in its penultimate year with Alcindor (now long since renamed Kareem Abdul-Jabbar), would muster enough brilliant offensive play of its own to extend Heinsohn's men to the full seven final-round championship games. Included was a double-overtime Game 6 in which Abdul-Jabbar stunned the Boston Garden crowd with a decisive hook shot in the final three seconds. In the rubber match, however, Cowens outpointed Abdul-Jabbar by a bucket (28 to 26) and Boston coasted 102–87 to reclaim its first banner in five years.

Boston's second title of the decade came in the bicentennial year of 1976 and featured a dramatic postseason series with Phoenix that even topped the seven-game shootout with Milwaukee and also included one of the single most dramatic playoff games ever witnessed. Game 5 in the Garden with the series deadlocked was a tense contest that seemingly refused to end and one that owned almost as much controversy (cf. "Richie Powers" in Chapter 6) as it did thrill-a-minute action. Jo Jo White and third-string Glenn McDonald hit the third-overtime shots that finally brought the Celtics out on top, but not before Curtis Perry saved Phoenix with a baseline jumper in the first overtime, Paul Westphal rescued the Suns with a heady time-out call at the end of the second extra session (Phoenix was penalized with a free throw because it was out of time-outs, but nonetheless gained the chance at a final desperation heave), and Gar Heard exploited Westphal's quick thinking by canning the most miraculous last-second bomb in playoff history. In the end, the exhausting June 4 slugfest in Boston Garden may indeed have been the league's most attractive moment of the entire downhill decade.

The end of the '70s brought a string of dramatic story lines in the form of highly competitive seasons featuring a brand new batch of first-time champion-

One of the brightest and most-traveled ABA stars was Mack Calvin, who performed backcourt magic for the Los Angeles Stars, Miami Floridians, Carolina Cougars, Denver Rockets, and Virginia Squires.

From the author's collection

ship franchises in West Coast Portland and Seattle and East Coast Washington, D.C. First, Portland enjoyed a near-miracle 1977 season that centered quite literally on Bill Walton's one largely injury-free pro season. The Trail Blazers were completing only their seventh campaign, enjoying their first winning season, and making their first playoff visit when they snuck by Chicago (2–1), Denver (4–2), Los Angeles (4–0), and Philadelphia (4–2) to collect the first-ever crown won by a post-1970 expansion franchise. Washington also emerged from two decades of dormancy during these same transitional seasons with one of the league's all-time noteworthy blue-collar teams. And Seattle scrapped to the top with the same hard-nosed work ethic that was now succeeding for the Bullets. Two straight springs the Dick Motta–coached Bullets and Lenny Wilkens–coached Sonics met for the NBA title with the two Cinderella clubs splitting their postseason clashes. Washington, especially, was a team of seasoned veterans who had long paid their dues before enjoying a first moment in the winner's circle. Wes Unseld summoned up the finest outing of his then-10-season sojourn in Washington with a 1978 playoff MVP performance. And Elvin Hayes, especially, proved his worthiness in the nation's capital after nine pro years and three college seasons played in the constant shadow of Kareem Abdul-Jabbar. Hayes emerged as perhaps the most effective pure power forward since Pettit, yet for all the scoring and rebounding numbers he was consistently compiling, he seemed to do so without the usual flamboyance and gate appeal of a normal NBA superstar.

The ambivalent star status of Elvin Hayes was symptomatic of a new malaise. By the end of the '70s the league was fading in public esteem and new stars seemed in distressingly short supply. Pro basketball had somehow failed in its quest to join football and baseball as a viable prime-time television spectacle. Much of the league's slide could be laid perhaps to the blandness of the few "stars" it still owned. The big guns were now Bob McAdoo in Buffalo, Billy Knight in Indiana, George Gervin in San Antonio, Hayes in Washington, and Lloyd Free in San Diego—not West in Los Angeles, Barry in San Francisco, Robertson in Cincinnati, or Wilt Chamberlain almost anywhere. Scoring leaders and other front-runners of the NBA hardly provided a list of recognizable household names, nor were they the types of inspiring heroes sports fans could get very excited about.

Part of the problem had been the short-lived American Basketball Association, which had first cut squarely into the available player talent pool and then provided a wide-open style of play for fans that seemed quite a bit more exciting— even if a bit more circuslike—than the predictable pass-and-shoot action offered by the long-established league. In the ABA the accent was on speed—running, jumping, getting the ball upcourt in a flash, and putting on playground "moves" around the hoop. There was also the colorful red, white, and blue ball, the revolutionary three-point bomb, and the sudden runaway popularity of the dunk shot. But there was also a new ABA prototype player to contend with—the muscular and gravity-defying power-scoring forward who was usually black (Rick Barry was an exception) and always gazelle-like in his flight down the court. The ABA had no Russells or Chamberlains or Nate Thurmonds to clog up the lanes. With the three-point shot spreading the action on the floor, a swift-moving breed of new athletic forwards was soon taking over the game in the rebel league and setting up new expectations for the old league in the process.

The birth of the ABA had been largely a lark for a group of overambitious investors and speculators who really wanted to start a second football circuit, but had been beaten to the punch in their original scheme by the American Football League. From the outset, the venture was surrounded with excessive hype and hoopla and much untoward optimism. And from the beginning the operators of the new league displayed their penchant for boldly taking risks in an effort to gain both media notice and a desperately needed ticket-buying audience. Retired NBA legend George Mikan was brought on board to lend the desired respectability, but even the NBA's most venerable name from the past quickly caught the refreshing spirit of innovation that was everywhere in the air. It was Mikan himself who came up with the league's most recognizable and lasting symbol, the red, white, and blue leather ball.

And most of the "colorfulness" resulted from much more than just the visible playing equipment. Carolina Cougars coach Larry Brown roamed the sidelines in farmer's overalls (today's blue jeans), while Wilt Chamberlain directed operations wearing sandals on the bench in San Diego. Artis Gilmore measured in with the Kentucky Colonels at 7'7", with five inches of height added by his spectacular Afro hairstyle. Marvin Barnes was more famous in St. Louis for having 13 telephones in his apartment and for consuming bags of cheeseburgers in the pregame locker room than for his nightly 24 points and 15 rebounds. Lefty Thomas played for the Denver Rockets with a ring adorning each of 10 fingers, while in Dallas Maurice McHartley earned the name "Toothpick" by always playing with one hanging from the corner of his mouth. And the Dallas franchise once made its draft day selections not according to playing talent, but in alphabetical order. The screwball league, nonetheless, had one unmatchable marquee player in Julius Erving, who sold most of its tickets, and one great team in the Indiana Pacers, which won the largest cluster of its championships (three out of nine).

The colorful nature of the new league was equally a matter of playing style, in part fostered by two revolutionary rules governing game action, but resulting equally from the bevy of young stars signed on to carry the league's banner. The rule innovations were a three-point field goal salvaged from the short-lived American Basketball League of 1961 and a longer 30-second shot clock, which permitted more freelancing on offense. Foremost among the earliest individual headliners were Connie Hawkins—an NBA reject who had been banned from NCAA play at Iowa and later from the pros merely for casual association with suspected game-fixers—and Rick Barry, who had abandoned the established league for more dollars and the lure of increased self-promotion. Hawkins came out of exile (he had played in the one-season ABL and with the Globetrotters) to be the new league's first big scorer and genuine crowd pleaser. Barry signed on with the Oakland club coached by his father-in-law (and former college coach), Bruce Hale, but had to sit out a full year by court order imposed with a lawsuit by his former NBA team, the San Francisco Warriors. When the new league opened up for operations with Hawkins on the court and Barry on the sidelines, it was altogether fitting that the first game was staged between the Oakland Oaks and Anaheim Amigos on Friday the 13th. From the moment of its birth the ABA was dogged by unusual events and strange happenstance.

There were other major ABA stars such as Artis Gilmore (shot-blocking paragon), Dan Issel, Larry Brown (MVP of the first ABA All-Star Game before taking up coaching duties with Carolina and Denver), Louie Dampier (three-point shooting nonpareil and record holder for points scored and games played), Byron Beck, Mel Daniels (rebounding pacesetter), George McGinnis, Roger Brown, and Doug Moe. The latter two players—both playground stars from New York like Connie Hawkins—had also been brushed aside by the NBA for alleged connections with scandal. Brown's career at Dayton was scuttled by connections with the 1961 college betting scare, and he was rescued by the Indiana Pacers (after being recommended by Oscar Robertson) while working in an Ohio auto assembly plant. Moe—the second-leading scorer behind Hawkins in the inaugural ABA campaign—had also been associated with 1961 betting shenanigans (though never convicted of any wrongdoing) while still a teammate of Larry Brown's at North Carolina. Now the new league provided a lucrative home and second chance for these and other previ-

ABA play featured high-flying forwards like George McGinnis of the Indiana Pacers, who here stuffs a bucket against the Spirits of St. Louis.

© Indiana Pacers

ous pro rejects. And it also created an intense talent war that doubled the number of pro basketball jobs and also drove salaries rocketing skyward to the delight of all players in both leagues.

ABA action brought a new helter-skelter, run-and-gun style that set a tone for the sport's future and also underscored almost everything that was wrong with the trouble-plagued NBA of the '70s. And no one embodied that style any better than a *wunderkind* who had provided little splash on the college level that might forewarn of his eventual greatness and unrivaled magnetism. Julius Erving broke in

Charlie Scott was one of a considerable collection of high-scoring college stars who first took their offense-minded acts to the fledgling ABA before earning later NBA stardom.

From the author's collection

with the Virginia Squires and flashed immediate brilliance in the freestyle profes-sional game. His college achievement had been solid enough as a member of an elite circle of only seven collegians (he was only the fifth at the time) who have ever averaged more than 20 in both points and rebounds for a full (two-, three-, or four-year) career. Once he relocated with the media-capital New York franchise and honed his high-flying skills, Julius Erving took full wing with achievements of mythic proportions. The impact was so great and the show so spectacular that for many observers "Dr. J" *was* the ABA. There were several scoring titles (1973, 1974, 1976). There was a one-on-one showmanship that made him the most exciting ath-lete in the land. There was a legendary performance in the league's new marketing gimmick known as a slam-dunking contest (unveiled in Denver at halftime of the 1976 All-Star Game and won spectacularly by Erving). But most important of all, there was nothing quite like Dr. J or his hang time brand of play over in the competing and more venerable NBA.

One vital event of the ABA years involved the two-year, two-league saga of Spencer Haywood, and it turned out to be a soap-opera affair with severe and long-lasting implications. Haywood had starred in the 1968 Olympics as a mere teenager (sparking USA victory after established stars like Alcindor, Bob Lanier, and Wes Unseld had boycotted the team) and looked to leave the University of Detroit after a single sophomore season to pursue his pro dream—two decades ahead of Jerry Stackhouse, Glenn Robinson, or Allen Iverson. NBA doors were not open under existing rules, and Haywood thus began his play-for-pay adventure in Denver with the lesser league. NBA clubs were still sticking fast to a self-imposed truce with the NCAA: they would not sign collegians until four years after their matriculation, and in return, the colleges would provide a convenient farm system for player development. The ABA moguls had no such qualms about college signings and rushed in to collar big-name collegians in order to gain the upper hand in a life-and-death struggle against the NBA, and thus to increase its own chances for marketplace survival. Haywood was inked first; soon there would be similar contracts for Erving at Massachuetts and Gervin at Western Michigan. The NBA struck back predictably with blows that eventually would kill off its younger rival. Haywood himself was soon lured away by bigger NBA paychecks and so was Charlie Scott, who was signed by Phoenix after winning an ABA scoring title in Virginia. Jim McDaniels was also grabbed by the senior circuit after starring briefly for the Carolina Cougars, and even Rick Barry (who missed the Bay Area when his ABA club transferred east) was enticed back to the NBA Warriors after four lost seasons in the hinterlands.

The big coup, and the one with the far-reaching implications, was, nonetheless, Haywood. After a spectacular rookie year in the ABA (top rookie, MVP, and leading scorer), Haywood longed for greener pastures (the green in this case being cash), and he was indeed such a huge talent and potential box-office draw that there were NBA owners (especially Sam Schulman of the expansion SuperSonics) willing enough to circumvent their own rules to gain his services. Seattle hurried to sign the talented youngster, and the matter immediately landed in the law courts when other NBA owners strenuously objected, since Haywood had never passed through an NBA draft. When the courts decided in favor of the Seattle signing (a judge ruling that drafts were illegal if they blocked players from turning pro whenever they want to), the NBA was left with no choice but to modify its ban on undergraduates, opening the floodgates on early signings under the thin guise of "hardship" exceptions. Haywood, by this route, found his way into the established league and, in the process, opened doors for generations of collegians who wanted far loftier and much more above-board paychecks than the colleges were secretly offering.

The ABA lasted far longer than almost anyone expected. Its own club owners likely had not anticipated true longevity, since most of the contracts they offered prized recruits involved deferred payments that stretched out long after the ball clubs and even the league itself would presumably be gone. Somehow the operation

Dan Issel's career ABA-NBA point total of more than 27,000 places him among the game's 10 most prolific all-time scorers. Here he is scoring against the Indiana Pacers in ABA action.

© Indiana Pacers

nonetheless held together for nearly a decade and then it inevitably collapsed, despite its bevy of star performers and glamorous run-and-gun "above-the-rim" formula for action. The downfall of the league actually unfolded over the painful course of several seasons, and although the collapse wasn't exactly immediate, it was always obvious enough in its coming. Alcindor's choice of the Milwaukee Bucks was as good a harbinger as any. Of course, as long as Julius Erving was on the scene the league still had a niche and a potential market. But that market had shrunk (attendance, which averaged about 3,000 leaguewide in the first season, sometimes was reported at less than 100 for some early '70s games), and the only remaining viable franchises by the mid-'70s were those in Indianapolis (with a winning tradition), Louisville (with Dampier, Gilmore, and Issel), and New York (with Dr. J). And eventually it was evident that this wasn't enough by itself to keep the entire ship afloat. Four ABA franchises bought their way into the NBA in 1976 (at $3.2 million apiece), and the New York ownership had to peddle Erving to Philadelphia in order to meet its additional entrance fees (an extra $4.8 million to the Knicks for territorial invasion).

Although the NBA was resilient enough to deliver a death blow to the ABA with its *tour de force* in signing Alcindor, and then forward-looking enough to pick up the pieces of the shattered competing league (absorbing not only Erving and a handful of other stars, but also the promising franchises in Indiana, New York, Denver, and San Antonio), nonetheless, the NBA had come on hard times of its own by the close of the 1970s. By the decade's final season, pro basketball could boast only a 5.6 Nielsen national television rating, compared with 16.9 for the NFL, 13.5 for major-league baseball, and 12.8 for college football. The NBA now trailed even auto racing (6.7), golf (5.7), college basketball (8.1), and horse racing (9.1) in video popularity. The sideshow of professional basketball—no matter how hard purists touted the star attractions and dramatic action of the game itself—had obviously not made any real inroads toward supplanting pro football as the nation's preferred spectator event. In truth, the bucket sport was unquestionably on the wane. Something drastic was clearly needed to fire the imaginations of the nation's increasingly apathetic pro hoops fans.

In the wake of an ABA collapse, it became clear what the NBA needed to revive its own sagging fortunes. It was the same thing the sport had always needed to jack up fan support. Glamorous stars were the first and foremost order of business, and unfortunately such stars were no longer very much in evidence. Clearly, there was a lack of the kind of superstars that had filled up the Celtics Era of the '60s and the "Big Man" era at the outset of the '70s. Abdul-Jabbar was still around, but the rookie glamour of sky-hooking Lew Alcindor in Milwaukee had eventually faded into the methodical veteran efficiency of a West Coast Kareem. Gervin had now been the league's scoring leader for three seasons running but lacked anything approaching pizzazz or true charisma. Truck Robinson in Phoenix had recently captured the rebounding title, and Detroit guard Kevin Porter was the current NBA leader in assists. Kids could hardly be expected to take to the alleys and school yards in droves, aping every move of nondescript hoopsters like Gervin, Robinson, or Porter. It was indeed a tall order now to be filled, but one that was about to be met with surprising suddenness and effectiveness.

Magic, Bird, and Air Jordan

Pro basketball had been rescued from oblivion once in its infancy by George Mikan and then once again in its adolescence by Bill Russell. Julius Erving had played a similar role when he came on board in the mid-'70s from the defunct ABA, bringing with him a popular new soaring style known as "hang time" as part of his considerable entertainment package. Now at the dawn of a new decade, two celebrated collegiate stars would arrive simultaneously to give the sport its biggest

Boston's Larry Bird brought new life to the NBA throughout the decade of the 1980s.

© Frank P. McGrath Jr.

shot in the arm ever. And they had perfect names for their role, names which reflected the sport's airborne and "showtime" modern-era images. Bird and Magic had paved the way for their NBA popularity with their spectacular NCAA Final Four showdown in Salt Lake City only months earlier. The Magic Johnson and Larry Bird NBA rivalry that was expected to spill over from their dramatic 1979 NCAA title chase was touted from the first tip-off of their mutual rookie season. And for once, the early hype was matched by the resulting realities.

Bird was the more mature in years and was christened by some with suppressed racist leanings as a "great white hope" in the face of the black-dominated NBA game. Johnson was only a college sophomore when he left for the pro ranks and was anticipated more for his flamboyance than his less obvious all-around court skills. Both would quickly mature in the pro game and fulfill every expectation and then some. Individually they would become two of the game's true legends. As a tandem, they would write a script that rekindled interest in NBA title races. And it also didn't hurt that the teams that they represented were the most celebrated and intense rivals of past decades—Auerbach's Boston Celtics and their pesky West Coast rivals, the Los Angeles Lakers.

Magic and Bird both enjoyed sensational rookie seasons. Both found the transition to the professional game was smooth and almost effortless; each actually improved under the freewheeling style of NBA play. Larry posted the larger numbers—21.3 scoring average, 10.4 rebounds per contest, a credible 4.5 assists from a frontcourt slot. He also walked away with coveted Rookie of the Year honors. Johnson's numbers were nearly equivalent (18 points, 7.3 assists, and a surprising 7.2 rebounds nightly at the guard slot) and his value every bit as noteworthy. But most of all, Magic proved beyond any shadow of a doubt in the early going that his size and flashy style would almost overnight revolutionize the league's standards for backcourt play.

But 1980 was not only a season for rookies. Julius Erving was still on the scene with a strong Philadelphia club that postponed the much-sought Bird-Magic championship showdown by blowing past Boston in an easy five games during the semifinal playoff round. With the first opportunity for a Bird-Magic reunion thus lost, fans would have to settle instead for the poetry of Dr. J versus Magic. And such a season's finale proved to be highly entertaining indeed. Abdul-Jabbar would lead the Lakers in the early going before seriously injuring his ankle (while scoring 40 in Game 5) and dropping from the fray. In the pivotal final Game 6, the Lakers, under coach Paul Westhead, would have to turn in desperation to a small lineup featuring Magic Johnson in his old familiar college low-post position as Abdul-Jabbar's emergency replacement. And the strategy somehow worked—Johnson (42 points, 15 rebounds, 7 assists from the center post) and his teammates were able to hold off the Sixers' final charge. At the end of his very first league campaign, Magic Johnson was already occupying center stage, boasting a league playoff MVP to cap his sensational rookie season.

The two new stars in L.A. and Boston would meet only a handful of times with the league trophy squarely on the line. Yet their head-to-head clashes and those of their storied teams were indeed some of the biggest chapters of the new decade. The pinnacle of the rivalry came with the NBA championship rounds of 1984 (Bird and Boston prevailing in seven) and 1985 (Los Angeles gaining revenge in six). In '84, Bird swept the individual awards with regular-season and postseason MVPs to spice his championship; a year later the Lakers finally broke a string of eight straight defeats by Boston in past championship series, and it was Kareem Abdul-Jabbar playing the starring role. Before those two clashes, Bird and Magic each already had at least one title under his belt, with Boston and Bird breaking through against Houston in 1981 and Magic and L.A. repeating against Philadelphia a season later. In all, Bird would only capture three championships across the full decade to Magic's more impressive five, although both had equal supporting casts; Boston six times posted the best regular-season record during the '80s, while Johnson's team could only boast this distinction twice. Each would also earn three season-long MVPs and Bird's would actually come in succession, the first such string since Chamberlain two decades earlier.

In the mid-'80s Boston featured a frontcourt that journalist Peter May, among others, has called the best ever in the NBA. Purists may argue for Mikan, Pollard, and Mikkelsen of Minneapolis in this category, or even for Chamberlain, Walker, and Jackson with Philadelphia, but there is little room to deny that Bird, Parish, and McHale provided a front wall that had little peer, especially during recent decades. Bird's injuries after only a decade would, unfortunately, cut the trio short while still in their prime. Parish would stick around nearly a half dozen seasons

Many called Boston's frontcourt of Larry Bird (33), Robert Parish (00), in photo at top, and Kevin McHale (32), in the bottom photo, the best ever in the NBA. Of the three, Parish lasted the longest as a player, overhauling Kareem Abdul-Jabbar for record longevity. He holds career records for both seasons and games played.

© Frank P. McGrath Jr.

© Frank P. McGrath Jr.

after Bird (bowing out with Charlotte and Chicago in the mid-'90s) to set a flock of NBA longevity records. And McHale would eventually become a successful front-office figure with the expansion Minnesota Timberwolves. Even Bird would eventually return to the league in the late '90s as coach of his home-state Indiana Pacers.

Bird and Magic didn't hold the center stage alone for very long. Michael Jordan soon loomed on the horizon, and with Jordan's debut in the fall of 1984, the NBA was unknowingly welcoming its biggest marquee attraction ever. In a few short years Jordan would be bigger (not necessarily better) than Mikan, Chamberlain, Robertson, and Abdul-Jabbar combined. Debate would one day rage over whether Jordan had actually outstripped either Oscar Robertson or Wilt Chamberlain as the best player of all time. But after less than three seasons it was already apparent that Air Jordan would be absolutely unrivaled in his ordained role as the league's—the entire sport's—most recognized figure and most celebrated superstar the world over. And in an age of runaway commercialism, Jordan would also become almost overnight the most marketed athlete ever to grace the planet.

The game's biggest all-time star arrived on the scene with a considerable bang in what constituted the worst NBA Draft Day gaff ever. Whatever successes the Portland Trail Blazers franchise might enjoy in the future, likely it will never quite outlive the blunder of bypassing Jordan in the June player lottery for the chance to select often-injured seven-footer Sam Bowie out of Kentucky. (Houston had actually picked first and opted for its own franchise player, Akeem Olajuwon.) Jordan immediately underscored the folly of the Portland choice with one of the best rookie-season performances since those of Chamberlain and Baylor in the '50s and Robertson and Rick Barry in the '60s. The tally for Jordan read: 2,313 points, 28.2 scoring average (third in the league), 196 steals (fourth). Bowie averaged an even 10 in scoring, which would also approximate his career mark over his remaining 450 games in the league.

Jordan had taken the league by storm as a rookie, even if Boston and Los Angeles (NBA champion) with Bird (NBA MVP) and Magic were still the biggest season-long winners. Air Jordan's second campaign was largely wiped out by injury, though there was a brilliant postseason burst to salvage something of the sophomore season. A broken foot bone shut down the regular season for MJ in game three and left Chicago clinging to only slim playoff hopes. MJ returned for part-time duty in the final month, then revved up his postseason comeback performance to new heights with a record-smashing 63-point game against Boston; but the Bulls lost that one in Boston Garden in two overtimes, despite Jordan's heroics, and didn't survive the opening round of the playoffs. A third campaign was enough to put the legend firmly in place as Michael ran up yearlong scoring numbers that only Chamberlain had ever registered before him. With his 37.1 points per game average and 3,041 total points, Jordan had suddenly entered a lofty realm previously visited only by the incomparable Wilt.

By the mid-'80s it had already been two decades since the league had seen a repeat champion. But the Lakers, with a maturing Magic Johnson and a senior statesman in Kareem Abdul-Jabbar, were emerging as something of a minidynasty. It was time for coach Pat Riley's version of West Coast "Showtime," and even Michael Jordan would have to take a back seat to the Lakers' two-year league domination. The string began at the end of 1987 with another title win against

Boston, the second in three seasons. Coach Riley enthusiastically guaranteed a repeat, which Magic and Abdul-Jabbar promptly delivered. But the road to the second title, as might be expected, was a good deal rockier. It took three straight seven-game series to survive the postseason title hunt. At the end of the marathon postseason chase, James Worthy provided the 11th-hour heroics. With his most sterling season and career performance, Worthy rang up 36 points (along with 16 rebounds and 10 assists) to nail the coffin shut against Detroit. The NBA now had a repeat champion for the first time in 19 springs.

Once the Lakers had finally broken the back-to-back title drought—a fixture for two decades—such winning consistency suddenly seemed to be in vogue. Detroit was next in line with two superlative seasons of its own as Los Angeles's "Showtime"

15 All-Time Greatest NBA Players

Michael Jordan (Chicago Bulls, 1985–93, 1995–98, Guard)—An unmatched showman, Jordan is the most celebrated and most commercially promoted American athlete ever, and ultimately, the most consistent scorer in NBA annals. He is the NBA career record holder for per-game scoring average (31.7) and cumulative individual scoring championships (10). He is the clear choice of many analysts and fans as the greatest all-around player in basketball history.

Oscar Robertson (Cincinnati Royals, Milwaukee Bucks, 1961–74, Guard)—The only player ever to average a triple-double for a full season (1961–62), Robertson is Jordan's single rival for enshrinement as the greatest all-around talent ever. He was an unstoppable offensive performer who single-handedly redefined the point guard stereotype from passer–floor general to prolific scorer–complete offensive weapon. His cumulative totals for his first five NBA seasons (1961–65) stood above triple-double standards: 30.3 ppg, 10.4 rpg, and 10.6 apg.

Wilt Chamberlain (Philadelphia Warriors, San Francisco Warriors, Philadelphia 76ers, Los Angeles Lakers, 1960–73, Center)—Wilt Chamberlain is the most dominating offensive force the game has ever known and one of only two NBA scorers to top 30,000 career points. He enjoyed an unprecedented dominance in 1961–62 with a 50.4 scoring average, 4,029 total points, and a single-game 100-point effort. He owns the only career 30-plus scoring average besides Jordan and the long-held record (before Jordan) for most consecutive individual scoring titles (seven).

Earvin "Magic" Johnson (Los Angeles Lakers, 1980–91, 1996, Guard)—Magic Johnson is perhaps the closest rival to Oscar Robertson for overall versatility and one of the game's most charismatic performers. He is second all time in NBA career assists. As the tallest point guard in NBA history he is responsible for revolutionizing the style of point-guard play. He is a three-time NBA MVP and the leader of five NBA championship teams. Along with Boston's Larry Bird, he revived the NBA's sagging popularity in the early 1980s. He was the first rookie ever named an NBA Finals MVP.

Bill Russell (Boston Celtics, 1955–69, Center)—Bill Russell is the only player ever to dominate with defensive performance alone, and also the sport's greatest winner of team championships. He is indisputably the greatest defensive center and shot-blocker in basketball history. He owns a record 11 NBA titles, including 8 consecutive. His career rebounding average (22.6) is second only to Wilt Chamberlain's (22.9).

Larry Bird (Boston Celtics, 1980–92, Forward)—The perfect prototype of the shooting forward, Larry Bird is arguably the best nonblack player ever. He is noted for his unmatched consistency, deadly shooting accuracy, and clutch pressure performances. He was an NBA Rookie of the Year (1980), three-time NBA MVP, once All-Star Game MVP, twice NBA Finals MVP, and a three-time winner of NBA team championships.

Julius Erving (Virginia Squires, New York Nets, Philadelphia 76ers, 1972–87, Forward)—Known as the prince of "hang time" Julius Erving was the grandest slam-dunker of all time. He redefined the forward position during 16 stellar ABA and NBA seasons. His combined ABA-NBA career point total (30,026) trails only Abdul-Jabbar and Chamberlain on the all-time list. He won three ABA MVPs, three ABA scoring titles, one NBA MVP, and one coveted NBA championship ring.

Bob Pettit (Milwaukee Hawks, St. Louis Hawks, 1955–65, Center-Forward)—Bob Pettit was the first NBA player to reach 20,000 career points. He was the pioneering big man who played facing the basket (revolutionary for centers of his era) and was the hardest on-court worker pro basketball has ever known. Pettit was Rookie of the Year (1955) and an NBA All-Star for all 11 seasons in his career. He retired (in 1965) as the league's highest career scorer and second-highest career rebounder.

was rapidly exchanged for the Motor City's colorful "Bad Boys" act. The Pistons, coached by Chuck Daly, would now win with a less glamorous hard-nosed workmanlike style of play that reminded one of the Washington and Seattle no-name ball clubs of the late '70s. Isiah Thomas was the catalyst, providing playmaking leadership and pacing the team scoring along with forward Adrian Dantley. Bill Laimbeer (rebounding), Dennis Rodman (sixth man and the league's field-goal accuracy leader), and Joe Dumars (Thomas's backcourt running mate) were the specialists.

Detroit was nearly perfect for two consecutive postseason rounds, sweeping three of four playoff series in 1989 and losing more than once in only a single series during the 1990 championships. The first Detroit title came with a storybook matchup against Los Angeles and Abdul-Jabbar, who was now closing the door on his 20th

Jerry West (Los Angeles Lakers, 1961–74, Guard)—Jerry West is known as "Mr. Clutch" and the best pure shooter in pro basketball annals. He has the fourth-highest career NBA scoring average (27.0) and 10th-highest point total (25,192), both achieved without benefit of three-point field goals. West appeared in 14 NBA All-Star Games (named MVP in 1972) and averaged 29.7 points per game across 153 playoff games. He was the best all-around playoff performer outside of Air Jordan.

George Mikan (Chicago American Gears, Minneapolis Lakers, 1947–56, Center)—The dominant player of the pre-shot-clock era, George Mikan was once chosen by the Associated Press as the "Greatest Basketball Player of the First Half-Century." He led the Chicago American Gears and Minneapolis Lakers to six pro titles (NBL, BAA, NBA), paced the NBA in scoring four times, and led the league in rebounding twice. He was so superior in his day that he forced college and pro rules changes (widened foul lanes and an NCAA ban on defensive goaltending) to control his dominance.

Elgin Baylor (Minneapolis Lakers, Los Angeles Lakers, 1959–72, Forward)—Elgin Baylor was the first true "skywalker" and the acknowledged inventor of black freelance "one-on-one" playground style. Described as "the man with a thousand moves" for his unprecedented abilities to suspend himself in airborne flight, he holds the third-highest career scoring average (27.4) and highest single-season average (38.3 in 1962) by anyone other than Chamberlain. He was an All-NBA First Team player 10 times and the first player to score 70-plus points in a single NBA game.

Kareem Abdul-Jabbar (Lew Alcindor) (Milwaukee Bucks, Los Angeles Lakers, 1970–89, Center)—Kareem Abdul-Jabbar is basketball's monument to longevity with 20 NBA seasons, 1,560 games played, and 38,387 career points. He is the all-time career NBA leader for points scored and perhaps the best-ever all-around post-position player during his early seasons with the Milwaukee Bucks. He retired as the leader in nine career statistical categories and is the owner of six NBA team championships, along with a record six league MVP honors.

Rick Barry (San Francisco Warriors, Oakland Oaks, Washington Capitols, New York Nets, Golden State Warriors, Houston Rockets, 1966–80, Forward)—Rick Barry is matched only by Jordan in competitive zeal and only by Bird for mythical distinction as the greatest all-time white player. Remembered for his unique but deadly underhanded free-throw shooting style, he owns the second-best career free-throw percentage in combined NBA-ABA history. He was an NBA Rookie of the Year (1966), NBA scoring leader (1967), NBA All-Star Game MVP (1967), and NBA Finals MVP (1975). He is the only player ever to lead the NCAA (1965), the NBA (1967), and the ABA (1969) in season scoring.

Dolph Schayes (Syracuse Nats, Philadelphia Warriors, 1949–64, Forward)—Dolph Schayes was the first player to cross the NBA's 15,000-point threshold. He was one of the most durable and intense competitors in pro annals, who retired with a league-record 1,059 games played. He held the iron-man mark of 706 consecutive games played between 1952 and 1961. He was a prolific scorer from inside and outside as well as from the free-throw line. A three-time NBA free-throw leader with a unique two-handed set-shot style, Schayes appeared in 12 straight NBA All-Star Games and won one NBA team title.

Bob Cousy (Boston Celtics, Cincinnati Royals, 1951–63, 1970, Guard)—The inventor of backcourt ballhandling magic, Bob Cousy is still acknowledged widely as the best pure playmaker of all time. He combined with Bill Russell to win six NBA championships for Boston. He paced the NBA in assists eight consecutive seasons, played in 13 straight NBA All-Star Games, earned one league MVP, and two All-Star Game MVPs. A brief playing appearance while coaching the Cincinnati Royals made him, at the time (1970), the oldest player in NBA history.

and final NBA season. Joe Dumars, normally more of a defensive mainstay, provided most of the Pistons' fireworks; the former McNeese State hotshot averaged better than 27 points per game in a short four-game sweep, which quickly dispensed with Abdul-Jabbar's dreams of a swan-song championship. One season later the defending champions had to climb past a tough Jordan-led Bulls team in a nail-biting seven-game conference finals. The trophy round with Portland proved much less strenuous, however, as Detroit captured three in a row on the road to coast against the already spent Trail Blazers.

As Bird, Magic, and finally Isiah and company made their successive miniruns at dynasty status, Michael Jordan, for his part, was taking over the game as perhaps the greatest individual talent of all time. Jordan had already amassed a string of scoring honors by the late '80s and was even Defensive Player of the Year in 1988 (to complement his second scoring title). But MJ had not yet escaped from the stigma of being a yearly bridesmaid during the postseason. Detroit was too big a mountain for Jordan's Bulls to climb for several seasons, and Michael simply didn't have enough reinforcements to get the late-season job done against the league's other strong-arm teams. Nor did his electrifying game and take-charge personality quite mesh with Chicago coach Doug Collins. It was obvious that in any tug-of-war between Collins and Jordan it would not be the coach who would find many sympathizers, and Doug Collins's career with the Bulls was not expected to survive the close of the decade.

Two dramatic changes in Chicago put the Jordan-led Bulls on a fast-track route toward an eventual championship as the 1990s and Jordan's sixth NBA season finally dawned. Phil Jackson replaced Collins for the 1989–90 campaign and rapidly posted the second-winningest ledger in franchise history. And Scottie Pippen emerged as a superstar in his own right at just about the same time. The official trumpeting of Pippen perhaps began only with his 1994 All-Star Game MVP performance in Minneapolis. But his game had already arrived with a noticable jump in offense (21.0 points per game) two winters earlier. Pippen had come to the Bulls in a 1987 Draft Day snafu that had almost rivaled the one involving Jordan. (His draft rights were acquired from the Seattle SuperSonics in exchange for journeyman center Olden Polynice and an additional second-round pick.) Steadily, the acrobatic 6'7" forward from Central Arkansas revealed raw talents (especially electrifying moves to the basket) that soon were surpassing all expectations both in Chicago and everywhere else around the circuit.

The Bulls would be next to stake repeat claims on the NBA championship banner. The breakthrough title came with the 1991 postseason and involved a celebrated championship matchup with Magic Johnson. Chicago's club-record 61 victories were extended with a 15–2 playoff ledger. After the Lakers captured Finals Game 1 on a last-minute three-pointer by Jordan's former North Carolina teammate Sam Perkins, Chicago coasted to the title that finally elevated Jordan from the status of superstar to the level of living legend. A second banner was hung in Chicago Stadium after another club-record season (67–15) and a year-end romp past the Portland Trail Blazers during a series that was billed as a showdown between the game's two highest flyers—Jordan and Clyde "The Glide" Drexler. It was not surprisingly almost all Jordan during a six-game series that featured two road victories by the Bulls and a miraculous home-floor comeback

© Frank P. McGrath Jr.

No NBA act has ever been bigger or more sensational than the one featuring Chicago's Michael "Air" Jordan.

in the final quarter of deciding Game 6. The anticipated three-peat came a year later in a Finals matchup with league MVP Charles Barkley and the Phoenix Suns. The Phoenix title series was highlighted with one of the longest and most entertaining postseason games ever, a triple-overtime Phoenix win at Chicago in Game 3. (Phoenix had also been featured in the only other Finals three-overtime match when it lost at Boston Garden in 1976 Game 5.) The NBA Finals of 1993 turned out to be one of the rarest in league annals, with the home team winning only once (Chicago took Game 4). The real significance of the Suns-Bulls shootout, however, was that Chicago had now joined Boston (1959 through 1966) and Minneapolis (1952 through 1954) as the only franchises ever to capture as many as three uninterrupted NBA titles.

The NBA had become a phenomenal growth industry between the arrival of Bird and Magic and the domination of Air Jordan. Clever marketing as well as raw athletic talent were the keys to such image enhancement, and the ultimate marketing guru was, of course, league commissioner David Stern. There were also some apparent drawbacks to the league's new strategies for selling itself on the sole basis of glamorous image and raw celebrity appeal. The NBA's single-star promotion of first Magic and Bird and later Jordan and Shaquille O'Neal was laced with inevitable pitfalls, as was discovered when 1989 All-Star Game television ratings plunged with Bird and Magic both on the sidelines with injuries, and then again in 1994 and 1995 when Bird, Magic, and Jordan had all stepped aside and were missing from the showcase midseason game. And the rush to create instant replacements for Jordan meant media-molded synthetic stars like O'Neal, Penny Hardaway, and Grant Hill, who, for all their potential talents, were draped with hype and hoopla that far outstripped their early development as on-court monster talents.

The NBA had now also gone international under Commissioner Stern's ambitious expansion plans. There was, foremost, the selling of the game throughout Europe as a lucrative television spectacle. There were NBA-style European feeder leagues (with Spain, Yugoslavia, Italy, and Greece as the primary venues) that provided an informal farm system. The McDonald's Open—a joint venture between the NBA and the International Basketball Federation (FIBA)—was launched in 1987 and for a decade has matched selected NBA clubs with top European pro squads in a weekend tournament format. And there were now even crack European players making their presence felt on NBA rosters. Among the best were Drazen Petrovic (Portland, New Jersey), Vlade Divac (L.A. Lakers, Charlotte), Arvydas Sabonis (Portland), Gheorghe Muresan (Washington), Zydrunas Ilgauskas (Cleveland), and Toni Kukoc (Chicago). And during 1992 (Barcelona) and 1996 (Atlanta), the much ballyhooed "Dream Team I" and "Dream Team III" catapulted the NBA game onto a worldwide Olympic stage with embarrassingly easy gold-medal victories against outclassed and awestruck international competition.

But even with Stern's ingenious hand on the tiller, there would nonetheless be numerous potholes to circumnavigate. Bird was eventually crippled by a back injury and would soon be gone from the scene after only a short dozen-plus seasons. And more shocking and disrupting still was the sudden and unexpected retirement of Magic Johnson, who had contracted the dreaded AIDS disease. Johnson had tested positive for the HIV virus, and doctors had advised against the further physical stress of pro basketball competition. Magic had announced his departure during the first week of the 1991–92 season, then returned for one final dramatic encore with a 25-point MVP performance during the midseason All-Star contest at Orlando. Boston's Bird had also been once more elected as matter of course for the All-Star squad, but for the second straight year, Bird sat out with injury during what was his own swan-song season. Suddenly the two biggest drawing cards of the '80s were gone almost overnight.

A still bigger shock now also lay in store. Michael Jordan next caught the nation's sports scene and the world at large off guard when he announced his own early retirement at age 30 in the wake of his father's brutal murder on the eve of the 1993–94 season. With his triple NBA titles and the tragic loss of his father, Jordan had seemingly lost all motivation to continue. Within a few short months, however, basketball's biggest icon was chasing another personal dream when he signed up with Bulls owner Jerry Reinsdorf's Chicago White Sox franchise as a minor-league baseball player. The Bulls, meanwhile, were suddenly an average ball club, and the league as a whole took a huge public relations hit.

Commissioner Stern's marketing specialists and NBA image makers rushed to fill the vacuum left by Jordan's premature exit with a hastily propped up image of the giant-sized Shaquille O'Neal. While the second-year Orlando Magic center was a considerable playing talent in his own right (1995 scoring leader and David Robinson's major rival as the best all-around big man) and a celebrity of almost Jordanesque proportions off the court (with movie appearances, rap music recordings, and numerous television commercials already to his credit), nonetheless, the effort was doomed to minimal success. As a complete ballplayer and personable pitchman, Shaq could not quite "be like Mike." Nor could another heir apparent, Detroit Pistons rookie phenom Grant Hill, who more closely resembled Jordan as a player and even accomplished a feat of recognition and popularity denied to His Airness. Hill became the first rookie ever to rank as top vote-getter in the fan All-Star Game balloting when he earned a starting spot on the 1995 Eastern Division squad. But for all his talent and marketing appeal, Grant Hill also was far from being Michael Jordan. For one thing, he was not yet a serious threat to win scoring titles. For another, he could not single-handedly carry a youthful Detroit team to postseason respectability. And for a third, for all his offensive flair, he was not yet in the same league with Jordan or Julius Erving when it came to highlight-reel aerial solos.

So colorful and flamboyant had the Bulls been with Jordan during their "three-peat" reign that the back-to-back champion Houston Rockets team that replaced them looked flat and brutish by comparison. Fans and even league luminaries fussed about the ugly 1994 championship series between Houston and New York, which was marred by excessive fouling and dulled by plodding and low-scoring action. Overly aggressive defensive tactics in that first post-Jordan series even led to some minimal rule changes for the subsequent year. Hand-guarding was outlawed on defense, but after a few weeks under the new rule, fans could hardly perceive a difference in the way the game was being played. Houston's repeat-performance title series against Orlando and the bulky Shaquille O'Neal was not as much of a street fight, yet neither team played with much of the pizzazz Bulls watchers had come to expect from Jordan, Pippen, John Paxson, and crew. Houston defended its championship in a four-game sweep, and for the first time since the arrival of Bird and Magic in 1980, the entire NBA postseason inspired more yawns than excitement.

Jordan's return—as sudden as his departure—thus gave the entire league a huge shot in its collective arm. The moment came in mid-March 1995 in Indianapolis and created an immediate media frenzy. Jordan's reemergence also lit as large a fire under his own team as it did under the fans and media. MJ's presence in the lineup was more than enough to lift Chicago squarely back on the fast track toward dynasty status. With one partial season (17 games plus the Orlando play-offs, where the Bulls were eliminated by New York) to get his legs back and his on-court timing fine-tuned, Jordan was as good as ever and perhaps even more competitive the second time around. Not missing a beat as the league's top scorer as well as its top showman, Jordan led his teammates to an unprecedented 72-win 1996 campaign and a laughably easy romp through the postseason, culminating with a six-game skunking of the Seattle SuperSonics for title number four. A year later both the club and the superstar sustained enough momentum to prove that the 72-win season had not been a mere fluke. While Chicago fell ever so short of repeating the 70-win mark in 1997 (finishing a game short at 69–13), Jordan, Pippen, and crew had little difficulty in mowing down Utah in yet another six-game romp during the championship finals. This fifth Chicago championship was perhaps the sweetest for Jordan, who had been edged out in regular-season MVP balloting by Utah's Karl Malone, yet consistently dominated Malone during the title-round matchup. The season's highlight came when Jordan, weakened by the flu, nonetheless unleashed still another spectacular MVP performance during the deciding sixth game.

The Chicago Bulls of the mid-'90s were no longer Michael Jordan's team exclusively. Phil Jackson had developed on the bench into a coaching guru almost as celebrated in the '90s as Red Auerbach had been in the '60s. Jackson also claimed a record-book distinction for himself by reaching 500 career victories faster than any of his predecessors; but unquestionably, the professorial Zen-spouting mentor of the world champion Bulls had enjoyed his five world titles far more than any such individual milestones. On the night of his landmark 500th victory (December 23, 1997) against the L.A. Clippers in Chicago, Jackson put the matter in final perspective: "It's wonderful to have won a lot of games in regular-season play, but the ones that count are those playoff victories. Each one I value 10 to 1 over the regular-season wins, since they're so much more difficult to capture."

Chicago's Scottie Pippen—a versatile scorer and outstanding defender—had also now emerged as a true superstar in his own right, and an injury, which kept him out of the lineup for nearly half of the 1997–98 season, revealed the vincibility of any Chicago lineup featuring Jordan as a solo act. Further support came from basketball's top bad boy, Dennis Rodman, who brought to Chicago in time for the 1996 season a reputation for rebelliousness balanced by the league's top rebounding skills. Rodman's flamboyant off-court lifestyle and punk-rocker appearance consisting of numerous tattoos, nose rings, and constantly changing hair colors—as well as an intimidating but tantrum-marred on-court presence—actually paid surprising dividends by taking Jordan somewhat out of the constant limelight and thus allowing the superstar to concentrate more on his spectacular game. Rodman, for all his antics, was also a unique rebounding presence in the modern age who strung together a league-record seven straight individual rebounding titles, beginning in 1992 and split evenly between seasons in Detroit (1992, 1993), San Antonio (1994, 1995), and Chicago (1996, 1997, 1998). Leave aside the fact that competition was now considerably watered down and improved shooting percentages had made obsolete those per-game averages in the mid-20s once posted by Chamberlain, Russell, and Nate Thurmond. In his own era Rodman was an equally impressive board-sweeper who averaged in the high teens and—like Russell in a bygone age—was able to impact on victories while making almost no contributions to offense. Other mainstays of unbeatable Chicago lineups in the mid-'90s were additional role players like 6'11" Croatian import Toni Kukoc, 7' Australian center Luc Longley, flashy ball handler Ron Harper, and consistent three-point marksman Steve Kerr.

Although some experts predicted that Utah might be capable of unseating the Bulls as NBA champions, the Jazz, led by Karl Malone (top) and John Stockton (bottom) were unable to break Chicago's grip on NBA supremacy, falling in six games in both 1997 and 1998.

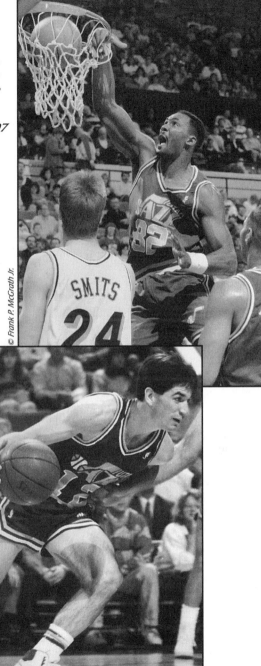

© Frank P. McGrath Jr.

© Frank P. McGrath Jr.

With such depth during an age of watered-down league rosters, Chicago's Bulls had no peers other than Boston under Auerbach when it came to compiling successive world championships. The lineup of Jordan, Pippen, Rodman, Kukoc, Longley, and coach Jackson was a strange and colorful mix—recalling baseball's '70s-era Oakland A's under owner Charlie Finley—yet one that worked in spectacular fashion. One immediate result was the greatest two single seasons on the NBA ledgers with record victory totals of 72 and 69 games. If the Bulls of 1996 and 1997 were not the best team ever, they were nonetheless enshrined by the accumulated numbers as the winningest all-time NBA outfit.

Jordan still held the center stage as the league enjoyed its Golden Anniversary season amidst considerable 1997 fanfare. While baseball simultaneously marked 50 years since the debut of Jackie Robinson and racial integration, the NBA celebrated the same half-century anniversary of its own founding with the inaugural 1947 BAA season. (Fifty seasons under the NBA label would not be complete until the millennium.) Central to the self-congratulatory hoopla that surrounded the anniversary season was the formal naming of the league's 50 greatest all-stars. Air Jordan punctuated his own presence at the top of the illustrious roster of immortals with a record ninth scoring title and his fifth team championship. Inclusion on the list of other current stars like Scottie Pippen, Karl Malone, John Stockton (now the career assists leader), and Robert Parish (who the same season was overhauling Kareem Abdul-Jabbar's longevity milestones for games and seasons played) clinched the widespread feeling among both fans and league public relations mouthpieces that the 1990s was truly a zenith era for the National Basketball Association.

The 1990s with Jordan, David Robinson, Karl Malone, Scottie Pippen, Barkley, Olajuwon, Alonzo Mourning, Penny Hardaway, Grant Hill, and Shaquille O'Neal had indeed collected the greatest pantheon of inspiring stars since the early 1960s era of Wilt, Oscar, Jerry West, and Elgin Baylor. Recent expansion cities of Miami, Orlando, Minneapolis, and Charlotte have built competitive and even exciting teams in but a few short years, and the league has now also gone international with vibrant franchises in eastern and western Canada. The placement of an NBA club in Toronto also brought the league full circle just in time for its Golden Anniversary season with a return to the locale of its first-ever game of a half-century earlier. Most vital of all, fan interest by any conceivable measure—television ratings, popularity polls, ticket sales, merchandise demands—has never been higher. The pro sport that had once limped and crawled a half-century earlier is now soaring ever higher on the fullness of its newfound wings.

If the NBA was looking for new corners to turn in the wake of Air Jordan, it had already stumbled on at least one in the guise of the newfound interest in the women's side of the sport. Pro basketball now seemed ready for the ladies in the mid-'90s, just as college basketball had been ready for the women's game during the mid-'80s. Thus the 1996–97 season would witness not one but two simultaneous efforts to get a professional women's league off the ground and into the marketplace. The American Basketball League (with U.S. Olympians Teresa Edwards, Dawn Staley, and Nikki McCray among the headliners) began its first eight-team 40-game season in November 1996. The NBA-sponsored WNBA enjoyed even more visibility resulting from a hefty television deal when it opened its own doors for action in June 1997. The WNBA not only held a slight upper hand with NBA arenas for its games and the biggest Team USA Olympic stars under contract (Rebecca Lobo, Sheryl Swoopes, and Lisa Leslie), but even reached into the past to ink 39-year-old former legend Nancy Lieberman-Cline (who suited up for the Phoenix Mercury) and 37-year-old ex-Globetrotter Lynette Woodard (who appeared with the Cleveland Rockers). The WNBA also corralled Hall of Famer Cheryl Miller as a coach and former UCLA legend Ann Meyers as a television broadcaster.

Women's pro circuits had been tried before, yet had never been very successful after an initial splash of novelty. In 1992 the short-lived Women's Basketball Association (WBA) was launched with six Midwestern franchises and drew little sustained notice. Only a season earlier an unprecedented experiment known as the Liberty Basketball Association attempted to operate with shorter courts, lower rims, and unitards for uniforms; not surprisingly, it too folded, after a single preseason exhibition game. A much more successful experiment in the form of an eight-team circuit calling itself the Women's Professional Basketball League (WBL) took the floor for three campaigns in the late '70s, staging its first contest between the Chicago Hustle and Milwaukee Does in December 1978. But even though the women's college game had attracted a large enough following by the early '80s to spawn its own NCAA-sponsored postseason tournament, the ticket-buying fan base was still quite small for women's play once college loyalties were stripped from the picture.

By the mid-'90s, however, the odds seem stacked much more favorably for the women's cage game. The USA Basketball Women's National Team had only recently achieved a fair measure of media attention with its 52–0 record against NCAA and international competition, and especially with its sweep to a gold medal at the Atlanta Olympics. And college women's action was rapidly becoming a prime-time television event during springtime March Madness season. Against this promising backdrop, both the ABL and WNBA completed highly successful and surprisingly visible inaugural seasons. There was not a single franchise collapse, and several of the top women players (especially Jennifer Azzi, Sheryl Swoopes, Rebecca Lobo, and Lisa Leslie) were even soon appearing in frequent TV commercial spots. The ABL underscored its opening-year successes by entering a second campaign with its first expansion franchise and with marquee-name Celtics star K. C. Jones coaching its New England–based team. One further important spinoff was a pair of female referees who debuted in the NBA in time for the 1998 men's season. Still another was a complete overhaul of the NBA All-Star weekend, one which replaced the once-popular Saturday slam-dunk contest with a staged shootout competition featuring a handful of WNBA headliners paired with male NBA stars from the corresponding league cities.

The NBA enters its second half-century with fans, league executives, and marketing gurus all flushed with the knowledge that the sport cannot look to Jordan to carry its banner single-handedly any longer. By the 1998 playoffs MJ was already hinting at another retirement if coach Phil Jackson was forced by Bulls management to seek a bench role elsewhere after 1998. At the end of the 1998 season, Jordan retired. And the league's overriding successes of the past decade were now also widely acknowledged to be fraught with inevitable and predictable dangers. Those dangers included, but were not limited to, all the following: overexpansion of both player salaries (thus dulling competitive hunger) and league franchises (diluting available talent), overreliance on the marketing potential of budding megastars rather than on proven on-floor achievements to sustain star images, and the gambling strategy of selling the game with individual celebrities rather than with the achievements of victorious teams or (more logically) with the inherent beauties of the roundball game itself.

In search of further danger signs, one could point—as have numerous recent commentators on the NBA scene— to the methods by which club managements now build their franchises. Owners want quick fixes and are rarely patient with the slow rebuilding process necessary to nurture solid championship rosters. Young college stars are brought on board for flair and flash (guaranteed ticket sales) and are themselves loath to accept (just like their owners) a shift in roles that might reduce their individual visibility (i.e., playing time) in the cause of building a solid winning unit. NBA coaches are thus not given the tools and strategies to win consistently, and fan interest eventually wanes in most of the league's 29 cities. And fan enthusiasm is also dulled by increasingly one-dimensional ballplayers, whose games seem focused on little more than showcase dunks and individualized playground moves, who appear to disdain fundamentals like foul shooting and hardnosed defense, and who sleepwalk through an excessively long schedule, which provides few incentives for maximum nightly effort.

Against this backdrop, is there still room for optimism about a sport that was as recently as two or three seasons ago the unrivaled kingpin among athletic entertainments? The evidence from both the deep past and recent past on balance points to a positive answer. New stars have always emerged to fill the void (Wilt and Oscar trailing Cousy, Alcindor/Abdul-Jabbar in the shadows of Chamberlain, Jordan on the heels of Bird and Magic), and the NBA horizon is already full of young luminaries like Grant Hill and Kobe Bryant seemingly poised to take Jordan's throne. An eventual slide in the dynasty status of the Bulls might at first deflate interest (as did the inevitable collapse of the even greater Boston Celtics dynasty of the '60s), but the game has always been full of the stuff of overnight renewal. Pro basketball NBA-style thus enters its sixth decade on a crest of successes that only seem to portend larger triumphs around the next corner and larger (and more international) audiences than ever before poised to thrill to the spectacle.*

*For more exhaustive retelling of pro basketball's colorful history—from George Mikan to Wilt Chamberlain and Oscar Robertson, and then on to Magic, Bird, Jordan, and Shaq O'Neal—readers are referred to the author's comprehensive book, *The History of the NBA* (Random House, 1992).

Chapter Three

Basketball's Dozen-Plus
Most Significant Players

Basketball, as much as any sport, has had its larger-than-life arena heroes equipped with enough charisma and magnetism to rival any of baseball's or football's most substantial icons. In the modern era names such as Air Jordan, Shaq, Magic, and Bird—and more recently Penny Hardaway and Grant Hill—stand at the pinnacle of fan idolatry. In earlier epochs our court stars were perhaps not so visible nor such common currency, since basketball itself lagged far behind the gridiron game and the diamond sport in the public imagination. But from Hank Luisetti to George Mikan to Wilt Chamberlain and on down to Oscar Robertson, Lew Alcindor, Larry Bird, and Michael Jordan, each passing decade has boasted its full complement of legitimate cage heroes, all standing quite tall (often quite literally) among the sports world's biggest frontline attractions.

Before Luisetti in the late '30s there were admittedly few, if any, basketballers who might be called true matinee idols. The college game was largely regional in its appeal previous to the Second World War, and professional players were, in turn, almost invisible on the nation's sports entertainment stage. Most cage stars were known widely, if at all, only within their own sectors of the country—Chris Steinmetz of Wisconsin and Pat Page of Chicago in the teens, Paul Endacott at Kansas or Vic Hanson at Syracuse in the '20s, Johnny Wooden and Stretch Murphy with Purdue in the '30s. Luisetti himself was able to gain a national following only on the strength of his two remarkable New York City performances during his junior and senior seasons. Had Luisetti not unleashed his one-handed bombs before a packed Madison Square Garden in 1936, basketball might have waited another decade or more for its first glamour-boy hero.

First with Mikan in the late '40s, however, and then with the coming of the dozens of great black stars of the '50s and '60s, all this would change, and change rather dramatically. In the decade immediately after World War II, George Mikan almost single-handedly brought the fledgling sport of professional basketball squarely into the public limelight. Mikan easily did as much to launch basketball into the main public arena alongside football and baseball as Jordan has now done in the '90s to elevate the cage game to its current position as unrivaled No. 1 fan favorite. Black superstars such as Robertson, Baylor, and Chamberlain in the '50s and '60s not only opened racial doors for cage players as Jackie Robinson, Larry Doby, and Don Newcombe and company had done a full decade earlier on the diamond, but also pioneered an entirely new style of basketball play; along with Oscar and Elgin, entered a new brand of raw excitement that, as much as anything, was responsible for basketball's exploding appeal once slam dunks and one-on-one playground "moves" supplanted set shots and crisp passes as the true essence of the game.

Today, there is little argument that the top basketball stars occupy a center stage once reserved almost exclusively for heroes from the baseball diamond. Yet, the spotlight held over the past two decades by players like Magic, Bird, Jordan, and Shaq casts a somewhat distorting image. It is easy for modern fans to assume that their favorite contemporary stars have never been matched in raw skill across the game's long history, since they have never been matched in hype or fan hysteria. Yet, at least a handful of the nonpareils of the '50s and '60s boast legitimate claims for skills as large as any of today's multimedia megastars. Even Air Jordan may well not surpass Oscar Robertson for all-around talent (see the Epilogue for full discussion). Chamberlain, in turn, was, at his peak, an offensive force never since equalled or even imagined, and the same claim can be made for Boston's Bill Russell on defense. Elgin Baylor anticipated virtually all the airborne moves that brought far greater fame during another era to Julius Erving and to Jordan, both of whom were blessed by their own eras with larger audiences, but not necessarily with greater talents. And the pioneering roles of Luisetti and Mikan—the men who together brought the sport its first broad fan appeal—will never again be approached in a spectator sport that has now fully come of age.

Elgin Baylor—The First Prince of Flight

Before Michael Jordan there was Julius Erving soaring above the rim as basketball's wing-footed master of solo flight. And a decade before Dr. J, there was also the remarkable Elgin Baylor, the true progenitor of basketball's airborne hang time moves. Baylor had every ounce the skill and every inch the showmanship of today's latter-day NBA high flyers. And what made Baylor so special among soaring dunkers and airborne acrobats of the hardwood was the irrepressible fact that he was first upon the scene. What Elgin Baylor lacked in the end was only the widespread audiences to marvel at his unprecedented "smooth-as-silk" offensive style. For a dozen seasons he was the highest-scoring forward in the game. And for the same 12 years he was basketball's most explosive and entertaining spectacle to boot.

Elgin Baylor was not only basketball's innovator of flight and paragon of body control, but also the game's greatest hard-luck victim. He was also perhaps the sport's grittiest survivor—toppling scoring records, setting eye-popping milestones, and leaving behind an indelible image as the most spectacular one-on-one player of his era, all despite just about every injury, setback, and bad break that might possibly beset a professional athletic career. Baylor was certainly the first

A decade before Dr. J and a quarter-century before Michael Jordan, there was the remarkable Elgin Baylor, the true progenitor of basketball's airborne hang time moves.

Transcendental Graphics

great exponent of "showtime moves" and "hang time" exploits. In fact, when Elgin Baylor first arrived on the NBA scene, the league's fans and players alike were largely unprepared for the innovative nature of his spectacular game: "Either he's got three hands or two basketballs," mused New York Knicks guard Richie Guerin. "Guarding Baylor is like guarding a flood!"

But for a series of bad breaks, Baylor's unparalleled talents might have been enough to establish a string of personal scoring records and team championships that would have placed him alone on a pedestal as the all-time best. As it is, Baylor ranks near the top as a scorer: first, he toppled Joe Fulks's unthinkable record of 63 in a single NBA game; later, he was the first to tally 70, lighting up the Knicks for 71 points in 1960; his career average of 27.4 points per game trails only the marks of Chamberlain (30.1) and Jordan (32.7); and his 23,149 total points were also third-best in league history at the time when he finally called it quits.

When it comes to standards for single-season scoring, only Wilt surpassed Baylor's 38.3 average logged during one abbreviated campaign of 48 games (which came, ironically, in the same point-crazy year when Wilt averaged 50.4 and Oscar Robertson averaged a yearlong triple-double). Baylor had been forced into military service that fall and was thus restricted by his fate to commuting only to weekend games. His career point totals, in spite of several such missed or shortened seasons, eventually positioned him as the 14th-best scorer of all time (entering 1997), yet only Wilt and Oscar outstripped him at the time of his 1971 retirement.

When it came to explosive single games, only Wilt and Jordan have soared above Elgin Baylor's level, although Jordan never has reached the 70-point plateau, which is shared exclusively by Chamberlain (four times), Baylor (the only forward), and Denver's skywalker, David Thompson. And Baylor was more than just a mechanical scorer. His soaring athletic ability and amazing body control made him an unparalleled rebounder as well, and his career total of 11,463 is still the second-most ever among forwards, trailing only the 12,851 boards compiled by Bob Pettit (who actually played not infrequently in the center position during his own 11-year NBA career).

Elgin Baylor's injury-riddled career, in the end, reminds one of the fate of Ted Williams in baseball. Had not injury and wartime military service intervened, "Teddy Ballgame" would likely have smashed 700 homers to rival Ruth and Aaron and won a half dozen more batting titles to also stand in the company of Ty Cobb. Baylor similarly lost a significant chunk out of a prime season to the military in the very year that he was at his uncanny best as a scorer (and the year when scoring records were falling like flies everywhere around the league). And then injuries wiped out several more stretches: knee troubles reduced his effectiveness on almost a nightly basis after 1963, worsening knees limited him to 54 games in 1969–70 and then wiped out the following campaign altogether, and at one point he played a full month with a steel plate on a finger of his shooting hand, yet still averaged 30 points per game.

But it was not only injuries (especially tattered knee muscles) that victimized Baylor. For one thing, his poor academic standing in high school had early prevented a more glorious collegiate venue at one of the country's prime basketball powers. Elgin's only apparent ticket to athletic fame was, at first, a football scholarship to tiny College of Idaho, where a perceptive coach noticed his basketball talents during a pickup game and engineered a fortuitous switching of sports. Eventually transferring to yet another small-time institution, Seattle University, Baylor made the best of his increased opportunities by averaging 31 points per game as an academic senior (he still had another year of basketball eligibility after the transfer), pacing the nation's collegians in rebounding and leading the unheralded Seattle Chieftains straight to an NCAA title matchup with vaunted Kentucky. Baylor, almost overnight, had put himself and his school squarely on the nation's basketball map. His was seemingly too much spectacular athletic talent to get lost in any further shuffles—no matter how many times the fates chose to intervene.

But fickle fortune was not altogether done with Baylor's erratic athletic career. Once reaching the pros with the Lakers, Elgin was victim of yet other stroke of misfortune that would have kayoed lesser talents. He came to a glorious team (winner of four titles in the first nine NBA seasons) at the very hour when it had fallen on the hardest of lean times. Elgin's first several seasons—including a spectacular 1959 Rookie of the Year performance, which led a sub-.500 Lakers ball club all the way into the playoff finals against Boston—were wasted on a losing outfit that he alone made competitive with his unstoppable offensive fireworks.

When the Lakers franchise moved westward and Baylor picked up a running mate appropriately also named West, things got only slightly better. Baylor, like West and like Wilt, saw his title dreams postponed time and again by an invincible

Elgin Baylor Career Profile

College Teams: College of Idaho, Seattle University
College and Amateur Achievements:
- One of seven players to average 20 ppg and 20 rpg for entire collegiate career (31.3 ppg and 20.0 rpg)
- Unanimous First-Team All-American (1958)
- NCAA Final Four Most Outstanding Player (1958)
- NCAA National Rebounding Leader (1957)

NBA Teams .... Minneapolis Lakers, Los Angeles Lakers
NBA Points .... 23,149 (27.4 ppg)
NBA Games .... 846 (1959–72, 14 seasons)
NBA Assists .... 3,650 (4.3 apg)
NBA Rebounds .... 11,463 (13.6 rpg)
NBA Field Goals (Pct) .... 8,693 (.431)
NBA Free Throws (Pct) .... 5,763 (.780)
NBA All-Star Game MVP 1959
NBA Rookie of the Year 1959
Naismith Memorial Basketball Hall of Fame (1976)

Boston Celtics juggernaut and by the defensive exploits of Bill Russell. There were some near misses, however, and several of those misses were a direct result of Baylor's lingering and nagging injuries. The Lakers lost seventh-game matchups in the title round in both 1969 and 1970, both times with an injured Elgin Baylor either hobbled on the court or sitting on the sidelines. And then when Wilt was added to the roster and the Lakers eventually broke into the winner's circle, Baylor was an unwitting victim yet one more time. Nagging injuries had finally forced the longtime Los Angeles star to the sidelines (as still a relatively young man, even by athletic standards) only a single season before Jerry West and his teammates hoisted their very first West Coast championship banner.

Larry Bird—Boston's Great White Hope

Bird and Magic are names likely to be forever linked throughout the remaining aeons of basketball's unfolding epic saga. Their mano-a-mano duel in the last NCAA Finals of the '70s was the undisputed highlight of a college basketball decade that had also included the zenith seasons of John Wooden's UCLA dynasty. Together the two 6'9" rookie phenoms seemingly rescued pro basketball from near-oblivion at the outset of the 1980s—a time when fan interest had sagged and genuine stars were as scarce as at any point in league history—then carried out their continued personal warfare in three of the most exciting NBA Finals matchups of all time. Bird in Boston and Johnson in Los Angeles were perfect joint saviors for the NBA in one of its bleakest hours.

If Bird and Magic were destined to be linked by fate, they were also two of the most different ballplaying heroes in NBA annals. Johnson, as a stylish black player, was the epitome of pure grace personified—a direct descendent of Elgin Baylor, Oscar Robertson, and Julius Erving. He was also the new prototype for perfection at the guard position. Bird, by stark contrast, was a small-town white paragon who didn't look quite so cool (he lacked pure foot speed and seemingly couldn't even jump), yet possessed enough hidden proficiencies to ultimately make him, arguably, the best forward ever to play the game.

Larry Bird was a small-town white paragon who didn't look quite so cool (he lacked pure foot speed and seemingly couldn't even jump), yet he possessed enough hidden proficiencies to ultimately make him, arguably, the best forward ever to play the game.

© Frank P. McGrath Jr.

Bird's statistical legacy alone seemingly makes him the game's supreme figure at the forward position. While he never won an individual scoring title (no Boston Celtics player ever has), he scored with deadly proficiency throughout the full decade of the '80s. His 30.3 collegiate average at Indiana State remains one of the loftiest in history; he ranks 10th within the tiny circle of a mere dozen college players who have posted 4,000 career points and rebounds; he once topped 60 in a single NBA game and averaged better than 25 points per game on four different occasions; his nearly 22,000 career points rank second in Boston history (behind only Havlicek). But scoring proficiency aside, Bird did other things even better. He was the best passing forward ever to pick up a basketball: his full-court heaves on the fast break rivaled those of Russell, and his over-the-shoulder blind feeds were

Larry Bird Career Profile

College Team: Indiana State University
College and Amateur Achievements:
- NCAA National Player of the Year (1979)
- Naismith Award (1979) and Wooden Award (1979) Winner
- Unanimous First-Team All-American (1978, 1979)
- Member of 1992 USA Olympic Team

NBA Team	Boston Celtics
NBA Points	21,791 (24.3 ppg)
NBA Games	897 (1980–92, 13 seasons)
NBA Assists	5,695 (6.4 apg)
NBA Rebounds	8,974 (10.0 rpg)
NBA Field Goals (Pct)	8,591 (.496)
NBA Free Throws (Pct)	3,960 (.886)
NBA MVP	1984, 1985, 1986
NBA All-Star Game MVP	1982
NBA Rookie of the Year	1980
NBA Championships	1981, 1984, 1986

the equal of Cousy's. He shot the ball from the outside like no towering corner man before him, ranking in the career top 10 in three-point goals and free-throw percentage, and barely missing out on that distinction in career scoring average when his lifetime mark dipped below 25 points per game during his final season. Bird even specialized in three-pointers ("home runs" in the current NBA lingo) as Erving had specialized in rim-rattling dunks. It was Bird, surprisingly, who captured the first three NBA All-Star Saturday Long Distance Shootout trophies. He controlled games like a guard and flaunted an unmatched intelligence and unmatched set of physical reflexes that made him one of the most dangerous all-around offensive performers ever to step on the court.

And above all else, Larry Bird was a proven winner. With his pinpoint blind passes delivered softly to the open man, and his uncanny sense of every movement on the court surrounding him, Bird ran the Boston offense from his forward slot like a true point guard; and like most great players, he always made his teammates better as well. Perhaps the most deadly outside shooter of any era (save perhaps Jerry West or Bill Sharman), Bird always wanted the ball when the game was on the line. It was for this reason alone that the wisest of all basketball talent judges, Red Auerbach, pronounced Bird as the one player he would choose above all others if he were building a franchise from scratch. "If I had to start a team, the one guy in all of history I would take would be Larry Bird," Auerbach once pronounced at a charity banquet. "This is the greatest ballplayer who ever played the game."

Auerbach may well have grown slightly nostalgic and effusive in his senior years. Bird, above Robertson or Chamberlain or Jordan, is perhaps a bit of a stretch; and it was Auerbach himself who built an even greater team on Russell's shoulders than on Bird's. But it is a strong endorsement, nonetheless, and one not to be taken altogether lightly. There is indeed a long line of superstars in the annals of the Boston Celtics. But only Russell today remains a brighter star in the Celtics' firmament than does Indiana's Larry Joe Bird.

Wilt Chamberlain—Basketball's Enigmatic Goliath

Jordan aside, a perusal of the record books or even a casual review of the NBA's middle decades makes it difficult to arrive at any conclusion but one—the conclusion that promotes Wilt Chamberlain as the most dominating presence ever to step upon a basketball floor to guard goals at one end of the arena and stuff them with dunk shots at the other end. If there is a downside to Chamberlain's storied career, it is the wildly unaccountable fact that he was simply too good, too much in a class by himself. It is seemingly a reasonable criticism that Chamberlain hardly ever played at more than about half speed. He dominated whatever statistical categories he chose (most often those of scoring and rebounding), yet had trouble emulating Russell by carrying teams on his back into the winner's circle. And such a critique is both the sharp thorn in the side of his reputation and the indisputable badge of his ultimate and unmatched greatness.

For most of his career Chamberlain was frequently bored by a sport that was so easy for him that he could even accomplish the unthinkable when he simply put his mind to it. And the "unthinkable" (here) is not merely a term of unrestrained hype. While still motivated as only a third-year NBA player, Wilt decided to score at will and averaged 50 points per contest for an entire season. Such a figure is so far above the norm, that it cannot even be assessed, standing more than 25 percent higher than the next loftiest season average anyone else ever recorded—Jordan's 37 in what was, ironically, his own third NBA season. Chamberlain once scored an even 100 points in a single contest—not against podunk schools such as Presbyterian College (Frank Selvy's opponent in his 100-point game) or Hillsdale Institute (the team against which Bevo Francis once racked up 113)—but against the NBA's New York Knicks. His rebound average year in and year out was double that of most of the game's other classic board-sweepers (his career-long 22.9 mark barely edges Russell at 22.5 but dwarfs modern-day paragons like Moses Malone, Olajuwon, and Rodman who win league titles with 60 to 70 percent of that number). And when he was once stung by constant criticism of his all-too-easy scoring, Wilt took personal offense one season near the end of his career (1968) and paced the circuit in assists from the center slot (besting the great Oscar Robertson in total dishes if not in per-game average). A season later he set his mind on pacing the circuit in field-goal accuracy and canned a never-to-be-matched 72.7 percent of his shots. On the court Wilt Chamberlain could do just about anything he wanted, and he did so with abandon on the few occasions when he was truly motivated.

The degree of Chamberlain's career-long boredom (and often frustration) with the game was best revealed in his two collegiate seasons at Kansas. No collegiate star had (or has since) come on center stage with loftier and thus more impossible-to-fulfill expectations, unless possibly it was Kareem Abdul-Jabbar (nee Alcindor) at UCLA. Phog Allen had already placed a hefty onus on his prize recruit (as well as on his own coaching successor, Dick Harp) even before Wilt's first college season had opened. Facing mandatory retirement and thus unable to enjoy the fruits of the "big prize" he had landed, Allen announced to the national press on the eve of the 1957 postseason (where Wilt as a sophomore "rookie" would carry Kansas into the NCAA championship game) that his former team could undoubtedly coast to an NCAA trophy with "Wilt, two sorority girls, and two Phi Beta Kappas" in the lineup.

Air Jordan aside, a perusal of the record books, or even a casual review of the NBA's middle decades, makes it difficult to arrive at any conclusion save one—a conclusion that promotes Wilt Chamberlain as the most dominating presence ever to step upon a basketball floor to guard goals at one end of the arena and stuff them with dunk shots at the other end.

Transcendental Graphics

Not that he failed to live up in large part to the loose predictions of awesome individual skill. In his debut sophomore campaign, Wilt was the nation's fourth-leading scorer (29.6) and fourth-best rebounder, and carried the Jayhawks to within mere seconds of a national title. But his opponents, from the first, bent the rules in pulling out every stop to defeat him with rugged and harassing play. Wilt was banged and bruised on the court (by triple-teaming defenses) and subjected to relentless criticism away from the arena (by overanxious alumni and an unrealistic media). He carried his team immediately to the top rung yet lost a championship game by an unlucky bounce or two in triple overtime against one of the best teams in collegiate history (North Carolina was only the second undefeated NCAA champion). A year later, as a battle-worn junior, he struggled through a season where the opposition simply wouldn't let him play under normal conditions, hacking and mauling him whenever he was fed the ball. In short, college basketball quickly turned out to be anything but fun for the biggest talent that had ever come along. The result was an inevitable early escape into the pro circuit—first with the barnstorming Harlem Globetrotters for a year, until his class graduated and he was eligible for an NBA contract. What Wilt Chamberlain never could quite escape, however, was his seeming ambivalence toward the game at which he so easily excelled.

Wilt Chamberlain Career Profile

College Team: University of Kansas
College and Amateur Achievements:
- Unanimous First-Team All-American (1957, 1958)
- NCAA Final Four Most Outstanding Player (1957)

NBA Teams	Philadelphia Warriors, San Francisco Warriors, Philadelphia 76ers, Los Angeles Lakers
NBA Points	31,419 (30.1 ppg)
NBA Games	1,045 (1960–73, 14 seasons)
NBA Assists	4,643 (4.4 apg)
NBA Rebounds	23,924 (22.9 rpg) NBA Record
NBA Field Goals (Pct)	12,681 (.540)
NBA Free Throws (Pct)	6,075 (.511)
NBA MVP	1960, 1966, 1967, 1968
NBA All-Star Game MVP	1960
NBA Rookie of the Year	1960
NBA Scoring Leader	1960, 1961, 1962, 1963, 1964, 1965, 1966
NBA Championships	1967, 1972
Naismith Memorial Basketball Hall of Fame (1978)	

After his short sojourn with the Globetrotters, Wilt took up residence in NBA arenas where he would at least be free from zone defenses and noxious offensive stalling tactics. It was hard at first to conclude that the giant "Big Dipper" was holding back much, if at all, since he scored and rebounded with such unprecedented profundity. But Wilt's teams didn't win titles and—with Russell and Boston parked in the same four-team Eastern Division—they didn't even get into championship-round showdowns. Wilt and the Warriors (first on one coast and then the other) lost repeatedly at year's end to Russell and Boston. After just three headline-grabbing seasons in Philly, Chamberlain was soon bouncing from team to team and city to city, as first the Warriors relocated in San Francisco, then traded Wilt back to Philadelphia and the 76ers (nee Syracuse Nats), who in turn unloaded him after only three more seasons to the Los Angeles Lakers. One complaint about Chamberlain, as seasons unfolded, was that he appeared to hold back during fourth-quarter action to protect his cherished record of never having fouled out of a game. Another was that he quibbled frequently with his coaches and either shot the ball far too much (early in his career with the Warriors) or far too little (later in his career with the 76ers and Lakers). And if he sometimes seemed painfully bored (especially during endless midseason contests), he also often appeared to be held back by an awkward fear of his own unmatched physical strengths. Wilt rarely angered, undoubtedly knowing that he was so strong he might actually maim or even kill an opponent if he ever unleashed his full wrath.

If there is some reasonableness to the argument that Chamberlain never approached his obvious potential for complete domination, it is also equally true that any view which contends he was not a winning player (and many have contended this) is largely also an overblown distortion. Wilt would never boast eight straight NBA titles like Russell, but then neither would anyone else. What is so conveniently overlooked by Wilt-snipers is the obvious fact that Chamberlain was the dominant force on two of the greatest single-season teams in league history. First came a Philadelphia 76ers team in 1967 that set new standards for NBA domination with a record 68 regular-season victories plus a postseason interruption of

Boston's decade-long dynasty run. Second was a Los Angeles Lakers outfit in 1972 that rang up the longest winning streak of any major sports franchise when it posted 33 unblemished games between early November and early January. And Wilt also took three different franchises into the NBA championship round, logging as many title-round appearances as Jordan. The problem was simply that everyone always judged that Phog Allen had been right all along and that Wilt Chamberlain was supposed to win every title, every year, no matter who his teammates were or how stacked the opposition was. (One might ask how many rings Jordan would sport today if he played the heart of his career in an eight-team league that boasted roadblocks like the Russell-Cousy tandem in Boston, the Pettit-Hagan duo in St. Louis, and the West-Baylor combo out in L.A.) No other NBA or collegiate superstar has ever carried quite so heavy a burden and yet fared so well for quite so long a tenure. And no other behemoth of the hardwood was ever quite so clear a showcase for the old adage that, indeed, no one ever loves Goliath.

Bob Cousy—Houdini of the Hardwoods

Bob Cousy was basketball's first spectacular wizard of ballhandling. He was also one of the most intense and focused athletes to grace the pages of American sports history. Cousy was driven by an almost maniacal will to succeed and to win. And once he had shot-swatting Bill Russell at his side, he would indeed win time and again with the greatest offensive weapon pro basketball has ever known. That weapon was the Boston Celtics' fast-breaking attack—conceived on the chalkboard by Red Auerbach, unleashed on the hardwood court by Russell's rebounding and shot-blocking exploits, and directed down the Boston Garden parquet floor (and those of a couple dozen other NBA arenas) by Cousy's unparalleled ballhandling and dribbling skills.

Few fans today remember precisely what Cousy's original razzle-dazzle showmanship looked like. Today, a behind-the-back dribble or blind pass is almost commonplace; before Cousy, these maneuvers were simply unheard of and even unthinkable. As an All-American at Holy Cross, Cousy had fine-tuned his skills and already earned a reputation as "The Houdini of the Hardwood." Playing only a minor role as a freshman member of the Holy Cross team that captured the NCAA title in 1947, the Queens, New York, native was a much-heralded star for a Crusaders team that won 26 straight in 1950 before slumping badly in its postseason performance.

Yet despite this lofty status as local legend at the nearby Massachusetts college, a new Celtics coach named Auerbach did not see any particular value in a 6'1" professional player, no matter what his collegiate scoring exploits (19.4 points per game as a senior) or passing antics might have been. Auerbach stirred considerable controversy by ignoring the popular Cousy in the college draft, refusing to take the local star under the Celtics' territorial draft option. "Am I supposed to please the local yokels or win ball games?" Auerbach groused when pressed about not signing Cousy. But fate immediately conspired to put Cousy in a Boston uniform despite Auerbach's unpopular slights; the team originally drafting the deft guard (Tri-Cities) traded him immediately to the struggling Chicago franchise; when that club folded without playing a game of the new season, the

Bob Cousy Career Profile

College Team: Holy Cross College
College and Amateur Achievements:
* Unanimous First-Team All-American (1950)
* NCAA National Championships, 1947

NBA Teams	Boston Celtics, Cincinnati Royals
NBA Points	16,970 (18.4 ppg)
NBA Games	924 (1951–63, 1970, 14 seasons)
NBA Assists	6,959 (7.5 apg)
NBA Rebounds	4,794 (5.2 rpg)
NBA Field Goals (Pct)	6,168 (.375)
NBA Free Throws (Pct)	4,624 (.803)
NBA MVP	1957
NBA All-Star Game MVP	1954, 1957
NBA Championships	1957, 1959, 1960, 1961, 1962, 1963

Naismith Memorial Basketball Hall of Fame (1970)

ex-Holy Cross ace—behind-the-back passes and between-the-legs dribbles and all—went straight to Boston via a dispersal-draft coin flip. (Boston had chosen seven-footer Charlie Share and black Duquesne star Chuck Cooper over Cousy in June and now coveted either Max Zaslofsky or Andy Phillip of the three available Chicago players; but Boston lost the three-way toss and was stuck with Cousy.) Bob Cousy—despite the best-laid plans of Red Auerbach himself—backed into his role as a key ingredient in Auerbach's new style of relentlessly running and relentlessly winning basketball.

Cousy could do more than merely dribble and pass and amaze with his bag of ballhandling tricks. He was an effective scorer as well, and often ranked at the top of his team and near the top of the league before the superscorers (Wilt, Oscar, Baylor, and Jerry West) came along at the end of the '50s and outset of the '60s. For four straight seasons, between 1951 and 1955, he paced the Boston offense, twice averaging a hair over 20 and twice a fraction under; in 1954 he was second in the league behind Neil Johnston; he once rang up 50 in a playoff game (admittedly an overtime contest); and his point total reached 17,000 before his 14-year career had closed.

But Cousy's true badge was delivering the ball, even in the days before Russell was available to reconstitute Auerbach's fast-

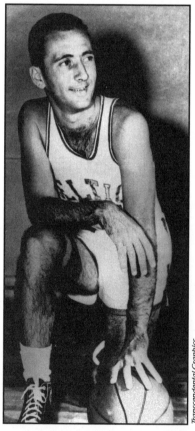

Transcendental Graphics

Bob Cousy was basketball's first great wizard of ballhandling and was also one of the most intense and focused athletes ever to grace the pages of American sports history.

break attack. Eight times he was the NBA assists champion, and he still ranks seventh lifetime in that category three full decades after retirement. Cousy was also an intelligent student of the game, one who became a longtime coach after playing days ended, and also one who was truly a "coach on the floor" while he ran the versatile Boston offense for more than a dozen seasons.

But Boston's immortal "number 14" was also a ruthless perfectionist who could endure nothing less than 100 percent effort, total victory, and perfect execution—from himself and all others around him—and in the end, excessive intensity sabotaged Cousy's coaching effectiveness with the Boston College team, as well as with the NBA Cincinnati Royals. As a player, however, Cousy's burning intensity (along with a giant assist from Auerbach and Russell) made him a tireless winner as well as one of the game's greatest innovators. None ever delivered a pass better or with more crowd-pleasing finesse and eye-popping invention—not Magic Johnson or John Stockton, or even Joe Montana or Joe Namath. Cousy was to passing a basketball what Jordan was to dunking it, or Rick Barry and Jerry West were to shooting it. He was the combined Picasso, Rembrandt, and Dali of the ballhandling art.

Julius "Dr. J" Erving—Inventor of Hang Time

Few events have impacted NBA history like Dr. J's arrival in the league back in the bicentennial year of 1976, precisely at the crucial moment of the landmark NBA-ABA merger. Perhaps only the coming of Wilt Chamberlain or the tandem arrival of Bird and Magic had quite the same earth-shaking significance. Wilt lifted the NBA into a new era of spectacular offense, just as Babe Ruth had done for baseball with his home run blasts in the wake of the Black Sox scandals. Erving would, in similar fashion, save the run-and-shoot game, which had become an NBA trademark, from boring predictability with his patented hang time dunking style and his previously unimagined playground "moves" against hapless defenders. Facing the onslaught of runaway football popularity in the '70s, baseball needed to introduce its designated-hitter rule to generate more scoring and thus provide desperately needed upscale excitement. The NBA needed only the fabulous Dr. J to accomplish essentially the same result.

Erving's legend today derives as much from ABA exploits as from NBA achievements despite one NBA championship with Philadelphia and years of all-star status. For within the ABA the phenomenon of Dr. J seemed almost more the stuff of myth than of substantive athletic history. As a rookie he averaged 27.3 as a scorer and 15.7 as a rebounder (third-best in the league) and teamed with Charlie Scott to turn the Virginia Squires from an also-ran into a showcase ball club. Over the four following seasons (three in New York), his scoring average never dipped below 27.4, he paced two championship teams, won three scoring titles, and captured two league MVP trophies. More importantly still, he replaced Connie Hawkins as basketball's premier high-flying sideshow, and in the process, established the airborne "wingman" (forward) as the sport's new glamour position. ABA Commissioner Dave DeBusschere would once credit the famous "doctor" with "carrying the whole league" on his soaring shoulders; others would eventually credit Erving with almost single-handedly forcing the eventual merger of the two competing pro circuits.

Julius Erving's larger-than-life legend today derives as much from ABA exploits as from NBA achievements, despite one NBA championship with Philadelphia and years of all-star status.

© Frank P. McGrath Jr.

Veteran NBA-ABA coach Kevin Loughery (Erving's mentor with the New York Nets) has put Dr. J's ABA playing days into helpful perspective: "He had the biggest and best hands in basketball. It was like he was playing with a grapefruit. I honestly believe that Doc did more for pro basketball than anybody, on or off the court. He wasn't just 'the franchise' with the Nets—he was the league."

Julius Erving, in essence, made Michael "Air" Jordan and all other such airborne, slam-dunking, "in-your-face" intimidators entirely possible. He sent the game moving in a direction that culminated with Jordan and with other current skywalkers such as Drexler and Pippen and Shawn Kemp. He, more than anyone, changed the level of expectations about what basketball could potentially be like. And he introduced "flamboyant style" and with it, thrills that had turned on play-

Julius Erving Career Profile

College Team: University of Massachusetts
College and Amateur Achievements:
- One of seven players to average 20 ppg and 20 rpg for entire college career (26.3 ppg and 20.2 rpg)

ABA-NBA Teams	Virginia Squires (ABA), New York Nets (ABA), Philadelphia Sixers (NBA)
ABA-NBA Points	30,026 (24.2)
ABA-NBA Games	1,242 (1972–87, 16 seasons)
ABA-NBA Assists	5,176 (4.2 apg)
ABA-NBA Rebounds	10,525 (8.5 rpg)
ABA-NBA Field Goals (Pct)	11,818 (.506)
ABA-NBA Free Throws (Pct)	6,256 (.777)
NBA MVP	1981
NBA All-Star Game MVP	1981
ABA Scoring Leader	1973, 1974, 1976
ABA Championships	1974, 1976
NBA Championships	1983

ground aficionados for years but had not yet impacted on the more conservative professional game. And with his new, made-for-television brand of soaring from the key to the rim, he set the expectations for the next generation of basketball fans. Thus, Erving's position in the game is now legendary. Dr. J is seemingly the world of slam dunk personified, an athletic personality so unique that it was not even perceived as excessive hype when Philadelphia General Manager Pat Williams crowed to the press in 1976 (after dishing out $3 million for Erving's NBA rights and another $3.5 million for his playing contract) that "we just got the Babe Ruth of basketball."

Erving has left a huge statistical legacy as well as an indelible image of soaring flight. His combined ABA-NBA scoring totals rank him with the top handful of scoring stars. He is, in fact, one of only three 30,000-point men, and the only one who was not seven feet tall. And those 30,000 points were—incredible as it may seem—even more notable for the flair and grace with which they were delivered. Erving seemingly had all of Jordan's immense skills (some would contend that the Doctor was a more flamboyant dunker); but in an era before the NBA was mainstream and fashionable, he would never enjoy Jordan's crushing media following. In the wake of Air Jordan one can only imagine what celebrity-crazed advertisers of the 1990s might have made of a fabulous showman and unparalleled athlete like Julius Erving in his prime. Today's Madison Avenue likely could not have held him any more effectively than did the measured dimensions of the ABA and NBA courts on which he once so dramatically performed. In brief, there was little to separate Erving in his prime from Jordan in his—save the wildly disparate decades in which they played.

Tom Gola—Greatest College Player Ever Invented

The argument is not unreasonable that Tom Gola was, inch-for-inch, the greatest college basketball player of all time. For those of us who saw him play, he would always remain fixed in the permanence of youthful memory as the rarest of all players—a perfectly agile small man blessed with residence in a big man's over-

Tom Gola Career Profile

College Team: La Salle College
College and Amateur Achievements:
- UPI NCAA National Player of the Year (1955)
- NCAA career leader in combined points/rebounds (4663)
- Unanimous First-Team All-American (1954, 1955)
- NCAA Final Four Most Outstanding Player (1954)
- NIT Tournament Most Valuable Player (1952)
- NCAA National Championships, 1954

NBA Teams .... Philadelphia Warriors, San Francisco Warriors, New York Knicks
NBA Points .... 7,871 (11.3 ppg)
NBA Games .... 698 (1956–66, 10 seasons)
NBA Assists .... 2,953 (4.2 apg)
NBA Rebounds .... 5,605 (8.0 rpg)
NBA Field Goals (Pct) .... 2,964 (.431)
NBA Free Throws (Pct.) .... 1,943 (.760)
NBA Championships 1956
Naismith Memorial Basketball Hall of Fame (1975)

powering body. One of the game's best historians has uttered the final words on one of the sport's most memorable early superstars. Neil Isaacs, perhaps better than any other writer, has captured the essence of Gola's immense talents: "He had the strength and timing to rebound with the biggest centers, the ballhandling and passing and outside shooting to play backcourt with the best, and the speed and inside moves to play All-American forward." It is true enough that when he took his game to the NBA, Gola never lived up to the hoopla surrounding his stellar college play. There were perhaps reasons enough for this: his size (at 6'6"), the role he would play with the Warriors (sixth man alternating between frontcourt and backcourt service), the different nature of the evolving professional game. But it is all immaterial, at any rate, since Gola's collegiate career alone was of earthshaking proportions.

The most cogent explanation for the apparent drop-off in Gola's game with the Philadelphia Warriors was the makeup of Gottlieb's powerful team of the mid- and late '50s. The Warriors relied on towering Wilt Chamberlain and crack-shooting Paul Arizin for the bulk of their offense; Gola, meanwhile, was a vital and versatile cog at the guard and forward posts: he excelled on defense, rebounded with tenacity, and handed out nearly 3,000 career assists (the bulk to Chamberlain and Arizin). Philadelphia's most cherished basketball legend was one of the earliest prototypes of the tall NBA guard and also one of the last players to be drafted under the NBA's territorial rights ruling.

In short, Gola indisputably owned perhaps the greatest all-around skills of any college hoopster before and probably since. And he also was the subject of one of the strangest recruiting sagas in the sport's history. One can search long and hard through the annals of college sport and never uncover a stranger recruiting story than the one that attaches to the signing of Tom Gola to play basketball for La Salle College. Certainly no school has ever found a bigger superstar any closer to its own backyard—or in this case right in the middle of its own backyard. Gola, it turns out, attended high school classes and played high school games in the very same building that housed the basement gymnasium of the college team that would eventually recruit his services.

It is not unreasonable to argue that Tom Gola of La Salle College was, inch-for-inch, the greatest college basketball player of all time.

Transcendental Graphics

Gola was already a star during his freshman season, a rare opportunity handed him by the eligibility rules still in effect at the time. Gola had been allowed onto the varsity roster in fall 1951 only because of a technicality then on the NCAA rule books: the tiny Philadelphia college enrolled less than 1,000 students and was therefore granted an exemption from the edict banning four years of college play (regular freshman eligibility was still two decades away). With the freshman hotshot already pacing his team in both scoring (17.2) and rebounding (16.5), the Explorers, playing out of the loosely knit Middle Atlantic Conference, built up a 20–5 season record before posting a string of surprising victories over Eastern powers Seton Hall (with seven-footer Walter Dukes), St. John's (upset winner earlier in the year over No. 1 Kentucky and No. 2 Illinois), and Duquesne (the nation's fourth-ranked team) that put coach Ken Loeffler's upstart Explorers into the NIT championship game opposite Dayton, another top-20 club. Gola shared tourney MVP honors with teammate Norm Grekin while inspiring a 75–64 La Salle victory in what was still the nation's most prestigious year-end tournament.

The biggest prize and the biggest headlines, however, would come at the end of Gola's third winter at La Salle. There was, of course, a huge break along the way in the form of the postseason absence of Adolph Rupp's undefeated Kentucky Wildcats, who had thrashed Gola's Explorers 73–60 back in December in Lexington. (Rupp's team elected to sit on the sidelines for the tournament after a ruling that its three top stars—Cliff Hagan, Lou Tsioropoulos, and Frank Ramsey—had already completed their NCAA eligibility.) But when the door was left slightly ajar, Gola and his teammates moved in for the inevitable kill. After narrowly escaping an opening-round overtime showdown with Fordham and Ed Conlin (Gola's chief rival as the nation's best rebounder), La Salle ran by N.C. State, Navy, Penn State, and finally Bradley, to complete a Cinderella trek to a shocking national championship. Despite accumulating four fouls early in the second half of the title game and being forced to spend most of the second stanza setting up his teammates for easy baskets, Gola earned a Final Four MVP trophy to go along with his team's surprising set of championship rings. And a year later there was almost a second straight title when tiny La Salle carried its second straight 26–4 record into another NCAA championship showdown, this time with San Francisco and its ace defender, Bill Russell. It was only the superior force of Russell (23 points and 25 rebounds) teamed up with K. C. Jones (who smothered Gola like a blanket and held the All-American to only 16 points) that blocked Gola and his teammates from wearing an unlikely repeat NCAA crown.

If Gola's final campaign unfortunately ended in defeat, there would also be many memorable milestones before that last season had run its full course. His UPI plaudits as National Player of the Year came largely on the strength of another 600-plus rebounding season and his highest scoring average (24.2) in four brilliant years. A new system for ranking rebounders (in effect from 1956 through 1962, and based on highest percentage of individual recoveries out of the total rebounds by both teams in all games) saw Gola slip from third place in the national rankings as a junior to eighth during his senior season. But the four-year star, who had never managed to lead the nation in any individual season, nonetheless, now became the first man ever to reach the 2,000-rebound career total. Only George Washington's Joe Holup (the very next season) would ever join him in that most select circle in all the years that have subsequently passed. More impressive still is Gola's combined total for points (2,462) and rebounds (2,201), which at 4,663 is still the highest ever logged across a full collegiate career.

Tom Gola thus left behind a mind-stretching four-year legacy. His career rebounding totals by themselves stand as perhaps the most secure record in all of sports. Rebound numbers simply can never be as high today (in an era of greatly increased shooting accuracy and thus elevated field-goal percentages) as they were in the '50s or '60s. Chamberlain (22.9) and Russell (22.5) completed their entire NBA careers with lifetime averages above 20 in this department, and even Bob Pettit logged a 10-year career average well above 15 (16.2). Today's fans and writers are enthralled when Dennis Rodman paces a single NBA season with an average slightly above a dozen. And it also must be remembered here that Gola was not a big man—he checked in at 6'6", played forward for most of his college games, and was later a fixture at the guard position when he signed on with the NBA Warriors. What is truly amazing is the actual percentage of loose shots the tenacious Gola snagged, no matter how many of those available errant shots there may or may not have been. Could those now so enamored of Rodman have only seen Gola in action, perhaps even once, a substantial reality check certainly would have set in.

In the end the real legacy of Magic Johnson—like that of Bill Russell and Bob Cousy in Boston—comes down to the matter of winning coveted NBA championships.

© Frank P. McGrath Jr.

Earvin "Magic" Johnson—Reinventor of Guard Play

Magic Johnson's grandest among numerous legacies has to be his role in destroying the ruling stereotypes concerning size on the basketball court. Magic Johnson stood the same height as Bill Russell and weighed nearly as much; yet Johnson would run the backcourt end of a fast-breaking offense à la Cousy and not the shot-blocking and board-clearing end of the operation à la Russell. Whereas Russell invented defense and Erving and Baylor invented flight, Johnson obliterated all notions that physical stature dictated positions on the court. It was Magic who first brought the agile big man into the backcourt and thus rewrote the rules on how point-guard play was to be performed. But there were other "Magic" legacies as well. One had to do with bravery and inspiration off the court, once Magic's active playing career was cut short in 1991 by his tragic infection with an AIDS-producing virus. As spokes-

Magic Johnson Career Profile

College Team: Michigan State University
College and Amateur Achievements:
- Unanimous First-Team All-American (1979)
- NCAA Final Four Most Outstanding Player (1979)
- Member of 1992 USA Olympic Team
- NCAA National Championship, 1979

NBA Teams	Los Angeles Lakers
NBA Points	17,707 (19.5 ppg)
NBA Games	906 (1980–91, 1996, 12 seasons)
NBA Assists	10,141 (11.2 apg)
NBA Rebounds	6,559 (7.2 rpg)
NBA Field Goals (Pct)	6,211 (.520)
NBA Free Throws (Pct)	4,960 (.848)
NBA MVP	1987, 1989, 1990
NBA All-Star Game MVP	1990, 1992
NBA Championships	1980, 1982, 1985, 1987, 1988

man for HIV-positive victims, Johnson would become an all-too-rare modern-day athlete who turned his powerful celebrity status into a major force for public good. And not the least of the legacies of Magic Johnson was the one that had to do with reviving pro basketball's sagging fortunes at the end of the wasteland 1970s and thus charting a bold course for the halcyon days of pro basketball as America's emerging new national pastime in the 1980s and beyond.

Few rookies have held a starring role on an NBA team; fewer still have been the dominant factor in bringing a league title to their brand-new team. The list of such "rookie winners" contains exactly two names—Bill Russell and Earvin "Magic" Johnson. And the list grows shorter still when we speak of rookies who have claimed NBA playoff MVP status—Magic Johnson. Averaging 41 minutes, 18.3 points, 10 rebounds, 10 assists, and three steals—and subbing at the center slot for an injured Kareem Abdul-Jabbar (posting 42 points and 15 rebounds in the process) in the Game 6 clincher—Magic simply stole center stage of the 1980 NBA season's finale. And that was only to be the first act of one of the most brilliant all-around careers in NBA history.

Only one player truly comes close to Oscar Robertson in the mythical race for "all-time" most-skilled all-around player—at least if one is to judge by the record-book numbers alone—and that player is also Earvin Johnson. There can be little argument that Magic Johnson (with a boost from Larry Bird) saved the NBA in 1980 with his inspired play and infectious personality, arriving as he did at the very time when NBA hoops needed a large image upgrade in time for the coming video era. Magic (with Bird and also Jordan) is as responsible as anyone for the current revival of the league and its ultimate takeover of the American sporting scene at the outset of the 1990s. And a strong argument can be made as well that Johnson is indeed the finest "total-package player" of the past decade and a half. Bird was a better offensive show; Jordan did more to turn on the crowds with his rim-rattling moves. But no one did any more (Bird and Jordan included) to win basketball games.

Magic Johnson's numbers indeed compare favorably to those of Oscar Robertson, especially when it comes to assessing balanced overall performance.

Here was the game's second-greatest career-long triple-double man. While a slide in late-career totals left Oscar a tad short of lifetime triple-double numbers in the rebounding and assists departments, Magic, in the end, missed out in only a single category—rebounds. Johnson owns the only career-long double-figure average in the assists category (among retired players: John Stockton's playing days are far from over and his own double-figure numbers are not yet safe from the onslaught of late-career slumps). And Magic also posted rebound numbers from the guard slot that miss Oscar's by only a mere fraction (7.2 to 7.5 rebounds per game).

In the end, however, the real legacy of Magic Johnson—like that of Russell and Cousy in Boston—comes down to the matter of winning coveted NBA championships. Jordan's Bulls may flaunt their impressive and nearly unprecedented pair of three-peats, but Magic's Lakers also remained in the league's upper echelons for an entire decade, and they did so when the NBA could boast better balance and more competitive rivals to the reigning title holder. Magic owns a collection of world titles that nearly equals MJ's stash and surpasses Larry Bird's haul by three. Only Bill Russell seems to have done more to win more championships over the course of a career. Cousy and Tom Heinsohn each owned more championship rings, but both have Russell to thank for that. Jordan never won without Pippen, arguably the second-best player of the '90s. Magic Johnson rode to five world titles on nobody's coattails but his own.

Michael "Air" Jordan—True Sultan of Space-Age Slam

It can be hotly contested whether or not Michael Jordan of the Chicago Bulls is the game's greatest all-time player. (The Epilogue of this volume debates the issue in full detail.) There certainly are rivals to the throne, even if most are lacking Jordan's full battery of press agents. And the argument is substantial that Jordan receives advantages from the current era (such as almost total abandonment of the traveling rule), which work to pad his stats and thus inflate his mythic status. There is, however, no argument whatsoever that Air Jordan is the roundball sport's loftiest icon and, unarguably, its biggest media celebrity of all time. Perhaps only Babe Ruth remains a rival to Jordan for the mythical title of "supreme icon" of American sports history. The one thing that might still tip the balance slightly in Ruth's favor is the simple fact that the Babe's universal celebrity seemed far more naive and spontaneous; that is to say, that it arrived without any orchestrated media campaigns by corporate giants such as Nike (or by Major League Baseball) and without the benefits of the "global village mentality" of today's electronic age.

Jordan's claim as the best of all time can nonetheless be bolstered with an impressive array of statistics and an even more persuasive list of less "measurable" achievements. Only Chamberlain shares the distinction of scoring more than 3,000 points in a single season, yet Jordan is far more entertaining to watch than Wilt ever was. No one else has ever so thoroughly dominated league scoring, yet at the same time won a simultaneous nod as the NBA's top defensive player. Jordan's hang time moves can indeed be favorably compared with Baylor's or with Julius Erving's; he falls slightly (but only slightly) short of Robertson when it comes to combining passing and rebounding with prolific scoring, yet he is quicker, more

Michael Jordan Career Profile

College Team: University of North Carolina
College and Amateur Achievements:
* Unanimous First-Team All-American (1983, 1984)
* NCAA National Player of the Year (1984)
* Naismith Award (1984) and Wooden Award (1984) Winner
* Member of 1984 and 1992 USA Olympic Teams
* NCAA National Championship, 1982

NBA Team	Chicago Bulls
NBA Points	29,277 (31.4 ppg) (NBA PPG Record)
NBA Games	930 (1985–93, 1995–98, 13 seasons)
NBA Assists	5,012 (5.4 apg)
NBA Rebounds	5,836 (6.3 rpg)
NBA Field Goals (Pct)	10,962 (.505)
NBA Free Throws (Pct)	6,798 (.838)
NBA MVP	1988, 1991, 1992, 1996, 1998
NBA All-Star Game MVP	1988, 1996
NBA Rookie of the Year	1985
NBA Scoring Leader	1987, 1988, 1989, 1990, 1991, 1992, 1993, 1996, 1997, 1998 (NBA Record)
NBA Championships	1991, 1992, 1993, 1996, 1997, 1998

deceptive, and certainly more flamboyant than Oscar; he nearly matches Bill Russell for monomaniacal single-minded dedication to victory, even if he still falls a bit short of the Boston legend in aggregate league championships. Twice MJ has scored more than one third of the Chicago Bulls' total points and, of the five largest margins between the first and second-leading scorers on an NBA team, Wilt owns three (with the Philadelphia and San Francisco Warriors, 1962–64) and MJ has the other two (1987 and 1988).

Jordan's career can now be seen in two neatly packaged segments, and it is the latter segment, unquestionably, which has finally clinched his true greatness. In the early seasons (1985 through 1990) Jordan was deified as an unsurpassed showman and an unparalleled athlete, but certainly not anointed as a relentless winner. The latter crown belonged squarely on the head of Magic Johnson, Larry Bird, or even Detroit's Isiah Thomas by decade's end. Jordan did finally climb to the heights of an NBA championship before his first retirement in 1994, however, and by leading the Chicago Bulls to the first three-peat since Boston's dynasty a quarter-century earlier, he was indeed able to depart the game with credentials that assured his immortality.

Then came the saga of Jordan the baseball player, followed immediately by the most successful return from retirement in American sports history. Jordan's baseball failures in some ways enhanced his appeal by adding an element of previously absent humanness. If Mike couldn't hit a curveball, he was—finally after all—just like the rest of us; if he could not fulfill any athletic dream that was his whim, that made his glorious achievements all the more momentous and all the more something to be envied. The ill-fated baseball venture also served to keep the nation's most talked about and coveted athlete at least partially in the limelight during the 17 months he was away from the basketball arena. But it was once back on the hardwood court that Jordan magically transformed his time away from the game into the richest chapter of his still burgeoning legacy.

© Frank P. McGrath Jr.

In the end, all arguments about basketball's most dominant player today must begin and end with comparisons to Michael Jordan.

Some star athletes manage to return from self-imposed exile and even manage to retain some semblance of their former brilliance. When Jordan—as basketball's most beloved performer—came back to face the loftiest expectations imaginable, it was universally assumed that he would overnight resurrect Chicago's championship status, that he would again be totally invincible, that he would even save the entire NBA from its recent slump in the public eye—and somehow, he even outshone expectations that were perhaps the most unrealistic ever facing a returning ballplaying hero.

Upon his return to the NBA Jordan would write a second chapter to his ever-expanding legacy that miraculously topped even his seemingly unmatchable earlier achievements. Jordan's comeback would soon read like a Hollywood script almost too success-bound to be believable. Not only would he lead the Bulls back to the Promised Land of another NBA title, but he would become the linchpin of the most wildly successful two-season dynasty in NBA history. The Bulls would set records for team winning that might well be attributed to a weakened league, but were also a reflection of Jordan's renewed dominance. MJ, of course, now had the reinforcements he had lacked in early and midcareer. Scottie Pippen had become one of the all-around best in the league, and the duo of Jordan and Pippen was soon to be basketball's equivalent of Ruth and Gehrig or Mantle and Maris. The sport's new "bad boy," Dennis Rodman, made his own colorful impact, rebounding profusely, but also deflecting some of the hype from MJ with his own headline-grabbing antics and thus freeing Jordan to go about business. And the perfect coach in Phil Jackson and perfect role players in Toni Kukoc, Luc Longley, Steve Kerr, Jud Buechler, and others were also now on hand. The results were surprising, though not shocking. Jordan won three more scoring titles (for a total of 10) plus a handful of new MVP trophies; Chicago became the first team to win 70 games in a single season and narrowly missed doing so twice; another trio of championships were won with surprising ease and a second three-peat elevated Jordan's Bulls to a plane with Auerbach's Celtics.

There is, of course, an inevitable downside to the renewed floodtide of Jordan mania. Our self-serving need as a society to worship celebrity and attribute greatness wherever it might take root has both obscured Jordan's true on-court achievements and, at the same time, badly overvalued his uniqueness. It is not enough for the sporting press and the product pitchmen to place Jordan at the top of the Pantheon; instead, he must be touted as its sole occupant, and after a while, the relentless din of praise begins to numb its captive audience. Since everyone "wants to be like Mike" (as the Nike refrain suggests), a generation of young imitators have focused their own games on solo moves, artistic slams, and in-your-face styles, which have slowly robbed basketball (at both collegiate and professional levels) of fundamental skills (long-range shooting for one example) and the patterned team play which is still the sport's ultimate aesthetic appeal.

More perceptive viewers eventually also tire of Jordan's excessive "protection" by the league's on- and off-court policemen—he travels on most drives to the hoop, palms the ball repeatedly, and fouls with impunity; his blatant exploitation by the league's hired pitchmen—he not only dominates game-long action when the Chicago Bulls are the television fare but appears on a half dozen commercial spots during almost every televised NBA game, whether the Bulls are playing or not—and the media circus that, even in his retirement as a player, surrounds his each and every move. There is something insidiously unbalanced and ominously foreboding for the game's future about the reigning popular view that Michael Jordan *was* and, in many ways, still *is* the National Basketball Association.

In the end all arguments about basketball's most dominant player—complaints about commercial overkill cast aside—today must begin and end with comparisons to Michael Jordan. As much as Mikan or Erving or Robertson or Magic, the reigning superstar of the 1990s has altered the style of play of his contemporaries and raised the level by which we measure on-court greatness. Now that he has retired, there are few pages of the record book he will not own outright—MJ is a good bet to retain the record of career scoring average; his combined total of NBA, playoff, and All-Star MVP trophies will assuredly be unsurpassed; and he will possess nearly all the postseason scoring records (per-game average, total points, high-point games, etc.). The winning legacy of Russell will likely not ever be reached (certainly not by Jordan), and Michael may not overhaul Abdul-Jabbar at the summit of the point-making list, or even Chamberlain in the second slot. Jordan will likely remain for decades into the future as basketball's equivalent to Babe Ruth wrapped up in the same package with Ty Cobb, Willie Mays, and Mickey Mantle. Indeed, had his career truly ended with his first "retirement" in 1994, this might well have already been the case.

Bob Kurland—Forgotten Giant from the Foothills

The prime factor distinguishing the career of Bob Kurland from that of George Mikan seemingly was the decision of the former to opt for a safe and secure postcollegiate career with the Phillips Oil Company (as part-time executive and full-time AAU-circuit basketball star), while the latter gambled on a risky barnstorming existence with the fledgling pro cage circuit that would soon turn itself into the NBA. The results would mean obscurity for Kurland and immortality for Mikan once AAU competitions slid to the back of the sports page and pro basketball exploded in the glow of a postwar economic boom era. As collegians, Kurland always had something of the upper hand over Mikan and certainly shared equal billing as one of the game's first two effective giants of the hardwood. While Mikan paced the country in scoring in 1945 and 1946, Kurland was picking up a pair of NCAA championship rings and a pair of NCAA Final Four MVPs during the same two seasons. And while Mikan was twice tabbed as Helms Foundation National Player of the Year (1944 and 1945), Kurland garnered the same honor once (1946).

The first true leviathan star of the college game was indeed the towheaded seven-footer fresh off the plains of Oklahoma. While Kurland and his Oklahoma A&M teammates enjoyed several fine seasons for coach Hank Iba out in the Missouri Valley Conference (despite the fact that official league play was suspended for two seasons during the war), it would be in the postseason and in Madison Square Garden tournament competitions that both would hone their national reputations. A&M (now Oklahoma State) would first explode on the national scene in the mid-'40s with a series of heralded performances in Madison Square Garden tournament play, which included a semifinals loss in the NIT to DePaul and George

Bob Kurland Career Profile

College Team: Oklahoma A&M University

AAU Team: Phillips 66ers

College and Amateur Achievements:
- NCAA Consensus First-Team All-American (1944, 1945, 1946)
- NCAA Final Four Most Outstanding Player (1945, 1946)
- Member of 1948 and 1952 USA Olympic Teams

NCAA Points .... 1,669 (14.1 ppg)

NCAA Games .... 118 (1943–46, 4 seasons)

NCAA Field Goals 675

NCAA Free Throws 319

NCAA National Championships 1945, 1946

Naismith Memorial Basketball Hall of Fame (1961)

Mikan in 1944, a pair of NCAA titles in '45 and '46, and a convincing post-tournament exhibition rematch victory in 1945 over Mikan and DePaul to close Kurland's productive junior season.

Kurland, for his own part, was a rare physical specimen and talented all-around player who brought a new dimension to the evolving cage game. And that dimension for the first time pointed straight up and over the net-draped rim. In the days when shot-blocking (the net-guarding type) was still perfectly legal, the giant center would make his reputation as an intimidating defender, setting up near the hoop and swatting away enemy bullets almost at will. But Kurland was soon a talented performer at the offensive end of the floor as well, and averaged a shade under 20 points per game as a senior. Phog Allen of Kansas would be quick to refer to the first agile and athletic seven-footer as a mere "glandular goon" destined to cheapen the game; but Kurland was, in reality, an inspired athlete who worked endlessly to develop his motor skills and build up his leg speed and stamina. By the time he was an experienced senior, and then later as an incomparable AAU and Olympic performer, Kurland could handle himself around the basket with much the same facility as the more agile sub-seven-foot players who stood deep in his shadow.

Today Bob Kurland remains the forgotten figure of basketball's early modern era. That his reputation is not far larger reduces, of course, to the fact that he chose not to follow his collegiate career with a tour through the barnstorming leagues that then constituted professional basketball. While Mikan bet his entire future on the pros, Kurland, in turn, would perform for a decade largely out of the limelight with the AAU champion Phillips 66ers team (also simultaneously earning a handsome salary with the Phillips Petroleum firm as a competent front-office executive). And in 1948 and 1952 Kurland would be the towering force who would dominate international Olympic play, earning his nation's gratitude (plus a pair of precious gold medals), but little in the way of front-page personal glory. It certainly seemed a solid decision at the time, and one tainted only by the vagaries of history. Had he chosen differently, of course, Bob Kurland might well himself have been the George Mikan and even the Bill Russell of pro basketball's remarkable breakthrough decade.

Perhaps the most memorable single image of college basketball at the height of the war years was the handful of titanic head-to-head collisions between Kurland

The first true leviathan star of the college game was a towheaded seven-footer fresh off the plains of Oklahoma named Bob Kurland.

Transcendental Graphics

and his rival, Mikan. The highlight matchup would come in the spring of 1945. That year Oklahoma A&M would complete the season with a No. 2 ranking in most of the "unofficial" nose counts; DePaul was generally ranked third. When top-ranked Iowa declined an NCAA invitation (the Hawkeyes were sensitive to wartime restrictions), the door was left wide open to national prominence for both A&M with one giant center and DePaul with the other.

Hank Iba's Oklahoma team ran unfettered through the NCAAs, edging lo-cal favorite NYU, with its young star Dolph Schayes, in the finals, when Kurland banged home 22 and himself held Schayes to only half a dozen. DePaul, in the meantime, manhandled the competition in the NIT, drubbing West Virginia and Rhode Island State, and coasting against Bowling Green. Mikan set a school record with 53 points in the semifinal against Rhode Island State. Then came the much-heralded showdown between the two behemoths during a postseason extra session known as the American Red Cross War Fund Benefit Game (a Ned Irish creation that lasted four years and matched NCAA and NIT winners). The Blue Demons led early, but Mikan fouled out after only 14 minutes with his team still up 21–14. Kurland would hang on to pace the win and collect 14 points in Mikan's absence, though neither giant was the game's star (a role reserved for A&M's Cecil Hankins who bagged 20 points on a variety of corner set shots and running one-handed hooks).

Kurland's most memorable achievement would not be his showdown victory over Mikan and DePaul, but rather his rare double in postseason play. The boys from Oklahoma would become the first repeat champions a season later when the NCAA staged its title matchup in New York City for the fourth straight season. This time the Aggies would win a close one from North Carolina by a 43–40 count with Kurland alone now dominating the scene. The seven-footer would be the only one of Hank Iba's players to score in double figures in any of the Aggies' three tourney games, and he would, in fact, become the only player in NCAA history to log more than half of a championship team's total points throughout an entire postseason's play. The giant dropped in and hooked in 72 points in the three matches to record 51.8 percent of the A&M point total. So one-dimensional indeed was the Aggies' attack that, during semifinals and finals action, only three of Iba's men could score more than five points in either contest. It was not surprising, then, that it was again Kurland who walked off with the NCAA MVP trophy.

Hoops fans fed a steady diet of NBA fare or born in the century's second half perhaps have never heard the name Bob Kurland nor heard stories of the very first seven-footer to dominate midcourt actions and thus set the stage for more bally-hooed big men such as Mikan, Chamberlain, and Alcindor. Yet, if Kurland's legacy is today an obscure one, it is a substantial legacy, nonetheless. No player of any era can boast of a more relentless winning legacy. Wherever he played, Kurland carried teams to championship celebrations. As a collegian he won the first back-to-back national titles earned on the proving grounds of an "all-comers" tournament. In AAU arenas his teams compiled a six-year 369–26 record and earned another three national championships. In Olympic play he brought home a pair of gold-medal victories, without losing a single contest in either London or Helsinki. "In Bob's day, he was simply the best around," admitted Mikan's own coach, Ray Meyer of DePaul. And few who witnessed the Mikan-Kurland era never took issue with Meyer's astute assessment of the game's very first dominant post-playing giant.

Hank Luisetti—Basketball's First Matinee Idol

When ballots were cast by leading sportswriters of the early '50s to select the great-est basketball player of the first half-century, it was George Mikan who pulled a wide majority of the votes. This was not surprising since Mikan, along with Bob Kurland, had been the biggest story of college basketball during the war years and also the grandest attraction in the pro ranks that had first thrived in the war's aftermath. The second-place vote-getter, more surprisingly, was a star of the late '30s who had never had the opportunity to perform on the stage of the newly popular professional league. Angelo "Hank" Luisetti of Stanford University had flashed brilliantly on the American sports scene as the nation's first recognized basketball matinee idol. He took the East Coast by storm in December 1936 with his revolutionary one-handed shot and, in the process, radically altered the popular style of play. But the lack of a viable professional league and the intervention of the war in the early '40s conspired to rob the flashy Stanford grad of a chance to further display his wares on the national sporting scene. And then a rare illness intervened to cut short a budding career in its prime—a mere handful of seasons before the two postwar pro leagues were born that might have given Hank Luisetti an even larger slice of basketball fame.

The NBA prejudice today built into the assessment of all-time cage greats (Mikan over Kurland, or Russell over Gola) was never clearer than in the case of one of basketball's earliest collegiate heroes. While the game's certified experts at midcentury assessed Luisetti's talent and impact to surpass those of any but Mikan, more recent historians have seemingly lost sight altogether of one of the sport's most important pioneers. In a recent book (*One Hundred Greatest Basketball Players of All-Time*) authored by pseudo-official NBA historian Alex Sachare, published by the Naismith Basketball Hall of Fame itself, and devoted to profiling the game's immortals, Luisetti shockingly is omitted altogether from the list. Lesser lights from the sport's first half-century like Benny Borgmann, Joe Brennan, Charles "Tarzan" Cooper, Harry Gallatin, Harry Hough, and Bobby McDermott, as well as the modern era's Adrian Dantley, Bob Lanier, Jo Jo White, and Joe Dumars all claim their sanctified spots in Sachare's list of paragons. Yet the man who originally catapulted the college game into the national limelight and popularized the shooting style that was pillar and post to modern-day basketball is utterly ignored. It is an act of egregious omission that again glaringly reveals the blinders worn by many a modern-day basketball historian.

Hank Luisetti is remembered almost exclusively by old-time fans for a single memorable visit to Madison Square Garden in December 1936, midway through the West Coast star's scintillating junior season. But Luisetti's brilliant tenure at Stanford included far more than a single headline-grabbing East Coast swing. His sophomore team raced to a 22–7 record and won the league title in the Pacific Coast Conference. Luisetti made his own mark that first season by tossing in 416 points (nearly 15 per game when such levels of offense were almost unprecedented) during his first varsity season. Included were some eye-popping outbursts against Oregon (20 points from the inside post position) and Southern Cal (a game-winning 24 during the final 11 minutes after his exasperated coach urged him to stop passing and start shooting). Such scoring would continue throughout two final seasons as he posted 410 points (17.1) as a junior and 465 more (17.2) as a senior. The biggest single-game outburst game in Cleveland Auditorium was on New Year's Day of 1938 versus Duquesne when the Stanford star reluctantly became headline news with a then-incredible 50-point outpouring (it was a night when Stanford players

Angelo "Hank" Luisetti of Stanford University flashed brilliantly on the American sports scene in the late '30s as the nation's first recognized basketball matinee idol.

Transcendental Graphics

decided to pad their teammate's totals by returning every pass and leaving the embarrassed All-American little option but nonstop shooting). At career's end Luisetti, not surprisingly, held the national record for point-making, although numerous earlier histories incorrectly pad the official total (1,596) by counting points tallied in freshman games along with the varsity total. The three-year varsity ledger of 1,291 was, in its own day, impressive enough, however.

In both his final two seasons, the West Coast shooting wizard was also the acknowledged National Player of the Year (later sanctioned by the retroactive Helms Foundation Award). And in a return trip to the famed Garden as a senior, he and his team were again twice victorious, edging Nat Holman's powerhouse CCNY team 45–42 in a draining contest and two nights later again flattening Clair Bee and LIU, this time by 14 points. When the pesky 6'3" Luisetti uncorked his one-handed bombs against CCNY, the conservative Holman was aghast at such unorthodox play. He would be singing a very different tune only a decade later when his own star, Irwin Dambrot, would be winning games with an almost identical one-handed push.

But the birth of Hank Luisetti as a national star, as well as the emergence of the West Coast game as rival to Eastern-style play, all unfolded on that single

Hank Luisetti Career Profile

College Team: Stanford University

AAU Teams: San Francisco Olympic Club, Phillips 66ers

College and Amateur Achievements:
- NCAA Consensus First-Team All-American (1936, 1937, 1938)
- NCAA National Scoring Leader (1936, 1937)

NCAA Points .... 1,291 (16.1 ppg)

NCAA Games .... 80 (1936–38, 3 seasons)

Naismith Memorial Basketball Hall of Fame (1959)

memorable evening at New York's Madison Square Garden during Stanford's first trip to test the East Coast basketball waters. Luisetti would quickly prove himself, once and for all, to a doubting sporting press and a nay-saying Eastern coaching establishment. Luisetti wowed the LIU starters from the opening whistle with his one-handers and thus wowed the partisan crowd as well. And he dazzled them as much with his tough defense and stellar passing to open teammates as he did with the shooting that had earlier made his reputation. The Stanford star did unleash some of his patented one-handers, and these left All-American Art Hillhouse and other Blackbird defenders amazed and outmatched. Luisetti would score 15 on the night and the visiting Indians would end the Blackbirds' two-year unbeaten streak, 45–31. It was a solid offensive display by the West Coasters for such a low-scoring era. The game was played, remember, during the final season of the jump ball after each and every made basket.

With his first New York visit, Luisetti irreversibly established the direction of basketball's future. That future, of course, took the form of the one-handed running shot. The pioneering steps (and shots) Luisetti had taken in Madison Square Garden would soon enough be followed by other crack Western teams and their hot-shooting stars out of places such as Oregon (Slim Wintermute and the first NCAA tourney winners in 1939), Oklahoma (Kurland and the great Oklahoma A&M squads of the mid-'40s), Wyoming (Kenny Sailors with the 1943 NCAA champion Cowboys), and Utah (Arnie Ferrin and the Utes 1944 NCAA victors). It would all begin to happen almost overnight once postseason tournaments became the year-end rage with the dawn of the 1940s. But Hank Luisetti had already been there first.

For all the successes that surrounded Luisetti's three years at Stanford, there were also elements of disappointment attached to his fairy-tale career. If he benefited from good timing in one sense, he was, at the same time, equal victim of ill-fated coincidence. For starters, the college game's greatest showcase event—the postseason national tournament—would be launched with the first NIT and NCAA matches during the first two seasons immediately following his own graduation. And of course there were no existing national-scale pro leagues (they would come a half decade in the future) in which he could star for years to come and earn a comfortable living in the process. Luisetti was, at the same time, too early and too late for the national stages that might have provided a larger piece of individual glory. Like Bob Kurland, a few seasons down the road, he would be forced to turn instead to the AAU circuit, where he starred in the early war years for both the San Francisco Olympic Club and the same Phillips 66ers outfit for which Kurland would soon be suiting up.

A final stop in the postcollege gypsy basketball life that Luisetti now inherited would be the Navy's St. Mary's Pre-Flight team, on which he starred for two years after his wartime enlistment. It was here that his overall game reached perhaps its greatest heights, and on several occasions, he clearly outplayed another ex-Stanford star and future NBA Hall of Famer named Jim Pollard. It was also during his Navy service in 1944 that Luisetti tragically contracted a case of spinal meningitis that left him in a coma for a week and soon spelled an unfortunate end to his brilliant competitive athletic career. There would miraculously be a full recovery from the affliction, yet recovery would be accompanied with a stern warning from doctors that he must now give up the tough, competitive AAU and pro-style levels of competition. Only in his early 30s at decade's end, a healthy Luisetti might well have still popped in his running one-handers with one of the talent-hungry teams in the newly formed Basketball Association of America. And had fate only treated him a bit more kindly in the end, the legend might well have loomed even larger than it already did.

George Mikan—The Original "Mr. Basketball"

First Julius Erving and later Michael Jordan revolutionized the public perception of how basketball was supposed to be played. From a game of long-range shooting, pinpoint passing, and organized team flow, these two masters of hang time turned the sport into one-on-one displays of high-flying rim-rattling acrobatics. More than any others, "Dr. J" and "MJ" made the slam dunk the glamour piece of basketball's high-speed spectacle, just as the home run stands supreme in baseball and the long touchdown pass rules in football. And others also had major impacts on the sport that, in turn, were truly revolutionary in scope. Bob Cousy seemingly invented fancy dribbling, Houdini-like ballhandling, and magical "no-look" passing. Bill Russell first established shot-blocking and lane-cramming defense as the game's most unbeatable weapons.

But no one ever had quite the same degree of impact on basketball, by his very presence on the floor, as did the game's first widely recognized superstar, George Mikan. It was Mikan who once caused the entire strategy of play to shift in drastic ways. Elaborate defensive schemes (some pushing the limits of legality) were first designed, both on coaches' chalkboards and in front-office conclaves, exclusively to stop him. And when all these ploys failed to keep down Mikan's relentless scoring, the men controlling basketball's management were next forced to alter the rules shaping the game's on-court actions.

Because the bulky and bespectacled 6'11" Mikan would set up under the basket and simply make layups that were unguardable in an age of smaller players, teams first fouled ruthlessly, then took to holding the ball and stalling the clock, hoping to win on a last-second bomb after first neutralizing the big man for much of the game. The result was, first, a widening of the foul lanes in 1951–52 from 6 to 12 feet. Then came the 24-second shot clock at the start of the 1954–55 season. It was as if today's rules makers should have to raise the bucket to 14 feet to stop Shaquille O'Neal's power slams. Or if regulations on traveling were changed (perhaps ruling that each player was allowed but one step and one dribble) in order to eliminate Michael Jordan's drives toward the bucket. (It is a measure of how the game has changed, of course, that in today's atmosphere such runaway scoring, which threatens

Transcendental Graphics

No one ever had quite the same degree of impact on basketball by his very presence on the court as did the game's first widely recognized superstar, George Mikan.

competitive balance, is always rewarded and promoted, not shunned and stifled, since this is the very element that now draws the ticket-buying public.) Such drastic rules alterations were exactly what the rules makers did to George Mikan when they stretched out the lanes and forced teams to speed up offense with the ever-ticking shot clock.

History still records Mikan's impact on the rule book. But what often gets forgotten, after nearly half a century of drastic change and evolution in the game, is exactly how good a player George Mikan actually was during his own heyday. And also how big a star he was for the long-struggling sport and the three new leagues (NBL, BAA, NBA) he helped put squarely on the sporting map. Mikan was pro basketball's one showcase talent in an era when he alone was a sure-bet gate attraction—although perhaps as much for his freakish size as for his predictable scoring. The original Mr. Basketball was indeed a truly dominating scorer, outdistancing all competitors in point-making his two initial seasons with the NBL, outpointing the phenomenal jump-shooter Joe Fulks (though never approaching Fulks's remarkable 63-point single-game effort) during his one BAA campaign, and then earning the first two scoring titles in the history of the newly constituted NBA.

George Mikan Career Profile

Elected "Greatest Basketball Player of First Half-Century"

College Team: DePaul University

College and Amateur Achievements:
- NCAA Consensus First-Team All-American (1944, 1945, 1946)
- NIT Tournament Most Outstanding Player (1945)
- NCAA National Scoring Leader (1945, 1946)

NBL–BAA–NBA Teams .... Chicago American Gears (NBL), Minneapolis Lakers (NBL, BAA, NBA)

NBA Points .... 11,764 (22.6 ppg)

NBA Games .... 520 (1947–56, 9 seasons)

NBA Assists .... 1,245 (2.8 apg)*

NBA Rebounds .... 4,167 (9.5 rpg)*

NBA Field Goals (Pct) .... 4,097 (.404)

NBA Free Throws (Pct) .... 3,570 (.777)

NBA All-Star Game MVP 1953

NBL–BAA–NBA Scoring Leader 1947, 1948, 1949, 1950, 1951

NBA Championships 1950, 1952, 1953, 1954

BAA Championships 1949

NBL Championships 1947, 1948

Naismith Memorial Basketball Hall of Fame (1959)

* = NBA record only (no assists or rebounds recorded for NBL)

Mikan's moves were primitive by today's standards and perhaps would be easily enough defended in the modern era. He simply camped within four feet of the hoop, waited patiently for a lob pass (which his mates would take forever delivering in the pre-shot-clock era), elbowed defenders aside, and dropped in an easy layup or short-range hook. No one dunked in those days—there didn't seem to be any point to such extra expenditures of showy energy. Yet, in his own era, Mikan was more unstoppable than almost any scorer before or since. And with Mikan in the lineup the Lakers were equally unstoppable. Mikan would lead his team to seven championships in eight seasons. These would come in three different leagues as the vagabond Minneapolis club first jumped from the National Basketball League (1948 champions) over to the Basketball Association of America (1949 champions), which then reconstituted itself into the renamed National Basketball Association (1950, 1952, 1953, 1954 champions). Mikan's first team, the Chicago American Gears, also reigned as NBL titleholders for the 1946–47 season. Only Bill Russell touts a winning legacy that can surpass this one.

The winning of team championships and individual scoring titles at an unprecedented rate, the unparalleled impact on the game's reshaped appearances and rewritten rules, the magnetism of basketball's first oversized one-man spectacle, all conspired to write a lasting legend. When the ballots were counted in 1950, George Mikan was named "The Greatest Basketball Player of the First Half-Century" in an unsurprising landslide.

Oscar Robertson—The Incomparable "Big O"

Oscar Robertson was not quite the most remarkable scorer in college basketball annals, though as the first sophomore scoring champion and first triple scoring leader in NCAA record books, he comes close to qualifying even on this count.

Frank Selvy had already set loftier standards a half decade earlier with a yearlong 40-plus average and an unmatchable 100-point single-game effort. And "Pistol Pete" Maravich would soon outreach Oscar with his own three-peat of national scoring titles and his considerably loftier 40-plus-point career average. When it came to winning national titles, Robertson also fell far short of phenomenal. While he carried his teammates to the NCAA Final Four twice, he never got past the semifinals (losing both times to California with Darrall Imhoff); by contrast, cross-state rival Ohio State with Jerry Lucas was in the title game three years running. Walton, Alcindor, and Russell—not Oscar—merit the clear nod when it comes to collegiate stars who seemingly guaranteed championships and team invincibility with their very presence on the floor.

Once he reached the pros Oscar would also fall a bit short of the top rung as a premier offensive force (he never captured the league scoring crown while playing in the elongated shadows of Wilt Chamberlain) and also considerably short as a championship linchpin (his only title came as a veteran adjunct to Kareem Abdul-Jabbar in Milwaukee). Whatever Oscar's true greatness, it was not to be measured by a slot at the top of the record books or a spot in the winner's circle. His career scoring total has continued to slide from his once-lofty spot in second slot behind only Chamberlain; he now stands sixth all time, having been overhauled by Jordan only this past season. But if Oscar was not quite the greatest scorer ever, it is also true that no six-time league assists leader (9.5 assists per game) ever logged quite so many career points (25.7 points per game) or garnered quite so many career rebounds (7.5 rebounds per game). It can be reasonably argued that Oscar's yearlong triple-double (30.8 points, 12.5 rebounds, 11.4 assists) posted in 1961–62 still constitutes the single greatest overall one-year performance in pro annals, outstripping even Wilt's 50-plus scoring average in the very same campaign. And while Oscar lacked the NBA teammates in Cincinnati to rack up league championships, he did make the league's annual All-Star classic his own special showcase; in 12 appearances "O" logged 246 points (20.5 points per game)—a record total that even Jordan did not reach—while earning three All-Star MVP trophies (1961, 1964, 1969)—a record he still shares with Bob Pettit.

Before Jordan there were few, if any, serious rivals to Robertson for the mythical title of the game's single greatest all-around performer. Wilt may well have dominated the floor when he chose to (something he didn't always do), but Oscar also took complete control of both ball and game action each and every time he stepped upon a collegiate or professional court. His teams may not have always won, but it always took a "gang effort" to overcome him, and it was never quite possible to overshadow him. Certainly, none could match the "Big O" for pure artistic grace, for single-handed control of the playing floor he inhabited, or for all-around shooting, passing, and playmaking abilities. In brief, there was never a more complete package for a basketball player put together within a single human frame.

Robertson was also destined to play a role in American sports history that would hold far greater import than the measure of his scoring numbers or other remarkable record-book statistics, and one that would cast a far greater shadow than even his remarkable image as the most polished and balanced player ever to lace up a pair of sneakers. For Oscar's role in opening doors for black athletes

Oscar Robertson Career Profile

College Team: University of Cincinnati
College and Amateur Achievements:
* NCAA National Player of the Year (1958, 1959, 1960)
* Unanimous First-Team All-American (1958, 1959, 1960)
* First Three-Time NCAA Scoring Leader (1958, 1959, 1960)
* Member of 1960 USA Olympic Team

NBA Teams	Cincinnati Royals, Milwaukee Bucks
NBA Points	26,710 (25.7 ppg)
NBA Games	1,040 (1961–74, 14 seasons)
NBA Assists	9,887 (9.5 apg)
NBA Rebounds	7,804 (7.5 rpg)
NBA Field Goals (Pct)	9,508 (.485)
NBA Free Throws (Pct)	7,694 (.838)
NBA MVP	1964
NBA All-Star Game MVP	1961, 1964, 1969
NBA Rookie of the Year	1961
NBA Championships	1971
Naismith Memorial Basketball Hall of Fame (1979)	

was nearly as large as Jackie Robinson's had been a decade and a half earlier in baseball. Oscar was far from the first black college star (Jackie Robinson himself had been a paragon of the hardwoods at UCLA while a Pacific Coast Conference scoring leader in both 1940 and 1941); nor did he bring about the black revolution single-handedly. Russell and Baylor and Chamberlain all played roles nearly as significant earlier in the same decade. But Oscar, with his multiplicity of talents and his thorough reflection of black "street cool," was nonetheless steps ahead at the vanguard of the movement.

One huge breakthrough for the emerging black ballplayer came with Oscar Robertson's debut in Madison Square Garden on January 9, 1958. Oscar would play a flawless game that night—only the 11th contest of his collegiate career—and would etch his image forever into the lengthy collective history of basketball's greatest mecca. In a lopsided 118–54 shelling of Seton Hall, Oscar rang up a new Garden scoring mark of 56 points with his explosion of 22 field goals and perfect 12-for-12 free-throw shooting. It would be only the first of four 50-plus NCAA games for the All-American rookie. And while the "Big O" was setting an eye-catching new record that night, he was also accomplishing something else of far greater significance with the very same performance.

Chamberlain and Russell had already drawn considerable attention to the black hoops star, but neither played what could be considered a textbook game. Oscar, by contrast, was true master of textbook basketball as it had always been played by the best white stars. This was no freelancing and undisciplined playground leaper whose flash and flamboyance outshone his few scattered fundamentals. As black culture historian Nelson George has so precisely phrased it (in *Elevating the Game*, 1992), Oscar did absolutely everything the classroom coaches always loved. He dribbled equally well with either hand, muscled inside for rebounds, passed with uncanny intelligence and accuracy, and always shot unerringly from any spot within 30 feet of the hoop. The difference was he did it all much better than anyone else ever had.

Oscar Robertson was not quite the most remarkable scorer in college basketball history, though as the first sophomore scoring champion and first triple scoring leader in NCAA annals, he comes close to qualifying even on this count.

Transcendental Graphics

In one of the finest textbook histories of college cage play, Neil Isaacs (*All the Moves*, 1975) isolates and personifies five major evolutionary elements of basketball: freelance one-handed shooting (Luisetti was both the originator and the prototype), the big-man offense (Mikan, Kurland, Chamberlain, and the other giants who occupy the paint), dribbling and passing magic (invented by Bob Cousy), the defensive shot rejector and rebounder (vintage Bill Russell), and finally the all-around offensive intimidator (Oscar Robertson above all others). It is the legacy of the latter element that has been fulfilled primarily by the great black stars of the past three decades—in a direct line of evolution through Earl Monroe, Julius Erving, and David Thompson down to Magic Johnson, Dominique Wilkins, Scottie Pippen, and Michael Jordan. Oscar Robertson was indeed the spiritual fountainhead of what would soon prove to be basketball's final great evolutionary movement.

Bill Russell—First Chairman of the Boards

More than any other imposing figure among basketball's true superstars, Bill Russell has always had his numerous doubters and detractors, naysayers, and negators. As a high school and a college recruit, he was hardly outstanding and struggled to make a varsity squad; Russell was cut from tryouts for his junior high school team in Oakland and barely made a junior varsity squad as a high school sophomore. Once he began to dominate opponents at the University of San Francisco, he was nonetheless still viewed as a one-dimensional performer and thus something of a gamble as a pro prospect. And after establishing his hold over the NBA as the driving engine of Auerbach's Boston dynasty, Russell was nonetheless never an extremely popular icon among Boston fans or league fans as a whole.

A mixed reaction to Bill Russell is all the more surprising when set against the backdrop of his simply unrivaled impact on the sport of basketball. On the occasion of the NBA's 35-year anniversary in 1980, it was Russell and not Chamberlain, Mikan, or Oscar Robertson whom members of the Professional Basketball Writers Association tabbed by a wide margin as "the greatest player in the history of the NBA." Russell was among that truly rare handful of athletes—Babe Ruth comes immediately to mind in baseball—who dominate their sport so thoroughly that they actually change the way the game is played and perceived by future generations. Russell's dominance was, of course, of a far different order from Wilt's or Oscar's or Air Jordan's. Russell set few individual records (none for offense) and spent remarkably little time holding on to the basketball. Yet in 13 NBA seasons Russell's Boston team won the league championship on 11 occasions (it would have been 12 of 13 if an ankle injury hadn't sidelined Russell for the final three games of the 1958 postseason); his USF college team was two-for-three in winning NCAA tournament championships and won 55 straight between the outset of his junior season and the close of his career. He was also one-for-one in Olympic gold-medal triumphs. It was not at all surprising that while Wilt Chamberlain captured seven straight individual scoring titles in the '60s and obliterated nearly every NBA offensive record along the way, it was Russell whom sportswriters picked as Player of the Decade by nearly a three-to-one landslide margin.

Bill Russell Career Profile

College Team: University of San Francisco
College and Amateur Achievements:
* One of seven players to average 20 ppg and 20 rpg for entire college career (20.7 ppg and 20.3 rpg)
* UPI NCAA National Player of the Year (1956)
* Unanimous First-Team All-American (1956)
* NCAA Final Four Most Outstanding Player (1955)
* Member of 1956 USA Olympic Team
* NCAA National Championships, 1955, 1956

NBA Team	Boston Celtics
NBA Points	14,522 (15.1 ppg)
NBA Games	963 (1957–69, 13 seasons)
NBA Assists	4,096 (4.3 apg)
NBA Rebounds	21,721 (22.6 rpg)
NBA Field Goals (Pct)	5,687 (.440)
NBA Free Throws (Pct)	3,148 (.561)
NBA MVP	1958, 1961, 1962, 1963, 1965
NBA All-Star Game MVP	1963
NBA Championships	1957, 1959, 1960, 1961, 1962, 1963, 1964, 1965, 1966, 1968, 1969 (NBA Record)

Naismith Memorial Basketball Hall of Fame (1974)

Yet if Russell was a nonpareil, he was never an unconditionally beloved icon even among hometown boosters. Part of the problem, of course, is that, while dominating defense wins games and even wins championships, it hardly ever wins over a majority of the fans. Russell's style could inspire admiration and even awe, but it did not attract legions of worshippers and imitators. As a college and pro star Russell never dominated when it came to numbers: even in college, where he carried more of the offensive burden, he nonetheless barely averaged 20 a game (though he does remain one of only seven in history to average 20 points and 20 rebounds for a full career); his lofty totals for NBA rebounds still fell short of numbers posted in the same seasons by Chamberlain; a search of the NBA career top-10 lists reveals his name only in the total rebounds and minutes played (eighth) categories. The areas in which he did prove matchless—blocked shots and defensive rebounds—were not even acknowledged in the stats columns of his era. And when he went head to head with Chamberlain, he would usually lose the individual battle, yet gain the war of team victory. The Celtics maintained their seven-year NBA winning streak in 1965, for example, even though Wilt outplayed Russell in Game 7 of the Eastern Division finals, and Russell's errant inbounds heave in the closing seconds handed Philadelphia a rare chance to capture the series and scuttle the streak; Boston and Russell were miraculously saved on this occasion by Havlicek's memorable last-second pilfering of Hal Greer's own inbounds toss.

It was also Russell's personality that forever got in the way of unconditional acceptance. Bill Russell was, from the start, a proud and private man, and that pride—both in his on-court play and in his oppressed black race—was also key to his championship successes, while at the same time fuel to his unpopular image. Boston's most dominating cage star was also the first black superstar in professional basketball, and he occupied this role during a decade when racial segregation was still the law of the land in nearly a quarter of the nation, as well as an unspoken custom in other areas, including Boston itself. More importantly,

Eight straight NBA championships—all attributed in lion's share to Bill Russell's presence on the court—is a monument beside which even the individual achievements of Jordan, Oscar, Baylor, Chamberlain and all the game's greatest offensive stars seem somewhat pallid.

Transcendental Graphics

like Jackie Robinson in Brooklyn, Russell was always outspoken and thus controversial, unwilling to repress or conceal his rage about racial injustice. In Boston of the '60s Russell was thus destined to be a figure who personified unpopular and distasteful racial rebellion despite all his athletic heroism. Boston's greatest star on Boston's greatest-ever team (likely the NBA's greatest-ever team) was thus also a painfully controversial figure who robbed that very team of a far greater audience than the surprisingly slim one it enjoyed. The Boston Celtics and Bill Russell owned the NBA in their heyday, but they were always a backroom act in Boston—poor cousins to the ever-popular Red Sox in baseball and NHL Bruins with whom they shared the spotlight.

The same mixed review also clouded stage two of Bill Russell's basketball life, the one that came after his playing days had ceased at the end of the '60s. As a coach in Boston he accomplished what perhaps no other figure could possibly have accomplished. He successfully replaced the legend that was Red Auerbach and stretched out Boston's winning grip on the NBA through the end of the decade. (Cynics contended at the time that Russell was Auerbach's only possible choice as coaching replacement simply because Bill Russell the coach was the only man who could possibly control and motivate Bill Russell the player.) Yet when he took his act to Seattle a few seasons later, he was to be victim of his own growing disrespect for modern-age players and the modern-era game. As coach and general manager with Seattle from 1974 through 1977, Russell posted losing records in both regular-season (162–166) and postseason (6–9) action before wearing out his welcome with players, management, and fans alike. Returning to a similar role with the Sacramento Kings a decade later, Russell again bombed on the bench and was relieved early in his second campaign with the Kings, owning the league's fourth-worst record at the time. Whatever magic Russell exerted in Boston Garden throughout the '60s was clearly not still part of his act out on the West Coast in either the late '70s or late '80s.

Russell had one more public role to play, and that was behind the microphone. As a pro basketball television analyst—first with ABC's *NBA Game of the Week* and later with NBA broadcasts on Ted Turner's WTBS cable network—he would prove to be one of the most honest and insightful color commentators the business has ever known. But the broadcast career was short-lived as the private Russell withdrew even further from the public limelight. Over the past decade he has remained largely detached from his own towering legend, making few appearances at NBA functions and shunning fans. Russell has never signed autographs, for one thing, viewing the popular practice cynically as a bothersome symbol of the American sports fan's misplaced values. Given this history of unpopularity and standoffishness with fans, both during his playing days and after, and the somewhat one-dimensional nature of his on-court presence, it is truly remarkable that Bill Russell's star still looms today as large as it does in the basketball firmament. But then, eight straight NBA championships—all attributed in lion's share to Russell's presence on the court—is a monument beside which even the individual achievements of Jordan, Oscar, Baylor, Chamberlain, and all the game's greatest offensive stars seem somewhat pallid. Add on 55 straight college victories and the first-ever undefeated NCAA championship team with the University of San Francisco, and Bill Russell remains a monument as large as any in the game's century-long history.

Chapter Four

Basketball's Dozen-Plus Most Significant Nonplayers

Across hoopdom's first full half-century it was indisputably the coaches—almost exclusively the college coaches—who stood squarely on basketball's center stage. Joining them in notoriety were a smaller contingent of sideline administrators, most notably a pair of farsighted *New York World Telegram* sportswriters-turned-promoters—Dan Daniels and Ned Irish—who first launched college cage "spectaculars" in the big-time venue of Madison Square Garden. It was the college coaches, above all others, who behind the scenes shaped and reshaped the sport during its long evolutionary period. A small handful of these coaches even left their own indelible marks upon the outward face of Dr. Naismith's sport. Some of the game's early movers and shakers operated in the offstage shadows; but most were as visible and as large as the sport itself.

For a few opening decades basketball had little in the way of formalized coaching, of course, and almost nothing in the way of coaching personalities. For a dozen years or more after the game began appearing on college campuses, most teams had perhaps a student manager and certainly a playing captain for some semblance of leadership; the latter figure (usually a star player) sometimes stayed on after his graduation (or during his graduate studies) to arrange practices and schedules and guide a school's team for a few additional winters. It is not so surprising, then, that basketball was a most chaotic and often rough-and-tumble sport across its first several decades.

When it came to the professional venues for cage play, some of the game's earliest innovative organizers and administrators (Lew Wachter, founder of the barnstorming Troy Trojans; Jim Furey, organizer of the famed New York–based Original Celtics; and Abe Saperstein, with his Chicago-born Harlem Globetrotters) held far greater influence over the sport's future evolutionary course than did any of the pioneering ballplayers (Troy's Ed Wachter; Celtics stalwarts Johnny Beckman, Dutch Dehnert, and Davey Banks; Inman Jackson of early Globetrotters fame) who served under their tutelage and benefited handsomely from their business savvy. Forrest "Phog" Allen in Lawrence, Kansas, as much as any single individual, invented the respectable profession of full-time college basketball coaching in the '20s. Ned Irish, Gotham sportswriter turned wildly successful sports promoter, conceived a breakthrough approach to main-event roundball promotion (twin bills matching the local college ball clubs against attractive intersectional rivals) that transformed a popular '30s campus game into an even more profitable big-city fund-raising event in the '40s. And as the cage game labored into its second half-century, plagued by recent game-fixing scandals at the college level and bogged down by sluggish blood-spilling play in its pro venues, Syracuse Nats NBA team owner Danny Biasone dreamed up single-handedly (and quite overnight in 1954), a piece of innovative rule tinkering that not only lent the infant NBA its distinctive flavor for years to come but literally also saved the fledgling professional game from looming threats of total extinction.

While America's earlier national pastime of baseball remained for almost a century and a half free of any serious modification—in terms of either its on-field playing rules or the game's professional organization (the same two major leagues and 16 charter teams remained unmodified for exactly half a century)—basketball recast itself continually and in most dramatic ways throughout each passing decade. Archive videos and photos of game action in both sports from decades past clinch the point. While Ty Cobb (through some imaginary conjuring) might come alive on the major-league playing fields of the 1990s and still feel largely at home in such hi-tech surroundings, George Mikan would find his one-dimensional shot-blocking skills and plodding playing style largely useless against modern-era hardwood opponents. And college basketball of the 1930s—with center jumps after every basket, two-handed set shots, and five-man weaves as the reigning offensive ploys, and coaches banned from communicating with their players during time-outs—would hardly be recognizable as the same game that so thoroughly thrills us today.

Basketball's very essence has been its penchant for constant change (while baseball's defining feature has been its obdurant stasis), and all the most important and dramatic alterations in basketball rules and playing styles can almost, without exception, trace their origins directly to the individual genius of a handful among the game's most gargantuan off-court figures.

Even across basketball's modern era, which followed on the heels of the midcentury birth (in 1946) of the BAA and NBL (the NBA's progenitors) and which has been an unrivaled showcase for the individual star athlete, the basketball head coach (both pro and college) has steadfastly remained a significant—even predominant—figure. A handful of larger-than-life (or at least in the cases of Rupp or Auerbach or Wooden, larger-than-the-game-itself) coaches have thrived and prospered even during the recent epoch dominated by celebrity star players, and some of these popular sideline figures stand among the biggest names the sport has ever boasted. Arnold "Red" Auerbach of the NBA Boston Celtics and John Wooden with the NCAA UCLA Bruins together dominated the turbulent '60s as flesh-and-blood personifications of two of the greatest dynasty teams in American sports history. No other such dynasties—not the Yankees in baseball nor the Canadiens in hockey nor Notre Dame in college football—have been so narrowly identified with a single mentor who stood at the team's helm across an entire decade-plus dynasty reign.

And while Auerbach owned the '60s era in the NBA and Wooden ruled the late '60s and early '70s in the NCAA wars, two other star-quality college coaches also made their lasting marks throughout the middle and final portions of the century, mainly through their remarkable penchants for memorable longevity, which cut across any singular decade. At the time of his 1972 retirement, Adolph Rupp had amassed a near half-century victory total of 876 games that seemed for years (even decades) to be altogether untouchable. Across the next quarter-century, Rupp's fellow Kansas alumnus and fellow Phog Allen disciple, North Carolina's Dean Smith, has slowly but surely himself approached and finally overhauled Rupp's once unmatchable winning legacy.

Similarly, if Michael Jordan, Magic Johnson, and Larry Bird have most visibly carried the torch for the wildly popular NBA during its recent epoch of relentlessly spectacular inroads on the nation's sporting scene, it has nonetheless been the savvy behind-the-scenes efforts and unprecedented business acumen of '80s–'90s league commissioner David Stern, who most knowledgeable observers would justly credit for masterminding and sustaining basketball's miraculous late-century explosion. The global cable-television hookups, which have made Michael Jordan (and with him the NBA) a household name in every corner of the planet, were Stern's brainchild alone, and also the sport's grandest and most vital step toward seizing lasting prominence on the nation's sporting scene.

The players may today be basketball's frontline marquee attraction for legions of adoring fans. But in historic terms it has always been the men who wrote the rules, evolved the strategies, and managed the game from the bench, the owner's box, and the press box who have stood closest to the heart of basketball's ongoing growth and ceaseless evolution. Without Phog Allen or Red Auerbach or Danny Biasone—or most assuredly without Maurice Podoloff and David Stern—the game that launched Magic Johnson and Michael Jordan might today still be played only in back alleys and bandbox school gymnasiums and worshipped only on inner-city playgrounds. Basketball, without its off-court manipulators, might today remain nothing more than what Jim Naismith had originally envisioned it to be—a school grounds, leisure-time, participant-oriented, and low-pressure recreational sport. If basketball has its Michael Jordans and George Mikans and Wilt Chamberlains to salute for its modern-day broad-based fan appeal, it also has its Phog Allens, Danny Biasones, David Sterns, and John Woodens to celebrate most heartily for its miraculous dozen-decade survival.

Forrest "Phog" Allen—Father of Basketball Coaching

Canadian Dr. James Naismith and Kansan Dr. Forrest Allen never saw eye to eye when it came to almost any philosophy about the meaning or purpose of the peach basket game that Naismith had accidently launched in Springfield back in 1891, a mere six years after Allen's birth. In reality the views about the sport held by the two men in the vanguard of its leadership were almost diametrically opposed on just about every count. For Dr. Naismith, basketball was nothing more (or less) than a leisure-time activity that belonged to the players alone and was thus to be engaged in for the purpose of gaining the moral advantages of healthy exercise. It was not at all an activity to be indulged for the impure purposes of intense competitions or the side benefits of popular spectator entertainment.

Allen had quite different notions, of course. The legendary Kansas University coach, who took over the school's basketball team from Dr. Naismith briefly in 1908 and then returned as full-time coach at his alma mater in 1920, saw basketball from the first as an exacting science to be sternly mastered and also a competitive challenge to be totally indulged and savored. Allen loved the sport's competitive thrills above all else about the game; Naismith, in stark contrast, never saw anything in his brainchild beyond another form of healthful Christian "recreation." Nonetheless, the man called "Phog" would lean most heavily on Naismith and his invention as the source of his own career niche and his own ultimate fame. And "The Father of Basketball," for his own part, would provide his young disciple with a lasting and much-merited designation as "The Father of Basketball Coaching." Allen's more commonplace moniker—"Phog"—had resulted from a student's attention-calling to the young coach's "Foghorn" voice while umpiring a baseball contest. While the first nickname stuck like glue, the loftier epithet ("Father of Basketball Coaching") was seemingly far closer to the mark.

Before the arrival of Baron Rupp and Dean Smith—both his students and thus both his "spiritual" progeny—Phog Allen reigned as basketball's most imposing bench genius and certainly its most enduring coaching legend across the years separating the two world wars. It was Allen's record for all-time winning that Rupp would eventually have to overhaul. (Allen's actual victory total has often been misreported in the standard histories and should stand at 746 games and not 771.) And it was Allen who did as much as any man, both on the court and off, to insure the sport's continuing growth and also its burgeoning national popularity. In 39 seasons he would capture 24 conference titles, earn (retroactively) two Helms Foundation national championships (1922, 1923) as well as a 1952 NCAA tournament title, and climb to the very top of the heap as college basketball's winningest coach (later passed only by his own students, Adolph Rupp and Dean Smith). Off the court he would impact even further on the game as founding president of the National Association of Basketball Coaches and as leading proponent of a movement in the '30s to make basketball an "official" Olympic sport. In the latter role Allen was instrumental in bringing about the debut competitions for basketball during the 1936 summer games staged in Berlin, Germany.

But if Allen carved out the sport's future direction across the 1920s and 1930s, he almost always did so against a constant backdrop of raging controversy. Away from the basketball court an ongoing successful career as a practicing osteopath rankled the medical community occupying his own campus. Doc Allen, throughout his coaching career, treated the muscular and skeletal injuries of his own players and scores of other high school, college, and pro athletes (the list includes Casey Stengel, Ralph Hoak, and Johnny Mize) who found their way to his Lawrence office. When it came to basketball matters, the man called "Phog" (short, recall, for his bellowing voice) made enough noise of another sort to constantly stir the ire of much of the rest of the national coaching community.

There were small matters, like his preference for aggressive football players on the basketball squad and his experiments with the unpopular zone defense. But what turned off most fellow coaches was the constant harping about a foul smell that Allen detected coming from the sport's big-city arenas back East. Allen long suspected that gamblers maintained a hand and a foot in the game and were sowing

Transcendental Graphics

Phog Allen (left) compares notes with Topeka sportswriter Stu Dunbar during Allen's final season in 1956. In 48 seasons at Kansas Allen won 746 games.

the seeds of its eventual destruction, a message the purists around him simply didn't want to hear. In the end, of course, the country's coaching dean would also prove something of a clairvoyant by nosing out the betting scandals that would wrack (and nearly wreck) the sport during the late '40s and early '50s. Yet throughout much of the late '40s Allen proved a lone unheeded voice crying in the wilderness when he tried to alert others to growing compromises with the game's integrity.

The immortal Kansas coach was ironically thus destined to be remembered almost as much for his testy personality and his off-the-court crusades—not always related to the game of basketball—as he was for his role in institutionalizing Naismith's popular form of wintertime recreation. But nevertheless, it was basketball that was always Phog's main calling card, and in the final years of his career, the records and milestones begin to pile up with impressive regularity. A high point finally arrived with the rock-solid early '50s team built around giant All-American Clyde Lovellette, and with the wild 1952 NCAA championship run that team would make during Lovellette's senior year. Kansas drubbed Santa Clara in the semifinals and pounded St. John's in the finals. Lovellette became the only player to this day to pace the nation in individual scoring and also pace his team to an NCAA trophy, and coach Allen at long last had his one and only national championship won directly during a postseason tournament shootout.

A final ironic twist to Phog Allen's half-century coaching career involved the strange saga of KU's most famous player and the disappointments of high-expectation seasons that followed promptly in Allen's immediate wake. Wilt Chamberlain arrived at the Lawrence campus under shadows of the most heated recruiting war ever, signing on with the Jayhawks primarily because of Allen's own presence there. The aging mentor would never be permitted to coach his biggest and best recruit, however, since retirement was forced upon Allen a single season before Wilt's landmark sophomore debut. And Allen was not the only loser in this strange scenario. Unfortunately for all concerned in the Kansas basketball family, the always outspoken Phog would utter fateful words in the aftermath of his recruiting coup that would go a long way toward scuttling both Chamberlain's upcoming Kansas career and that of Allen's coaching successor, Dick Harp, in equal measure. Coach Allen observed for delighted reporters that "with Wilt, two sorority girls, and two Phi Beta Kappas" anyone ought to be able to bring home a national championship. This perhaps well-meaning (and certainly almost true) boast put such unwarranted pressure on the 20-year-old Chamberlain and the inexperienced Harp that neither could ever quite crawl all the way out from under the spell, even though Chamberlain did carry Phog's old school to the very doorstep of another national title (a draining three-overtime title-game loss to North Carolina) at the end of his debut sophomore season.

Arnold "Red" Auerbach—Author of Celtics Mystique

Arnold "Red" Auerbach's NBA coaching career, in hindsight at least, will forever be bound up with two legendary athletes who contributed mightily to his Boston Celtics dynasty and its almost unimaginable successes, yet who also serve today to diminish somewhat unfairly his own immense two-decade coaching achievements. There is little doubt that the often irascible Auerbach would not have won quite so relentlessly in Boston without the sleight-handed Bob Cousy to run his offense or without towering Bill Russell to anchor his unique model for a fast-breaking offensive machine. Naysayers have long contended that Auerbach's victories can never be separated out from Russell's. And those same nigglers are quick to point out that Auerbach only ended up with Cousy quite against his wishes and despite his own best efforts to block the local hero's presence in a Boston uniform.

The story of Auerbach's unplanned acquisition of Cousy and his painstakingly orchestrated acquisition of Russell, together reveal much about the combined role of rare luck and unmatched acumen in shaping his own coaching and administrative career. Cousy was one player Auerbach had seemingly little use for in the beginning. The newly arrived Boston mentor tried to avoid the popular favorite on draft day of 1950, and was clearly annoyed by the hounding he at first received from the Boston-area press to draft the local hero and Holy Cross All-American. Auerbach even squared off with the hometown media in his earliest press conference when he uttered words that were among his most famous. "Am I here to win games," chided Auerbach, "or to please the local yokels?"

Auerbach opted for 6'11" Charlie Share from Bowling Green, while Cousy was a draft choice of the Tri-Cities Blackhawks. But the Hawks immediately dealt

Despite his rough edges and unpopularity with opposing fans and coaches, the record of Arnold "Red" Auerbach stands for itself: eight straight NBA titles and a long-standing record of 938 career victories only recently overtaken by Lenny Wilkens.

Transcendental Graphics

Cousy to Chicago, which almost as immediately folded its own franchise operations. Cousy was then thrown into a dispersal draft with popular veterans Max Zaslofsky and Andy Phillip and went by default to Boston, which owned the last of the three available "special" picks. In the end, then, Bob Cousy wound up in the Boston camp despite Auerbach's best efforts, but then again the stubborn coach was quick to demonstrate that he was quite wise enough to exploit the new talent once he owned him.

With Russell it was a different matter altogether. Here the ingenious Auerbach had done his homework thoroughly, knew precisely what he wanted and how to manipulate other owners and GMs to get it, and saw in the rough-cut gem that was Bill Russell what other club directors failed entirely to see. That fortuitous insight was soon to give the victory-minded Auerbach all the edge he ever needed. Auerbach was alerted early (tipped off by his former George Washington University coach Bill Reinhart) to the raw potential in the San Francisco University defensive star, and from the beginning, seemed to see in Russell's latent talents the key to reshaping his own unbalanced team and thus altering the entire NBA's future course in the process. Auerbach envisioned the fast break (learned from Reinhart at George Washington) as the key to turning around his middling ball club, but he also knew precisely the kind of player he needed to make his scheme work. That player was built perfectly in the image that corresponded to Bill Russell. With Ed Macauley in the center slot and Cousy and Sharman in the backcourt, Boston already boasted plenty of shooting power (it was the NBA's highest-scoring team) but little defense (it gave up the most points) and less rebounding. The fast break would work as a strategy only if it was anchored by a stellar rebounder and shot-blocker who could

Pro Basketball's Ten Winningest Coaches (1998)

Coach	Teams	Record (Pct.)
Lenny Wilkens	Seattle, Portland, Cleveland, Atlanta	1,120–908 (.552)
Bill Fitch	L.A. Clippers, New Jersey, Houston, Boston, Cleveland	944–1,106 (.460)
Red Auerbach	Boston Celtics	938–479 (.662)
Dick Motta	Chicago, Washington, Dallas, Sacramento, Denver	935–1,017 (.479)
Pat Riley	L.A. Lakers, New York Knicks, Miami	914–387 (.703)
Larry Brown	Carolina (ABA), Denver (ABA), New Jersey, San Antonio, L.A. Clippers, Indiana	884–638 (.581)
Don Nelson	Milwaukee, Golden State, New York Knicks, Dallas	867–679 (.561)
Jack Ramsay	Philadelphia, Buffalo, Portland, Indiana	864–783 (.525)
Cotton Fitzsimmons	Phoenix, Atlanta, Buffalo, Sacramento, San Antonio	832–775 (.518)
Gene Shue	Baltimore, Philadelphia, San Diego, Washington, L.A. Clippers	784–861 (.477)

sweep the defensive boards and deliver lightning-fast outlet passes to a streaking Cousy. Russell fit the job description to a tee.

Once he had deemed Russell the answer to his plan, the clever Boston mentor still had to do some fancy manipulating to bring the future star to Boston. Rochester owned the top 1956 draft pick, but was almost certain not to pursue Russell for purely financial reasons. Sihugo Green thus became the answer to a classic trivia question (who was drafted ahead of Russell in 1956). St. Louis, in second slot, likely would not grab Russell either, but the risk here was far greater. Auerbach knew that Russell would not be a saleable item in racially tense St. Louis. But Hawks owner Ben Kerner was not about to let him go to Boston without plenty of "appropriate" compensation. The deal that was finally made (sending All-Star Ed Macauley and hot prospect Cliff Hagan to the Hawks) not only cemented Boston's future, but it also strengthened a prime rival—Kerner's Hawks—and in the process, created block-buster postseason confrontations with St. Louis over the next half decade that would remain one of the league's showcase events of its first quarter-century.

It is not surprising to find such carping about Auerbach's achievements in Boston—claims that he gained his first true star, Cousy, against his own will and best judgment, and also that he won only because Russell and Cousy were regularly in the lineup—since in his own day he was one of the least-popular coaches on the scene—with fans, media, and even rival players—and especially with his rivals in the coaching fraternity. Auerbach, from the start, had as much of a knack for alienating the general populace (especially his bench rivals) as he did for winning championships. Especially despised was his on-court behavior during Boston's many triumphs across the decade known for "Celtic Mystique." Red's flaunted victory

Transcendental Graphics

Red Auerbach, in what became a familiar scene in Boston, celebrates yet another NBA championship with Bill Russell. This was Auerbach's ninth and final league title in 1966.

cigar—which he would light on the bench in closing moments of games when victory was in the bag—remained throughout the late '50s and '60s the most universally hated sight to be found anywhere around the league.

But despite this veneer of broad-based unpopularity, Auerbach's record for 16 seasons as a Boston head coach speaks eloquently for itself. No NBA coach has won so much, so consistently, and for so long a string. (Lenny Wilkens's victories now exceed Auerbach's by 200 and counting, but Wilkens's winning percentage is 100 points lower and his championships (1) are minuscule.) Red's teams dominated an era that may well have been the league's most balanced and most competitive despite all the Boston winning. If it can be claimed that Boston won only because it had Russell and, to a lesser extent, Cousy or Heinsohn or Sharman, then the credit must again nonetheless fall in large part to Auerbach and not merely the star players themselves. It was the coach's genius, after all, that had envisioned the new directions the game would inevitably take with a player such as Russell. It had also been Boston's boss man who arranged the coup that brought Russell to Boston in the first place and then molded the elements of a winning team around the game's greatest defensive player. And if Auerbach was at first skeptical about Cousy, nonetheless, he knew precisely how to exploit the great ball handler and stellar playmaker once he had the other pieces of his powerhouse team set into place.

Even when his coaching time ran out, Auerbach continued to display a unique flair for organizational genius. First, he would select Russell to replace himself on the bench, thus choosing rather fortuitously the only man who could possibly have done the job properly at the time. Auerbach, of course, again immediately saw what others may well not have seen, and this time it was the fact that no one else could have stepped in to manage the equally cantankerous Russell but Bill Russell himself. Then in the 1970s, having retained control of the club as general manager, the still-fiery Auerbach would once more rebuild Boston's fortunes around the latent coaching skills of one of his former players. This time it would be Tom Heinsohn who would be the exceptional beneficiary. Having built two powerhouse teams in two different decades, Auerbach was not quite done as he entered his fourth decade at the helm of franchise fortunes. As Boston's performance again seemed about to sag in the wake of Heinsohn's era (as coach) and then the Dave Cowens era (as star player), Auerbach would pull off yet one final coup that would bring Boston its most popular and talented player ever—Larry Bird—and establish in the process yet another remarkable chapter of Boston NBA invincibility.

The ingenious move that brought Bird to Boston and reopened the Celtics Mystique was, in reality, a series of transactions that not only landed Bird but brought on board at the same time both Robert Parish and Kevin McHale. The key this time was a deal with Golden State, not unlike the earlier deal with St. Louis involving Russell. Auerbach had first plucked Bird from the 1978 draft, even though the Indiana State star was only a junior and would not join the club until another full season had passed. Now, with the 1980 draft, he shipped veteran Bob McAdoo to Detroit for the No. 1 pick, then swapped that pick to Golden State (which coveted Purdue center Joe Barry Carroll) in exchange for established center Parish and a lower draft selection that was penciled in to be McHale.

The Warriors would get what they wanted, even if it was not by any stretch what they needed. The trio brought to Boston by Auerbach's latest maneuvers—Bird, McHale, Parish—would eventually comprise what many still believe to be the greatest front line in the history of the sport. The immediate victims this time around were thus the Golden State Warriors, who had gambled in a big way on seven-foot prospect Carroll and ultimately lost in an even bigger way for their boldness. Acquiring McHale and Parish was a big enough coup in itself, but the capturing of Bird had been without question the league's biggest deal of the first half of the new decade. Much of the credit again would fall to Auerbach's rare insight into players whose potential was even greater than commonly perceived. McHale and Parish would provide championship backbone. Bird would shine for a decade and more and even turn out to be Red Auerbach's final on-court legacy.

Auerbach might well have extended his own reputation and the Boston dynasty record still a bit farther if another draft-day gamble—that involving Maryland star Len Bias—had not taken a bizarre 11th-hour tragic turn that even basketball's most astute front-office genius could never have anticipated. (Auerbach plucked Bias with the No. 2 pick in 1986, but the All-American died two days later of a cocaine overdose.) With the Len Bias fiasco, the great Boston mastermind would finally be beaten by fate's cruel hand. But one such loss in five (Russell, Bird, Parish, McHale, Bias) still left Auerbach miles ahead of the pack when it came down to an unmatched lifetime track record for building charismatic championship teams around true franchise superstars, stars for whom others were not quite so willing to mortgage their own front-office futures.

It is not an insignificant fact that, while Auerbach owned some of the sport's best team-oriented and championship-driven players, he never had a league scoring champion, something that Boston to this day has never enjoyed. In the end this rare insight into team-concept individual talent was Auerbach's greatest genius. It was getting Cousy, Heinsohn, Russell, K. C. Jones, Sam Jones, Cowens, and finally Bird, into Boston uniforms in the first place that was Red Auerbach's special calling and also his indelible claim to future fame.

Danny Biasone—Inventor of the NBA Shot Clock

Among basketball's most enduring landmark names, none is more narrowly associated (except perhaps for Naismith himself) with a single achievement than is the name Danny Biasone. Nor is any individual among the game's founding fathers today so little recognized or so rarely remembered as a living, breathing personality, alive behind the single seminal idea that brought its creator such lasting fame. But even if it had not been for the 24-second shot-clock innovation, which today remains his narrow claim to notoriety, Danny Biasone would nonetheless still merit a page or two in the early history of the NBA, if only for his considerable achievements as one of the most influential among the first decade of ball club owners.

Biasone had come to the NBA through the back door as a by-product of the merger between NBL and BAA clubs. As owner of one of the NBL's more successful franchises, he was viewed by fellow owners as a persuasive if soft-spoken voice of reason; he was also not part of the clique of wealthy owners—Brown in Boston, Irish in New York, Sutphin in Cleveland, Uline in Washington—who were the big-city arena managers and hockey magnates standing behind the more financially stable BAA. With the Syracuse Nationals ball club, Biasone had nonetheless built and maintained through lean times one of the young league's most respectable and durable organizations. It was Biasone's Syracuse team that had won the first regular-season title in the merged league, which had been newly christened in 1949–50 as the National Basketball Association, posting a runaway 51–13 Eastern Division mark before succumbing to the George Mikan–led Minneapolis Lakers (another NBL import) in the six-game league championship finals. It was also Biasone's club that boasted one of the game's first true superstars in tenacious Dolph Schayes, offered one of the fledgling NBA's finest small-town arenas in the Syracuse War Memorial Coliseum, and boasted perhaps the league's most vocal and fervent hometown fans.

The story of the 1954 rule change that saved the shaky NBA from imminent death has been frequently told in academic histories of the sport, and yet retains little common currency for the modern-era fan. The NBA shot clock appears to stretch so far back into the sport's Dark Ages that—like baseball's ball-and-strike count and football's three-point field goal—its seems a holdover from some long-lost prehistoric epoch. That was certainly not the case, however, and the struggling league of the early '50s—dominated by George Mikan and his Minneapolis Lakers and filled with scrappy veterans of years of industrial league and barnstorming professional play—was a circuit that knew no such legislation to control the tempo of play and restrict rough-and-tumble tactics, ploys that often won

Among basketball's pioneering front-office executives, none is any more narrowly associated with a single achievement than Danny Biasone. Owner of the Syracuse Nats during the first decade of league history, Biasone made his lasting mark by dreaming up one of the game's most distinguishing features—the 24-second shot clock.

Transcendental Graphics

games, but sapped the sporting spectacle in the process. The BAA-NBA for seven seasons after its 1946 founding was a league that seemed to be disintegrating rapidly into a style of play that emphasized on-court brutality and deadly ball-hogging inaction, a combination that was by 1953 sending fans scurrying for the exits or snapping off their TVs in a fit of mass boredom. A radical solution was needed if the game was to survive and even perhaps seize the stage left vacant by the recent floundering of the college sport in the wake of disastrous 1951 game-fixing scandals.

Enter Danny Biasone and the piece of legislation that saved the pro game from premature extinction. Biasone presented his fellow owners with a radical alternative to slowdown basketball, and it was an alternative that seemed well worth the gamble. With the opening of the 1954–55 season, the odd-looking box-shaped 24-second shot clocks were stationed along the sidelines, and with their use, the game suddenly transformed itself overnight. Both the number of shots taken and the resulting scoring totals soared in the new season, and many games saw one or both teams topping the century level in point-making. Fans warmed rapidly to the new level of shot-making action and filled arena seats, a fact which, in turn, spurred one of the nation's major TV networks to bid for expanded rights to televise league games. And with this sudden upturn in scoring, return of disaffected fans, and unprecedented media attention came other signs of improving health as well. The undercapitalized Baltimore franchise would collapse early in the same 1954–55 season, reducing the circuit to eight teams. But there the attrition would finally stop, or at least slow to a mere trickle. In coming decades clubs would move from small-market cities (Biasone's own Syracuse team included), and new teams would be added, but never again would an NBA franchise falter altogether and go out of business. Biasone's innovation had seemingly worked a miracle in saving the beleaguered circuit. And ironically, the innovation seemed to pay immediate dividends for its inventor as well, since his own Syracuse Nationals team would surprisingly win the first league championship played under the new set of working rules.

The shot-clock idea was one that Biasone had arrived upon without anything that approached a magical formula. The method of calculating the time allotted for shooting the basketball had stemmed from pure logic and nothing at all mysterious or even the least bit sophisticated. Biasone had calculated that NBA teams of the past several seasons had fired up an average of 120 shots nightly (60 per team), one shot approximately every 24 seconds. In the past season, Biasone noted, the per-team shot totals had already soared to nearly 80 per game. By legislating 24 seconds as a mandatory shooting time, the rules-makers would only be requiring teams to do what they did under normal circumstances most of the time anyway; what would be banned would only be intentional slowdowns for strategic purposes.

Once the experiment was in place it proved an immediate success, so much so that, within a few short years, it seemed as though the procedure was so natural that it must have always been around. There were also other rule changes that accompanied the shot clock and worked with equal effectiveness to put the game on a fast-track correction course. The most important was a piece of legislation lifted from the college game in order to discourage intentional fouling, certainly one of the banes of the plodding professional sport. Under the new requirements personal fouls would be counted against the teams and not just individuals (who were banned after six violations); only six "team fouls" would now be permitted in a quarter, and after that, an additional penalty free throw would also be awarded (three chances to make two on a two-shot foul). Since the extra foul shot (and potential extra point) was a stiff price to pay, strategic fouling was now also discouraged. But the notion that Biasone had advanced regarding the shot clock had more than anything else given the league its much-needed new identity. It was also the notion, of course, which would provide Biasone himself with his own historic niche and lasting claim to fame with generations of basketball fans to come.

Eddie Gottlieb—Philadelphia's Feisty Mr. Basketball

A careful search of the NBA record books or the league's official encyclopedias today turns up Eddie Gottlieb's name in two rather obscure locations. One is in the league's championship listings as the first coach to win a league title in the inaugural NBA season over 50 long winters ago, even though the circuit was not yet called the NBA at the time. The second place to encounter Gottlieb's name is attached to the league's annual Rookie of the Year trophy, a fitting, if somewhat small, recognition of one of the pro sport's most important early groundbreakers.

Gottlieb's first associations with basketball administration and with basketball coaching came during the hectic barnstorming era of the 1920s and early '30s. As early as 1918 he had helped organize the Philadelphia SPHAs ball club and remained closely associated with that team for the next several decades. While the South Philadelphia Hebrew Association, which originally provided sponsorship and uniforms, soon withdrew its support, both the name and Gottlieb himself remained as fixtures; when the powerful local club defeated New York's Original Celtics in 1922, the team's fame was off and running and so was Gottlieb's career as unparalleled sports promoter. The popular SPHAs would eventually capture 11 pro championships (mostly in the Eastern League and ABL) and thus remain a featured attraction in arenas everywhere around the country. In addition, Gottlieb was also active along with Abe Saperstein in promoting black baseball throughout the nation's heartland. One of the defining features of Gottlieb's exceedingly long and productive career was, indeed, the fact that he was a relentless promoter of professional sporting events whose scope stretched far beyond the basketball arena. He was business advisor to Saperstein's touring Harlem Globetrotters basketball outfit with whom he often traveled; at the same time, he backed pro wrestling events throughout the Philadelphia area; and he arranged an all-black baseball all-star game in Yankee Stadium during 1929 that may have been the first such event ever held in a major-league ballpark. Gottlieb's remarkable tenure would finally come to a quiet but profit-laced end only in the early 1960s when the majority owner of the Warriors (for which he had paid $25,000 in the early '50s) sold his interest (for $875,000) to a group prepared to move his Philadelphia NBA franchise and its star, Wilt Chamberlain, to the West Coast city of San Francisco. Gottlieb accompanied his former ball club to California in 1963, but only in a semiofficial advisory capacity.

The greatest fame for Eddie Gottlieb, however, would come with his role as a driving force in the formation of the early NBA. The diminutive promoter-turned-coach would compile only a lackluster 263–318 nine-year NBA bench record, yet he nonetheless pasted together one of the best ball clubs of the three-season BAA. He would bring on board for the opening league season (on recommendation of Pete Rosenberg, one of his players with the old SPHAs outfit) an unheralded ex-collegian from Murray State Teachers College, who would quickly prove one of the game's first offensive stars, and who would also bring to basketball the important innovation of the running jump shot. He would subsequently fill his roster with local Philadelphia phenoms like Paul Arizin (Villanova), Tom Gola (La Salle), Ernie Beck (Pennsylvania), and Guy Rodgers (Temple), who could provide local fan appeal as well as a potent front-running ball club. And he would also help steer the eventual merger of the rival BAA and NBL into the lasting circuit known finally after 1950 as the National Basketball Association.

Gottlieb's first championship team was one of the more flamboyant outfits in the three-year life of the BAA. It was a team that featured jump-shooting pioneer and ultimate basketball flake Joe Fulks and that rode Fulks's hot hand to surprising postseason victories over Eastern Division leader Washington (coached by Auerbach) and Western Division pacesetter Chicago, during the first BAA playoff round-robin. With his penchant for local talent as a motivating factor, Gottlieb enjoyed his largest success by persuading fellow NBA owners to allow him to claim Wilt Chamberlain of Philadelphia's Overbrook High School as a future "regional" draft choice. It was Chamberlain's arrival as the league's biggest showpiece in 1959 that allowed Gottlieb to remain highly competitive during the final years of the Warriors' residence in Philadelphia. With Wilt in the fold, Gottlieb enjoyed an intense Eastern Division rivalry with Boston and Red Auerbach that was one of the most attractive showcases (Chamberlain and Arizin versus Russell and Cousy) across the league's first two decades.

At the end of his reign he would also play a key role in opening up of the sport's westward expansion by moving the league's biggest star and one of its marquee teams into a potentially lucrative California venue. But perhaps Gottlieb's most lasting contributions came during his numerous years as an innovative thinker on the sport's powerful NBA Rules Committee. He rarely resisted any idea that would improve the NBA as a fan-pleasing spectacle and was thus an enthusiastic supporter of Biasone's revolutionary shot-clock scheme, as well as of legislation to ban zone defenses and award bonus penalty shots for excessive fouling.

He also promoted the idea of NBA doubleheaders (providing fans with a chance to see four teams and twice the stars for a single admission price) and experimented with games in small-city venues such as Hershey, Pennsylvania, or Binghamton, New York, that spread the league's exposure and increased a then-tiny throng of NBA boosters. One of Gottlieb's "NBA road shows" ironically turned out to be one of the league's most memorable and historic games, the one in which Chamberlain poured in 100 points before a sparse but highly appreciative crowd at a converted hockey arena in backwater Hershey. For years Eddie Gottlieb also worked 12 hours a day for several summer months to arrange with pencil and paper the NBA's upcoming official season's schedule. It was in this final capacity as NBA legislator and watchdog that Gottlieb would author and support several of the bold moves designed to increase the cage sport's appeal to the much-needed fan base still located largely within a handful of Eastern Seaboard NBA cities.

Nat Holman—New York's Original Mr. Basketball

Like Johnny Wooden a decade later, Nat Holman earned Hall of Fame credentials as both pioneering player and innovative coaching giant. Unique to Holman's case, however, was the rather amazing fact that some of his best years as both professional ballplayer and collegiate mentor overlapped during basketball's formative decades of the 1920s and 1930s. As a barnstorming professional player, the New York City native earned lasting recognition as a key member of the Original Celtics aggregate that also featured Johnny Beckman, Dutch Dehnert, Pete Barry, and Joe Lapchick. During the rough-and-tumble days of one-night stands and fly-by-night leagues, Holman etched his immortality by devising the pivot play along with Dehnert (at least in one version of the legend) and inventing as well the man-to-man defensive switch, maneuvers destined to become essential staples of the game for generations to come. As a sideline coach, he built a three-decade career at CCNY that would culminate in a unique pair of simultaneous postseason tournament crowns during March 1950, smack on the eve of disastrous point-shaving scandals that would drive a stake in the heart of his own career and nearly deflate the sails of college basketball as a whole. Holman's early coaching career was also supplemented with a prestigious basketball teaching assignment for the State Department, which found him instructing neophyte players during the 1930s in such far-flung foreign posts as Israel and Japan.

A quarter-century before Nat Holman coached CCNY to the only postseason double sweep in collegiate history, the barnstorming star of the Original Celtics had already earned lasting fame as a player by pioneering the pivot play and inventing the man-to-man defensive switch.

Transcendental Graphics

The playing career that Nat Holman appended to his longer coaching stint would find him eventually attached to a half dozen of the best-known barnstorming outfits of his era. Primary contributions came with the Original Celtics and the New York Whirlwinds, but he also played at the end of the Roaring '20s with ABL ball clubs stationed in Syracuse, Brooklyn, and Chicago. His forte was his considerable ability as a deft passer and creative playmaker who concentrated on feeding more proficient scorers like Dehnert, Lapchick, and Beckman. Yet he did also once lead the Brooklyn ABL club (that particular season's manifestation of the Celtics) in scoring with a then-respectable 8.8 points-per-game average during the 1926–27 campaign.

Holman's coaching career with CCNY began long before his playing days had closed, commencing with a part-time assignment as early as 1920. By 1932, however, in the wake of the Great Depression and the collapse of the ABL, he would concentrate exclusively on his coaching role, one that would produce some of the finest collegiate teams of the '30s and '40s in the basketball mecca which was New York City. The zenith for Holman as coach arose with the team he fielded for the final season of the 1940s. That outfit starred Ed Warner and Floyd Layne, alongside Ed Roman and Irv Dambrot, a pair of black stars teamed with a pair of white stars. While the roller-coaster season strung together by this team throughout the winter of 1949–50 was at best an inconsistent one—no more than a 17–5 won-lost record in regular-season contests with late-year upset losses to Niagara, Syracuse, and Canisius—it was solid enough, in the end, to earn berths in both postseason playoffs. Both college round-robins were, at the time, stationed in New York's Madison Square Garden (the NCAA held its Finals there), which also served as the CCNY Beavers' own part-time home floor. With this decided advantage, the local favorites didn't disappoint: they first rallied behind their veteran coach for a series of startling upsets, including a thorough routing of highly favored Kentucky and Adolph Rupp in the NIT quarterfinals; Holman's Beavers then salted away a pair of convincing victories over the same Bradley ball club (69–61 and 71–68) to clinch both tournament titles. It would thus be the one and only time that an identical winner would be crowned for both the NCAA and the NIT, although Rupp's Kentucky squad had barely missed the same honor a single season earlier. NCAA rules makers, fighting for inroads against the still more popular NIT, soon took drastic steps to make certain that such dual participation would not again be possible, eventually demanding that schools invited for NCAA participation reject all other post-season bids.

What might have been Holman's greatest hour of glory, however, almost overnight tragically turned into his worst possible private and public nightmare. The following season—with CCNY returning a near-identical roster of players—had only partially run its course, when the shocking college betting scandals finally broke, first in New York and then nationwide, and Holman's crew was one of the prime targets of the unfolding investigation. Agents from the District Attorney's office first broke the news to the stunned CCNY coach aboard a train, which was returning his team from an important 1951 road victory at nearby Rutgers. Holman hastily gathered his troops and urged that all involved simply tell the truth and maintain faith in the honesty of their deeds. Yet, with little honesty underpinning the players' earlier actions, both they and their coach's trust quickly went up in a cloud of sickening scandal. Two of CCNY's top stars (Warner and Roman) were eventually convicted for their roles in widespread game-fixing and score-rigging during the 1949 and 1950 seasons.

Holman himself was never touched by even a hint of scandal; he had remained in the dark about his athletes' despicable actions. But the whole affair now explained his team's regular-season inconsistencies during the previous year's double-championship campaign. (Also revealed eventually were the reasons behind Kentucky's upset loss to Loyola-Chicago, which had prevented an earlier two-tourney sweep for Rupp's men in 1949, as well as Bradley's poor play against CCNY during both 1950 title matches, something which seemed as an afterthought to cheapen further the Beavers' two tarnished championships.) A disillusioned coach Holman resigned in 1952, and the program that he had so painstakingly built over decades was largely dismantled over the next several seasons as CCNY de-emphasized the popular roundball sport. Holman would return briefly to coach losing teams in 1955, 1956, and 1959 (he had known only two such losers during his first 31 years on the job) before saying his final farewell four games into the 1959–60 campaign.

Despite this premature end to his tenure in the early '50s, Nat Holman had left behind an impressive CCNY record that included 422 career wins and one of the best all-time college victory percentages anywhere on record. At the time of his somewhat tragic retirement, Holman ranked second only to Adolph Rupp (then still active) in career winning percentage. In 1964 Nat Holman's immortality was officially sealed with election to the Naismith Memorial Basketball Hall of Fame in Springfield. But Gotham's grand old "Mr. Basketball" would live on for yet another three full decades, revered as a local legend in all corners of the sport's acknowledged capital city, and finally succumbing in 1995 near the end of his ninth decade.

Ned Irish—Basketball's First Great Promoter

No single nonplayer or noncoach performed any larger innovative role in assuring basketball's solid future than did a *New York World Telegram* sportswriter-turned-promoter named Edward "Ned" Irish. Irish earned his indelible spot in history as the sport's first large-scale professional promoter—the first, that is, who took advantage of big-city venues and staged marquee events designed to bring the nation's top college teams directly to the doorstep of one of basketball's potentially most enthusiastic audiences. This was promotion of a far different order than that earlier practiced by the barnstorming pro clubs and their owner-entrepreneurs, who sought to take their one-night shows on the road and play whomever would have them in even the most cramped of dance halls or local school gymnasiums. As a promoter with big ideas Irish did almost as much to launch the winter game of basketball into the nation's consciousness as did James Naismith himself. It is reasonable to assume that, in truth, he did far more than Naismith, a visionary who had planted the seed, but then did little to till the soil or gather the harvest. Basketball of the college variety found its first true mecca during the Roaring '20s and turbulent '30s in the arenas and on the playgrounds of New York City, and that mecca was largely the product of the promotional genius of a single man—Ned Irish.

The stroke of genius for Ned Irish came with his sudden insight into the future potential of college basketball as a main venue spectator sport. The story is told often how Irish first seized on the potential of college cage play as a marketable commodity during his early days as an itinerant sportswriter. Legend has it that Irish tore his trousers one night in 1933 while trying to crawl through a locker-room window to gain access to a sold-out Manhattan College gymnasium where he was slated to cover a local college shootout. The story is likely apocryphal—as all such charming stories are—but it is historical record, nonetheless, that Ned Irish soon harbored a belief that the burgeoning college game could easily be better promoted and profitably sold to willing spectators, if occasionally staged in larger arenas such as the spacious Madison Square Garden. Irish could not have helped but notice, during his journeys around the metropolitan college scene, that tiny gyms were overflowing and enthusiastic fans were being turned away nightly by the hundreds. The '20s boasted a number of fine teams in New York City—the St. John's "Wonder Five" coached by Buck Freeman, Howard Cann's competitive NYU clubs, Nat Holman's stellar CCNY contingents—and fans were hungry to see them do battle.

The true genius and lasting contribution of New York's arch-promoter Ned Irish came with his rare insight into the future potential of the college cage sport as a marketable entertainment spectacle.

Transcendental Graphics

And there was stiff competition throughout other sectors of the land—especially the Midwest and Pacific Coast—while the notion of cutthroat intersectional rivalries had barely yet been tested. Irish gained a further boost for his idea when he recalled witnessing the gate successes enjoyed with such heated college intercity matches in the newly built Philadelphia Palestra (opened in 1927) during his own undergraduate days at Penn.

Irish was soon staging special college basketball nights, featuring doubleheader matchups between the local schools and imported intrasectional rivals. There had been one earlier trial run (January 1931) when Mayor Jimmy Walker sponsored a most successful tripleheader affair headlining the St. John's "Wonder Five" as a fund-raiser for his Mayor's Unemployment Relief Fund designed to benefit the city's Depression victims. Young Irish had helped *World Telegram* sports editor Dan Daniel stage that first landmark event and had been convinced by the turnout (15,000-plus) that New Yorkers truly loved their basketball. The first such MSG doubleheader handled exclusively by Irish (December 1934) drew a surprising crowd of well over 16,000, thus setting the table for future roundball extravaganzas, which soon became a trademark of the exploding sport. In that first historic Ned Irish twin bill, NYU tussled with Notre Dame, while powerhouse Westminster (Pennsylvania) with its star, Wes Bennett, lined up against local favorite St. John's. During the 1934–35 season the now-encouraged Irish booked eight more doubleheaders into the Garden, and the result was a total draw of 99,528 basketball-hungry fans. Among the imported attractions over the next few seasons were

Hank Iba's crack Oklahoma A&M squad and Stanford University, with its charismatic revolutionary one-handed shooter, All-American Hank Luisetti.

The momentum gained by Ned Irish's popular intrasectional games was soon paying other huge dividends as well, the grandest being the formation by Irish and his backers in 1938 of the first National Invitation Tournament at season's end. The first such multiteam gathering was followed immediately, a mere year later, by still another, as the National Collegiate Athletic Association (NCAA) announced formation of its own "official" championship tournament, although the NIT round-robin staged entirely in Madison Square Garden would remain the showcase of college basketball for at least another full decade. As college basketball grew in popularity during the 1930s and 1940s, in large part due to the New York promotions of Irish, interest also ballooned in the appearance of a large number of touring semiprofessional and professional ball clubs traveling the countryside to play amateur club teams in rented local gymnasiums. Many of these touring pro outfits featured marquee ex-collegiate players whose fame had already spread a few years earlier with the growing luster of the college-level game.

The true heyday for Irish-arranged collegiate doubleheaders in Madison Square Garden would come with the boom-era years that were the 1940s. Under Irish's guiding hand the continued tradition of MSG doubleheaders drew better than a half million paying customers between 1942 and the decade's final winter. And while he was enjoying the richest fruits of his labors on behalf of the college game, Irish also turned his attention and considerable skills to a lesser role in launching the postwar professional version as well. It was Irish who represented the New York interests when hockey club owners banded together at the end of the war to patch together the BAA experiment that would rival and soon overtake the more established Midwest-based NBL. Irish's final legacy was the stable NBA ball club in New York that won no league titles early on in its history, yet nonetheless provided one of the young league's most profitable and necessary pioneering franchises.

Joe Lapchick—Bridge Between Early and Modern Epochs

Only John Wooden and Nat Holman can boast more honor-filled and historically significant dual careers as both player and coach than can the New York City native who first starred (with Holman) for the famed Original Celtics during the Roaring '20s barnstorming era, then built a bench legacy in the same city with both St. John's University (first in the '40s and again in the '60s) and the BAA-NBA Knickerbockers (during their earliest NBA days). Joe Lapchick was neither the winningest nor the most long-lived coach of college basketball annals—he came nowhere near getting into the running for either distinction. The argument can be made, however, that no other coach from the sport's formative years boasted more pure charisma, certainly none was more intense, and few were any more innovative or consistently successful. Lapchick's teams never showed double figures in the loss column during his first St. John's tenure and were permanent features of the prestigious NIT during the era of World War II.

Lapchick's itinerant playing career was launched several years before he first joined up with Jim Furey's touring Celtics for the 1923–24 season. Robbed of a high school education by impoverished family circumstances, the lanky youngster was already earning cash on the city's hardwoods at the age of 15, pulling down $5 a game with the touring Yonkers Bantams. By age 17 a frame that had stretched out to 6'5" was bringing him $7 per contest with the more highly regarded New York Whirlwinds. And over the next couple seasons he was found playing for several teams at the same time in and around the metropolitan New York City area. Soon the fees for his services had soared to $1 per minute, and eventually (when he had grown to 6'6"), even to $75 per game with a prestigious team like the Troy Trojans outfit of the semipro New York State League, one of many short-lived barnstorming circuits of the era.

It was with Jim Furey's Original Celtics, however, that Lapchick blazed the most significant trails as the game's first truly coordinated big man and thus the sport's pioneering post-position player. The trend-setting New Yorkers boasted the first players retained with seasonal salaries (rather than paid for individual games), won five of every six outings against all comers, and ran roughshod over the handful of pro circuits they slipped in and out of. Furey's team was also as remarkable for its revolution of playing styles as for its domination of competition during basketball's formative years. Among the Celtics' groundbreaking and widely imitated tactics were their switching zone defenses, "give-and-go" offensive weaves, and the soon-famous post-pivot ("give-and-go") play. And Lapchick, as much as any of the team's numerous stars (which included Nat Holman, Dutch Dehnert, and Johnny Beckman, among others), was always at the hub of such early innovations. A giant at six and a half feet, he was also both a talented shooter and accomplished leaper. He consistently controlled the center taps that were held after each basket (thus proving invaluable to any team with his services). With these talents he would also star for a number of campaigns in the American Basketball League once the Celtics joined that circuit for its second season in 1927. When ABL honchos decided the New Yorkers' total domination was simply bad for business and disbanded the Original Celtics, scattering Furey's star players, Lapchick took up residence with the powerhouse Cleveland Rosenblums—alongside former Celtics teammates Pete Barry, Dehnert, and Beckman—and continued his winning influence unfazed with still another pair of ABL championships during 1929 and 1930.

It was Lapchick's fellow Hall of Famer and former teammate Nat Holman who was most responsible for bringing the trailblazing giant into the collegiate coaching ranks. Holman, already head coach at CCNY, recommended Lapchick—at the time still barnstorming with a team known as Kate Smith's Celtics—to the administration at rival St. John's University. Without any formal education of his own, Lapchick was nonetheless brought on board at St. John's as head coach in 1937, on the very eve of basketball's abandonment of the center jump after each basket and also on the eve of the birth of both the NIT and NCAA postseason tournaments. Joe Lapchick thus launched his accomplished coaching career at precisely the moment when basketball of the college variety was about to enjoy its own major transition from infancy into a full-blown modern era. New York was destined to be a focal point of this first important decade of the game's newfound identity, and Lapchick and his St. John's teams were destined, as well, to stand at the forefront of New York City basketball throughout those same wartime years. The Redmen would win 181 games during Lapchick's initial 11-year tenure, enjoy-

Only John Wooden and Nat Holman can boast more distinguished dual careers as both player and head coach than St. John's University and New York Knicks mentor Joe Lapchick. Lapchick's Hall of Fame playing career featured performances with the remarkable barnstorming team known as New York's Original Celtics.

Transcendental Graphics

ing seven NIT visits, only twice losing as many as seven contests in a season, and posting the first-ever back-to-back NIT crowns (1943, 1944).

But the pull of the still-less-prestigious pro game was always there for Lapchick, and in 1948 he would gladly accept an invitation from Knicks president Ned Irish to take over the reins of the city's struggling BAA entry, at the same time turning down $12,000 in salary to stay on at St. John's. It would prove a fortuitous move for the New York franchise, which under Lapchick emerged as one of the league's toughest clubs over the next 10 seasons. Lapchick was never quite able to pull his team past the potent Lakers with Mikan, Mikkelsen, and Pollard, but on several occasions he came tantalizingly close. For three straight seasons in the early '50s the New Yorkers found themselves in the NBA Finals and each time lost out on the championship by the narrowest of margins. In one of those losing series only a referee's error may have cost them a coveted NBA title: a made basket by Knicks reserve Al McGuire (future Marquette coach), immediately before a foul call, was missed by officials in the 1952 opening championship-round game between the Knicks and Lakers, costing New York the game (which went overtime) and eventually perhaps the seven-game series.

The pro game soon wore heavily on the super-intense Lapchick, and the already thin (even gaunt) giant would, over the next few years, take on the emaciated appearance of a skeleton by each season's end. Finally, the stress became simply too great, and New York's most famous sideline face would be forced to step away from the pro game for reasons of failing health. But Lapchick was still not ready for full retirement and within a month ended up back at St. John's, where his second tenure in the college ranks would last for another nine long seasons. It would include 154 more victories, but a single losing season, four campaigns of 20-plus wins, and two more NIT championship crowns.

By the time a series of heart attacks forced retirement for a second time, Joe Lapchick owned the second-best college winning percentage of his day (the leader being, of course, Rupp). If Lapchick the player had been an offensive stalwart, Lapchick the coach was foremost a defensive genius. As a coach, his greatest skill seemed to be a knack for watching enemy teams intently and immediately detecting weaknesses in their strategies that could be turned to his own team's advantage. But in the end, Joe Lapchick is perhaps better remembered as the relentless innovator who, more than any other player-turned-coach, effectively bridged gaps between basketball's earliest barnstorming days and its later postwar modern-day era.

Dr. James Naismith—Father of Basketball

Some founding fathers become the heroes of history, even when their enshrinement is altogether unwarranted. When it comes to sagas of American sport, Abner Doubleday is, of course, the prototype example, given the fact that baseball's long-reputed inventor never did touch a horsehide ball nor heft an ashwood bat, and thus had about as much to do with the founding of our national pastime as Casey of Mudville did with setting early slugging standards. Both Doubleday (a real-life figure but no baseball inventor) and Casey were the pure stuff of myth upon which the game's essential folklore would so richly feed. And when it comes to recording the evolution of the roundball sport that today enthralls a nation's winter spectators, James Naismith is another whose legend far outstrips his practical contributions. Dr. Naismith most certainly did hang his revolutionary peach baskets in the YMCA gym at Springfield, and in that sense, he merits far more credit than the undeserving General Doubleday. Yet Naismith had in mind no more than a healthy exercise for his off-season football players, who needed a little indoor muscle toning at the height of winter. He hardly envisioned his new form of indoor gymnastics as providing a potential native American game that would some day rival and surpass even baseball in its ascendancy.

There is little evidence, in fact, that Naismith first saw his new game of "baskets" as anything more than a healthy diversion from more serious outdoor sports. And his concept was not an entirely original one at any rate. The game he designed—while strikingly like the one already played for centuries by native tribes in Mexico and in the mountainous Central American regions farther south—was certainly imaginative, though light-years removed from the whirling circus of athletic entertainment that comprises today's hardwood spectacle of modern basketball. Yet it would be left for numerous disciples of Naismith to envision a game with true potential as America's foremost action-packed sporting event. Many of those disciples—men with names like Lambert, Meanwell, Podoloff, Biasone, Gottlieb, Reinhart, and Newell—emerged on the eve or in the midst of the leisuretime revolution which followed on the heels of World War II, a decade after Naismith's own death, and few have received anything more than the occasional footnotes in history that their contributions so richly deserve.

The game invented in Springfield in December 1891 contained only the unwatered seeds of the modern "basket" sport. And Naismith's own conception of his new game had almost nothing to do with the attractions of the modern-day thrill-a-minute version. Dr. Naismith's early personal history in Kansas is perhaps the best barometer to his ongoing relationship with his foster-child creation today known universally as basketball. Naismith introduced the sport to the college campus in Lawrence, and he was indeed the varsity program's first coach there. But the game's inventor seemed anything but an intercollegiate coach—as we know the prototype today—at least not in his practice-time and game-time behaviors. He set up schedules for games with rival schools and held occasional formal practices. But he rarely traveled with his team when it played out of town. If he attended games at all, it was to referee and not to guide his ball club from the sidelines. He had no interest in winning basketball contests, and competition itself always seemed an anathema to the full-time teacher and part-time coach.

And Naismith hadn't even come to Kansas because of basketball in the first place. His official role on campus was first to lead mandatory student prayers in the campus chapel; later his assigned task became that of administering physicals to new freshmen arriving in Lawrence. Eventually, he took charge of the physical education classes, where basketball took no precedence over any other games he instructed. Wrestling, not basketball, seemed to be Dr. Naismith's preferred teaching assignment.

When he did continue a mild interest in the basketball team as Phog Allen's assistant in later years, he barely seemed to approve of his protégé's competitive practices and game tactics. There was also little that was competitive about Dr. Naismith's own first team at Kansas, which opened its "official" schedule on March 2, 1900, by suffering a 48–8 drubbing at the hands of the neighboring University of Nebraska five. Naismith's biographer, Bernice Larson Webb, reports that, at Kansas after the turn of the century "basketball advanced by its own momentum more than by Naismith's propagandistic efforts, for he never became very excited about the game" (*The Basketball Man: James Naismith*, 1973, p.120). Fifty-five victories and 60 losses over 12 years under the school's first head coach seem to verify Webb's rather cold assessment. It is thus a wonderful piece of historic irony that, while Naismith did mentor the Kansas team, he also logged the only losing record in the school's rich basketball history.

Yet Naismith's place in history is nonetheless assured by his almost accidental invention. No other major sport can trace its origins in quite the same way to a single inventive genius. There is no question that Naismith was the sole visionary

James Naismith remains the unquestioned "father of basketball," despite the fact that the game he invented in Springfield, Mass., contained only the seeds of the modern sport we know today, and the additional fact that most of Naismith's adult life knew only a tangential relationship with the popular game he had launched as a young YMCA instructor.

Transcendental Graphics

behind one of America's greatest sporting institutions. The rules of the game he laid down in 1891 contained little that would be recognized as basketball today. Naismith's 13 original rules contained but half a dozen that are still active in anything like their original form. There was no space in the original game for dribbling, for free-throw shooting, for movement that would suggest a patterned team game. Yet in these rules is nonetheless found the true essence of the modern-day game. And in Naismith's original conception of shooting at goals suspended high in the air was already apparent the genius of a game best attuned to a space-age world that would eventually dawn a near-century later. Naismith may not have envisioned the physicality and speed of today's basketball play. But he was inspired, nevertheless, to create a game like no other, one where the movement was vertical, the ball tosser's aim was always upward, and the challenge was to break free from the bonds of gravity.

The inventor of basketball lived a long and full life after his moment of pure inspiration in 1891, and most of that life knew only a tangential relationship with the sport he had launched as a young and idealistic educator. It was left to his legions of disciples to shape and promote the game he casually birthed, and then just as casually abandoned. In later years Naismith's relationship with basketball was at times almost bittersweet and at other times almost bitter. He did travel

Naismith's Original 13 Rules for Basketball

Naismith's original rules were printed in the Springfield YMCA School of Christian Workers newspaper (*The Triangle*) on January 15, 1892. Rules are abbreviated here, with the boldface rules being ones largely still in effect today.

1. **The ball may be thrown in any direction with one or both hands.**
2. **The ball may be batted in any direction with one or both hands, but never with the fist.**
3. **A player cannot run with the ball, but must throw it from the spot where he catches it.** Allowance is made for a man who catches the ball when running at a good speed.
4. The ball must be held in or between the hands; the arms or the body must not be used for holding the ball.
5. **No shouldering, holding, pushing, tripping, or striking of an opponent shall be allowed.** The first infringement of this rule by any person shall count as a foul, the second shall disqualify him until the next goal is made. If there is evident intent to injure an opponent to put him out of the game, no substitute shall be allowed for the disqualified player.
6. A foul is striking at the ball with the fist, violations of Rules 3 and 4, and such violations as are described in Rule 5.
7. If either side makes three consecutive fouls, this shall count as a goal for the opponents. Consecutive means without the opponents in the meantime making a foul.
8. **A goal shall be made when the ball is thrown or batted from the ground into the basket and stays there, providing those defending the goal do not touch or disturb the goal.** If the ball rests on the edge and the opponent moves the basket, it shall count as a goal.
9. When the ball goes out-of-bounds, it shall be thrown into the field (onto the court) and played by the person first touching it. In case of a dispute, the umpire shall throw it straight into the field (court). **The thrower-in is allowed five seconds. If he holds it longer, it shall go to the opponent. If any side persists in delaying the game, the umpire shall call a foul on them.**
10. **The umpire shall be the judge of the men and shall note the fouls** and notify the referee when three consecutive fouls are made. He has the power to disqualify men according to Rule 5.
11. **The referee shall be the judge of the ball and shall decide when the ball is in play, in bounds, to which side it belongs, and shall keep the time. He shall decide when a goal has been made, and keep account of the goals, with any other duties that are usually performed by a referee.**
12. **The time shall be two 15-minute halves, with 5 minutes' rest time between.**
13. **The side making the most goals in that time shall be declared the winners.** In case of a draw, the game may, by agreement of the captains, be continued until another goal is made.

(thanks to Phog Allen who raised funds for the purpose) to the 1936 Olympics to witness personally the first tentative step of his sport (however minor it was at the time) toward full-fledged international recognition. Only three years later Naismith passed away, late in the same year (1939) that had housed the first hodgepodge effort at an NCAA postseason championship tournament. It was perhaps yet one final irony that the year of Naismith's departure coincided with the very moment in which basketball was making its own most important departures from the past—departures such as the advent of postseason college tournaments and the elimination of constant center-court jump balls—that would transform it for the very first time into a mass-appeal spectator sport nearly on a par with football and baseball. Naismith must have been more than slightly bemused when he saw the game he had invented presented in the format it took during the Berlin Olympics. He likely could never have imagined (nor would he likely have approved of) what would soon become of his invention in the first few years after his death.

Maurice Podoloff—The Man Who Built the Pro Game

If there had been no Maurice Podoloff in the late 1940s, it is likely there would be no pro basketball as we know it in the late 1990s. The recent Golden Anniversary celebration of the nation's foremost sports league would not likely have happened if it had not been for the puckish Russian immigrant who hardly knew a basketball from a hockey puck when he first took charge of the sport on the eve of an American "Boom Era," which itself followed on the heels of World War II. It was not so much Mikan or Cousy or Pettit or Russell or Auerbach who kept the NBA afloat across its dozen seasons of hit-and-miss trial and error. It was Maurice Podoloff who deserves the lion's share of credit for pro basketball's near-miracle coming of age.

The native of Elizabethgrad, Russia, (he was raised in New Haven, Connecticut) hardly boasted a background that foreshadowed success in the world of professional basketball. But some of the sports world's greatest leaps forward are given a fortuitous push in the right direction by the most unaccountable of circumstances. Podoloff's background was first in law and later in the administration of professional hockey. He earned degrees at Yale University and much later fortuitously purchased the half-finished New Haven Arena. He developed a hockey franchise to play in the newly acquired building as a member of what was then known as the Canadian-American Hockey League, and by 1935 had risen to an administrative position as president of the thriving renamed American Hockey League.

Al Sutphin, owner of the Cleveland Arena and a fellow AHL franchise owner, first approached Podoloff with the speculative plan for a fledgling basketball circuit to compete head-to-head with the established but still struggling Midwest-based National Basketball League. Podoloff was to be president of the new circuit, and it would thus be the first time that one person would head two pro leagues simultaneously, since Podoloff would retain his old AHL hat as well. The idea behind the entire scheme was to capitalize on a new booming interest in basketball, attract the hordes of Americans with disposable income and a lust for entertainment in the years immediately following the second world war, and solve the need to increase arena revenues by occupying the empty hockey buildings on nights when AHL games or visiting ice shows were not penciled in.

The first BAA season began with a small bang, but the opening campaign was never more than a moderate success. The New York Knicks battled the Toronto Huskies in the opening game, staged on Canadian soil. Toronto, however, would be one of four franchises (along with Cleveland, Detroit, and Pittsburgh) that would not stick around long enough to see a second season. Philadelphia grabbed the first championship in a postseason playoff system that was ill-conceived and marred severely by the most ridiculous of possible round-robin formats. Division first-place finishers, second-place finishers, etc., played each other in opening-round matches, assuring immediate elimination of one of the two best teams. It was at the end of the BAA's first chaotic year, however, that the rookie commissioner came up with his first stroke of genius in the form of a college player draft that would distribute new talent equally among the league's teams.

But it was Podoloff's campaign to pull the foundations out from under the rival NBL and force eventual merger of the two competing circuits that was most responsible for his own legacy and for the league's survival and even its eventual solid footing. At the outset, the older NBL seemed to have the upper hand. Podoloff's circuit had the bigger arenas and more populous Eastern cities to exploit for its desperately needed fan base. But the NBL clubs had easily the best players and, by extension, all the best ball clubs—particularly those in Rochester, Syracuse, and Minneapolis. Most especially, they had George Mikan and his Minneapolis Lakers team that also boasted playmaker Herm Schaffer and Stanford All-American Jim Pollard. And there was also seven-footer Don Otten with Tri-Cities, ballhandling whiz Bob Davies and crack center Arnie Risen at Rochester, long-range bomber Bobby McDermott with first Fort Wayne and then Chicago, and, eventually, durable Dolph Schayes with Syracuse. It was precisely here—with the NBL's few attractive franchises—that Podoloff would strike his devastating blow, convincing both the Rochester and Minneapolis teams that they would find a much better showcase for their games (and thus better opportunities for revenues) if they were playing in Madison Square Garden, Boston Garden, or Providence Arena, and not in rundown high school gyms at Sheboygan or Oshkosh or Anderson, Indiana. The hijacking of the NBL's two best clubs (Fred Zollner's Fort Wayne Pistons team and the NBL ball club in Indianapolis also came on board for the 1949 season) inflicted a fatal blow on the BAA's faltering rival and started the snowball rolling downhill toward a quick and life-sustaining merger. Podoloff, of course, had been a main architect of it all.

The largest legacy of Maurice Podoloff is today the thriving NBA itself. No individual outside of David Stern is owed more credit for the modern-era health of the nation's most thriving professional sports league. But Podoloff's memory and name have today been preserved by other postcareer honors of a more formalized nature. The annual NBA Most Valuable Player trophy is now known as the Podoloff Cup. And pro basketball's first great administrator was duly inducted into the Naismith Hall of Fame in 1974, 11 years after his retirement as NBA Commissioner and another 11 years before his death at the eye-popping age of 95.

Adolph Rupp—Kentucky's Baron of Bluegrass

For nearly half a century Adolph Rupp stood unrivaled as true dean of collegiate basketball's coaching fraternity. Phog Allen may have been the acknowledged and officially sanctioned Father of Basketball Coaching, anointed in that role by none other than Dr. James Naismith himself. But Kentucky's Baron Rupp was long the sport's most favored son, and eventually also its most overshadowing legendary figure. Having learned the game's intricacies as a part-time player (1919 through 1923) and always-attentive student under Phog Allen in his native Kansas, Rupp represented a direct link (through Allen and hence also through Naismith) back to the college game's very roots and foundations. As an often cantankerous and always overbearing teacher-coach in his adoptive state of Kentucky, the living legend soon to be universally known as "The Baron" would build throughout the '30s, '40s, and '50s the college sport's longest-lasting dynasty (UCLA under Wooden reached greater heights for the short haul, yet fails to boast the consistency that has left Kentucky, North Carolina, and Kansas in a near dead heat for all-time wins), produce several of the most dominant teams in college basketball history, and eventually set records for longevity and annual winning that were long assumed to be utterly unmatchable.

Rupp's glorious run at Lexington began in the midst of World War II, though Neil Isaacs and other respected cage chroniclers have repeatedly pointed out that the decade and a half which preceded wasn't too shabby, either. It is not quite true, as some of his rabid Kentucky fans often preached, that Rupp invented the fast-break offensive style; nor is it true either, as diehard Bluegrass boosters might have long convinced themselves, that Rupp invented the sport of college basketball itself. Yet it is not that much of a stretch that the Baron came surprisingly close on both counts. Across 15 seasons at Lexington before 1944, Rupp won at an 80 percent clip and claimed half of the dozen Southeastern Conference postseason titles contested. More lasting in its effect was the Baron's predilection for regional play that, in the long run, helped to cement the game of college basketball as a truly national game. The first of these intersectional sorties by Rupp and his charges came with an ill-fated trip to Madison Square Garden in 1935, where Howard Cann's NYU team administered a bruising physical beating for 39 minutes and then stole victory in the closing minute on a disputed (at least by Rupp) foul call. So outrageous was the hacking permitted by officials against Kentucky center LeRoy Edwards, that this game strongly influenced soon-enacted three-second foul lane legislation. And the frustrations of the outing (Notre Dame coach George Keogan had earlier warned Rupp to bring his own officials if he wanted a fair shake in New York) only whetted Rupp's appetite for taking on the best teams from other quarters of the country.

The dominance of Rupp-coached outfits crested, however, in the World War II years and their immediate aftermath. The true peak came with Rupp's marvelous Fabulous Five three-year team (veterans Ralph Beard, Alex Groza, Cliff Barker, Wallace "Wah Wah" Jones, and Ken Rollins) that would leave its lasting mark as one of the true legendary outfits in the game's annals. The first postwar UK team (1946) was comprised of freshmen Beard, Jones, and Joe Holland alongside veterans Jack Parkinson and Jack Tingle, and was backed up by bench riders (like Wilbur Shue) who would have perhaps been All-Americans anywhere else in the land. A year later Groza, Bob Brannum (who soon transferred to Michigan State), Rollins, Barker, and Dutch Campbell all returned from military service to strengthen the already awesome forces of a squad, which failed to defend its NIT crown of a year earlier only when upset in the title game by the defending NCAA champions from Utah.

With an NIT title (1946) and back-to-back NCAA crowns (1948, 1949), as well as an Olympic championship (1948) to its credit, the miraculous "Fabulous

Five" unit was indeed so good it was even able to manipulate game scores and game results and yet remain, in the process, nearly unblemished against even the heftiest opposition. Only after the two top stars, Beard and Groza, had left Lexington did scandal break around Rupp's program, as well as around college basketball in other quarters of the country. Kentucky players had (with or without Rupp's knowledge) fixed game scores for the benefit of unscrupulous gamblers. Beard, Groza, and Dale Barnstable were the chief wrongdoers. The shocking NIT loss in 1949 that had blocked dual titles had resulted from a botched effort to manipulate the spread against Loyola of Chicago. The holier-than-thou Rupp, who had boasted at the first hint of betting scandals that no one could "touch my boys with a 10-foot pole," was left floundering in a sea of embarrassment. A proud UK program was suddenly in pieces. But not, of course, before another national title had been salted away in 1951 by a 32–2 team headed by seven-foot All-American Bill Spivey and also boasting Shelby Linville and future All-Americans Cliff Hagan, Frank Ramsey, and Lou Tsioropoulos (all sophomores).

Kentucky's program and Rupp's reputation were simultaneously dealt a severe blow by the whole affair of the 1951 college betting and point-shaving scandals. Nonetheless, the veteran coach, who was now himself a rock-solid institution, miraculously persevered and soon returned to the first ranks with a vengeance. Waiting in the wings for the smoke and fire to clear from the betting scandal was another flock of Kentucky recruits as good or better than the one that had included Groza, Beard, and Wah Wah Jones. Rupp's 1952 team (of Hagan, Ramsey, and Tsioropoulos) battled gamely in the face of scandal surrounding the UK program, and eventually fell off its pedestal only at the end of the season (losing to St. John's in the Regional Finals), even though it remained top dog in the sportswriters' balloting. The 1953 season had to be canceled, however, when the NCAA and SEC levied a yearlong ban based on irregular expenditures by Rupp's program. Rupp simply used the year to further train what would soon prove his best unit ever.

When the UK juggernaut reemerged in 1954 it would be to race pell-mell through an entire season undefeated and unchallenged, along the way pummeling eventual NCAA winner La Salle and its superstar, Tom Gola. But Hagan, Ramsey, and Tsioropoulos were subsequently ruled ineligible for postseason tournament play (as fifth-year seniors they had been granted eligibility only for the 1954 regular season), and the finest Kentucky team ever sat home in Lexington with the pride of a marvelous comeback and the bitterness of an NCAA title (what would have been Rupp's fourth) denied by a technicality. The golden era that began with the arrival of Groza, Beard, and Wallace Jones in 1945 ended finally with the graduation into the pros of Hagan, Ramsey, and Tsioropoulos nine seasons later.

Rupp would return to the summit twice more, once at the end of the '50s with his championship "Fiddlin' Five" squad of overachievers (Vern Hatton, Johnny Cox, John Crigler, Adrian Smith, Ed Beck) and again with his NCAA runner-up "Rupp's Runts" (Louie Dampier, Pat Riley, Thad Jaracz, Larry Conley, Tommy Kron) a half dozen seasons before retirement. His most bitter defeat would be the one that came at the hands of Texas Western University in the finals of the 1966 NCAA national shootout, a loss which cost a fifth national title and also held even larger symbolic significance. It was that 1966 game which saw the emerging play-

© University of Kentucky

Baron Rupp poses with the most famous and accomplished of his many juggernaut teams. The 1948 NCAA champions include: Wah Wah Jones (27), Alex Groza (15), Cliff Barker (23), Ken Rollins (26), and Ralph Beard (12). All were also members of the 1948 gold-medal–winning U.S. Olympic team.

ground style featuring freelancing black athletes defeat Rupp's highly disciplined and all-white standard bearers ("Rupp's Runts") in a showdown involving clashing playing styles and distinct evolutionary eras. But despite this final failure, Rupp had now amassed enough victories to assure his immortality. Two seasons later (December 1967) he overtook his mentor, Phog Allen, as the winningest college coach of all time.

Rupp's successes were not based primarily on a new coaching style per se, or any innovative approaches to winning, but rather merely upon a drive and perseverance that was nearly unmatched in college coaching annals. Arriving at Kentucky in 1930 Rupp had fully adopted the fast-breaking style of his predecessor, John Maurer. His uniqueness came rather in his unsurpassed ability to promote UK basketball, and his unrivaled passion for winning that attracted endless streams of top-flight athletes to his solid program. As much as anyone he would make the growing game a national attraction in the century's three middle decades. And during his own final two decades of a 42-year career, he managed to overcome two embarrassing black marks severe enough to scuttle the reputation of almost any other coaching genius. The first was the point-shaving scandal during which he faced widespread insinuations of complicity and from which he never escaped entirely unsullied. It seemed unlikely that the Baron had never smelled a rat or never attempted to deflect attention from his own players' distasteful involvement with a gambling crowd. And equally as distasteful were the ongoing suspicions of racist attitudes that kept the Kentucky program "lily white" until after the end of Rupp's reign, long after talented black players had been thoroughly integrated into the sport elsewhere. Rupp assuredly never campaigned openly against blacks. But neither did he pursue the black athlete even when it became both expedient and fashionable to do so.

Yet if the Baron was not above reproach on some counts even in his adopted home state, he was nonetheless a living legend in his own time, and that legend would only grow after his departure from the scene. Rupp set standards for winning that only Dean Smith has been able to match in a quarter-century that has followed. He dragged the game onto the national stage with some of the greatest teams ever to emerge from the Deep South, or from any other quarter for that matter. And in the end, he built a passion for basketball in the hills and valleys of Kentucky that yet remains unrivaled in any other sector of the nation, even down to the present day.

Dean Smith—College Basketball's Winningest Coach

Every corner of the nation seems to have its local choice for college basketball's truest coaching genius. Fans in the Midwest continue with surprising frequency to cast a ballot for Indiana's Bob Knight, despite the more recent seasons and mediocre Hoosier teams that have tarnished a once-bright legend. Kentuckians see a direct lineage from Adolph Rupp to Rick Pitino with almost nothing or no one in between. The West (and much of the rest of the land to boot) still stands behind an irreplaceable John Wooden two decades after his Westwood retirement. Duke's Mike Krzyzewski was also a popular choice during his spectacular, but now-aborted, postseason run (five consecutive Final Four visits) of the late '80s and early '90s. But throughout most of the Southland's Tobacco Road country—where basketball is undisputed king—there is no true rival to Carolina's Dean Smith nor has there ever been one for the past quarter-century.

Dean Smith's 879 career victories (three better than Rupp) are indisputably his living legacy, and his overhauling of Rupp's record will almost certainly remain Smith's crowning career achievement. But there have been many additional milestones and many other treasured accomplishments that flesh out the details of Dean Smith's ongoing North Carolina legend. So many, in fact, that the head spins during any attempts to order or even recount them all. In 1993, for one example, the most remarkable of all ACC mentors was tabbed as league Coach of the Year for a record eighth time. He has several times also been celebrated as National Coach of the Year (1977, 1979, 1982, 1993), and he has guided Team USA (1976) to the matchless glories of an Olympic gold-medal victory. He was already enshrined within the

College Basketball's Winningest Coaches

Coach	Schools (Years)	Record (Pct.)
Dean Smith	**North Carolina (1962–97)**	**879–254 (.776)**
Adolph Rupp	**Kentucky (1931–72)**	**876–190 (.822)**
Henry (Hank) Iba	NW Missouri, Colorado, Oklahoma A&M (1930–70)	767–338 (.694)
Ed Diddle	Western Kentucky (1923–64)	759–302 (.715)
Forrest (Phog) Allen	Kansas, Baker, Kansas (1906–56)	746–264 (.739)
Ray Meyer	DePaul (1943–84)	724–354 (.672)
Bobby Knight	Army, Indiana (1966–98)	720–270 (.727)
Norm Stewart	Northern Iowa, Missouri (1962–98)	711–366 (.660)
Don Haskins	Texas–El Paso (1962–98)	703–341 (.674)
Jerry Tarkanian	**Long Beach St., UNLV, Fresno St. (1969–98)**	**688–158 (.813)**
Lefty Driesell	Davidson, Maryland, James Madison (1961–97)	683–335 (.671)
Lou Henson	Hardin-Simmons, New Mexico St., Illinois (1963–98)	681–343 (.665)
Ralph Miller	Wichita, Iowa, Oregon St. (1952–89)	674–370 (.646)
John Wooden	**Indiana State, UCLA (1947–75)**	**664–162 (.804)**

Ranked by total victories; coaches with winning percentage over .775 in **boldface**

Naismith Memorial Basketball Hall of Fame (1982) with only two-thirds of his illustrious coaching career logged into the record books. And his ledger for relentless winning stretches far beyond the mere bulk of his nearly 900 total career victories. It includes unmatched marks for NCAA tournament victories, all-time and active career regular-season triumphs, active career winning percentage (before his retirement on the eve of the 1997–98 campaign), all-time NCAA tournament appearances, and just about every imaginable ACC standard for coaching victories currently on the books.

The most success-saturated coach in ACC history may still receive niggling criticisms in some quarters for failing to win a larger number of NCAA championships than he has (two, in 1982 and 1993, with three losses in the NCAA Finals and six in the Semifinals, including his final game against Arizona in 1997). For those jealous of success and those who can find nothing else to harp on regarding Smith's impeccable career, there is always the charge that he took his teams to endless rounds of postseason play but almost always failed to advance to the championship match. Or that he failed to bring home the coveted trophy once he did get his teams into the celebrated title bout. This accusation of underachievement has most often been based on the glaring fact that Smith, for years, always owned a team listed high among pretourney (even preseason) championship favorites (a condition quite obviously stemming from Carolina's annual ACC successes), yet only once previous to the 1990s delivered the ultimate NCAA prize. If the venerable Dean's presumed lack of Final Four successes says anything meaningful at all, it is perhaps merely a demonstration that this coaching paragon (unlike Wooden) has enjoyed far less tournament-time raw luck than he has demonstrated season-long proven skill. A 1993 national title certainly did something—although perhaps not quite enough—to allay the bulk of these mean-spirited and nit-picking criticisms.

None, however, can ever challenge Smith's sparkling record as a teacher and as a molder of basketball talents. Graduation rate for his players over three and a

The Roots of Success

Is it coincidence that the two all-time winningest coaches in college basketball can trace their successes back to the roots of basketball itself? Dean Smith of North Carolina and Adolph Rupp of Kentucky were both schooled in the college game at the University of Kansas by Phog Allen, who, at the time of his retirement in 1956, was the college game's winningest coach. Allen spent much time with James Naismith, the game's inventor, who was the original coach at Kansas and was a longtime professor after giving up his short-lived coaching duties. Another of Allen's students, Ralph Miller, is also on the list as the 11th-winningest NCAA coach.

Adolph Rupp (top row, far left) was coached by Phog Allen (second from left, second row) at Kansas where James Naismith (third from left, second row) was a professor. Also in this 1923 picture is Kansas All-American Paul Endacott (with ball).

© University of Kansas

© University of Kansas

After becoming a successful coach at Kentucky, Rupp planned to play Allen and Kansas in the dedication game of the new Allen Fieldhouse. The game never happened, however.

© University of North Carolina

Dean Smith's 879 career victories were his true living legacy, and his overhauling of Adolph Rupp's record for victories will remain his greatest career achievement. But North Carolina's biggest coaching legend was far more of an imposing monument to everything good about the sport of college basketball than even his matchless record might suggest.

half decades stands at 96.6 percent; four dozen of his top stars eventually played in either the NBA or ABA; 13 of his alumni became Olympians; and the "All-Dean Dream Team" of former UNC players Michael Jordan, Billy Cunningham, Sam Perkins, Phil Ford, and James Worthy can only be matched perhaps by a mythical "All-Westwood Wizard" starting-five culled from Wooden's 27 UCLA seasons (Alcindor, Walton, Sidney Wicks, Walt Hazzard, Gail Goodrich).

As Exhibit A on Smith's behalf there is, of course, the incredible list of top-of-the-line performers his program has regularly produced. The list of NBA stars and quality role players who are Carolina alumni is inarguably as extensive as that from any other single institution. Names such as Brad Daugherty, Hubert Davis, Rick Fox, Eric Montross, Sam Perkins, J. R. Reid, Clifford Rozier, Kenny Smith, Scott Williams, Joe Wolf, James Worthy, Jerry Stackhouse, Rasheed Wallace, Michael Jordan (to begin only with the most-recent NBA performers) fill up the Carolina alumni roster. Among them are candidates for the greatest pro player ever (Air Jordan), the best ACC backcourt man of all time (Phil Ford), and some of the NBA's and ABA's most relentless winners (Walter Davis and Worthy) and prolific scorers (Charlie Scott and Bob McAdoo). And as Exhibit B there is also the lengthy list of banquet-circuit honors earned by the No. 1 Tar Heel for his role as coach and educator of young men. There was the Gold Plate Award from the American Academy of Achievement, which honors leaders from all service fields and not just the worlds of sports and entertainment. There have been several honorary doctorate degrees from institutions of higher learning (Eastern College in Pennsylvania and Catawba College in North Carolina). There was also a Distinguished Service Citation (the highest individual award that institution bestows for humanistic activities) from Smith's own alma mater, the University of Kansas.

Dean Smith's preeminence can be largely established with a mere listing of NCAA records and ACC achievements. There is no one else, save perhaps Wooden, who can boast quite so otherworldly a record of on-court achievement. The Dean Smith legend has now been officially canonized, of course, with the overhauling of Adolph Rupp's once seemingly untouchable standard for all-time winning. In the end, however, coach Smith's most remarkable legacy on the basketball court will have to be his domination of regular-season and postseason ACC competitions that, in the end, now has stretched beyond a third of a century. The Carolina coaching legend ranks so far ahead of all past and current league mentors in games and titles won and tournament victories and trophies garnered, that there is no one else even in his class. And in all likelihood, it may just be that no one will ever quite be in his class again.

David Stern—Godfather of the Modern-Era NBA

If first NBA commissioner Maurice Podoloff deserves a lion's share of the credit for a fledgling circuit's survival during its formative seasons, so too does most-recent NBA commissioner David Stern merit the largest segment of the plaudits for authoring the league's runaway successes during the modern era stretching from Magic Johnson and Larry Bird to Michael Jordan and Shaquille O'Neal. Podoloff labored behind the scenes to construct an appropriate stage on which George Mikan pranced and strutted as the game's first superstar; similarly it has been Stern whose business acumen and promotional savvy have constructed a global market in which Michael Jordan has become basketball's greatest-ever paragon and pitchman. Podoloff painstakingly captured a legitimate American market for professional basketball; David Stern has thrust the NBA into living rooms in nearly every corner of the rest of the world.

Stern's impact on the NBA stretches back to the late '70s—several seasons before Magic and Bird arrived on the scene—and has, from first to last, involved the league's penchant for successful television deals. As the youngest partner in the law firm of Proskauer, Rose, Goetz, and Mendelsohn, which represents the NBA, Stern worked on a key mid-'70s case, which became known popularly as the "Oscar Robertson Settlement" and culminated a decade of benefits-related disputes between the league and its past and present players. The future league commissioner would also play a crucial role in negotiations that brought the 1976 merger of the four remaining ABA franchises into an expanded NBA. One reward for this service was appointment in September 1978 as the NBA's first general counsel. In his newfound role as league business lawyer Stern would subsequently negotiate a pioneering NBA-wide cable network contract with USA Cable, related follow-up agreements with both the USA Network and ESPN, and a landmark contract with Turner Broadcasting System, which provided 75 game broadcasts annually and a new audience for the league in 30 million cable-subscribing homes. Stern's climb up the NBA corporate ladder included the newly created position of executive vice president for business and legal affairs (1980) and the eventual expansion of that position to include full responsibility for marketing, broadcasting, public relations, and development of NBA properties and merchandise licensing.

Over the past decade and a half the NBA's fourth and most innovative commissioner (he succeeded Lawrence O'Brien to the post in November 1983) has guided the wildly successful professional circuit through some of its choppiest and most tempestuous seas, while at the same time negotiating some of its loftiest peaks. While his most visible impact has come in the realm of television coverage and the league's huge global growth in both popularity and prestige, his heavy hand has been felt equally in other organizational areas. He formulated a collective bargaining agreement—one establishing a team salary cap, while at the same time guaranteeing players a percentage of exploding NBA revenues—that is the basis for the NBA's current labor stability. He has pioneered with substance abuse policies that have addressed one of the most volatile issues of modern professional sports. The NBA's antidrug program provides counseling and assistance for players with drug abuse problems, yet also mandates drug testing and threatens lifetime bans for policy abuses. It first made headlines in January 1987, when Commissioner Stern suspended Houston Rockets players Lewis Lloyd and Mitchell Wiggens after both tested positive for cocaine use. Stern has also directed an expansion plan that has brought six new teams into the NBA fold (those in Miami, Minneapolis, Charlotte, Orlando, Vancouver, and Toronto), has converted the league into an international enterprise with two Canadian franchises, and perhaps has set the stage for future global expansion into Europe, Latin America, or Asia. At the heart of the league's nonstop growth under Stern, however, have been the lucrative television deals with USA, CBS, NBC, and TBS, which have led to dramatically increased league revenues. There has also, of course, been the internationalization of the league's television rights which has expanded the burgeoning audience for league games to more than 50 nations and counting.

In the long haul David Stern has loomed over the past decade and a half as the near-perfect prototype of the business-savvy modern-age sports executive. He has achieved media megadeals that have constructed rock-solid foundations for the most popular and successful sports-entertainment business operation on the national landscape. He has also, however, authored moves and fostered plans that have lessened any naive notion that American professional sports is anything less than a cutthroat bottom-line business venture, which is far more sensitive to owners' profit margins than it is to the fans' sense of tradition or vital competitive spirit. With Stern at the helm today's NBA seems only a step or two away from such inevitable anathemas as team uniforms bearing corporate logos, arena tickets far beyond the financial reach of most everyday fans, watered-down competitions among teams filled with spoiled prima-donna athletes lacking fundamental basketball skills, and an endless and near-meaningless regular season, which stretches from late September to mid-June in order to eliminate only a half dozen or so ball clubs from playoff contention. Under David Stern the NBA has gained its long-overdo economic maturity, while at the same time sacrificing forever its attractive veneer of sports-world innocence.

John Wooden—The Wizard of Westwood

Ask any fan—casual or diehard—to name the game's three greatest all-time coaches, and John Wooden, without fail, will always make the list, though numerous candidates will pop up beside him. Auerbach, Rupp, Meanwell, Lambert, Phog Allen, Dean Smith, Pat Riley, Hank Iba, even Bobby Knight, John Thompson, Ed Diddle, or Rick Pitino, will often be chosen, but few, if any, will leave Wooden off their highly selective first-blush list. And the result is not at all surprising, since Wooden's track record for domination of the sport is still quite without parallel. The championship record speaks quite eloquently for itself. There would be 10 NCAA championships won in only a dozen years, 7 without any interruption. There would be two of the most dominating three-year teams in the sport's annals (one 88–2 with three NCAA titles in its pocket, and the other 86–4 with the bulk of an 88-game unbeaten streak to its credit) and two of the most dominating big men ever. And there would be a winning percentage (.804 over a full 29-year career and .938 during the dozen-year career-closing dynasty) that is Wooden's legacy, even if his career ended a little too soon for him to challenge many of the sport's longevity milestones.

Often forgotten in the mix is the one-time stature of John Wooden, the college and professional player. Wooden is, in fact, the first and to date the only man ever to be voted into the Naismith Pantheon in Springfield in recognition of both his on-court and his sideline achievements. As a player "The India Rubber Man" (an epithet earned during Purdue playing days because the hustling backcourt star bounced off the floor so often in pursuit of loose balls) was first enshrined in 1960, four years before his first national title as UCLA coach. Wooden, the sideline genius, was again enshrined in 1972 near the end of his seven-year total domination of the sport's coaching profession. As a player he was one of the first backcourt

John Wooden's Winning UCLA Legacy

NCAA National Championships: 10 (1964, 1965, 1967, 1968, 1969, 1970, 1971, 1972, 1973, 1975).

NCAA Final Fours: 12 (with 21–3 record, including 3rd-Place Consolation Games). **NCAA Tournament Appearances:** 16 (47–10 record, including Consolations). **PCC (AAWU, PAC-8) Championships:** 18 (including several division titles).

National Coach of the Year Awards: 19 awards over six seasons (1964 UPI–USBWA, 1967 AP–UPI–USBWA, 1969 AP–UPI–NABC, 1970 AP–UPI–USBWA–NABC, 1972 AP–UPI–USBWA–NABC, 1973 AP–UPI–USBWA) Note: AP = Associated Press, UPI = United Press International, USBWA = United States Basketball Writers Association, NABC = National Association of Basketball Coaches.

Awards as Purdue University Player (1930–32): First-Team All-American in 1930, 1931, and 1932; Helms Foundation National Player of the Year in 1932

Consensus First-Team All-American Players Coached: 13, with 8 players (Walt Hazzard, 1964; Gail Goodrich, 1965; Lew Alcindor, 1967, 1968, 1969; Sidney Wicks, 1971; Henry Bibby, 1972; Bill Walton, 1972, 1973, 1974; Keith Wilkes, 1973, 1974; David Meyers, 1975)

National Player of the Year Award Winners Coached: Seven, with four players (Walt Hazzard, 1964; Lew Alcindor, 1967, 1969; Sidney Wicks, 1971; Bill Walton, 1972, 1973, 1974)

stars of basketball's just-dawning fast-break era while performing for Piggy Lambert at Purdue University. During three seasons as the Boilermakers' "floor guard" (playmaker), Wooden made All-American three times, while his team earned two Big Ten championship banners and was consensus pick as the nation's top team in 1932. As a successful high school coach for a dozen winters after Purdue graduation, the future Hall of Famer was also a part-time pro star with the NBL Indianapolis Kautskys, once making 138 consecutive free throws in league competition (the modern-day NBA record stands at a mere 84 in a row).

The UCLA career of coach Wooden is best remembered for the unparalleled teams he built around his two superb big men, Lew Alcindor (later Kareem Abdul-Jabbar) in the late '60s and Bill Walton in the early to mid-'70s. These were unquestionably two of the best—if not the best—multiseason teams in the history of the college sport. Between them they lost but a single clutch championship game (the defeat of Walton and company by N.C. State in the 1974 national semifinals) over a six-year cumulative span. But several other Wooden-led championship squads were perhaps even better reflections of the Hoosier native's unparalleled coaching genius. One was the 1964 team, his first national championship squad. Riding the All-American backcourt duo of Walt Hazzard and Gail Goodrich, the harassing strategy of a zone press defense, and the superb sixth-man play of Kenny Washington, Wooden's smallest and most surprising champion sprinted through 30 games unchallenged before drubbing Duke in the NCAA Finals. Another typical Wooden squad was his early '70s outfit sandwiched between the departure of Alcindor and the arrival of Walton. For two more championship seasons the Bruins parlayed a pair of superb forwards (Sidney Wicks and Curtis Rowe), a much-underrated transitional center (Steve Patterson), and a dynamic point guard (Henry Bibby)—plus plenty of hard work and coaching genius—into adequate replacements for the indomitable force that Alcindor had once provided and Walton would soon provide once again. These teams of 1964, 1970, and 1971 clinched the often-overlooked point that Wooden was foremost a guard-oriented mentor and also the arch-disciple of an uncompromising team concept of championship play.

A three-time All-American guard for Purdue (1930–32), John Wooden was first to be elected to the Naismith Memorial Basketball Hall of Fame as both a player and a coach.

© Purdue University

Johnny Wooden's success in manufacturing his own mythical persona as coach and inspirational leader was almost as complete as his decade-plus run at manufacturing NCAA championship victories. As other respected historians of the sport have already noted, the methods that coach Wooden piously espoused once he stood atop the sports world were not always exactly those methods that originally had gotten him there. The coach's advocacy of patience, faith, and self-control seemed always at odds with his own personal impatience with losing, his not-infrequent sideline temper-laced outbursts, and his constant scathing cajoling of officials and opponents during heated game action. The carefully crafted image was always more real than the man himself. And yet that image is easily the most luminous in the entire history of a sport seemingly always built upon larger-than-life personalities.

The UCLA teams that Wooden produced indeed reflected his own image—both real and perceived. These were teams noted for great discipline and a flawless work ethic; there would be no oversized egos or selfish concentration on personal statistics; even such giants as Alcindor and Walton would mold their games within a fixed team concept. And these were also teams that won relentlessly and against all odds. Wooden's Bruins rarely, if ever, defeated themselves. (In this sense they provided the starkest possible contrast with that other great dynasty outfit built by Adolph Rupp in Kentucky under the shadows of World War II.) Almost as rarely were they beaten by anyone else. During the three-year reign of Alcindor and the three-year epoch of Walton, it was almost never a question of whether or not Wooden's teams could repeat national championships; the issue was only if they would ever lose a single game.

John Wooden does not rank near the top of the heap in total career coaching victories, yet his 7 straight NCAA titles and 10 in 12 years is a standard for excellence almost certain never to be equalled.

Transcendental Graphics

It is a virtual certainty that college basketball will never see another dynasty like the one built in Westwood by Wooden, or also another uninterrupted run of national championships like the one UCLA and Wooden manufactured between 1967 and 1974. No other string in college or professional sports is quite as miraculous as the one pasted together by Wooden and his Bruins. Championship runs by the Yankees in baseball behind Casey Stengel or the Celtics in basketball under Auerbach hardly carry the same impact when it is recalled that pro teams (at least in an era before rampant free agency) kept winning rosters intact for a half dozen years or more, while college teams are forced to turn over personnel completely every few seasons. And Wooden's national titles were all won in tournament formats, under a single-elimination system that failed to allow for even a momentary slipup across all the many seasons.

John Wooden contributed mightily to basketball's legacy of near-mythical figures who loom above the sport—with either their landmark achievements or their innovative roles—and who have thus either redefined long-held standards for excellence or even reshaped entirely the very essence of the game. Like Phog Allen, Baron Rupp, Red Auerbach, Nat Holman, and a handful of others before him, Wooden would once again establish that basketball, above all other sports, was a game that left the largest openings for the individual athlete-hero or the clairvoyant pioneer. Allen arguably invented the profession of basketball coaching, Rupp and Auerbach first defined the standards for dynasty rule in the cage sport, but it was the Wizard of Westwood who fashioned the greatest winning legacy of them all.

Chapter Five

Peach Baskets to Jump Shots

Basketball's First Half-Century (1891–1954)

Basketball, from its immaculate conception with Dr. James Naismith in Springfield until the onset of the Second World War a half-century later, was a game dominated almost exclusively by coaches and officials, men, and a handful of women, whose off-court activities shaped the sport for those thousands of athletes who met its on-court challenges. It was during this pioneering period that the college sport held clear sway, and it was in the college version of the sport, in particular, that the major personalities and important innovators were almost without exception all coaches. There were a handful of playing stars of course. In the teens, Steinmetz built a small legend at Wisconsin, as did Schommer and Page at Chicago. Purdue boasted John Wooden in the early '30s, and coach Phog Allen won a mythical national championship at Kansas a decade earlier with the exploits of Paul Endacott. In the East there were famed athletes such as Vic Hanson who tried the cage game. The first approximation of a true star with national reputation, however, did not appear until Hank Luisetti unleashed his one-handed shooting for Stanford at the end of the 1930s. Before that, basketball heroes, where they existed, had only a regional appeal and even this paled compared to campus football idols. It was perhaps precisely the absence of recognizable individual stars that, more than anything, kept basketball out of the limelight as a major national sport.

The coaches were the recognizable figures of the game, and their pioneer roles in shaping the direction of the sport were often enough to earn national reputation among their contemporaries and a place in sports history as well. Phog Allen inherited the cage game from Naismith himself in Kansas, and over the next four decades became the "father of basketball coaching" in the shadow of the "father of basketball" who preceded him as Kansas coach. Allen's greatest impact was perhaps in his mentoring of two other future coaches who played for him as reserves—Adolph Rupp and Dean Smith, eventually the game's all-time winners. Doc Meanwell up in Wisconsin developed a style of play that molded the game's earliest decades as a major college sport. Soon, Meanwell had rivals such as Ward Lambert at Purdue, Doc Carlson at Pittsburgh, and Raycroft at Chicago. In the East there were Clair Bee at LIU, Lapchick with St. John's, and Holman at CCNY. And the West Coast—with "Slats" Gill at Oregon State, Hec Edmundson at Washington, Sam Barry at Southern Cal, Johnny Bunn at Stanford, Vadal Peterson at Utah, and Hank Iba at Oklahoma A&M—also had its coaching pioneers in the sport's formative period.

There were lesser lights among the stars of the professional barnstorming game, but without a lasting pro league on the national level, the play-for-pay version never became well enough established to sustain stars with national visibility. The closest approximation were a few early barnstormers like Barney Sedran and the half dozen regulars who made up the rosters of the greatest pre–World War II barnstorming teams—the Harlem Renaissance Five (Harlem Rens for short) and the Original Celtics of New York. The earlier-mentioned group featured names such as "Fats" Jenkins, Bill Yancey, and "Tarzan" Cooper. The latter and more familiar team boasted Holman, Lapchick, Johnny Beckman, and Dutch Dehnert among others. But even among these pioneering stars, the ones who maintained lasting reputations did so by becoming important and innovative college coaches. Holman carved out his legend at NYU, while Lapchick began teaching the game at St. John's. Both played crucial roles in two of the sport's defining moments—"the last great dribble debate" of 1927, and then the movement to eliminate the repetitious center jump 10 years later.

It was the one-handed shooters like Luisetti and Sailors, the jump-shooters like Fulks and Arizin, and the agile giants like Mikan and Kurland—all products of the years surrounding World War II—who finally brought basketball into its modern era and at the same time established the proficient scorer as a true basketball matinee idol. Once the game could potentially be dominated on any given night by the flashy or strong-armed performance of a single individual player, only then did basketball merit superstars and at the same time front-page status. Coaches never would relinquish their role at the game's controls entirely, but by midcentury they were regularly being squeezed from the limelight by the athletes they trained and then unleashed for public display. And with a new breed of cage stars, basketball was ready to compete squarely with baseball and football as a first-rate American sporting spectacle.

Clara Baer

Within a year of Naismith's invention of basketball in Springfield, women college students were playing the game with every bit the same enthusiasm as the men. Women's teams were reported on California campuses at Stanford and Berkeley by autumn 1892, and Senda Berenson had introduced the game to her female students at Smith College (a few miles from Springfield) by the following spring. A gaping gulf in the mode of play would soon, however, separate the male and female versions of Naismith's game and unfortunately keep them widely divided for more than three-quarters of a century. The cause of such a gulf in rules and playing styles was at least partially accidental and perhaps only secondarily a product of reigning notions during the late Victorian Age that it was neither socially appropriate nor physically possible for young women to enter into the strenuous sports, exercises, and games enjoyed by their male counterparts.

The consequential accident occurred in early 1895, when a young physical training teacher in New Orleans named Clara Baer wrote to Dr. Naismith for an explanation of the new recreational game she had been hearing about. Naismith was deluged with such inquiries from teachers in many sectors of the country and obliged Baer as he had others with a set of printed materials that included a diagram for the playing area and rules of organized play. Baer—to the likely dismay of generations of women basketballers to come—simply misread Naismith's diagram and assumed that players were strictly confined to one of three court areas sketched in Naismith's blueprint. Acting on her false impressions, Ms. Baer drew up rules for a drastically modified game she labeled as "Basquette" and introduced to her own students at Newcomb College (later a branch campus of Tulane University). Clara Baer's rules themselves were soon being widely disseminated to other campuses as part and parcel of the chaotic spread of Naismith's new game during its explosive first decade.

Don Barksdale

Chuck Cooper of the Boston Celtics may have received too much credit as a pioneer of basketball's integration. Don Barksdale, also a Boston Celtic, has never received enough. It has recently been clarified in the better histories of early NBA play that Cooper may have made headlines as the NBA's first draft selection from his race, but he did not earn a unique niche as the league's first-ever black man to step upon the court (Earl Lloyd was there first, and Dolly King pioneered even earlier in one of the two NBA forerunner leagues, the NBL). What has remained buried in the back pages of history is the list of pioneering achievements accomplished by UCLA's earliest basketball All-American, Don Barksdale. The 6'6" collegiate center and pro forward would cross the racial barriers of his sport first on several different occasions. In 1947 (ironically the same year that ex-UCLA basketballer Jackie Robinson integrated major-league baseball), he became the first African-American named to an NCAA consensus All-American squad. His appearance on the 1948 Olympic Basketball roster, alongside Bob Kurland of Oklahoma A&M and the "Fabulous Five" contingent from Kentucky, earned him distinction as the first black U.S. Olympic basketballer. And Barksdale was also the first black in an NBA All-Star Game when he suited up for the third classic played in 1953 at Fort Wayne. The sum total of Don Barksdale's pro career was two seasons with Baltimore and two more in the uniform of the pre–Bill Russell Boston Celtics. He scored less than 3,000 points, but he left a groundbreaking legacy that deserves far more recognition and credit than it has so far ever spawned.

Frank Basloe

Basketball's roots are not as purely American as popular lore would have us believe. The game's founding father was a Canadian, and it was in Canada that the first game was played in the inaugural season of the National Basketball Association, the game's professional showcase league. It was also a native-born Hungarian who did as much as anyone to spread the basketball gospel during the infant sport's first two decades. Budapest-born Frank Basloe grew up in Herkimer, New York, and embarked on a career of promoting the new game of basketball at the raw age of 16, only a dozen winters after Naismith had drawn up the first set of rules at the Springfield YMCA. Basloe's young team consisted of himself, Lew Wachter (eventual founder of the Troy Trojans), Jimmy Williamson, and two long-forgotten fellow Herkimer teenagers who each received $5 per game for their services. The first nine-game tour consisting of contests held in local dance halls and theaters around upper New York State earned the teenage entrepreneur $300 and launched a popular practice of mercenary barnstorming clubs that roamed the countryside in search of any game that could turn them a small profit. Over the next decade Basloe's teams continued to tour New York and New England, and in 1911 his club representing the National Guard of Herkimer gained a large measure of notoriety by snapping the 111-game winning streak of the most potent early barnstormers, the Buffalo Germans. In subsequent seasons Basloe's teams played under such names as Oswego Indians and Basloe's Globetrotters, expanded their routes to include the Great Lakes region and Upper Midwest states, compiled a reported 1,324 victories against only 127 defeats, and traveled close to 100,000 miles in just short of 20 seasons. His basketball road show would dominate the infant sport in those years before the emergence of the New York Original Celtics and Harlem Rens at the outset of the Roaring '20s. Basloe's 1952 autobiography, co-authored with Gordon Rohman and entitled *I Grew Up with Basketball*, was published a decade and a half before his death and today provides an invaluable, if highly personal, perspective on lost early days of professional basketball barnstorming.

Ralph Beard

Kentucky All-American backcourt ace Ralph Beard was brilliant in his years with Adolph Rupp, a potential Hall of Famer during his NBA cup of coffee, and as tragic a figure as the game of basketball has ever produced. In four postwar seasons with Kentucky, the 5'11" Louisville ace won three first-team All-American honors, was second-leading scorer (behind fellow All-American Alex Groza) on a repeat pair of NCAA championship teams that won 68 games and lost but 5, starred in two straight NIT title matches and hit the game-winning free throw in one, earned a 1948 Olympic gold medal, and crowned it all with a first-round NBA selection by the Chicago Stags. Regrettably, he also succumbed to temptation and accepted gamblers' monies to shave points during Kentucky's most heavily wagered games.

Beard's tragically short NBA tenure was not destined to unfold in Chicago with the Stags (a franchise which itself would soon fold), but rather was fated to open in Indianapolis, where he and four Kentucky teammates (including Groza) had been offered not only roster spots on a brand-new team in the spanking new league, but also a shared ownership of the franchise. With the Indianapolis Olympians of the first two NBA seasons (1950 and 1951), Ralph Beard was one of the league's stellar backcourt performers, earning All-Star selection and ranking among the leaders in assists and overall offense. Then on the very eve of his third season,

Ralph Beard

© University of Kentucky

the collegiate betting scandals broke wide open. Beard and Groza were taken into custody while watching a college all-star contest in Chicago, and two of the struggling league's brightest up-and-coming stars were quickly banned for life by Commissioner Maurice Podoloff and thus exiled into lifetime obscurity. Ralph Beard might well have been the near clone of Bob Cousy or Bobby Davies; instead, he was little more than a tragic recycling of baseball's Shoeless Joe Jackson.

Johnny Beckman

Professional basketball had few household names before Mikan and the explosive growth of the NBA in the century's middle decade. The few star players on the basketball barnstorming circuit that did make more than back-page news were almost all members of the New York–based Original Celtics who reached their peak of popularity throughout the '20s and early '30s. While the roster of this legendary team shifted with the seasons, there were half a dozen mainstays, each with his own narrow claim to fame. Dutch Dehnert is reputed to have pioneered the pivot play and is widely credited as the sole inventor of that strategy. Nat Holman first envisioned the man-to-man defensive switch and often receives dual credit with Dehnert for the first pivot play. Joe Lapchick was the game's first truly coordinated big man and specialized in controlling center taps, which were held after every basket. And Johnny Beckman was widely renowned as the greatest foul-shooter of his day. Standing well ahead of his time when it came to deadly accuracy from the free-throw stripe, Beckman averaged nearly 90 percent accuracy on his charity tosses, a considerable and valuable feat in the early '20s when many courts were surrounded by netting, preventing missed shots from going out-of-bounds. There were no backboards, and free-throw misses remained in play. Jim Furey's Original Celtics did not become dominant until the 1921 season, when Beckman, Dehnert, and Swede Grimstead first joined the team. In September 1959, Johnny Beckman joined former Celtics teammates Dehnert, Pete Barry, Holman, and Lapchick as the very first inductees into the Naismith Memorial Basketball Hall of Fame.

Clair Bee

The infamous 1951 college basketball point-shaving scandals produced no more tragic victim than legendary LIU coach Clair Bee, an altogether innocent bystander but a casualty nonetheless. Bee had been as responsible as any single individual for making college basketball of the '30s and '40s—at the very least New York City college basketball—one of America's most popular spectator-sport attractions. At the same time he was grooming and directing some of the finest college teams in the land at LIU, the indefatigable Bee was combining coaching with administrative and writing duties, authoring numerous instructional and fictional books, including the widely successful series of Chip Hilton juvenile novels. In his 20 seasons at Long Island University between 1931 and 1951, Bee's teams compiled a record of 357 victories against only 79 losses—the best performance of any program in the land at the time—and emerged as a national basketball powerhouse and showpiece of basketball's New York City mecca. In the mid-'30s Bee's Blackbirds won 43 in a row, a string ended by the memorable showdown with Hank Luisetti and Stanford in Madison Square Garden. LIU posted another undefeated season in 1939 and won the then-prestigious postseason NIT that season and again two years later. Coach Bee also pioneered with black athletes, including Dolly King (later the first black in the NBL) and All-American Sherman White. But it was the team on which White starred in 1950 and 1951 that sowed the seeds of Clair Bee's tragic and premature demise from college coaching circles. When the point-shaving scandals of 1951 broke around New York City basketball, several of Bee's players, including Sherm White, were culpable of wrongdoing. The university temporarily dropped its basketball program, and a devastated Bee resigned from his post. He would coach briefly with the NBA Baltimore Bullets in 1953 and 1954, but after the heartbreaking events at LIU, Bee would devote most of the remainder of his professional life to conducting basketball clinics and camps and continuing his writing career. In the latter capacity Clair Bee would earlier contribute an introduction to the only textbook on the sport ever written by the game's inventor, Dr. James Naismith.

Senda Berenson (Abbott)

Women's basketball as a formal collegiate and scholastic sport has spent the better part of the century catching up with what long remained a more streamlined, athletic, and visually exciting version played by the boys and men. Most of the blame can be placed squarely on the shoulders of Smith College physical education director Senda Berenson, one of the pioneers of organized female play who set up teams and contests at her own Northampton (Massachusetts) campus after communication with Naismith about the new form of recreation as early as March 1893. Controversy surrounded female competitions during the first several winters following Naismith's invention, after an early misunderstanding of the rules for play (initiated at first by Clara Baer, physical education administrator at Newcomb College in New Orleans) left some women's competitions using stationary players who were restricted to prescribed areas of the court. The slower women's version played in places such as Smith, Bryn Mawr, and Vasser—allowing no player movement or ball stealing, and permitting only three players at one end of the court to shoot the ball—also fed a popular belief (especially among women's physical training instructors such as Berenson and Clara Baer) that standard play was far too rough and dangerous for lady athletes.

The issue came to a head in 1899 when a four-woman committee headed by Berenson drew up standardized women's rules that indeed forbade ball stealing, outlawed holding the ball for more than three seconds, and banned players from crossing out of their assigned areas on the floor. In the view of Springfield College athletic director Luther Gulick (one shared by many players and fans for decades to come), such women's restrictions "seriously handicapped the most skillful, interesting, and valuable plays of the game." A certain result of the actions by Berenson and her committee was that women's college and high school play was everywhere restricted to a dull and uninspired (as well as unathletic and unartistic) mode of play from which it would not recover until collegiate women's sports were drastically streamlined in the face of a growing feminist movement in the early 1970s.

Ernest Blood

Wooden's Bill Walton–led team captured 88 consecutive games; Phil Woolpert with Bill Russell and K. C. Jones at San Francisco piled up 60 uninterrupted wins; Clair Bee and LIU had a 43-game string on the line before Luisetti came along, and Honey Russell duplicated that feat a few seasons later at Seton Hall. None even comes close to the mark for endless winning posted between December 17, 1919, and February 6, 1925, by Ernest Blood and his Passaic (New Jersey) High School ball clubs today known as "The Wonder Teams." No evidence exists for a longer winning skein anywhere in roundball history, at least at the schoolboy, college, or professional levels. Blood actually earned a 200–1 composite record over his total nine-year tenure with Passaic High and was on board for all but the final dozen games of the incredible winning streak. Over the stretch his teams also picked up seven state championships, won by competing against high school, college, and local amateur opponents. One key to Blood's phenomenal success was his forward-looking approach to using wide-open and freelancing offenses. His players employed hooks and one-handers for shooting long before these then-novel techniques were widely accepted or even tolerated by other coaches.

Benny Borgmann

One of the best-known names of basketball's barnstorming epoch was a multisport athlete, who actually spent the largest part of his career in professional baseball as a minor-league player, coach, manager, and longtime big-league talent scout. It was Benny Borgmann's own insistence throughout his minor-league playing days that he be allowed to report late for spring training, at the conclusion of the basketball season, that probably cost him a chance at making the majors with either the Boston Red Sox (he played in their farm system from 1923 to 1931) or later the St. Louis Cardinals (who he also served as a minor-league manager throughout the '40s, '50s, and early '60s). His barnstorming basketball career took the 5'8" offensive whiz to stops with such teams as the Kingston Colonels (New York State League), Fort Wayne Hoosiers (ABL), Paterson Legionnaires (Metropolitan League), Paterson Whirlwinds (ABL), Chicago Bruins (ABL), and the famed New York Original Celtics (when they operated as the Brooklyn Celtics of the ABL during the 1926–27 season only). While Borgmann's induction into the Naismith Hall of Fame was based, in large part, on his membership with the Original Celtics, the bulk of his career was spent elsewhere and featured numerous offensive landmarks, including: NYSL scoring leader in 1923, star of the 1924 Kingston Colonels team which claimed a world championship by defeating the Original Celtics,

ABL scoring leader with Fort Wayne in 1927 and then again in 1929, the third-time ABL point-making champion with Paterson in 1930. The well-traveled star closed his barnstorming basketball days in the late '30s with the Brooklyn Americans, Newark Mules, and New Britain (Connecticut) Mules, and was a fourth-time ABL scoring pacesetter at the advanced age of 38. Borgmann's own estimate is that his playing career included 3,000 pro basketball games and more than 2,000 baseball contests, and he did not retire from baseball as an active scout (with the Oakland A's) until after his 75th birthday.

Carl Braun

Wilt Chamberlain was not the first pro rookie to post eye-popping league scoring records. Twenty-year-old Carl Braun of the New York Knicks poured in 47 points early in the 1947–48 campaign for a single-game BAA record that stood only until Joe Fulks of the Philadelphia Warriors pushed scoring into the stratosphere with an incredible 63 points in February 1949. The 6'5" backcourt set-shot specialist had starred at Colgate University along with Ernie Vandeweghe, before dropping out of school to sign a pro baseball contract with the World Champion New York Yankees. An arm injury quickly ended Braun's minor-league pitching prospects, but his basketball career blossomed throughout the late '40s and the entire decade of the 1950s. He was the Knicks' scoring pacesetter in each of his first seven BAA-NBA seasons (four times in the league's top 10) yet never averaged more than 16.5 in any season. Late in his career the five-time all-star's role changed to that of a playmaker, and three times he ranked among the NBA's top 10 in assists. Braun also served briefly as a player-coach with New York before closing his 13-season NBA sojourn as a reserve with the 1962 champion Boston Celtics.

Frank Brian

While a handful of grand marquee stars like Mikan, Fulks, Schayes, Alex Groza, and Bobby McDermott dominated the first few postwar pro basketball seasons, there were numerous blue-collar players who labored in the trenches to win ball games and thrill hometown fans. In later eras they would have been notable stars, but in basketball's infancy they played mostly in the shadows. None was any more valuable than 6'1" guard-forward Frankie Brian, a hefty tough-as-nails athlete who performed admirably for the Anderson Packers, Tri-Cities Blackhawks, and Fort Wayne Pistons of the NBL and later the NBA. A college star at LSU a half decade before Bob Pettit, Brian poured in nearly 6,700 pro points and averaged better than a dozen for 561 career games. This was modest scoring by today's standards, yet productive enough to trail only Mikan and Alex Groza (with a 17.8 average) in the first NBA season of 1949–50. A year later only Mikan, Groza, Boston's Ed Macauley, and jump-shooting Joe Fulks outpointed the slick and versatile Brian, who ranked in the league's top 10 in scoring the following season as well. During the 1990s the league's No. 3 scorer (say Charles Barkley or David Robinson or Scottie Pippen) would be an instant multimillionaire and fixture as television endorsement celebrity; in the early 1950s Frankie Brian, like most of his fellow NBA players, worked for little more than laborer's wages and occasional hometown headlines buried deep in the back pages of the sporting news.

Walter A. Brown

The man who was co-owner and president of the Boston Celtics during their remarkable dynasty seasons and also one of the original founders (along with other National/American Hockey League arena owners) of the Basketball Association of America, which soon became the NBA, was, in addition, one of the major individual influences on the direction of pro basketball's boom-industry development during the two rapid-growth decades immediately following World War II. For a handful of the game's innovators, one pure inspiration would constitute a lifetime's work. One example of this narrowness of inventive genius would be Danny Biasone with his shot-clock concept, and another would be James Naismith himself, with his peach baskets and his indoor noncontact game. Walter Brown, on the other hand, had at least four such moments of pure inspiration and each one radically altered the pro basketball scene.

It was Brown, first off, who had conceived the original idea for a true national professional league that could pack arenas in larger cities and exploit the national hunger for high-quality pro sports entertainment. The fledgling league into which he dragged such fellow sports moguls as Ned Irish in New York, Al Sutphin in Cleveland, Lou Pieri in Providence, and Mike Uline in Washington would over only a handful of winters evolve as the infant NBA. Secondly, Brown brought Arnold "Red" Auerbach to Boston as his coach for the Boston Celtics team he owned and directed. Third, he boldly drafted the first black player into the NBA with his second-round 1950 pick of Duquesne's Chuck Cooper (after bypassing local favorite Bob Cousy in the first round to grab Bowling Green center Charlie Share). And finally, as if all his earlier strokes of pure genius were not already quite enough, Walter Brown also inaugurated the institution known as the NBA All-Star Game. Attracted to the concept dreamed up by NBA publicist Haskell Cohen, the risk-loving Boston owner gambled his reputation and much of his team's thin coffers by agreeing to host and cover all expenses for the first All-Star event to be staged at Boston Garden in March 1951. Walter Brown also put into place basketball's greatest-ever dynasty team consisting mainly of Cousy (eventually acquired in a special dispersal draft from the defunct Chicago Stags), Russell, Sharman, Heinsohn, Frank Ramsey, K. C. Jones, and Sam Jones, although this last achievement was, perhaps more than anything else, the doing of his hand-picked coach, Red Auerbach.

Ernie Calverley

If Ernie Calverley is remembered by the nation's few aficionados of early basketball history, it is likely because of a single sensational shot uncorked in the 1946 NIT. That rare moment would perhaps be reason enough. But the talented and diminutive guard, who starred at Rhode Island State (now the University of Rhode Island) and with the BAA Providence Steamrollers, was noteworthy for far more than that one miraculous heave of the basketball, which to this day remains the most sensational in college basketball postseason history. Calverley's moments in the sun came with two games of the 1946 NIT. In the opening-round encounter with Bowling Green the Rhode Island ace uncorked his 58-foot bomb with only seconds remaining to tie the contest and force overtime. In the championship match with Kentucky he performed brilliantly against Wildcats backcourt ace Ralph Beard, although the game and the tournament went to Kentucky on Beard's last-minute foul shot. Although Calverley's performances were not enough to bring victory to coach Frank Keaney's Rams, they were enough to earn tournament MVP accolades. But Ernie Calverley had already made his substantial mark on the college basketball world two seasons earlier. His 26.7 scoring average paced the nation in 1944 and established a national record that stood for seven years. The figure is still a school single-season record and as such remains the longest-standing NCAA season's scoring mark on record. To further his résumé, Calverley became the first collegian to record at least 45 points twice in the same season with 48 logged versus Northwestern and 45 poured home against Maine.

Henry "Doc" Carlson

Doc Carlson of Pittsburgh stands alongside Doc Meanwell (Wisconsin), Phog Allen (Kansas), and Piggy Lambert (Purdue) when it comes to the most imposing giants from the 1930s-era college coaching ranks. While Meanwell pioneered tactical offenses based on a short-passing game, and while Lambert fine-tuned an early prototype of the fast break, Carlson developed the first true patterned offense, one he called his "Figure 8" or "continuity" and began using in the mid- and late '20s. The style was simple enough in concept; it involved three men moving in a figure eight shape with their two teammates remaining stationary. It was a weapon that broke down enemy defenses and led to easy layup baskets with enough regularity to be widely copied by other schools that had been its victims. It also generated enough victories for Carlson to guide his team through the entire 27-game 1927 season unbeaten and thus to claim an unofficial national championship. Other groundbreaking achievements by this coach, who held a medical degree, involved taking his team on the first-ever western barnstorming swing by an eastern college and establishing the first formal basketball clinics at the University of Pittsburgh. It was the pioneering western odyssey in 1932, however, which may well have been Carlson's biggest contribution. Victories on that memorable junket over powerhouse teams such as Colorado and Stanford went a long way to restoring the then-sagging reputation of East Coast college basketball.

Everett Case

No one merits any more individual credit for the birth and prosperity of college basketball's most successful conference—the ACC—than does North Carolina State coaching legend Everett Case. A native of Indiana and owner of a previous legend in that state's high school basketball annals, Case arrived in Raleigh when N.C. State was still a member of the old Southern Conference and not much of a factor in the annual basketball wars that entertained fans of the Deep South in the region already known as Tobacco Road. Before he retired a couple of decades later, Ev

Case had put not only the school, but indeed the entire region and the new conference that was its showcase, squarely on the nation's basketball map.

It is not an exaggeration to claim that Indiana's native son, Everett Case, single-handedly transformed North Carolina State into a legitimate national basketball dynasty. It would also hardly be an overstatement to boast that it was Ev Case alone who put Naismith's wintertime sport squarely on the map everywhere along Tobacco Road. The one-time Indiana high school coaching legend worked his transformational magic during a postwar era when cage play had already reached a zenith of popularity in the Northeast, Midwest, and West Coast regions of the nation. Everett Case, in reality, did nearly as much to claim the Southland for basketball with his decade of Wolfpack domination during the final seasons of the expansive Southern Conference as Adolph Rupp simultaneously did over at Kentucky with his own reign of terror around the Southeastern Conference.

Case made his lasting mark with an initial string of triumphs at the close of the Southern Conference era, which amounted to a total stranglehold on the league's regular and postseason trophies. During his first seven seasons he won both titles five times and at least one of them every time out of the gate. In the '50s he would quickly extend his domination into the new venture known as the Atlantic Coast Conference without skipping a beat. Sparked by its pair of repeat All-Americans, Dick Dickey and Sam Ranzino, the Wolfpack ran off its stretch of six regular-season Southern Conference titles in seven years (losing only in 1952) and an equal number of conference tournament titles over the same span (dropping a single title match to Wake Forest in the final pre-ACC season). Over these same first seven seasons under Case, the victory total never dropped lower than 24 and once reached as high as 30. Entry into the new ACC alignment saw nothing in the way of immediate drop-off, as Case's teams, with new All-American star Ronnie Shavlik, captured all three inaugural ACC postseason affairs and two of the first three regular-season banners. It was the best 10-year stretch in school history and one that put N.C. State smack at the heart of the collegiate basketball world.

The legacy of Everett Case in the annals of Tobacco Road basketball rests upon more than a mere string of Southern Conference and ACC regular-season and postseason triumphs. There was also the state-of-the-art Reynolds Arena, which opened its doors in 1949, for which Case was the spiritual architect, and which soon became the regular showcase home for ACC postseason tournament play. The "House that Case Built" was, of course, Wolfpack-friendly and would also soon be site to four ACC tournament titles for the home team. And there was also the midseason holiday tournament known as the Dixie Classic, another brainchild of Ev Case, that was as responsible as anything else for putting Tobacco Road basketball fever on the national map. Reynolds Coliseum would, soon after its opening, become regular host to the Dixie Classic, an event launched in 1949 which pitted the "Big Four" of State, Duke, Wake Forest, and North Carolina against four top-ranked teams drawn from other sectors of the nation. The popular December affair would remain a decade-long showcase for the strength of the local Carolina teams (especially Case's own Wolfpack squads) and would not be discontinued until the 1961 reforms that followed a second outbreak of nationwide collegiate point-shaving scandals.

Al Cervi

One strategy implemented by founders of the Basketball Association of America in 1946 was to compete with the established National Basketball League by drawing on the popularity of the college game (especially in the big East Coast cities of New York, Boston, Washington, and Philadelphia) by recruiting graduating college standouts with marquee names. The league's first season quickly demonstrated, however, that traditional styles of play practiced by the already experienced and game-hardened pros (physical aggressiveness, rough fouling, intimidation on defense, slow deliberate offense) were more effective for game winning than a more wide-open and aesthetic college style. College hotshots who didn't adapt to the rough-and-tumble pro style weren't worth much in a league (two leagues counting the NBL) filled with savvy and battle-weary itinerant pros, many of whom had little or no college playing experience, but years of bangs and bruises earned on military service teams or during barnstorming professional play.

One of the latter was rugged 5'11" high school dropout Al "Digger" Cervi, who debuted briefly in the NBL with the Buffalo Bisons during the league's first season of 1938, then returned in postwar years to star as an all-purpose backcourt ace, team captain, and eventual player-coach with both the NBL Rochester Royals and NBL-NBA Syracuse Nationals. Before his career would wind down in the mid-'50s, Al Cervi would become not only one of the toughest competitors in NBA annals but also the top player-coach of all time. Cervi's earliest accolades included All-NBL first-team selection through all three seasons of NBL-BAA rivalry, selection as the NBL's best defensive player, consistent ranking among the top NBL scorers, and a widespread reputation as an unmatched clutch performer. Cervi was a regular playmaker on the Rochester team that captured an NBL title in 1946; the following season his club lost to Mikan and the Chicago American Gears in the championship playoffs, yet Cervi was the league's top point-maker (Mikan led in scoring average) and also the MVP. Hired away by Syracuse as a player-coach in 1948, Cervi enjoyed considerable coaching success throughout his final five NBA playing seasons. In his first year with additional bench responsibilities, he scored a career-high 695 points (12.2 points per game) and brought his team home second in the Eastern Division to garner Coach of the Year honors. A year later the Nats posted the best regular-season mark (51–13) in the newly constituted NBA and lost out in the championship round to Mikan's Lakers. Cervi also coached the East All-Stars to victory in the second NBA All-Star Game at Boston in 1952.

The high point of Al Cervi's spectacular career came two years after his retirement as an active player, when his 1955 Syracuse team starring Dolph Schayes finally broke the Lakers' stranglehold on the league and earned an NBA championship banner during a dramatic, hard-fought seven-game series with Fred Zollner's Fort Wayne Pistons. Additional NBA Coach of the Year honors were garnered in 1952 (when Syracuse lost to New York in the Eastern Division Finals) and 1955 (the championship season). Cervi's final NBA coaching record was a most-impressive 366–264, including three division titles and one league championship. But Al Cervi's lasting claim to fame indisputably remains the fact that his 266–127 record as an NBA player-coach is, by wide margin, the best in league history and may well also be the best in all of basketball history.

Nat "Sweetwater" Clifton

One of the first black athletes to perform in the NBA, Sweetwater Clifton owns a major piece of basketball history, though not necessarily the piece sometimes assigned to him. The facts surrounding NBA integration have long been a jumble of error and oversight (to an even greater extent than the facts surrounding Jackie Robinson's debut in major-league baseball as the first 20th-century African-American, but not the first nonwhite or first professional ballplaying Negro). Ofttimes, Nat Clifton is assigned the honor of crossing the NBA color line. More frequently, Boston's Chuck Cooper is tabbed as the first black pro basketballer to appear, but few standard histories mention Earl Lloyd, who most merits the honor. The true facts are that Duquesne's Cooper was selected in the 1950 NBA lottery by Walter Brown and the Celtics as the first African-American drafted by an NBA ball club. Later the same day Lloyd, out of West Virginia State, was selected by the Washington Capitols. Before either had reached a deal with his new team, the New York Knicks inked Clifton, property of the Harlem Globetrotters, as the first NBA black ballplayer to sign an official contract. The technicality of "first in uniform" clearly belongs, however, to Earl Lloyd, whose Washington team opened the season two nights before either Boston or New York. Overlooked in all this historical minutiae is the fact that the NBA's direct ancestor, the National Basketball League, had already featured a number of black ballplayers in the final seasons of the 1940s, including LIU star Dolly King with the Rochester Royals in 1947 and a whole team of Dayton Rens (including again King, future major-league baseballer George Crowe, and ex-Rens star Pop Gates) in 1949.

For his own part Sweetwater Clifton did enjoy the most on-court success among the handful of pre-1951 NBA-NBL racial pioneers. As a 28-year-old rookie the 6'8" forward was an important role player on the 1951 Knicks team that made the first of three straight appearances in the NBA Finals. His eight-season pro career was played out almost entirely with New York (he played his final season with the Detroit Pistons) and included 5,444 points, 544 games, and a perfect 10.0 scoring average. Nat Clifton also appeared in one NBA All-Star Game in 1957, scoring eight points and pulling down 11 rebounds. He was not the first black to appear in the league classic, however, as Don Barksdale (1953) of the Boston Celtics—as well as Ray Felix (1954) of Baltimore and Maurice Stokes (1956) of Rochester—had already beaten him there by several seasons.

Charles "Tarzan" Cooper

While big-man pivot play didn't really begin in the college arenas until the arrival of agile behemoths like Bob Kurland and George Mikan in the World War II years, it had its handful of ancestors among the barnstorming pros a decade earlier with the likes of Original Celtics star Joe Lapchick and New York Rens headliner Charles "Tarzan" Cooper. The 6'4" Cooper performed 11 years with the legendary Rens (1929 through 1939), during a period when that invincible basketball road show won more than 1,300 games and lost barely 200, and in the process, earned a reputation that would gain Naismith Hall of Fame recognition for the team's entire starting five. Cooper was a towering figure in his era, and the Rens' offense during his tenure consisted largely of long-range shots by smaller players such as Fats Jenkins, Bruiser Saitch, and Bill Yancey, with Cooper hovering near the basket to toss back or tap in any misses. Contemporary Hall of Fame center Joe Lapchick, who frequently played against the Renaissance Five with the rival Original Celtics, called the black giant the finest inside player he had ever seen. Late in his career Cooper would enjoy one final moment of glory while leading a second team, the Washington Bears, to the 1943 world's professional title. But his identity forever remains entwined with that of teammates Saitch, Jenkins, Yancey, Wee Willie Smith, Pappy Ricks, and Casey Holt as a central member of the Harlem Renaissance "Magnificent Seven"—the most storied outfit of early basketball's romantic, if hardscrabble, barnstorming era.

Chuck Cooper

Jackie Robinson's singular and universally acknowledged credit for integrating major-league baseball is improperly attributed only on a technicality—or at worst a small string of such technicalities. Robinson was indeed the first 20th-century African-American to set foot in the majors; he was not, of course—despite popular mythology—the first-ever big-league black man (Fleetwood Walker and several others had already been there in the 19th century), nor for that matter, the first present-century major-league man of color (several Cubans, Venezuelans, and Puerto Ricans can lay claim to this latter distinction).

When it comes to NBA integration, however, one man has wrongly received all the credit, albeit credit that has had little popular hold on the consciousness of even the most rabid sports fans. What happened in the NBA in the early '50s was about as noteworthy as peasant uprisings in Outer Mongolia. Most formal and informal NBA histories point to Chuck Cooper of Duquesne University as the first black to set foot inside the NBA, based on the bold move of Boston owner Walter Brown in plucking Cooper out of the April 1950 college draft. The actual facts are that Cooper was indeed the first man of his race to be formally drafted by an NBA team, followed closely by Earl Lloyd of West Virginia State on the same day. What weakens Cooper's case as the true first NBA black, however, are all of the following related events and circumstances.

First and foremost, the NBA had already experienced occasional blacks several seasons earlier, even if it wasn't yet calling itself the NBA. In at least one of the two leagues that were to become the NBA after the 1950 merger, blacks had already appeared on several occasions. Dolly King (Rochester Royals) and Pop Gates (Tri-Cities Blackhawks) together broke racial boundaries in the NBL as early as 1947, the exact year that baseball welcomed Robinson and basketball experienced its first "Negro" collegiate All-American in Don Barksdale of UCLA. The same league had also already had a contingent of other blacks (on the 1943 roster of the Chicago Studebakers), but this was well before the 1947 season, usually considered the launching year for the NBA (thus allowing a Golden Anniversary season in 1997). Also, a whole team of blacks would play under the banner of the Dayton Rens in the NBL season of 1949, that league's final year before NBA merger. Finally, while Cooper was first to be drafted, minutes ahead of Lloyd, Lloyd was the first actually to play in an NBA regular-season game. And Sweetwater Clifton of the Harlem Globetrotters had signed a contract with the New York Knicks before either Lloyd or Cooper had "officially" joined the league with his own contract signing. These latter two players—Earl Lloyd and Nat Clifton—thus deserve equal credit alongside Chuck Cooper as the NBA's recognized troika of earliest black pioneers.

Howie Dallmar

Only one player can boast of winning an NCAA Final Four MVP trophy with one school and then later earning All-American honors with yet another institution. Howie Dallmar's highly unusual list of accomplishments doesn't stop there, however. The star player at both Stanford and Penn and longtime Stanford coach was also the only NCAA MVP to later coach a school other than his alma mater to the postseason playoffs (he took his second school, Penn, to the tourney in 1953, but never made it back during 21 years as headman at Stanford, thanks mainly to the presence of John Wooden at UCLA). The list of rare accomplishments continues: he played with the BAA Philadelphia Warriors in 1949 while at the same time coaching collegiately at Penn (Bob Davies pulled off the same rare double with the Rochester Royals and Seton Hall University two seasons earlier). And to clinch his uniqueness, Dallmar was the prototype of the oversized assist-dishing guard (at 6'4", which outstripped some centers of his era) three decades before Earvin "Magic" Johnson.

Dallmar earned his first spot in history when his game-high 15 points and outstanding floor game allowed Stanford to overcome the loss of flu-stricken leading scorer and future pro star Jim Pollard to defeat Dartmouth 53–38 in the 1942 NCAA championship match. When the navy shipped the ex-Stanford star to Philadelphia to attend flight-training school at the end of World War II, Dallmar was able to enroll at Penn to complete both his undergraduate course and collegiate basketball eligibility, earning a consensus All-American nod in 1945. His subsequent pro career, which lasted only three BAA seasons with the Philadelphia Warriors, was filled as well with distinction. Dallmar was a league first-team selection and assists leader in 1948 with the defending BAA champions one season before pulling off his unique playing-coaching double with the city's pro team and its Ivy League college contingent.

Irv Dambrot

Stellar sophomore forward Ed Warner earned one of the two postseason MVP Awards (NIT) during CCNY's improbable double-championship feat of 1950, while durable senior Irv Dambrot walked off with the other (NCAA). In the Bradley-CCNY rematch for the NCAA trophy Dambrot was not only Nat Holman's leading scorer with 15 (he had trailed Warner and Ed Roman in scoring average during the season), but also a last-minute hero as he stripped the ball from Bradley All-American Gene Melchiorre in the closing seconds and looped a long pass downcourt to Norm Mager for the basket that sealed victory. There would soon transpire, of course, the shocking developments that unfolded during the year following CCNY's emergence at the top of the college basketball world and worked to assure for Irv Dambrot and Ed Warner far different roles in the pages of history. Despite his territorial draft selection by the hometown Knickerbockers, Dambrot was simply not talented enough to play his way onto any NBA roster. Only a junior the following season, Warner, by contrast, remained a highly touted pro prospect until the college betting scandals breaking in midseason 1951 implicated Holman's two top scorers (Warner and Ed Roman) and wiped out all dreams of future NBA glories.

Bob Davies

Today we remember Bob Cousy as basketball's original ballhandling wizard, yet during the same college and NBA decade (1940 through 1950), Bob Davies of Seton Hall University and the NBA Rochester Royals wasn't far behind—if he even trailed Cousy at all. Davies' collegiate career was certainly a shade or two more distinguished than Cousy's, even if the latter was fortunate enough to play on an NCAA title team and the former was not. Davies was brilliant at Seton Hall and also innovative in his style of play. Twice he was an All-American, twice team captain, three times team MVP. He also led the Honey Russell–coached Pirates to 43 straight victories and an NIT appearance and was named MVP of the 1942 College All-Star Game staged in Chicago. Even before Cousy owned a near-identical label, Davies had been dubbed "The Harrisburg Houdini" on account of his sophisticated dribbling and his heretofore unseen behind-the-back maneuvers.

At the pro level the difference between basketball's two greatest ball handlers of the wartime and postwar eras was largely in the supporting cast. Cousy was blessed with a super troupe of Boston teammates—Russell, Heinsohn, Sharman, and Frank Ramsey for starters. But the team Davies played with in Rochester wasn't weak either and grabbed an NBL crown in 1946 and an early NBA title in 1951. Davies' pro career was thus only a step or two behind his collegiate days. Among other honors and achievements were eight All-Star selections, BAA assists champ (1949), an NBL MVP (1947), and a postcareer selection to the prestigious NBA Silver Anniversary Team announced in 1970. Most

Bob Davies,
Seton Hall University

Transcendental Graphics

remarkable of all was the "double" he pulled off in 1947 by playing full-time with Rochester in the NBL, while at the same time coaching his alma mater to a stellar 24–3 record on the college hardwoods. Bob Davies' landmark contribution will likely always be his widely copied behind-the-back dribble. But as if this were not enough, the handsome and hardworking athlete also served as the real-life role model for Clair Bee's fictional sports hero, Chip Hilton. Like Chip, after all, Bob Davies was truly "the All-American boy" during an era when that squeaky-clean image still had all its considerable glitter.

Dutch Dehnert

If the Original Celtics of New York City were the most popular road show of barn-storming basketball in the "Roaring '20s" era, then Dutch Dehnert was the prime drawing card. Many handbills advertising local appearances of the famed troupe (such as one printed in 1928 for a Celtics match in the Columbus, Ohio, Civic Center versus the Rochester Ebers, Western New York League champs) carried billings such as the following: "See The Original Pivot Play Starring The One and Only 'Dutch' Dehnert!" Standing a then-imposing 6'1" and weighing well over 200 pounds, the athletic Dehnert boasted considerable speed, unparalleled ballhandling skills, clever passing skills, and tenacious defensive efforts. Through the early '30s when the Celtics played briefly in the ill-fated American Basketball League, the biggest Celtics star remained one of the game's best-known and top-paid performers; and by career's end, he had participated in 1,900 victories in a Celtics uniform alone. But it was the invention of the "pivot play" as a new offensive strategy that remained Dehnert's calling card with future generations. The genesis of Dehnert's innovation is usually placed in Chattanooga, Tennessee, during either the 1924 or 1925 season, though some legends cite Rochester (New York) or Jacksonville (Florida) as the locale and place the moment at various points in the early '20s.

The essence of the legend is that the innovative Celtics, always searching for ways to advance their winning edge, were troubled by a host team's standing guard (a popular strategy of the day) who blocked the center of the foul lane and prevented drives to the basket. Dehnert reputedly foiled the strategy by taking a position in front of the pesky opponent, blocking him from defending the Celtics' passing lanes. Dehnert, who backed into the defender, accepted a pass from Nat Holman or perhaps Johnny Beckman, then passed back to one or the other as he streaked past the befuddled defender who was now screened by Dehnert's positioning. The practice was so effective it became an immediate team calling card and a major gate attraction when executed to perfection by its original practitioners. It was also so widely adopted by teams everywhere that, in short order, it was one of basketball's staple patterns of offense.

Ed Diddle

Ray Meyer (DePaul, 1943 through 1984) had George Mikan looming at one end of his seemingly interminable coaching career and Mark Aguirre and Terry Cummings waiting at the other end, with 20 NCAA tournament appearances and 12 NIT visits strung across the four decades that intervened. Ed Diddle (Western Kentucky, 1923 through 1964) nurtured two lesser-known All-Americans (Jim McDaniels and Clem Haskins) and visited the postseason dances far less frequently (two NCAAs and eight NITs). Yet together they share one of the most noteworthy landmarks in college basketball coaching annals—42 consecutive seasons as headman with the same school. And with all their longevity, the two Hall of Famers posted almost identical records for relentless success. Diddle's 759–302 (.715) lifetime mark leaves him fourth on the all-time list (first at the time of his retirement, with Rupp nipping at his heels), behind only Dean Smith, Adolph Rupp, and Hank Iba. Meyer at 724–354 (.672) today still stands sixth.

Robert Douglas

Sandwiched between Jim Furey (founder of the Original Celtics in 1920) and Abe Saperstein (organizer of the Harlem Globetrotters in 1927) came Robert Douglas, organizational genius behind the third most memorable road show of basketball's great barnstorming era. A native of the British West Indies, Douglas himself played with the New York Spartans in the Harlem Commonwealth Arena before forming his own club in 1922. His patchwork team would be called the New York Renaissance after the Renaissance Casino ballroom in Harlem, which Douglas rented as a local playing site and shared during the Big Band era with such notable music entertainers as Count Basie and Jimmy Lunsford. But most of the Rens' games were played on the road as the team built a national reputation by traveling most of the eastern half of the country throughout the '20s and '30s to play any team—black or white—that would host it. Leading stars signed to contracts over the years by Douglas were Clarence "Fats" Jenkins, James "Pappy" Ricks, Eyre "Bruiser" Saitch, John "Casey" Holt, Bill Yancey, Charles "Tarzan" Cooper, and Wee Willie Smith (an immortal lineup known during the zenith seasons of the early '30s as the Rens' "Magnificent Seven"). The highlight moments for Douglas's famed club were the end of the 1931 season, when the Rens captured the World Professional Championships by defeating Saperstein's Globetrotters, and also the 1934 season, when Douglas's Magnificent Seven would boast 88 straight victories and a final 127–7 cumulative record.

Walter Dukes

Had Walter Dukes come along a decade or two later, he might well have been a household name. Had he stayed around for an additional college season, he might have owned a much larger piece of collegiate roundball lore than he does. And had his drive and dedication on the hardwood court matched either his immense physical skills or reported native intelligence, Walter Dukes might have even been a first coming of Wilt Chamberlain—a dominating behemoth with an unstoppable offensive arsenal—close to a decade before the ultimate Big Dipper swept into the college and professional basketball world.

Dukes enjoyed a spectacular college career at Seton Hall, which had as its main drawback the fact that it didn't last as long as it should have. There was enough awesome raw talent in the sophomore seven-footer for veteran coaching legend Honey Russell to crow on the eve of the 1951 season that "with Dukes we'd still be

Transcendental Graphics

Walter Dukes, Seton Hall University

tough even if the other four were from Singer's Midgets." With All-American candidate Rich Regan also in the lineup, Russell's 1952 squad lost but two games (both close enough to have made an undefeated season plausible) before being ousted in the NIT opening round by eventual champion La Salle with freshman Tom Gola. A year later, with Clyde Lovellette graduating at Kansas, Dukes was the cream of the nation's big men. Seton Hall returned to the NIT to reign as champion, and the hulking seven-footer, with 70 points in three games, was the NIT MVP. The Seton Hall team of 1953, which Honey Russell had fashioned around Walter Dukes, was indeed one of the most memorable of the era.

The numbers posted by Dukes in his two fabulous Seton Hall seasons stand among the handful of best individual career performances during the decade. With amazing maneuverability for his size, Dukes drew bushels of fouls and converted a remarkable 503 in his two seasons. His NCAA record one-year rebound total of 734 remained unequalled until 1991. Most impressive of all, he was one of but seven players in NCCA Division I history to post 20-point and 20-rebound career per-game averages. It was not surprising with such stats in his résumé that the Rochester native was a player expected by many experts to be a force who would radically alter the NBA upon his arrival in the pros; nor was it surprising that the New York Knicks tabbed Dukes as their "territorial" draft pick at the end of his junior campaign. The trouble was that Walter Dukes did not burn with competitive fire: bored with the college game, which seemed almost too easy for him (shades of Chamberlain), the All-American left school early for two barnstorming seasons with the Harlem Globetrotters before arriving in the Knicks' camp as a tardy rookie for the 1956 season. Once on board in the NBA he was indeed an awesome physical force for those who had to face him in the paint night after night. Yet across single seasons in New York and Minneapolis and a half dozen more in Detroit, Dukes proved a huge disappointment. His career numbers were average (10.4 points per game, 12.1 rebounds per game, 37 percent shooting) even for a man a foot shorter, and his destined legacy was that of a durable journeyman rather than that of a Hall of Fame legend.

Dwight "Dike" Eddleman

There was plenty that was glitzy—even if short-lived—about Dwight "Dike" Eddleman's injury-shortened pro hoops career, which blipped across the sports pages in the early days of the NBA, as well as about his marquee collegiate sojourn at the University of Illinois in the aftermath of World War II. Few more versatile athletes have tried their hands at basketball, and fewer still are those who have possessed basketball skills that so closely matched their prowess in other athletic endeavors. When it came to track and field, Eddleman was exceptional enough in the high jump to capture fourth place in the 1948 London Olympics, win an NCAA title in the event that same summer, and tie for second place in the collegiate championships a year earlier. On the gridiron the Illini multisport star still holds a flock of school records almost half a century after graduation: highest season punting average (43 yards per kick), longest punt (88 yards), best punt return average in a season (32.8), and longest punt return (92 yards). He still found time and focus to lead the Illini cagers in scoring in 1948 (13.9) and 1949 (13.1) as a 6'3" guard-forward and a Converse first-team All-American (1949).

As a professional Dike Eddleman opted for his best sport, basketball, and enjoyed four NBA seasons (the league's first four campaigns under the NBA label) with the Tri-Cities Blackhawks, Milwaukee Hawks, and Fort Wayne Pistons. The durable and spring-legged forward logged highs of 15.3 points per game (his second season with Tri-Cities) and 69 games played (his final league year with Fort Wayne). As a Blackhawk he played alongside such NBA notables as Frankie Brian, Harry Boykoff, and John Logan; in Fort Wayne he teamed with Larry Foust, Andy Phillip, and Fred Schaus. But Eddleman's highlight moment came during his rookie season when he appeared for the losing West squad in the first-ever NBA All-Star Game staged in Boston Garden.

LeRoy "Cowboy" Edwards

Pro basketball had few individual stars in the decades before World War II and George Mikan, especially among athletes who didn't play for the renowned barnstorming Original Celtics, the Harlem Renaissance Five, or Saperstein's Harlem Globetrotters, but plied their trade instead in one of the several regional professional leagues that popped up from time to time in the Midwest or along the Northeastern Seaboard. One such rare cager of prominence (if not wide notoriety) was LeRoy "Cowboy" Edwards, who gained consensus All-American status in 1935 with Rupp's Kentucky Wildcats before departing early for the increased perks of playing in the National Basketball League with the Oshkosh All-Stars. While Cowboy Edwards provided Rupp's program with its first widespread national publicity as a bona fide All-American, he also dealt the program a severe blow by deciding to abandon college after his sophomore season in order to compete for cash (reportedly receiving a $2,400 salary, which nearly equalled Rupp's) with an AAU industrial league club in his hometown of Indianapolis. It didn't make many headlines back in 1935, but Edwards's defection was one of basketball's earliest unofficial "hardship case" undergraduate flights to the pro ranks anywhere on record.

The 6'4" rugged center-forward posted then-lofty season scoring averages of 16.2 (1938), 11.9 (1939), and 12.9 (1940) that were good enough to cop three straight NBL individual scoring titles in the immediate prewar years. His one 30-point single-game outburst (in the days before Joe Fulks and Paul Arizin popularized jump-shooting) was enough to raise eyebrows among the small hardcore of pro basketball watchers in America's heartland. And his flamboyant assortment of fakes and short drives provided enough offensive firepower to lead Oshkosh to a pair of league titles, as well as a sterling .860 winning percentage (14–2) during the brief 1938 season. Edwards stayed only one season with Rupp in Kentucky, but it was long enough to figure in one landmark intersectional game in which the Baron took his charges into Madison Square Garden. There Edwards was mauled by NYU frontcourt thugs and victimized by hometown refereeing to such an extent that this single contest later was motivation for revamping of roughness rules and spurring enactment of the three-second lane violation rule.

Paul Endacott

The Helms Foundation (based in Los Angeles and founded in the mid-1930s) employed its board of basketball experts to carefully compile contemporary records and retroactively select top players and teams back to the onset of the century. The first Helms Player of the Year (1901) was Chris Steinmetz of Wisconsin, and the first top-ranked team was Yale. The selections for 1923 were Kansas under fourth-year coach Phog Allen and its star 5'10" guard and defensive specialist Paul Endacott. Allen's assistant coach for that team (which repeated the mythical national championship also earned a season earlier) was none other than James Naismith, and a seldom-used reserve player was Adolph Rupp (kept on the bench his entire Kansas career by the stellar play of Paul Endacott). In leading the Jayhawks to the first-ever undefeated Missouri Valley Conference season in his senior year, Endacott also earned his second straight selection as first-team all-star in the MVC. Although he rarely scored in double figures, Endacott controlled games with his ballhandling and defensive prowess and was the most famous player on one of college basketball's most memorable early-era championship teams.

Bob Feerick

Among a half-century of pro basketball deadeye shot-makers, only one has ever led the NBA in both field-goal percentage and free-throw percentage during the same season. This rarest of feats occurred during only the second season of the infant pro league (still known at the time as the Basketball Association of America) and was authored by journeyman guard-forward Bob Feerick. Feerick would enjoy only five pro seasons before becoming a highly successful coach at his alma mater, Santa Clara—one with Oshkosh in the NBL and four playing for Red Auerbach's Washington Capitols. Admittedly, Feerick's unique double was partially aided by the extremely low field-goal percentages that were the norm of his day—his league-leading 34 percent would hardly rate a passing notice in the modern era. But the feat was hardly a fluke since the Capitols' stalwart was also the league's field-goal shooting leader a season earlier (1947), as well as its free-throw percentage pacesetter a season later (1949). And his 16-point scoring averages in 1947 and 1948 left him second in the league (behind Joe Fulks) during the lid-lifting BAA season and fourth during the season of his memorable deadeye double a year later.

Ray Felix

One of the earliest black NBA players, towering 6'11" Ray Felix out of Long Island University, crossed a number of pro basketball racial barriers in the company of Boston's Chuck Cooper and Don Barksdale, New York's Sweetwater Clifton, and Syracuse's Earl Lloyd. Only on one occasion, however, did the gentle giant lay a unique claim to "first black" and that came with his selection (in 1954) as the pioneering member of his race to be tapped as NBA Rookie of the Year. Beginning but two seasons later blacks would capture the honor six out of seven seasons strung between 1956 and 1962 (beginning with Maurice Stokes, ending with Walt Bellamy, and including Woody Sauldsberry, Elgin Baylor, Wilt Chamberlain, and Oscar Robertson). Felix also trailed only Barksdale as the second member of his race to play in an NBA All-Star Game (appearing in the fourth gala as a rookie). Ray Felix would remain in the league nine seasons, score slightly more than 10 points a game, and spend the bulk of his career with the New York Knicks (six seasons, sandwiched between one with Baltimore and two with Los Angeles).

Arnie Ferrin

Michigan's "Fab Five" unit was not the first all-freshman lineup to reach the NCAA tournament finals despite widespread media reports touting it as such. It had been beaten to the punch by almost half a century by the Vadal Peterson–coached Utah team of 1944 that won a surprise championship behind star Arnie Ferrin and his contingent of fellow academic rookies. Utah featured a wartime lineup of freshmen Ferrin, Herb Wilkinson, Bob Lewis, Wat Misaka, and Dick Smuin, along with sophomore and top substitute Fred Sheffield—a contingent that averaged barely 18 years of age and barely six feet in height. The gritty Utes were known as "The Blitz Kids" for their whirlwind play. The ironies of that team and its highlight first season were at least twofold. Because of wartime restrictions the Skyline Conference had closed down, and the military had appropriated the Utah field house. Forced to play a schedule of mostly service ball clubs that included only three college teams, the Utes nonetheless were 19–3 before a tough loss to Rupp's Kentucky knocked them from the NIT. But the wet-behind-the-ears Utes would receive a second chance at glory when an automobile accident wiped the Arkansas team from the NCAAs, and Ferrin and Company were called in as a last-second substitute. Utah next rolled by Missouri and Iowa State and nipped Dartmouth in overtime to claim the NCAA version of the national championship. Ferrin, with 22 of his team's 42 points in the finals, was an easy choice for tourney MVP honors.

Arnie Ferrin would catapult from that eye-popping triumph to a wildly successful college career that stretched three more seasons (with a one-year break for military service) and a pro sojourn equally as productive of postseason victories. The college ledger included three All-American selections and an NIT championship as a senior in 1947. The pro achievements included only three seasons with the George Mikan Minneapolis Lakers, yet two of them ended with NBA championship laurels. Arnie Ferrin was never among those star-quality players who posted the highest attention-grabbing individual numbers for scoring or rebounding. But here was a player who usually managed to be on a winner (two-for-four in collegiate postseason titles and two-for-three in NBA titles), and perhaps no other player can boast a better seasons-to-championships ratio than the 6'4" forward out of Ogden, Utah. Perhaps it would be more accurate still to claim that Arnie Ferrin usually contributed most mightily to making winners out of each and every team on which he ever played.

Larry Foust

Larry Foust was one of the finest early prototypes of the agile modern-era basketball big man. He was also the author of one of the most famous and indeed unusual game-winning shots in pro basketball history. But above all else, Foust was one of

Larry Foust, St. Louis Hawks

the most valuable team players in NBA basketball's early rough-and-tumble epoch of strenuous, physical, and often ruthless play. He had played his college basketball at La Salle in the years immediately before Tom Gola and the NIT and NCAA championship teams from that school. As an NBA stalwart he logged a dozen seasons that began with the pro league's "integration" season of 1950–51 and ended the year that Wilt Chamberlain averaged 50 and Oscar Robertson posted a season-long triple-double. With Fort Wayne (mostly), Minneapolis, and finally St. Louis, Foust

recorded 11,198 points (13.7 points per game), played in eight straight All-Star Games, and led the NBA once in rebounding (1952) and once in field-goal percentage (1955). At 250 pounds and 6'9" he was bulky and aggressive off the boards but also agile and adept at handling the ball. Foust's moment in the sun came early in his rookie season, when he tipped in a field goal with six seconds remaining to give the Fort Wayne Pistons a 19–18 victory over Mikan and the Lakers at Minneapolis. The stall-plagued game ended a 29-game home-court winning streak by the Lakers, was the lowest scoring in league history, and was a major impetus for the introduction of the NBA shot clock several seasons later.

Clarence "Bevo" Francis

The 1953 college basketball season was bumping along without mighty Kentucky—Rupp's top-ranked team was serving out a one-year NCAA suspension—and without any reigning superstars—Duke's Dick Groat had graduated, Kentucky's seven-foot Bill Spivey had been expelled in the aftermath of the 1951 game-fixing scandals, and three lesser lights named Frank Selvy (Furman), Larry Hennessey (Villanova), and Johnny O'Brien (Seattle) were pacing the nation in scoring. No other time in the sport's annals could have been more ripe for a folk hero with an odd-sounding name like "Bevo" Francis and his equally strange-sounding school to first grab headlines on the nation's sports pages.

What Bevo Francis did during that 1953 season—for all the doubts surrounding the achievement—was unprecedented and only slightly short of miraculous. He scored points as no one ever had before and no one else ever likely would again (with the single noteworthy exception of Wilt Chamberlain in the NBA a decade later). The 6'9" center with perhaps the deadliest pure shooting eye ever owned by a man his size threw in basket after basket against a motley array of business school and two-year college rosters that were helpless to corral him. His freshman season's average was an unthinkable 50.1, amassed with 1,952 points in 39 contests. One incredible night against Ashland College he totaled 116 of his team's 150; twice more he scored more than 70, an additional half dozen times more than 60, and on four occasions he outscored the entire opposing lineup. Rio Grande College, for whom Francis played, of course didn't lose a single game that season.

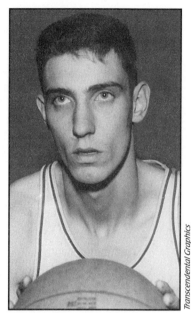

Clarence "Bevo" Francis

Transcendental Graphics

If basketball has a single magnificent folk hero during its formative years, that figure is thus the gangly Clarence "Bevo" Francis at tiny Rio Grande (pronounced Rye-O Grand) College of southeastern Ohio. That Francis is not a larger folk hero of the American sporting scene has mostly to do with the fact that basketball does not nurture its mythical past to the same degree as the long-preferred national pastime of baseball. It also didn't help that Bevo's records as a freshman were quickly thrown out as illegitimate, since they were not posted against a schedule of accredited four-year schools. A season later, however, with an improved schedule (including Villanova, Providence, Wake Forest, Butler, and Arizona State) and increased public scrutiny, Francis checked in with a 47.0 average and 1,318 points. Again he logged a 100-point game, this time posting 113 versus Hillsdale College of Michigan. And Rio Grande compiled a 20–8 season's mark before falling in the NAIA tournament when Bevo was rendered ineffective by injury. Then the legend just as suddenly ended. Bevo, with a wife and family to support, dropped out of school, turned down a tryout with the NBA Philadelphia Warriors, and faded into obscurity after signing on for a barnstorming career with Abe Saperstein and the Harlem Globetrotters' companion touring team known as the Boston Whirlwinds.

In the end it was hard to get an accurate reading of the Bevo Francis legacy. His records were clearly doomed to permanent disregard once they were labeled as "illegitimate"—at least in the eyes of NCAA record keepers and most of the nation's basketball press. After a two-year circus-wagon campaign, which had totaled an amazing 67 games (Rio Grande was 59–8 over the span) against obscure opponents with strange names like Ashland, Alliance, Bluffton, Mayo State, Cedarville, Sue Bennett, and Wilberforce, Bevo Francis was merely a blip on the screen of basketball history.

Buck Freeman

The glory days of New York City college basketball began in the late 1920s with a St. John's University team known widely as "The Wonder Five" and coached by James "Buck" Freeman. Over a four-year period the unchanged roster of 6'5" center Matty Begovich, forwards Mac Kinsbrunner and Max Posnack, and guards Rip Gerson and Allie Schuckman would post 86 victories against a mere eight defeats. Half the losses came in the first season, which meant that, for its final three campaigns, the Freeman squad was a brilliant 68–4 against all comers. Freeman's novel system that produced such relentless winning was one of cautious ball control on offense, stinginess of shot selection, and tenacious defense. During the final year of "The Wonder Five," only one team—an all-star contingent of St. John's alumni—was able to score as many as 30 points against the crack Redmen outfit. Once their eligibility was finally exhausted, the famed quintet remained together as a touring team and later together entered the American Basketball League, first as the Brooklyn Jewels and later as the New York Jewels.

Buck Freeman and his style of play first introduced with his Wonder Five roster not only put New York City basketball squarely on the map; more importantly, it also forced rules makers to introduce some radical pieces of legislation, namely the midcourt time line and the backcourt 10-second rule. The relentless winning of the Wonder Five had been built upon Freeman's successful adaptation of a monotonous passing-style game practiced by such renowned pro outfits as New York's Original Celtics. Freeman's own disciplined passing game was combined with a tough switching defense to make it doubly effective. With the original center jump rule still in effect, after each scored basket the Redmen would rely on Matty Begovich to control the ensuing tap. They would then slowly work the ball into position for the perfect set shot, usually taken by Schuckman. If the shot didn't emerge as planned, they would retreat to the far end of the court and launch still another painstaking passing attack. There was no center-court line at the time and backcourt violations did not exist. Max Posnack was the unparalleled ball handler, and Mac Kinsbrunner as superb dribbler would maintain control of the ball for as much as 10 minutes at a time with a shot rarely, if ever, taken. It was a ploy effective enough for generating frustration and usually defensive collapse by the opposition. But it was hardly a crowd-pleasing spectacle, and new rules rendered it obsolete only a single season after the graduation of Buck Freeman's most famous team.

"Jumpin' Joe" Fulks

This skinny 6'5" cornerman popularized the jump shot (called his "ear shot" because that's where he released the ball), which revolutionized the pro game and impacted dramatically on the college sport as well. Ample publicity for the new offensive style came when the flamboyant Philadelphia Warriors forward tossed in an incredible 63 points during a single BAA game versus Indianapolis in February 1949, a full decade before Wilt's arrival and during an era when 20 points was still a truly high-scoring evening. There was little question among those who saw him that the charismatic Fulks was basketball's first great pure shooter. But close observers noted also that here was one of the indoor sport's pioneering "flakes" as well. And a sure bet as an early drawing card. His whirling turnaround jumpers from 20 feet and more were launched high enough to bring rain or at least appear on radar screens.

Among basketball's dozen or so most important playing pioneers, Joe Fulks may well be the most easily overlooked and thus the most fully shortchanged by the course of history. The recent Golden Anniversary season of the NBA (1996–97) found the league public relations arm paying some "official" lip service to early stars from the sport's formative period. There was acknowledgment of Mikan and Dolph Schayes and even some recollection of the two separate leagues (BAA and NBL) that struggled for recognition in the three seasons before merger and the adoption of the NBA label. But there was no mention of Fulks, though the potent bomber who played for the Philadelphia Warriors during the same time frame when Mikan toiled with the Minneapolis Lakers was one of the fledgling NBA's biggest drawing cards and certainly its most important playing-style innovator. Fulks dominated league scoring in the years of the forerunner BAA: his league-leading 23.2 average was more than 30 percent better than his closest rival during the league's first

Joe Fulks, Philadelphia Warriors

Transcendental Graphics

season; he was tops in per-game average during two BAA campaigns and trailed only the newly arrived Mikan in the third; his record 63-point game surpassed the previous league mark by better than 25 percent. More importantly he pioneered a shooting style that dramatically altered the nature of the sport and, in the process, set the pattern for the game's growing popularity in the years soon to come.

Joe Fulks arrived on the postwar pro basketball scene like a fanciful figure straight from the murky legends of fiction: his college career at Murray State (where he averaged 13 points in 47 games) was a black hole, his unorthodox playing style was unprecedented, and his personality and demeanor were any sportswriter's pure delight. Jumpin' Joe Fulks's approach to shooting a basketball was not only unique but deadly effective as well. He wowed fans with his jump-shooting technique, but he also floored opponents with his scoring onslaughts and even paced his team straight to a memorable championship victory in the process. But like many such mythical figures, Fulks was destined to be only an all-too-brief comet in the basketball heavens of the postwar years. His ephemeral NBA career (1947 through 1954), of course, only added to his already legendary qualities.

Jim Furey

Basketball's barnstorming kings of the years between the wars came into being when New York promoter Jim Furey, along with his brother Tom, attempted to reorganize a locally renowned New York Celtics ball club that had folded only a few seasons earlier. The first Celtics unit had been formed in 1914 and represented a settlement house in one of the roughest Manhattan neighborhoods. Pete Barry (a later star with Furey's revamped team) and Johnny Witte had been the mainstays of the first club, which chose to disband with the onset of World War I. When the founder of the first club, Frank McCormack, refused to hand over rights to the team name, the Furey brothers simply altered the designation for their team to "Original Celtics" and set up operations in 1920 by signing Barry and Witte and picking up an additional roster of seasoned pros, which included Mike Smolick, Joe Trippe, Eddie White, and Ernie Reich. A year later, with the additions of Dutch Dehnert, Johnny Beckman, and Nat Holman, Furey's ball club became the best touring team in the New York region. Over the next dozen seasons, with the further addition of players like Joe Lapchick, Chris Leonard, Horse Haggerty, Carl Husta, and Davey Banks, the Original Celtics dominated several of the short-lived pro circuits of the day, including the Eastern League, the Metropolitan League, and the American Basketball League.

What clinched Jim Furey's place in basketball history, as well as that of his Original Celtics team, was a bold business innovation that marked the inauguration of stable professional basketball teams as we know them today. Furey was the first to sign up his players with full-season contracts, not on the nightly cash basis used by other clubs. With the revolutionary move came the first signs of roster stability. Players (at least Furey's players) would no longer switch teams and leagues weekly as higher-paying offers came their way. It was Jim Furey's abilities to keep his team together over time—not just his original founding of the ball club—that dramatically changed the course of professional basketball history.

William "Pop" Gates

Of the numerous talented black athletes who filled out the roster of the barnstorming Harlem Renaissance Five during their peak years in the '30s and their waning years in the '40s, none enjoyed a more productive debut or experienced a more significant curtain-call season. A New York City high school star, Pop Gates signed on with the Rens in late 1938 for a salary of $125 a month and immediately became a star on one of the nation's best touring pro outfits. In Gates's inaugural season of 1938–39 the Rens finished a brilliant 111–22 for the winter-spring campaign and defeated the NBL champion Oshkosh All-Stars in the title match of the first World Professional Tournament in Chicago, with the 6'3" rookie leading the scoring. Seven years later Gates and former LIU standout Dolly King integrated the NBL when they were signed by Rochester Royals owner-coach Les Harrison. King broke into the lineup with Rochester at the opening of the 1946–47 season, while Gates was sold to the Buffalo franchise, which relocated that same year as the Tri-Cities Blackhawks. With Tri-Cities Pop Gates was a starter (7.6 points per game) at forward throughout the 1947 season, then moved to the Dayton Rens' NBL franchise (which featured other blacks including Dolly King and future baseball big-leaguer George Crowe) as player-coach for 1948–49, his final professional season. One of the last significant stars to perform with the famed New York Rens of basketball's heyday barnstorming era was also one of the first of his race to integrate professional basketball at the dawn of its modern post–World War II era.

George "Blind Bomber" Glamack

Big-league baseball has had its pair of one-handed ballplayers (Pete Gray and Jim Abbott) to add a touch of the bizarre and the unnatural to the diamond sport. Pro basketball, in turn, once had its blind—or nearly blind—scoring star who made a considerable mark in both the college and pro ranks. George Glamack, despite his handicap, was the first-ever basketball All-American at the University of North Carolina, a prolific scorer who once narrowly missed Hank Luisetti's record of 50 points in a single game, and even a double-figure scorer for six seasons in the pre- and postwar National Basketball League.

Glamack was one of the most colorful cagers in storied North Carolina Tar Heels roundball history. The "Blind Bomber" sobriquet resulted from an actual visual impairment severe enough that the talented athlete could barely see the basket a few feet above his head. If his poor vision made him something of an inspired success story, however, this quite real handicap should in no way detract from Glamack's considerable raw basketball skills. He owned a deadly, if surprising, foul-line-range left-handed hook shot that was the scourge of enemy defenses. The shot was guided in the direction of the hoop by the resourceful player's intelligent use of the foul-line stripes painted on the gym's floor. Glamack's rugged pivot play and 20-plus scoring average brought not only two All-American honors but also back-to-back Helms Foundation Player of the Year recognitions. The Carolina star was only the second player (after Hank Luisetti) ever to receive such a repeat distinction as the nation's individual best.

Joe Graboski

Joe Graboski was an NBA workhorse who labored valiantly in the trenches with the BAA Chicago Stags, NBA Indianapolis Olympians, and NBA Philadelphia Warriors for the bulk of his 13-year professional career. He posted nearly 10,000 points and 6,000 rebounds before retirement in 1962, and earned a championship ring as a front-line mainstay and rebounding dervish for a high-scoring 1956 Philadelphia Warriors team, which featured Paul Arizin, Neil Johnston, Tom Gola, and Jack George. But what made Graboski unique was the fact that he entered the BAA in 1948–49 without having ever attended college, a feat which would later earn considerable notoriety for Moses Malone, Darryl Dawkins, Bill Willoughby, Kevin Garnett, and Kobe Bryant.

Dick Groat

To dedicated sports fans old enough to recall the 1950s and 1960s, Dick Groat is certainly a recognizable name. Yet few among such readers may have much recol-

Dick Groat, Duke University

Transcendental Graphics

lection of Groat as a basketball star, and some may not even know that the 1960 baseball World Series hero and National League Most Valuable Player once owned a reputation every bit as big for college cage play as the one he possessed for his big-league diamond heroics.

Only two things stood between Dick Groat and a much larger piece of college basketball immortality. One was Groat's own more impressive legacy on the major-league baseball diamond, and the other was the fact that the crack guard had the mis-fortune of performing at Duke a handful of seasons before the new ACC confedera-tion brought Tobacco Road campuses into the national sports spotlight. Groat led the nation in scoring in 1951 with a lofty total of 831 points (his 25.2 pace left him fourth in per-game average); he averaged more than 25 points per game over his final two seasons and accumulated enough points (1,886) to briefly hold the national career record; and to prove that he wasn't merely a one-dimensional scoring machine, the Duke ace also posted the top total in the land for assists in 1952 and set a new free-throw mark (261 of 338) a season earlier. It was all good enough to lead his Blue Devils teams to 20–13 and 24–6 records, earn several All-American selections, and garner the Helms Foundation National Player of the Year trophy for his senior season.

Groat seemed to lean toward baseball from the start (though he would later tab basketball as his true favorite) and had come to Duke in the first place because of the school's lofty status on the springtime diamond. It was an irony of his Duke sojourn that the nation's premier cage player would never appear in NCAA or NIT postseason events but would instead pace his team in baseball's College World Series. A series of fortunate breaks on the hardwood, however, were enough to launch him toward considerable collegiate fame as a cager. Red Auerbach made a short stopover as assistant at Duke and tutored the ace guard in offensive funda-mentals. Harold Bradley also came on the scene in time for Groat's junior season and engineered the first steps toward a quality winning program. Groat would learn from both men and polish his game under their combined tutelage. Perhaps the largest piece of good fortune, however, was the emergence during his career of the Dixie Classic midseason tournament, which quickly became the showcase event of Deep South basketball. It was in that tournament during his junior campaign that Groat would enjoy his most memorable single performance. A torrid second-half shooting display resulted in a game-high 32 points and enabled Duke to overcome a seemingly insurmountable 56–27 halftime deficit against Tulane in the consolation game; it was one of the most remarkable comebacks in Southern Conference history. While Sam Ranzino of N.C. State captured the Dixie Classic MVP that year for the victorious Wolfpack, Groat's three-game 71-point outburst nonetheless stood as the crown jewel of a stellar three-year Blue Devils career.

Alex Groza

What will likely always be remembered about Alex Groza is the painful tragedy of a promising NBA career washed away by foolhardy conspiracy with gamblers to fix scores of Kentucky games in 1948 and 1949. Groza was indeed a budding superstar during his two seasons (inaugural NBA campaigns of 1950 and 1951) with the Indianapolis Olympians. He trailed only Mikan in scoring both years, and both winters he led the entire circuit in field-goal accuracy. He was also high scorer for the West squad in the first-ever NBA All-Star Game of March 1951. What has largely fallen out of view after half a century, however, is the true brilliance of

Alex Groza,
University of Kentucky

© University of Kentucky

Groza's collegiate career in Lexington, one of the most honor-filled in storied Kentucky Wildcats history. The 6'7" center was a two-time NCAA tourney MVP, leading scorer on two NCAA title winners and an Olympic gold-medal team, and a three-season All-American selection. An important piece of trivia attached to one of basketball's most tragic figures was the additional fact that he was also the brother of all-time NFL placekicking great Lou Groza.

Luther Gulick

If Naismith is the game's father, the godfather is Luther Gulick. It was Gulick—Naismith's supervisor as the head of physical education at the YMCA training school in Springfield—who issued the order for his young protégé to come up with playing rules and design for a new indoor game that would provide healthy exercise, Christian discipline, and raw entertainment for a rowdy class of trainees who had grown altogether bored with calisthenics during off-season months between fall football and spring baseball. Gulick had planted the seed which under Naismith's persistent tending would bear such rich fruit. Not unsurprisingly, Dr. Gulick maintained almost as little insight into the new game's explosive and competitive future—once Naismith had designed it—as did the inventor himself. Only six winters later, in 1897, the future founder of both the Boy Scouts and Camp Fire Girls movements would loudly complain that the version of Naismith's game being already widely played by women (with stationary players and no dribbling) was constructed with entirely different rules and thus shouldn't even be called by the same name ("basket ball") as the men's more strenuous version. It was a statement true enough at the time it was spoken—and one that remained largely accurate for nearly three-quarters of the coming century—yet it was a complaint that today rings quite hollow in an era filled with fast-paced collegiate and professional women's cage action.

Vic Hanson

The All-Time All-American Team selected by legendary sportswriter Grantland Rice in 1952 contained four names that even casual fans would likely recognize—George Mikan, Bob Kurland, Hank Luisetti, and John Wooden—and one name that even many modern roundball aficionados would be at pains to identify: Vic Hanson of Syracuse University. When Rice made his selections at midcentury, however, Hanson was still very much a basketball legend, especially in eastern sectors of the country. A three-time All-American forward during the late '20s, Vic Hanson captained the 1927 Syracuse team coached by Lew Andreas that claimed a mythical national championship. The Helms Foundation committee would later retroactively proclaim him National Player of the Year for that same season. A year earlier he set a school scoring mark with 280 points that would stand for 20 years. Over three seasons with Hanson in the lineup, Syracuse compiled a dominating 48–7 record. Most remarkable of all about this 5'10", 160-pound athlete, however, is the fact that, in the fall of 1926 he also earned All-American tribute as a Syracuse football end, was subsequently elected to the National Football Foundation College Football Hall of Fame, played minor-league baseball in the New York Yankees farm system, performed as a basketball pro with the ABL Cleveland Rosenblums, and finally served his alma mater for seven seasons as its head football coach.

Bob Harrison

George Mikan, Bob Pettit, and Dolph Schayes were arguably the three most consistently potent offensive forces in the NBA during the first three or four seasons that followed the NBL-BAA merger in 1949. One underrated feeding guard (today's point guard) had the fortunate distinction to play in the same lineup with all three. Launching his NBA career in 1950 with Minneapolis, Bob Harrison earned three championship rings (in only four years) with the invincible Lakers frontline trio of Mikan, Pollard, and Vern Mikkelsen. Traded to the Milwaukee Hawks in late 1954, he arrived in the nick of time to spend two campaigns feeding a young Bob Pettit in both Milwaukee and the ball club's new home at St. Louis. Two final NBA seasons were spent alongside Schayes as a backcourt starter for the Syracuse Nats, a team which had won its only championship two seasons earlier.

Lester Harrison

Les Harrison, and not Walter Brown, may well deserve the bulk of the credit for being basketball's version of Branch Rickey. It was Harrison, as owner (and also bench coach) of the Rochester Royals, who signed up Long Island University star Dolly King as the first black pro basketball player in the NBL. King's one-season appearance in 1946–47 with the Royals preceded the NBA debuts of more celebrated black pioneers Chuck Cooper, Nat Clifton, and Earl Lloyd by four years and rates consideration as the true start of pro basketball's integration after World War II. History has seemingly bypassed the moment largely because—despite the NBL and BAA roots in NBA history—today's surviving professional league inappropriately recognizes only the later circuit as part of its true parentage. At the time of Harrison's bold move, however, the NBL's only eastern ball club experienced considerable discriminatory treatment inside and outside of league arenas simply because of Dolly King's presence in the Rochester lineup.

Dickie Hemric

Wake Forest unquestionably owned the Atlantic Coast Conference's first legitimate superstar and already had him on board for the initial launching of the newly constituted league. Dickie Hemric would rule the ACC during its two maiden seasons, pacing Wake to first-division finishes both winters, topping all league rebounders, ranking second (1954) and then third (1955) among conference scorers, and engraving his name on the first two league MVP trophies. The only true rivals to Wake's powerful 6'6" pivotman were Virginia's hot-shooting Buzz Wilkinson (owner of the league's first two scoring titles) and Clemson's talented backcourt ace Bill Yarborough. Len Rosenbluth and Ronnie Shavlik were waiting in the wings at North Carolina and North Carolina State, respectively, during Hemric's senior season, but both were still a season away from glory.

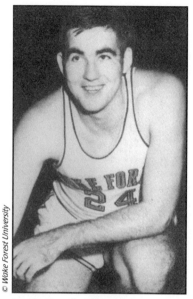

© Wake Forest University

Dickie Hemric, Wake Forest

Hemric's dominance sprang in part from his uniqueness: as an aggressive board-crasher who could also shoot with a soft touch, he was a rare phenomenon for his era. But the rules then governing play also added a strong assist for a hard-nosed player of his size. The foul lane was still at 6 feet and not 12, thus allowing the mobile but not exceptionally large Hemric to take up a spot next to the hoop without fear of drawing three-second violations. Another rule aberration allowed each team an inside foul-line position on foul shots (today both go to the defense); Hemric thus had plenty of extra opportunity to score off tap-ins of missed free throws by his teammates. A special 1954 provision also allowed players a second bonus free throw after a first miss; thus teams with strong offensive rebounders, like Hemric, would often intentionally miss the second charity toss by aiming it toward their own rebounder's side of the bucket.

With these considerable assists from the rules makers plus his own superior talents, Hemric posted outstanding numbers during the first two league seasons, and he still owns several pages in the Wake Forest basketball record book. He is not only the school's first great scorer—still holding the career four-year records for total points and overall scoring average—but also the greatest rebounder in Wake Forest history. In the final two seasons of his career Hemric would altogether dominate statistical play in the new Tobacco Road conference with combined rebound and point totals that outdistanced the rest of the league field by a country mile. And very few have matched his numbers in the four full decades that have since followed.

Art Hillhouse

Art Hillhouse never made much of a dent on the NBA: two seasons (both with the BAA Philadelphia Warriors after he was already in his 30s), 71 games, less than a six-point scoring average—not at all impressive numbers for a 6'7" former star of one of the most potent college teams of early modern-era college basketball history. But a decade earlier the same Art Hillhouse was one of the biggest names in the basketball mecca of New York City as a mainstay performer with Clair Bee's finest couple of LIU teams ever. Bee had become himself the toast of New York college roundball during his third season in Brooklyn, when his Blackbirds finished 27–1 losing only to St. John's and piling up a remarkable 1,000 points for the season. Two years later with a lineup featuring sophomore center Hillhouse—alongside Marius Russo (future big-league hurler with the Yankees), Willie Schwartz, Leo Merson, and Jules Bender—Bee's powerhouse quintet posted an unblemished mark in 26 games. The streak stretched to a then-record 43 before LIU bowed to Stanford and

Hank Luisetti in a memorable Madison Square Garden match the following December. That was the game in which Luisetti launched his one-handed shooting style on an incredulous New York audience and launched a basketball revolution that overhauled the pace at which the game was played. It was All-American Hillhouse who was fated to guard Luisetti on that historic night, and thus to be the befuddled victim of one of basketball's landmark offensive performances.

But Art Hillhouse was hardly a basketball goat. During his final season at LIU in 1939 (he graduated in February, a month before the Blackbirds' NIT championship), Hillhouse was the pillar of yet another undefeated team, this time playing alongside All-American Irv Torgoff and one of New York City's first black collegians, Dolly King. All told, the four varsity teams on which Art Hillhouse played compiled a combined record of 79–8 and were twice undefeated, one of the finest career records in college basketball history.

Tony Hinkle

Bobby Knight is only the most recent oversized figure in a considerable history of legendary college coaches who have plied their trade in the basketball-crazed state of Indiana. Ward Lambert at Purdue was perhaps the prototype, but even before Lambert, there was already Tony Hinkle at Butler University in Indianapolis. As a three-sport mentor Hinkle won a combined 1,000-plus college basketball, football, and baseball games and is one of but seven NCAA coaches to have earned a tenure that stretched for more than 40 years. Only Ed Diddle at Western Kentucky and Ray Meyer at DePaul coached more seasons at a single school than Hinkle's 41 campaigns with Butler. A 1920 All-American during his playing days at Chicago under legendary Joseph Raycroft, Tony Hinkle began his Butler career a season later when hired as a coaching assistant by his former Chicago teammate, Pat Page. He would not leave the Butler scene for 50 seasons, retiring in 1970 after 600-plus cage victories posted over 44 seasons of varsity coaching. Hinkle's illustrious career also included nearly 100 victories as coach of the Great Lakes Naval Training Station team during World War II, chairmanship of the National Basketball Rules Committee (1948–50), presidency of the National Association of Basketball Coaches (1954–55), and one mythical Helms Foundation basketball national championship earned with his 17–2 1929 team. Today Butler's best-known athletic figure is immortalized in the Tony Hinkle Memorial Fieldhouse, a longtime location for Indiana state high school basketball championship games and also a site for filming of the popular 1985 Hollywood film *Hoosiers*, the nostalgic cinematic portrayal of legendary "Hoosier Hysteria"-style Indiana high school basketball.

Howard Hobson

Every college coach's fondest dream is likely to be the winning of the NCAA postseason tournament and thus the coveted basketball national championship. Twenty-three-year mentor Howard Hobson got there first when his "Tall Firs" contingent of Oregon Ducks capped a 29–5 1939 season with a title-round 46–33 victory over Ohio State in Evanston, Illinois, to walk off with the prize of the inaugural NCAA postseason playdown. Only eight teams made up the field of an event that was far from the monthlong extravaganza it is today, and Oregon had only to defeat Texas and Oklahoma to make it to the title game. Hobson only made it back to the "big dance" once again, in 1949 when his Ivy League champion Yale club lost both its opening-round and regional consolation matches. His teams at three schools did capture 401 games, and his Oregon club helped pioneer intersectional play with several East Coast road swings. Hobson also served as president of the National Association of Basketball Coaches, contributed heavily as a distinguished member of both the U.S. Olympic Committee and National Basketball Rules Committee, and was elected to the Naismith Basketball Hall of Fame in 1965.

Red Holzman

It was never much of a secret that NBA league brass long coveted a championship team in New York, the media capital of the nation and thus a key location for touting the image of a league striving to gain the kind of public attention enjoyed by the more popular major-league sports of baseball and football. When that New York championship season finally arrived in 1970, the NBA's 23rd season, it was won by a Knicks team coached by Red Holzman, a veteran of NBL, BAA, and NBA campaigns stretching back to the end of World War II. Holzman had taken over the Knicks' bench job halfway through the 1968 season, would win titles there in both 1970 and 1973, remain on the scene for a decade, enjoy winning campaigns his first seven seasons in New York, and make the playoffs during the first eight. Previous to his New York tenure he would also coach the Milwaukee and St. Louis Hawks for two full seasons and parts of two others, and during that first tenure would nurture the talents of young Bob Pettit, eventually one of the greatest frontcourt players in basketball history. As a player the 5'10" carrot-top guard spent eight of his nine seasons with Rochester (the first three in the NBL) and was a backcourt fixture on two championship Royals teams—the one that defeated Fort Wayne and Sheybogan in the 1946 postseason and the one that beat out the New York Knicks in the 1951 NBA Finals. But the 1970 NBA Coach of the Year will always be best remembered not as a pesky guard who helped block a Knicks title run in the early '50s, but rather as the taciturn coach who guided New York to its first NBA title banner precisely two decades later.

Bob Houbregs

If James Naismith was Canada's first important gift to basketball, Bob Houbregs was the second. While Ken Sailors and Joe Fulks were busy popularizing the jump shot during and after World War II, Bob Houbregs, during the same epoch, was perfecting the picture-perfect hook shot. The sweeping heave he eventually developed is still considered by old-timers to be the most deadly ever launched. In fact, Washington University's Houbregs may well be basketball's only true hook-shot specialist down to this very day. Certainly no other player (including Kareem Abdul-Jabbar) has relied on the hook quite so exclusively as the main thrust of his offensive game. Playing before freshmen were eligible (1951 through 1953),

Houbregs racked up 1,774 points (a school record until 1988, and still the three-season mark), garnered two All-American selections, averaged 25.4 (sixth in the nation) as a senior, and was the leading scorer and rebounder for a national third-place team with a 30–3 record. Houbregs's marks for single-game scoring, season's average, and career average still stand unscathed at Washington. During five NBA seasons with the Milwaukee Hawks, Baltimore Bullets, Boston Celtics, and Fort Wayne and Detroit Pistons, Houbregs was several times among the league's field-goal percentage leaders. But it was the potent and graceful hook shot that foremost gained Naismith Hall of Fame honors for Washington's greatest-ever basketball star. His Washington coach, Tippy Dye, boldly called him "the greatest pivotman ever in college basketball" and a more neutral judge, John Wooden, contended that Bob Houbregs had "even a better hook shot than George Mikan."

Hank Iba

The list of winningest college coaches only has two names etched in stone above Hank Iba—Dean Smith and Baron Rupp. Bobby Knight of Indiana is the only sure bet to bump Iba down a notch before another decade passes. Along with 767 career victories, mostly at Oklahoma State (originally Oklahoma A&M), there were 14 Missouri Valley Conference crowns, one Big Eight title, and the first back-to-back NCAA tournament trophies in history. But the list of unique and special achievements hardly stops there. No coach has duplicated Hank Iba's feat of leading two different U.S. Olympic Teams (1964, 1968) to gold-medal victories. His pair of NCAA postseason titles in 1945 and 1946 was encored with another trip to the championship game in 1949. His entire starting lineup filled out the 1946 Missouri Valley All-Star honors. And had it not been for the controversial last-second loss to the Soviet Union in the 1972 Olympic gold-medal game (Iba's last coaching appearance), the Olympic medal count would have stood at three. Lost perhaps in all this overachievement is also the significant fact that it was Iba who nurtured and developed the raw talent of seven-foot Bob Kurland, pillar of the two NCAA championship squads and rival to George Mikan for the distinction of being the sport's first agile and effective dominant seven-foot center.

Buddy Jeannette

Few coaches have enjoyed a more successful long-term tenure in the NBA (or any of its immediate forerunner leagues) or done so under any more arduous circumstances than those found in the tumultuous days of the struggling postwar BAA and NBL. Certainly few, if any, ever led a more surprising championship team than Jeannette's 1948 Baltimore Bullets of the BAA. And fewer still have captured a league title when they themselves were the championship team's star player. This rugged 5'11" Washington and Jefferson College alumnus played seven seasons with an array of NBL clubs, which included the Warren (Pennsylvania) Penns, Cleveland White Horses, and Detroit Eagles; finished off his career with three seasons as player-coach of the Baltimore BAA-NBA franchise; and made the all-tournament team at both the 1941 and 1942 World Professional Championships. He also logged playing time with the Sheybogan and Fort Wayne NBL clubs in a career that stretched from the low-scoring era of center jumps to the run-and-gun era of fast-breaking offenses and a 24-second shot clock. His career-defining moment came in the 1947 BAA campaign when his Baltimore team was brought into the league at the last moment in the wake of several franchise collapses and then proceeded to capture the league postseason championship after limping through most of the season as little more than a break-even club. In addition to his bench duties Jeannette was also a starting guard and third-leading scorer on that charmed Bullets team, which surprised the defending champion Philadelphia Warriors with high-scoring Joe Fulks and dependable Howie Dallmar. In the precisely half-century of seasons that have followed, only one other man—Boston's Bill Russell (1968 and 1969)—has directed an NBA champion while wearing a pair of seemingly incompatible hats as both player and coach.

Clarence "Fats" Jenkins

Of the barnstorming heroes who made up the legendary "Magnificent Seven" lineup of the New York Rens during their four peak years between 1932 and 1936, it was Clarence "Fats" Jenkins who earned the biggest measure of fame away from the basketball court. The slim 5'7" fleet-footed athlete doubled as a talented baseball outfielder for two decades and made his mark with such famed Negro League ball clubs as the New York Black Yankees (Negro National League), Harrisburg Giants (Eastern Colored League), Philadelphia Stars, and Brooklyn Eagles among others. Amassing a 20-year career batting average usually credited at .331, Jenkins was known everywhere among black ball aficionados as the ideal leadoff hitter of the Negro baseball circuit. But it was basketball that remained his best sport and also his eventual ticket to Hall of Fame immortality. The Rens' Magnificent Seven lineup had barely a weakness to be exploited by opposition ball clubs, even powerful and polished ones such as the rival Original Celtics with Dehnert, Holman, and Lapchick. Towering 6'4" Tarzan Cooper and 6'5" Wee Willie Smith manned the interior basket region; Bill Yancey and Bruiser Saitch were the deadly set-shooting outside threats, while John Holt and Pappy Ricks ably filled in off the bench. But the fuel for the Rens' attack was the lightning-quick Jenkins—"the fastest man in basketball" by all accounts—who tirelessly ran the devastating Rens fast break and wore out opponents in the process. With their unparalleled lineup the best of barnstorming teams was 473–49 for the four-year span of its peak seasons and also one of the biggest shows anywhere to be found on the professional or amateur basketball circuit.

Frank Keaney

Frank Keaney didn't invent the fast-break offense, but he did perhaps as much as anyone to popularize it. And his teams were once the terror of New England basketball at a time when New England enjoyed almost its only moment in the national limelight. Throughout the three decades that spanned the two world wars, the well-rounded Keaney coached all major sports and found time to teach chemistry as well in his Rhode Island State College faculty post. But it was as an architect—architect of modern "run-and-shoot" basketball play—that Keaney found his niche and left his indelible print. His very first team in 1921 would tally 87 points in a single contest, an almost unheard of total at the time. By 1927 the Rhode Island club first reached the near point-a-minute level of scoring with a 40.5 per game average. In 1936 it was again Keaney's team that climbed above the 50-per-game plateau before all other collegiate outfits. But it was in the late '30s and early '40s that Keaney's system reached its greatest fruition and unleashed the game's first contingent of big-time college scorers. Chet Jaworski, the school's first All-American, was the first in line and was followed closely by two-time national scoring leader Stan "Stutz" Modzelewski. A team peak was reached in 1947 when Rhode Island's scoring proficiency reached an all-time high at 82.4 points per game. The Rams reached the NIT finals versus Kentucky (where they lost a heart-breaking one-point decision to one of Rupp's best-ever teams), and All-American Ernie Calverley (later an accomplished Rhode Island coach himself) earned honors as the NIT MVP. When he retired in 1948, Keaney's .765 (403–124) overall winning percentage was one of the loftiest on record. But it was the wide-open style of play and not just the results that earned Frank Keaney his deserved piece of coaching immortality.

Junius Kellogg

From a distant vantage point of nearly five decades Junius Kellogg, one-time Manhattan College star of the early '50s, emerges as one of the most heroic figures gleaned from the saga of midcentury New York City basketball. It was Kellogg, the 6'8" center for a mediocre 1951 Manhattan College team and one of the first blacks to play at that school, who turned his back on lucrative cash offers for point shaving and reported his contacts with gamblers (specifically an offered $1,000 bribe to rig the score of an upcoming game with DePaul) to Jaspars head coach Ken Norton and other school officials. Kellogg's actions helped bust open the scandals that swept the sport during the 1950 and 1951 seasons. Less than a month after the January incident, members of Nat Holman's defending NIT and NCAA champions were arrested and charged with an earlier game-fixing conspiracy. In the Manhattan case two of Kellogg's teammates and three gamblers were arrested and tried. The exploding scandals that crippled the game's image throughout the remainder of 1951 and into 1952 would wipe out potential NBA careers for such recognized college stars as Kentucky's Ralph Beard and Alex Groza, Bradley's Gene Melchiorre, CCNY's Ed Warner and Ed Roman, and LIU's Sherm White. Kellogg himself never made it into the NBA (due to lesser talent and not legal actions), yet he was hailed everywhere as a shining symbol of what remained of honesty and integrity in the world of increasingly sullen college sports. Now 70 and confined to a wheelchair for four-plus decades by a tragic auto accident suffered in 1955 while touring with the Harlem Globetrotters, Junius Kellogg was recently remembered at his alma mater with a special tribute dinner called "A Night to Remember" and staged to honor a single player's courageous stance during one of the sport's darkest hours.

Pat Kennedy

A standard chunk of wisdom is the observation that the best basketball referees, baseball umpires, and football officials are the ones whose presence goes entirely unnoticed. Yet like most pithy "truisms" this one doesn't always hold up to historical record. The most colorful and animated pro cage referee of all time was, by all accounts, also one of the unrivaled best at his trade. And Pat Kennedy usually did much on the hardwood floor to call attention to himself. Kennedy began his career as a hardwood arbiter in the ABL of the late '20s when he had barely reached 20 years of age. He was eventually hired by former ABL star and then CCNY coach Nat Holman to work a Madison Square Garden contest between Holman's squad and Rutgers, a professional break that led to several decades of work officiating the top intersectional college attractions that were soon a Madison Square Garden staple. Throughout his long tenure Kennedy never failed to display fairness, honesty, and—most of all—intense showmanship, which often surprised players and never failed to entertain spectators. Flailing arms, red face, and bulging neck muscles were always part of the act during Kennedy's delivery of foul calls and other violations. One widely circulated and perhaps apocryphal story involves Kennedy and legendary Stanford All-American Hank Luisetti. After a particularly histrionic display in making a traveling call in the Garden against Luisetti the All-American responded in hushed voice. "I heard you were crazy, Pat," quipped the Hall of Fame player, "but no one ever told me you were that crazy!" In another incident during a pro exhibition game between the Original Celtics and Brooklyn Visitations, an enraged player responded to a Kennedy foul call by literally ripping the shirt off the offending referee's back. Kennedy retaliated by docking the offender with three more rapid-fire fouls, but insisted on working the entire remainder of the match shirtless.

George Keogan

Being a basketball coach at Notre Dame University has long been something akin to being a backup first baseman with the New York Yankees of the early '30s, (behind iron-man Lou Gehrig) or perhaps third chair in a symphony orchestra's string section. Yet, if there is anywhere a true giant looming above Fighting Irish basketball history who merits enshrinement in the school's pigskin-oriented sports annals, it would have to be two-decade cage mentor George Keogan, who served in South Bend from just after the close of the First World War (1923) to the middle of the second (1943). Keogan posted winning seasons (he never had a losing campaign) and winning streaks (his last half dozen teams never lost more than six games in any season) throughout the 1930s that rivaled those that Knute Rockne was posting on the gridiron. He tutored some of the school's most memorable stars, including 1930s All-Americans Walter "Moose" Krause, John Moir, and Paul Nowak. And he was also one of the college game's more notable innovators, utilizing pivots and cuts copied from the barnstorming pros and pioneering the shifting man-to-man defense. Keogan's legacy might have been much greater than it was, but the 300-game winner (with a remarkable .773 win-loss percentage in South Bend) tragically died while still in his post during the middle of the 1943 college basketball season.

Dolly King

If there is a lost name in the history of basketball integration, it is most certainly the name of LIU's Dolly King. King pioneered as an early black in New York City while playing at LIU under Clair Bee in the late '30s. The first notable black star in what had previously been an all-white college game, King was in the starting lineup for an undefeated 1939 team that captured the second-ever NIT postseason trophy. He was also a fixture on Clair Bee's crack team the following season that pushed its winning streak to 34 games, one game late in the streak against defending NCAA champion Oregon being saved by Dolly King's last-second overtime scoop shot. More significantly, King was the first black to integrate a team in the National Basketball League once that league began to presume major-league status. Signed by Les Harrison to play the 1946–47 season for the eventual champion Rochester Royals, the 6'4" center-forward crossed the pro basketball racial lines several seasons ahead of recognized NBA pioneers Chuck Cooper (in Boston), Sweetwater Clifton (in New York), and Earl Lloyd (in Washington). King's career lasted but one winter in Rochester, yet he did reappear (alongside several other blacks, including Pop Gates and George Crowe) two seasons down the road in the lineup of the NBL Dayton Rens.

George King

Future NBA All-Star guard George King became the first college player at any level to average more than 30 points per game for a complete season when he paced the nation's small-college scorers (31.2) in 1950 for Morris Harvey College. It was not the last moment of glory for the five-season Syracuse Nats guard (1952 through 1956) who, half a dozen years later, sank a clutch free throw in the closing moments of Game 7 of the 1955 NBA Finals and then seconds later stole the ball to preserve a 92–91 championship victory over Fort Wayne. King also coached Purdue, with Rick Mount, to the NCAA championship game in 1969 versus Lew Alcindor and John Wooden's UCLA Bruins, and was also mentor for several stellar West Virginia University teams in the same decade.

Red Klotz

The Baltimore Bullets were one of the surprise teams of pro basketball history when they climbed out of a second-place regular-season slot in the weak Western Division to emerge as BAA champions during the 1948 season. They also boasted the league's smallest player at the time in 5'7" Louis "Red" Klotz out of Villanova. The diminutive guard didn't hang around long in the league that became the NBA, appearing in only 11 games that 1948 season and collecting only 15 regular-season points and 6 more in the playoffs. Klotz would nonetheless prove more durable in other venues of barnstorming basketball, stretching his career for another three full decades, first as a player and later as coach and eventual owner of the Washington Generals contingent, which provided regular opposition and nightly foils and whipping boys for the famed Harlem Globetrotters. BAA fans had only the briefest glimpse of Red Klotz, but literally millions of other spectators who crammed makeshift indoor and outdoor arenas spread from London to Hong Kong knew his face all too well. Potential NBA superstars such as Kentucky's Ralph Beard and Alex Groza and Bradley's Gene Melchiorre tragically lost lucrative careers in the early

'50s due to their efforts at purposely losing ball games. Red Klotz ironically built himself a satisfying career out of his own nightly and equally conscious efforts at intentional losing.

Walter "Moose" Krause

A handful of remarkable scorers stood out in the era of center jumps, set shots, ball control, zone defenses, and low-scoring plodding basketball. One of the most remarkable was Walter "Moose" Krause, three-time Helms All-American (1932 through 1934) in both basketball and football at Notre Dame. During three seasons of playing for Hall of Fame coach George Keogan, Krause and his teammates posted a 54–12 won-lost record and resurrected sagging Notre Dame basketball fortunes. In the process the bulky 6'3" Irish star became the first collegiate player to average more than 10 points per game since the sport's earliest days, when free-throw specialists padded their totals by taking all of a team's charity tosses. Before he was finished in South Bend, Krause would post records for single-game, single-season (10.1 points per game in 1933), and career points (547, 8.8), all of which would stand for more than a decade. Although his later Notre Dame coaching career (98–48 overall, but marked by poor teams in his final several seasons) was only moderately successful and sometimes soiled by campus dissension, Moose Krause remained of sufficient stature as one of the sport's earliest offensive stars to earn 1975 election into the Naismith Memorial Basketball Hall of Fame.

John Kundla

Red Auerbach coached pro basketball's most renowned dynasty, but it was the lesser-known John Kundla who directed the sport's first dynasty unit. A star player with the University of Minnesota's 1937 team that won a Big Ten championship, Kundla was plucked from an obscure position as coach of the local College of St. Thomas team to manage the new NBL outfit known as the Lakers, which had just been added to the National Basketball League. Handed such players as George Mikan, Jim Pollard, Swede Carlson, and Herm Schaefer (and later Vern Mikkelsen, Arnie Ferrin, Slater Martin, and Bob Harrison), Kundla hit the ground running in the pro ranks with six championships in his first seven seasons at the helm (one NBL crown, one BAA title, four NBA banners), certainly the fastest coaching start in post–World War II pro history. His NBA career ended in 1959, one season before the franchise was relocated to Los Angeles, and his final pro mark stood at 423–302 and also included six Western Division titles. Kundla also later coached his alma mater in the Big Ten, winning 110 of 216 contests, as well as the champion United States team for the 1965 World University Games.

Ward "Piggy" Lambert

More than a half-century after his retirement as Purdue coach in 1946, Ward Lambert's glowing basketball record is still largely unchallenged. For years Lambert owned seemingly unapproachable records for Big Ten coaching excellence: 29 seasons, 228 conference wins, 371 overall victories at a conference school, 11 Big Ten (then Western Conference) titles, and a stable of nine consensus All-American players. Before Bob Knight at Indiana University, only the Hoosiers' Branch McCracken had joined Lambert in reaching the conference 200-victory plateau. In recent seasons Knight has begun overhauling Lambert's records—foremost those for career (596 at Indiana) and conference (323) wins and for league championships (they are now tied at 11 apiece). Today it is Knight as symbol of the modern era and Lambert as standard-bearer for the past who together remain the greatest exemplars of winning in Big Ten basketball history. Closing in as well is Purdue's Gene Keady, who, during the 1998 season, himself overtook Lambert's record for Purdue victories.

*Ward "Piggy" Lambert,
Purdue University*

But Lambert's legacy—like Meanwell's at Wisconsin or Woolpert's out on the West Coast—had to do with far more than just winning countless games and a near-dozen league titles. Piggy Lambert was one of that small contingent of most influential pioneers who worked to shape the modern-era game of racehorse-style run-and-shoot basketball. When Lambert first came on the Purdue scene in the receding shadows of World War I, it was the "pass-and-plan" philosophy of Wisconsin's Walter Meanwell that still ruled the world of collegiate basketball play. Lambert held a far different vision of court tactics, however, and once he could recruit a small stable of athletes good enough to absorb and execute his looser version of the game, basketball was well on its way to undergoing radical changes that would alter the game forever.

Lambert's game would soon come to be known as "racehorse-style basketball" and was built on a delicate balance of size (for controlling the defensive boards) and speed (for running the ball up the court without set plays and careful shot selections). All-Americans John Wooden and Lloyd Kemmer (the speedsters) and Charles "Stretch" Murphy (the rebounder and feeder) soon enabled Lambert to take racehorse basketball off the drawing board and put it directly onto the hardwood. The era (and the league dominance) of Doc Meanwell was suddenly at a close, and that of Piggy Lambert was now off the ground and (quite literally) running. Although Lambert would know lean seasons from time to time over the next quarter-century, he would never go more than three successive campaigns without a Western Conference championship—at least not until the final five years of his lengthy career. But Lambert had also launched more than a winning tradition for Purdue; he had launched a revolutionary style of play that would eventually give birth to Red Auerbach, to Bill Russell, to Bob Cousy, and eventually to all the slam-dunking stars of today's more athletic version of James Naismith's once painfully slow-moving indoor game.

Tony Lavelli

A three-time All-American (1946, 1948, 1949), owner of a graceful sweeping hook shot and soft foul-shooting touch, and leading scorer of the then-prestigious Ivy League, Yale's Tony Lavelli was nonetheless overrated as a future pro and thus symbolic of Ivy League basketball's late '40s status as "a noncontact activity for effete intellectuals." Lavelli was at the time widely considered New England's best player, despite the simultaneous presence of both Bob Cousy and George Kaftan at Holy Cross. The 6'3" guard out of Somerville, Massachusetts, did enjoy the national limelight as the country's top college scorer (22.4) during his senior (1949) campaign, edging Villanova's Paul Arizin for the honors, and also maintained a 20-plus scoring average across four varsity seasons. Yet he was nonetheless a Boston Celtics draft pick who lacked speed as a guard and size as a forward and thus predictably labored through a pair of mediocre NBA campaigns with Boston and New York. What makes Lavelli memorable, despite such shortcomings and overblown reputation, was a rare backup talent with which he also entertained roundball crowds in both Yale Payne Whitney Gym and the venerable Boston Garden (during his stint as one-year Celtics benchwarmer). Lavelli—incredible as it seems—doubled as a skilled accordion player who regularly left the team locker room at intermissions to provide spectators with bonus halftime entertainment.

Bob "Slick" Leonard

The complete basketball career is likely to be one combining heroic college moments with significant pro impact, then rounded off with coaching luster in either the college or professional ranks. By this standard no one did it all any more completely than Indiana's Bob "Slick" Leonard. As a collegian Leonard was a two-time All-American, led a national championship team as an Indiana University junior, and even canned the key pressure-packed free throw to steal an NCAA tournament trophy. As a pro he turned in solid seasons with one of the legendary franchises of NBA history, unfortunately joining the Minneapolis Lakers several seasons too late to win championships with George Mikan and Company, yet nonetheless logging seven respectable pro seasons, which also included stops in Los Angeles and Chicago. And when it came to coaching Bob Leonard was a genuine legend of the American Basketball Association, directing the Indiana Pacers for a dozen seasons (eight in the ABA and four in the NBA), winning 529 games with that franchise (a club record), and masterminding three ABA championships. Leonard was the winningest mentor and also the longest-tenured bench fixture of the short-lived red, white, and blue American Basketball Association. Fifteen years beyond retirement as pro head coach, Bob Leonard has remained a fixture of the game in his new role as a colorful veteran broadcaster (currently in his 14th season) with the now-NBA-based Indiana Pacers. His infectious "Boom Baby!" call after hometown three-point baskets (especially those by Pacers star Reggie Miller) has become a popular rallying cry for Pacers fans throughout his home state of Indiana and the signature piece by which Leonard is now widely known to a whole new generation of Hoosier cage fans.

Earl Lloyd (11), Syracuse Nats

Transcendental Graphics

Earl Lloyd

October 30, 1950, perhaps should be a date that resonates loudly in the pages of American sports history. It was that evening when 6'6" forward Earl "Big Cat" Lloyd—freshly drafted from West Virginia State—took the floor for the Washington Capitols and thus became the first black ballplayer to appear in a professional basketball circuit that was itself beginning only its second season under the label of the National Basketball Association. Yet the date marking NBA integration is certainly not one boasting a similar impact on the public psyche as, say, April 7, 1947 (Jackie Robinson's debut with Brooklyn's National League Dodgers); and indeed the moment has been largely lost altogether to this nation's historical consciousness. It is hardly a surprising occurrence, since both the moment and its implications were largely unnoticed even at the time they unfolded.

There are at least four factors that have contributed mightily to the obliteration of Earl Lloyd and his pioneering moment in the integration of American sports. Foremost is the fact that basketball already had a more visible black presence at the time Lloyd, along with Chuck Cooper and Sweetwater Clifton, entered the league. Black and white barnstorming pros had often met head-to-head over the preceding decades. And the more popular college game had been slowly moving toward a black presence for more than 20 years. Jackie Robinson himself was a college star at basketball, among other sports, leading the Pacific Coast Conference in scoring for UCLA (1940, 1941). Secondly, few were paying much attention to basketball of the pro variety at the time (as opposed to baseball, which was almost "the only game in town"). What happened in arenas, gyms, and field houses didn't matter much to the American sports fan and (outside of a few NBA cities) was never truly front-page news. Thirdly, there remains the confusion over what constitutes NBA history (as opposed to NBL history or BAA history). One of the two forerunner leagues known as the National Basketball League (NBL) had already experienced black ballplayers, singularly and in groups: Dolly King appeared with the Rochester Royals in 1947, as did a whole team of Dayton Rens in 1949, plus an integrated Chicago Studebakers team a half dozen seasons earlier.

A fourth factor involved a matter of historical accident and a large measure of callous injustice to boot. Considerable attention was understandably paid to Walter Brown's drafting of Chuck Cooper for the Boston roster in April 1950, and thus for years Cooper would improperly be credited as the first man to integrate the league, totally overshadowing both Lloyd (first to actually play in an NBA game) and Nat "Sweetwater" Clifton (first to sign an official NBA contract). But in the end a major contributing factor is also the lackluster nature of Lloyd's own career. It would last a reasonable number of seasons (nine, more than either Cooper or Clifton), but would involve little more than role playing and nothing of true significance in individual statistics (8.4 points per game, 6.4 rebounds per game, 560 games). While his achievements were grander than those of Cooper (who had been the better college player), they don't measure up to those of Clifton (who at least averaged double figures and earned a single All-Star Game selection). And they would be quickly dwarfed by an explosion of black stars over the next few seasons—namely Maurice Stokes, Elgin Baylor, Oscar Robertson, and Wilt Chamberlain.

Ken Loeffler

Posting winning seasons was a regular habit for Hall of Fame coach Ken Loeffler, whether it was with one of the four college teams he served between the late '20s and late '50s, or with his two BAA clubs (St. Louis Bombers and Providence Steamrollers) in the late 1940s. But nowhere was that winning habit quite so easy as when Loeffler was at La Salle University in the early '50s and thus benefited from a one-man team named Tom Gola in his nightly lineup. During this 1952 through 1955 stretch Loeffler's Explorers copped an NIT crown (1952, with Gola as a freshman), encored with an NCAA title (1954, Gola's junior season), and then again reached the NCAA final game (1955, in Gola's last year). It was a four-year stretch run that only a handful of coaches (namely UCLA's John Wooden, Ed Jucker at Cincinnati in the early '60s, Mike Krzyzewski with Duke in the late '80s and early '90s) have ever matched or even come reasonably close to equaling.

Ken Loeffler, La Salle University

Even without Gola, however, Loeffler possessed a winning touch almost everywhere he went that was regular enough and long-lived enough to merit a 1964 induction into Springfield's Naismith Hall of Fame. In seven seasons at Geneva the Beaver Falls, Pennsylvania, native never knew a losing campaign and won two small-college conference crowns; at Yale he had only two winning clubs, but also much less serviceable talent; the half dozen years at La Salle brought 20-plus victories and postseason tournament invites in each and every campaign of his tenure; he coached winning teams in two of his three pro seasons (both with St. Louis); only at Texas A&M at career's end did he suffer a pair of humiliating campaigns in which his teams were regularly and soundly drubbed. The total NCAA count for Ken Loeffler was 310–198, a .610 winning ledger. The winning percentage with Gola in the house, however, stood above 85 percent, and it is likely that, without the three Final Four appearances (two NCAAs and one NIT) of those Gola-led seasons, there would have been little chance for Loeffler earning a prestigious plaque on the hallowed walls in Springfield.

Dutch Lonborg

Adolph Rupp and Dean Smith—college basketball's two all-time winningest coaches—both launched their masterful careers as undistinguished bench players on Phog Allen–coached Kansas University teams. Another of Allen's prodigies was a considerably more talented player, a somewhat less noteworthy longtime coach, yet nonetheless a heavyweight courtside figure who maintained his own major role in the sport's midcentury evolution. An all–Missouri Valley Conference football quarterback and end, as well as a baseball starting third baseman, Lonborg earned his primary playing laurels as second-team All-American and captain for a Phog Allen Kansas squad that preceded the Jayhawks' back-to-back consensus national championship teams by only two seasons. As a coach, Lonborg proved his mettle in the Big Ten Conference during 23 seasons at Northwestern, winning 237 games and a pair of conference crowns (1931, 1933). But it was back at his alma mater as athletic director after 1950 that the biggest impact was made. During 14 seasons under Lonborg's administrative hand, the Jayhawks reached national prominence, capturing an NCAA basketball championship in 1952, narrowly missing another with Wilt Chamberlain in 1957, and gaining national titles in several other sports as well. As an athletic administrator Dutch Lonborg would also leave his considerable mark by overseeing construction of the Allen Fieldhouse (one of the nation's largest campus basketball arenas at the time it was built), chairing the NCAA Basketball Tournament Committee (1947 through 1960) and the U.S. Olympic Basketball Committee (1957 through 1960), and serving as a distinguished president of the National Association of Basketball Coaches.

Clyde Lovellette

Clyde Lovellette owns one of the rarest of collegiate basketball bragging rights. To date, after almost six decades of postseason championship play, Lovellette remains the only man ever to win a national scoring title and simultaneously lead his team to an NCAA Tournament championship. The two-time consensus Kansas All-American and future journeyman NBA center-forward would accomplish this rarest of feats during the 1952 winter—his senior season—while filling a role as marquee player on Phog Allen's only tournament-era national championship team.

As a somewhat disappointing NBA journeyman, Lovellette would be most noted for his second-fiddle roles as backup to several of the game's most memorable starting centers—first George Mikan in Minneapolis, later Bob Pettit with St. Louis, and finally Bill Russell in Boston. When he was forced to step in as Mikan's

Clyde Lovellette,
University of Kansas

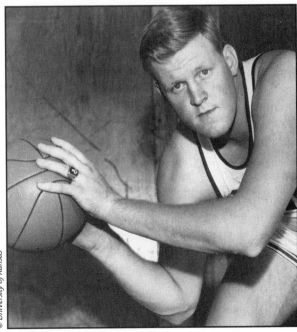

© University of Kansas

permanent replacement in 1955, however, it became clear that Lovellette possessed neither the quickness nor requisite ruggedness to stand on his own as a full-fledged NBA star. The gentle giant never held down an NBA starting role long enough to continue his prodigious collegiate scoring with Kansas. Yet he did log enough seasons and enough minutes to compile nearly 12,000 points as a pro and to register an 11-year 17.0 regular-season scoring average.

Branch McCracken

Branch McCracken still owns one record that can never be scratched from his impressive coaching résumé. It was McCracken (a Naismith Hall of Famer and Indiana University's first All-American player in 1930) who directed the very first NCAA championship team ever to emerge out of the Big Ten Conference, guiding his alma mater to a lopsided 60–48 triumph against Kansas in only the second year (1940) of the infant tournament's existence. Ohio State had represented the league in the very first postseason title fray in 1939 and had come home a 46–30 loser to Oregon. But McCracken and his Hoosiers did the nation's oldest conference proud a single season later. Jay McCreary, Marv Huffman, and Curly Armstrong combined for more than half the scoring output as McCracken's free-wheeling offense overwhelmed Kansas with its Phog Allen–taught controlled "pass-and-wait-for-the-perfect-shot" style of play. McCracken, unlike Allen, believed in putting the ball straight in the bucket and not in the hands of his playmakers, and it would be another full decade before any team would again top the 60-point level during an NCAA title game. In the interim McCracken's teams remained at the top of the Western Conference (as it was then still called) for almost all of the 1940s wartime era (finishing second for five straight seasons between 1939 and 1943) and the immediate postwar epoch (second again in 1947 and 1951) as well.

But despite his early successes, McCracken was never able to capture a conference crown during his first decade-plus of service in the league. That changed dramatically in the '50s—when the conference expanded by adding Michigan State University and officially renaming itself "The Big Ten," and when McCracken landed an unheralded prize in Hoosier state recruit named Don Schlundt. The wiry 6'9" player was able to shoot with either hand, used his elbows with recklessness under the basket, and was the most mobile big man the league had so far known. Behind Schlundt (a better than 25-points-per-game scorer over his final three varsity seasons) the supercharged Indiana team became an immediate powerhouse, and McCracken soon earned his long-awaited string of conference titles (1953, 1954, 1957, 1958) and another NCAA crown to boot. The national title would come at the conclusion of Schlundt's sophomore season, with forward-guard Bob Leonard sharing the offensive load (16.9 points per game and a key free throw to seal victory in the national title match) and Kansas again providing the futile opposition for the breathtaking 69–68 championship game showdown.

Arad McCutchan

Five national titles, two National Coach of the Year selections, several All-American players (including Jerry Sloan, Ed Smallwood, and Larry Humes), and even a Pan

American Games championship (1971) adorn the résumé of the most consistently successful college division coach in amateur basketball history. Arad McCutchan enjoyed his best single campaign when he led the 1965 University of Evansville Purple Aces (for whom he also played in the early 1930s) to a glowing 29–0 mark and defeated such national powers as Notre Dame, LSU, Northwestern, and Iowa in the process. McCutchan's career mark of 433–259 (compiled between 1947 and 1972) was also the winningest ever in college division play at the time of his retirement.

Robert "Bobby" McDermott

McDermott was one of the last of a breed—the tough-as-nails itinerant pro basketball journeyman who came to the game with no college experience and a blue-collar laborer's work ethic. He was also the last of the great two-hand set shooters, and his arching long-range bombs launched from anywhere inside the half-court line made him the most prolific scorer of first the ABL and then the National Basketball League in the years before hook-shooting George Mikan and jump-shooting Joe Fulks overhauled the game. And he also came at the end of the line for another dying pro basketball institution—the player-coach. In the dual capacity of bench boss and floor general he paced the George Mikan Chicago American Gears to the 1947 NBL title a season after leading the NBL Fort Wayne Pistons to a thrilling victory over the College All-Stars before a then-record 23,000-plus spectators.

But Bobby McDermott was hardly a dinosaur in his own era. His personal list of unique achievements is, in fact, almost staggering in its magnitude. He was the only player to lead three different pro leagues (ABL, New York State League, NBL) in scoring and one of the first two pros to average better than 20 points for a full season. He is also the only player-coach ever to guide two different teams

Bobby McDermott,
Chicago American Gears

Courtesy of Richard F. Triptow

(Fort Wayne in 1944 and Chicago in 1947) to league championships. Five consecutive times he was the NBL MVP; he ranked first all time in NBL scoring; and he was also second overall in NBL postseason scoring (54 points behind LeRoy "Cowboy" Edwards). In 1946 on the eve of the opening of the BAA and with it the modern era of pro basketball, NBL coaches and players joined with sports editors in a poll that named Bobby McDermott as the "Greatest Basketball Player of All Time."

Horace "Bones" McKinney

Among those basketballers who have first starred as players and later tried their hand at the coaching game, Horace "Bones" McKinney has enjoyed perhaps the greatest dual successes. This is true at least when it comes to the narrower list of combined player-coaches who have served exclusively at the Atlantic Coast Conference schools. McKinney would first parlay a successful playing tenure under Ben Carnevale at North Carolina into a substantial all-star career as a professional in the postwar Basketball Association of America. At Carolina the 6'6" McKinney plugged the center spot and provided scoring (9.8 points per game) and rebounding support for All-Americans John Dillon and Jim Jordan on a Tar Heels squad that reached the NCAA title game and fell just short of a first-ever national crown for the Chapel Hill school. The lithe frontcourt player (hence the nickname) was later a mainstay under a young coach named Auerbach for the BAA Washington Capitols of the late 1940s. He averaged a then-substantial 10 points over a six-season career (12 points per game as a rookie) that stretched out to more than 300 games. In 1947, the league's inaugural session, he ranked among the circuit's top point producers at a time when Joe Fulks was just beginning to boost scoring totals with his awesome jump-shooting displays. That same season McKinney was elected as a starter on the BAA's first-ever All-Star Team. The final season of BAA play (before merger with the rival NBL created a newly constituted NBA in 1950) would find McKinney and his front-running Washington team challenging legendary George Mikan and the dynasty Minneapolis Lakers in the championship finals.

McKinney's pro tenure ended with the Boston Celtics in 1952, after he had been reduced to limited service as a part-time role player. Half a decade later he was launched on a successful coaching venture at Wake Forest that would lead to a more-than-respectable eight-year winning percentage of better than 60 percent in league games, a regular-season league title in 1962 (when Wake with Len Chappell edged out Duke with Art Heyman by a single game), plus consecutive championships in the ACC postseason event in 1961 (besting Duke) and 1962 (beating upset-minded Clemson). In the first of these two highlight campaigns he would edge out another former star player—Duke's Vic Bubas, who had played under Ev Case at N.C. State and had also suited up for the NCAA Final Four in 1950—for the league's Coach of the Year honors. His overall 122 coaching victories would leave him, at the time of his departure, second only to his predecessor, Murray Greason, on the Wake Forest all-time list. He would later slide to fourth when passed by Carl Tacy and recent Wake mentor Dave Odom, and his 69 league wins would later also be rubbed out by both Tacy and Odom. For a span of eight years, nonetheless, McKinney's ACC win total stood as the Wake Forest benchmark.

McKinney's coaching tenure at Wake Forest would, of course, receive a huge boost from his one true star-quality player, repeat All-American Len Chappell. Chappell would not only carry McKinney and the rest of the Demon Deacons to consecutive ACC tournament crowns; as a senior he would almost single-handedly lift the Deacons all the way to an NCAA Eastern Regional title (with a 10-point victory over Villanova) and cherished Final Four berth against Ohio State in Louisville (the game in which Jerry Lucas suffered a leg injury that cost the Buckeyes a national title). That trip would make Bones McKinney only the second coach in ACC history—after North Carolina's Frank McGuire—to reach college basketball's ultimate championship showdown. It was the feather in the cap that topped a sterling, if brief, bench career for one of the most versatile basketball men ever to arise from the rich cage foundations already being embedded everywhere along Tobacco Road.

Walter "Doc" Meanwell

No one ever launched a coaching career with a faster route to the top of the heap than Walter "Doc" Meanwell. Not even Michigan's Steve Fisher—winner of an NCAA title game before he ever copped a regular-season victory as a head coach—

Transcendental Graphics

Walter "Doc" Meanwell,
University of Wisconsin

can boast a quicker jump out of the blocks. Nine of Meanwell's first dozen seasons (seven at Wisconsin, interrupted with two at Missouri) resulted in conference titles; his first three years on the job translated into Western Conference crowns for Wisconsin, and the Badgers lost only one game in the process (a road game at Chicago on the final date of the 1912 campaign). Meanwell's coaching record was an astounding 44–1 after just three winters on the job in Madison and Columbia.

Like Fisher, Meanwell would also coach a national championship club in his rookie campaign. For Meanwell, it was a Helms Foundation national title (retroactive), one that rang with slightly less authority, since there was no tournament at the time to settle the issue of the nation's best overall cage squad. Meanwell's impressive victory skein continued for much of the next two decades in Wisconsin, though the championship pace abated somewhat after the first dozen seasons. In all, Meanwell's teams would claim the Western Conference (Big Ten) championship banner in 9 of his 20 seasons at Madison, nearly a .500 average.

But, like Ward "Piggy" Lambert at Purdue, it was more than winning championships that etched Meanwell's nationwide reputation, though admittedly it was the year-in and year-out winning that first drew attention to his soon-to-be-renowned coaching philosophies. In short order Doc Meanwell was established as the most influential coach in the land. His methods were copied by other head coaches from East Coast to West Coast and everywhere in between. Meanwell's game was one of disciplined offensive patterns built around crisp, short passing and precisely rehearsed set offensive plays. It was Meanwell in Wisconsin, more than any other figure, who entrenched the earliest notions of the basketball coach as an artistic choreographer.

Ironically, Doc Meanwell's greatest legacy to the modern game of basketball, in the end, involved the battle he lost with the sport's national rule-making body and the dramatic backward-looking overhaul of the sport, which he tried but failed to provide. Although Lambert's fast-breaking style at Purdue was beginning to hold sway by the late '20s, Meanwell would make one last-ditch effort to move the game back in the direction of the pass-oriented sport he admired and taught. In what has become known to basketball historians as "the last great dribble debate" of 1927, Meanwell convinced the Collegiate Joint Rules Committee to vote by a slim margin (9–8) in favor of eliminating the dribble as a legal offensive maneuver. After adjourning to witness a professional championship game in which the famed Original Celtics of New York defeated the Cleveland Rosenblums by using a perfected version of Meanwell's passing style, the committee reconvened to hear an impassioned plea from CCNY coach Nat Holman, himself also a player with the Original Celtics. Holman's message that college players needed the dribbling game to successfully compete convinced the august committee to reverse its earlier stand and seal modern basketball's futuristic-looking direction.

Don Meineke

Sometimes a pioneering honor is misattributed and a single claim to fame evaporates in the face of revisionist (or in this case "correctionist") history. A 6'7" forward out of Dayton and top draft pick of the Fort Wayne Pistons, Don Meineke put together an all-around solid, if not spectacular, debut season (10.8 points per game, 460 rebounds, 78 percent free-throw accuracy) that assisted in lifting the Pistons from a losing ball club to an entry in the Western Conference Division Finals and also gained Rookie of the Year honors for Meineke. It was long assumed that Meineke's honor was the first of its type in the NBA, since the league's "official" encyclopedia (edited by Zander Hollander) for years began its rookie award lists with the 1953 season. More thorough research into early campaigns of a league with little sense of historical heritage has recently revealed that the NBA began making this trophy presentation (later called the Eddie Gottlieb Trophy and, most recently, the Coca-Cola Classic Trophy) as early as 1948, with Paul Hoffman of the Baltimore Bullets being the true first recipient. Others to precede Meineke in the honor were: Howie Shannon (Providence, 1949), Alex Groza (Indianapolis, 1950), Paul Arizin (Philadelphia, 1951), Bill Tosheff (Indianapolis, 1952 tie), and Mel Hutchins (Milwaukee, 1952 tie). Robbed of his unique distinction, Meineke nonetheless still boasts a five-year NBA career, which also featured stops in Rochester and Cincinnati, as well as a more stellar collegiate career in which he played for two NIT champions at Dayton, led the Flyers with seasons of 27 (1951) and 28 (1952) victories, and paced the nation in field-goal percentage as a senior.

Ray Meyer

Ten seasons might easily have been the full span of Ray Meyer's college coaching career and he still would have earned a rare and lasting niche in coaching lore. For it was Ray Meyer of DePaul University who discovered and nurtured (in some sense, actually created) basketball's first superstar—George Mikan. Mikan came to the DePaul campus as an uncoordinated giant and was turned into a skillful athlete by hours of strenuous practice and conditioning under the guidance of a young coach just launching his own Hall of Fame career. One immediate payoff was the best player in the country during the war years and an NIT championship behind Mikan in 1945. Meyer's tenure and record of solid achievement did go on for decades after Mikan and he inevitably produced some other excellent teams along the way. He also nurtured other high-profile star players—Dick Triptow on the same team with Mikan, Mark Aguirre and Terry Cummings in the '70s, and a slew of NBA-quality players in his final decade to prove he wasn't losing his touch after nearly 40 seasons on the job. By the time he retired in 1984 he ranked high among the all-time winners—currently sixth all time with 724 victories. His teams posted a most remarkable 37 winning campaigns, 20 20-win seasons (7 consecutive), 13 NCAA tournament visits (1 Final Four), and 7 NIT entries (1 title). When DePaul University finally fired Ray's son and successor Joey in 1997, the school, as a consequence, would be forced to embark on its first cage season in 53 years without a coach named Meyer.

Vern Mikkelsen

Mikkelsen earned the small measure of immortality that early pro basketball allowed as a member of perhaps the greatest front line of the game's first three decades. As a linchpin of the NBA's first great dynasty team in Minneapolis, Mikkelsen joined with Mikan and Jim Pollard to create a frontcourt trio that was known around the league as the Minneapolis Mountain Range and that was, by physical standards alone, the strongest frontwall trio ever assembled. Vern Mikkelsen arrived on the pro scene as a little-known 6'7" center out of local Hamline University who had recently led the small-college Pipers to three straight NAIA tournaments and a 1949 national championship in the lesser school division. Over 10 seasons in a Lakers uniform (all in Minneapolis) he would establish new standards for rugged floor play setting a benchmark for career foul disqualifications that still stands today, starring on four of the five Minneapolis league championship teams, amassing more than 10,000 points, and consistently ranking near the top of the league's rebounding leaders.

But the defining moment in Vern Mikkelsen's career (and one of the defining moments of NBA history) came on Christmas Day of 1949, one-third of the way into Mikkelsen's rookie season. Coach John Kundla, seeking a way to reverse his team's slow start and also trying to take advantage in the same lineup of both Mikan and his talented rookie backup, introduced for the first time a "double-pivot" frontcourt that had Mikan at his normal center post and Mikkelsen moved to a forward slot, but stationed near the basket. The result was basketball's first "power forward," with Vern Mikkelsen's role now redefined as that of grabbing rebounds, setting screens and picks, and collecting "garbage baskets" off of misses by Mikan and Jim Pollard. Over the subsequent decades the newly designed lineup slot became a staple of NBA play.

Bill Mlkvy

Wilt Chamberlain was immortalized by his superhuman size and strength, Elgin Baylor captured a piece of history with his unprecedented gravity-defying airborne antics, and Bill Mlkvy owns a piece of the sports history books on account of a spelling oddity. This 1951 unanimous All-America selection will always be remembered for his unique name and moniker—"the Owl without a vowel"—earned in a handful of high-scoring seasons at Temple University. What first got his unique name into the nation's sports pages, of course, was a single sensational season in which Mlkvy averaged a shade under 30 (29.2) to pace all collegiate scorers (he was also second in the land that year in both rebounds and assists). That one year (he failed to average 20 his one previous and one following campaign) was enough to earn a 1952 NBA draft selection from Eddie Gottlieb's hometown Philadelphia Warriors. During a mere 31 games among the pros (1952–53), the slim 6'4" forward unfortunately lacked more than simply vowels on the lineup card; he also displayed little, if anything, in the way of scoring punch or other compensating big-league talents.

Bill Mlkvy, Temple University

Transcendental Graphics

Stan (Stutz) Modzelewski

Lew Alcindor changed his name in midcareer for religious reasons and dozens of others have followed the pattern, from Kareem Abdul-Jabbar to Mahdi Abdul-Rahman (Walt Hazzard) and Zaid Abdul-Aziz (Don Smith) to Mahmoud Abdul-Rauf (Chris Jackson). But early 1940s Rhode Island State College star Stan Modzelewski decided on a name alteration for no other reason than the troublesome matter of spelling and the thorny issue of pronunciation. Stan Stutz compiled an impressive college résumé at Rhode Island, where he was a second-team All-American in 1941 and 1942. There he led the nation in scoring all three of his varsity seasons, aided considerably by playing under legendary coach Frank Keaney's famed "firehouse" fast-break offensive system. Within the pro ranks his achievements were far less spectacular: three BAA seasons with New York and Baltimore

*Stan "Stutz"
Modzelewski,
Baltimore Bullets*

Transcendental Graphics

and a modest 7.1 points per game average. He did flash brilliance, nonetheless, and once held the Knicks' playoff single-game scoring record with 30 points against the Cleveland Rebels in April 1947. Stutz was never on the cutting edge of basketball innovation nor (outside of his three national scoring titles) was he first to cross any important landmarks for individual statistical achievement. But decades before Abdul-Jabbar and his numerous imitators, Stan Stutz was the first basketballer of national note to overhaul his identity by means of a midcareer name change.

Charles "Stretch" Murphy

Charles Murphy once had his considerable cage fame linked to that of his teammate Johnny Wooden and his coach, Ward Lambert. Six decades later, however, he is a forgotten man whose name rarely appears even in reputed survey histories of the sport. During the first decade of racehorse basketball, however, Stretch Murphy was a giant, both on the court and in the sports pages. For Murphy played something of the same role in coach Lambert's early version of run-and-gun basketball at Purdue that Bill Russell would later play in Red Auerbach's Boston Celtics scheme. The 6'6" Murphy would clear the ball from the boards, and Lloyd Kemmer would lead the charge down the floor on 1928 and 1929 Purdue teams that didn't yet win conference titles but revved up their unique offensive style enough to outscore their closest Big Ten rivals by more than 100 points for the season. It was only the arrival of Johnny Wooden in the backcourt during Murphy's senior season that catapulted Ward Lambert's team to a mythical national championship and to legendary status as one of the first completely successful running-style teams. For his own part Stretch Murphy was a first-team All-American in 1929 and 1930 and eventually received Naismith Hall of Fame recognition for his pioneering position in the game's evolution.

Pete Newell

Naismith wasn't the only Canadian who impacted grandly on America's favorite indoor sport. Pete Newell's mark as a coach was not made with impressive longevity of service or overwhelming numbers in the victory column. He served only a modest total of 14 seasons as a head coach, 4 each at San Francisco and Michigan State and 6 with California, and his victory total reached only 234 games. Among those victories, however, were NIT (in his third season at San Francisco, 1949) and NCAA (his penultimate year at Cal-Berkeley, 1959) crowns plus an Olympic gold-medal win (1960) as mentor of one of the finest amateur teams ever assembled (Oscar Robertson, Jerry West, Jerry Lucas, Bob Boozer, Terry Dischinger, Darrall Imhoff, and Walt Bellamy). More im-

Charles "Stretch" Murphy, Purdue University

© Purdue University

portant for Newell's living legacy than any championships, however, was his oversized contribution as an inventive strategist and tactician: a forward-thinking approach to the game inherited from his playing days and coaching internship under pioneering James Needles at Loyola–Los Angeles College. Newell burst on the scene as a head coach at San Francisco between 1947 and 1950, where he pioneered a system of tight, aggressive defense and disciplined, patterned offense; his 1949 NIT championship team featuring John Benington, Rene Herrerias, and Ross Guidice not only shocked the eastern basketball establishment with their successes, but also set the stage for those later fabled NCAA championship teams with Bill Russell and K. C. Jones coached by his successor Phil Woolpert.

The pinnacle of Newell's coaching success came during the 1959 and 1960 seasons, when his University of California Golden Bears achieved two consecutive appearances in the NCAA championship game. A tension-packed victory over West Virginia (with Jerry West) in 1959 for the school's only national title was encored with a disappointing 20-point loss to the Ohio State Buckeyes featuring Jerry Lucas and John Havlicek the subsequent season. Newell's memorable accomplishments of those two glorious seasons included successive NCAA Final Four victories over the University of Cincinnati Bearcats, led by the incomparable Oscar Robertson. And during this same heady period Newell coached Team USA to its six-game sweep and gold-medal championship at the 1960 Olympic Games in Rome, Italy. That final event (overhyped Dream Teams aside) provided Americans with perhaps their finest moment ever in the international basketball arena.

Johnny and Eddie O'Brien

It was not Elgin Baylor who first put backwater Seattle University on the nation's basketball roadmap. That event occurred five winters before Baylor showed up in Washington State (imported from D.C.) and involved a diminutive backcourt star who was also a recruit from the East Coast and just as much of a giant killer as was the basketball team of Seattle University itself. During the 1951–52 season Seattle's 5'8" sharpshooter Johnny O'Brien (playing alongside his twin brother Eddie) became the first collegiate player to top 1,000 points in a single season. To underscore the feat, O'Brien also captured national attention that winter with a 43-point game (while playing in the pivot against the famed Goose Tatum) during his team's surprising exhibition upset of the world-renowned and seldom-defeated Harlem Globetrotters. A year later, as a senior, O'Brien posted a second 28-plus scoring average to finish third in the nation in that department (he would have paced the nation's scorers as a junior but Seattle was still only a Division II school). It was good enough to enthrone one of college basketball's most prolific scorers ever (25.8 career average) as the leading point-maker at the time of his graduation (he would be overhauled at the end of the decade by Oscar Robertson). And if this were not enough, Johnny O'Brien remains, to this date, the only player to score more than 40 points (42 versus Idaho State in 1953) in his first-ever NCAA postseason game.

Basketball was not the only talent for the amazing O'Brien twins, as together they joined the roster of baseball's Pittsburgh Pirates at the end of their college cage careers. But Johnny O'Brien's fame—for all his other scoring feats—will always rest upon the memorable 84–81 defeat of Tatum and the Globetrotters. The Trotters at the time were still playing serious basketball and generally ranked with the NBA champion Minneapolis Lakers as the world's best pro outfit. The January 1952 fund-raiser (aiding the 1952 U.S. Olympic Team) was at the time touted as one of the greatest upsets of both college and pro cage history. The contest drew a packed house into the University of Washington Pavilion and featured famed jazz musician Louie Armstrong as half-time entertainment. But the show, in the end, belonged entirely to the phenomenal Johnny O. Not only did the versatile O'Brien sink the 'Trotters with a hefty scoring barrage, but he did so by challenging the much taller Tatum at the big man's own pivot position. Goose Tatum had some choice words about his diminutive rival after the 5'8" New Jersey native dazzled him with his unstoppable scoring from directly under the bucket: "That Johnny O'Brien's no little man," grinned Tatum. "He's nothing but a big man!"

Harold "Ole" Olsen

If Naismith is the founding father of basketball and Phog Allen the spiritual father of basketball coaching, then it is longtime Ohio State University coach Harold Olsen who merits designation as "father" of college basketball's greatest showpiece—the NCAA postseason tournament. Trained as a player under the legendary Doc Meanwell at Wisconsin, Olsen set up shop at Columbus in 1922 after brief stops at Bradley and Ripon College and didn't depart until lured to the new BAA pro league in 1946 for a brief three-year tenure with the Chicago Stags. His 30-year college ledger in the end would contain 305 victories, five Big Ten Conference titles, three trips to the Regional Finals (then the tourney semifinals), and another to the championship game of the NCAA tournament, which he himself was most responsible for orchestrating. It was Olsen's lobbying that convinced the National Coaches Association to stage its own year-end playoffs in 1939 in direct competition with the National Invitation Tournament organized for Madison Square Garden by Ned Irish and the New York Metropolitan Basketball Writers Association a mere season earlier. Coach Olsen also sought and received permission of his fellow coaches to stage the deciding game between East and West Regional winners at the Patten Gymnasium on the Northwestern University campus. When the dust of that first historic event had settled, it was perhaps only fitting that Olsen's own Ohio State Buckeyes team was there to meet Oregon of the Pacific Coast Conference for the first NCAA trophy. But poetic justice would not pay off for Olsen, in the end, as Oregon's "Tall Firs" team scored a convincing victory over their game Eastern rivals. Olsen was thus owner of a dubious distinction as the first coach ever to lose an NCAA tournament championship game. Far more important, however, it was largely through Olsen's almost single-handed efforts that the pioneering 1939 NCAA postseason event ever became a reality in the first place.

Don Otten

This 6'11" giant out of Bowling Green University (Ohio) managed to hang around in the NBL and early NBA for a half dozen seasons with nothing much to distinguish his career beyond an individual league scoring title in the final campaign of the much-depleted NBL. That questionable pacesetting performance resulted from a 14-points-per-game average that was mediocre even by the standards of the day. What made Don Otten stand out on both the basketball court and in the sports pages was merely his immense size that was still a badge of uniqueness in the years immediately following World War II. The first agile and athletic seven-footers (or near-seven-footers) had appeared on the college cage scene in the mid-'40s with the likes of Bob Kurland at Oklahoma A&M, Mikan at DePaul, and George Kok of Arkansas, and Bowling Green's Don Otten (sometimes listed at seven feet) was among them. Otten's two most memorable moments on the basketball floor came during collegiate days in back-to-back NIT appearances at the ends of the 1945 and 1946 seasons. In the first, he lost a hard-fought personal and team duel in the championship game with DePaul's George Mikan. A season later he stood in stunned disbelief along with his teammates when a miracle last-second 58-foot heave by Rhode Island's Ernie Calverley spelled first-round defeat.

Fred Padderatz

Few modern-day fans have the slightest clue why basketball players are often referred to by sports columnists and announcers as "cagers" (many using the term may be equally as clueless) or why Naismith's game is repeatedly labeled the "cage" sport. The origins of the term hark back to basketball's misty past, to the earliest decades of barnstorming professional play, when courts were often enclosed in a hanging mesh of chicken wire or nylon rope—an innovation designed in part to keep rude fans (especially those in coal mining towns of Western Pennsylvania) from jabbing, poking, or pelting visiting players with foreign objects, and also, in part, to keep the basketball in play during an era when the rule still read that possession went not to the team opposite the last one to touch it in play but rather to the first team that could retrieve it out-of-bounds. The vicious scrambles for possession often led to the flattening of spectators, even those in balconies hanging above the floor.

The "cages" that marked early basketball play—like almost everything else in the sport from Naismith on down—can be traced to a known innovator and even a single moment of inventive inspiration. It was the very first acknowledged pro club—the Trenton Basketball Team in New Jersey, which had been ejected from its YMCA quarters in 1896 and began staging exhibitions in the local Masonic Temple— that takes full credit. Team manager Fred Padderatz, a carpenter by trade, strung and nailed the first chicken wire mesh in the Masonic Temple to keep both his players and the ball itself restricted to the wooden playing surface. One delightful legend reports that Padderatz conceived the innovation after a local sportswriter penned an account of a team exhibition match that quibbled that "these fellows play like monkeys and should be put in a cage." The cage idea, whatever its inspiration, soon received widespread popularity and was not entirely outlawed until the close of the 1920s. Padderatz's strange invention is no longer a part of the game we watch today, but the term it spawned is still very much with us a century later.

Andy Phillip

When it comes to selecting ultimate examples of the perfect "team player," World War II–era collegiate All-American and early NBA journeyman Andy Phillip may have to stand at the top of almost any list. Phillip's earliest fame came as floor leader of the legendary University of Illinois "Whiz Kids" club, which was the best in the nation at 17–1 in 1943 but disbanded before postseason tournament action so that all five starters could volunteer for military duty. The 6'3" versatile guard and forward set a Western Conference (Big Ten) scoring record for the first-place Illini as a sophomore, erased his own mark during the repeat championship year of 1943, and repeated his previous two All-American honors after returning from the war for his senior season in 1947. But his 11 pro seasons in the BAA and NBA with Chicago, Philadelphia, Fort Wayne, and Boston were known more for quick defensive hands, agile passing, and fiery play as a tireless competitor than for big-time scoring or individual stardom. He was twice a league leader in assists (with Philadelphia) and four times the league runner-up (twice with Chicago and twice with Fort Wayne). And it was Phillip and not Bob Cousy who in 1952 became the first NBA player to register more than 500 assists in a single season.

Two incidents in Phillip's career, however, are far better yardsticks of his esteemed value than any raw statistics. When the Chicago Stags franchise folded on the eve of the 1951 season, three top Chicago players—Phillip, Max Zaslofsky, and Bob Cousy—were placed in a special dispersal lottery involving New York, Philadelphia, and Boston. All three clubs coveted Phillip and Boston was especially disappointed when Cousy's name rather than Phillip's came up under its banner. Five seasons later Auerbach talked Andy Phillip out of retirement, and when the aging playmaker joined the Celtics' lineup as a top substitute his presence was as responsible as anything else (including the arrival of rookies Bill Russell and Tom Heinsohn) for Boston winning its first NBA crown.

Jim Pollard

"Kangaroo Kid" was his unusual nickname, and his leaping and soaring style of play seemed years ahead of the rest of the league. If Jim Pollard was a major star with one of the great teams of the late '40s and early '50s, he might have been far more luminous had he come along a decade or two later. The nickname came from an extraordinary leaping ability that the 6'4" Pollard had already demonstrated as a 1939 high school All-American in Oakland, California. The slim and agile natural athlete repeated his All-American accolades at Stanford University in 1942 and was the leading scorer on a Stanford team that captured the national championship with an NCAA Finals victory over Dartmouth, despite the fact that the star junior forward himself missed the title game due to a bout with influenza. Pollard's largest notoriety, however, came during an eight-season NBA career in Minneapolis, where he anchored one of pro basketball's great frontlines alongside George Mikan and Vern Mikkelsen, contributed to one NBL championship, one BAA title, and four NBA crowns, made the NBA All-Star squad on four occasions, and was high scorer during the 1954 NBA All-Star Game in Madison Square Garden. Pollard's deadly jump shot was once called the best corner shot ever, and in 1952 a poll of former and active BAA, NBL, and NBA players surprisingly selected Pollard over Mikan and Dolph Schayes as the best individual player who had yet appeared in the still-infant league.

Art Quimby

The first man to play in the NBA owning a last name beginning with *Q* was unfortunately not Art Quimby; the early '50s Yankee Conference rebounding and scoring ace at Connecticut never played in the league, though he was a middle-of-the-pack draft choice by Rochester after his 1955 senior season. Quimby was not big enough nor mobile enough for the pros, yet the tenacious 6'5" center was an excellent board-sweeper from an era when the rebounding specialist was still a center-stage feature of the college sport. An extraordinary set of athletes plus an era of low shooting percentages (usually hovering around the high 30 percent range) combined to convert the mid-1950s into a veritable rebounding sideshow. Seven of the eight top NCAA career rebounding totals still belong to players who graduated in either 1955 or 1956. Joe Holup of George Washington, Charlie Slack of Marshall, and Eddie Conlon of Fordham trail directly behind La Salle's incomparable Tom Gola on the all-time career list. Not far off the pace stand Dickie Hemric of Wake Forest and Connecticut's Art Quimby. With exactly 40 caroms versus Boston University, the UConn ace became one of only four major-college players ever to grab 40 or better in a single game. Quimby was also the main reason why Hugh Greer's perennial Yankee Conference champions set a still-standing 1955 NCAA single-season record for highest rebounding average with 70 per game.

Sam Ranzino

Sam Ranzino came onto the scene in Raleigh at the height of that marvelous string of years in the wake of World War II that established the Deep South coaching legend of Everett Case, while at the same time closing the door on a final marvelous chapter of N.C. State's participation in the venerable Southern Conference. He teamed up with Dick Dickey to give the school its first pair of multiple-year All-Americans. It was a combination that grabbed victories as well as headlines, and the Case-led Wolfpack amassed a sterling 111–24 overall record during the four seasons that Ranzino suited up (51–4 in Southern Conference league play and 14–0 in league tournament action). As a remarkable scorer during an era still marked by modest team point totals, the 6'1" guard-forward rang up the school's first 20-plus scoring average when he crossed that plateau as a senior in 1951. His 2,237 career field-goal attempts and 479 successful free throws surprisingly have never been surpassed in four subsequent decades. And his 744 successful field goals also still rank him in the Wolfpack career top five, as do his numbers for free-throw attempts and total career points. It is a remarkable legacy for a cager who performed in an era when the jump shot was a brand-new innovation, when dunking was considered showboating, and when the game's pace of action was still nothing short of glacial by today's racehorse standards.

Mel Riebe

Among the professionals performing in stable leagues in the years during and immediately after World War II, it was a stocky 5'11" Wooster College alumnus playing with Cleveland of the NBL who logged the very first 20-points-per-game season's scoring average on record. The lofty total, accumulated across 30 games, came during the 1945 season, giving "Mouse" Riebe his second straight league-leading honors in only his second season in the circuit. Playing with Cleveland teams two more seasons (the NBL Allmen Transfers and BAA Rebels) and then wrapping up his pro career with Boston and Providence of the BAA over yet two more campaigns, the agile dribbler and uncanny outside shooter never again crossed the 20-point scoring barrier. But in this case once was enough to assure a small but lasting piece of the professional basketball record book.

Arnie Risen

Today Arnie Risen is a forgotten figure, but in the early '50s he was a highly recognizable fixture for the first generation of NBA followers. He was also a constant thorn in the side of some of the more prominent big men such as George Mikan, Alex Groza, and Larry Foust. In 13 seasons with the Indianapolis Jets (NBL), Rochester Royals, and Boston Celtics, the slim but extremely agile 6'9" pivotman collected two NBA titles (1951, Rochester, and 1957, Boston), tallied 9,000 points and 5,000 rebounds (the true figure was likely one-third higher, since no rebound numbers were recorded during his first five pro seasons), ranked high among league scorers and rebounders in his earliest seasons, and proved an able bench player with Boston in his final three campaigns. Perhaps only Mikan, Neil Johnston, Ed Macauley, and Alex Groza were more polished at the pivot position during the NBA's first half dozen seasons. Risen's career year came with Rochester in the final year of the BAA (1949) when the former Ohio State star paced the circuit in field-goal percentage, trailed only Mikan, Fulks, and Max Zaslofsky in scoring, shouldered his team's rebounding responsibilities (though no official league stats were yet kept in this category), and was voted second-team all-league center behind the incomparable George Mikan.

John "Honey" Russell

The Boston Celtics didn't actually launch their franchise history with Arnold "Red" Auerbach at the reins, although sometimes it seems that way in retrospect. In reality the doors swung open on the first several seasons of BAA action with Auerbach running the show for the short-lived Washington Capitols franchise and another future Hall of Famer entrenched on the bench for Walter Brown's club in the Boston Garden. John "Honey" Russell suffered two painfully long losing seasons with the fledgling Celtics, a tenure that was hardly a fitting middle chapter to what had already been a somewhat brief but altogether spectacular college coaching career during the late '30s and early '40s at Seton Hall University. Russell took over the Pirates' cage program in 1936 and quickly built it into one of the strongest in the nation. His teams won a then-record 43 straight games between 1939 and 1941, a stretch when he had as his centerpiece player one of the great college backcourt men of all time in future pro star Bobby Davies. But when Seton Hall dropped its basketball operations during World War II, Russell's college coaching career ended abruptly and quite unexpectedly.

Russell would next return to the ABL, where he had already been a star player during the league's heyday between 1925 and 1931 and had paced the Cleveland Rosenblums to the ABL title during the league's inaugural season. On returning to a now watered-down ABL in the mid-'40s, the 40-plus-year-old mentor again saw service as an active player in addition to his coaching duties. And he also pulled a rarest of doubles for one stress-filled season, coaching both an ABL club in Trenton, New Jersey, and Manhattan College simultaneously. Russell would return to Seton Hall in 1950 (on the heels of his Celtics debacle) and would prove, in the process, that he was still a master of the college game, producing another series of fine teams and another string of All-American stars. Especially potent were the clubs featuring Walter Dukes at center and Rich Regan in the backcourt, both future successful NBA warriors. A 1953 Russell-coached team featuring Dukes and Regan captured an NIT crown by blitzing St. John's and also sat second in that year's final AP and UPI national polls. By career's end his 17 years at Seton Hall had produced an impressive 294–129 winning record. But most important about Russell's split college tenure was the manner in which it offered a microcosm of basketball's evolution. In the professional game he had begun as a barnstorming player (with the Original Celtics) and would close by serving as first coach (at Boston) for what would turn out to be the modern sport's most legendary team. In the college ranks he stood squarely at the fountainhead of the sport's midcentury explosion into a major-arena big-time entertainment spectacle that rivaled even the national game of baseball.

Ken Sailors

Stanford's Hank Luisetti is widely credited with inventing one-handed shooting in the mid-'30s; a closer approximation to the truth would be that Luisetti spread the popularity (especially on the East Coast with his several visits to Madison Square Garden) of a shooting style that had been experimented with from time to time in western and southern sectors of the country and even mentioned in the *Spalding Guide* as early as 30 years previous. Joe Fulks similarly gets his share of credit for

Ken Sailors (4),
University of Wyoming

Transcendental Graphics

pioneering the one-handed jump shot, but in reality that style also had at least several practitioners before Fulks brought it to the BAA in the late '40s. The most memorable of Fulks's predecessors was 5'10" guard Ken Sailors, whose dazzling exhibition of dribbling and leaping one-handed tosses earned an NCAA tournament MVP trophy and also lifted Wyoming to the 1943 national title over Georgetown in a headlining Madison Square Garden matchup.

Sailors, who was a junior at the time of his sensational 1943 splash in New York, had caused little previous national notice of his unique talents. He was the Cowboys' second-leading scorer (behind 6'7" center Milo Komenich) in the championship season and never earned All-American honors. While he would make a small mark with seven different BAA and NBA teams across seven seasons (three seasons averaging double figures and a 12.6 career scoring average), there was nothing consistently brilliant about his pro career, either. About the most that can be said in the way of underscoring distinction is that the deft passer and ball handler was an All-BAA selection during his rookie season with Providence and ranked but one time in the league's top 10 in both points and assists. Ken Sailors was nonetheless an important pioneer of the revolutionary one-handed jump-shooting style that would alter basketball's fortunes in the 1940s and pave the way for the wide-open and high-scoring modern version of Naismith's once-plodding game. At the time of his brief glories, however, he was recognized more for unorthodoxy than for pacesetting. "If your feet left the floor," Sailors once recalled about his playing days, "you were definitely considered a freak."

Abe Saperstein

Barnstorming days of basketball's middle-age years provided no more memorable name or charismatic figure than colorful Abe Saperstein. Of the many ingenious promoters who built the sport from scratch in the teens and '20s, by organizing traveling squads of itinerant hoopsters who would play in dance halls, high school gyms, converted outdoor arenas, or absolutely anywhere a game might be had against local opposition for a night's paycheck, it was Saperstein with his Chicago-based Harlem Globetrotters that captured the nation's and eventually even the entire world's imagination. Saperstein's pioneering team—with its boatload of charismatic stars such as Reece "Goose" Tatum, Marques Haynes, and Meadowlark Lemon, and its unique blend of basketball skill with comic routine and pure entertainment spectacle—spread American basketball to all corners of the globe with their whirlwind tours around the globe and across the decades of the 1930s, 1940s, and 1950s.

Saperstein began his fairy-tale career by managing local semipro outfits in Chicago and out of these grew first his Savoy Big Five team and later his Harlem Globetrotters, who played their first road game in Hinckley, Illinois, on January 7, 1927. Early members of the team, which won 101 of its 117 first-season matches, were Toots Wright, Fats Long, Kid Oliver, Andy Washington, and Runt Pullins. The misleading name for a team with Chicago roots was carefully chosen as a promotional gimmick orchestrated by a brilliant novice promoter. Along with its popular suggestion of Negroes, Harlem (New York as a whole) owned a far greater aura of importance and worldliness and would be likely to sell a few more tickets to easily duped audiences. The 'Trotters first gained widespread recognition with their triumphs in the World Tournament competitions at the end of the '30s, reaching the semifinal round and beating the Rens in 1939 and winning the whole affair a year later. They gained considerable visibility also with tours versus college all-star squads and with a series of games staged with the NBA champion Minneapolis Lakers. Both promotional tours produced big gates and even grander hard-court excitement. And the renowned troupe soon became a world fixture with regular summer European tours throughout the 1950s. By the 1940s, with Goose Tatum and Marques Haynes in the fold, the Globetrotters spectacle turned more and more toward crowd involvement, featured stunts designed to interact with the courtside spectators, introduced wholesale slapstick comedy, and provided something of a three-ring-circus atmosphere. Despite Saperstein's death in 1966, the Globetrotters have continued on for three more decades and for hundreds of thousands of additional miles, remaining active down to the present day. In the process they have further extended Saperstein's living legacy as well as their own unique niche as basketball's original international ambassadors.

Abe Saperstein's promotional sports career extended beyond the scope of the 'Trotters and barnstorming basketball. He was a promoter as well of Negro-league baseball in the '30s and owned financial interests in numerous Negro-league teams. He maintained other basketball and baseball ownership interests as well, including those with the major-league St. Louis Browns and the NBA Philadelphia Warriors. But the Globetrotters are his truest legacy and perhaps still stand as the greatest single ongoing sports promotion venture of all time. The team Saperstein launched has now played beyond 20,000 games over a half-century of touring, appeared in more than 100 countries, and performed before an estimated 100 million spectators. Even Michael Jordan, operating in the era of the electronic village, has never amassed quite so extensive and lasting an audience.

Dolph Schayes (NBA "Top 50" Selection)

Five men can boast the rare distinction of having, at one time in their lives, been the most prolific scorer in NBA history. George Mikan was the league's first point-making star and entered retirement in 1955 with 11,764 total points stuffed into his résumé. Wilt Chamberlain would begin obliterating all existing scoring records from the moment he first entered the professional league as a rookie in the fall of 1959; by the time Wilt's own career enjoyed its final curtain call in 1973, "The Big Dipper" had posted a seemingly unchallengeable career total of 31,419. Chamberlain's mountain of points was built largely on the strength of his incomparable seven-year run between 1960 and 1966 during which he averaged a phenomenal 39.5 per game across the entire stretch. But even Wilt's lofty mark was not safe from future assaults and has since been overhauled by basketball's flesh-and-blood monument to longevity, Kareem Abdul-Jabbar (Lew Alcindor), who amassed a stratospheric 38,387 total across his own 20-season NBA sojourn. And for a brief period a few seasons before Chamberlain overwhelmed all earlier point totals, Bob Pettit would also reign supreme, becoming the first to cross the career 20,000-point plateau in his 11th and final campaign. The fifth, and usually overlooked, member of this quintet of career record holders was a gritty workhorse who never averaged more than 25 for any single season of his career and

*Dolph Schayes (4),
New York University*

Transcendental Graphics

only reached the 20-points-per-game watermark in 6 of his 16 NBA seasons (1 in the NBL). Yet it was Dolph Schayes of the Syracuse Nationals who first climbed past Mikan in 1957, and whose 19,249 career total (after retirement in 1964) was the standard that Pettit overtook in 1965.

Never a scoring champion, yet nonetheless a true scoring machine of the NBA's first decade, Schayes was a slashing driver and adept free-throw shooter who specialized in breaking to the basket for a bucket and an inevitable "fouled-in-the-act-of-shooting" charity toss. He was thus the game's first "three-point" specialist back when three points were still earned the hard way—on a bucket and a free throw. And he earned enough of these "hard-way" points to become the first NBAer ever to cross the 15,000 career points plateau.

The distinguishing features of Schayes's unique game were three-fold—his adept driving ability, an accurate two-handed outside set shot (also used for free-throw tosses), and his rugged durability during the sport's rough-and-tumble age. Schayes took a continued battering due to his aggressive style and often played with severe injuries that never seemed to slow his remarkable shooting performances. It was, in fact, the injuries (broken right wrist, fractured left wrist, broken nose several times) that likely indirectly contributed to Schayes's remarkable shooting prowess. Schayes himself would later comment that the two broken wrists were probably "the two best breaks I ever had"—a fracture to the right wrist led to his consciously developing a deadly left-handed shot; a broken left wrist two seasons later spurred the resourceful All-Star to perfect his patented two-handed set shot.

Two additional claims to fame for Dolph Schayes were his role as perhaps the greatest-ever Jewish professional player and his distinction as half of the NBA's best-ever father-son combination. As the former, he was the last of a line of impact Jewish cage stars (mostly out of the playgrounds of New York) of the '30s and '40s, a list that includes such names as Moe Becker, Sonny Hertzberg, William "Red" Holzman, Harry Boykoff, Ralph Kaplowitz, Dutch Garfinkel, Sid Tanenbaum, Hy Gotkin, Max Zaslofsky, and Ossie Schectman, among others. Today he cheers on his son, 6'11" Danny Schayes, longtime role-playing forward-center with the Denver Nuggets and several other NBA clubs in the late '80s and throughout most of the 1990s.

Ossie Schechtman

Ossie Schechtman's span of notoriety didn't even last the reputed 15 minutes. It hardly spread over as much as 15 seconds. The LIU grad, who played under legendary Clair Bee on the undefeated 1939 NIT champions (alongside Irving Torgoff and Dolly King), did appear in 54 BAA games (although these were all crammed into a single season) and recorded 435 career points (better than 8 per game). Yet Schechtman might be one of the most forgettable among the hundreds of journeymen who have trod the floors of the NBA, BAA, NBL, and ABA across the past half-century had it not been for one of the most egregious sports-world examples of someone being precisely in the right place at the right time. When the New York Knickerbockers and Toronto Huskies tipped up the first ball in Toronto's Maple Leaf Gardens on the night of November 1, 1946, inaugurating a new sporting enterprise known ambitiously as the Basketball Association of America, history was about to be made in a momentary flash of action. That opening tip was corralled by Knicks guard Leo Gottlieb; Gottlieb broke downcourt with several dribbles and fed a perfect lead pass into the hands of Schechtman breaking down the opposite sideline, who in turn matter-of-factly dropped in the driving layup. In an instant that had passed even before its full significance had sunk in for those who had witnessed it, Ossie Schechtman had scored the first field goal of NBA history.

Don Schlundt

Indiana University's Don Schlundt was a basketball player well ahead of his time. As formidable as he was, perhaps a decade or two later he would have been even greater. Here was a rail-thin 6'9" center who moved like a point guard, shot from a variety of angles and with both hands, outmaneuvered all inside defenders, and used his blade-like elbows with merciless efficiency to cut his path clear to the basket. By the time Schlundt arrived on the Indiana University scene in 1951–52, the era of the lumbering immobile center (à la George Mikan or Bob Kurland) had passed, and the era of the mobile pivotman as a vital cog in a nonstop fast-breaking offense (à la Bill Russell with the Boston Celtics) was just around the corner. Schlundt pioneered the new prototype within the Big Ten Conference with great efficiency while starring for one of Branch McCracken's finest-ever Hoosier teams. Bolstered by Schlundt's three years of high scoring (25.4, 24.3, 26.0), the McCracken-coached Hoosiers ran to a pair of league championships and the school's second-ever NCAA postseason crown.

It was in the 1953 NCAA title match with defending champion Kansas, coached by legendary Phog Allen, that Schlundt and his Hoosiers enjoyed their finest hour. Schlundt was only a sophomore, yet had burst into the nation's top 10 in scoring and carried the club to a 23–2 record and top national AP and UPI rankings. Junior teammate "Slick" Leonard canned the decisive free throw to preserve a thrilling 69–68 championship victory, but Schlundt led all scorers in the title match with 30. The performance would also earn an ironic distinction: Don Schlundt is, to date, still the only player to average better than 20 for a team reaching the national finals and yet not later play in either the NBA or ABA after college days. Don Schlundt's IU career unfortunately ended with something of a huge disappointment two seasons later, despite its many early successes. Stripped of his backcourt running mate, Bob Leonard, the senior captain was surrounded with little in the way of a

Don Schlundt, Indiana University

supporting cast. Schlundt's final season thus resulted in his third-straight individual conference scoring crown, but Indiana as a team tumbled to 8–14 overall and limped home with an embarrassing ninth-place conference finish as belated encore to its 1953 national championship banner.

John Schommer

No more imposing figure arises from the first three decades of college basketball action than University of Chicago four-time All-American John Schommer. The 6' center was later a retroactive selection (in the 1930s) for the Helms Athletic Hall of Fame All-Time All-American Team, he also led all Western Conference (later Big Ten Conference) scorers for three consecutive seasons (1907 through 1909), a feat only duplicated in nine subsequent decades by Don Schlundt (Indiana), Terry Dischinger (Purdue), and Rick Mount (Purdue). Schommer once scored 15 field goals in a game against Illinois (in an era when an entire team would only score half that many) and on another occasion, held all opposing centers to a grand total of four baskets over a stretch of nine games. But Schommer's most imposing feat of all was the 80-foot desperation shot he heaved in for a last-second victory over Pennsylvania that clinched a mythical national title in 1908 for Chicago's Maroon. It remains by far the longest title-clinching game-winning basket in the entire century-plus history of college basketball.

Fred Scolari

Nine-year BAA-NBA veteran and two-time All-NBA selection Fred Scolari owns one of those rare and much-touted "first-ever" labels as the inaugural NBA free-throw accuracy champion. This distinction came for the Washington Capitols' backcourt ace during the opening campaign of the Basketball Association of America (BAA), when he poured home more than 81 percent of his charity tosses, a dead-eyed proficiency that would hold up well in almost any season of the league's subsequent half-century history. Scolari was also a double-figure scorer in all of his pro seasons but two (the final two, when he saw only part-time service), played with five clubs including the Fort Wayne Pistons and Boston Celtics, and even served one "double-duty" season in Baltimore (1952) as a player-coach.

Ken Sears

During the mid- and late '50s the list of imposing and durable NBA big men included the likes of Bill Russell, Bob Pettit, George Yardley, and Maurice Stokes, as well as New York's slender 6'9" pivotman Ken Sears. In his best seasons of 1959 and 1960 the Santa Clara grad averaged 21.0 and 18.5, respectively, and was a member of the Eastern Division squad in two consecutive NBA All-Star contests. With 15 points Sears trailed only Philadelphia's Arizin (16) as top point man for the East during the 1959 game in Detroit. Over eight NBA campaigns (including one with San Francisco), the Knicks' "Big Cat" would log more than 7,300 points and average only a fraction under 14 points per game in career scoring. Despite all these positives, however, Ken Sears's name will perhaps always be linked with one of the NBA's most infamous lists, that of the string of disappointing and underachieving top draft choices squandered annually in the '50s by badly managed and ill-starred Knickerbockers clubs. The list between 1953 and 1963 included all of the following in annual order: Walter Dukes (1953), Jack Turner, Ken Sears (1955), Ronnie Shavlik, Charles Tyra, Mike Farmer, Johnny Green, Darrall Imhoff, Tom Stith, Paul Hogue, and Art Heyman (1963).

Barney Sedran

Numerous star athletes doubled as playing coaches in the early days of pro basketball at midcentury and also at the dawn of the century in the college ranks. Few have ever claimed the distinctions on the high school court, even in the sport's earliest days. One who did was pioneering Barney Sedran, one of the most prominent scholastic, collegiate, and barnstorming pro stars of the teens and '20s. Standing only 5'4" and feather light at 115 pounds, Sedran was agile and talented enough to pace a championship team at New York's DeWitt Clinton High School (1905 through 1908), earn numerous college all-star honors while playing at CCNY (1909 through 1911), and earn major billing on the barnstorming circuit with the New York State League team at Utica. The career highlight came for the "Mighty Mite of Basketball" in 1914, when he paced Utica to a World Pro Championship banner, scoring 34 points in one tournament game along the way without benefit of a backboard. Sedran also later starred with the famed New York Whirlwinds ball club and scored an estimated 3,500 career points over two decades, although few, if any, statistics are available from many of his grandest seasons.

George Senesky

It is still a select circle of men who have won NBA titles as both a player and a coach: names such as Bill Russell, Tom Heinsohn, Bill Sharman, and Phil Jackson come most readily to mind. Excluding player-coach Buddy Jeannette (Baltimore, 1948), who accomplished both ends of such double victory at one and the same time, it was 1956 Philadelphia Warriors first-year coach George Senesky who first stepped across this rare milestone. Senesky was a backcourt starter on a Philadelphia team coached by Eddie Gottlieb and starring Joe Fulks that ran off with the very first BAA championship in 1947, routing the Chicago Stags in five games for the trophy. Nine seasons later he inherited from Gottlieb a Warriors team loaded with scoring punch that included Neil Johnston (No. 3 in the league in points and best in shooting percentage), Paul Arizin (the league's second-best scorer and second-best percentage shooter), prized rookie Tom Gola, and a deep backup roster including Jack George, Joe Graboski, and Ernie Beck. Again it took Senesky's team only five games of a championship series to sprint to victory, this time over the Fort Wayne Pistons. The championship in 1956 not only clinched a rare first for Senesky, but it also closed out the league's pre-Celtics era, marking the last campaign before Boston had Bill Russell and thus owned a lock on league championships for most of the next decade and a half.

Bill Sharman (NBA "Top 50" Selection)

Bill Sharman was unquestionably one of basketball's greatest pure shooters of any epoch. He was also one of the most adept athletes at making foul shots (he led the NBA seven times in this category, five times consecutively), one of the game's most relentless winners (four NBA championships as a player and three pro titles as a coach), basketball's most fanatic proponent of relentless physical conditioning, and also one of the sport's cleverest and most fate-charmed coaches. As a player Sharman rained his deadly jumpers first at Southern California (twice Pacific Coast Conference MVP) and then in the Boston Garden during the earliest seasons of Red Auerbach's Boston Celtics dynasty. He teamed with the Hardwood Houdini, Bob Cousy, for the finest NBA backcourt of the league's first decade. His foul-shooting numbers during those Boston years were marvelous, especially when considering the conditions that prevailed in early NBA seasons.

Bill Sharman,
Boston Celtics

Transcendental Graphics

Balls were not always perfectly round, playing floors were often warped and rarely allowed for true bounces, and arena temperatures in Rochester, Syracuse, Fort Wayne, and elsewhere were often in the low 40s (since windows were left open to combat smoke-filled gymnasiums) and shooters' hands often nearly turned blue as a result.

Throughout his playing days Bill Sharman maintained a physical conditioning regime that crossed the boundaries of the obsessive. When it came to coaching, Sharman had a knack for being in the right place at the right time. He first enjoyed a championship team in the ABL (with Cleveland in 1962) and later another in the ABA (with Utah in 1971). His best stroke of fortune, however, involved taking over the 1972 Los Angeles Lakers team that featured Wilt Chamberlain, Gail

Goodrich, and Jerry West and won a still-record 33 straight games. Sharman thus stands as the only coach to win titles in three pro leagues (NBA, ABA, ABL) during the second half of the century. And this knack for timely positioning also showed up on the baseball diamond where Bill Sharman once starred as a promising late-1940s outfield prospect with the Brooklyn Dodgers organization. Called to the big leagues for the final month of the 1951 season (his last month in pro baseball), the future basketball Hall of Famer would be in uniform on the Brooklyn bench when Bobby Thomson cracked the most famous homer in baseball history to win a renowned pennant playoff at the Polo Grounds. Weeks earlier the same Bill Sharman—who would never appear in a big-league game—was tossed from the Dodgers' bench for umpire-baiting, thus making him the answer to one of the most famous among baseball trivia questions. Bill Sharman is perhaps the only ballplayer ever ejected by umpires from a major-league game, while at the same time never having appeared in a big-league lineup.

Ronnie Shavlik

Ronnie Shavlik (a pain-wracked victim of cancer in 1983) is today remembered among that fortunately small handful of past N.C. State basketball legends whose personal lives were scarred by ill luck and even weighty tragedy. In happy undergraduate days, however, Shavlik was one of the first legitimate cage stars of the dawning ACC era. Ronnie Shavlik played in an epoch of truly impressive rebounders, and among those early giants of the backboards, he was certainly one of the very best and undeniably one of the most consistent. His career rebounding total (1,598) stands more than 50 percent above the school's closest challenger in this department, lanky future NBA star Tom Burleson (with only 1,066). His career rebounding average (16.8) also far outstrips all earlier and later N.C. State challengers and ranks among the highest in ACC history (second only to his contemporary, Dickie Hemric of Wake Forest). And Ronnie Shavlik was also a proficient scorer—his point totals and per-game average both remarkably still hold down the No. 6 spot in

*Ronnie Shavlik,
North Carolina State
University*

© North Carolina State University

the Wolfpack career derby. In the two maiden seasons of ACC competition State's first modern-era star was forced to perform largely in the long shadows cast by Wake Forest legend Dickie Hemric and Virginia gunner Buzz Wilkinson. But by his senior season Shavlik blossomed as a full-blown legend in his own right, inheriting both the league rebounding lead and the coveted ACC Player of the Year trophy from the finally graduated Hemric. And the fact that Everett Case's team was able to take up where it left off in Southern Conference domination, with three straight inaugural ACC tournament championships, was in large measure due to the powerful play of Ron Shavlik.

Myer "Whitey" Skoog

Mikan's Minneapolis Lakers were the scourge of the BAA-NBA's first decade, entering the circuit (as welcomed escapees from the NBL) in 1948–49 and winning championship banners in five out of the next six seasons. With its championship ledger standing already at three out of four, it was seemingly business as usual in springtime 1953 for the team coached by John Kundla and boasting the towering forward line of George Mikan, Jim Pollard, and Vern Mikkelsen. The 1953 title matchup once more pitted the expected entrants from Minneapolis against the almost equally regular New York Knickerbockers ball club, now itself a three-time participant in the league's final series. Again this time around there would be no surprise in the results; there would, however, emerge a most unexpected hero for the league's showcase year-end playoff fest.

New York had celebrated early with a series-opening victory in Minneapolis and had pressed the hometown Lakers (losing only 73–71) throughout the second game as well. When the showdown moved into New York's 69th Regiment Armory, however, unheralded backcourt reserve Whitey Skoog quickly went on an unexpected tear for the steamrolling Lakers. Handcuffing Knicks scoring ace Ernie Vandeweghe throughout Game 3, Skoog next proved he could be an offensive star to boot, collecting two much-needed buckets to preserve victory in crucial Game 4. The "Tall Timbers" front line of Mikan flanked by Pollard and Mikkelsen was the true backbone of Kundla's Lakers dynasty. And in the backcourt 5'10" Slater Martin was the deft playmaker who always oiled the frontline machine. Yet, when the very championship series, which Mikan himself would later label his "sweetest victory ever," was squarely on the line, it was unheralded reserve Myer "Whitey" Skoog who rose to the occasion and sealed another Lakers NBA championship trophy. Skoog never made an NBA All-Star team and rarely cracked a starting lineup; he averaged less than double figures in scoring throughout his half dozen seasons. Skoog rarely struck fear into the hearts of NBA opponents; on one crucial occasion, however, he struck a mighty blow for all the sport's rarely appreciated journeymen and little-heralded bench-riding role players.

Bill Spivey

It is common knowledge (among diehard devotees of NBA history, at least) that the promising NBA careers of two of Kentucky's greatest stars—Ralph Beard and Alex Groza—were torched by the firestorm that swept the basketball world when the

*Bill Spivey,
University of Kentucky*

© University of Kentucky

college gambling scandals exploded in 1952. It is not often remembered that another Kentucky All-American with limitless NBA potential also suffered dearly for his connections with the entire sordid game-fixing mess. Seven-foot Bill Spivey might well have been a household NBA name before the '50s were over had he not also been victimized by a lifetime NBA ban. And what makes Spivey's fate even more tragic than that of Groza or Beard was the fact that, by all apparent accounts, his only sin was not informing on his teammates. Spivey, in short, was something of a basketball version of baseball's Shoeless Joe Jackson.

Spivey, unlike Beard and Groza, never made it to the NBA even for a partial career; he did play long enough after his alleged connections with gamblers, however, to enjoy a national championship with Rupp's 1951 Wildcats. The towering junior led the 'Cats to a 28–2 season with a 19.2 scoring average and one of the top rebounding marks in the country. He poured in 28 in the NCAA semifinal versus Illinois and another game-leading 22 in the title match with Kansas State. He completely overshadowed such talented teammates as future NBA greats Frank Ramsey and Cliff Hagan. Yet when the investigations began concerning possible Kentucky game fixing during the 1949 and 1950 seasons, Spivey was among the host of Wildcats called upon to defend themselves in criminal proceedings. His testimony would conflict with that of several teammates, he would plead innocent, and his own case would end in a hung jury (which voted 9–3 for his acquittal of all charges). But Spivey's fate was to be finally settled by the NBA commissioner alone, and with any hint of scandal being a likely death knell for the new pro circuit, Spivey was as quickly served with a lifetime ban as were the convicted NBAers, Groza and Beard.

Amos Alonzo Stagg

The name Amos Alonzo Stagg resonates with nearly the same pioneering overtones for the sport of football as does Abner Doubleday in baseball circles and James Naismith with regard to basketball; one would hardly expect to find Stagg popping up in a basketball history. A fellow instructor at the YMCA Training School in Springfield between 1890 and 1892, the future pigskin coaching great played a not insignificant role in helping Naismith develop the nascent sport of basketball. Stagg was a participant in the historic first demonstration that Naismith staged for his experimental new game in the Springfield basement gym. Little more than a year later Stagg would introduce "basket-ball" at the University of Chicago, where he had become director of physical culture in late 1892. And on January 16, 1896, it was again Stagg who coached the Chicago "five" against a YMCA team comprised of Iowa University students in what is today widely acknowledged as the first-ever intercollegiate basketball contest (five men to a team). If Stagg's pioneering contributions to basketball's foundations are a bit surprising, they are nonetheless entirely fitting, since it was none other than Dr. James Naismith who, in turn, during Springfield YMCA days, designed and used the very first football helmet.

Chris Steinmetz

There may be room for debate about who qualifies for labeling as college basketball's first scoring star. Hank Luisetti's eye-catching point totals in the late '30s—including a single effort of 50 points against Duquesne—were arguably the first such events that sports fans sat up and took notice of on a nationwide scale. But when one judges individual point-making feats from the game's earliest decades against the standards of their day, then Chris Steinmetz of Wisconsin back in 1905 and 1906 might well boast the best credentials for selection. In an era when few teams reached 30 points in a contest (sometimes not even 20), the diminutive 5'9" all-around athlete was the first collegian on record with better than 1,000 career points, although his career consisted of fewer than 40 games total. In his junior season the prodigious Steinmetz collected 462 points, 23 more than the entire seasonal total for Wisconsin's opponents. That remarkable point total was padded by 238 of 317 free throws in an epoch when a single designated player took all of a club's charity tosses. In one game against Sparta College Steinmetz totaled 50, in another versus Beloit he logged 20 field goals, and in a third contest he bagged 26 of 30 free throws—all remained Wisconsin school records into the present decade at the opposite end of the century.

Reece "Goose" Tatum

No single athlete among Abe Saperstein's World War II–era Harlem Globetrotters was more popular worldwide or more emblematic of the Globetrotters' incomparable blend of skilled roundball play with side-splitting comic routine than was Reece "Goose" Tatum. The colorful nickname derived from Tatum's enormously long arms and neck, but especially from his uncoordinated appearance when catching a football. A gifted performer in all three major sports, Reece Tatum was first signed up by Saperstein in 1941 as a hard-hitting and glue-gloved outfielder for the Globetrotters' barnstorming black baseball team based in Minneapolis and St. Paul. Goose's act on the diamond was so popular with fans that he was quickly moved to first base, a position that placed him closer to the grandstand crowds. But after only a couple of seasons Tatum's baseball days were ended when he became an equally popular member of Saperstein's world-famous touring basketball troupe. Here Goose Tatum teamed with dribbling wizard Marques Haynes to become basketball's greatest single worldwide drawing card throughout the entire decade of the '40s and the early 1950s. Although a consummate showman, the top Globetrotter was an even more gifted basketball performer who set individual scoring records in Chicago Stadium (55 points) and the San Francisco Cow Palace (64 points). A falling out with Saperstein over a series of unexcused absences led to the marquee player's departure from the 'Trotters in 1955 and his subsequent formation of his own popular club—the Harlem Magicians—on which he was joined by Marques Haynes.

What made Goose Tatum special as both an on-court actor and hard-court virtuoso were enormous hands that allowed him to grip and manipulate the basketball with a single mitt. Also instrumental in establishing his fame were a series of Globetrotters routines that he pioneered and which included both "the swing" (Tatum would whirl the ball around his hips to confuse and tantalize defenders) and "the roll" (Tatum would roll the ball to teams while passing, rather than tossing or bouncing it). Tatum's most widely copied signature move, however, was his practice of holding the ball one-handed above his head when passing or launching his trademark hook shot. Wilt Chamberlain and Connie Hawkins both adopted the move as their own recognizable calling cards.

Chuck Taylor

The fact that Indiana native Charles "Chuck" Taylor never played varsity college basketball did not stop him from enjoying an 11-year career as a player in the early professional leagues. Taylor's special contribution, however, came as a basketball entrepreneur and equipment salesman. He developed the first specialized basketball shoe in 1921 and spent the remainder of his active life expanding what had begun as a business venture into a career of promoting the game he so loved. In 1922 Taylor presented his first organized basketball clinic at North Carolina State University. Subsequent instructional clinics took him to far-flung cities throughout the United States and abroad, including Hawaii, South America, Mexico, Puerto Rico, Canada, Africa, and Europe. Taylor also continued specialized instruction in the roundball game by inaugurating the popular *Converse* [Rubber Company] *Basketball Yearbook* in 1922. But it was the earliest footwear (Converse named its most popular model in his honor) that stood for years to come as the Chuck Taylor signature.

Bertha Teague

Three women were enshrined before all others in the Naismith Memorial Hall of Fame during 1985 induction ceremonies—Senda Berensen, founder and rule-shaper of the women's game; Margaret Wade, legendary Delta State (Mississippi) mentor whose name is today attached to the trophy honoring the nation's outstanding women's collegiate player; and Bertha Teague, Oklahoma high school coaching immortal who retired in 1969 as the sport's (men's and women's versions) winningest coach with 1,152 victories. Teague spent all but one season of a career that began at Cairo High School in 1926 with Byng High School, where 18 of her teams bettered the 30-win plateau, 38 editions captured conference titles, 27 were district titlists, and 7 reigned as state champions. In one stretch between 1936 and 1938 Bertha Teague's Byng team captured 98 straight games. Women's basketball may well have been played in the shadows for much of the century, yet even in the shadows there loomed some impressive giants of the game.

David Tobey

Few basketball careers were any more diverse than the one David Tobey enjoyed from his years as three-sport star at DeWitt Clinton High School (New York) in his mid-teens through his retirement as Cooper Union College head basketball coach in 1960. During the intervening half-century Tobey starred on amateur, semipro, and professional barnstorming clubs in the teens and '20s, officiated top professional and eastern college games for 24 seasons, and compiled an impressive 715–331 lifetime record as high school and college coach. It was as a game official, however, that Tobey blazed new ground for Naismith's sport. He worked the first-ever game to experiment with three referees (Georgetown versus Columbia), the initial East-West College All-Star Game in Madison Square Garden, and also many of the top-draw college events at Madison Square Garden during the 1930s and 1940s. Tobey's landmark, however, remains his book entitled *Basketball Officiating* (1944), the first full-length tome ever written on the whistle-blowing profession.

Oswald "Ossie" Tower

A 1942 presentation of the Harold M. Gore Award—given at the sport's half-century celebration to the living individual who had done the most for basketball—carried the following inscription: "The game was born in the mind of Dr. Naismith, but nourished in the mind of Oswald Tower." It was fitting tribute to a former college player, coach, and referee who long played a dominant role in the formation and development of the cage sport as a 50-year member (1910 through 1960) of the National Basketball Rules Committee. A charter member of the Naismith Hall of Fame in 1959, Tower succeeded George Hepbron in 1915 as editor of the NBRC's *Basketball Guide* and in that capacity served also as "official rules interpreter" until his 1960 retirement. One of several to wear the title "Mr. Basketball" as his recognized moniker, Tower was both the captain and coach for a Williams College team that captured the 1907 New England Conference championship, and he earned first-team All-American selection that same season.

Dick Triptow

Dick Triptow was a starter and even a minor star in the National Basketball League for four seasons, played another full season in the BAA, teamed with the immortal George Mikan with both DePaul University and the NBL Chicago American Gears, was a 1944 collegiate second-team consensus All-American, and was widely considered to be the fastest and flashiest backcourt ace of the mid-'40s NBL pro circuit. Triptow also was a key performer on one NBL championship team (1946), played in one NIT final (with DePaul) plus several World Professional Tournament championship games (with the American Gears), and performed in the 1944 College All-Star Classic against the NBL Fort Wayne Zollner Pistons. It was quite enough to leave a not insignificant mark on pre-NBA pro basketball history. Triptow's larger contribu-

*Dick Triptow,
Chicago American
Gears*

Courtesy of Richard F. Triptow

tion, however, would not come until a half-century later, and when it did arrive, it would be one for which each and every former NBL or early NBA player would one day be eternally grateful. For years Triptow nursed a passion for the forgotten saga of the league in which he had once played. He thus set out in the early 1990s to record NBL history (especially that of the American Gears team, which had been Chicago's first pro champion a half-century before Michael Jordan's Bulls) for a generation of modern-era cage fans with little or no appreciation of the sport's ancient roots or past-era heroes. Triptow's informative 1997 book entitled *The Dynasty That Never Was* has done much to provide a sorely needed record of one of the most overlooked yet necessary chapters in the history of James Naismith's ever-popular roundball sport.

Paul Unruh

When CCNY met Bradley University twice during the same postseason with national championships on the line both times (in the NCAAs and NIT), only one All-American took the floor for both of these rarest of historic tournament championship shootouts. Unanimous 1950 first-team selection (Bradley's first-ever All-American) 6'4" forward Paul Unruh was leading scorer (12.8 points per game) for a 32–5 Forddy Anderson–coached team that was national tournament runner-up ironically twice within a single week's span, held top spot in the final AP national poll, and also featured Gene "Squeeky" Melchiorre in the frontcourt and Elmer Behnke at center. Unruh would be selected in the second round of the NBA draft that same spring by the Indianapolis Olympians, yet never played a minute in the pro league. This latter fact had nothing to do with the soon-breaking college betting scandals, which snared teammate Melchiorre in a web of guilt but left Bradley's top star, Unruh, free of any accused wrongdoing.

Ernie and Kiki Vandeweghe

College and pro basketball have featured numerous noteworthy father-son combos, but perhaps none more memorable than late '40s and early '50s Colgate and New York Knicks star Ernie Vandeweghe (later a successful medical doctor) and his offspring Kiki Vandeweghe, high-scoring UCLA and NBA headliner of the late '70s and early '80s. Both were sharpshooting forwards, and while Kiki's 13-season scoring average (19.7) and point totals (15,980) dwarf Ernie's 6-season career ledger (9.5 average, 2,135 points), differences in their respective eras narrow the gap considerably. While Kiki posted bigger pro numbers by a wide margin, Ernie played a significant role on three Knicks teams that reached the NBA Finals (1951, 1952, 1953) and also earned the pair's only All-American selection (second team, 1949), which was also the first and only such honor in Colgate's cage history.

Robert "Fuzzy" Vandivier

Among Indiana roundball heroes of past eras, Fuzzy Vandivier has few peers. The inaugural 1962 class of Hoosier greats inducted into Indiana's Basketball Hall of Fame would include Vandivier alongside immortals John Wooden, Ward Lambert,

Griz Wagner, and Homer Stonebraker. The honor was topped perhaps only by eventual selection in 1975 for inclusion in the Naismith Hall of Fame at Springfield. Three legendary basketball figures of the early decades of the current century—Vandivier, Stonebraker, and Wooden—are even today considered by longtime observers to be unparalleled stars of the Indiana hardwood sport. Numerous supporters also tab Vandivier as the finest of the trio. In leading Franklin High School (coached by Griz Wagner) to Indiana's state championship an unparalleled three consecutive years (1920, 1921, 1922), he was also a three-time all-state selection. Vandivier also captained that team, which became known in Indiana sports annals as the Franklin "Wonder Five." All five members of the local squad entered hometown Franklin College, leading the small-school Grizzlies to their finest basketball achievements in history over the next four seasons. Fuzzy Vandivier also later enjoyed a successful coaching career at his high school alma mater, crowned with a 1939 state championship victory that came against Frankfort High—coached by future North Carolina State mentor Everett Case—and was earned by a team starring Indiana's first "Mr. Basketball" honoree and future major-league baseball star, George Crowe.

Ed Wachter

Basketball's finest center of the early barnstorming era was a player so dominant that he forced the disbanding of one early professional league and an innovator so insightful and persuasive that he influenced many of the sport's most significant rules innovations. He was also a successful college coach for 25 seasons (Albany State Teachers College, Rensselaer Polytech, Williams, Harvard, and Lafayette), despite never having attended high school or college himself. Ed Wachter made his biggest mark on the game as a pro player between 1901 and 1924, scoring 1,800 points, mostly with the Troy Trojans (New York State League) team that was so successful between 1910 and 1915 that the one-sided league was forced to suspend operations. Forced to barnstorm after the NYSL collapse, Wachter's Troy club won 38 straight road games in a single winter and pioneered numerous innovations in playing styles and techniques, including tipoffs leading to driving layups, dribbling, short and long passing games, fast breaking, shot blocking, five-man offensive weaves, and man-to-man switching defenses. In 1912 Wachter (along with his brother Lou, organizer and manager of the Troy team) introduced the current free-throw rule (requiring the man fouled to take the free toss, and not a single designated free-thrower as in the past). Later, in his career as a college coach, Wachter would also continue fighting for unified rules governing all pro and college play. He was also a strong voice at the forefront of the 1927 movement to ward off Walter Meanwell's proposal to limit legal dribbling to a single bounce.

Bobby Wanzer

Few Naismith Hall of Famers from the NBA's first decade are today as little remembered as the five-time league All-Star who teamed with Bobby Davies to give the Rochester Royals the league's most effective backcourt duo of the early '50s. Part of the reason is the fact that today's "official" *NBA Encyclopedia* lists season's

MVP honors beginning with the institution of the Maurice Podoloff Trophy in 1956 (Bob Pettit was the first winner). The forerunner of this award was captured by Bobby Wanzer in 1953 when he paced the second-place Royals in offense and was one of the league's top 10 scorers (as was teammate Davies). Wanzer excelled in all areas of the game (deadeye outside shooting, smart playmaking, skilled ballhandling, and pesky defense) was a six-time team leader in free-throw accuracy, and paced the Rochester club in scoring twice, despite sharing the long-range shooting load and scoring burden with skilled teammates like Davies, Arnie Risen, and Jack Coleman. Wanzer's notable career also included an NBA championship with Rochester (1951), a coaching stint with the team both in Rochester and after their relocation to Cincinnati, retirement of his uniform number by Seton Hall University, and election in 1987 to the Naismith Basketball Hall of Fame.

Ed Warner

When CCNY under coach Nat Holman pulled off its unparalleled dual-title season in 1950, the MVP performer during the team's NIT championship victory was 6'4" sophomore forward and high-post player Ed Warner. The gifted and versatile Warner was the club's second-leading scorer (14.8 to Ed Roman's 16.4) that season and a solid pro prospect with his impressive assortment of feints and moves from his post position. He was also one of the earliest black New York City college stars along with teammate Floyd Layne and LIU ace Sherman White. The most impressive single game of CCNY's late-season run through two championship tournaments was perhaps the 89–50 NIT rout of Rupp's Kentucky Wildcats, a major upset, which featured a surprising bit of strategy by Holman. Inserting Warner rather than Ed Roman in the low post against Kentucky's towering Bill Spivey, Holman proved a genius when the more agile Warner streaked through the lane time and again for a game-leading 26 points. Ed Warner's promise was never fulfilled, however, as his conviction in the wake of the 1951 game-fixing scandals meant a lifetime NBA ban and thus only a handful of misspent seasons in the shadowy semipro Eastern League as the remaining remnants of a squandered if once-brilliant cage career.

Clifford Wells

The first executive director of the Naismith Memorial Basketball Hall of Fame was also one of the most relentlessly successful coaches of all time at both the college and high school levels, and, in addition, served as one of the sport's most tireless and influential teachers and international promoters. In the latter capacity Clifford Wells orchestrated and delivered countless clinics, wrote prolifically on techniques and coaching strategies, and remained an extremely active long-term member of the National Basketball Rules Committee. Wells's high school coaching career was restricted to his home state of Indiana, where between 1919 and 1934, his various schoolboy teams won more than 600 games and better than 50 regional, sectional, and invitational tournament titles. In 18 seasons at Tulane University he tacked on another 250 wins, hiking his overall ledger to a near-unimaginable 885–418 career mark. The coaching tally itself was enough to justify 1971 induction at Springfield;

additional efforts as a promoter and proselytizer of basketball left Cliff Wells as one of the grandest legends of secondary school basketball history.

Sherman White

Sherman White is the Buck Weaver of college basketball, a substantial player in his day with all-star credentials and an almost certain major-league professional career laid out for his future. Like baseball's Weaver of Chicago Black Sox infamy, White let it all slip away through a distorted sense of values, greed for quick dollars, and underhanded dealings with gamblers, which wrecked his own career and almost brought an entire sport to its knees as well. White was a second-team All-American selection in 1950 and also backbone of a strong Clair Bee–coached LIU club that finished 20–5 and ranked 13th in the land while its star center trailed only future NBA stalwarts Paul Arizin of Villanova and George Senesky of St. Joseph's among the country's top scorers. Only a season later LIU—long one of New York's powerhouse teams under Hall of Fame coach Bee—would drop its basketball program in the wake of a nationwide game-fixing scandal centered on New York teams. Along with stars from NCAA-NIT dual-champion CCNY and several other metropolitan schools, three of Bee's regulars, including White, were named in the plot to control point spreads and outcomes of as many as 86 games. White, who had once scored 63 in a single game against John Marshall College a year earlier, was prosecuted for his crime and spent eight months in prison for conspiracy to commit bribery. All that was left of a promising NBA career was a handful of later appearances in the shadowy semipro Eastern League, the result of a lifetime NBA ban, which had also swept up Kentucky stars Ralph Beard and Alex Groza, and Bradley ace Gene Melchiorre.

Murray Wier

Murray Wier of the University of Iowa is perhaps the best-kept secret (or at least the most quickly forgotten legend) of Big Ten cage history. Wier's once rather noteworthy accomplishments have today been reduced to the stuff of barroom trivia and perhaps little more. When the NCAA began to recognize national scoring champions after 1948, it was Wier who walked off with the very first honor in that category. Never again would a national scoring leader have so few points (399) or average so few (21.0 points per game), but it was a scoring title nonetheless and one of only three (the others belonging to Purdue's Dave Schellhase, 1966, and Glenn Robinson, 1994) ever packed away by gunners from the proud Midwestern circuit. To further the delight of trivia buffs, at less than six feet tall, Wier was also the shortest NCAA scoring champ of all time.

Unable to stand comparison with today's towering, high-flying aerial specialists, Murray Wier was nonetheless one of the finest ballhandling and pure shooting talents ever produced in the basketball-crazy state of Iowa. His averages of 15.1 and 21.0 his final two seasons were approximately a third of his team's total output; Iowa averaged 56.9 points per game for the 1948 season when Wier ripped the nets for his own 21-points-per-game average. His first-team All-American status was also the first accorded to a Hawkeyes player in the winter sport. Wier was indeed a throwback to an earlier age of cage play when two-handed set shots, slow-moving and deliberate offensive patterns, and earthbound dribbling tactics were the full order of the day. But in that ancient post–World War II era of men named Mikan (DePaul), Kurland (Oklahoma A&M), Ferrin (Utah), and Cousy (Holy Cross), Iowa's Murray Wier, even at 5'9", was a true giant of the game.

Buzz Wilkinson

Virginia's Richard "Buzz" Wilkinson was the first college player with back-to-back 30-points-per-game seasons. He was also a big enough story on the Charlottesville campus in the early '50s to overshadow the birth of what would eventually become the nation's premier conference for collegiate basketball competitions. It was certainly true enough that the launching of a new smaller league (the old Southern Conference had grown by the early '50s to a nearly unmanageable 20-plus member schools) with its already established traditional intrastate and interstate rivalries infused plenty of immediate basketball excitement into the Charlottesville campus—just as it did in Winston-Salem, Durham, Chapel Hill, and elsewhere around the circuit. But despite this first taste of ACC mania, the debut of league play was not exactly the biggest basketball story on the Virginia campus during the winters of 1954 and 1955. That honor was usurped instead by the first Cavalier cage superstar, a deadeye shooter and flamboyant perimeter player named Richard "Buzz" Wilkinson. The most talented Virginia basketballer to date would light up scoreboards for three seasons in Memorial Gymnasium while he constructed a rash of individual school and conference point-making records destined to long remain unchallenged by the erosions of time. Popular number "14" thrilled Cavaliers fans and hassled Virginia opponents with a relentless varied arsenal of long-range bombs and deadly accurate jumpers launched from just about every imaginable angle on the court.

The exceptionally quick 6'2" athlete with an unerring shooter's eye performed in both the frontcourt and the backcourt and was equally unstoppable from either post. A 22.7 scoring pace as a sophomore was the first notch for Wilkinson in the school record book, and that first varsity season served notice that Virginia's entry would be entertaining, at the very least, even if not quite competitive in the first few seasons of the new ACC confederation. Scoring averages of 30.1 and 32.1 posted by the Virginia hotshot during the first two ACC campaigns not only far outdistanced all other individual scorers in the new league (he enjoyed a six-point margin over the runner-up one season and a four-point spread the next), but also made Wilkinson the first cager in the country to log consecutive 30-plus season averages. Only the previously unheard-of 40-points-per-game pace and single-game 100-point performance by Furman's superhuman Frank Selvy in 1953–54 prevented Virginia's Buzz Wilkinson from being the biggest offensive show found anywhere throughout the Southland.

Urgel "Slim" Wintermute

This oversized and lumbering center was no different from a huge collection of similar one-dimensional cage stars of the World War II era—a lanky, relatively immobile, and slow-footed titan who could be counted on to drop in 10 points nightly from short range and also to methodically push and shove enemy intruders from under the offensive and defensive backboards. This he did with enough efficiency to earn 1939 consensus All-American status during his senior season for coach Howard Hobson's University of Oregon Ducks. Yet "Slim" Wintermute stood out from the crowd largely because of the equally oversized contingent that surrounded him and the unique spot in history which they together enjoyed as champions of the inaugural NCAA postseason tournament. With the 6'8" Wintermute flanked by a pair of 6'4½" forwards—Laddie Gale (leading scorer of the Pacific Coast Conference) and John Dick (hot-handed hero of the national championship game)—Oregon boasted one of the tallest teams in the country, notoriously dubbed the "Tall Firs" by *Portland Oregonian* sports editor L. H. Gregory. Early in that championship season Hobson's charges had embarked on a nationwide tour (New York, Philadelphia, Buffalo, Cleveland, Detroit, Chicago, Peoria, Des Moines, San Francisco) that left them seasoned for postseason battles in the first tiny eight-team NCAA playoff field. With the championship match at Evanston (Illinois), Ohio State and All-American Jimmy Hull focused defensive strategy exclusively on Wintermute and Gale, exposing in the process the Ducks' considerable scoring balance and freeing John Dick for a memorable 15-point outburst that turned the tide and salted away victory. Wintermute and Company had thus launched a "March Madness" tradition that would one day be a true showpiece of the national sporting scene.

Bill Yancey

Few major-league baseball players doubled as pro basketballers during winter months in years previous to World War II, perhaps for no better reason than the fact that professional basketball circuits—or even barnstorming clubs where a decent off-season wage could be made—were few and far between in that pioneering era. Pro baseballers who were also cagers were not quite so rare among the nation's shadowy community of talented black athletes. And few were better in such dual roles than was Bill "Yank" Yancey, crack baseball shortstop and also headliner for basketball's famed New York Renaissance Five. Yancey's baseball career spanned most of the '20s and '30s with such Negro League outfits as the Philadelphia Giants, Hilldale Daisies, New York Lincoln Giants, New York Black Yankees, Brooklyn Eagles, New York Cubans, Atlantic City Bacharach Giants, and Philadelphia Stars. The well-traveled diamond defensive specialist was also a solid right-handed hitter and swift base runner and later served also as a field manager of some repute. Despite his diminutive size at 5'9", it was his basketball career with the Harlem-based Renaissance Five that carried true Hall of Fame credentials.

Yancey teamed up on the Rens with fellow Negro-leaguer Clarence "Fats" Jenkins in the early '30s as part of that team's devastating fast break. He developed over time into a crack playmaker with a special knack for delivering the ball to teammates cutting toward the basket. At the same time he became an effective long-range shooter, despite his penchant for tossing set shots with an underhand flipping style. Yancey and Jenkins were part of the "Magnificent Seven" Rens unit, which between 1932 and 1936 alone won 473 games (including 88 in a row) and lost but 49, and which also was inducted as a unit (in 1963) into the Naismith Memorial Basketball Hall of Fame.

Max Zaslofsky

If there was a notable rival in the scoring department to George Mikan (who took two individual titles in the NBL and one in the BAA) and Joe Fulks (twice BAA scoring pacesetter) during the three years that the two fledgling NBA ancestors went head-to-head, it was 6'2" backcourt whiz Max Zaslofsky of the Chicago Stags. One season (1948) the former St. John's collegian (who played only 18 college games) topped Fulks in point totals due to several missed games of the latter (Fulks won out in per-game average, 22.1 to 21.0). Two other winters "Slats" ranked high among league offensive stalwarts finishing third in points average and second in free-throw accuracy in 1949 and checking in as the league's fifth-leading scorer as a 1947 rookie. Zaslofsky's 10-year career would continue through 1955 with the New York Knickerbockers (whom he joined in 1950–51) and the Fort Wayne Pistons (1954 through 1956), and he would amass nearly 8,000 points and average a shade under 15 for the duration. While Philadelphia's Joe Fulks specialized in the jumper, and other star guards such as Boston's Cousy and Rochester's Bobby Davies made their marks with ballhandling and passing magic, Zaslofsky was distinguished for his deadly outside set shooting.

But Max Zaslofsky's name has been most often mentioned in recent decades— when he has been remembered at all—for his central role in the strange transaction at the outset of the NBA's second season that brought Bob Cousy to the Boston Celtics, despite Red Auerbach's stated intentions to pass on the popular Boston-area (Holy Cross) All-American. Cousy had gone to Tri-Cities in the June 1950 draft and then been rapidly dealt away to a struggling Chicago franchise. The Stags, however, folded operations before the opening of the new season, and their three top stars were placed by the league in a special lottery for distribution among the Boston, Philadelphia, and New York ball clubs. With the first pick New York's Ned Irish got the player he coveted—Zaslofsky. When the Warriors drew next, Eddie Gottlieb had his choice as well in hot-shooting Andy Phillip. Boston owner Walter Brown and the red-faced Auerbach were thus stuck with Cousy as the consolation-prize leftover. While Zaslofsky was enough of an addition to assist the Knicks in reaching the next three straight NBA Finals (where they lost once to Rochester and twice to Mikan and Company), that was hardly a mark of accomplishment that could compare with Cousy's six NBA titles (five in a row) up in Boston.

Fred Zollner

Among the early NBA franchises none was any more colorful than the one that started out in Fort Wayne as a pre–World War II member of the NBL, moved into the BAA for the final season before the NBL-BAA merger, and finally put down firm roots in Detroit by 1958. It was this Fort Wayne–Detroit Pistons team that dressed the first player in league history (George "The Bird" Yardley in 1958) to pour in 2,000 points during a single season. It was also this franchise that enjoyed the dubious distinction of being the first and last team to have an NBA referee take over as head coach: seven-year officiating veteran Charlie Eckman was named surprise bench boss in 1955 and immediately took the team straight to the NBA Finals that season and the next. These would be the last two times any Pistons ball club came quite that close to grabbing a championship until more than three decades had passed. Most unusual of all, here was the only BAA-NBA club to have its owner's name emblazoned directly on the team's uniforms as part of the official franchise ball club name. For it was the Fort Wayne Zollner Pistons—named for Fred Zollner's automobile piston manufacturing business—that took up residence in the NBA Western Division before the final franchise relocation to Detroit. It was business interests outside of basketball, in fact, that were prime motives for millionaire owner Zollner to relocate his ball club (along with the rest of his operation) to the Motor City in the late '50s, a location that left him in more immediate contact with the automobile industry that bought his manufactured products and thus sustained his livelihood. For Fred Zollner, as for other NBA owners of the '40s and '50s, basketball profits alone rarely ever paid the bills.

Chapter Six

Jumpers to Slammers

Birth of the Modern Game (1955–80)

Basketball, at both the college and pro levels, charged headlong into its modern era during the second half of the Fabulous '50s. It has never looked back since in its steady climb toward eventual prominence at century's end as the nation's favored sport.

In the single decade that stretched from the end of World War II (1945) to the headline-grabbing scoring feats of backwater collegians Frank Selvy and Bevo Francis (1954), the college game had overcome the near deathblow of game-fixing scandals to emerge firmly entrenched as one of the nation's most popular entertainment spectacles. The drastic rule changes of the late '30s (especially the elimination of center jumps after every goal), the competition spurred by two national postseason tournaments that picked up steam in the early '40s, the emergence of new styles of offense-oriented play (especially the fast break) that accompanied arrival of the first agile seven-footers and the first accurate one-handed shooters, and the immediate postwar emergence of the black athlete in large numbers on campuses everywhere but in the Deep South—all contributed to a speedier and more entertaining brand of play that brought fans back in droves to the college-style game.

But perhaps more than anything it was the emergence in the decades of the late '40s and early '50s of a legitimate professional league to rival the big-league spectacles in baseball and football that really put basketball on a par with the two older and heretofore more respected national games. The BAA-NBA of the late '40s and early '50s was still a struggling venture that was largely regional in nature (all the teams were clustered in the Northeast and Midwest) and still also smacked of a bush-league operation. But there was now in the guise of the BAA-NBA an emerging stage for college stars (Mikan, Kenny Sailors, Carl Braun, Alex Groza, Ralph Beard, Bones McKinney, "Easy Ed" Macauley) to remain in the limelight long after their campus days and also for many unheralded college performers (Paul Arizin, Bob Cousy, Joe Fulks, among others) to mature into full-fledged national cage heroes. And with the coming of televised sports, the possibility of professional games to supplement college action promised a heretofore unprecedented exposure for the winter sport at the very time when basketball was first unveiling its more rapid-fire pace and thrill-a-minute spectacle.

Basketball thus burst on the American scene in the mid-'50s with its greatest appeal to date. As the NBA first struggled for survival in the 1950s and then matured with the invincible Boston Celtics dynasty teams of the 1960s, and as the college version grew in attractiveness as well—with the NCAA year-end tournament increasingly demanding attention as the most exciting among extended sports venues—Dr. Naismith's indoor sport year in and year out produced a larger list than ever before of individual cage stars to capture public fancy.

It was, above all else of course, the increase in talented individual players during this epoch that provided the strongest underpinnings for the game and its newfound popularity. The prototype black school-yard ballplayer with his irrepressible one-on-one freelance style learned on Northeastern ghetto playgrounds had the most notable impact. Just as baseball was changed dramatically in the '50s by dozens of black superstars who dominated yearly MVP selections (Jackie Robinson, Roy Campanella, Hank Aaron, Frank Robinson, Willie Mays, Ernie Banks), so too were basketball and football similarly impacted. Basketball quite obviously felt the largest invasion by the talented black athlete. All-American teams of the mid-'40s had been exclusively Caucasian; a decade later the collegiate all-star teams were heavily black in makeup. Compare the 1948 mythical team of five whites (Ralph Beard, Ed Macauley, Jim McIntyre, Ken O'Shea, Murray Wier) with a 1958 All-American squad filled only with blacks (Elgin Baylor, Bob Boozer, Wilt Chamberlain, Oscar Roberston, Guy Rodgers). By the mid-'50s players such as Chamberlain, Russell, and Baylor dominated first the college ranks and later the pros. Before the full decade was out Oscar Robertson had unquestionably become the biggest star ever. And in the '60s, as the nation struggled off the athletic field with racial integration, basketball increasingly accepted the black basketballer as a dominant force that now ruled the game outright.

Any list of the game's loftiest stars will today find its roster heavily tilted in the direction of those decades that comprise the past 50-odd years. At the century's midpoint George Mikan was an unrivaled choice of sportswriters as the game's greatest-ever performer. A similar ballot now taken at century's end would likely find Mikan left off many such all-star listings, even if they were stretched to include the sport's top two or three dozen all-time performers. If the decades between Naismith and Mikan had provided most of the true pioneers who shaped the cage game's recognizable modern form, it would be the nearly equal number of decades between Mikan and Air Jordan that would fill up most of the gallery of basketball's most luminous all-around stars.

Kareem Abdul-Jabbar (Lew Alcindor)
(NBA "Top 50" Selection)

Kareem Abdul-Jabbar, like baseball's Pete Rose, was a superbly conditioned and remarkably focused athlete who methodically extended his professional career long enough to assure immortality by statistical achievements alone. No one except Robert Parish played longer in the NBA, and no one played quite as long with so much effectiveness. Parish alone has logged more games (1,560 for Abdul-Jabbar) and more seasons (20 for Abdul-Jabbar); no one to date has more points, and Air Jordan would need five-plus more seasons to catch up. While baseball's Rose was never to be seriously considered as baseball's greatest hitter despite ownership of the record for total hits amassed, neither was Abdul-Jabbar ever to be seriously ranked with Jordan, Robertson, Gervin, Thompson, or even Karl Malone or Alex English among the pro game's most talented point producers. While often a lethal offensive machine, especially early in his career, Abdul-Jabbar won only a pair of league scoring titles (1971 and 1972). Like Rose, his numbers had more to do with longevity than profundity. And while the balding Los Angeles Lakers star, who captured five league titles as the rock-solid veteran leader of a team built around Earvin "Magic" Johnson remains freshest in our minds, it is this late-career Abdul-Jabbar that unfortunately somewhat clouds the image of an earlier and more potent edition. It was the young Alcindor who was indeed one of the game's most dominant one-on-one offensive forces ever.

As a collegian Abdul-Jabbar had another name and also another identity. UCLA's Lew Alcindor was the first of two great centers who provided the book-ends of John Wooden's remarkable UCLA dynasty story. The companion book-end—marvelous Bill Walton—would later carry the trophy of college basketball's longest unbeaten streak, yet would fall short of the total domination already authored by Alcindor several seasons earlier. In fact, no player in the annals of the college game has ever been more dominant. Oscar Robertson and Bill Bradley were per-haps the most versatile undergraduate stars ever to lace up sneakers. Jerry West and Hank Luisetti—from far different eras but with similar dominant skills—may rank only a half step behind Oscar and Bradley. And Pete Maravich is unparal-leled as a scorer and ballhandling wizard. Among the big men, Russell and Cham-berlain were unstoppable forces (one on defense and the other on offense) that struck terror into the hearts and game plans of opponents in the '50s the way Bob Kurland and George Mikan had in the '40s. Kurland and Russell were big enough forces on their own to accomplish repeat national titles for their teams; Mikan and Chamberlain fell short of the ultimate team victories, but may simply have lacked the sufficient supporting cast placed around Kurland at Oklahoma A&M and Russell at USF. But it took the arrival of Alcindor in Westwood for a big man to emerge, who was so unmatched in all phases of the game and so well supplemented with reinforcements and coaching guidance, that every other school in the country sim-ply had to throw in the towel and stand on the sidelines to witness three straight, almost ridiculously easy, marches to national championships.

Alcindor at UCLA was without question the most unbeatable one-man force the collegiate game has ever witnessed. As a freshman he debuted with a much-heralded knockout of the varsity team that was a two-time defending national champion. The performance was so impressive that it caused wags to write that Wooden's varsity Bruins were No. 1 in the country and No. 2 on the Westwood campus. It was also a performance that, on the one hand, scuttled the 1966 UCLA team in its drive to another title by wrecking its confidence, while at the same time lending a fever pitch to the entire 1966 NCAA title scramble with the widespread

Kareem Abdul-Jabbar, Los Angeles Lakers

© Frank P. McGrath Jr.

feeling among the nation's coaches that this was the final time before Alcindor would depart four years hence that anyone else would have much of a shot at national bragging rights. Once Alcindor hit the varsity scene in the fall of 1966, he proved precisely as unbeatable as everyone had expected.

Lew Alcindor's collegiate ledger is unmatched for team triumphs and almost without parallel for personal accomplishment as well. For starters, no player before or since would reign three straight years as NCAA tournament MVP. And none would ever enjoy three consecutive seasons of such total domination on the national championship scene. Even Alcindor's freshman season was marked by unparalleled achievements. While Wooden's varsity squad saw its championship string temporarily halted by a rare off-year, the rookie squad may actually have been the best anywhere in America. The UCLA freshmen, with a 21–0 record and a 113.2 scoring average (to 56.5 for opponents), would likely have been more than a match for varsity squads everywhere else in the land. Alcindor averaged 33, Lucius Allen 22, and Lynn Shackelford 21; the entire squad shot the ball at a remarkable 56.8 percent clip from the floor.

Alcindor left UCLA in 1969 surrounded by nearly the same insane recruitment circus that he had endured four years earlier. The most dominant college player ever was not surprisingly also the most desperately recruited player in the history of the professional draft. The titan who combined Russell's defensive prowess with Chamberlain's offensive threat became the focus in summer 1969 of a bidding war that would prove largely responsible for the eventual failure of an entire promising professional league—the now rapidly shriveling ABA. With Alcindor's ABA rights assigned to the circuit's New York franchise and his NBA rights already won in a coin flip by Milwaukee, the future franchise player insisted on a single sealed bid from each party and opted for the one couched in the NBA envelope. Once Alcindor was safely in the NBA fold, wearing the uniform of the expansion upstart Milwaukee Bucks, the seven-foot nonpareil again proved in only a handful of seasons to be just as dominant among the pros as he had already been among the overmatched collegians.

Mark Aguirre

Six consecutive 20-plus scoring averages, including a league second-best in 1984, contributed to making Mark Aguirre one of the most potent offensive forces in the NBA during the decade of the '80s. As a collegian the two-time DePaul All-American paced his team to the NCAA Final Four as a freshman, earned National Player of the Year distinction as a sophomore, joined the roster of the 1980 U.S. Olympic team, and earned the top NBA draft slot (Dallas Mavericks) at the conclusion of his junior season. With the expansion Mavericks franchise Aguirre topped the 20-points-per-game level in six of seven campaigns (missing only in his rookie season when he averaged 18.7) before being traded to Detroit in midseason 1989. With the Pistons the durable forward scored less prolifically, yet was nonetheless a key contributor to back-to-back NBA titles captured by that team in 1989 and 1990. Closing out his career with the lowly Los Angeles Clippers in 1994, Aguirre fell only 1,542 points short of the milestone career 20,000-point plateau.

Lucius Allen

The backcourt complement to Lew Alcindor on two of John Wooden's finest UCLA teams, this dynamic leaper was, for two brief seasons, one of the showcase performers of the decade-long Bruins dynasty run atop the college basketball world. Recruited in the same sterling freshman class with Alcindor, forwards Lynn Shackelford and Ken Heitz, and guard Bill Sweek, Allen anchored the best all-around class of recruits on a single team in college hoops history. Allen also teamed for two seasons in the UCLA backcourt with Mike Warren, was the team's second-

© Sacramento Kings

Lucius Allen, Kansas City Kings

leading scorer both seasons behind the incomparable Alcindor on a pair of squads that earned an overall 59–1 record and two national titles, and was the third overall draft pick of the Seattle SuperSonics in 1969 after sitting out his entire junior season as a result of academic problems and a brush with the law (a second arrest for marijuana possession). While Allen's 10-year NBA career (split among Seattle, Milwaukee, Los Angeles, and Kansas City) was respectable—a 13.4 scoring average and nearly 10,000 points—it hardly measured up to his brief but spectacular résumé at UCLA as a linchpin of one of the most awesome collegiate juggernauts ever assembled. And while the Allen-Warren tandem came close to rivaling the great Hazzard-Goodrich duo of a few seasons earlier, Lucius Allen's most memorable performance perhaps came in a preseason exhibition match when he teamed with Alcindor to pace an unmatched UCLA freshman squad to a 75–60 thrashing of the Bruins' varsity team, which was the defending national champion.

Nate "Tiny" Archibald (NBA "Top 50" Selection)

Nate Archibald was hardly a one-season wonder, yet his single peak campaign of 1973 so far outstripped the rest of his 13-season pro sojourn and so heavily contributed to his Hall of Fame status as to almost make it seem that way. In just his third NBA season and his first with the Kansas City Kings (after the Cincinnati Royals relocated to the Midwest), the 6'1" backcourt flash would become the first and only performer to pace the pro circuit in both points (34.0 points per game) and assists (11.4 assists per game) in the same season. Archibald's milestone offensive performance that season was not enough to earn him league MVP honors, with the nod going to Boston's versatile center Dave Cowens. It was enough, however, to earn a place in the record books and lasting immortality for the rail-thin guard, who was durable enough to also play a league-leading 46 minutes per game during his remarkable career campaign. Archibald would post scoring averages above 20 in four other seasons and also serve as an important bench player for Boston in the early Larry Bird years at the outset of the 1980s, yet never again would he control the entire league as he had from end to end of one incomparable dream season in Kansas City.

Paul Arizin (NBA "Top 50" Selection)

"Pitchin' Paul" huffed and puffed up and down the NBA courts of the 1950s (he was a suffering asthmatic) and pumped in an endless array of undefendable jumpers that made him a two-time league scoring champion, a 22-plus–point scorer, a member of the league's mythical silver and golden all-time anniversary teams, and eventually a Naismith Hall of Famer. If his teammate, Joe Fulks, earns the bulk of the credit for introducing the running jumper as an offensive weapon of choice in the NBA, then Arizin merits the lion's share of acknowledgment for most fully perfecting the deadly tool. At Villanova he was the nation's scoring leader, and he once pumped home 85 points in a college contest (versus a non-NCAA-sanctioned team from the Philadelphia Naval Air Materials Center). In the NBA he reached the 10,000-point scoring plateau faster than any man before him (Dolph Schayes got there first by a few seasons, but not quite so rapidly in terms of career games) and became the most effective 6'4" forward ever to mix it up inside with the game's front-wall giants. And all this despite a very late start with the sport and a debilitating physical ailment that would have kayoed the career of just about any less-dedicated athlete.

Arizin entered Villanova University without any plans to devote himself to a basketball career, enrolling as a commuter student and focusing exclusively on his studies in chemistry. As a freshman he was playing his occasional basketball in the city recreational league rather than in college arenas stuffed with thousands of alumni fanatics. But this obscurity was not destined to last very long for a player with such remarkable natural talents. Diamonds, even in the rough, cannot remain hidden for very long, especially in a basketball hotbed like Philadelphia at the end of the 1940s. Arizin's 30-plus nightly scoring feats on the local amateur circuit had soon caught the attention of both Wildcats coach Al Severance (who was stunned to discover that the city's best "unknown" player was already enrolled on his own campus) and Warriors owner Eddie Gottlieb (who was impressed enough to be ready to offer an immediate NBA contract). Gottlieb would eventually garner Arizin's talents, but he would first have to wait a spell while Severance enjoyed rightful first dibs on the local phenom.

It was Arizin's ongoing battle with asthma that made his basketball accomplishments so remarkable, especially his ability to survive and even star within the brand of rugged play for which he was so renowned in the rough-and-tumble professional circuit of his day. Arizin not only left a flock of scoring records behind in Philly, but also an indelible image as one of the league's most proficient but most unorthodox scorers. Here was one of the rarest talents of early NBA days, one of those ugly duckling gangly ballplayers of basketball's pioneer era, cut in the same rough-hewn mold as teammate Joe Fulks and rival George Yardley. The apparent asthmatic condition (Arizin himself claimed it was only sinus problems) kept "Pitchin' Paul" huffing and puffing as he labored up and down the court and made him the only ballplayer around who labored like a freight train while simply running around in sneakers. But an uncanny sense of timing (prompting him to exploit any momentary relaxation by a defender) and quick-release jumper allowed him to drill points in machine-gun-like fashion from all over the floor. His national scoring title as a senior at Villanova was won by a comfortable margin of almost three points per game over the nearest rival. With Eddie Gottlieb's Warriors Arizin was soon exploiting his quick mind and even quicker jump shot to compete effectively up front against such opposing big boys as Mikan of Minneapolis, Arnie Risen in Rochester, and Alex Groza with Indianapolis. He played in nine All-Star Games during his 10 seasons, was three times an All-NBA selection, and earned a championship ring with Gottlieb's 1956 squad. Only a personal decision not to accompany the relocated franchise to San Francisco in 1962 kept the career numbers from being considerably higher and the honors from being even more numerous still.

Jesse Arnelle

Jesse Arnelle may have been the greatest student-athlete in Penn State history. The first-ever Nittany Lions basketball All-American also lettered four times in football, and off the athletic field served ably as president of the school's student body. While earning distinction as the earliest black cage star for the Nittany Lions, Arnelle was also posting school career scoring and rebounding totals, which still stand unchallenged nearly half a century later. National exposure first came to the Penn State basketball program in the early '50s with Arnelle playing the starring role. Between 1952 and 1955 the rugged Arnelle would set the school career scoring mark (2,138 points over four seasons) as well as posting career records for field goals and points, plus season records in scoring and field goals, that have never since been matched. The bulky 6'5" center would also prove to be the most proficient rebounder in school history and would be the only first-team

All-American selection in Penn State basketball history. A true student-athlete, Arnelle not only served as student body president but was a four-year football letter winner whose record for pass receptions (33 in 1952) would also stand unmatched for 13 seasons at the football-rich Pennsylvania school. Arnelle also briefly tested NBA action as one of the league's early black performers when he rode the bench (4.7 points per game in 31 games) for a single season (1955–56) with the Fort Wayne Pistons. In subsequent decades Arnelle would continue his penchant for minority leadership as founding partner of one of the first minority-owned national corporate law firms and as vice president of the Penn State board of trustees.

Al (Alvin) Attles

Few NBA figures boast better dual careers as tenacious player and durable coach than does Philadelphia and San Francisco Warriors mainstay Al Attles. Joining the Warriors as a 6'1" backcourt reserve out of tiny North Carolina A&T a season after Wilt Chamberlain, Attles was a valued role player who served alongside Wilt, Nate Thurmond, and eventually the outstanding scoring phenom, Rick Barry. His own playing career was known mainly for stellar defensive play and boasted only four double-figure scoring seasons and more than 750 league and postseason games. Taking command of the Warriors as player-coach in late 1970, in the twilight of his own playing career, Attles would survive as Warriors bench mentor for 13 seasons as the club relocated to Oakland as the Golden State Warriors. The highlight of that long bench career would be an NBA championship earned behind the stellar offense of Barry and a balanced bench during the 1974–75 campaign, culminating in a Finals four-game sweep of the Washington Bullets. Upon retirement from coaching in 1983 Attles could boast a lifetime winning record (.518) and more victories (557) than such notable coaching legends as K. C. Jones, Alex Hannum, and Joe Lapchick.

Dennis Awtrey

Some long-tenured NBA journeymen earn their yearly roster spots and modest paychecks with clutch shooting, nerveless ballhandling, or hard-nosed defense. A few (especially the lumbering backup centers) are kept around mainly as practice players to bang heads in preseason drills with the team's star pivotman. And a few are kept around as defensive intimidators and rugged enforcers, whose role is mainly to soften up opponents under the boards and earn respect for themselves and teammates in the heat of vicious rebounding and inside scoring action. No one was any more effective in this role than 12-year veteran 6'10" center Dennis Awtrey, who carved a league-wide reputation with a half dozen different teams (Philadelphia, Chicago, Phoenix, Boston, Seattle, Portland) across the decade of the '70s as one of the baddest "bad boys" on the modern-era NBA circuit. Awtrey's hard-nosed banging style of play under the bucket was indeed a throwback to the league's pre-shot-clock era when every rebound was an all-out war and every rebounder or inside shooter an endangered species. Never averaging double figures in scoring despite his size, Awtrey ended his career with a lifetime total for personal fouls (1,702) that was nearly half that of his accumulated career points (3,516) and more than half his aggregate career rebounds (3,342). Assigned the role of wearing down star big men of opposing teams, Awtrey once threw a knockdown punch at Kareem Abdul-Jabbar, which some NBA watchers at the time credited with earning enough league-wide respect to extend his career a half dozen seasons.

Jim "Bad News" Barnes

Some players' nicknames have a greater hold on immortality than do any of the accumulated stats, honors, or achievements of their actual playing careers. Such was seemingly the case with Jim "Bad News" Barnes, whose stellar scoring (29.8 points per game over two junior college seasons and 29.1 as a senior at Texas Western) never earned All-American honors and whose first overall selection by the New York Knicks in the 1964 NBA draft never resulted in anything beyond colossal disappointment in the professional ranks. As a two-year collegian the agile center-forward peaked as the nation's ninth-leading scorer in 1964 and also enjoyed an Olympic team berth that same season, sharing the pivot position with Mel Counts for the gold medal-winning United States squad in Tokyo. In the first round of that season's NCAA tournament, Barnes enjoyed a career outing when he logged 61.8 percent of his team's offense with 42 points in Texas Western's 68–62 victory over Texas A&M. One game later he was held to but four points while fouling out early in a season-ending defeat by Kansas State. As a pro Barnes managed to bounce around the NBA for half a dozen seasons, none of them distinguished after his 15.5-points-per-game scoring performance as a Knicks rookie in 1965. In retrospect, the best justification for Barnes's colorful nickname was perhaps the ill tidings he brought to Madison Square Garden fans as yet another in a long list of squandered New York Knicks first-round draft selections, a disappointing lot, which began with Walter Dukes in 1953 and never abated over the next dozen seasons.

Marvin Barnes

The talented ballplaying Barnes, hung with the colorful moniker "Bad News," was the one named Jim who played collegiately with Texas Western and flopped as a pro in the NBA with the New York Knicks. The nickname would have been far more appropriate had it been instead attached to the accomplished All-American named Marvin, who starred at Providence College before squandering his almost limitless talents in the professional arenas of the short-lived ABA. For three seasons in the early '70s the 6'9" Marvin Barnes was one of the biggest stars ever produced at basketball-rich Providence. The nation's leading rebounder in 1974, Barnes averaged 20-plus in scoring for his three college seasons and was second-leading scorer (behind Ernie DiGregorio) on a team that reached the NCAA Final Four a season earlier. It was a dislocated kneecap suffered by Barnes in the first half of the national semifinal game with Memphis State that may well have cost Providence a shot at that season's national championship matchup with UCLA and Bill Walton.

An ongoing penchant for poor judgment and flaky behavior, however, would dull Marvin Barnes's pro career despite the considerable natural talents and lengthy

*Marvin Barnes,
Detroit Pistons*

© Detroit Pistons

résumé of achievements that added such luster to his college tenure. First came the
decision to sign with the backwater ABA despite a No. 2 overall NBA draft selection by the Philadelphia 76ers. Barnes did manage two seasons of 24-point scoring averages with the ABA Spirits of St. Louis, despite off-court and off-color
behavior that drew more back-page commentary than his cage performances. These
behaviors included a much-publicized lust for flashy mink coats, pool halls, expen-
sive imported automobiles, and an entourage of attractive women companions, as
well as a debilitating habit of wolfing down huge meals of steak, potatoes, and
cheese nachos in the clubhouse moments before game time. During two seasons in
St. Louis Barnes missed numerous games, practices, and personal appearances due
to his unprofessional lifestyle. Things didn't get much better during four NBA seasons which followed, and during his final two campaigns in Boston and San Diego,
Marvin Barnes had tragically been reduced to an unwanted part-time benchwarmer
who was little more than a shadow of the awesome All-American talent of a few
short seasons earlier.

Dick Barnett

Dick Barnett is best remembered as a mainstay of the New York Knicks' first championship squad of 1970, starting at guard alongside Walt Frazier and supplying the team's third most productive scoring threat (14.9 points per game) behind Frazier and Willis Reed. But there are other notable features of Barnett's lengthy NBA and less-celebrated college career. In 13 full NBA seasons, the smooth-shooting guard climbed into the select circle of 15,000-point scorers and peaked in 1966 by posting a 23.1 season's average, by far the best offensive display during his nine-season New York tenure. At Tennessee State under coaching legend John McLendon, Barnett logged a collegiate career that ranks him alongside those of Willis Reed (Grambling), Lucious Jackson (Pan American), Earl Monroe (Winston-Salem), Sam Jones (North Carolina College), and Travis Grant (Kentucky State) among the all-time small-school black-college legends. During his three varsity seasons at Tennessee State, Barnett paced McLendon's squad to three consecutive NAIA national championships and a sterling 94–8 overall won-lost record.

John Barnhill

When Tennessee State swept to three straight NAIA tournament championships under coach John McLendon in the late '50s, it was only continuing a pioneering role begun earlier in the decade as the first historically black institution to compete in postseason competitions. The original historic moment had come in 1953 when the tiny Nashville school (then still known as Tennessee A&I) had ironically defeated the same McLendon and his also nonwhite North Carolina College squad; the victory earned a trip to Kansas City and made A&I the first black team to take

From the author's collection

the floor in an integrated national collegiate tournament. When Tennessee State later captured its three NAIA titles under a transplanted McLendon, the team's high-scoring stars were future NBA regulars Dick Barnett and John "Rabbit" Barnhill, both former high school stars from the basketball-rich state of Indiana.

The 6'1" Barnhill (13.8 career average) completed his Nashville collegiate career as second-leading scorer behind backcourt running mate Barnett, captained the Tennessee State squad all three of his varsity seasons, eventually joined the NBA St. Louis Hawks in 1963 (signed by super scout Marty Blake, who the same year drafted Zelmo Beaty and Bill Bridges for St. Louis), and ultimately enjoyed a 10-year journeyman NBA-ABA sojourn during which he twice averaged in double figures as a scorer. But it was in Nashville in the '50s that Barnhill had his

John Barnhill, St. Louis Hawks

299

biggest impact on the sport. With deadeye Barnett and speedy Barnhill at the controls, McLendon's three-year NAIA title winners exploited racehorse fast-break basketball, building a minidynasty that would precede both Auerbach's in Boston and Wooden's at UCLA. And when McLendon's team ran over Southeast Oklahoma 92–73 in March 1957 for its first NAIA crown, it was indeed a landmark moment—the first time any African-American college team (one with all five black starters) had ever won a national title against all-white competition in any sport or at any collegiate level.

Rick Barry (NBA "Top 50" Selection)

There have been few phenomenal shooters in the game's history who were not also prolific scorers. But basketball has known its share of phenomenal point-makers who were not exceptionally classy pure shooters. They are known respectfully as "garbage men"—persistent offensive workhorses who will always find a way to get the ball into the hoop for two points even if the effort isn't necessarily pretty—and at the head of the pack stands Rick Barry. Evidence for Barry's rank among the great scorers is everywhere in the pages of both the college and professional record books. For starters, the New Jersey native, who played college ball at Miami (Florida) and performed in two pro leagues, is the only man to claim the distinction of having led the NCAA, ABA, and NBA in season's scoring average. His 25,279 combined ABA-NBA career points and 25 points per game average in more than 1,000 regular-season games place him in the select dozen top career scorers. Four times he topped the 30-point barrier for a season, and it was Barry as a 22-year-old second-season novice who was able to put an end to Wilt Chamberlain's remarkable and then-record seven straight individual scoring titles.

If Barry's scoring came far more from dogged persistence around the hoop than from any soft-as-silk jump-shooting touch, this did not mean that the 6'8" tenacious forward did not perform with a memorable graceful style. It might well be claimed that Rick Barry's flashy style was in some ways responsible for hiding and even burying his considerable substance as a player. And if Barry's place in history was somewhat diminished by his flamboyant style (something that would have elevated him in the modern era), it was perhaps also hurt by his reputation as a malcontent and also as one of the game's supreme flakes. Certainly the gypsylike career that took the skilled point-maker from one league and franchise to another could not help but cut into Rick Barry's NBA statistical legacy in the long run.

Some would contend that Rick Barry still edges out Larry Bird as the game's greatest pro forward; certainly Barry must rank somewhere among the half dozen best pure scorers and right at the top of the list among efficient free-throw shooters. Losing parts of some of his earliest and best ABA and NBA seasons to nagging injuries and bitter contract holdouts, Barry nonetheless still stands 14th on the all-time ABA-NBA scoring list with more than 25,000 points (18,395 in 10 NBA seasons). Among those who were strictly forwards, only Erving, Dominique Wilkins, Alex English, and Karl Malone have outpointed him. And the story of basketball's first modern-era contract-jumping gypsy barely seems to begin there.

© Sacramento Kings

Rick Barry (with ball), Houston Rockets

Gene Bartow

The most difficult assignment of the basketball coaching profession is that of replacing a living legend. Joe B. Hall suffered that fate at Kentucky and escaped surprisingly unscathed with a remarkable career of his own. Longtime North Carolina assistant Bill Guthridge faces just such a thankless task while inheriting a super-talented Tar Heels squad in the wake of Carolina institution Dean Smith. And Gene Bartow was handed perhaps the most thankless task of all when asked to step in for the retiring John Wooden in the fall of 1975 in the wake of 10 national championships over the course of the previous dozen years. Bartow could, of course, do nothing but fail, no matter how well his teams might have played in the first handful of post-Wooden seasons. It was in the beginning a failure of rather limited proportions, of course. Bartow's first Bruins team did no less than win the Pacific-8 Conference title, post an overall 27–5 record, and climb back into the NCAA Final Four before losing a national semifinal game to eventual champion and undefeated Indiana. But it was failure nonetheless, and a season later Bartow would walk away from college basketball's hottest pressure seat and seek quieter waters to ply his trade at Alabama-Birmingham. Over 34 seasons Bartow would enjoy enough success to post 646 career wins and climb into the top 20 among all-time winningest college coaches.

Zelmo Beaty

Only a handful of players have scored more than 60 points in a single NBA or ABA game, and Zelmo Beaty stands among that select group of super scorers. Beaty's career night came with 63 points for the Utah Stars during his ninth overall season and second campaign in the ABA. It was an encore performance to Beaty's fabulous opening ABA campaign when he contributed heavily to the Stars' championship season by pacing the rebel league in field-goal percentage. Beaty posted a number of fine pro campaigns after being plucked from Prairie View A&M College (where he had averaged nearly 25 points per game) by the St. Louis Hawks in the first round of the 1962 collegiate draft. Five times he averaged better than 20 points per game, his combined NBA-ABA point totals reached above 15,000, and, in

From the author's collection

Zelmo Beaty, St. Louis Hawks

his best NBA campaign with the Hawks in 1966, he finished in the league's top 10 in points, rebounds, and field-goal percentage. Beaty not only owned one of the cage sport's most offbeat names, he also featured one of the most enduring reputations for consistently rugged all-around offensive play.

Byron Beck

Three men alone—Byron Beck, Louie Dampier, and Freddie Lewis—performed in every season of the colorful American Basketball Association. Only Dampier and Beck served the entire stretch with one and the same team. And Beck, for his part, was not only one of the league's rare survivors but also one of its most talented and durable performers. In each season but his first (1968) and last (1976), he averaged double figures as a scorer (only missing by less than a point in each of the other two campaigns), twice he hit the double-figure mark in rebounding (with a career high

11 per game during his second league season), and he was once second (1970), once fourth (1973), and once fifth (1976) among league pacesetters in field-goal accuracy. If one NBA season (his last) was largely a bust for the 6'9" University of Denver alumnus, it was likely small distraction from a stellar career as one of the red, white, and blue league's most durable frontcourt figures.

Ernie Beck

Rebounding is largely a lost art in today's version of both college and professional basketball. Hard work in the trenches (Dennis Rodman aside) is rarely a point of pride for the modern-day hoopster. And improved shooting percentages over the years have also cut down on carom opportunities and thus on the lofty numbers once regularly posted in the early NBA years and during postwar college seasons. Board clearing was at its zenith for NCAA play in the early and mid-1950s, and one of the best at the trade was Pennsylvania's 6'4" All-American forward Ernie Beck. It was Beck who led the nation in the very first season (1951) that the NCAA kept official statistics and crowned a national rebounding champion. And career marks of 22.3 points per game and 19.0 rebounds per game left the future NBA role player (seven seasons, six with the hometown Warriors) only ever so short in the rebounding department of joining (actually preceding) the seven elite players (Walter Dukes, Bill Russell, Elgin Baylor, Paul Silas, Julius Erving, Artis Gilmore, and Kermit Washington) who have posted 20-plus career marks for both bucket filling and backboard tending.

Walt "Bells" Bellamy

An important addition to the list of colorful basketball nicknames as well as the list of colorful basketball characters is found with Indiana University All-American and NBA mainstay Walt "Bells" Bellamy. The nickname reputedly came from the rugged 6'11" center's affinity for talking to himself aloud during the course of game action (he always addressed himself as "Bells" during such bouts of self-directed trash talking). But for all his eccentricity Bellamy was a player to be taken most seriously. For starters, he was the starting center for what remains the most talented amateur team ever to take the floor—the 1960 gold-medal–winning Olympic squad with a starting lineup also boasting Oscar Robertson, Jerry West, Jerry Lucas, and Terry Dischinger. He broke into the pro ranks with one of the greatest rookie offensive seasons ever when he trailed only Wilt Chamberlain in scoring the very year Wilt averaged his unthinkable 50 per game. While that early scoring binge (31.6) was a tough act to duplicate, Bellamy long remained a durable force in the league. He would post consistently remarkable numbers over the course of his career for points scored and rebounds snared, crossing the 20,000 barrier in the former category and nearly reaching the 15,000 threshold in the latter. But in the end his most impressive and most treasured numbers were those for total game minutes played (38,940). And when it came to the issue of on-court durability, Walt Bellamy could boast another rare distinction as the only NBAer ever to play in 88 games during a single NBA regular season. The rare record (the league then and now plays only 82-game schedules) transpired when a 1968 trade from New York to Detroit (the Pistons had not yet played as many contests as the Knicks) allowed Bellamy to log the six extra court appearances.

Kent Benson

It's hard to think of a greater riches-to-rags story than that involving the star center of the national champion 1976 Indiana Hoosiers. Indiana's NCAA championship season of 1976 was truly Benson's banner year and a year like few other collegiate stars have ever known. The junior pacesetter on the undefeated Hoosier "dream team" was dubbed the outstanding player of the Final Four weekend, earned unanimous first-team All-American honors, led the nation's top club in both rebounding and scoring, and stretched his two-year NCAA tourney record to 7–1 (with 19.6 points and 10.9 rebounds per game). For an encore, Benson capped his career with a senior season filled with similar achievement—consensus first-team All-American, leading Indiana scorer (19.8 points per game) and rebounder (for the fourth straight year), and No. 1 NBA draft selection by the Milwaukee Bucks. NBA stardom appeared almost automatic for the greatest Hoosier big man since Walt Bellamy.

But it never happened at the pro level for Benson. In fact, no first overall pick of the NBA draft has ever proven a larger disappointment. With his confidence eroded by a rookie-season fight with the Lakers' Kareem Abdul-Jabbar, Benson floundered for two seasons in Milwaukee (7.7 points per game as a rookie) and then for nine more in Detroit, Utah, and Cleveland. His career scoring average in the end was under double figures (9.1), his rebounding barely proficient enough to earn his salary or keep him in the league (8.7 per game in his best season of 1982). Kent Benson had apparently left his once dominant game back in Bloomington, a place where he also left a slew of memories surrounding some of the most cherished moments of Indiana University cage history.

Henry Bibby

The 1997 March Madness tournament season found the name of Henry Bibby suddenly back in the headlines of the college basketball news. The occasion was the showcase play of Bibby's estranged son, Mike Bibby, freshman backcourt spark plug for the 1997 NCAA champion Arizona Wildcats. An accomplished college and NBA star in his own right, the senior Bibby posted All-American seasons (1971, 1972) with Wooden's UCLA Bruins and modest seasons with the NBA Philadelphia 76ers (twice averaging double figures as a playmaker). As a collegiate champion Bibby provided floor leadership for three UCLA national champions (one undefeated) that spanned the years between Alcindor and Walton. But Henry Bibby also owned a special championship distinction that would distinguish his career for all time. He would become the second of only four players in basketball history to play for NCAA and NBA championship teams during successive seasons (1972 UCLA and 1973 Knicks). Only Bill Russell (1956 San Francisco and 1957 Celtics) preceded Bibby in this achievement. And only Magic Johnson (1979 Michigan State and 1980 Lakers) and Billy Thompson (1986 Louisville and 1987 Lakers) have achieved the rare double since.

*Dave Bing,
Syracuse University*

Transcendental Graphics

Dave Bing (NBA "Top 50" Selection)

It was a relentless work ethic and a nose for excellence that infused both the basketball life and postbasketball life of one-time NBA great Dave Bing. As an NBA performer Bing would merit endless accolades across each of his 12 seasons. More than 18,000 career points and a 1968 NBA individual scoring title clinched his reputation as one of pro basketball's greatest midgeneration offensive stars. As a collegian at Syracuse University he had also been a stellar performer (25 points per game for three seasons, unanimous first-team All-American selection) who may have been the best ever at the tradition-rich upstate New York school. And in postbasketball life Dave Bing would also prove to be a proud and relentless warrior and thus also an unflappable winner.

The heart of Dave Bing's on-court game was always his unstoppable offense. But he was more memorable still for his grit and courage in the face of bigger defenders, seemingly long-shot odds, and the inevitable bad breaks of both sports and everyday life. Bing overcame two serious eye injuries along the road to becoming an NBA scoring champion. A childhood fall left permanent blurred vision in one eye, which made his later athletic achievements all the more remarkable. A poke to the opposite eye during NBA action years later—resulting in a detached retina and several weeks of near total blindness—required further courage and still another painstaking midcareer comeback. Decades later that same relentless work ethic, which served the talented athlete, would also propel Bing straight to the top in yet another arena, this time as the nation's Black Businessman of the Year. From start to finish Dave Bing was always one of the NBA's most inspirational success stories.

Carol Blazejowski

Among the earliest legends of women's college and professional play, Carol Blazejowski ranks almost without peer. Her reputation was forged at Montclair State College in New Jersey in the mid-'70s when she burned up the nets as one of the most prolific scorers of modern-era women's college play. Twenty years after her final college game, "Blaze" still owns the all-time records for career scoring average (31.7 over four seasons) and single-season average (38.6 as a senior), and her career total of nearly 3,200 stands among the all-time best. Blazejowski's scoring marks remain technically "unofficial" since they preceded the beginning of NCAA-sanctioned record keeping in the early 1980s. Nonetheless, Blazejowski's 3,199 career tallies were enough to leave her third on the all-time overall list (behind only Lynette Woodard of Kansas with 3,649 and Tennessee's Cindy Brogdon with 3,240), and her senior-season total of 1,235 has never been bettered since the onset of NCAA-sanctioned play. Since Carol Blazejowski's Montclair State team never earned an AIAW championship, the 5'11" scoring machine was destined to fill a spot as the women's version of LSU great "Pistol Pete" Maravich. Still considered the best women's jump-shooter ever, the incomparable "Blaze" also once pumped home 52 points on basketball's most noteworthy stage, venerable Madison Square Garden.

Ron Boone

Much hoopla was created in the early weeks of the 1997–98 NBA season over the new iron-man record of Dallas Mavericks forward A. C. Green. In mid-November 1997 Green reached his 907 uninterrupted games to overhaul the somewhat tainted NBA longevity milestone held for better than 14 seasons by Buffalo Braves and Cleveland Cavs guard Randy Smith. Green's record hardly seemed to compare with the more celebrated baseball mark of a few seasons earlier established by Baltimore's Cal Ripken Jr. Baseball pays more attention to such primacies, for one thing, and Ripken's string was not only more than twice as lengthy but compiled in a sport that demands daily game appearances. But cheapening Green's achieve-

Two of basketball's iron men meet face-to-face, as Ron Boone of the Kansas City Kings drives against Randy Smith of the Buffalo Braves.

© Sacramento Kings

ment still further, of course, was the fact that it was not, after all, the true pro basketball longevity standard that it was advertised to be by the NBA's ever-ready public relations pitchmen. The true basketball iron man, after all, is not A. C. Green but ABA-NBA veteran Ron Boone, whose string of uninterrupted games outstretches Green's by more than a full season in length. Boone launched his own durability skein back in the ABA during his 1969 rookie season and stretched it to 662 contests before the league's 1976 demise. The durable 6'2" former Idaho State guard would then sign on with the Kansas City Kings and protect the ongoing iron-man mark for nearly five more seasons in the more established circuit, running his string to 1,041 games before finally sitting down for good with the Utah Jazz midway through the 1981 campaign. The most remarkable feature of Ron Boone's incredible iron-man run was that its 1,041 games represented exactly the number of games logged over a 13-year two-league career. Boone never visited the disabled list for even a single game, nor did he ever walk out of the locker room for a professional game that he didn't eventually play in.

Sid Borgia

If NBA ballplayers of the '40s and '50s were second-class citizens of the American sports world, NBA referees of that era were little more than an unrecognized and often abused peasant class. As one of the pioneering NBA officials, Sid Borgia experienced not only the hardships of travel in the league's more primitive days but also the wrath of arena crowds that were far more unruly than today's urbane upper-crust spectators. Two memorable and unfortunately altogether typical events involving Sid Borgia stand in testimony to the battlefield existence suffered by even the finest among the game's pioneering referees. One occurred in Syracuse sometime in the early '50s, when Borgia and John Nucatola needed the escort of a cordon of city policemen to the visiting team locker room to avoid a postgame physical thrashing threatened by several thousand local rooters whose Nats had just lost a close game. Eventually, an unmarked squad car had to whisk the still-threatened game officials directly to the train station for a hasty exit from town. On an earlier occasion in the same arena Borgia's call in favor of the Boston Celtics brought an enraged fan directly onto the floor for an exchange of blows with the embattled arbiter. The fan lost several teeth in the exchange and later served Borgia with a $35,000 lawsuit over the incident.

If these moments were not nightmarish enough, Borgia was also involved in yet another forgettable moment of early league history in which his controversial call in the heat of playoff action had a not-unnoticeable impact on an entire postseason championship series. In the opening contest of the 1952 NBA Finals between the Minneapolis Lakers and New York Knicks at St. Paul Auditorium, the underdog New Yorkers were unwitting victims of one of the greatest injustices of NBA Finals history. Late in the opening stanza with the Knicks nursing a 13–9 lead, Al McGuire (the future college coaching icon) drove the lane and was fouled. Somehow both officials—the irascible Borgia and former player Stan Stutz—missed the important fact that McGuire's shot had gone through the hoop seconds after the foul was called. McGuire made but one free throw and the Knicks eventually lost in overtime. The game that might have gone New York's way had Borgia made the right call (that additional point meant a Knicks victory at game's end) proved crucial in what eventually turned out to be a seven-game series, decided in favor of Mikan and company. Borgia, on this particular occasion, was rescued from further humiliation and inevitable fan wrath (especially back in New York later in the series) by another notable gap in basketball's pioneering era—absence of large television audiences and of the uncompromising judgments of television's instant replay.

Gary Bradds

Gary Bradds was the basketball equivalent of Halley's Comet. He appeared as a slight glimmer in the background during his sophomore season and was hardly noticed in the grand shadows cast by All-Americans Jerry Lucas and John Havlicek. That was until a devastating injury to Lucas in the year's penultimate game suddenly catapulted Bradds into the limelight during the 1962 NCAA Finals. An emergency substitute for the felled Lucas, the spindly sophomore battled gamely (5-for-7 shooting and a team-high 15 points), yet could not prevent a second straight bitter

NCAA title loss to the cross-state rival Cincinnati Bearcats. When Lucas and Havlicek departed for the pros, the lanky center who had averaged but 4.4 points per game his first season literally exploded unannounced upon the college basketball scene. First his scoring numbers zoomed to 28.0 in 1963, then to more than 30 per game as a seasoned senior. He was 1964's National Player of the Year, Ohio State's third recipient in only four years (Lucas had the other two). Few, in fact, have ever enjoyed a season more spectacular than the one with which Gary Bradds rang out his OSU career.

And then, suddenly, one of the brightest stars in the basketball heavens dimmed once more. Bradds suffered through a short-lived and mostly unproductive pro cage career. He hardly distinguished himself in 45 games spread over two seasons with the NBA Baltimore Bullets (44 games and a minuscule 3.3 scoring mark). Next, the OSU All-American escaped to the fledgling ABA but fared little better in the red, white, and blue circuit with Oakland, Washington, Carolina, and Texas. The numbers for a six-year pro sojourn were far less than impressive even for a journeyman ballplayer: 254 games, 3,106 points, 12.2 points per game. The legend was quickly forgotten everywhere but at the point of origin in Columbus. Worse yet, it was not just basketball skills that would prove fleeting for one-time superstar Gary Bradds. Life itself was destined to be a brief burst and then eternal silence. By age 40 Gary Bradds had prematurely succumbed to cancer in July 1983, an untimely death that cut short a promising career as an elementary school principal in Bowerville, Ohio.

Bill Bradley

Michael Jordan may be the most hyped and hurrahed (certainly the most marketed) athlete in American sports history, and some are in accord that Oscar Robertson was the greatest pure basketball player ever, at least on the college scene. But no basketballer of any era has enjoyed a fuller and more memorable life both on and off the court than Princeton All-American Bill Bradley. Bradley's NBA career may have been something of a disappointment to some, given the impossible expectations he carried as part of his baggage when he left Princeton. But a pair of NBA championship rings and a double-figure scoring average over a 10-year pro career are trophies that few cagers anywhere can boast. As a collegian Bradley was almost without peer, and even though he played for a basketball-poor Ivy League school and overlapped with a bevy of '60s all-stars and the launching of the Wooden UCLA dynasty, nonetheless Bradley has his numerous supporters as the grandest talent ever to suit up for the collegiate game. When the arena cheering stopped, the Ivy League intellectual and Rhodes scholar launched a career in politics that would eventually make him one of the nation's most respected and articulate United States Senators.

Bill Bradley's NBA sojourn does indeed now seem altogether moderate by the yardstick of the remainder of his academic, athletic, and professional career accomplishments. Coming out of Princeton as one of the most touted collegians ever, the 6'5" phenom immediately signaled that pro sports was hardly a No. 1 priority. Bradley spurned the rebuilding New York Knicks for a two-year retreat to the campus of Oxford University. When he returned to the pro hoops limelight, the college sensation was anything but an immediate impact player. And yet

Bill Bradley,
New York Knicks

Transcendental Graphics

Bradley's career was hardly without its unique achievements and stellar moments. Through it all, however, Bill Bradley seemed only a shadow of the incomparable collegian who had once terrorized the NCAA ranks for three seasons.

It was as a collegian, indeed, that Bill Bradley was almost without adequate comparison. Luisetti, Russell, and Chamberlain may have attracted as many head-lines in their respective eras, but none had so crowded a field to contend with when it came to hogging the spotlight. Bradley played in the immediate shadow of Oscar Robertson, and this somewhat tempered the praises that were heaped upon him. And he battled Michigan's Cazzie Russell across three seasons for the honor of the best overall player in the land. His stay at Princeton in the mid-'60s also came at a time when the college scene was crowded with other stellar achievers with names like Jerry Lucas, Gail Goodrich, Dave Stallworth, etc. But no player of that period or any other carried an unheralded set of teammates to such national heights exclusively on his own broad shoulders. And none of any era displayed a wider arsenal of unmatched all-around basketball skills that were more fully developed and unleashed night after night in the arenas of competition. Bradley may indeed have been—next perhaps to Oscar—the most complete college basketball machine ever developed.

There were very reputable voices in the mid-'60s who touted Bradley as without rival when it came to tabbing the "best ever" to play the game. One was former NBA star, and later coach, Carl Braun, who never hesitated in claiming that "Luisetti and Oscar Robertson were unbeatable, but Bradley is the greatest!" Another was Hall of Fame player and coach Joe Lapchick, who was nearly as effusive on Bradley's case. For even less-schooled critics, there seemed to be few other performers in basketball's first "golden age" of the '50s and '60s who ever authored such memorable single-game performances. Tops among these were the Holiday Festival showdown with Michigan and Cazzie Russell during Bradley's senior season. Also his swan-song game in the NCAA consolation matchup with outmanned (by Bradley alone) Wichita at the end of that same season.

Bill Bridges

Many modern-day fans remember nothing of the American Basketball Association, a not-so-surprising fact in light of the dim knowledge of NBA stars and events before

From the author's collection

Bill Bridges, St. Louis Hawks

the era of Magic Johnson and Larry Bird. The two-season history of a third rival professional league—the American Basketball League, which survived only the 1961 and 1962 campaigns—provides a complete black hole in pro basketball annals. While little about the ABL is worth remembering (outside of the fact that Connie Hawkins began his pro career in that backwater league), one future NBA star did make a considerable mark there. Before joining the St. Louis Hawks late in the 1963 season for what would become a productive 13-year NBA career, Bridges proved the biggest individual star in the ill-fated ABL, pacing the circuit in scoring with a 29.2 average one season, logging a single 55-point game, and also winning both ABL rebounding titles. As a longtime St. Louis and Atlanta Hawks star Bridges posted identical 11.9 rebounding and scoring averages over his dozen-plus NBA seasons. The two-time All-NBA defensive selection closed out his pro career with a championship ring earned as a backup forward on the 1975 Golden State Warriors ball club.

John Brisker

A handful of high-scoring ABA stars also became comparable or even bigger legends once they switched from bouncing a red, white, and blue ABA ball to shooting a brown NBA sphere. Among that number were all seven individual ABA scoring champions—Connie Hawkins (1968), Rick Barry (1969), Spencer

Haywood (1970), Dan Issel (1971), Charlie Scott (1972), Julius Erving (1973, 1974, 1976), and George McGinnis (1975). Such was not at all the case, however, for 6'5" Pittsburgh Condors backcourt gunner John Brisker. For a couple of heady seasons Brisker ranked among the second league's most prolific point-makers when he averaged 21.0, 29.3 (third in the league), and 28.9 (fourth) points per game, respectively. Then it was off to a handful of mediocre seasons with the NBA Seattle SuperSonics where the best Brisker could manage was 12.8 points per game (1973), where his final campaign saw him slip below double figures, and where his three-year total was a mere 11.9 points per game. Fortunately for rival league boosters, it was a plethora of players like Barry, Erving, Charlie Scott, and Dan Issel, and not ones like John Brisker, who stood as the true standard for judging the quality of leftover ABA basketball talent.

Nat "Feets" Broudy

While Danny Biasone deserves full credit for dreaming up the NBA's 24-second shot clock, an invention that both revolutionized and saved the pro version of the game, it is one-time scout, NBA public relations man, and confirmed basketball junkie Nat "Feets" Broudy who deserves much of the credit for monitoring the innovation across the first four decades of its successful life span. Over a three-decade-plus career (beginning in the late '50s and stretching to the early '90s) as official Madison Square Garden timekeeper for both pro and college games, Broudy alone operated the shot clock and game clock that controlled game action for hundreds upon hundreds of NBA contests staged in the league's most notable arena. Broudy became a more public figure for basketball fans of the '60s and '70s when for years he wrote an annual *Basketball Magazine* column rating each and every NBA player. He used a five-category rating system he had designed himself based on driving, shooting, playmaking, defense, and foul shooting, and awarding a possible four points in each category. Oscar Robertson was the only player ever to receive a perfect score of 20 in one of Broudy's popular annual ratings (Elgin Baylor also once got a 19.5 mark). Broudy's colorful nickname derives from his Yiddish first name *Nisel*; neighborhood boyhood chums called him *Nisel fissel*, with the Yiddish term *fissel* translating directly as "feets" and eventually sticking in its English form.

"Downtown" Fred Brown

A frontline star in Seattle for 13 seasons, Fred Brown blistered the nets repeatedly as one of the NBA's premier long-range marksmen of the 1970s and early 1980s. A 6'5" All-American guard out of Iowa who averaged 27.6 his final season, Brown once scored 58 points in a single NBA game, retired in the top 10 in NBA career free-throw shooting (85.8 percent), and accumulated 14,000-plus career points. A leader of the Sonics' 1979 league champions, Brown was the 1980 NBA three-point field-goal champion and the league's third most proficient free-throw shooter a season earlier. So distinctive was Brown's long-range shooting ability that this single defining feature of his playing style was soon forever fixed in public perception with one of pro basketball's most memorable and fittingly descriptive nicknames.

Larry Brown, left, and Lenny Wilkens are two of the NBA's high-profile coaches. Both were outstanding players, Brown in the ABA and Wilkens in the NBA.

© Frank P. McGrath Jr.

Larry Brown

One of the most talented passing guards of the ABA era, the 5'9" backcourt ace crammed five teams (New Orleans, Oakland, Washington, Virginia, and Denver) into his brief pro playing career. It was a nomadic pattern that would continue throughout a 25-year pro and college coaching career noted for high winning percentages as well as frequent changes of address. Brown's greatest successes have come with the NBA Indiana Pacers, where he led two editions to the Eastern Conference Finals and became the winningest franchise coach (NBA seasons) in only four campaigns; the ABA Denver Rockets, where he won two league Coach of the Year honors and posted two of the best regular-season won-lost records; and the University of Kansas, where he won an NCAA championship and Naismith Coach of the Year honors. Brown also reached the NCAA Final Four on two other occasions (with Kansas and UCLA), coached the ABA Carolina Cougars, and mentored NBA clubs in Denver, New Jersey, San Antonio, Los Angeles (Clippers), and most recently, Philadelphia. His combined NBA–ABA–NCAA victories have now stretched beyond 1,000, and his pro total of 853 entering the 1998 season was good enough for seventh place on the all-time combined NBA-ABA career list. A lifetime winning percentage of over .600 (.592 in the NBA-ABA) is testimony enough to Larry Brown's legitimate rank among the game's all-time coaching greats. And yet naysayers continue to point to two detectable blots on Brown's résumé: the fact that he has yet to take a pro team all the way to a league championship series and (more damning still) the widespread assumption that the intense coach's frequent job shifts are in no small measure related to the ease with which he quickly wears out his welcome with each new roster of initially enthusiastic ballplayers.

Roger Brown

Roger Brown was not only one of the ABA's biggest stars, but also the kind of player for which the league was seemingly invented. Brown's career would, in many ways, parallel that of the legendary Connie Hawkins. Implicated along with Hawkins in the 1961 college betting scandals (though never convicted of any wrongdoing beyond "guilt by association"), the New York City playground star was booted from Dayton University and received a lifetime NBA ban for his troubles. Like Hawkins, Brown eventually found his way back to the big-time sport through the largesse of the upstart and talent-hungry American Basketball Association. The disgraced cager had been working a dead-end job in a Dayton manufacturing plant when he was signed on by the league's new Indiana ball club. He had come to the attention of the Pacers when founders of the new team had attempted to lure Indiana native Oscar Robertson away from his contract with the NBA Cincinnati Royals. Oscar was not at all interested in casting his lot with the shaky new league, but he did urge the Pacers to locate and sign Brown. The 6'5" power forward was promptly offered a contract as "The Original Pacer" and overnight became one of the league's biggest stars and most valuable properties. His eventual accomplishments would include the team's third all-time career scoring total (10,058 points), the club's third-highest ABA single-game total (53), and a 1971 first-team All-ABA selection.

Vic Bubas

Vic Bubas inherited the Duke coaching job from Harold Bradley at the close of the ACC's first decade and quickly launched the school's first unbroken ascent to the apex of the collegiate basketball world with three quick-succession Final Four appearances. His Blue Devils teams would capture third-place consolation games in 1963 (drubbing Oregon State) and 1966 (nipping Utah), and in between lose a 1964 NCAA title game that signaled John Wooden's very first championship at UCLA. This run at the top by Bubas and his potent mid-'60s teams is, of course, memorable for far more than the trivial distinction of being the first in a long line of endless victims led to slaughter before Wooden and his invincible Bruins. It was a stretch that produced two of the greatest Duke stars of all time in Art Heyman, another New York import enticed into Tobacco Road country and 1963 National Player of the Year, and Jeff Mullins, Kentucky-bred scoring and rebounding star of the squad that faced UCLA a season later. The Bubas era was also one noted as a training ground for coaching assistants destined for stellar bench careers of their own. The roster of Bubas's aids would include future NBA headmen Hubie Brown and Chuck Daly. Other Bubas assistants who eventually became successful collegiate head coaches included Fred Shabel (Connecticut) and Bucky Waters (West Virginia).

Bubas, like Bones McKinney, owns a Tobacco Road history that plants its roots in more than one of the area's great basketball institutions. As a player Bubas was a native son of Raleigh, wearing Wolfpack scarlet and white. As a coach he would trade in his Wolfpack colors for the rich blue traditions of Duke University. At N.C. State under Everett Case, Bubas played on a Wolfpack team that reached the national semi-finals before bowing to Nat Holman's later scandal-wracked CCNY ball club that was on a steamroller path to its never-to-be-duplicated simultaneous NIT and NCAA titles. When he arrived at Duke to replace Harold Bradley a decade later, he was nonetheless an unknown quantity as a bench boss and thus very much a surprise choice by athletic director Eddie Cameron. But Bubas would not remain anonymous in coaching circles for very long. During the 1961–67 years that marked the heart of his tenure, his Blue Devils teams posted a 159–37 record that was the best to be found anywhere in the nation. During all six of these glorious seasons, the Devils finished the season ranked in the nation's top 10, twice holding down the year-end No. 2 spot in 1963 and 1966. Exclude Coach K's recent five Final Four visits, and no other single Duke era has seen quite so much success for quite so long a spell.

The Duke coaching career of Vic Bubas would, in the end, span exactly a decade, just long enough to climb into second spot (now third) on the all-time Duke coaching register behind the legendary Eddie Cameron, whose own '30s-era career outreached Bubas by merely four seasons. His overall winning percentages in both conference games (.768) and overall games (.761) have never been matched at Duke and are rivaled elsewhere in the league only by Dean Smith. Bubas's 106–32 ACC record, however, remains unchallenged as the best ever for a long-term tenure in the league. Blessed with the superbly talented Heyman and Mullins during the first half of his tenure and with additional All-Americans like Jack Marin (1966), Bob Verga (1966, 1967), and Mike Lewis (1968) during the second half, Bubas always seemed to have the horses to survive during one of the league's most balanced and competitive decades. And there was little doubt that during the entire stretch of the '60s, it was the Bubas-coached Blue Devils who always seemed to be the toughest kids on the ACC block. Perhaps the best measure of this continued excellence was the conference tournament where Bubas and company won 22 games while losing only 6. Just twice during the entire reign did a Bubas team fail to make it into the league's year-end championship game.

Mack Calvin

Starring in a league universally known for its soaring and slamming power for-wards, Mack Calvin was arguably the most potent backcourt performer in ABA history. The super-quick ball handler and deadly outside shooter was a four-time all-league performer who combined lofty scoring totals with some of the league's best numbers for dishing out valuable assists. Calvin's best all-around year came with the Miami Floridians in 1971, when his 27.2 scoring mark was fourth-best in the circuit and his assist total barely missed pacing the league. The second-year backcourt ace out of Southern California trailed New York's Bill Melchionni by 53 assists spread over 81 games. But it was consistency as much as anything that was

Mack Calvin's true forte. With five ABA clubs (he later served an equal number of NBA outfits), the well-traveled journeyman maintained a near 20-points-per-game mark during his seven ABA campaigns and could be counted on for a half dozen assists nightly across the same long stretch. An 85 percent career NBA free-throw shooting percentage (87 percent with the ABA red, white, and blue ball) was mere icing on the cake and money in the bank for one of the most dependable pro backcourt performers found anywhere in the '70s.

Austin Carr

When it comes to pure scoring genius two figures loom far above all others in the history of college basketball. LSU's Pete Maravich with his 40-plus career average (44.2) and 3,667 total points stands in an unrivaled class of his own. But Notre Dame's Austin Carr trails "Pistol Pete" by only a length or two. Carr's résumé includes the second highest career average (34.6) in college annals, two of the top 10 single-season per-game marks (38.1 and 38.0), and one of the most durable of NCAA tournament scoring records (41.3 points per game in seven tourney games between 1969 and 1971). The fact that Carr never led the nation in scoring is attributed solely to the fact that his three varsity seasons unfortunately overlapped with three of the five campaigns when the nation's pacesetter (twice Maravich and once Johnny Neumann of Mississippi) checked in with astronomical averages above 40. NBA numbers of the first overall pick of the 1971 draft (Cleveland Cavaliers) were more mortal than godlike. The 6'4" guard averaged more than 20 his first three pro campaigns before tailing off to a mere 15.4 mark for his 10-year career. But as a collegian Austin Carr's bucket-filling performances in South Bend were always suggestive of something straight from Mount Olympus.

Len Chappell

Few players corralled more individual trophies signaling personal glory than did Len Chappell during his three seasons with Wake Forest. He was the school's first consensus All-American and a double winner of ACC Player of the Year honors. Only Hemric, Danny Ferry, Bias, Larry Miller, Sampson, and David Thompson, with three, have matched the latter feat. He was only the third (also the last) ACC player to average 30 or better for a full season. He tallied enough points in only three seasons to still rank third on the school's all-time point-making list. He was a three-time all-conference first teamer and also earned a place on the NCAA Final Four first team. Few league alumni can boast a more consistently excellent career. And when it came to a subsequent pro career, he was a good deal more durable and productive (10 years, 591 games, 5,621 points, 9.5 points per game) than some of the earlier ACC first-decade stars like Hemric, Wilkinson, and Art Heyman.

Yet unlike Wake's first star, Dickie Hemric, Chappell was also able to boast considerable team achievements during his three-year stay with one of the earliest ACC powerhouse outfits. Chappell was not only the equal of his predecessor Hemric in native talent, but he was also blessed with somewhat better teammates. Yet for all the help from the likes of Billy Packer (the future TV analyst and hoops guru) and Dave Wiedeman, among others, it was clearly Chappell who was always the main man for the Deacons. On the 1962 Final Four club, for example, Chappell's 30.1 average more than doubled that of his best-scoring teammate; his rebounding totals also doubled those of the remaining Wake Forest starters combined. As a senior he was thus able to lead the Deacons to their first and only NCAA Final Four appearance. In the semifinal game—famous as the contest in which Jerry Lucas suffered a leg injury that perhaps cost Ohio State a second national title—it was Chappell who was the game's unquestioned star, scoring 27 and hauling in 18 rebounds. Despite falling to OSU 84–68 the Deacons returned a night later to eclipse UCLA 82–80 for the third-place consolation prize.

Chappell's three varsity teams also achieved far more within normal league play than any of those anchored by Hemric. First came the school's initial ACC regular-season banner. The record in regular-season ACC games was 35–7 for Chappell over three seasons and 16–10 for Hemric across two (Hemric's first two years anticipated the league). And there were also several trips into the finals of the ACC tourney that remain perhaps the highlight of Chappell's red-letter career. Few have carried their team on their backs any farther or any more single-handedly than did Wake Forest pioneer Len Chappell.

Gene Conley

Gene Conley stands alongside Dave DeBusschere, Dick Groat, Bill Sharman, and Danny Ainge as one of the handful of accomplished baseball professionals to make an equal or even larger marks on the indoor game of basketball. Among NBA two-sport stars, perhaps only DeBusschere can surpass Conley when it comes to a player's impact on postseason championship play. Yet, even here, Conley seems to hold the upper hand: of the numerous talented athletes who have reached the big time as both cagers and baseballers, it is only Gene Conley who can boast of playing in both sports on world championship teams. As a lanky major-league fastballer Conley was able to keep his head above water (91–96, 3.82 ERA) over 11 seasons (1952–63) with the Braves, Phillies, and Red Sox; pitch in three All-Star Games; and make one ineffective World Series appearance with the 1957 World Champion Milwaukee Braves. During a half dozen NBA seasons with the Celtics (1953, 1959–61) and Knicks (1963–64), he earned three championship rings as a backup forward and center, occasionally giving the great Bill Russell a few moments of bench rest. But for all the fastballs he lobbed and rebounds he wrestled, Gene Conley was destined to be remembered by sports fans more for his flaky diamond behavior than for any athletic prowess. Conley's moment of greatest infamy would come when he and reserve infielder Pumpsie Green left a Red Sox team bus stalled in Manhattan traffic after a loss at Yankee Stadium and hailed a cab for LaGuardia Airport with the plan of boarding a flight to Israel. Lack of passports foiled the plot almost immediately and the wayward athletes returned to the team only after several days of AWOL Manhattan bar hopping.

Kresimir Cosic

Foreign-born players are no longer a rarity on the North American basketball scene, but they were a distinct oddity in the early 1970s when Kresimir Cosic became the first foreign-born athlete to win basketball All-American honors. Today the hulking center with the foreign-sounding name is a standard feature of both the collegiate and NBA scenes (Zaire's Dikembe Mutombo, Nigeria's Hakeem Olajuwon, Holland's Rik Smits, Australia's Luc Longley, and Lithuania's Arvydas Sabonis, to mention the most prominent). The way for these "foreign" invaders of America's most native game was paved in the 1971, 1972, and 1973 college seasons by Croatia's towering Cosic. A trim 6'11", 195-pound center, Cosic averaged 19.6 points and 11.6 rebounds per game across a three-year varsity career at Brigham Young, seasons in which he paced his school in both point-making (as a junior and senior) and board-sweeping (all three years). It was more than enough to earn All-American selections from both the national coaches association (fourth team) and UPI (third team as a junior). While Cosic never brought the Cougars very far in the NCAA tournament (they fell to UCLA in the regional semifinals in 1971 and slipped in the opening round a year later), he did pace the Yugoslavian national squad to an Olympic gold medal in 1980, the very summer the United States contingent boycotted the Moscow Games in protest of a Soviet invasion of Afghanistan.

An adept passer and fluid ball handler for his size, Cosic played with an infectious passion that caused some later-day observers to muse that he seemingly was Magic Johnson a decade before Magic's own arrival on the scene. Kresimir Cosic bypassed pro offers from the Los Angeles Lakers and ABA Carolina Cougars to return to his homeland, headlining first as an international star player (first-team All-Europe seven times) and later as a renowned coach responsible for molding such future NBA notables as Drazen Petrovic, Toni Kukoc, Dino Radja, and Vlade Divac. A 1997 induction into the Naismith Basketball Hall of Fame followed by two years Cosic's tragic death in May 1995 from cancer.

Larry Costello

Twelve long NBA seasons, a career scoring average above 10 (12.2 points per game), eight straight double-figure offensive seasons, five NBA All-Star Game appearances, and a bench support role on the phenomenal 1967 Philadelphia 76ers team, which many still consider the best one-season outfit in league history—these were all considerable achievements, and yet nothing of the sort that would place a true stamp of uniqueness on Larry Costello's basketball-playing career. As a college junior playing for Niagara in 1953, however, the 6'1" rugged guard fashioned a feat that indeed was unique, playing all 70 minutes of a six-overtime 88–81 Purple Eagles victory against Siena. This marathon game still remains the longest in college basketball history and featured two additional bizarre events that mark it as a night never to be duplicated. Future NBA journeyman Ed Fleming (1956–60) barely missed equaling the iron-man stint of teammate Costello when he himself logged 69 minutes of playing time; more noteworthy, Fleming pulled off the best sleight of hand of the endless evening when he was forced to urinate into a bucket during a sideline huddle (there was no time for a needed locker room visit) as the clock approached midnight and teammates gathered around to block the crowd's view of the emergency act. Also, future Utah Jazz NBA coach and general manager Frank Layden (a rarely used Niagara benchwarmer) would collect 8 of his slim 12-point career college scoring total during this memorable evening.

Dave Cowens (NBA "Top 50" Selection)

It is widely acknowledged that there have been four pivotal on-court figures in the storied history of the Boston Celtics, America's most cherished team. Bob Cousy brought the first measure of respect to the team that struggled for its first decade of existence. Bill Russell launched Auerbach's dynasty. Larry Bird would resurrect Boston's supremacy in the '80s. The fourth figure is, of course, Dave Cowens, the bridge between the Russell era and the Bird era. Cowens was likely the most unusual star in NBA history. He revolutionized play at the center position as completely as had Russell. He possessed a unique personality that made him not only one of the game's special characters but also the most beloved Celtic of all. Russell was deadly efficient but personally cold; Russell perfected his game but revealed himself only to his teammates. Cowens was relentless, if undisciplined, and always refreshingly accessible. He never polished his offensive game, mainly because he loved rebounding and defense. But there were no deceits about him, on or off the court. He never let up a minute and he was ruthless in his play. The Boston fans loved him for it.

Transcendental Graphics

Dave Cowens, Boston Celtics

Cowens replaced Russell after a brief hiatus in which the Celtics and new coach Tom Heinsohn had almost totally collapsed in the wake of Russell's retirement. He came on board in Boston as almost a complete unknown. Because of NCAA sanctions his Florida State team had no visibility. As he had done with Russell and would later do with Bird, Auerbach had stumbled on this treasure and then ingeniously pulled strings to get him in the fold. The story has been widely circulated how Auerbach once scouted Cowens and then stormed out of the arena as if disgusted. But Red knew what he needed to rebuild his team for Heinsohn, and on draft day—as usually was the case—Auerbach got what he coveted. The Celtics had the fourth pick and waited patiently while Detroit plucked Lanier, San Diego collected Rudy Tomjanovich, and Atlanta traded for San Francisco's third selection in order to score with LSU scoring sensation Pete Maravich. When Boston finally grabbed Cowens it had perhaps the greatest No. 4 selection ever made.

Cowens's uniqueness consisted of three factors. There was his ability to leap. One black official commented on how amazed he was that a white man had such skying abilities. There was also his mobility. Cowens, like John Havlicek, simply ran bigger opponents into the ground. He would race around the floor for 45 minutes knowing that the final 3 minutes or so he would finally own his opponent. The result of this exhausting style, along with his innate intelligence, allowed great success against the other great centers of his era. He was rarely beaten by Abdul-Jabbar. He dominated Lanier. And he held his own with Chamberlain, Thurmond, and others as well. When he couldn't beat them inside, he took them outside. The final factor tipping the balance in Cowens's favor was his relish for rough-and-tumble physical play. He was one of the most aggressive players ever, which made him far bigger than his physical stature. The result of his style was a history of foul trouble. But it was also a history of dominating his opponents no matter what size or talent level.

In the end Cowens proved one of the greatest Celtics warriors of all—the franchise player of the '70s (an epoch also housing Havlicek), and undoubtedly the best center in club history after the immortal Russell. Auerbach was able to build a new Boston powerhouse around the most mobile and unconventional pivot player the league had ever known and ever would know. When Cowens arrived in camp as an unheralded rookie off the campus of Florida State in the fall of 1970, he immediately revolutionized inside play (aided by the strategy of his coach, Tom Heinsohn) by moving the conventional pivot position a full 20 feet from the basket. The strategy soon proved infallible, as Cowens utilized his rugged style of play to transform the Celtics from a dull and lifeless outfit (1970 record 34–48) into the fast-breaking thoroughbred of old, a team suddenly capable of seizing two more championships (1974 and 1976) and also posting the best regular-season winning mark on the franchise ledgers (68–14, ironically compiled in 1973 when the team failed to bring home the title once Havlicek was injured during the playoffs). Boston won in the '70s as exclusively because of Cowens as they had won in the '60s because of Russell and in the '80s because of Bird.

Billy Cunningham (NBA "Top 50" Selection)

If Billy Cunningham had a basketball weakness, it was only his off-court sense of timing; he took up residence on several of the weakest Carolina teams of the four-decade Dean Smith era. Cunningham was coach Smith's very first bright Carolina star, but, unfortunately for the Brooklyn native, the Tar Heels didn't have much else in the way of ammunition to go along with the "Kangaroo Kid" who performed so brilliantly in Smith's second, third, and fourth seasons. Cunningham did, nonetheless, extend the tradition of great New York imports at Chapel Hill (he may in fact have been the best of them all) launched in the mid-'50s by Frank McGuire. Carolina teams, with Cunningham setting the pace, finished in the middle of the ACC pack three years running and didn't taste a single round of postseason championship play. But it wasn't for lack of skill or effort on the part of the spring-legged Cunningham, who was the league's leading scorer in two of his three years (finishing second to National Player of the Year Art Heyman as a sophomore) and the rebounding pacesetter all three of his varsity seasons. Not surprisingly, Cunningham was also an ACC Player of the Year selection as a senior. His team's absence from the NCAA postseason, however, kept the spectacular leaper well out of the national limelight, at least until he moved on to his fabulous long-term (11 seasons) pro career that began with NBA Rookie of the Year accolades. In the end a painful irony attached itself to one of the best rebounders in school history: Carolina basketball's first Naismith Hall of Famer (1985) was also the school's only major star never to set foot in an NIT or NCAA year-end tournament game.

Louie Dampier

Dampier owns—along with Byron Beck—a rare distinction in ABA history, that of playing out the league's entire nine-year span with a single franchise. But that was only a start in the "milestones" department, since Dampier holds more record-book entries than any of the short-lived circuit's more glamorous stars like Julius Erving, Artis Gilmore, David Thompson, or Mel Daniels. He also boasts a knapsack full of the league's all-time marks for offensive productivity and supplemented such pacesetting with one of the league's loftiest reputations as a pure deadeye shooter. Career mileposts for the 6' Kentucky Colonels playmaker included games and minutes played, total points scored (13,726), playmaking assists, and field goals, both made and attempted. Foremost among novel ABA contributions to basketball culture, of course, was the exciting three-point field goal shot, and foremost among the league's original three-point launchers was again the former University of Kentucky star who had once teamed with Pat Riley on Baron Rupp's 1966 national runners-up. The ABA marks for career (794) and single-season (199) long-range bombs (as well as the lifetime and one-year "attempts" records) are also both personal property of the slick-shooting Louie Dampier.

Mel Daniels

Discussion of pro basketball's greatest centers rarely includes Indiana Pacers franchise star Mel Daniels, a fact attributed most directly to the fact that Daniels labored for eight of his nine seasons in the rebel ABA and thus never enjoyed any marked successes within the better-recognized NBA. During his 600-game ABA junket, however, Daniels was one of the truly dominating players of that lesser-advertised yet nonetheless every bit as competitive pro circuit. Daniels's ABA impact was immediate and came in the league's inaugural campaign when, fresh off the New Mexico University campus, he paced the circuit in rebounding for the Minnesota Muskies (a one-year franchise) by edging Connie Hawkins, garnering both first-team all-league honors and a Rookie of the Year trophy. Rebounding remained Daniels's forte in subsequent seasons as he ruled the league's backboards along with Artis Gilmore, twice more won the individual title in that department, and emerged as the league's all-time leader in both total caroms (9,494) and per-game average (15.1). But the mobile 6'9" pivotman was also a substantial point-making threat, with his opening six seasons of averages around 20 points per game and his career record for ABA All-Star Game scoring. The grandest achievements, of course, came in Indianapolis with the Indiana Pacers, where he won three championships (1970, 1972, 1973) and two league MVP Awards (1969, 1971). Currently Indiana's director of player personal, Mel Daniels is also one of only three Indiana Pacers (along with George McGinnis and Roger Brown) to boast a retired uniform number.

Dave DeBusschere, Detroit Pistons

© Detroit Pistons

Dave DeBusschere (NBA "Top 50" Selection)

Dave DeBusschere was not the only overly talented and overly ambitious athlete who tried to cram two professional sports seasons into a single calendar year. "Rifleman" Chuck Connors, Bill Russell–caddy Gene Conley, National League baseball MVP Dick Groat, and more than a handful of others (Ron Reed and Danny Ainge most recently) have attempted to balance exhausting dual lives as major-league baseball heroes and pro basketball warriors. But only DeBusschere was fool-hardy enough to attempt to toss professional coaching into the mix.

DeBusschere was a promising major-league pitching prospect in the early '60s and even earned some limited mound time with the Chicago White Sox (3–4, 2.90 ERA during 1962 and 1963). He was a far better cager, however, eventually one of Hall of Fame caliber. It was on the hardwood where his drive and intensity were matched by leadership qualities that were exceedingly rare in so young a player. Detroit attempted to exploit these abilities by making DeBusschere the league's youngest-ever player-coach (at 24) when they handed him the reins early in the 1964–65 campaign. It was a career move that immediately ended the versatile athlete's baseball efforts, even if it quickly convinced him that playing, and not coaching, was his principal basketball gift. DeBusschere would reach his greatest heights as an aggressive defensive forward with the championship New York Knicks teams of the early 1970s. His overall cage skills and intangible leadership qualities proved deep enough to carve out a career that ended in Naismith Hall of Fame recognition, despite a scoring average that never reached 20 and a distinct absence of individual statistical titles or MVP and all-star selections. Even after playing days were over in 1974 Dave DeBusschere was still demonstrating his penchant for unique leadership roles. He would eventually serve as two-season commissioner of the dying ABA as well as a longtime NBA front-office executive and general manager for two different league teams.

Ernie DiGregorio

New England has enjoyed its small but lively contingent of homegrown basketball legends—Jack "The Shot" Foley, Bob Cousy, Calvin Murphy, Johnny Egan—and Ernie DiGregorio was one of the flashiest and most promising of the entire lot. "Flash"

From the author's collection

Ernie DiGregorio, Buffalo Braves

is indeed probably the best description for Ernie Di, whose heady NCAA performances for home-town Providence College were encored with a promising NBA career that first rose like a rocket and then just as suddenly crashed like a flaming meteorite. DiGregorio was a much-celebrated local Providence schoolboy sensation, who, in 1970, already looked like a second coming of Bob Cousy grafted onto an undersized version of Pistol Pete Maravich. And it wouldn't be long before the latest pint-sized floor general would indeed prove nearly the equal of Boston's Cousy as a playmaker, even if he—like absolutely everyone else—fell considerably short of Maravich as a prolific scorer.

During his sophomore season Ernie "Dee" almost single-handedly engineered an earlier-than-expected revival in Providence College cage fortunes. The upstart Friars of coach Dave Gavitt were dumped in the second round of the NIT by eventual champion North Carolina. Yet for three winters DiGregorio (with a huge assist from 6'8" power player Marvin Barnes) kept his school near the top of the national rankings (fourth his senior year) and even lifted it to a 1973 Final Four appearance. The pro ranks were another matter, however, as the third overall pick of the NBA's 1973 draft scored productively only as a rookie (15.2 points per game with Buffalo) and lasted a mere five seasons before disappearing into a haze of lost legends. Before being sacked by nagging injuries and less than lion-sized personal drive, DiGregorio did, nonetheless, ring up one NBA milestone: he remains to date the only rookie ever to lead the NBA simultaneously in both assists and free-throw shooting percentage.

Terry Dischinger

Terry Dischinger ("Dish" to the faithful at Purdue University) was a phenomenon the likes of which may never again be seen in college basketball. For starters, he may well have been the greatest all-around offensive player in Big Ten history. If Dischinger's point totals fell a slight whisker's length short of Rick Mount's, his total offensive game was a quantum leap better than that of the all-time Big Ten scoring average leader. The inherent superiority of Dischinger's game over Mount's was proven beyond any shadow of a doubt once the two all-time Purdue Boiler-makers stars graduated to the subtler challenges of the professional ranks.

Dischinger is remembered by the basketball world at large as an NBA Rookie of the Year in 1963 and as a starting member—with Oscar "Big O" Robertson, Jerry West, Jerry Lucas, and Walt Bellamy—of the greatest amateur Olympic squad of all time. Dish enjoyed an outstanding rookie season as a pro and posted one of the highest rookie scoring standards (25.5 points per game) ever. But the Purdue stalwart's considerable pro career (nine seasons and 9,000 points) still pales beside his collegiate accomplishments. The unanimous two-time first-team All-American never played in an NCAA or NIT tournament game nor won a Big Ten championship (Lucas and Havlicek at Ohio State saw to that); and despite averaging more than 30 points per game his senior season and 28 as a junior, Dischinger never led the nation in scoring. He did, however, match the feat of Don Schlundt as a three-time Big Ten scoring champion. The final individual crown was earned by an eyelash over Indiana's Jimmy Rayl and is surrounded by a unique personal story. On the eve of the season's closing contest at Michigan, Dischinger received a heart-warming telegram from 1960 Olympic buddies Lucas and Havlicek. "Don't worry about Rayl," was the simple message. With the Buckeyes holding the IU forward below his season's average, the door was wide open for Dischinger to close out his career as one of the last three-time Big Ten scoring leaders (only Rick Mount has done it since) as well as one of the highest three-year point producers in that conference's lofty annals.

Wayne Embry

Wayne Embry's lasting place in the pages of hoops history will assuredly be attached to his role as the NBA's first black general manager. Yet, as a player, Embry was also a significant pioneering figure, first in Cincinnati with the Royals, later briefly in Boston with Red Auerbach's Dynasty Celtics, and also in Milwaukee with the expansion pre-Alcindor Bucks. As a muscular 6'8" center-forward Embry launched his pro career in Cincinnati, where he played alongside Oscar Robertson, Jack Twyman, and Jerry Lucas, logged seven of eight seasons as a double-figures scorer, and was team captain between 1962 and 1966. His two seasons in Boston (1967–68) included his only NBA championship, earned during a brief tenure as a front wall reinforcement alongside Russell, Bailey Howell, Satch Sanders, and Don Nelson. Embry will perhaps be remembered as much as anything else in his career for his role as one of the long list of great Boston short-term "pickups"—a list that also includes Clyde Lovellette, Andy Phillip, Willie Naulls, Don Nelson, and Bill Walton. Taken by Milwaukee in the 1968 expansion draft, he concluded his playing career as the Bucks' inaugural team captain and expansion-season second-leading rebounder. It was three seasons after his retirement that Wayne Embry broke new ground (in 1972) when named vice president and general manager for the still-young Milwaukee franchise. In June 1986 Embry became vice president and general manager of the Cleveland Cavaliers, a position that again underscored the ex-player's exceptional administrative talents. Cleveland would make six playoff appearances in the first eight seasons of Embry's tenure, a string of successes that led to the honoring of Cleveland's top front-office figure as *The Sporting News* 1991–92 NBA Executive of the Year.

Wayne Estes

Two decades before Len Bias and a quarter-century before Hank Gathers, basketball fans witnessed the tragic circumstances surrounding the premature death of Utah State star Wayne Estes. Runner-up to Miami's Rick Barry in the individual scoring race of 1965, the fluid 6'6" pivotman had just scored 48 points against Denver on February 8 to become the first Utah State cager ever to cross the 2,000-point barrier. En route to a campus restaurant with a teammate for a postgame meal, the pair of athletes came upon a car wreck and stopped to inspect the scene. In a freak accident the lofty basketball star brushed his head against a downed power line and was killed instantly by an electric charge of 2,700 volts. One result of the unhappy event was the postseason election of Estes as the first-ever posthumous All-American. Another was the shocking loss of a most promising athlete and the unfortunate short-circuiting of a near-certain NBA career for one of the most touted collegiate stars of the talent-rich 1960s.

Ray Felix

Disappointing college draft choices were long a New York Knickerbockers franchise legacy. The first of the exemplars certainly didn't seem to be so initially, since Ray Felix was a 1954 Rookie of the Year, the league's fifth-leading scorer and fourth-leading rebounder, and an impact player who immediately turned around the fortunes of one of the worst teams in the league. The problem was that New York had drafted lanky Walter Dukes and not towering Ray Felix, and it was the Baltimore team and not the New York team that Felix had revived. Dukes meanwhile played a single season with the Globetrotters before joining New York in 1956 and demonstrating immediately that he indeed had not been worth the pick. But Ray Felix soon would be able to contribute directly to the New York tradition of Draft-

Day busts when he was traded to the Knicks after his rookie campaign. Never again in six-plus seasons would the LIU alumnus flash the brilliance that had marked his first season in Baltimore. Ray Felix did leave a special mark on the sport, however, as the second black (after Don Barksdale) to perform in an NBA All-Star Game—the first to start—when he suited up as the East team's center for the fourth annual classic (1954) in New York's Madison Square Garden.

Phil Ford

Phil Ford was one of those memorable team-concept players whose stature is measured far more by championships captured under his steady brand of unselfish play than by any laundry list of individual honors pocketed or statistical titles garnered. Ford would lead his late '70s Tar Heels squads to three ACC regular-season titles and two league tournament championships. The first ACC postseason victory for Ford came as an unseasoned freshman, when he walked off with the league's tournament MVP Award after executing Dean Smith's "Four Corners" attack to perfec-

Phil Ford,
North Carolina

© University of North Carolina

tion against Clemson in the semis and drilling N.C. State with 24 points in the finals. It was the first time any freshman had ever captured the Everett Case Award for tournament excellence. For a belated encore the talented 6'2" guard would also take his team all the way to the NCAA Finals as a junior. By almost any measure Phil Ford was one of the league's biggest all-time winners as well as one of its rarest natural talents.

Individual honors and achievements were certainly not lacking, either, for the finest ballhandling guard ever grown on North Carolina soil. His 2,290 career points overhauled Lennie Rosenbluth's school mark, which had lasted for 21 years. At the end of his career club marks for lifetime assists (now held by Kenny Smith) and field goals had also been salted away. The culmination was Ford's senior season when he would capture both national and league Player of the Year plaudits. But there would also be two All-American selections and the freshman-year ACC tourney MVP plaque. And beyond the hardware and the numbers, Ford played with the poise and polish of one of college basketball's most expert floor generals. But if there is a single claim to fame that outranks all others, it would have to be his role as executioner in charge of Dean Smith's famed "Four Corner's Offense." It was versatility at the point guard position that made the Four Corners (called the "Ford Corners" by some weary opponents) work so effectively. Ford could hit the jumper with deadly regularity, drive the lane if left unguarded for even an instant, and penetrate before passing with blind accuracy. He exercised surgeon-like precision in dissecting defenses with both his laser shooting and pinpoint feeds. The strategy was so effective, some have written, that when Ford crossed midcourt with the ball and raised four fingers to his teammates, it was the equivalent of Red Auerbach's Boston victory cigar. There may have been some flashier guards on the league scene over the years. Yet there was never a more effective or dangerous one anywhere to be found.

Walt "Clyde" Frazier (NBA "Top 50" Selection)

No one—except maybe Air Jordan—has ever played as well on both ends of the court as did the man equally well known in the late '60s and early '70s for setting a championship pace on the basketball court and a standard for natty appearance away from the playing floor. Walt Frazier arrived on the NBA scene precisely at the time when the league needed a drastic boost in image, and he provided that needed lift with both his off-court tailored aura of "urban chic" and his on-court air of unflappable coolness. He also enhanced both the league's stature and its gate receipts by finally lifting a team from the league's biggest media market of New York into the postseason winner's circle. The nickname "Clyde" (provided by a Knicks trainer) was an obvious reference to the central character of the popular gangster film *Bonnie and Clyde*; his creative and aggressive defensive tactics were an even more obvious natural gift that combined with parallel offensive skills to provide the most complete NBA guard of the 1970s. An unparalleled playmaker, he also scored proficiently enough himself to average more than 20 points per game for six straight seasons. As an offensive force Frazier was always a deadly shooter from the playmaking guard slot with any ball game squarely on the line. As a defender he also had no parallel among backcourt men of his own or perhaps any other era. He aggressively overplayed his opponents and was a master at closing off passing and driving lanes. Walt Frazier was heart and soul for the early '70s New York Knicks championship teams (1970 and 1973) and a regular member of the NBA All-Defensive First Team for seven straight seasons. Better yet, he was also one of the most colorful and engaging personalities ever to grace the game of professional basketball.

Robin Freeman

Robin Freeman could fill the bucket and take it to the hole with the best of them. Ohio State stands second only to Purdue among Big Ten entrants when it comes to production of high-scoring court stars, and Freeman owns his place of prominence right next to Dennis Hopson, Bill Hosket, Gary Bradds, and Jimmy Jackson. Freeman was one of the smallest of Big Ten stars, but his diminutive stature was measured in inches, not heart or statistics or intangible star quality.

This 5'11" guard from the mid-1950s was the first Buckeye to include the newfangled jump shot as the primary weapon of his offensive bag of tricks and perhaps none (outside of Rick Mount, at any rate) has ever used it more effectively since. Freeman's legend began with a sensational junior season in which he played in just 13 contests because of assorted health problems. But a 31.5 points per game average in his abbreviated campaign was good enough to outscore his teammates (many of whom played twice the minutes) and most of the other shooters around the country as well, and bring him All-American honors in the bargain. A season later a healthy Freeman continued his scoring onslaught (32.9), pacing the Buckeyes to a 16–6 mark and becoming the school's first repeat All-American and the league's first repeat 30-points-per-game man. In the decades that have followed only Dennis Hopson and Gary Bradds have scored more points in a single season for OSU, but Freeman's 28-point career average is still the best in school annals. Those who saw him play still consider Robin Freeman the most exciting Buckeye of them all.

Harry "The Horse" Gallatin

Harry Gallatin was the NBA's first iron man, not missing a league game from his career debut in 1949 until his swan song in the 1958 season. This achievement was all the more remarkable for the era in which it was accomplished. Pro basketball of the pre-shot-clock era was a hardscrabble game of bangs, bruises, and gang-style warfare under the boards and in the foul lanes. One of the most successful battle-scarred warriors of this early style was nine-year New York Knicks veteran Harry "The Horse" Gallatin. While not a high scorer by modern standards (he averaged 13 points per game for his decade-long tenure, which ended in Detroit in 1958), Gallatin was nonetheless a key element in a number of outstanding Knicks teams of the early '50s. Durability, mental and physical toughness, polished rebounding talents, and an aggressive opportunistic style were keys to Gallatin's prowess on offense. While at 6'6" he was not a giant even by the standards of the league's first decade, he dominated board play against loftier opponents with a remarkable sense of timing and a ruthless refusal to be bullied or worn down. Gallatin did most of the bullying, and a key to both his leaguewide respect as well as his apt nickname was the fact that the durable Knicks forward played almost 10 seasons of the NBA's most ferocious era without ever missing a single game.

Gail Goodrich

It was about the highest praise one could ever get. The stamp of greatness was affixed to Gail Goodrich when John Wooden (also mentor to Bill Walton and Lew Alcindor) called him the best all-around player he had ever coached. Goodrich teamed with Walt Hazzard to provide the first truly talented Wooden-coached backcourt at UCLA, earn the first two NCAA titles of the Wooden-era Bruins Dynasty, and constitute one of the most memorable odd-couple guard duos of collegiate basketball's lengthy and colorful saga. On his own account Goodrich was eventually also one of the most potent offense threats in the history of the talent-rich Los Angeles Lakers NBA franchise. In addition to performing for one of the top college units of all time, Goodrich was also a member of one of the greatest single-season NBA teams ever, the 1972 edition of the Los Angeles Lakers coached by Bill Sharman, which featured Wilt Chamberlain and Jerry West and garnered 33 victories in a row. The single complaint on Goodrich from high school days onward was that he simply wasn't rugged enough and lanky enough (at 6'1") for big-time basketball wars. It might have been a sensible scouting report to the superficial observer, but never one that could stand up long against the Goodrich record of boundless achievement. In college that achievement included two national championship teams (one undefeated), unanimous first-team All-American status, and a territorial NBA draft selection by the hometown Lakers. As a pro the ante was even upped somewhat to include four straight All-Star selections, still another championship ring, nearly 20,000 career points, and some of the loftiest NBA scoring averages of the early and mid-'70s. Goodrich was hardly basketball's first overachiever, but he was certainly one of its most outrageous.

Travis "The Machine" Grant

One of basketball's least publicized dynasty teams was the Kentucky State University unit of 1970 through 1973 coached by Lucias Mitchell to three straight NAIA small-college national championships, and featuring two future NBA draftees in Elmore "Big E" Smith (one of the players eventually traded from Los Angeles to Milwaukee for Kareem Abdul-Jabbar) and Travis "The Machine" Grant. Smith soon developed the low-post moves under Mitchell's tutelage that made him an imposing inside rebounding and shot-blocking force. The lanky 6'8" Grant was a remarkable pure shooter who possessed that true gunner's fearlessness when it came to launching bombs from any angle on the court and almost any time he could get his hands on the ball.

Travis Grant would earn his lasting moniker in the first game of his sophomore season when he launched 70 shots (nearly half of them in the game's final 13 minutes), canned 35 baskets, and totaled 75 points in his team's 141–93 thrashing of Michigan's Northwood Institute. This was only the starting bell for three years of racehorse team play and relentless individual scoring (by Grant) that marked three straight national titles and a rash of individual scoring marks for the team's star forward. Over his four-year career Grant would pour in an incredible 4,045 points (making him the only collegian at any level to top the 4,000 mark), average 33.4 (also a career record for Division II), log an almost unimaginable 63.8 field-goal percentage (as a long-range shooter, not an inside basket stuffer), and also set the NAIA tournament single-game record of 60 against Minot State in 1972. Grant would bomb badly in the pros during a brief appearance with the NBA Lakers and ABA teams in San Diego, Kentucky, and Indiana (though he did average 25.2 during his penultimate ABA season). But that fact was hardly enough to diminish his performances as the most prolific small-college scoring machine ever to take to the hardwood floor.

Sihugo Green

One way to gain immortality in sports is to become the answer to an especially intriguing trivia question and none took this route more directly than Duquesne All-American guard Sihugo Green. It was Green who was drafted ahead of Bill Russell in the 1957 NBA college lottery, undoubtedly the career highlight moment for a highly touted college star who never became much of an NBA impact player. Si Green was twice a 20-point college scorer, a unanimous All-American first teamer, and the spark plug of an NIT championship team back when the NIT was still the most prestigious postseason venue. But it was raw economics and not talent projections that gave Green his unusual draft day prominence. The dollar-poor Rochester Royals owned the lottery's first selection and were unwilling and unable to meet the rumored $25,000 bonus Bill Russell would request for signing. Rochester management was content, therefore, to gamble on a lesser and far cheaper court talent to supplement its own roster reconstruction. The Royals would, of course, get just what they paid for—a journeyman who lasted less than two seasons with the ball club. Meanwhile, Boston's Red Auerbach would be left free to wheel and deal with St. Louis management for the No. 2 draft slot. As almost every veteran NBA watcher knows, it would be the deal that would clinch Auerbach's own immortality, and also the one that would guarantee the most sought after collegiate star and future Celtics dynasty linchpin for the Boston franchise.

Hal Greer (NBA "Top 50" Selection)

A deadly shooter who specialized in 15-foot jumpers, this durable guard topped the 20,000 career point mark, scored 20 or better per game for seven straight years (1964–70), and fed enough assists to Wilt Chamberlain alone (not to mention Chet Walker or Dolph Schayes) to account for nearly another couple thousand points. But what most identified this all-star performer was his picture-perfect jumper with its low arc and quick release. It was a leaping shot that was so smooth and effective that Greer even used it when he shot his free throws. But the remarkable jumper was only slightly more of a Greer trademark than the unparalleled ballhandling and unmatched yearly and nightly consistency, which also marked his career.

Upon retirement after 15 pro seasons Greer held an NBA career mark for games played (since broken several times) and had appeared in at least 70 games every season in the league save his first (1959) and last (1973) campaigns. It is a rare piece of ironic fate that the Philadelphia 76ers franchise could, for years, boast both the best team (1967 with 68 victories) and worst team (1973 with 73 losses) on record, and also that Hal Greer played for both. The 1967 ball club, featuring a newly minted, defense-minded Wilt Chamberlain, rode the Big Dipper's rebounding and Hal Greer's playmaking to interrupt Boston's decade-long league stranglehold. A half dozen seasons later the pathetic 1973 team amazed even basketball curmudgeons by failing to break double figures in the win column; Greer could take little of the blame for that disaster, however, as he logged only 38 games and less than 900 minutes as a seldom-used backup to one of the league's worst-ever backcourts (Fred Carter and Freddie Boyd). Greer, like the franchise itself, had peaked back in 1967. The rock-solid 76ers team that upset Boston's apple cart had its offense fueled by Hal Greer (22.1) as well as the always prolific Chamberlain (24.1). And during the postseason championship run, the Philadelphia backcourt ace was even better, leading the ball club with a 27.7 average and outscoring everyone in the entire playoffs except San Francisco's Rick Barry.

Hal Greer is today not often well remembered in an era of spectacular superstars that began with Bird and Magic and peaked with Air Jordan. Nonetheless, he was a franchise-leading scorer with a team that for three and a half seasons owned Wilt Chamberlain, and one that also boasted the lengthy career of the league's first 15,000-point scorer, Dolph Schayes. Greer surprisingly outstretched Schayes in career scoring (they played an identical number of seasons and nearly the same number of games), though the latter and not the former is universally recalled as one of the most talented point-makers in NBA annals. Unlike today's visible stars, Greer was hardly flashy and certainly not flamboyant. But in an epoch when consistency was the byword, he was one of the best night-in and night-out performers to be found anywhere in the entire league.

Richie Guerin

Largely forgotten today, Richie Guerin was a fixture on NBA All-Star teams of the second half of the '50s and early seasons of the '60s, making five straight appearances in the midseason classic, starting in the backcourt with Cousy three times and canning 23 points in the 1962 classic at St. Louis. It was in that 1962 campaign that Guerin reached his peak as an offensive player, averaging 29.5 (sixth in the league but miles behind Chamberlain who averaged 50.4) while also posting the league's fourth-best assists total. A mobile 6'4" ball handler with balanced shooting and passing skills, Guerin lasted 13 NBA seasons, topped 20 points per game in scoring on four occasions, logged just short of 15,000 points, and ranked in the league's top five in assists on three separate occasions. Finishing out his career with the Hawks in both St. Louis and Atlanta, Guerin also coached that team for eight winters, five of these in the dual role as player-coach.

It was as a head coach in St. Louis and Atlanta that the always tough Guerin proved to be remarkably durable, surviving a whim-driven owner, Ben Kerner, who had fired 16 coaches in the previous 15 seasons. Kerner's list of casualties had included legends Red Holzman, Red Auerbach, and Alex Hannum, a tandem that eventually owned 13 NBA championships between them. Guerin not only lasted eight winters under Kerner's scrutiny but also took his team to the playoffs each of those years, captured two division titles, and posted a new franchise mark of 327 career victories, a record that has survived for more than a quarter-century.

Cliff Hagan

Cliff Hagan's pro career began as the throw-in figure in one of pro basketball's most significant trades, indeed perhaps the single trade that more than any other altered the entire course of NBA history. Hagan not only survived the famous 1956 Russell-for-Macauley (with Hagan added on as a bonus to the Hawks' take) predraft

Cliff Hagan,
University of Kentucky

deal to post a productive NBA career of his own, but he earlier also enjoyed one of the true storybook tenures in all of college basketball annals. A couple of seasons before coming to St. Louis and the NBA, Hagan was one of the top stars of a Rupp-coached University of Kentucky five, which still ranks among the small inventory of the best NCAA teams ever. He is equally memorable as owner of a graceful, sweeping hook shot that was one of the most destructive offense weapons of the '50s and '60s in both the collegiate and professional ranks. It was that masterful hook that enabled Hagan to dominate much taller opponents as a potent center and forward at Kentucky, where he twice earned All-American honors and led Rupp's teams to an 86–5 three-year record and a 1951 national championship. During his sophomore season Hagan sparked UK in a stirring second-half rally that clinched the NCAA title game with Kansas State. As a senior, he was the leading scorer on the 25–0 squad that abandoned postseason play because its top three stars (Hagan, Frank Ramsey, and Lou Tsioropoulos) had used up their eligibility at the end of regular-season play. Chosen by the Boston Celtics in the third round of the 1953 NBA draft (a year before his college eligibility expired), Hagan would play another college season and serve two years in the military before the famed trade which sent him on to St. Louis. While his pro sojourn never earned top billing in St. Louis (where he played alongside Bob Pettit), nor garnered headlines equal to those attached to his former UK teammate Frank Ramsey with the Dynasty Celtics, nonetheless the 10-year pro was twice All-NBA Second Team and five times an All-Star. And his 1977 Hall of Fame election was given a healthy assist by his half dozen seasons of high scoring alongside Pettit in one of the most potent NBA line-ups of the golden era '50s and '60s.

Alex Hannum

Alex Hannum is one of the forgotten coaching geniuses of the NBA's first chaotic decade; he was also one of the league's better role players during the formative years of the struggling infant pro circuit. And when it comes to logging unique distinctions across the game's considerable annals, Hannum totes one of the rarest accomplishments among the entire pro league coaching fraternity—he is the only coach ever to win championships in both the NBA (St. Louis in 1958 and Philadelphia in 1967) and ABA (Oakland, 1969) as well as be named Coach of the Year in both circuits. Hannum's two NBA titles ironically formed the bookends for Boston's eight straight crowns that spanned most of the '60s. It was also no small badge of Alex Hannum's pro coaching career that he tutored such future accomplished bench bosses as Larry Brown, Doug Moe, Larry Costello, Billy Cunningham, and Matt Guokas (all of whom played for him at some point) and also earned Wilt Chamberlain's praise as "the best coach I ever had."

Hannum's own playing career spanned the NBL and NBA from 1949 through 1957 and included stints with Oshkosh, Syracuse, Baltimore, Rochester, Milwaukee, St. Louis, and Fort Wayne. As a journeyman rugged 6'7" forward who had played in college with Bill Sharman (Southern California), his contribution was more pronounced as a tenacious rebounder and hard-nosed forecourt defender than as a scorer (six points per game career average). It was with his last stop in St. Louis, during the 1957 campaign, that the muscular bench player launched by rather novel circumstances what would quickly become an exceptional tenure as an NBA-ABA mentor. Hawks owner Ben Kerner tabbed star guard Slater Martin as his new coach that year after a midseason firing of Red Holzman. But since Dugie Martin was not genuinely interested in the new role (his energies were still going into full-time playing), and his roommate, Hannum, seemed to do most of the directing from his spot on the bench anyway, Martin eventually urged Kerner to formally hand the position over to the team's most enthusiastic benchwarmer. It was a fortuitous move indeed for the St. Louis franchise as Hannum immediately directed

Alex Hannum, St. Louis Hawks

From the author's collection

the team to two Western Division crowns and one NBA title before moving on to Syracuse, San Francisco, Philadelphia, San Diego, and the ABA (Oakland and Denver). NBA Coach of the Year honors came in 1964 with San Francisco when Hannum guided the Warriors to the league finals versus Boston and also (and more remarkably) converted Wilt Chamberlain from a one-dimensional offensive force into a defense-conscious team player. His coaching apogee, however, came in Philadelphia three seasons later when his 76ers ball club, also built around a revamped Chamberlain, set a mark for winning percentage (68–13, .840) and fielded one of the best outfits in all of league history.

Lusia Harris (Stewart)

Delta State (Mississippi) star Lusia Harris closed out her brilliant four-year career (1974–77, 2,979 points, 25.9 points per game) as the first acknowledged superstar of the women's sport, and also a player whose future brilliance in the eyes of history was clouded only by the primitive record keeping and almost nonexistent recognition system in place during her own pioneering era. There were no women's All-American teams until Harris's sophomore season (1975) and the National Player of the Year Award would unfortunately not be instituted until a season after her own 1977 graduation.

But Harris's legacy is brilliant enough nonetheless. She would reign as MVP of the AIAW tourney for three straight seasons; would average more than 30 points per game her junior year (thus becoming the first woman to crack the 30-point barrier) and 25.9 for her career; and as the top scorer on the 1972 silver-medal Olympic team, she would also carve a rare piece of history by dropping in the first points ever registered by a woman player in Olympic competition. Most importantly of all, however, in 1992 Lusia Harris would also become the first female college player inducted into the Naismith Memorial Basketball Hall of Fame. Her talents were also given something of a backhanded tribute when the Delta State star was tabbed by the New Orleans Jazz in the NBA draft. The selection was little more than a cheap publicity stunt by the fan-hungry Jazz franchise, yet it did, nonetheless, speak unintentional volumes about the talent level of this memorable pioneering female star.

John "Hondo" Havlicek (NBA "Top 50" Selection)

There was never a better sixth man nor a more thoroughly team-oriented player than this Boston Celtics and Ohio State University Hall of Famer. Nor have there been many before or since who might qualify as a more effective clutch scorer, a more tenacious defender, a more versatile athlete at any spot on the floor, or a more dedicated "winner" than Hondo Havlicek of Red Auerbach's Boston Celtics. Havlicek is the only man in the game's full history to combine a career of "role playing" and "backup status" with frontline stats that rank among those of the all-time greats. He stands fifth all time for NBA games played (1,270), fourth in career minutes (46,471), ninth in points scored (26,395), and sixth in field goals made (10,513). And there are only a few who own more combined NBA and NCAA championship rings. And none can lay claim to a single moment more deeply etched into the sport's mythology—the dramatic closing seconds of the unforgettable 1965 Boston-Philadelphia divisional series when *"Havlicek Stole The Ball!"* and thus miraculously kept a dynasty championship string alive.

The greatest "sixth man" of NBA history was also the greatest understudy ever to lace up high-tops in the collegiate game. Havlicek played smack in the shadow of Jerry Lucas, and together they were the most unbeatable combo in Big Ten history (78–6, three league titles, one NCAA crown, three Final Fours). Despite his role as "second banana" the player called "Hondo" was, nonetheless, a recognized franchise player from the start and was twice tabbed All-Big Ten and once as a first-team All-American. His outstanding play in his first and third of three national title games won Havlicek a spot each time on the NCAA all-tourney team.

But if Hondo Havlicek never quite emerged from Lucas's shadow during college days, he soon dwarfed his teammate's considerable stature when the two reached the professional ranks. Havlicek would first enjoy a near-miss tryout with the NFL Cleveland Browns (despite not playing football in college) and then settle on a career with Auerbach's Celtics, which brought eventual accolades as one of the sport's true immortals. Havlicek's reputation in early NBA seasons (the '60s era featuring Bill Russell) was that of the most valued bench player and greatest hustler in all of pro cage history. A decade later he was a mainstay starter and club leader for a two-time championship team coached by Tom Heinsohn and bolstered by Dave Cowens. The NBA numbers that he would amass in the end (for games played, points, scoring average, minutes played, field goals, and a host of other offensive categories) have never been even approached by any other Big Ten Conference alumnus. His eight NBA championship rings are also a boast that only Celtics teammates Russell (13), Satch Sanders (8), K. C. Jones (8) and Sam Jones (10) can share.

Connie Hawkins

There are dozens of players with more impressive pro résumés than the one boasted by Connie Hawkins. Nowhere is found, however, a player who embodies a more incomparable myth. Connie Hawkins was unquestionably the greatest playground legend ever to arise from New York's poverty-ridden ghettos. He was also basketball's most egregious victim of a corrupt college-athlete recruiting system gone awry. And despite years of blind injustice, which kept him on the outside of the NBA looking in during what should have been his prime seasons, he was also for a brief late-career span a most memorable NBA star who still dominated opponents at a time when he was perhaps but a mere ghost of the cage phenom he had once been during his shadowy prime. Most of Connie Hawkins's most stellar moments were

Connie Hawkins

never captured on video; his best pro seasons were played in renegade leagues in half-empty arenas; and his Hall of Fame election in the early 1990s was the best acknowledgment on record that all of basketball's finest moments are not necessarily played exclusively in NCAA or NBA facilities.

As a playground legend and incomparable star at Brooklyn Boys High School (where he paced two straight city championships in the late '50s) Hawkins was the subject of an intensive recruiting war that eventually brought him to the campus of the University of Iowa. Barely able to read and write but unparalleled in cage talents, "The Hawk" was in 1960 an appropriate symbol of outrageously misplaced values in collegiate athletics. But he was also soon a clear victim rather than a ruthless victimizer of the system. When the 1961 college game-fixing scandals shattered the cage sport for the second time in a decade, Hawkins was one of those implicated for acknowledged contacts with known gamblers on New York playgrounds, though never charged with anything worse than guilt by association. Hawkins had accepted a loan from Jack Molinas, the former college and pro standout at the center of the game-fixing ring, and had also introduced Molinas to other playground talents. It had all been innocent, as far as Hawkins was concerned, and it was clear that the Iowa recruit had no involvement with actual game tampering. The result for Hawkins, however, was not only immediate suspension from Iowa but also a lifetime NBA ban. The still struggling professional circuit could not afford even the slightest hint of scandal.

While he waited vainly for reinstatement throughout the entire decade of the 1960s, Connie Hawkins played in the lesser pro leagues, first tearing up the short-lived ABL (1961–63), which collapsed out from under him after less than two seasons, and later dominating the somewhat more stable ABA when the red, white, and blue league came on the scene in 1967–68. In the first season of the ABL Hawkins was the league MVP and scoring leader, though only 19 at the time. In the ABA six years later "The Hawk" again emerged from the shadows as the inaugural scoring champion and MVP while lifting Pittsburgh to the league's first title. In between came four long years of country-hopping with the barnstorming Harlem Globetrotters. The nightmare of exile ended when NBA Commissioner Walter Kennedy removed the ban on Hawkins in the face of a multimillion-dollar lawsuit brought by the outlawed superstar and his battery of lawyers. Finally Connie Hawkins had won his courtroom battles and eventually had a taste of NBA life, though only when many of his skills had eroded. The 28-year-old rookie broke in with the Phoenix Suns by averaging nearly 25 points per game in 1970, then remained in the league for a half dozen more years before closing out his career in Los Angeles and Atlanta. Even as a brittle shell of what he once was, Connie Hawkins was still good enough during his much-belated NBA years to play in four All-Star Games, earn All-NBA First Team honors for his rookie campaign, and even turn enough heads to merit Naismith Hall of Fame election in 1992.

Elvin Hayes (NBA "Top 50" Selection)

One of only three rookies (along with Chamberlain and Joe Fulks) ever to pace the NBA-BAA in scoring, Elvin Hayes closed out a glorious 16-year career second in all-time minutes played (with an even 50,000), third (now fourth) in total games (1,303), fourth in total rebounds (16,279), and sixth (now seventh) in career scoring (27,313)—third in the latter category if only NBA points are admitted to the cumulative tally. With an unstoppable turn-around jumper, both along the baseline at close range and outside of the paint at long range, Hayes was likely the finest shooting big man in all basketball history. Perhaps only Bob McAdoo might raise a challenge in some circles for such a distinction.

Durability seemed the hallmark of Hayes's professional career and only a handful of high-scoring big men ever lasted longer or performed at such an elevated level for quite so long. The result was some of the loftiest career numbers in the NBA record books and a certain ticket into the Naismith Memorial Hall of Fame in Springfield. Besides nearly 30,000 career points and the records or near-records for games, seasons, and minutes logged, there was also the unmistakable impact that Hayes had on the opponents of every team for which he played. During a first brief four-year tour with the expansion Rockets in San Diego and Houston, Hayes had little teammate support that might supplement his own efforts. He dominated as a rookie with league-best totals in scoring average (28.4), points (2,327), minutes played (a league record), and field goals made and attempted, while at the same time his team languished as an NBA also-ran. Once hooked up with the Bullets of Baltimore and Washington in the '70s, and teamed with fellow workhorses such as Wes Unseld, Mike Riordan, Phil Chenier, and Kevin Porter, it was altogether a different matter. Hayes proved himself a durable winner at midcareer when he carried the Bullets (along with Unseld) to three NBA Finals (against the Warriors in 1975 and the Sonics in 1978 and 1979), earned one championship ring (1978), and in the process emerged as the all-time franchise leader in both scoring and shot blocking.

As remarkable as Hayes was in the NBA, he was even more of a superstar during his years in the collegiate ranks. There is no more storied instance of one-on-one duels in college annals than the one involving Elvin Hayes and UCLA's nonpareil franchise center Lew Alcindor. The two locked horns for the first and most memorable time on January 20, 1968, during a much ballyhooed contest staged for a national television audience in the mammoth Houston Astrodome and attracting a record arena audience of 52,693. Houston would emerge on top on the strength of game-long domination by Hayes, which included 39 points (29 in the first half) and a pair of game-deciding free throws. Despite the injury that slowed Alcindor that night and scuttled a true test between the two superstars, the game was, nonetheless, one of the most memorable of the college sport's full first century. Had Alcindor not been around for two of the same seasons, Elvin Hayes might well have been remembered as the dominant collegiate player of the entire decade of the '60s. As it was, Hayes posted a campaign his senior season (36.8 points per game) that was sufficient to corral National Player of the Year recognition and thus block Alcindor from joining Oscar Robertson and Bill Walton with a rare three-year sweep of that coveted honor.

Marques Haynes

"Harlem Globetrotters" is a label still capable of conjuring up a small handful of names and images that remain, for all time, synonymous with the ancient ball club's indelible barnstorming legacy. Promoter Abe Saperstein and the Harlem Globetrotters are, of course, nearly one and the same entity; and when it comes to players sporting 'Trotters red, white, and blue-spangled jerseys, the same can likely be said for Reece "Goose" Tatum, Meadowlark Lemon, and Marques Haynes. Haynes differs from both Lemon and Tatum in that his particular memorable image is more one of rare athletic skills than one of slapstick comic talents. Marques Haynes may indeed have been the most gifted dribbler in all of basketball's long and crowded annals. It was a talent he had learned under the tutelage of a brother, Wendall Haynes, who doubled as his junior high school coach. Applied to serious basketball at first, the youngster's remarkable ballhandling skills contributed to a state high school championship in Oklahoma in 1942 and paced a Langston University all-black team to a 112–3 four-year record, two conference titles, and a victory over Saperstein's touring 'Trotters outfit.

Signing first with a Kansas City affiliate of the famed Saperstein barnstorming team, Haynes was promoted to the Globetrotters in January 1947 and shared the team's top billing with Tatum for the next seven years. A staple of the Harlem Globetrotters' almost nightly shows was the special dribbling acts that Marques Haynes performed before and during games. In 1953 Haynes left the Globetrotters in a dispute over salary and formed his own rival troupe known as the Harlem Magicians. Twice over the next three decades he would return to the Globetrotters fold and then again depart once more to form or join competing road acts. In 40 years of continuous road life Haynes would log more games (over 12,000), miles (more than 4 million), and venues (every state in the United States, 97 countries, and six continents) than any other basketball player in history. During his lengthy life on the road Marques Haynes surely contributed as much as anyone to a proud sporting tradition of barnstorming basketball, a tradition that was once the sport's essential lifeblood, but in recent decades has served only as one of its more entertaining forms of window dressing.

Spencer Haywood

Haywood was a memorable Olympic star at age 18 and an accomplished pro by the time he was barely 20. As a raw teenager the 6'8" gazelle had enjoyed a single junior college season (28.2 points and 22.1 rebounds at Trinidad in Colorado) and one varsity campaign (32.1 points per game and the nation's rebounding lead at Detroit), which were truly the ingredients of a small-college legend. If this were not enough, he was destined to have an impact on the game which stretched far beyond his immense playing talents. For it was also Spencer Haywood who first brought modern-era free agency to the play-for-pay version of the game. Haywood left college (University of Detroit) as a mere 20-year-old sophomore and hooked on with the ABA circuit unfettered by any rules banning undergraduate signings. After an incredible first season (when he led the league in just about everything and was dual MVP and top rookie) Haywood decided that the NBA was both more glamorous and better paying, and thus inked a new contract with the older league, which as yet did not enjoy any such signing exemptions. When other NBA teams balked, the Seattle ownership announced plans for a court battle, and the league quickly reversed its restrictions on undergraduate contracts.

The contract squabble between the ABA's Denver Nuggets and NBA's Seattle SuperSonics over Haywood's services in 1970 would lead directly to an undergraduate "hardship" early-signing provision, which has since been both boon and bane to the existence of several subsequent generations of starry-eyed ghetto-bred African-American ballplayers. The newly instituted "hardship clause" (the sport's most ludicrous euphemism) more than ever transformed college basketball into a mere stepping-stone for talented (largely black) athletes seeking an elusive dream of NBA instant riches. College basketball, now more than ever, would become a transparent "meat market"—especially for hordes of black ghetto athletes. It all began with Spencer Haywood, whose own dozen remaining seasons of NBA play (despite some heavy scoring in Seattle and a single NBA title with Los Angeles in 1980) would never again quite reach the instant stardom and remarkable achievement of a single knockout ABA campaign.

Tom Heinsohn

Tom Heinsohn is one of those giants of the cage sport who deserves equal billing in the history books for each chapter in his tripartite career—first as collegiate All-American player for Holy Cross, later as year-in and year-out NBA All-Star with Auerbach's Celtics, and finally as championship-winning professional coach with the post-Russell Boston ball clubs of the mid-1970s. As though this three-decade association with the on-court game were not enough, Heinsohn today continues his affiliation with the Celtics in his second decade as a popular play-by-play television and radio announcer. In the latter capacity Heinsohn still teams with his former on-court running mate Bob Cousy. But it was way back in the late '50s and early '60s that Heinsohn and Cousy first teamed up to write some of the grandest legends of the early NBA saga.

Heinsohn was known foremost as a relentless shooter who earned the sarcastic nickname "Ack-Ack" for his machine-gun-like firing up of shots from any angle and almost any time he had the ball in his hands and gained a half-step advantage on his overmatched opponent. Putting in a full season with Auerbach's first championship outfit (while Russell only logged a partial campaign due to the 1956 Olympics), the touted territorial draft pick earned top rookie honors for the regular season and then poured in 37 points in the deciding seventh game of the title round with St. Louis to ice the first NBA banner of Boston's dynasty era. For his nine-season career as an active player, Heinsohn would walk off with eight championship rings. And he assuredly contributed as heavily as anyone else to each of those postseason triumphs. Within Auerbach's tightly orchestrated scheme Heinsohn was the designated scorer while Cousy was the playmaker and Russell was the defender and board-sweeper. When he took over bench duties as successor to Auerbach and Russell in 1970, he would continue his hero status by earning for the proud Celtics two more titles (1974, 1976) and garnering for himself both a coveted NBA Coach of the Year designation (1973) and a place in history as perhaps the league's most successful coach for the decade separating Bill Russell and Larry Bird.

Art Heyman

Multitalented Duke forward Art Heyman is perhaps as good a candidate as any to wear the mythical crown of the ACC's showcase player. Barely edged out in both the conference Player of the Year race (by Wake Forest phenom Len Chappell) and the individual scoring race (again both times by Chappell) during his first two varsity seasons, Heyman peaked with his senior outing for one of the most dominant single campaigns in ACC annals. As a senior Heyman would again have to settle for second spot in the league's individual rebounding race (trailing Carolina's Bill Cunningham), but would have to settle for second place in little else. He dominated the scoring race over UNC's "Kangaroo Kid" Cunningham, finishing up with a 24.9 average (a bit below his 25.3 junior mark) to clinch a second straight spot in the nation's top 10. Between them, Heyman and Cunningham had further extended the tradition of New York imports among the league's loftiest stars. Heyman's senior rampage was also convincing enough with the sportswriters to guarantee landslide selection over Princeton's Bill Bradley and Ohio State's Gary Bradds as AP, UPI, and USBWA National Player of the Year.

Behind Heyman's all-around play, a Duke team that also featured Jeff Mullins (No. 3 ACC scorer) and 6'10" Jay Buckley would race to a 27–3 season that was the school's finest ever prior to the 1990s-era of Final Four dominance under Coach K. The Blue Devils would first ride Heyman's potent scoring and rebounding to an undefeated league season, an ACC tournament sweep (68–57 over Wake Forest in the finals), and a successful postseason NCAA run, which culminated in the Eastern Regional crown and a spot in the national semifinal game against eventual sur-

*Art Heyman,
Duke University*

Transcendental Graphics

prise champion Loyola-Chicago. The Loyola Ramblers were themselves a charmed outfit in 1963, however, and would prove too much for Heyman and company in their Final Four showdown. Leslie Hunter matched Heyman with 29 points and all five starters for the Ramblers cracked double figures.

In the end Heyman's great senior season and his two brilliant earlier campaigns assured his large measure of league immortality. Some of the charm was unfortunately worn off in coming years by a disappointing and even lackluster pro career consisting of six NBA-ABA seasons and including seven teams and only a cumulative 10.3 scoring average. Teammate Jeff Mullins far outshone Heyman as an NBA performer (four of Mullins's 12 seasons boasted 20-plus scoring averages), and this fact further diminished Heyman's tarnished image back home on Tobacco Road. Part of the problem was undoubtedly the hell-bent style with which Heyman had always played: his flaw as a collegian had been shot selection (he was barely a 45 percent shooter at Duke), and this was a factor that had also haunted him during earlier year-end tournament action. Yet, when three years of collegiate play are the sole standard by which a career is judged, then Art Heyman was perhaps as good in the short haul (certainly as statistically dominant) as any Tobacco Road star has ever been. No league player ever had a greater hunger to win, a better facility for owning the ball with games on the line, or a greater knack for improvising around the offensive bucket. Art Heyman was a winner, and with Heyman in the lineup, Duke was a proven winner as well.

Paul Hogue

In the six-decade history of March Madness Paul Hogue deserves his rightful spot alongside such legends of the game as Bob Kurland, Bill Russell, Lew Alcindor, and Bill Walton. These are the handful of dominant centers who have carried their teams against all odds to consecutive NCAA title games and have also come away with a pair of national titles for their own considerable efforts. Jerry Lucas came within an eyelash of expanding the group, but it was Hogue himself who twice, almost single-handedly, kept the Buckeyes legend from joining the select number. The 6'9" wide-body center overlapped a single season with Oscar Robertson and succeeded the Big O as the Bearcats' top gun. But unlike Oscar, Hogue saved his greatest efforts for year-end tournament play and was a far bigger factor in championship games than he ever was in season-long conference play. Hogue averaged 18.4 points and 13.3 rebounds in a dozen NCAA tournament games between 1960 and 1962 (his team went 11–1 in that stretch), a significant upgrading of his three-year scoring (15.3) and board-sweeping (12.0) averages. In the final game of his career (the 1962 71–59 championship victory over Ohio State) he thoroughly outplayed the hobbled Buckeyes star (22–11 in points and 19–16 in rebounds), a triumph that can only partially be attributed to the fact that Lucas was partially slowed by injury. A season earlier, although Lucas was the one to dominate and capture the tourney MVP, Hogue was enough of a force to hold his own and contribute mightily to the Bearcats' five-point overtime victory. Paul Hogue was never an All-American nominee, but his All-NCAA tournament team selection in 1962 and overall stellar play in three straight sessions of the NCAA Final Four were still enough to earn him a position as the second overall pick (New York Knicks) in the 1962 NBA draft.

Bailey Howell

Had the ugly specter of racism not surrounded the Mississippi State University basketball program over the two decades following World War II, Bailey Howell's glorious Southeastern Conference cage career might have boasted even a good deal more glitter on the national scene than it did. As it turned out, Howell seemed to make a career out of being second best (which is not always bad, especially when it comes to the star-studded worlds of college and professional basketball). This penchant for being an overlooked runner-up began with the 6'7" forward's stellar senior season at Mississippi State, when the SEC's premier player finished second in the land among major college players in both rebounding (15.2) and scoring (27.5 behind Oscar Robertson). It was all to little avail, however, as Howell's 24–1 SEC championship squad withdrew from the NCAA postseason chase due to the presence of black players. As a sophomore, he rebounded at nearly 20 per game and also paced the nation in field-goal percentage. By the time of his graduation Bailey Howell ranked among the all-time all-around collegiate greats, joining Tom Gola and Elgin Baylor as the only players up to that time to log as many as 2,000 career points and 1,000 career rebounds. It was a sterling enough record to be the top draft pick of the NBA's Detroit Pistons.

Howell's grip on second-best status continued through much of his considerable NBA career, which spread over a dozen seasons split among Detroit (five years), Baltimore (two years), Boston (four years), and a final swan-song season in Philadelphia. While he managed to pace the Pistons in scoring four times and rebounding three times, he later occupied his familiar runner-up spot for those team categories while with Baltimore in 1965 and 1966. Traded to the champion Celtics for Mel Counts, Howell trailed only John Havlicek in scoring and Bill Russell in rebounding for three straight Boston campaigns (the three that Russell served as head coach). It was also in Boston that Bailey Howell finally reached championship status when the dynasty Celtics won their final two NBA banners of the Auerbach–Cousy–Russell era. And if Howell was often only second-best when it came to league or ball club statistical categories, nonetheless his long-term consistency was sufficient to eventually make a deep impact on the NBA record book. Mississippi State's most productive NBA performer retired in 1971 ranked among the top 10 in 11 different career statistical categories. It is not surprising, given his reputation as a punishing rebounder and bruising defensive player, that the highest of these rankings fell in the area of personal fouls committed, a dubious category in which Howell once stood entrenched as the fifth most notorious hacker in NBA annals.

Rod "Hot Rod" Hundley

Basketball's clown prince was one of the sport's most uniquely gifted all-around players. He was also one of college basketball's all-time flakes, and as a result, its greatest crowd-pleasing sideshow. "Hot Rod" Hundley didn't log anything like the lofty point totals of Furman's Frank Selvy, Temple's Bill Mlkvy, or Villanova's Paul Arizin—other relentless scorers of the 1950s. Nonetheless, the entertaining gunner from the Mountaineer State of West Virginia was perhaps the most outrageously colorful athlete ever to come down the pipe in the '50s or any other decade for that matter.

If Rod Hundley didn't fill the nets at the same dizzying pace as some of the top gunners turning up at other hoop-crazed campuses during the same decade of scoring excesses, he indeed had no peer when it came to pleasing crowds who paid admissions to see him play. So sensational were his shooting and ballhandling skills in high school, in fact, that the Charleston native stirred an all-out recruiting war among more than 100 colleges coast to coast. An apparent born showman who delighted in turning on crowds with his dribbling and passing antics, Hundley at first leaned toward attending powerhouse North Carolina State, the dominant team in the just-formed Atlantic Coast Conference. Yet, when the Wolfpack program was suddenly slapped with both NCAA and ACC sanctions for numerous recruiting violations, longtime N.C. State coach Everett Case nobly advised Hundley against casting his lot with a program that might now doom his promising career even before it got off the ground. Hundley wisely swallowed the advice, opted to stay closer to home, and signed up with coach Red Brown in Morgantown, just before Brown turned over the West Virginia program to ex-Mountaineers star and NBA performer Fred Schaus.

The decision was not only a boon to the West Virginia schoolboy star but to the state's leading institution as well. "Hot Rod" Hundley would overnight become a Mountaineers legend whose catchy nickname as fittingly captured his flaky personality as it did his deadeye basket-making.

"Hot Rod" Hundley,
West Virginia University

A proficient enough scorer, Hundley would average a shade under 25 a game during his three WVU seasons. But clowning on the court always seemed to take precedence over honing almost limitless offensive skills. In a few short seasons a pair of other sensational Mountaineers forwards, Jerry West and Rod Thorn, would win games, league titles, and even postseason honors in droves for West Virginia's growing cage program. Rod Hundley instead expended most of his own energies on winning the crowd with his outrageous antics.

A cross between the Harlem Globetrotters and Houdini, this original "court jester" played seriously enough to pace his team to 19 wins and its first-ever Southern Conference title as a sophomore rookie, racking up 711 points in the process for a sophomore-season NCAA record. As a junior he averaged 26.6 points per game, brought WVU to a second league title, and completely outgunned Frank Selvy's shot-happy Furman College successor Darrell Floyd in a head-to-head matchup (Hundley had 32 in the first half alone). As an experienced senior he garnered All-American honors, a third conference team crown, and the individual top spot in the first round of the NBA player draft.

And through all the glory, Hot Rod lived up to his growing reputation for pure show business on the hardwoods night after night. With his team safely in the lead (which it frequently was) he would shoot with either hand, spin the ball on his fingertips Globetrotter style, dribble with his knees and elbows, and punch layups into the hoop volleyball style with a closed fist. Frequently he offered the ball to a defender with one hand while dribbling downcourt then flipped it over his shoulder and caught it behind his back with the opposite hand. He launched his "praying mantis" long-range set shots from his knees, hooked in foul shots, and refused to shoot at all if his team built too large a lead. Another crowd-pleasing feature of the Rod Hundley sideshow was to shoot free throws blindly over his shoulder with his back facing the basket.

College basketball had never before seen anything quite like the Hot Rod Hundley Show and would never again quite find his equal. (Nor do the recent NBA antics of the modern anti-star, Dennis Rodman, rate for comparison. Rodman's act has always detracted from his court presence and never served to heighten or embellish it.) It was rare enough to have a court star who seemed to double as the team's public relations officer; it was rarer still to have a full-fledged on-court clown talented enough to twice win All-American honors and even check in as the No. 1 overall draft pick (by the Cincinnati Royals) of the win-at-all-cost professional league.

Darrall Imhoff

Darrall Imhoff was never an NBA household name, though he was hardly a bust in the professional circuit, either. The 6'10" center known as "Big D" survived a dozen pro seasons in New York, Detroit, Los Angeles, Philadelphia, and Cincinnati (bowing out with a handful of games in Portland); he scored slightly less than 6,000 points and pulled in slightly more than 6,000 rebounds (averaging more than 7 per game in both categories); and in 1970 he ranked second in the league in field-goal percentage. But when it comes to a memorable and accomplished collegiate career, the huge and agile Cal-Berkeley center came within reaching distance of the accomplishments of Bill Russell, Lew Alcindor, Bill Walton, and Paul Hogue. Imhoff carried his University of California team to one NCAA title in 1959 (edging Jerry West and West Virginia by a point) and got within a single game of duplicating the effort a season later. But ironically, just as Cincinnati's Paul Hogue would later block Ohio State star Jerry Lucas from joining the ranks of centers who lifted their teams to repeat NCAA titles, a year earlier it was Lucas himself who had managed to keep Imhoff out of that highly select fraternity. The Pete Newell–coached Golden Bears with Imhoff in the post as the team's leading scorer (13.7) and rebounder (12.4) battled back to the NCAA Finals in 1960 with excellent prospects to defend their 1959 NCAA crown against the high-scoring Buckeyes. Lucas, however, shut down Imhoff effectively (holding the Cal standout to eight points and five boards, half of his own totals) as Ohio State romped over the outclassed Berkeley team by 20.

Dan Issel

Among the dozens upon dozens of legendary All-Americans spawned and shaped by Baron Rupp at Kentucky, few outreach the accomplishment of 1970 First Team All-American Dan Issel. Perhaps only Alex Groza does so, and then only when professional tenures are put aside and college accomplishments are the sole standard for measuring. During three seasons in Lexington the 6'6" versatile for-

Dan Issel,
Denver Nuggets

© Indiana Pacers

ward-center improved from a 16-point scorer as a sophomore to averages of 26.6 points per game (junior season) and finally 33.9 (fourth in the nation behind Maravich, Carr, and Mount). He left Kentucky as the leading scorer (2,138 points) in the proud history of Wildcats basketball. A first-round 1970 ABA draft selection of the nearby Kentucky Colonels, Issel was not only an ABA Rookie of the Year, but also the league scoring champion (29.9 points per game) during his debut season. Before being acquired by the Denver Nuggets in the final season of the short-lived ABA, Issel also led the Louisville-based Colonels to a 1975 league championship and earned league All-Star honors in every one of his half dozen ABA campaigns. Moving into the NBA with the Denver franchise in 1977, Issel would log nine more pro seasons and average above 20 points per game in six of them. In the early 1980s he teamed with Alex English and Kiki Vandeweghe to form one of the most productive front walls in NBA history. The high-scoring trio combined for an unparalleled composite scoring average of better than 75 per game during the 1983 season.

As both a collegian and a professional Issel made his mark not by flash or finesse (he didn't jump well and had little raw speed), but instead by tenacious hustle and a relentless work ethic. He was also a durable workhorse who missed only 24 games across his entire 15-year career split between the two pro circuits. A deadly outside jumper from the 20-foot range was a vital facet of his game, which set up a most effective drive to the hoop, and the combination was effective enough to produce one of the highest composite ABA-NBA point totals in history. Dan Issel's 27,482 career scoring total is today topped only by Abdul-Jabbar, Chamberlain, Julius Erving, Moses Malone, and Michael Jordan, a fact in itself sufficient to explain his status as a member of the Naismith Memorial Basketball Hall of Fame.

Neil Johnston

It would be difficult to come up with a more underrated or more overlooked figure from the first decade of NBA play than the hook-shooting center of the Philadelphia Warriors, who won a trio of NBA scoring titles (1953, 1954, 1955) and proved year in and year out to be one of the most talented offensive forces from the league's first dozen seasons. The string-bean-like Johnston dominated NBA inside play in the few short seasons between Mikan's heyday in Minneapolis and Russell's arrival in Boston. But once Bill Russell was on the scene Johnston's career would take an almost immediate and irreversible nosedive. The hoopla surrounding Mikan in the early '50s and Pettit at the end of the decade obscures the fact that Johnston ripped off three straight individual scoring titles during his first three full seasons in the league. Somewhat surprising is the fact that he did most of his damage during that stretch with his sweeping classic hook and not with the power inside moves that characterized other board crashers of the epoch like Mikan, Pettit, Foust, Mikkelsen, or Alex Groza in Indianapolis.

Neil Johnston teamed with Paul Arizin to give the Philadelphia club a virtual grip on the individual scoring honors, winning the honor four years running (Arizin took the crown in 1952, then departed for a two-year military stint). But for all their scoring punch in the persons of Arizin and Johnston (along with Joe Fulks, Andy Phillip, and Joe Graboski), Philadelphia could not make much of a dent in the league title races under coach Eddie Gottlieb. The 1952–53 Philly squad even set a new league standard for futility, boasting the top scorer with Johnston but managing to win only a mere dozen games. The critical blow had been the loss of Arizin, who didn't return to the scene until the 1955 campaign. And for all his point-making, Neil Johnston himself was really not much of a game-winning force. His offense was entirely one dimensional, which became altogether apparent once the shot-blocking Bill Russell came onto the scene. Russell so intimidated Johnston and so shut down his offense in head-to-head confrontations, that the Philadelphia ace quickly faded away into early retirement, leaving off as an active player in 1959 and taking up as the Warriors' head coach the following season. In only his fourth pro game Russell had 34 rebounds against Johnston; a week later he held Johnston scoreless over 42 minutes.

In the end Neil Johnston owned a small piece of fame as a three-time scoring champ, yet, nonetheless saw his career squelched by a double stroke of misfortune. The first bad break was Bill Russell's arrival up in Boston, which hastened Johnston's retirement. The second was Chamberlain's arrival in Philly immediately on the heels of Johnston's departure. Once Wilt started scoring nightly in the 40- and 50-point range and rang up his remarkable string of seven uninterrupted scoring crowns—also making the Warriors a league force in the process—hardly anyone was about to remember the soft-shooting Neil Johnston, even in the City of Brotherly Love itself.

K. C. Jones

The man who played in the shadows of Bill Russell, in both San Francisco as a collegian and Boston as a professional, was indisputably one of the sport's most talented background role players. He was also one of its most enduring winners, who, as collegiate and professional player and later as an NBA coach, amassed a collection of championship rings that has been matched by only a mere handful of All-Americans and Hall of Famers. K. C. Jones also won those rings (eight as a player and two as a coach with Boston) with legitimate contributions and not just because he happened to sit on the bench for the right team at the right time. More than Russell, it was Jones who shut down phenomenal Tom Gola of La Salle and brought USF the first of its back-to-back NCAA titles in 1955. A decade later Jones was also contributing heavily to a number of Russell's most hard-earned NBA titles, first as a backup to playmaker Bob Cousy and later as a backcourt tandem with Sam Jones. It was the "Jones Boys" who made Boston partisans quickly forget the once incomparable duo of Cousy and Sharman and who keyed the final three of Boston's eight straight banners in the wake of Cousy's retirement. When K. C. replaced Cousy alongside Sam Jones in 1964, he inherited the playmaking role and paced the ball club in assists the next three seasons. He also contributed heavily as a ball-hawking defender who pressured opposing quarterbacks relentlessly and whose disruptions at the defensive end were as vital as any part of the vaunted Boston attack. Playing days (he retired in 1967) were followed by 10 years of NBA head coaching spread over two decades, which brought seven division titles and two additional NBA championship rings (again with Boston, in 1984 and 1986). And as a coach (with Washington, Boston, Seattle, and the ABA's San Diego Conquistadors), his quiet style brought not only deep respect from all the athletes who played for him, but a continued winning tradition as well.

Sam Jones (NBA "Top 50" Selection)

While black stars at large (and thus largely white) colleges were beginning to grab some share of the national headlines in the mid-1950s (Walter Dukes at Seton Hall, Sihugo Green at Duquesne, Bill Russell at USF, and Wilt Chamberlain at Kansas), there was another tradition simultaneously being sustained in the backwaters of the college sport. This was the tradition of the great black college teams, which often dominated NAIA small-college action. Coach John McLendon, for one, had pioneered both fast-break basketball and the small-college black powerhouse team during his journeyman career that took him from North Carolina Central to Hampton Institute to Tennessee State and finally on to Kentucky State. McLendon, at his height, would capture three consecutive NAIA titles with Tennessee State, while at the same time recruiting and shaping players like Dick Barnett, Jim Barnhill, and Ben Warley.

The first notable individual talent to emerge from this arena and make his lasting mark on the national hoops scene would be Sam Jones, backcourt ace with the Auerbach-coached Bill Russell Celtics of the mid- and late 1960s. Jones would first carve out his reputation at North Carolina Central College under McLendon's successor, Roy Brown. And he would enter the Celtics' lineup as a top June 1957 draft choice already sporting his later reputation as a phenomenal "carom" shooter and (in the words of Boston teammate Bob Cousy) "the fastest thing ever seen" charging up and down a 90-foot basketball floor.

Of all the memorable superstars to wear the uniform of the Boston Celtics, none was more of a surprise find than was Sam Jones. For one thing, Jones arrived in Boston for his 1958 rookie season as a completely unknown quantity, a player whose college career had transpired in almost total obscurity. In four seasons at North Carolina Central (spread over six years due to military service), Jones averaged nearly 18 per game after turning down a scholarship at more visible Notre Dame, but in the mid-'50s few scouts and fewer fans were attuned to the small-college cage scene. It wasn't long, however, before the lesser of Boston's "Jones Boys" (K. C. Jones joined the squad a year later after his own military stint) had established a personal style and list of accomplishments that would rank him right alongside Cousy and Sharman as part of Boston's unforgettable triumvirate of all-time backcourt immortals. Most eye-catching was his shooting style and his shooting proficiency, which eventually outstripped even that of the deadeyed Bill Sharman. With a key spot on 10 Boston championship teams, Sam Jones compiled enough outstanding postseason playing time to eventually rank second in total NBA playoff games (at the time of his 1969 retirement), fourth in playoff points, and third in Celtics career scoring. More importantly the rangy 6'4" marksman, who once collected a club-record 51 against Detroit in 1965, was an early prototype of the tall shooting guard, which would become an NBA staple a full quarter-century later. With Sam Jones and K. C. Jones inheriting the backcourt in the mid-'60s from Cousy and Sharman, Auerbach's dynasty was destined to steamroll on for several more seasons without as much as a single missed step.

Billy Keller

The nine-season ABA produced far more than Julius Erving and a small, if much-publicized, stable of soaring and slamming black power forwards among its legacy of super-talented athletes. It was also incubator to some of the sport's finest long-range shooters encouraged to refine their talents by the league's revolutionary three-point field goal. Foremost among ABA bombers was Kentucky's Louie Dampier and not far behind was Indiana's Billy Keller. Keller's slick shooting was accurate enough to twice capture the league's three-point field goal crown and also to produce one phenomenal free-throw shooting mark over 90 percent (1976) and six others above the 87 percent accuracy level. Serving as a playmaker for an Indiana

*Billy Keller,
Purdue University*

© Purdue University

Pacers front line that featured George McGinnis, Roger Brown, and Mel Daniels, the former Purdue standout also played on three ABA championship ball clubs in Indianapolis and was one of the key fixtures in Indiana's early ABA dominance. Keller's three-point shooting legacy is anchored by the fact that, with 506 career "home runs," he stands alongside Dampier (794) and Glen Combs (503) as the only three ABA marksmen with more than 500 lifetime three-pointers to their credit.

Johnny "Red" Kerr

Red Kerr was pro basketball's version of baseball's Everett Scott—a player who wore "iron-man" laurels years ahead of the writing of latter-day iron-man legacies.

(It was Scott who held baseball's consecutive games record at 1,307 before Lou Gehrig and Cal Ripken Jr. ever came along.) Years before Randy Smith, Ron Boone, and A. C. Green were building their own modern-era legends for durability, Kerr had already established a remarkable skein for future generations to shoot at. And given the rough-and-tumble era in which Kerr's original iron-man accomplishments were logged, the pioneering center's achievements—like those of Lou Gehrig versus Cal Ripken—seem far more impressive than the slightly longer stints of more pampered modern-era players. Kerr—currently a long-tenured broadcaster with the Chicago Bulls franchise—took up the center post for the Syracuse Nats at the outset of his rookie 1955 season and never missed a night's work in the trenches during the dozen seasons that followed. His mind-boggling string of uninterrupted games would reach 844 (917 including playoff games) before he finally sat out a night with Baltimore early in his final campaign of 1966; it was a record for matchless durability that would last all the way until the 1982–83 season, before being finally overhauled in a far gentler age by San Diego guard Randy Smith.

Hal Lear

Temple backcourt great Hal Lear flashed brilliantly for one single NCAA season, a campaign in which he proved to be a true basketball David who stole thunder from some of the college game's most formidable Goliaths. Bill Russell was the toast of the college basketball world in the spring of 1956 when he led the San Francisco Dons to a repeat NCAA title as the first undefeated national champion of the postseason tournament era. But while Russell owned just about every other conceivable boasting right of that season, he was surprisingly not the Final Four MVP, despite a 26-point, 27-rebound performance against Iowa in the title game. The trophy for individual excellence went to 5'11" dervish Hal Lear who encored a 32-point scoring outburst in the semifinal match against the same Hawkeyes with a then-record 48-point explosion versus SMU in the consolation shootout. Lear, who teamed up with outstanding sophomore Guy Rodgers in the Owls' talented backcourt and averaged 24 for the season, had authored an even loftier virtuoso performance earlier in the same tourney against overmatched Yankee Conference champion Connecticut. In that regional semifinal match Lear made 18 of 27 from the floor and 4 of 5 from the charity stripe to tally two-thirds of his team's baskets and 40 (61 percent) of its 65 points in the 65–58 victory. Lear's final total of 160 tournament points (32 per game) has only subsequently been surpassed on four occasions: Glen Rice (183 in 1989), Bill Bradley (177 in 1965), Elvin Hayes (167 in 1968), and Danny Manning (163 in 1988).

"Meadowlark" Lemon

Harlem Globetrotters on-court clowning didn't begin (or even end) with Meadowlark Lemon, star performer for Saperstein's barnstorming troupe from the mid-1950s until the early 1970s, a span which included almost 5,000 games. But world-famous Globetrotters high jinks are today almost synonymous with barnstorming basketball's most popular drawing card. Lemon (whose real name is Meadow George Lemon III) coaxed a tryout with Saperstein's team while serving with the military in Germany and was impressive enough to earn a contract with the outfit after completing his army tour in 1954. Capitalizing on a number of unforeseen opportunities for top billing with Saperstein's barnstormers—Goose Tatum left unexpectedly to form the Harlem Magicians with Marques Haynes, Showboat Hall was felled with pneumonia, and Sam Wheeler broke a knee—Lemon quickly seized the spotlight and added the colorful "lark" to his given name as part of his new center-stage identity. Featured in such familiar trademark routines as the medicine ball–basketball switch, the rubber-banded foul shot, and wild heaves of buckets of confetti at startled spectators, Lemon in short order became a world-renown entertainment figure in his well-earned and self-styled role as "The Clown Prince of Basketball."

"Jungle Jim" Loscutoff

Basketball has had few "enforcers" whose singular role on the floor seemed to be physical intimidation of more talented opponents. Unlike hockey, basketball is not structured to allow for such a role or such a style of knockdown, drag-out play. Yet with the tal-

"Meadowlark" Lemon, Harlem Globetrotters

Transcendental Graphics

ent-rich Boston Celtics of the Russell-Cousy era, nonetheless, "Jungle Jim" Loscutoff provided the NBA's closest-ever model for such a muscle-bound prototype. The Oregon graduate debuted with Auerbach's crew in 1956, a year before the championship run began, and lasted through nine campaigns until 1964, a year after Cousy bowed out. Through more than 500 NBA games and more than a decade of action, he only once averaged double figures (10.6, 1957) and most often scored at only half that rate. While a ferocious rebounder who played more than 1,100 minutes in five different seasons, his rebounding average also reached double figures on but one occasion (the same 1957 season). Loscutoff was on the floor most of the time simply to wear down opposing centers and forwards and to protect the rest of the Boston front line that consisted over the years of Heinsohn, Frank Ramsey, Lou Tsioropoulos, Jack Nichols, Gene Conley, Clyde Lovellette, and Gene Guarilia. It was a job he did proficiently enough to have his number eventually retired, though since that same number (18) was later worn more distinctively by Dave Cowens, it was actually Loscutoff's nickname ("Loscy") and not his numeral that was eventually hoisted into the Boston Garden rafters.

Jerry Lucas (NBA "Top 50" Selection)

He may well have been the most dominant college player of all time—at least outside of Bill Walton, Lew Alcindor, Tom Gola, and Bill Russell. We are not talking here about huge offensive numbers à la Pete Maravich, Johnny Neumann, Nick Werkman, or Glenn Robinson; nor is future NBA stardom the appropriate yardstick, as in the case of Magic Johnson, Cazzie Russell, or Isiah Thomas out of the same Big Ten Conference. At issue here is the rare combination of skilled, crowd-pleasing offensive and defensive play coupled with the ability to lift the team around him to championship heights. For three seasons the Ohio State Buckeyes (despite their talented supporting cast of Havlicek, Siegfried, and others) largely rode the shooting and rebounding of Jerry Lucas—and they rode it all the way to the NCAA championship game three straight years, winning the title in 1960 and suffering heartbreaking near misses in their two encores. Only Walton (winner of two out of his three Finals) and Alcindor (never beaten in the championship game) carried their teams to equal championship heights in quite the same fashion or with quite the same regularity.

Lucas's college numbers are solid enough, yet they are more moderate than outstanding. For three seasons he averaged more than 20 points per game (though descending slightly each campaign). He owns no school or Big Ten scoring records, however. The latter fact is attributed to the coincidence that Terry Dischinger (Purdue) was in the league at exactly the same time. Rebounding was Lucas's true forte, and he paced the nation in that department for two seasons running. For three seasons he was a unanimous first-team All-American and for two years the nation's clearcut Player of the Year. Only a handful of roundball's greatest stars share the first distinction. Only Alcindor, Oscar Robertson (thrice), Walton, and David Thompson divide the latter honor.

But perhaps the truest (and most costly) measure of the impact of Jerry Lucas at Ohio State came with the most disappointing game in Buckeyes cage history. The national title won by OSU during Lucas's sophomore season was rudely ripped away by an inspired University of Cincinnati club in a tense overtime match a year later. Poised to regain their crown during the senior season of Lucas and Havlicek, the Buckeyes rode the scoring and rebounding prowess of the nation's top player through a 26–1 campaign into an expected NCAA Finals rematch with the cross-state rival Bearcats. But disaster struck when Lucas suffered a severe leg injury in the semifinal match with Wake Forest. The hobbled Lucas gamely tried to perform the next night but had to be spelled for much of the contest by promising, though inexperienced, sophomore Gary Bradds. Without their workhorse at full strength, the Big Ten champs were again no match for the national champion Bearcats. Cincinnati won for a second straight season—this time even more convincingly to the one-sided tune of 71–59. Thus Jerry Lucas bowed out in most uncharacteristic fashion with only the sixth loss of his collegiate career, yet his second in the prestigious year-ending championship game.

John Lucas

The athletic career of Maryland's John Lucas carries several boasting points beyond what the athletic guard was ultimately able to accomplish on the collegiate basketball court. As a high schooler and collegian Lucas displayed world-class talent as a tennis player, in the end earning plaudits on two different courts by also reigning as the ACC's singles tennis champion. His later pro basketball career would be a roller-coaster ride punctuated by battles with substance abuse and by a series of inspirational comebacks in the aftermath of suspensions and on-court failures. As an NBA mainstay Lucas was never an All-Star but almost always a solid performer and later also an inspirational coach for both the San Antonio Spurs and Philadelphia 76ers. But as a basketball player Lucas reached his greatest heights during four seasons in the ACC. Twice he was a first-team All-American, and all four years his Maryland team played near the top of the conference heap, winning one regular-season title, twice finishing as the runner-up, and once copping a third-place slot. Lucas started all 110 of his games for Lefty Driesell, and with the quick guard at the controls, the Maryland four-year record was 92–23 overall. Three times the talented and versatile guard was also on the all-league first-team roster, and twice he finished third in the conference in individual scoring. His 2,015 points and 514 assists were both school records at graduation time, though they have both since been broken. But Lucas's overall flash and flair in those years was even more impressive than his raw numbers. In the end he left Maryland as perhaps the greatest all-around backcourt performer in Terrapin history.

Al McGuire

Al McGuire was one of college basketball's most enduring coaching legends. He also long served as an astute and entertaining television commentator, and also as a pro player who enjoyed a brief three-season sojourn with one of the more colorful teams of the NBA's first pioneering decade. It was while playing for one of those memorable New York Knicks teams of the early 1950s that McGuire also gained lasting legend by launching one of the most unforgettable and unusual shots ever witnessed (or in this case not witnessed!) during NBA playoff action. That shot came in the first game of the 1952 championship finals versus Mikan and Minneapolis and was long credited (though not entirely accurately) by New York Knicks faithful with turning around an entire series and robbing New York of a league title that should have (or at least could have) been theirs. The opening game of the league's sixth-ever championship series was staged in St. Paul (a scheduling conflict had evicted the Lakers from their normal home in the Minneapolis Auditorium) and was filled with first-quarter controversy when the pesky McGuire drove the lane and launched a shot that went in and simultaneously drew a foul. But officials Sid Borgia and Stan Stutz never saw the made basket (it was an era long before television and instant replays), and thus awarded two shots rather than allowing the basket and a free throw for what could have been a three-point play. McGuire made only one of his two charity tosses—a crucial loss of a point for the Knicks when the game eventually went into overtime and turned out in the Lakers' favor. Not only did that stolen game (coupled with a Game 2 New York victory) prevent the Knicks from building a perhaps insurmountable series lead, it also proved vital when the series (which might well have ended with New York's Game 6 victory) stretched out to the ultimate seven games.

McGuire's brief pro playing career (he was used mainly off the bench as an unofficial "designated fouler") contained little else as memorable as the remarkable lost shot versus Minneapolis. It was only during his final coaching seasons at

Marquette University that the flamboyant McGuire, with his colorful personality, became something of a familiar basketball icon. As a college coach McGuire would eventually serve 20 seasons, 7 at tiny North Carolina-based Belmont Abbey and 13 with Marquette; he would record 405 victories, grab three National Coach of the Year honors (1971, 1974, 1977), visit both the NCAA and NIT final fours twice, and run off 11 straight 20-win seasons to close out his brilliant career. And even in retirement Al McGuire would remain a fixture on the college basketball scene by turning to a second career as an extroverted and entertaining announcer for NBC coverage of college court action. Never was his image more prominent for a nation of hoops fans, however, than it was in the closing moments of his final game. A nation of television viewers gawked as the embarrassed coach buried his face in his hands in a vain effort to conceal tears of joy at the end of the Marquette bench while the final seconds clicked off a 67–59 1977 NCAA championship victory over legendary Dean Smith and his North Carolina Tar Heels. Thousands of fans at the Atlanta Omni and millions more watching at home thus witnessed an ironic unguarded display from a coach who had expended as much energy over the years building a carefully manicured public persona as he had patching together some of the most talented collegiate teams of the era. Even more ironic, however, was the circumstance that an instance of perhaps far too much public exposure rang out the final career moments for a basketball giant whose earlier career was perhaps most noted for an instant (a vital made but uncounted shot) that unaccountably somehow went tragically unseen.

Dick McGuire

Today the less-noted and less-remembered member of a famed basketball sibling duo, "Tricky Dick" McGuire was a gritty, durable backcourt performer on those New York Knicks teams of the early 1950s which regularly provided the strongest postseason opposition for the Mikan–Mikkelsen–Pollard dynasty Minneapolis Lakers. Performing for both St. John's and Dartmouth (as a transfer in the Navy wartime V-12 program), he was a collegiate second-team All-American (1944) and also the first freshman to win the New York Basketball Writers Association award as the outstanding college player in the New York metropolitan area. As an 11-year pro with the Knicks and Detroit Pistons he was widely acknowledged as one of the greatest assists men and flashiest playmakers of his era. His unselfish backcourt play and clever ballhandling wizardry made him a consistent league All-Star, though he never scored in double figures (four times missing that mark by less than a point per game), and he still owned the New York franchise career assists mark more than two decades after his 1960 retirement. And Dick McGuire shares as well a rare piece of history with his younger sibling, Al McGuire (also a St. John's standout and Knicks backcourt regular in the early 1950s). Together they are the only brother duo today residing in the Naismith Memorial Basketball Hall of Fame.

Frank McGuire

Frank McGuire's ACC coaching legacy comes in two neatly divided chapters. One is the North Carolina chapter (164–58), which involves one of the greatest individual teams and gutsiest postseason runs of league history. The second is the South

Carolina chapter (283–142), which boasts its own remarkable story of comeback followed by renewed triumph. And in the larger scope of McGuire's career there was a third opening chapter as well, one that would string together three brilliant 20-win seasons as replacement for the legendary Joe Lapchick at St. John's University. For preface and epilogue the durable McGuire also debuted with 11 successful campaigns at the helm of St. Xavier High School (126–39) in his native New York and later interrupted his two ACC tenures with an NBA stint that left him as coach of the Philadelphia Warriors during the 1961–62 campaign when Wilt Chamberlain unleashed his almost unimaginable scoring feats of a 100-point game and 50-point season-long scoring average. Wherever Frank McGuire took his coaching act, plenty of success seemed inevitably to follow. So much so that McGuire still clings to the rare distinction of being the only mentor ever to top the century mark in victories at three different college stopovers.

If McGuire's victory totals were far greater at South Carolina (283 of his total 550 wins), nonetheless his name for the bulk of ACC and college hoops fans will always be linked indelibly to the Tar Heels' program in Chapel Hill and not the Gamecocks' fortunes in Columbia. This despite the fact that he remains the latter school's winningest coach ever (a rank he fails to hold at Dean Smith–ruled North Carolina), and the fact that his name today graces the new basketball arena on the South Carolina campus. Not only is McGuire associated in the mind's eye of all fans with a single school (despite his numerous successes elsewhere), but also with a single season and single team—perhaps even a single NCAA tournament game—despite a number of other highly successful campaigns in Chapel Hill. (His final two Chapel Hill teams, for example, finished atop the conference standings.) In the end McGuire's résumé will always boast on its top page the 1957 national championship year, the brilliant undefeated team paced by Len Rosenbluth, Joe Quigg, and Tom Kearns, and the dramatic three-overtime triumph versus Kansas and Wilt Chamberlain. It was indeed one of the most storybook scripts found in the chapbook of college basketball lore.

McGuire's achievements at North Carolina and elsewhere stretch far beyond the single NCAA title game and the single undefeated season that would become his lasting calling card in the public view. For starters, at St. John's, his alma mater, he coached the talented 1950 and 1951 squads to back-to-back NIT third-place finishes in the final two years before betting scandals at the New York schools stripped the Madison Square Garden event from its place of prominence among postseason venues. At South Carolina he added a fourth ACC title to his three at North Carolina; it would be the only ACC crown earned by the Gamecocks before their departure from the nation's premier cage conference. And if his championships and cumulative victories at Chapel Hill would soon enough be buried in an avalanche of winning by his UNC successor, Dean Smith, McGuire nonetheless owned an even more important Carolina legacy that Dean Smith would never erase. This was the practice of flooding ACC basketball with brilliant New York–area recruits, which McGuire launched as a tradition at Chapel Hill in the mid-'50s and later continued to foster at the Columbia campus through to the end of the school's league tenure in 1971. It would start with Rosenbluth, Pete Brennan, and Joe Quigg, who provided the backbone of a 1957 championship squad that also featured a half dozen other New York and New Jersey imports. It would continue with later Chapel Hill recruits like John Crotty, York Larese, Doug Moe, Donnie Walsh, and Larry

Brown (the latter three renowned for their own pro coaching exploits). And it would extend to McGuire's South Carolina tenure with ace rebounder Frank Standard in 1966 and 1967, backcourt scoring star Skip Harlicka the same two seasons, and John Roche, Bobby Cremins, and Tom Owens with the powerhouse Gamecocks teams of the late '60s and early '70s. It was indeed the New York pipeline and not just the breakthrough 1957 national title that would, in the end, rank as McGuire's most important Tobacco Road legacy.

"Easy Ed" Macauley

Today Ed Macauley is the stuff of trivia questions. Who was the first Boston Celtic to average 20 points for a season? What Celtics immortal has his retired uniform hanging in the rafters in Boston, yet never earned a championship ring with the green-clad occupants of Boston Garden? Who was the "other" player in the most significant trade in NBA history? But during his heyday Macauley was a talent awesome enough to merit every ounce of his Naismith Hall of Fame plaque in Springfield. Despite a brilliant All-American collegiate career at Saint Louis University—AP National Player of the Year recognition in 1949, as well as 1948 NIT MVP honors, and a 1947 national field-goal percentage leadership—Macauley gained his greatest renown in the early 1950s with the Boston Celtics, when he teamed with Cousy and Sharman to produce one of the greatest scoring combinations in league history (the first team to average better than 100 points per game for a full season). Nonetheless, it was destined to be Macauley's departure from Boston and not his debut there that would clinch his true measure of lasting fame.

Boston had acquired Macauley only after the sudden folding of the St. Louis Bombers franchise for which he debuted, and also only after the New York Knicks offered unsuccessfully to purchase the entire defunct franchise just to obtain Macauley's stellar offensive talents. But the player known as "Easy Ed" for his soft playing style was—for all his scoring skills—something of a liability as a post-position player at 6'8" and less than 200 pounds. Once Auerbach arrived in Beantown with his vision of a fast-breaking offense fueled by aggressive frontcourt rebounding, it was clear that Macauley's Boston tenure would be severely limited. The end came in spectacular fashion when one of the league's most versatile scorers (along with draft property Cliff Hagan) was peddled back to his hometown of St. Louis in 1956 for the draft rights to coveted USF All-American Bill Russell. Macauley, for all his talent, was not Russell, and in future years the Hawks, for all their victories, were never quite the Celtics. But Macauley did play well enough in the remainder of the decade to wrap up Hall of Fame certification nonetheless. And when he was chosen by the Naismith Memorial Basketball Hall of Fame in 1960 (merely two years after retirement) Ed Macauley earned yet another special distinction by becoming the youngest man or woman ever elected for permanent enshrinement in Springfield.

Pete "Pistol Pete" Maravich (NBA "Top 50" Selection)

Pete Maravich rarely is mentioned in serious discussions of basketball's greatest individual players. Perhaps this has most to do with his reputation as an outrageous "gunner," or perhaps it is simply the result of his failures to prop up any of the teams he ever played for. But when the issue is showmanship, Pete Maravich of LSU is rarely assigned anywhere except at the top of the list. And in the NCAA record books Maravich—after more than a quarter of a century of challengers—still merits nearly an entire page on his own. Maravich was a true 1960s phenomenon if there ever was one. He wore floppy socks that dusted his shoe tops, featured a rock 'n' roller's floppy hairstyle, and was the hardwood court's supreme individualist. He was a player who was truly the stuff of mind-stretching myth and larger-than-life legend.

In the same colorful package hoops fans here had not only the most prolific college scorer ever, but also the most flamboyant ball handler to boot. "Pistol Pete" could do things with a basketball that no one else had ever done—not even Bob Davies at Seton Hall with his behind-the-back dribbling or Bob Cousy at Holy Cross with his behind-the-back no-look passing. But most of all, Pete could flat-out shoot the pill. If Julius Erving (whose sophomore year at Massachusetts overlapped Maravich's senior season at LSU) would, by the mid-'70s, redefine the game played above the rim, Maravich would, at the outset of the '70s, already have redefined the game being played below the rim.

Pete Maravich left a scoring legacy in his wake that has never yet been matched. While other schools boast their

"Pistol Pete" Maravich,
Louisiana State University

Transcendental Graphics

select lists of career 1,000-point scorers, with Maravich, LSU had a shooter who would top the four-digit figure in each of his three individual varsity seasons. He scored more than 50 points in 28 different games and registered high games of 66 and 69. Three straight times he reigned as national scoring champ, something that only Oscar Robertson accomplished before him and no one has duplicated since. He would average a phenomenal 44.2 for an entire three-year career and do this, not against phony competition like Bevo Francis had at tiny Rio Grande, or inconsistent competition like Furman's Frank Selvy had, but instead against defenses from one of the premier conferences (SEC) in the land. No one except Francis and Selvy had ever before scored quite like this. And neither Bevo Francis nor Frank Selvy ever had to face nightly opponents from conference rivals named Kentucky, Tennessee, Vanderbilt, Georgia, or Mississippi State, or intersectional rivals named Southern Cal (against them Pete scored 50), UCLA, or St. John's (Pete once outscored the entire St. John's opposing team in the second half of a Rainbow Classic tournament matchup).

The one thing Maravich did not do was win championships—in either the college or pro ranks (where he did capture one individual scoring title but never a league MVP or even Rookie of the Year)—and it was at LSU that the surrounding overall team ineptitudes were most glaring and inexplicable. LSU with Maravich was barely an above-average team, posting two .500 campaigns before finally going 22–10 in 1970 and enjoying a third-place NIT finish. The reason was quite obvious: Maravich did nothing to make his teammates better and perhaps quite a bit to make them worse. He played over their heads, bounced spectacular passes off their legs and shoulders, gambled and freelanced himself on defense, and soloed in search of big-scoring nights rather than hard-earned team victories. It was a style that would eventually earn a seven-figure pro contract at the end of the line but few team triumphs along the way. And for all his individual brilliance, Pete Maravich was never enough of a team player to earn himself or his supporting crew even a single visit to the college sport's main event, postseason NCAA tournament play.

Slater "Dugie" Martin

Four playmaking guards performed for as many as five NBA championship teams. Air Jordan, Magic Johnson, and Bob Cousy are the most celebrated members of this exclusive club. Less noted, but almost equally effective, was Slater "Dugie" Martin, who dished out assists and orchestrated plays for the famed Minneapolis Lakers front line of George Mikan, Vern Mikkelsen, and Jim Pollard. Across 11 NBA seasons split between Minneapolis (7 years) and St. Louis (4 years) with a brief 13-game stop in New York sandwiched between, Martin enjoyed five championships, four with Mikan and company and one with a frontline tandem of Pettit and Hagan. This amounts to half his career in the championship circle, a remarkable percentage for someone not playing with the Boston Celtics in the 1960s or the Chicago Bulls in the 1990s. Five times he also earned All-NBA second-team honors and regularly scored in double figures despite the fact that his main contributions came as a playmaker and not as a shooter. If there was any '50s-vintage NBA player who truly merits distinction as forerunner of the modern point guard, it would most likely have to be Slater Martin. And the fact that the 5'10" Texas native was consistently rated as the best small-man defender in the league also goes a long way toward explaining his key role with Minneapolis in building the first true dynasty team in NBA annals.

Scott May

Scott May was the best all-around player on what may arguably have been the best-ever college team not coached by John Wooden. It is therefore hard to think of a more talented player ever to represent Indiana University. Calbert Cheaney had more raw skill as well as a higher career point total. Steve Alford was a better shooter and Isiah Thomas was a more accomplished magician with the basketball.

But May did it all at both ends of the court and was also a proven big-game player and unflappable winner. While 6'11" junior Kent Benson anchored the inside for the 1976 national champions from Indiana, 6'7" senior May provided the emotional leadership, the clutch offense, and the rebounding assistance that solidified one of the best NCAA title teams ever. May was National Player of the Year for coach Bob Knight's most deeply talented club and also was a first-team All-America selection in both his junior and senior seasons. While it was May's outstanding tournament play that keyed the 1976 championship drive, it was an injury to the Hoosier star (broken arm) that had stalled a similar run in 1975 and left Knight's charges a single game short (a two-point defeat by Kentucky in the regional finals) of reaching the Final Four a season earlier than they actually did. Although Scott May was back in the lineup for the regional showdown loss to the Wildcats (92–90), the layoff caused by his injury had left him rusty, ineffective, and capable of only a single bucket in the losing cause. It was the only loss May and his Hoosiers would suffer during his final two seasons on campus.

Scott May was also a Hoosier standout who went on to represent school and conference with distinction on the higher level of professional play. A second overall selection of the Chicago Bulls in 1976, May strung together a half dozen creditable, if not stellar, NBA campaigns, collecting 1,050 points (14.6 points per game) in his rookie season and averaging double figures during two later campaigns as well. By almost any standard of choice—Naismith College Player of the Year (1976), Olympic team starter (1976), NCAA All-Decade Tournament Team for the 1970s (1979), or NBA regular—Scott May shares the center-stage limelight alongside Cheaney and Thomas as the best trio of versatile cagers ever bred in Bob Knight's stable of championship thoroughbreds.

Tom Meschery

pro basketball players
live in bat caves
upside down
hotel rooms
minds pointing
to darkness . . .
–Tom Meschery

Baseball is more noted for its flakes and certified weirdos than is professional basketball. Daffy port-sider moundsmen and incorrigible masters of bullpen and locker-room mayhem are a more notable breed than are zany power forwards or goofy point guards. Yet the cage sport has also known its eccentrics, and the list is topped by 1960s-era San Francisco Warriors mainstay Tom Meschery. A rugged and always competitive leader of several Chamberlain and post-Chamberlain Warriors ball clubs, Meschery merged the seemingly incompatible personas of a nasty hardwood enforcer and a thoughtful, sensitive poet. It was in the latter capacity that the one-time St. Mary's College star fashioned a rare collage of road-trip musings and on-court experiences and distilled wry word portraits of his nightly NBA rivals (immortalizing Bill Russell, for one, as "an eagle with a beard"); Meschery enrolled, after his athletic career, in the prestigious University of Iowa writer's program and published a 1971 volume of his verse with the *Saturday Review Press*. In the former capacity he etched a reputation for bulldog aggressiveness, fouled out of 20 of his first 100 NBA contests, and probably "unofficially" lost more fights than any player in pro basketball history. Although he never scored more than 16 points per game in a single season and only once made an NBA All-Star squad, Meschery's legend looms so large in the Bay Area— where he played exactly half of his 10 seasons—that his uniform number (along with those of Al Attles, Rick Barry, and Nate Thurmond) has been retired by the Golden State Warriors.

Cyndi Meserve

Georgeann Wells of West Virginia University was the first female college cager to dunk a basketball in game action; Delta State's Lusia Harris pioneered as the first female collegian to gain entrance to the Naismith Hall of Fame; Ann Meyers was the first and only female cager good enough (or at least lucky enough) to earn a legitimate, if unsuccessful, tryout with an NBA team. But it was left for Cyndi Meserve to tread uncharted ground in 1976 as the first woman athlete to appear on the floor with a men's varsity collegiate basketball squad. The 5'8" guard would go scoreless in her debut game for New York's Pratt Institute and register only a pair of free throws in a second and final appearance of her aborted cage career. But it was nonetheless enough for a unique footnote in the NCAA record books.

Ann Meyers

Ann Meyers earned considerable notoriety as the first woman awarded an athletic scholarship to play basketball for the UCLA Bruins. That notoriety would accompany all four years of Meyers's collegiate career and then follow her into postcollege days as well. The brilliant passer and accomplished long-range shooter owned enough credentials and enough moves to become the first legitimate female draftee of an NBA team when her court skills earned a preseason 1978 tryout with the Bob Leonard–coached Indiana Pacers.

While the drafting of Delta State's Lusia Harris had unquestionably been seen as a profitable publicity gimmick by the NBA New Orleans Jazz a season earlier, the

Ann Meyers (left), UCLA

Transcendental Graphics

Pacers were willing not only to invite Meyers to their preseason camp (where she was quickly cut) but also to offer a guaranteed contract that specified broadcast duties if the UCLA cager didn't make the final playing roster. This deal was soon enough nullified when Meyers decided a women's league venture was more to her liking. She would instead play two seasons with the New Jersey Gems of the short-lived WBL (Women's Basketball League), earn both league MVP trophies, and also serve as television commentator for NCAA women's games as well as college and NBA men's games. A 1993 Naismith Hall of Fame inductee and widow of the late baseball great Don Drysdale, Meyers would thus also later earn even further distinction as half of the first married couple ever to be both elected into the halls of fame in their respective sports.

Larry Miller

When Dean Smith lost the remarkable Billy Cunningham to graduation, he immediately inherited Larry Miller, the first fruit of his maiden recruiting efforts. In retrospect it appears to have been equal or better compensation. For it was around Miller that Smith would be able to build his first successful team capable of making a dent on the national scene. Miller's sophomore season found the Tar Heels still in the middle of the ACC pack and thus still standing outside of postseason play, yet the new forward's offensive punch (he finished fourth in the league in scoring and second in rebounding) was at least a small sign of major improvement. And that

Larry Miller,
North Carolina

© University of North Carolina

improvement snowballed during the two coming seasons. Both years Miller was the league's dominant force, twice Player of the Year and twice everybody's All-American. His senior season he trailed only Clemson's Butch Zatezalo in the conference scoring race. More importantly, behind Miller's heavy scoring and with an eventual boost from sophomore Charlie Scott during 1968, the Tar Heels finally shot straight into national prominence. Both years the club climbed into the NCAA Final Four as well as into a season-final No. 4 wire service ranking. And in these sudden postseason triumphs Larry Miller was always the biggest part of the remarkable story. A surprisingly talented rebounder (9.2 career average) at only 6'4", he was also an indefatigably consistent scorer, reaching double figures a school-record 64 straight outings. He was also a left-handed shooter, which made him one of the most complete offensive machines ever to bleed Carolina blue.

William Mokray

Twenty-two members of the Naismith Memorial Basketball Hall of Fame have spent all or part of their careers with the proud Boston Celtics franchise, and of these nearly two dozen legends, only two have earned their place in some capacity other than that of player or coach. These two immortal special "contributors" to basketball's legacy are original Boston franchise owner Walter Brown and longtime NBA statistics guru Bill Mokray. Mokray was first smitten with a love for basketball numerology while attending Passaic (N.J.) High School during the era of Ernest Blood's "Wonder Teams" of the early '20s, a series of legendary squads that won 159 games without defeat. The young Mokray compiled statistics and detailed records for these teams thus fueling his early passion for the numerical side of the sport. A student at Rhode Island State College during the early years of coach Frank Keaney's race-horse fast-break basketball tradition, Mokray would sign on after graduation as the school's first sports publicity director and work arduously for more than a decade publicizing the Rams' colorful style of cage play.

But the true calling of Bill Mokray would be finally found after 1944 when he took over the post of basketball director for the Boston Garden, a position which led directly to a final assignment as public relations director for the Boston Celtics once that BAA franchise was established by Walter Brown in the shadows of World War II. While laboring in a variety of promotion-oriented positions for the Celtics over the next quarter-century, Mokray also voraciously collected NBA statistics and published numerous analytical articles for the Converse Rubber Company pioneering publication known as the *Basketball Yearbook*. But his greatest efforts in pioneering the field of basketball record keeping came with his founding and editing of the *Official NBA Guide*, his authoring of a history of basketball for *Encyclopaedia Britanica* (1957), and his writing of the 900-page landmark, *Ronald Basketball Encyclopedia* (1963). Years before baseball would discover Bill James, sabermetrics basketball had already found Bill Mokray.

Earl "The Pearl" Monroe (NBA "Top 50" Selection)

Backwater black colleges and the showcase NAIA postseason tournament in which many of them performed became a much-valued talent font for NBA teams of the

'60s. The biggest find of all in this newly mined talent vein was a deadly jump shooter recruited off the streets of Philadelphia who first left his calling card at a tiny North Carolina college playing its games in the shadows of the neighboring big-brother ACC schools. Earl Monroe in 1966–67 unleashed what remains unquestionably the greatest one-man single-season performance of collegiate roundball history (with 1,329 points and a 41.5 average) while simultaneously carrying Winston-Salem to a College Division national championship.

Playing under the tutelage of legendary coach Clarence "Big House" Gaines, Monroe elevated his entire team to a 31–1 record while time and again working offensive magic rarely seen on any level of college play. The smooth-as-silk ball handler with scoring moves not even invented yet would shoot better than 60 percent from the floor for an entire year (Maravich shot 45 percent when he tallied 1,300-plus points in 1970); and at the same time he would fire the ball up frequently enough to log the highest season's average ever posted in the small-college record books. The man known simply as "The Pearl" would, in the process, also conveniently erase several of the Bevo Francis College Division records that had created such a storm of controversy a single decade earlier. It was during his days at Winston-Salem that Monroe also garnered his colorful nickname. This came about when a local sportswriter penned a story referring to the star player's remarkable on-court "moves" as "Earl's pearls." The name would soon stick as permanently as the classic playground style that had inspired it.

It was at Winston-Salem that the future Baltimore Bullets and New York Knicks star would also uncover and perfect the flamboyant "shake-and-bake" one-on-one style that would soon be seen everywhere as the very paragon of "black-style" play during the coming decade and well beyond. Creaky legs prevented Monroe from ever being much of a jumper, yet his "feints" and "jukes" kept defenders so unbalanced that he could pop shots from almost anywhere on the floor without hardly ever having to leave his feet at all.

Behind the scenes of "big-time" college basketball, "The Pearl" was quietly anticipating what "Pistol Pete" Maravich would soon be accomplishing over at LSU and more squarely in the Division I limelight (Maravich's first season would immediately follow Monroe's last). But if there was any lingering doubt about Earl Monroe's talent against small-time competition versus Maravich's skills versus big-time opponents, this would be definitively answered (somewhat in Monroe's favor) when the two reached the professional ranks. Maravich won an NBA scoring title and wound up (largely due to his collegiate legacy) in the Naismith Hall of Fame; Monroe carried his teams to playoff glories and garnered a spot on the narrow list of the pro league's all-time greats.

In the NBA ranks Monroe achieved at a level that unquestionably equaled and even largely surpassed Maravich. He inevitably earned the ultimate recognitions that came with a plaque in the Naismith Hall of Fame and a slot on the 50th Anniversary All-Time Team announced at the outset of the 1996–97 NBA campaign. He debuted in sensational fashion with 1968 Rookie of the Year accolades and fueled a Baltimore fast-breaking offense (along with Wes Unseld and Gus Johnson) that propelled the ball club into four straight playoff appearances and Monroe himself into instant stardom. Traded to the New York Knicks in November 1971 his offense displays were suddenly and inevitably toned down on a balanced team that also featured Walt Frazier, Willis Reed, Bill Bradley, Jerry Lucas, and Dave DeBusschere. While Monroe was never again the same high-octane scoring machine (averaging 20-plus only twice) after joining the team-oriented Knicks, he nonetheless remained a flamboyant stylist who would contribute heavily to one New York championship (1973) and also continue to delight NBA crowds in Madison Square Garden and elsewhere around the league all the way to the end of the decade.

Johnny Most

Baseball's radio voices were once as much a part of the game's nostalgia as were the sport's colorful stars themselves. Mel Allen, Red Barber, Connie Desmond,

Johnny Most

Ernie Harwell, Bob Elson, Harry Caray, and Bob Prince were, for legions of fans in dozens of cities, the very soul of the game they daily described. Basketball has never been such a radio-oriented game, and few longtime broadcasters have enjoyed such an intimate connection with a cage team's evolving history. Johnny Most—longtime voice of the Boston Celtics—is almost a singular exception, though L.A. fans may have an argument that Chick Hearn is an equal prototype. Outside of Boston Most's immortality (like Russ Hodges in baseball) rests with a single momentary call of ephemeral action. When John Havlicek stepped in front of Chet Walker to pick off Hal Greer's wayward inbounds pass and preserve Boston's championship string during the 1965 Eastern Division Finals, he created a moment that would plant into the national consciousness not only his own legendary career but also that of the man who called the action for Boston radio listeners—"Havlicek stole the ball! It's all over! It's all over!"

The memorable moment came less than a third of the way into Johnny Most's long tenure (1953 through 1989) in the Celtics' radio booth and was only a small part of the legend for those who could tune in his broadcasts regularly during the Cousy-Russell dynasty years and the two up-and-down decades that followed. Like most sports broadcasting giants, Most seemed to have nothing in his on-air manner that fit him for the job. His voice was pure gravel, his style was annoyingly machine gun-like ("rat-a-tat-tat") in anything but small doses, his personality was always acerbic (he had long-running feuds with arena security forces that tried to limit his on-air smoking and coffee guzzling at courtside), and he wore his one-sided love for the home team squarely on his sleeve, for which Boston fans loved him all the more. But Most was genuine and passionate and brought basketball to full life on the airwaves for 36 long seasons. In an era when fans did not yet flood into NBA arenas in droves televised basketball was far more occasional than ubiquitous, and pro basketball—even in the dynasty city of Boston—was still only the third or fourth most popular game in town, Johnny Most remained a vital link to nightly action for New England rooters who followed the ebb and flow of one of America's most cherished dynasty ball clubs.

Dick Motta

Dick Motta lost far more games as a pro coach than he ever won. But this was never enough to sidetrack one of the most durable survivors in the profession from hanging around long enough in Chicago, Washington, Dallas, Sacramento, and finally, Denver to compile the fourth-longest NBA victory list on record. And Motta even managed to pick up a Coach of the Year plaque (with Chicago in 1971) and an NBA title trophy (with Washington in 1978) along the way. Motta's career, of course, didn't start off in the college ranks with quite the same penchant for repetitive year-in and year-out losing that marked most of his professional seasons. In a half dozen seasons at Weber State in the '60s, he won more than 20 games four times, and he had his teams in the 70 percent victory range for the additional two campaigns. Over a quarter-century span with the pros, however, Motta directed mostly also-ran teams that gave him losing ledgers 13 times and a near-record 1,017 career losses (only Bill Fitch has more) to go with his 935 total victories. The diminutive Motta surprisingly never played varsity basketball in either high school or college (Utah State). But despite his late introduction to the game (he started out as a Utah junior high school coach in 1954), few men ever sat on a bench at the highest levels of competition longer than did Dick Motta. And few ever lost or won quite as many times, either.

Rick Mount

Rick Mount was, admittedly, a one-dimensional player. But that single dimension was, nonetheless, spectacular almost beyond belief. For fans who want pure shooting as the staple of their favorite sport, Mount was the unmatched performer for all ages. And since Mount's game was almost exclusively one of firing the ball at the rim—from any angle, distance, position, or moment in the game—there isn't a great deal more to Mount's story than the scoring numbers that defined every corner of his memorable career.

Part of the reason for the paucity of ways to describe Mount falls to the nature of the game itself. There are just so many ways to describe or analyze a perfectly launched jump shot and most of them fall considerably short of the mark. In Mount's case one is better served by merely parading out the numbers and leaving the imagination to wrestle with reconstructing the ballet-like artistry from which they resulted. The numbers are a litany of raining rainbow shots and rippled nylon nets: 2,323 points in only 72 games, the only career average of more than 30 points per game found in the Big Ten record books, a still-unmatched 61-point single-game onslaught, the highest-ever season-long Big Ten scoring average (39.4), the only back-to-back individual league averages of more than 35 points per game, and a 30.5 average over four games in the 1969 postseason march to the Final Four.

And Rick Mount owns one other important distinction outside of the scoring barrages with which he is so thoroughly identified. It was Mount alone among the modern-era Purdue greats (not Dischinger or Schellhase or Joe Barry Carroll or

Rick Mount,
Purdue University

© Purdue University

Glenn "Big Dog" Robinson) whose fireworks propelled a Boilermakers team all the way to a cherished seat in the prestigious national championship game. Rick Mount may have been an undisciplined gunner, but he was a gunner who also carried squarely on his shoulders the finest one-season Purdue Boilermakers club ever assembled. No small boast for a school that has produced more Big Ten cage champions than any other.

Joe Mullaney

Joe Mullaney spent only 1 of his 22 college coaching seasons outside of the city of Providence (Providence College and Brown University, plus a debut season at Norwich College in Vermont). As a professional coach he was much more of a frequent flyer, making stops in the NBA (Los Angeles Lakers), ABA (Kentucky Colonels, Utah Stars, Memphis Sounds), CBA (Pensacola), and even briefly in the Italian League. But almost his entire reputation derives from a nine-season span (half of his total time there) as headman with the Providence College Friars during that school's greatest glory era between 1959 and 1967. Three of Mullaney's heyday-era players at Providence were highly successful future coaches—Johnny Egan, John Thompson, and all-time NBA victories leader Lenny Wilkens. His teams posted 20-win campaigns and enjoyed postseason invitations for each of those nine zenith seasons, beginning with the last campaign of the 1950s (Lenny Wilkens' junior year). The peak for the Providence College sojourn came with a pair of NIT titles earned in 1961 and 1963, seasons when the Providence reputation for stellar backcourt heroes peaked as well with Johnny Egan and Vinnie Ernst the first time around, and with Ernst and Ray Flynn the second.

Calvin Murphy

Inch for inch, Calvin Murphy was arguably the "biggest" talent ever to set foot inside an NBA arena. In the college ranks this 5'9" mighty mite built a legacy that was even grander than his professional achievements, though this may seem hard to imagine given Murphy's considerable impact on the NBA record books. When it comes to scoring and ballhandling, Murphy was every bit as phenomenal as LSU's Pete Maravich, especially if one considers his diminutive physical stature. Here was a player everyone judged too small to play successfully in the big-time college game when he first appeared on the scene at Niagara University. Here was

Calvin Murphy,
Niagara University

Transcendental Graphics

also a pint-sized shooting machine who was as talented a pure scorer as anyone who ever rattled the rafters of a local college gym or lit up a local playground scene. Like Maravich, Murphy entertained fans with lightning-quick change-of-direction dribbles, uncanny blind passes, and an array of off-balance bombs from anywhere within sight of the basket. At the same time he also devastated enemy defenses with bushels of points, including a phenomenal 68 against Syracuse University during his junior season.

Murphy, who was tutored in long-range marksmanship by his ballplaying mother (and was also a champion high school baton twirler), began setting eye-popping scoring marks at Norwalk High School in rural Connecticut (where he was a high school All-American in 1966). He averaged 38.2 as a college sophomore (second in the land to fellow rookie Maravich) and 33.1 for his full career at Niagara. And during his later stellar pro career with the Houston Rockets, the pint-sized hotshot would also set new standards for free-throw shooting accuracy (95 percent for a single season and above 90 percent in five others) that long remained untouched by subsequent NBA marksmen. Murphy's lifetime 89.2 percent from the NBA charity stripe trails only the 89.3 percent posted by Rick Barry.

Murphy would peak as a collegian during 1967–68 as an unknown first-year sensation, when he trailed only Maravich in the national scoring race. A year later, as a junior, he would be bested again by Maravich and also Purdue standout Rick Mount. But both Mount (at 6'4") and Maravich (6'5") had hefty height advantages over Murphy, a factor that made the midget guard seem even more phenomenal to those who saw him dominate a college or perhaps later a professional game. In the play-for-pay ranks he scored less (17.9, but still enough to become Houston's all-time scoring leader at retirement), but shot even better (setting league standards for one-season free-throw percentage and consecutive free throws made). As impressive as the tiny giant was in NBA circles, however, it was as a college sensation that he remains most memorable. To date only legends Maravich, Austin Carr, and Oscar Robertson own loftier three-year career scoring averages.

Johnny Neumann

Among basketball's true one-season wonders none looms larger than Mississippi's Johnny Neumann, the only man to average 40-plus for a season at the major college level and yet play for only one NCAA season. Neumann's one remarkable offensive campaign came at the height of college basketball's era of unbridled point-making and left him in the company of such late '60s and early '70s offensive wizards as Pete Maravich, Austin Carr, Rick Mount, and Calvin Murphy. The 6'6" offense-minded sophomore guard out of Memphis pumped in 923 points in 23 games (missing 2 with injury) for Kermit Davis's 15–10 Ole Miss team to lead the nation in scoring, outgunning Notre Dame's Austin Carr (a senior). The heavy bombing was enough to make Neumann the only Ole Miss player ever to earn first- or second-team All-American notice. It was also enough to make him the only sophomore other than Maravich to hit for more than 40, and Neumann might even have overhauled Pistol Pete's college rookie mark had he not slumped badly (29.5) in his last five contests. Fresh off his debut success Neumann signed with the hometown Memphis Pros of the ABA as an undergraduate free agent and, in the process, closed the door on his brilliant, if brief, college sojourn. While he did average near 20 his first two ABA campaigns in Memphis, Neumann quickly disappeared as a productive point-maker in five additional seasons of ABA (Utah, Virginia, Indiana, Kentucky) and NBA (Buffalo, Los Angeles, Indiana) journeyman wanderings.

Pete Newell

No other coach has packed quite so many achievements into quite so short a tenure on the major college cage circuit. Newell's résumé boasts only 14 seasons and 234 victories, but also trumpets NCAA (1959), NIT (1949), and Olympic (1960) championships. Only two other coaches (Dean Smith, Bobby Knight) have collected that particular much-coveted triple and both spent far more seasons in pursuit of such rare triple-crown glory. Newell's career highlight was neither the upset NIT victory with San Francisco at the end of the '40s nor the NCAA championship with California at the end of the '50s. It was, instead, his unique stature as coach of the acknowledged greatest amateur team of all time, which took the floor during the 1960 Rome Olympics. His was a starting lineup of Oscar Robertson, Jerry West, Jerry Lucas, Walt Bellamy, and Terry Dischinger (backed up by reserves Adrian Smith, Bob Boozer, and Darrall Imhoff) that dominated eight opponents by an average of 42 points per contest. Despite his early withdrawal from active coaching on the heels of his notable 1960 Olympic success, Newell has, in recent decades, remained close to the cage game, first as an NBA general manager (San Diego Rockets in 1969 through 1971, Los Angeles Lakers in 1972 through 1976), and later while operating behind the scenes as roving scout, talent consultant, and respected tutor to some of the modern game's most talented post-position big men.

Bob Pettit (NBA "Top 50" Selection)

Pettit replaced Mikan as the game's greatest offensive force and retired in 1965 at the top of the career lists in scoring (20,880) and rebounding (12,849), although Wilt Chamberlain (at the end of only his sixth season) was already nipping savagely at his heels in both categories. While a dozen players have now passed Pettit's career rebounding numbers, his legacy remains intact as the first ever to score 20,000 NBA points and also as the most talented rebounding forward of the league's first half-century. In the first 10 of his 11 pro campaigns this rugged clutch player never finished lower than fifth among league leaders in rebounding or scoring, a claim no other NBA player can make to this day. Such accomplishments would be remarkable enough for even the most gifted of athletes; they were simply overwhelming for a basketballer who was cut twice from his high school squad and later considered too frail physically to succeed in the NBA ranks despite two All-American seasons and a 27.4 career scoring average at LSU.

There was far more to Bob Pettit and his brilliant career, of course, than mere numbers. He was, for one thing, the most relentlessly driven and highly competitive star of his era, and also as much a champion of the model work ethic as he was of individual point-producing and rebounding. In fact, Bob Pettit was arguably the greatest "second-effort player" in all of basketball history. No one worked harder than the 1955 NBA Rookie of the Year, two-time NBA MVP, and 11-time league

Bob Pettit (9) battles for a rebound with Tom Heinsohn (15) and Bob Cousy (14).

Transcendental Graphics

All-Star. And no one could be more devastating to the opposition when it came to crunch time—in either crucial postseason games or less vital nightly regular-season games. No example of this outshines one memorable 50-point performance delivered in the deciding sixth game of the 1958 league championship series. Avenging a previous year's defeat by the Celtics, Pettit put Boston away with a torrid shooting display that included 19 of his team's final 21 fourth-quarter points, including the game-deciding tip-in with 15 seconds left on the clock. Pettit's 50 only tied the league single-game playoff mark by Cousy (which had been achieved with the help of 30 points from the foul line and four overtimes of extra clock time); but it was, nonetheless, the most stunning offensive display before or since in a postseason NBA game with the league title squarely on the line. With that one performance this franchise player delivered the Hawks their only title banner. But night in and night out for a full decade from the mid-'50s through mid-'60s, Bob Pettit almost single-handedly made the Milwaukee and St. Louis Hawks one of the league's most rugged challenges.

Richie Powers

It is a time-worn sports axiom that the best game officials are those who are never noticed while they ply their trade. Richie Powers was indeed one of the best ever to blow the whistle in the NBA, though at times he unfortunately grabbed far more than his share of the limelight. The most infamous moment for Powers came during the climactic seconds of perhaps the most famous game in NBA history—certainly the most memorable moment in the sparkling postseason annals of the storied Boston Celtics. On the night of June 4, 1976, the Celtics and Phoenix Suns locked horns in a three-overtime heart-wrencher during which Boston outlasted the spunky underdogs 128–126 and thus captured crucial Game 5 of the championship series, which proved a springboard to the club's 13th league championship banner. It was a game that would witness easily the most bizarre chain of events ever to unfold in an NBA title round (or anywhere else in NBA history for that matter), and Richie Powers stood smack in the middle of all that rapidly transpired.

A couple of dramatic shots by ex-Celtic Paul Westphal first knotted the game during regulation play. True fireworks, however, were saved for the close of the second overtime stanza, when an off-balance 15-footer by John Havlicek gave Boston a 111-110 margin as time seemed to expire. As joyous mayhem covered the floor, the unflappable Powers signaled that Phoenix had successfully called a time-out with but two ticks of the clock still remaining. The further complication—if one were needed—was that the Suns did not actually have a legal time-out remaining when Westphal signaled for the TO. In the melee that followed Powers was struck in the face by an irate fan who had rushed onto the floor, and a full-blown riot next broke out before police and players from both teams could restore some semblance of order. When both order and play resumed, the clever ploy by Westphal paid rich dividends: Jo Jo White sank a penalty free throw, but Phoenix had the ball at midcourt for a desperation shot that Gar Heard somehow sank to trigger the third nail-biting overtime period. Eventually Boston prevailed and Powers escaped with his life and reputation largely intact. Richie Powers had also been squarely on the firing lines for the tense deciding game of the 1970 New York and Los Angeles NBA title confrontation—an equally famous game in which Willis Reed made his dramatic and inspiring last-second appearance (returning from a serious Game 5 injury) and launched an emotional New York championship party. But what happened in Madison Square Garden in May 1970 was altogether mild compared to the wild night in Boston six postseasons later.

Jack Ramsay

Jack Ramsay didn't win many championships as either a college mentor at St. Joseph's (where he also played in the late '40s) or pro coach in Philadelphia, Buffalo, Portland, and Indianapolis. Yet the popular "Dr. Jack" nonetheless piled up victories at a near-record pace and also amassed friends and admirers with almost the same profundity. His two-decade 864–783 (.525) NBA record today ranks him eighth all time (in total victories) among professional mentors. An 11-season college ledger at St. Joseph's (234–72, .765) included seven 20-victory seasons and one of the highest winning percentages ever posted for more than 10 seasons of service in the collegiate ranks. While at St. Joe's Ramsay reached the NCAA Final Four in 1961 (with a team that featured future NBA coaches Jim Lynam and Paul Westhead) and also the NIT semifinals in 1956. As a pro head coach Ramsay enjoyed his career pinnacle in Portland at the end of the 1977 season (his first with that ball club) when the combination of a rare healthy season for center Bill Walton and Ramsay's perfectly orchestrated "team concept" resulted in a 14–5 postseason run and an NBA championship banner. Other career highlights for the ever-popular Ramsay include service as general manager of the 1967 NBA champion Philadelphia 76ers, an earned doctoral degree in education from the University of Pennsylvania (1963), authorship of a widely respected book on coaching techniques, standing as the second-winningest all-time NBA coach (behind Auerbach) at the time of his 1988 retirement, a spot in the Naismith Memorial Basketball Hall of Fame (1992), and a successful decade-long career as television analyst for both the NBA and the league's expansion Miami Heat.

Frank Ramsey

Today the "sixth man" is a basketball staple, especially in the professional ranks. Toni Kukoc has most recently filled the role admirably with the dynasty Chicago Bulls; more renowned exemplars were John Havlicek in the late '60s and Kevin McHale in the early '80s. For the past decade and a half (since 1983) the NBA beat writers and broadcasters have even selected a yearly recipient for an officially sanctioned league award in this category. The prototype, however, was actually invented four long decades ago—not surprisingly, by Red Auerbach in Boston— and Auerbach's first polished model was former Kentucky All-American Frank Ramsey, the progenitor of a long line of such super bench players that have resided in Boston over the subsequent decades.

Ramsey had been anything but a bench player for Adolph Rupp at Kentucky. As a sophomore sensation in 1951 Ramsey teamed with Cliff Hagan to spark Rupp's 32–2 national championship squad; as the quarterback of that team from a forward slot, the 6'4" Madisonville native was UK's second-leading rebounder. When Kentucky's basketball program fell on difficult times over the next three seasons (sitting out the 1953 season because of recruiting violations and missing the 1954 NCAA postseason despite the school's first undefeated record), things only got better for Ramsey on the personal level. He averaged nearly 16 a game in scoring for a 1952 squad that was stunned by St. John's in the NCAA regional finals, then earned second-team All-American honors and scored a shade under 20 for the 25–0 team that followed the 1953 probation year. Kentucky lost a shot at another national championship in 1954 when it voluntarily bypassed postseason play when seniors Ramsey, Hagan, and Lou Tsioropoulos (who had all been given an extra season of eligibility because of the 1953 suspension) were ruled ineligible for tournament competitions.

Ramsey (first overall pick) and Hagan (third selection) were both plucked by Auerbach in a surprise move during the 1953 NBA draft, though it was apparent that both would enjoy another year of NCAA eligibility. It was the first of the many ingenious lottery moves that would mark Auerbach's résumé and the one that is today least remembered in the wake of his later fortuitous selections of Russell and Bird and his draft-day-connected trades for McHale and Parish. While Hagan was traded for the rights to Russell before he ever put on a Boston uniform, Ramsey launched a Hall of Fame career with Cousy and company that was interrupted briefly for a one-year military stint after his rookie campaign, but then extended for eight more seasons that were all championship campaigns except one. While he only once failed to score in double figures (his final season of 1964), he excelled off the bench as a spark plug at the forward slot, where despite his limited height he was consistently able to outrun and outthink all of his bulkier and more offense-minded opponents. Ramsey's career pinnacle came earlier in his pro career when his final-second off-balance 20-footer clinched a Game 7 double-overtime victory against the St. Louis Hawks and brought Auerbach and Boston their inaugural NBA title.

Willis Reed (NBA "Top 50" Selection)

The career of Willis Reed is crystallized in a single uncharacteristic moment when the durable Knicks center was relegated to the sidelines by a disabling leg injury. In the hard-fought 1970 championship shootout between New York and Los Angeles the vaunted Knicks attack had suffered a severe jolt when Reed went down with a debilitating deep thigh bruise in Game 5, then sat helplessly on the sidelines while Wilt Chamberlain dominated for Los Angeles with 45 points in Game 6 to knot the series and force a Madison Square Garden rubber match for the NBA title. New York, still seeking its first league banner and boasting easily its best team ever (with Bradley and DeBusschere up front, Barnett and Frazier at the guards, and Riordan, Stallworth, and Cazzie Russell coming off the bench), was given a huge emotional lift when Reed hobbled onto the floor moments before the season's final contest and then took his place in the starting lineup. While the 6'9" wide-body center was able to contribute little to team offense (he scored four points on the team's first two baskets of the night), his emotional presence was enough to ignite New York to a 113–99 victory and thus keep Los Angeles frustrated in its own search for an elusive first championship. The irony here is that Reed's most memorable moment of incapacity today tends to overshadow all the rest of what was a most productive and accomplished 10-year professional career. The second-round draft pick out of Grambling had been an NBA Rookie of the Year and was a league All-Star for seven years running. Reed would also spark two New York championship teams (1970, 1973) and capture NBA Finals MVP honors on both occasions. On the first title team he was also the regular-season league MVP and yearlong emotional leader as team captain. Across a decade of seasons (1964 through 1974) he built a reputation for solid scoring (18.7 for his career), tenacious rebounding, and fearsome shot-blocking. The gutsy postseason return by the bruising New York center was also a moment that provided a stranger-than-fiction conclusion to what had certainly been one of the three or four most accomplished single seasons in NBA history. It was during the 1970 campaign that New York fielded one of the most balanced teams in league annals, posted a record winning streak of 18 straight early in the year, and established a still-standing franchise record with 60 total victories. In short, Willis Reed's heroic championship performance on May 8, 1970, was anything but a one-night stand.

Guy Rodgers

Philadelphia has produced a boatload of cage legends—beginning with Tom Gola and Paul Arizin and including along the way names like Bill Mlkvy, Wilt Chamberlain, Walt Hazzard, Lionel Simmons, and Guy Rodgers. Of all the talented athletes to emerge from the playgrounds of South Philadelphia in the immediate postwar

Guy Rodgers,
Philadelphia Warriors

Transcendental Graphics

years, only Gola and Arizin can match or surpass Guy Rodgers for a balanced array of superb basketball skills. Perhaps the flashiest (and certainly the fastest) ball handler the city has ever produced, the lightning-quick six-footer emerged from an all-city high school career as a dynamo destined to lead Temple University back down Glory Street. With Rodgers, the Owls would achieve their greatest heights as immediate successor to La Salle in the destined role as the Liberty City's biggest college cage boasting point.

In three years with Rodgers running the offense, Harry Litwack's Owls posted school-best records of 27–4 (1956), 20–9 (1957), and 27–3 (1958). Rodgers's sophomore campaign ended with a third-place NCAA finish sparked largely by teammate Hal Lear's record scoring feats during a semifinal loss to Iowa and a consolation triumph over SMU. His junior year brought another third-place postseason finish with a 67–50 consolation match triumph over St. Bonaventure, this time in

375

the NIT. And his final season was capped with a heartbreaking semifinal 61–60 loss to eventual champion Kentucky during a return to NCAA action. For the third year in a row Rodgers and the Owls would capture a third-place national slot by edging Kansas State and All-American Bob Boozer in the consolation match.

Guy Rodgers's three years at Temple ended with an overall 74–16 winning mark (.822) and a brilliant 9–3 postseason ledger, as well as the three tourney third-place trophies. His career 19.6 scoring average was supplemented with a 23.3 scoring pace in three NIT postseason appearances and a 17.9 average over nine NCAA tournament games. The crowd-pleasing backcourt ace also finished his senior season with school records for career scoring, field goals, and assists. During his final campaign he also chalked up a record 15 assists in a single game against Manhattan College and led the Owls to a midseason Holiday Festival Tournament championship in Madison Square Garden as a fitting encore.

Lennie Rosenbluth

Lennie Rosenbluth, like all his teammates on the 1957 North Carolina national championship team, will likely always be remembered for a single game—his last. That game was perhaps college basketball's most memorable postseason championship battle, even if it was played long before television made NCAA Final Four events into a true national experience. It was in that game that Rosenbluth and his teammates battled Wilt Chamberlain to a draw and then stole away a national title in dramatic three-overtime action. But that single epic contest was, ironically, far from a showcase performance for Rosenbluth himself. In fact, his biggest contribution to the game's lasting lore—despite pacing the Heels with 20 points—was the fact that he wasn't around for the nail-biting finish. Rosenbluth fouled out with 1:45 left in regulation and then held his breath with the rest of the spectators through three extra sessions while the remaining Tar Heels regulars held on for a victory clinched by Joe Quigg's pressure-packed pair of free throws.

Yet if the New York recruit didn't exactly propel the Cinderella Tar Heels team on its most memorable night, he did, in fact, carry that charmed outfit on his broad shoulders for much of the three seasons leading up to the showdown with Chamberlain. As high-scoring forward Rosenbluth was the centerpiece of Carolina's first New York–flavored team, specially imported by Frank McGuire to put Tobacco Road basketball on the coast-to-coast map. And he certainly lived up to expectations and then some with 25-, 26-, and 28-point season averages and a school-record point total that lasted for two decades. As a sophomore and rookie he cracked the league's top five in scoring and rebounding. A year later he was the leading ACC point-maker, edging South Carolina's Grady Wallace and ranking in the nation's top 10. As a senior he was ACC Player of the Year, the first one ever from Carolina, and swapped places with Wallace in the conference scoring derby. While he thus slipped behind Wallace, who had edged above 30, he nonetheless upped his own average to 28 per game. Rosenbluth was the Tar Heels' acknowledged "go-to" man throughout his three seasons. When the brilliant 1957 team made its memorable late-season charge, it was indeed Rosenbluth who carried the burden leading up to that final titanic battle with Chamberlain and the pesky Kansas Jayhawks. Frank McGuire's boldest shooter reached as high as 39

Lennie Rosenbluth of North Carolina (left) defends Wilt Chamberlain of Kansas in the most memorable NCAA championship game of all time.

© University of North Carolina

points in one regional contest (against Canisius) and also did considerable damage in the early first half, going against the Jayhawks defenders, even if he wasn't around for the closing stages.

Rosenbluth tried his hand at professional basketball but was never again a headline player after he left Chapel Hill. During an NBA cup of coffee he proved too short for NBA pivot play, too frail to operate at power forward, and too lead-footed to ever roam as a small forward. A jersey (No. 10) hanging from the rafters in UNC's spacious Dean Smith Center nonetheless makes it almost certain that Rosenbluth will never be entirely forgotten back on the Chapel Hill campus, the site where he had a major hand in landing the ACC's first national championship.

Cazzie Russell

Only Cazzie Russell can seriously challenge Jerry Lucas's entrenched position as the greatest all-around player in Big Ten history. Had Russell been blessed with a greater collection of teammates, he might today garner even more support for the honor of the league's all-time best than he usually does. When it comes to mere statistical comparisons Russell seems to overwhelm Lucas in all but rebounding and field-goal accuracy. Lucas logged 1,990 points, a 24.3 three-year average, a .624 field-goal percentage, a .777 free-throw shooting mark, and 1,411 rebounds. Russell boasts 2,164 points, 27.1 points per game, .505 field-goal accuracy, and .828 free-throw proficiency, plus 676 rebounds. But Lucas (who played with celebrated Havlicek and Siegfried, and unheralded Joe Roberts and Mel Nowell) owned a national championship and three Final Four visits. Russell (who played with Bill Buntin, Oliver Darden, Larry Tregoning, and George Pomey) lost a national title shot against UCLA in his one NCAA Finals, visited the Final Four a second time to be nipped in the semifinals by Duke, and lost as a senior in the regional finals to national runner-up Kentucky. In reality there wasn't a whole lot separating them beyond their teammates.

Cazzie Russell, New York Knicks

Transcendental Graphics

Cazzie Russell owned one of the most unusual and memorable first names (and thus one of the most colorful nicknames—"Jazzy Cazzie") found in the collegiate hoops record book. He also owned such special talent that his unique name was assured of being repeated in that record book with great regularity. Later a pro star with the New York Knicks and Golden State Warriors, Russell still stands among the Big Ten Conference's all-time leading scorers and was the third of only six Big Ten athletes ever to earn National Player of the Year selection. He is, to date, Michigan's only three-time basketball All-American and started his career with a bang by establishing a new school single-season mark of 670 points as a sophomore. That record would be eclipsed in each of his two subsequent seasons. As a senior Russell both broke his single-season standard (with 800 points) and established a touchstone (30.8) for single-season average that has remained unchallenged up to the present. And three of Russell's other high-water marks still remain etched in the Michigan record book—career scoring average (27.1), free throws made (486), and free-throw percentage (.828). It may well take another three decades to erase Cazzie Russell's name from that record book altogether.

Tom "Satch" Sanders

Satch Sanders was the quiet man of the dynasty Red Auerbach Boston Celtics. He was also one of the most underrated contributors to the regular Boston championships that stretched from one end of the '60s to the other. On a series of Boston teams noted for their defensive prowess, it was Sanders who was the most effective all-around defender, even while the headlines went to Russell and K. C. Jones. It was not a labor that went unrewarded since, in the end, Sanders owned more NBA championship rings than any man save Russell and Sam Jones—a total of eight. After playing days he blazed new trails as the first African-American coach at an Ivy League institution, in this case, Harvard. "Satch" Sanders also has another special distinction to boast: He may be the only NBA star who picked up his nickname from a Negro leagues baseball legend. As a youth he had first loved baseball, and his physical characteristics reminded his friends of the legendary Satchel Paige. Sanders's own favorite player, however, was Jackie Robinson. It was a more fitting choice of hero and more intimately connected with his own life, especially his own destiny as a pioneering black coach.

Woody Sauldsberry

Many former NBA Rookies of the Year are among the sport's largest icons and most familiar household names—Jerry Lucas, Willis Reed, Rick Barry, Dave Bing, Earl Monroe, Wes Unseld, Lew Alcindor, and Dave Cowens, to cite only one consecutive string of such novices from the early to late '60s. Others such as Don Meineke, Ray Felix, and Geoff Petrie are forgotten flashes in the pan whose moment in the spotlight lasted hardly beyond their single debut campaigns. One of the least remembered NBA novice stars was Woody Sauldsberry, 1958 honoree with the Philadelphia Warriors. Sauldsberry, a 6'7" soft-shooting forward out of Texas Southern, was talented enough to average double figures (with a 15.4 best as a second-year pro) and lucky enough to pick up one championship ring with Boston as a part-timer in 1966 (his last campaign). But his only real notoriety came when he was traded from Philadelphia to St. Louis at the end of the 1960 season, expressly to prevent an all-black Warriors lineup (along with Wilt, Guy Rodgers, Andy Johnson, and Al Attles) once the more talented Attles was plucked from the college draft.

Dave Schellhase

First there was Terry Dischinger (1960–62, 28.3 points per game), then Dave Schellhase (1964–66, 28.8 points per game), and finally Rick Mount (1968–70, 32.3 points per game). The turbulent '60s (also home to Maravich, Calvin Murphy, Elvin Hayes, and Spencer Haywood) was a talent-showcase epoch that unleashed college basketball's most memorable contingent of incredible scorers. And Purdue University of the Big Ten Conference seemed for a long while to have something of a clear corner on the market. Schellhase, a 6'4" forward and two-time All-American, led the nation in scoring as a senior—the last Big Ten athlete to earn this honor before a conference-wide dry spell of almost 30 years. Most notable about the Evansville, Indiana, native's point-making title, however, was the fact that it was earned in the closest individual race in major college history. Purdue's Schellhase nipped Idaho State guard Dave Wagnon by merely .04 points (32.54 to 32.50).

The NCAA rules makers had perhaps as big a hand in Schellhase's claims on the national point-making title as did the figure filberts. The very same winter as

Schellhase's triumph, sensational UCLA rookie Lew Alcindor was also racking up points at a 33.1-points-per-game pace while playing freshman-only games in the Pac-8, since first-year recruits were still being banned from varsity competitions. And a further set of ironies was added by circumstances in the Big Ten Conference itself. Schellhase actually paced the nation in scoring, yet still finished only second within his own league. The rare paradox came about when Michigan All-American Cazzie Russell outpointed his Purdue rival by 15 points in conference games alone. With nonconference games taken into the mix, however, Russell trailed Schellhase by nearly two points per contest (30.8 to 32.5). A final paradox was the fact that, despite Schellhase's impressive scoring, the Purdue Boilermakers finished dead last in the Big Ten race for the only time in the past 35 years.

Charlie Scott

As an 11-year pro star in two leagues Charlie Scott rang up five seasons of 25 points per game or better scoring and earned one significant record-book niche with the highest-ever single-season ABA mark (34.8 in 1972 with the Virginia Squires). But the pro achievements never outdid the college legacy already on the ledgers. Charlie Scott was, for one thing, the final noteworthy link of a '50s and '60s tradition of North Carolina–bound New York City playground imports—a potent pipeline that stretched from Lennie Rosenbluth to Larry Brown to Billy Cunningham and beyond. This particular 6'5" leaper from the Big Apple was a heavy-duty scorer who paced the ACC (27.1) during his senior season after working his way up from eighth slot (17.6) as a sophomore to fifth (22.3) as a junior. But he was also an anchor on the Larry Miller–led Carolina team that stretched its string of NCAA Final Four appearances to three straight during Scott's first two seasons on the squad. While it was Scott's senior season that posted the biggest individual numbers, it was his junior year that brought the most memorable team results: 12–2 in the ACC, fourth in the year-end AP national poll, an appearance in the Final Four, and a 27–5 record overall for Dean Smith's eighth season on the job. It was the postseason ACC shootout of that year, in fact, which brought Charlie Scott's supreme hour as a collegiate cager. In one of Carolina's best-ever comebacks Scott poured home 40 points against Duke, rallying the Dean Smith forces from a 9-point halftime deficit to an 11-point championship victory.

Frank Selvy

No major college star has ever scored more proficiently than Furman's Frank Selvy. Selvy's 100 points in a single game (versus Newberry College on February 13, 1954) have never been matched (or even approximated) in Division I NCAA play; the 6'4" forward was the first two-time national scoring champion (after "official" NCAA record-keeping began in 1948); and he was also first to register a single-season 40-plus scoring average (41.7, 1954). It is, therefore, a grand piece of unmatched irony that no NBA star is more narrowly remembered or vilified for a single important shot that he failed to make. Frank Selvy, unfairly, remains to this day the Bill Buckner of NBA championship play. Such are the rare twists of fickle fortune.

Frank Selvy's unaccountable moment of rare ignominy came in the waning seconds of championship Game 7 at the close of the 1962 NBA campaign. It was a game that rivaled the 1957 deciding match between Boston and St. Louis for moments of raw drama and bone-crunching intensity. With some last-second heroics by Jerry West in Game 3 and Elgin Baylor's 61-point explosion in Game 5, the ill-starred Lakers climbed within a single victory of their first West Coast title. But as always, Auerbach's Celtics were simply invincible (and also a little lucky) in the final stretch run and thus roared back for a pair of victories of their own, clutch wins that made them the first four-time back-to-back champions in NBA history. The true turning point of the memorable series came in the final seconds of the closing game. As it had in Game 3, L.A. charged from four points back during the final minute of play on two clutch goals by Selvy. Aiming to duplicate West's last-minute performance of several nights earlier, Selvy unleashed one final dramatic shot that glanced off the rim just as the regulation horn sounded. Had Selvy's missile connected with the game knotted at 100, the title would have been owned by the upstart Lakers, but it was simply not meant to be; an overtime session that followed was all Boston to the final tune of 110–107.

As painful as the 1962 championship loss was, it took on even further symbolic dimensions for West, Baylor, Selvy, and company. The L.A. defeat allowed Boston to extend its championship streak to four, besting the Lakers' own record set earlier (1952–54) when the franchise resided in Minneapolis. Also extended was Boston's mastery over the Lakers during the postseason that would continue for another full decade. And in a final touch of irony, Selvy's fateful miss came at the end of the very season in which Wilt Chamberlain had scored 100 in a single game (March 2, 1962), a feat which had duplicated on the pro level Selvy's own unprecedented collegiate effort of eight years earlier.

Bob Short

Bob Short is basketball's small-scale version of baseball's much-maligned, but nonetheless exceptionally farsighted, Walter O'Malley. Short, like O'Malley, fixed his place in history by pirating one of his sport's most glamorous franchises and transporting it for profit motive to greener pastures in Los Angeles. In the process he opened up the NBA to truly "national" status, just as O'Malley had done for baseball only two years earlier. Short was a local Minneapolis attorney, trucking and hotel magnate, and political maverick (he was onetime treasurer of the Democratic National Committee), who in 1954 had headed a group of 117 firms and individuals that had purchased the once proud, but now struggling, Minneapolis Lakers from original owner Ben Berger. Short rapidly gained control of the entire operation, hired and then fired Lakers legend George Mikan as his coach, gambled wildly in 1959 by drafting Elgin Baylor (an underclassman who many thought would either not forsake college eligibility or not sign with the struggling Minneapolis outfit), and presided over the disintegrating club's rapid swoon to the bottom of both the league's standings and attendance rankings. Facing extinction under their new ownership, the six-time champion Lakers were placed on financial probation by the NBA for the 1960 season.

By the time the last Minneapolis edition of the Lakers had succumbed to St. Louis during postseason play in March 1960, their fate as a ball club, a community resource, and a revenue-generating entertainment spectacle had already been permanently sealed. The team had suffered record losses on the court as well as at the ticket gate over the previous half-dozen seasons—the result largely of a series of inept draft choices (Elgin Baylor not withstanding), unwise trades (especially Clyde Lovellette to Cincinnati for much-overrated Hot Rod Hundley), and the poorest of coaching selections (first George Mikan in 1957, followed by ineffective John Castellani who lasted but 36 games in 1959). Bob Short had also already been testing the California waters with several league games scheduled into Los Angeles in the late winter of 1960. Thus it came as little surprise when the league fathers approved Short's petition to move his near-moribund ball club westward. Only New York Knickerbockers owner Ned Irish raised his voice in loud objection to the plan, and it was as plain as punch that Irish's protests were far from selfless. While the crafty Knicks boss feigned concern about added expenses for travel to West Coast games, few doubted that the true motive of the Knicks' brain trust was a hope that a financially stressed Minneapolis club could be forced to unload Elgin Baylor to New York if not given a fast franchise-saving escape route out of the Twin Cities.

Not satisfied with wreaking havoc with tradition in one sport alone, Bob Short would take his franchise-uprooting tactics over to baseball a mere decade later as owner of an expansion edition of the Washington Senators. Purchasing the second 20th-century version of the Washington ball club in January 1969 (he had sold the Lakers in 1965 to Canadian Jack Kent Cooke), the absentee owner was soon hard at work dismantling another franchise with hopes of transporting it to more lucrative pastures. Before claiming responsibility for transporting American League baseball to Texas, and in the process leaving the nation's capital stripped of its big-league credentials for the second time in slightly more than 10 years, Short purposefully scuttled his Senators in a manner reminiscent of his machinations in Minneapolis. Among his more notable moves were the hiring of Hall of Famer Ted Williams as field manager, a trade for scandal-plagued former 30-game winner Denny McLain, defaults on rent payments for Washington's Robert F. Kennedy Stadium, and the signing of outfielder Curt Flood at a time when baseball's most notorious free agent was still embroiled in a legal challenge to baseball's long-standing reserve clause.

Gene Shue

Some of the NBA's most victory-rich coaches have been anything but the league's most successful mentors. For these men the key to a place in history is seemingly the mere mastery of the art of survival. Bill Fitch is perhaps the most famous example and Cotton Fitzsimmons, Dick Motta, and Kevin Loughery are other noteworthy exemplars. And then there is also the case of Gene Shue, five-decade NBA veteran, who has made a lengthy career out of surviving even if he has never shown much aptitude for mastering the art of winning basketball games on a regular basis.

As a player Gene Shue was a playmaking standout of the late '50s who once produced a backcourt-record 1,712 points (with the Detroit Pistons in 1960) but

Gene Shue,
University of Maryland

Transcendental Graphics

always, nonetheless, remained in the shadow of flashier guards like Bob Cousy, Bill Sharman, and Oscar Robertson, who dominated his era. As an NBA coach Shue also knew several early successes, earning Coach of the Year honors in 1969 after rebuilding the lowly Baltimore Bullets into a division champion, and also guiding the Philadelphia 76ers to a 1977 NBA Finals showdown with the Portland Trail Blazers. But the bulk of his extended coaching saga, which stretched through the '70s and '80s, and also included stops with the San Diego Clippers, Washington Bullets, and Los Angeles Clippers, was little more than an indifferent journeyman's affair. Despite another Coach of the Year honor with Washington in 1982, Shue was destined to be known primarily for teams that always hovered around (usually slightly below) the break-even point and regularly generated little in the way of postseason excitement. While he did survive long enough to appear in more than 2,000 NBA games as either player or coach (at one time the league record), and also to amass 784 career coaching victories (still 10th-best all time), his 861 defeats also leave him fourth on the career ledger of relentless losers. Shue, in fact, shares with Bill Fitch and Dick Motta the ambiguous distinction of being career losing coaches who, nonetheless, also miraculously stand near the apex of the NBA honor roll for coaching lifetime victories.

Larry Siegfried

Almost completely lost in the dust bin of hoops history is the remarkable collegiate career of rock-steady understudy Larry Siegfried. Ohio State's Siegfried made a career out of playing in the shadows of John Havlicek and Jerry Lucas, and a handful of other Buckeye stars. He then repeated the stint at the professional level. Among basketball's endless list of important role players, however, none boasted any more awesome individual talents than did the guard who pocketed an NCAA championship with Ohio State and also collected several NBA rings with the Boston Celtics.

Siegfried had launched his schoolboy and collegiate hoops career as a rising star of the brightest magnitude; then suddenly, this can't-miss prime-time player was relegated to an unfamiliar and uncomfortable slot as backstage role player. Unlike most spoiled superstars of the modern era, however, Siegfried adjusted quite admirably to his new diminished stature. An immensely talented Ohio schoolboy star, Siegfried had averaged a thunderous 38 per game during his final high school season; as a Buckeye sophomore he maintained his spot as scoring frontrunner pacing the 11–11 1958–59 OSU team with a 19.6 average. Then sophomores Lucas and Havlicek suddenly arrived on the scene, and while the OSU team soared, Siegfried was just as suddenly forced out of the limelight.

It was a far different era, of course, and there was no whining from Siegfried about lost scoring chances and also no threats of transfer to another program. He would later admit that the new role as caddy to Lucas and Havlicek did not suit him at all well. Yet, through it all, he would, nonetheless, quietly accept his fate and continue to contribute more than adequately to the endless (and undoubtedly consoling) team victories. Siegfried was the second-leading point-maker (13.3) in the balanced championship lineup of 1960; as a senior he was again the No. 2 scorer (15.2) behind Lucas. And down the road there would still be a credible pro career, though one that also extended Siegfried's destined role in the supporting cast (as a member of seven editions of the "dynasty" Boston Celtics teams of the 1960s) and deep in the shadow of teammate John Havlicek. Larry Siegfried was drafted by Auerbach to be that type of semi-important bench player who always remains a key cog in the team wheel, yet nonetheless never quite manages to emerge as the blustery hero who can enjoy center stage.

Paul Silas

Long before Dennis Rodman made a professional career out of monomaniacal focus on pursuing rebounds to the exclusion of more celebrated offensive feats (i.e., scoring), Paul Silas had built a solid leaguewide reputation for precisely the same one-dimensional talent. Over 16 seasons the Phoenix, Boston, and Seattle star (he also played in St. Louis, Atlanta, and Denver) logged 1,250 games and 12,000 points, but also posted almost an identical number of missed-shot caroms. Silas was, in fact, one of the few pros in history actually to accumulate more rebounds (12,357, 9.9 per game) than points (11,782, 9.4 per game). Silas's rebounding totals, of course, do not stack up with the masters of the art like Chamberlain, Russell, Abdul-Jabbar, or Elvin Hayes, to mention but four of the dozen or so who far outdistanced his career totals. He never paced the league in this category, though he did crack the top five in 1976 and did average double figures seven years running in the decade of the 1970s. But there was never much doubt what Silas's role on the floor was, especially in Boston (1973–76) where he converted the team's famed sixth-man slot from that of heavy-artillery scorer (Frank Ramsey and John Havlicek) to efficient board-sweeper. Silas's most memorable niche as a rebounder, however, had already been earned as a collegian, where at Creighton in the early '60s (1962–63) he earned special stature as one of but seven athletes ever to complete a collegiate career with both scoring and rebounding averages lodged above 20.

Jerry Sloan

Jerry Sloan once ranked with Dave DeBusschere as the NBA's best defensive forward of the late '60s and early '70s era. Today he stands alongside the likes of Phil Jackson, Pat Riley, and Lenny Wilkens as one of the league's most respected and successful long-term coaches of the '90s. Before entering the pros as a player Sloan was a small-college superstar forward (15.5 points, 12.4 rebounds per game) at Evansville (Indiana) University, where he paced two NCAA Division II national champions, and where his senior season produced the first undefeated team (29–0) ever to capture the small-college postseason tournament. His pro playing career peaked with a single talented Chicago Bulls team in 1972, a 57-25 club that reached the Western Conference semifinals before being buried by a Bill Sharman–coached first-ever Los Angeles Lakers NBA championship outfit. It was as a long-term head coach in Utah, however, that the intense Sloan was destined to make his grandest mark.

Taking over from Frank Layden early in the 1989 campaign, Jerry Sloan has aptly guided a decade-long Western Conference powerhouse ball club featuring the league's best backcourt-frontcourt combo in John Stockton and Karl Malone. Sloan's potent Jazz teams regularly won 50 games or more throughout the 1990s, yet always seemed to wilt before Los Angeles, Portland, Phoenix, Seattle, or Houston in highly competitive Western Conference postseason action. Sloan and his Utah Jazz finally reached the NBA Finals at the conclusion of his 9th and 10th seasons, yet could offer little serious opposition to a defending champion Chicago Bulls team, which extended its own current dynasty string to six titles in eight seasons with Michael Jordan badly outclassing both Malone and Stockton during a pair of easy four-games-to-two romps. But if Utah has not made it into the championship circle under the gentlemanly Sloan, it has, nonetheless, remained under his even-keeled and soft-spoken leadership one of the most consistently successful NBA teams of the past decade.

Norm Sloan

A well-traveled basketball past attaches itself to Norm Sloan. Yet for all his other accomplishments on four different campuses (one of them twice), Sloan will always be intimately linked with one of the greatest of all ACC lineups—the '72-'74 N.C. State team boasting the league's premier player, David Thompson. For two full seasons the Wolfpack five, featuring Thompson as a sophomore and junior, maintained a nearly unblemished record against the best competition in the land—and all this during a time frame when college basketball talent was perhaps as rich and deep as it has ever been before or since. (This was still the John Wooden era at UCLA, remember.) Only an early-season collapse in a showdown with defending national champion UCLA at the outset of the 1973–74 campaign prevented back-to-back perfect ledgers. And only a year of NCAA suspension blocked the way to two title showdowns with John Wooden's Bruins, and perhaps also the first pair of consecutive national titles in ACC history. During the entire two-year span the N.C. State conference record (regular and postseason) remained spotless. And along the way were some of the most thrilling games in storied N.C. State basketball history.

Sandwiched between the legendary Everett Case and the charismatic Jim Valvano, Norm Sloan indeed had a tough road to travel when it comes to competing for the nostalgic affections of hordes of N.C. State boosters. Sloan owned neither Case's innovative mastery of the game nor Jimmy V's inborn flair for the dramatic and the theatric. But Sloan did have two things going for him over the long haul. One was David Thompson—consensus choice for the greatest ACC performer ever, and enough all by himself to make this brief era as memorable as any in school lore. The second was the greatest single team and most remarkable end-to-end season ever enjoyed by any ACC school. For raw achievement only the 1957 North Carolina national championship joyride can possibly match N.C. State's own 1974 championship trip. And Sloan's single great team had actually stretched over two seasons and not just one, doubling the pleasure, if not the number of NCAA trophies.

There is also a most rare trivial distinction that attaches itself to Sloan's remarkable coaching career. The oft-traveled mentor, in 1980, became the only ACC boss ever to serve as Olympic head coach for a team not representing the United States. This transpired when Sloan accepted an invitation to mentor the British Olympic squad preparing for the Moscow Games eventually boycotted by United States athletes. Such a rare happenstance could only seem somewhat appropriate for a coach who changed addresses quite so often, despite the high degree of success he knew at every stop along the way. At Presbyterian he launched a winning tradition with 21 victories in his very first campaign and 20 more, along with an undefeated league record, in his fourth and final winter. At The Citadel he inherited little talent, yet still built a competitive Southern Conference program in yet another brief four-year stint. In two stops at Florida he painstakingly constructed still another winning program that finally peaked with a rare SEC title for the Gators during the veteran mentor's 37th and final season on the coaching trail. But all these layovers were merely side routes, and it was at North Carolina State that Sloan unquestionably clinched his lasting reputation. There have been many highlights in Raleigh beyond the David Thompson era. But it was during that unforgettable winter and spring of 1974 that Norm Sloan briefly reached as high as any ACC coach has ever reached. It was truly a dream season and one that guaranteed its chief architect almost certain immortality.

Maurice "Mo" Stokes

Maurice Stokes is without doubt pro basketball's most tragic figure. No other career that offered such unlimited promise came to such an alarming and painful end. A bruising 6'7" forward at St. Francis (Pennsylvania) College, Stokes first grabbed headlines with 43 points in the 1955 NIT championship game. A 27-points-per-game scoring average as a college senior was followed with scoring and rebounding averages of 16-plus as an NBA rookie with Rochester. Early pro honors included NBA Rookie of the Year, one league rebounding crown and a second year as runner-up, and three straight NBA All-Star Game appearances. During his third year in the league—with his Royals ball club now relocated to Cincinnati—Stokes ranked third overall in both rebounds and assists (a rare combo indeed). There was thus wide agreement in the second half of the '50s that Maurice Stokes was headed straight for a spot in the Naismith Memorial Hall of Fame. And then cruel fate struck one of its most vicious blows.

In mid-March of the first Royals season in Cincinnati, Maurice Stokes would crash to the floor during the final regular-season game at Cincinnati Gardens and receive a severe blow to the head, rendering him unconscious and immobile. Three nights later the star forward would again collapse on a plane flight returning the team to Cincinnati immediately following an opening-round playoff loss in Detroit. A once-graceful athlete, Mo Stokes had unaccountably been struck down and left a lifelong paralyzed invalid by a rare form of brain damage to his motor control centers (official diagnosis was the disease encephalitis). Teammate Jack Twyman would have himself named legal guardian for his fallen comrade and would, for years to come, tirelessly organize an off-season charity game designed to raise funds for the crippled ex-star (and later for other needy former players from the game's earliest days). Twyman's involvement over the years with the wheelchair-bound Stokes (see Twyman's entry below) was itself one of the sport's most inspiring tales. The tragic circumstances of Maurice Stokes was a truly dark moment of NBA history (paralleling the fate of star Houston pitcher and stroke victim J. R. Richard in baseball annals) and one that would cast a lengthy shadow over the subsequent decade and a half of NBA play in the city of Cincinnati.

Fred Taylor

Three feats distinguish Fred Taylor's illustrious 18-year career at Ohio State University, and all came early in his remarkable Columbus tenure. The first was earning a national championship banner for the school and for the Big Ten Conference, as well as achieving a berth in the Final Four shootout three consecutive seasons. The second of Taylor's lasting monuments was the winning of five straight Big Ten titles, something no other conference coach has managed to accomplish. And the third landmark was Taylor's handling of both the greatest all-around team (1960) and the greatest individual star (Jerry Lucas) in Big Ten annals.

It was the unparalleled contingent of Lucas, Havlicek, Larry Siegfried, Mel Nowell, and Gary Bradds that would cement Taylor's reputation for postseason successes and build his string of landmark conference titles. Behind two-time Player of the Year Jerry Lucas (1961–62), the Buckeyes charged to a surprising national title in 1960 and then fell ever so short of repeating during the next two seasons. It was a streak of unmatched Big Ten glory. The five-year reign by Taylor and his Buckeyes over the rest of the Big Ten during the first half of the 1960s is the closest thing yet to a dynasty in one of the nation's oldest and most venerable campus circuits. Over the course of three seasons the Bucks dominated the conference in all facets of team play, losing but two league games over the three-year span. This domination occurred despite a number of other quality clubs, including a 20–4 Indiana contingent with Walt Bellamy in 1960 and Purdue teams featuring national scoring leader Terry Dischinger. Any team with Lucas and Havlicek was seemingly too strong for league opponents (or anyone else in the country, save downstate rival Cincinnati, which featured a hefty arsenal of its own). Despite NCAA championship game losses to Cincinnati in 1961 and 1962, the Buckeyes were clearly the nation's class team for three years running.

When Lucas and Havlicek finally departed, Taylor was still not quite done with his winning ways. His 1963 and 1964 clubs with Gary Bradds (the nation's top performer in 1964) tied for conference crowns. And he was back again with league champions in both 1968 and 1971 to run his personal collection to seven. By career's end Taylor had climbed atop the all-time list of OSU coaches, surpassing Harold Olsen in overall wins (297–255), league victories (158–154), and winning percentage (.753–.570). Taylor still sits firmly atop the list of Big Ten coaching success stories today, more than 20 years after giving up his coaching reins on the heels of a rare last-place finish during his 18th season on the job.

Tom Thacker

One of basketball's best-known trivia questions features the journeyman who collected championships with remarkable ease as both a collegiate and pro player and yet rarely grabbed any front-page headlines on his own. Tom Thacker was a versatile 6'2" guard who managed to hang around for seven pro seasons, three in Cincinnati, one with the Boston Celtics, and three more with the ABA Indiana Pacers. In only one of those campaigns, however—with Indiana in 1970—did Thacker manage to log as many as 70 games and post as many as 1,000 minutes of floor time. Only once—during only 18 games with Indiana the previous season—did his scoring average soar above five points per game. Yet if Tom Thacker was never the recipient of much playing time he was, nonetheless, a genius when it came to impeccable timing. Thacker's most active season in Indianapolis coincided with the Pacers' first ABA championship victory. One year in Boston also translated into a spot on an NBA championship roster as part of the penultimate chapter in the Celtics' 13-year dynasty run. As a starting forward and double-figure scorer on all three Cincinnati Bearcats Final Four teams of the early '60s, the fortune-blessed cager also picked up a pair of NCAA title trophies. This remarkable string of improbable victories would make Tom Thacker the sole player in history who could boast NBA, ABA, and NCAA championship credentials.

David Thompson

Art Heyman's only neck-and-neck rival for the mantle of the ACC's "best-ever superstar" would have to be N.C. State's amazing home-grown leaper who arrived on the scene in 1972 and left four years later as Tobacco Road's apparent answer to absolute perfection on the basketball court. On at least three counts David Thompson actually appears to have at least one leg up on Duke's Heyman. For one thing, the N.C. State immortal enjoyed a far better (even if somewhat disappointing in its own right) professional career. Thompson ran off a string of six 20-plus scoring seasons in Denver, barely lost a memorable 1978 NBA scoring race (the closest in league history) to George Gervin, joined Chamberlain and Elgin Baylor as the league's only 70-point single-game scorers, and stirred as much passion with his sky-walking moves in Denver as he had back in Raleigh. Secondly, N.C. State's three-time unanimous All-American would take his teammates not only to the Final Four, but also to the treasured national title. Heyman (assisted by Jeff Mullins) carried his own Duke clubs to the doorstep and no further; Thompson (aided by Tom Burleson and Monte Towe) delivered college basketball's biggest single door prize.

A third factor weighing in on the side of David Thompson would have to be the less tangible element of boundless charisma. Thompson owned all the flash and flair that distinguishes the super-athletic modern-era NBA superstar. He could slice through the lane and soar over the basket; his vertical leap allowed him to shoot over any size defender; his deadly accuracy from long range made him a complete offensive triple-threat. At his best the Shelby, North Carolina, native seemed a perfect foreshadowing of Michael Jordan and an exact memory trace of Julius Erving all rolled into one spectacular package.

In ACC play alone David Thompson's numbers and overall résumé were every bit as brilliant as his patented "hang time" moves. There was a three-year scoring average that outstripped even Art Heyman's (26.8 to 25.1); there were three years of unanimous first-team All-American selections; and there was a clean sweep of 1975 National Player of the Year honors (AP, UPI, USBWA, NABC, Naismith). There was also a Final Four Outstanding Player trophy to accompany the 1974 NCAA championship banner. And there was the fourth-highest scoring average (after Buzz Wilkinson, Grady Wallace, and Lennie Rosenbluth, but ahead of Heyman, Chappell, and Hemric) in conference history. But over and above the raw numbers it was the visual image of Thompson—especially when caught in hang time mode—that left the most lasting impression for all who witnessed his magic. Only Jordan flashed across the league with anything like this kind of boundless excitement. And even Air Jordan was never quite a David Thompson during his own undergraduate days. The Carolina controlled style fostered by Dean Smith always kept Jordan under tight wraps. At N.C. State, under coach Norm Sloan, David Thompson was fully unleashed to run, leap, shoot, and soar with abandon. The result was a spectacle that two decades of subsequent seasons have yet to either match or erase from memory.

Rod Thorn

Modern-era fans stumble on Rod Thorn's name several times each NBA season when the league front office is forced to discipline one of its wayward bad-boy stars such as Dennis Rodman, Allen Iverson, or Latrell Sprewell. As NBA director of operations Thorn is charged with policing on-court and off-court behavior of players and coaches and thus hands out fines and suspensions for unsightly and dangerous on-court brawls. Rod Thorn was also once a collegiate star of considerable stature at West Virginia, where he followed immediately on the heels of Hot Rod Hundley and Jerry West and kept alive a nine-year unbroken string of heavy artillery scorers. He was later also an

NBA journeyman with four teams across eight seasons, where he scored at barely half the rate and peaked his career at the outset with a 1964 All-Rookie Team selection. As the former he twice earned second-team All-American status and averaged 21.8 during a career that saw his Mountaineers teams twice reach the NCAA tournament. As the latter he was a first-round draftee of the Baltimore Bullets but played only fill-in roles with Detroit, St. Louis, and the expansion Seattle SuperSonics. The most unique facet of Thorn's much-traveled cage career occurred in his final high school season when he was officially designated as a state treasure by the legislature in the hope that he wouldn't leave West Virginia and take with him his considerable shooting and ballhandling talents.

Nate Thurmond (NBA "Top 50" Selection)

You need to know nothing more about Nate Thurmond's talents and hefty reputation as a potential NBA superstar than the fact that the San Francisco Warriors once traded Wilt Chamberlain in order to open up the team's pivot position for the powerfully built seven-time league All-Star who had been wasting away on the bench as Wilt's caddy. Of course—as always is the case in these matters—there was a bit

more to the story. Chamberlain simply couldn't put fans in the seats in San Francisco, which had never warmed up to "The Big Dipper" or appreciated his one-dimensional style of play; the drafting of Thurmond out of Bowling Green a season earlier had provided an adequate defensive replacement for Wilt; the financial benefits of the deal (which included cash from Philadelphia and the loss of Wilt's huge salary) would allow the Warriors to rebuild a weak ball club that hadn't packed in the fans with Wilt even when he had led them to a division title. Once Thurmond had inherited the post, he became one of the league's most consistent inside performers—a better defender than Chamberlain or Abdul-Jabbar and a better scorer than Russell. If he was fortune-crossed because he played in an era featuring so many other great centers, nonetheless he was respected widely by on-court peers and knowledgeable fans as the equal of any of the bigger names. Thurmond's unmatched versatility was capsulized in one milestone moment early in the 1974 season. Playing for Chicago against Atlanta on

Nate Thurmond, Cleveland Cavaliers

390

October 18 of that year, the mobile 6'11" giant would record a truly remarkable "complete game" while authoring the first quadruple-double in NBA history (22 points, 14 rebounds, 13 assists, 12 blocks). Only three times over the next two-plus decades has the feat ever been duplicated.

Jack Twyman

Jack Twyman is forever linked with Maurice Stokes as a result of his humanitarian efforts on the part of one of the sport's most tragic figures. But Twyman was not only a most decent human being; he was at the same time an immensely talented star who long rated as one of the NBA's front-ranking offensive players. The hardworking 6'6" Twyman became one of the best pure-shooting forwards in the first two decades of the NBA. He also became one of the most dedicated players in basketball history, practicing more than 100 foul shots, 200 jump shots, and 150 set shots per day during the off-season summer months. Twyman, a four-year starter at the University of Cincinnati, was the Ohio school's second all-time leading rebounder upon graduation and earned several All-American honors in 1954–55.

A second-round draft pick and the 10th player chosen overall by the Rochester Royals in 1955, Twyman enjoyed an 11-year pro playing career with the Rochester-Cincinnati franchise and never averaged below double figures in scoring until his final campaign. In his three most outstanding seasons as one of the best corner men in the pro game, Twyman registered scoring averages of 25.8, 31.2, and 25.3 points per game between 1959 and 1961. His 31.2 average in 1960 stood second in the league behind sensational rookie Wilt Chamberlain. Further honors included two All-NBA Second Team selections and six appearances in the NBA All-Star Game (1957 through 1963). Twyman finished his career among the all-time leaders in several offensive categories with 15,840 points, a 19.2-points-per-game scoring average, and 5,421 rebounds in 823 regular-season games.

Upon leaving the game Twyman enjoyed successful business careers as first an ABC-TV basketball color commentator and later a vice president of A. W. Shell Insurance Company of Cincinnati. Yet one of the sport's most prolific offensive stars of the late '50s and early '60s is best remembered for his considerable humanitarian acts on behalf of Cincinnati Royals teammate Maurice Stokes, stricken with a crippling and ultimately fatal illness in late-season 1958. When the Royals' ace rebounder was felled by encephalitis (a paralyzing brain disease), Twyman had himself declared legal guardian for his wheelchair-bound teammate in order to supervise treatment for the remainder of Stokes's shortened life. For 32 years Twyman would organize the NBA's Maurice Stokes Memorial Benefit Basketball Game held annually at Kutsher's Country Club in upstate New York to raise funds first for his fallen comrade and later for all needy ex-professional players from the game's earlier days.

Wes Unseld (NBA "Top 50" Selection)

Only two players boast the unique double coup of earning NBA Rookie of the Year and MVP honors in the same success-stuffed season. One is Wilt Chamberlain (1960) with Philadelphia and the other Westley Unseld (1969) with Baltimore. But

Unseld's brilliant performances and leaguewide impact didn't end there with his spectacular debut season. He would later earn further prestige as an NBA Finals MVP while leading a Washington Bullets team, which also featured Elvin Hayes, to the league championship in 1978, engineering a dramatic Game 7 victory on the road in Seattle. He was the heart and soul of one of pro basketball's hardest-working teams with the mid-'70s Bullets and captained those clubs during four different NBA Finals appearances. And he was eventually a long-term coach and popular general manager with the same Bullets franchise he has now served continuously for nearly three decades. But the most enduring image of the former University of Louisville great is that of one of basketball's most devastating wide bodies. Both a rugged rebounder at only 6'7" (leading the NBA in that department in 1975) and an efficient inside scorer despite limited mobility, Unseld left his lasting impression on countless opponents with bone-jarring picks and pinpoint outlet passes that fueled the Bullets' fast-breaking offense in both Baltimore and Washington for a dozen thrill-packed seasons.

Butch Van Breda Kolff

Butch Van Breda Kolff coached some of the sport's biggest pro stars as 1968 and 1969 mentor of the Los Angeles Lakers and also directed the fortunes of two of the NBA's most successful teams, but he will always be remembered above all else for his destructive relationship during that brief L.A. stint with one of basketball's biggest icons. A season-long war of personalities in Los Angeles between the control-conscious Van Breda Kolff and giant Wilt Chamberlain reached a crucial nadir during the 1969 Game 7 championship matchup, which also marked a final head-to-head confrontation between Wilt and longtime rival Bill Russell.

The Lakers were rallying desperately to narrow a hefty Boston fourth-quarter lead that threatened once more to crush the Lakers' championship hopes. When Chamberlain sustained what appeared to be only a minor leg injury, he removed himself from the game in a surprise move that shocked the Lakers faithful as well as the entire L.A. bench, while at the same time lifting Boston spirits considerably. With the clock winding down several minutes later and the game finally knotted, Wilt at last signaled his coach that he was ready to reenter the fray. Van Breda Kolff—obviously irritated by his star's apparent lack of dedication—ignored Wilt's signals and stuck with replacement Mel Counts until the final buzzer. The game, as well as the Lakers' title chances, evaporated when Boston's Don Nelson rattled home a short jumper just ahead of the final buzzer. Unmolested by the absent Chamberlain down the stretch, Russell closed out his career with a relentless 48-minute performance that included 21 crucial rebounds. Thus, while L.A. players and fans suffered yet another humiliating title defeat at the hands of the hated Celtics (the sixth of the decade), Boston's remarkable player-coach suffered the lesser disappointment of not having his arch rival on the floor to heighten the waning moments of their final shoot-out. And Van Breda Kolff would experience considerable regrets of his own in the face of the embarrassing incident when he soon learned that this final rift with his disgruntled franchise player had not only cost him a championship ring but had also lost him his plush coaching job.

Norm Van Lier

A hustling defense specialist, Norm Van Lier was one of Chicago's all-time fan favorites in an era when the Chicago Bulls remained one of the NBA's laughing-stock franchises. Van Lier was rarely among the league's statistical leaders in glamour categories such as scoring average or field-goal shooting, and he never collected a championship trophy. But he nonetheless had his legions of fans in the Windy City long before the city's NBA team was a Chicago institution of the same front-ranking stature as the baseball Cubs and football Bears. A defensive and playmaking specialist, the St. Francis (Pennsylvania) star frequently climbed into the NBA's top 10 in assists and steals and even captured the league's 1971 assists crown with one of the loftiest per-game averages (10.1) of the '70s. The eight-time All-Defensive Team selection was also a legitimate rival to New York's Walt Frazier as the NBA's best all-around backcourt defender during the near decade separating Jerry West from Magic Johnson.

Bob Verga

Two memorable eras have bolstered the reputation of Duke University basketball. The freshest in memory flowered at the outset of the 1990s and featured Christian Laettner, Bobby Hurley, Grant Hill, and the expert tutelage of current coach Mike

From the author's collection

Bob Verga, Carolina Cougars

Krzyzewski. The companion peak period came in the mid-'60s and boasted a string of phenoms that stretched from the trio of Art Heyman, Jeff Mullins, and Jay Buckley, who filled the lineup in 1963 and 1964, to the trio of Bob Verga, Steve Vacendak, and Jack Marin, who terrorized opponents in 1965 and 1966. While Verga never quite reached the stature of Heyman or even Mullins, he was, nonetheless, one of the most polished all-around backcourt performers ever to reside on the Durham campus. The six-foot New Jersey product debuted at the shooting guard slot on a 1965 ball club that captured a third consecutive ACC regular-season crown and missed by only a hair's breadth (a 91–85 ACC championship loss to the last Everett Case–coached North Carolina State team) of carrying on the NCAA magic that had just witnessed back-to-back Final Four entrants. It took Verga and company (strengthened by high-scoring and re-bounding sophomore center Mike Lewis) but one year to have Duke back in the limelight and also back in the Final Four. As the league's third-leading point-maker (21.4 points per game) in his initial campaign, Bob Verga was largely responsible—with an able assist from junior forward

Jack Marin (19.1 points, 10.3 rebounds)—for keeping coach Vic Bubas's championship machine straight on track toward a repeat ACC title. A year later there was a fourth regular-season crown, this time supplemented with a tournament trophy earned when the Blue Devils reversed the previous year's fortunes against the pesky N.C. State Wolfpack. Verga (18.5 points per game) was a junior that season and split team scoring honors with Marin (18.9) while repeating his rookie all-league first-team status. During his final trip around the league the future ABA star was barely nipped by Carolina's Larry Miller in a narrow vote for 1967's top ACC player (52 votes to 48), just as Verga's Blue Devils were caught at the wire by Miller's Tar Heels for the league's regular-season and postseason crowns. Verga himself shot to the top of the pack as the conference scoring leader (26.1 points per game), the first at Duke since Art Heyman earlier in the decade. Bob Verga eventually packed it in after the 1967 season as one of the highest-scoring guards in Duke annals, and also as the widely acclaimed heart and soul of one of the best three-year teams ever produced by a nearly always successful Duke University roundball factory.

Margaret Wade

Each spring the Wade Trophy is presented to the nation's outstanding women's collegiate player, and the list of honorees since 1978 reads something like a who's who of the modern-era women's game—Carol Blazejowski, Nancy Lieberman, Lynette Woodward, Cheryl Miller, Jennifer Azzi, and Rebecca Lobo are among the distinguished recipients. It is a fitting tribute to the six-year Delta State coach whose program captured three consecutive AIAW national championships in the mid-'70s, succeeded Philadelphia's Immaculata College at the top of the women's college basketball world, and produced Lusia Harris, the first female college player inducted into the Naismith Hall of Fame and the original prototype center of the modern-era women's game. Wade ran up a 453–89 record in 19 seasons at Cleveland (Mississippi) High School before reviving the Delta State program in 1973 and bringing it to national championship status in only two short seasons. During a brief half-dozen-year reign Wade's teams won 157 games (.872 winning percentage) and once rang up 51 consecutive victories, still the reigning women's NCAA record. Most fittingly, Margaret Wade was the first women's college coach honored with Hall of Fame status in Springfield.

Chet Walker

Chet Walker was a memorable point-making prodigy in an era known for its seemingly endless supply of great scorers and supreme one-on-one offensive showmen. First at Bradley University as a two-time All-American and later in the NBA with the Syracuse Nats and Chicago Bulls, Walker not only possessed a distinct nose for the basketball but also a deadly shooting eye (18,831 career points and 18.2-points-per-game career average) that was one of the most accurate of his era. Yet the single distilling fact of Walker's basketball career is the fact that he teamed with forward Lucious ("Luke") Jackson and center Wilt Chamberlain to form the formidable front line of a 1967 Philadelphia 76ers championship team that many experts still consider the most balanced individual squad in NBA history. Walker was third-best scorer (trailing Chamberlain and playmaker Hal Greer) on that powerhouse squad that won a then-record 68 regular-season games and ended Boston's championship skein at eight straight. Walker also led the NBA in free-throw percentage in 1971, played in seven All-Star Games, and played on playoff teams (one with Syracuse, six with Philadelphia, and six with Chicago) in all 13 of his NBA seasons.

Jimmy Walker

Another of the largely forgotten college scoring leaders of the prolific point-making decade of the '60s, Providence College great Jimmy Walker was once such an offensive force that he received numerous favorable comparisons with Oscar Robertson. Those comparisons were based more on style points and loose impressions of ballhandling artistry than on hard numbers: while Walker never approached Oscar's statistical impact on the record books, he did once pace the nation in scoring (besting Alcindor in 1967 at 30.4 points per game), average more than 25 points per game for a three-year career, and garner a top overall draft selection by the Detroit Pistons. As a nine-year pro Walker earned two 20-plus scoring seasons and compiled 11,000 points while also regularly ranking in the league's top 10 as a free-throw shooter. Yet his most lasting legacy to the game may well have been his out-of-wedlock son—Jalen Rose—who two decades later starred for the University of Michigan as the flashy backcourt ace of a celebrated "Fab Five" unit (including Chris Webber and Juwan Howard), which twice reached the NCAA Final Four championship game.

Bill Walton (NBA "Top 50" Selection)

If there is not easy accord concerning the two or three greatest players of college basketball history (my own vote would be cast for either Robertson, Alcindor, or Gola, or perhaps even Bill Russell) there is, nonetheless, fairly wide agreement about the two or three best-ever teams: the two invincible outfits in Westwood built around Lew Alcindor and Bill Walton, plus the San Francisco University juggernaut anchored by Russell. Walton's team didn't quite live up to impossible expectations as well as the other two, capturing but two NCAA titles instead of the universally anticipated three, and winning only 86 of 90 games, 2 less than Alcindor's talented group. But the second great Wooden dynasty ball club built around a single dominant player did post the longest winning skein (88 games) in college history, and if Walton was not the most dominant collegiate center ever to dunk basketballs, then he misses the mark by precious little. Walton was a three-time National Player of the Year while Alcindor only reigned twice (being edged out one season by Elvin Hayes); this seems adequately to balance the fact that Alcindor captured three NCAA Final Four MVPs while Walton garnered only two (losing both the individual trophy and the national title to David Thompson in 1974). And as dominant as Alcindor was for three seasons and Russell was for two, no one ever put on a championship performance that could rank with the one Walton authored as a curtain call to his junior season. It was in that memorable game against Memphis State that Walton dominated from opening tap to final horn, drilling 21 of his 22 field-goal attempts (most from close range) and adding a pair of free throws for a championship-game record 44 points. The incomparable redhead also hauled down 13 re-bounds in UCLA's almost effortless 87–66 championship romp.

While Walton and his team stumbled for a rare moment at the end of his final UCLA season, it was on the pro circuit that the often eccentric redhead's career seemed to come apart at the seams. Foot injuries that would plague the remainder of his uneven career would ruin a much-anticipated rookie season in Portland by lim-iting the top draft pick to 35 games and a 12.8 scoring average. An alternative lifestyle and anti-establishment attitude carried over from UCLA years added to the aura of disappointment. Yet despite the slow start there were several marvelous seasons with the Portland Trail Blazers that showed the brief domination that had been expected from Bill Walton. That honeymoon period lasted long enough for a spectacular championship season in 1977 in which the versatile Walton topped the league in rebounding and shot-blocking and, as hub of Jack Ramsay's patterned offense, logged one of his two 18-plus scoring averages (the other coming during an MVP campaign that followed in 1978). But then renewed injuries wiped out the brilliant future that might have been. There would be a few lesser milestones left along the way, and the biggest of these was the 1986 season in which Boston won a championship largely because a veteran Walton provided invaluable bench strength to supplement the powerful front line of McHale, Parish, and Bird. But Bill Walton's NBA career, in the end, would largely be a legacy of unfilled promise and vacuous dreams of what might easily have been. So large was the legend surrounding the 1977 championship season in Portland, however, and so weighty was the image of Walton at his occasional best, that Bill Walton was found among the privileged honorees when the league's "50 Greatest" were nominated to commemorate the NBA Golden Anniversary season.

Kermit Washington

Like coach Bill Musselman, Kermit Washington's career is marred forever by a single infamous moment of bad judgment and savage on-court behavior. Despite twice leading the nation in rebounding at American University and earning rarefied status as one of only seven collegians to average both 20 points and 20 rebounds for a career, Washington will nonetheless always be best (even exclusively) remem-bered for the ugly incident in which he smashed Rudy Tomjanovich's eye socket with an unprovoked sucker punch. It was an attack that nearly ended Tomjanovich's career and even threatened his life; it was also an assault that scuttled anything that was left of Washington's own once-promising NBA career.

Just as Juan Marichal a dozen years earlier nearly derailed a Hall of Fame-bound baseball career with his bat-wielding attack on John Roseboro, Washing-ton also paid dearly for his unwarranted and horrifying assault tactics. The inci-dent was ignited during a December 1977 contest with Houston when a scuffle broke out between Washington and hefty Kevin Kunnert. Tomjanovich rushed in to aid his threatened teammate and was floored by the crushing blow he didn't see coming. Washington, for his own part, was swiftly fined and suspended for 60 days, losing $50,000 in cash and also wearing out his welcome in Los Angeles. Before year's end the once-promising 6'8" forward and five-year L.A. veteran was peddled to Boston, where he lasted but 32 games before drifting through San

Diego, Portland, and Golden State over the final five seasons of his rapidly dete-
riorating NBA sojourn.

Richard Washington

Had this 6'10" forward-center played in any other program and labored for any
other coach, he might well be enshrined as an all-time great and enjoy status as
some school's best ever. The trade-off, of course, is that if Richard Washington had
played for some team other than John Wooden's UCLA Bruins, he would almost
assuredly never have won a national championship nor enjoyed trips to the coveted
Final Four in all three of his undergraduate seasons. Although he only managed one
campaign as a 20-plus scorer (his final season at 20.1), the 6'10" forward-center
was the second-leading scorer for Wooden's last team and top point-maker for the
Final Four outfit that launched the post-Wooden era at UCLA. His stellar performance as Final Four MVP of 1975 plus a hefty-scoring senior campaign were enough
to make him the NBA's third overall pick (Kansas City Kings) at the end of three
varsity seasons, leading to early exit from Westwood, and a mediocre half dozen
pro campaigns split among Kansas City, Milwaukee, Dallas, and Cleveland.

Nick Werkman

Few gunners can boast of scoring at a loftier rate than Larry Bird, Elgin Baylor,
Lew Alcindor, and Elvin Hayes, or of averaging more than 30 points per game in
each of three collegiate seasons. Rarely heralded Nick Werkman of Seton Hall
ranks in the first exclusive group and missed only by a hair's breadth of joining
Oscar Robertson, Pete Maravich, and Freeman Williams in the second. Averaging
33 points per game as a sophomore and 33.2 as a senior, the 6'3" deadeye forward
slipped to 29.5 his junior campaign, ironically the one season when he paced the
nation in scoring. A season later he would be edged out for individual honors by
Bowling Green's rubber-armed backcourt cannon Howie Komives (36.7 points
per game). Besides his unparalleled prolific point-making, Nick Werkman also
owns another rare distinction, that of being the highest scoring player ever to
perform at a major college and yet not make it onto either an NBA or ABA roster,
or even earn a single nomination for All-American honors.

Jerry West (NBA "Top 50" Selection)

Jerry West could flat-out shoot the basketball. From all distances and under all
imaginable conditions he pumped in shots with unflappable grace and relentless
regularity. He poured in tons of points across a 14-year NBA career, enough in fact
to stand ninth on the all-time scoring list (counting NBA points alone) and remain
the leading franchise scorer for a Los Angeles Lakers ball club that has also boasted
such superstars as Baylor, Chamberlain, Abdul-Jabbar, and Magic Johnson. (Abdul-
Jabbar and Chamberlain both outstrip West's career point totals, but not while playing exclusively in a Lakers uniform.) Jerry West today also still owns the fourth-
highest points-per-game average (27.0) in pro basketball history. Only Jordan (31.7
after 1996), Chamberlain (30.1), and Baylor (27.4) outdistance the shooting wiz-

ard who was known fondly in playing days as "Zeke from Cabin Creek" (a semiaccurate reference to his small-town West Virginia origins; West was born in Cheylan, but the closest post office was in Cabin Creek). In light of such impressive career numbers it was yet another popular Jerry West moniker—"Mr. Clutch"— that always seemed far more accurate in capsulizing one of the showcase performers in basketball history.

West was the Lakers' "Mr. Outside" to teammate Elgin Baylor's "Mr. Inside" role. A large enough percentage of his deadly missiles came from such long range that, had there been a three-point field goal at the time West played, his scoring totals would likely have been as much as 30 percent higher than they actually were. In other words, playing with today's standards, the all-time Lakers offensive great would likely have soared even above Jordan's totals and might well have owned rare distinction as the sport's most prolific point producer—certainly in total career points, perhaps in total number of league scoring championships, and even likely in career scoring average. As it was, West captured but a single league scoring crown, which came in 1970 (his 10th season) when he ripped the nets for 31.2 points per game. But the paucity of individual titles occurred simply because West, like everyone else in the '60s, experienced the bad timing of playing in the era of Wilt Chamberlain. In the face of Wilt's prodigious numbers Oscar Robertson (now the NBA's sixth all-time scorer but for decades ranked No. 2) never owned even a single point-making crown, either. In West's case, of course, he also had to share the ball and the offensive responsibility with first Baylor, later Chamberlain himself, and also Gail Goodrich, another hefty bomber of the early '70s. Such teammates naturally all demanded plenty of shooting opportunities of their own. Put West in another decade (even without the three-point rule) or on any other team and he would likely have won individual honors almost every season running, especially once Wilt's enthusiasms for offensive displays waned in the late '60s and early '70s.

West's scoring was easily as eye-popping as it was proficient. For starters, there was his spectacular 55-foot game-tying bomb against the Knicks in Game 3 of the 1970 Finals, which to date remains perhaps the most famous clutch shot of basketball history. "Mr. Clutch" earned his moniker time and again at season's end, for no one ever shot better (not even Bird, Magic, or Air Jordan) when the important games were squarely on the line. When it came to postseason playoff time Jerry West ranked squarely among the most unstoppable scorers in the game's annals. Twice he averaged better than 40 points per game for a playoff series, and his 46.5 in the 1965 Baltimore–L.A. matchup is an all-time mark; his 29.1-points-per-game overall playoff average trails only Jordan's, and his 4,457 postseason points were long second only to Kareem Abdul-Jabbar (Jordan has now also passed him here as well).

Jerry West's career was no pure joyride, however, despite his brilliant scoring onslaughts and numerous NBA milestones. Of course, there was the frustration of always playing second or third fiddle to Wilt and Oscar and Elgin Baylor in the individual scoring races (and also in the hearts of league fans). There was the physical abuse that he regularly took as a player of unmatched hustle and drive. Nine times over the years West would suffer painful broken noses as a price for his aggressive playing style. And above all, there was the ongoing

Jerry West,
West Virginia

Transcendental Graphics

frustration—especially acute for such a relentless competitor—of playing on a team that was itself always second-best in the championship standings. For West not only played in the epoch of Wilt, but also in the era of the unbeatable Auerbach-coached Boston Celtics. West's Lakers teams always seemed to get straight to the bridal altar only to become deeply disappointed bridesmaids. Seven aggravating times in West's first 11 NBA seasons his Los Angeles team was the loser in an NBA Finals series.

Even when the Celtics collapsed in the early '70s there would be several more seasons of frustration for West and for the snake-bit Lakers. Seemingly this was destined to be the case no matter how hard or how well West performed in postseason matchups—in 1970 he poured in 31.2 points per game in a losing Finals series with the Knicks; a year earlier his 30.9 average paced all playoff scorers, yet it couldn't stave off another seventh-game loss to Boston. Then finally—after seven uninterrupted defeats in the NBA Finals—the Los Angeles Lakers eventually broke through with a first title in 1972, with West this time again leading all postseason performers in assists and once more ranking high (second on the Lakers behind Goodrich) in the scoring column. The long-sought-after championship sadly came one year too late for Elgin Baylor, who had been forced into retirement by another round of painful injuries. But fortuitously, it didn't come too late for Jerry

West, who now finally possessed a championship ring to go along with all his other unmatched credentials.

West's career had other significant on-court and off-court moments that only add to the luster of his heady days in a Los Angeles NBA uniform. As a collegian he was one of the best ever, a relentless scorer and NCAA Final Four MVP who was never a National Player of the Year simply because his career overlapped with Oscar Robertson's. While never climbing out from behind Oscar's long shadow in the college ranks, West did, nonetheless, eventually take his own team farther (the national title game) only to suffer one of his several bitter postseason defeats. (The Mountaineers were one-point championship losers to California in West's junior season, then got bombed by NYU in overtime at the regional semifinals his senior year.) As a coach he was also accomplished, leading Los Angeles to playoff births in his three seasons at the helm before bickering with owner Jack Kent Cooke cut short his bench duties. And for much of the past two decades he has also been a fixture at the controls of the Lakers' front office, where he has served as general manager for 15-plus seasons. When it comes to one of the NBA's premier franchises—the one that holds more luster and more championships than any league club save Boston's—no one has contributed more than West Virginia's Jerry West.

Paul Westphal

At one point in his career Paul Westphal was considered the best at his playmaking position to be found anywhere in the NBA. An electrifying guard out of the University of Southern California, Westphal had dulled campus memories of Trojans great Bill Sharman and had also become a career 1,000-point scorer, although he never earned All-American honors or broke important school offensive records. Entering the pros as 1972's first-round pick of the Boston Celtics, Westphal quickly launched a red-letter pro career that easily outstripped his moderate collegiate credentials. Sharman's USC protégé was not destined to remain in Boston long, however, even if a solid rookie campaign off the bench in 1973 contributed heavily to the league's best regular-season record and a still-standing franchise mark of 68 victories. Contract squabbles arose on the heals of the team's 1974 NBA title, and Westphal was sent packing to Phoenix in exchange for Charlie Scott (who himself had earlier been dealt to the Suns for Paul Silas in one of Auerbach's most astute front office moves). The stage was set with the Westphal-Scott trade for a single great irony coloring the remainder of Paul Westphal's NBA career. Despite his early unhappy departure from Boston Garden, Westphal would, nonetheless, now be fated to become a feature player in what may well be the most storied moment of Boston Celtics postseason history.

That moment came in 1976 during the three-overtime Boston Garden NBA Finals thriller that saw the Celtics outlast a never-say-die Phoenix ball club 128–126 and thus turn the tide toward a second league title in three years. The pivotal Game 5 hung in the balance when Westphal came back to haunt his former mates by scoring 9 of his team's final 11 points to fashion a 95-all tie at the end of regulation play. Curtis Perry's jumper off a Westphal steal also gave the Suns a one-point lead in the final minute of the second overtime session. Havlicek's desperation shot next put the hometown team again in the driver's seat with only seconds left on the game clock. Amidst the pandemonium that followed Havlicek's heave, Westphal managed to call a time-out, which Phoenix no longer had, a brilliant ploy since, although it permitted Jo Jo White to sink a technical free throw for a 112-110 Boston lead, it also allowed Phoenix one last half-court possession that would result in a memorable game-extending desperation bucket by Garfield Heard. Westphal's heroics were not enough in the end to salvage the series or even to rescue the seesaw game. His brilliant time-out call would nonetheless be sufficient to secure his own lasting spot among the most memorable architects of indelible NBA postseason heroics.

Jo Jo White

Revival of the Boston Celtics NBA dynasty in the mid-'70s featured three Boston immortals—Dave Cowens, John Havlicek, and Jo Jo White—who together share almost equal billing with Cousy, Russell, Sam Jones, Larry Bird, and Kevin McHale in the expansive pantheon of all-time Boston Celtics greats. Like other indelible Boston legends from the four decades stretching between Red Auerbach and Rick Pitino, White was rarely found atop any of the NBA individual statistical categories. But he was, nonetheless, a regular fixture on league All-Star teams (seven selections) and also a frequent visitor to postseason NBA winner's circles (two NBA championships). Among the myriad Boston heroes, White was the ubiquitous "quiet man" who tended always to fade from the limelight and perform his on-court magic deeds in the shadows; not only was the former Kansas All-American doomed to play second fiddle to flashier NBA backcourt stars of the era such as Earl Monroe, Walt Frazier, and Pete Maravich, but he was also overlooked in his own backyard due to more attention-grabbing Boston teammates like Cowens and Havlicek. Nonetheless, he was a major contributor to two NBA championships (1974, 1976) in the mid-'70s as both a reliable playmaker and a dependable scorer, and he was even the NBA Finals MVP on the second of those winning ball clubs. Continuing a tradition of noteworthy Boston shooting guards that had debuted with Sharman and been extended with Sam Jones, White combined the role with more extensive playmaking duties. He nonetheless averaged 18 points per game in all but his first and last of nine Boston campaigns, and he led both championship teams in steals and assists while simultaneously also ranking among the team leaders in scoring.

Nera White

Among pioneers of women's basketball none ranks higher in stature than longtime Nashville (Tennessee) AAU star Nera White. The 1990s mark the first time that notable athletes among women basketballers—Olympians such as Rebecca Lobo, Jennifer Azzi, Dawn Staley, Lisa Leslie—are household names almost as recognizable as counterpart male NCAA and NBA stars. A dozen years back even the most talented women players on the international basketball scene were virtual unknowns, and this was the case even on their own college campuses or in their own sports-crazy hometowns. One of the most obscure yet accomplished of these hidden stars was Nashville Business College stalwart and 15-time AAU All-American Nera White. Between 1955 and 1969 the six-foot all-around playmaker, defender, rebounder, and shooter kept her Nashville teams at the pinnacle of AAU Women's

Tournament play. Two career highlights came in 1962, when her 28 points paced a national championship victory over Wayland Baptist College, and 1966, when her game-high 23 tallies in the title match secured another championship and also an undefeated season. Behind White, Nashville BC captured 85 percent of its games, 10 AAU championships, and 8 straight AAU crowns (along with 91 of 92 games) in the final seasons before the team was disbanded. Also a regular participant on national teams from the mid-'50s to mid-'60s, White keyed a 1957 world championship tournament victory over Russia, which also brought her a ballot box selection as that year's "Best Woman Player in the World."

Sidney Wicks

Among the endless stream of star players graduated from John Wooden's UCLA dynasty teams of the '60s and early '70s, only Lew Alcindor can boast a more productive long-term NBA career than the one fashioned by 1970 Bruins stalwart Sidney Wicks. A starring role on three successive NCAA champions, two All-American selections, and National Player of the Year and NCAA Final Four MVP honors might have been an impossible act to follow for most collegiate headliners. But the second overall 1971 draft pick of the Portland Trail Blazers maintained only a slightly diminished pace during 10 NBA campaigns split among Portland, Boston, and San Diego. The NBA ledger included four 20-plus scoring averages (and a fifth only a shade below), 1972 Rookie of the Year plaudits, and four All-Star nominations, plus one of the highest NBA career scoring averages among graduates of John Wooden's all-star training grounds. Former Wooden-coached UCLA greats and their lifetime pro scoring averages are as follows: Abdul-Jabbar (24.6), Marques Johnson (20.1), Gail Goodrich (18.6), Keith Wilkes (17.7), Wicks (16.8), Willie Naulls (15.8), Lucious Allen (13.4), Bill Walton (13.3), Walt Hazzard (12.6), Curtis Rowe (11.6), Dave Meyers (11.2), Richard Washington (9.8), and Henry Bibby (8.6).

Lenny Wilkens (NBA "Top 50" Selection)

A handful of mediocre NBA players have become stellar coaches (take Pat Riley, Phil Jackson, Red Holzman, and Fred Schaus as leading examples) while in still other rare cases, star players have flopped (no better illustration is found than Wilt Chamberlain) once they traded in their gym shoes for a seat at the top end of the bench. Few, however, have owned the successes at both ends of the bench that have been enjoyed by Lenny Wilkens across the last three-plus decades. As a player Wilkens was both a collegiate headliner and an NBA mainstay. He paced his Providence College teams to back-to-back NIT appearances and was the tournament's MVP for 1960. At the close of his pro playing career he owned the NBA's second-highest career assists mark; 15 seasons later he still stood third on the NBA all-time list (behind Oscar and Magic), and today he remains sixth in that hierarchy. As a player-coach he was the NBA's last member of a rare breed, with Seattle in 1971 through 1973 (where he was twice his own second-leading scorer) and at Portland in 1975. Finally, as an NBA head coach Wilkens has rolled up numerous new milestones for year-in and year-out winning. Currently serving in his fourth NBA coaching post, Wilkens has long since overhauled Red Auerbach in total victories (he entered 1997–98 with 1,170), has raced past the once-unthinkable 1,000-victory plateau, and assuredly will put huge distances between himself and the old record (Auerbach's 938) by the time he finally calls it quits.

During the summer of 1996 Lenny Wilkens crowned his coaching achievements with a coveted position as mentor of the fabulous gold medal–winning U.S. Olympic "Dream Team III," which featured Air Jordan, Karl Malone, John Stockton, Scottie Pippen, and its virtual all-world, all-star lineup. In a few more seasons—when he logs his required 25 campaigns as an NBA coach and thus qualifies for official selection—Wilkens is almost certain to join John Wooden as only the second man elected to basketball's Naismith Memorial Hall of Fame as both a player (Wilkens entered in that capacity in 1988) and again as a head coach. The only challenge remaining seems to be that of winning another NBA championship ring to duplicate the one captured two decades ago with his 1979 Seattle SuperSonics ball club. For it is only in the matter of winning championships that Wilkens's career coaching record fails to rank among the very best of all time.

Jamaal (Keith) "Silk" Wilkes

Sidney Wicks may have gotten more mileage out of his NBA years than any other John Wooden product save Lew Alcindor and Gail Goodrich, but Golden State Warriors great Jamaal Wilkes (Keith Wilkes at UCLA) wasn't that far behind. While earning his considerable NBA reputation as a high-powered offensive threat, Wilkes also found his way onto championship rosters almost as regularly as he had with John Wooden's invincible Bruins. The two-time All-American forward was second-leading scorer and rebounder (trailing Bill Walton on both counts) for the undefeated 1973 NCAA champions and third-leading point-maker (behind Walton and Henry Bibby) for the 1972 unblemished champions. An 11th overall pick in the 1974 NBA draft, Wilkes continued his winning ways with the NBA's 1975 champions, the Golden State Warriors (where he teamed with high-scoring Rick Barry), and with two NBA title teams (1980 and 1982) in Los Angeles alongside Kareem Abdul-Jabbar and Magic Johnson. Along the way he managed three 20-plus scoring seasons, nearly 15,000 career points, three league All-Star Game appearances (11.0 points per game), and three NBA All-Defensive Team selections. It was the five championship rings, however, and the rare ability to play unselfishly alongside such superstars as Walton, Barry, Abdul-Jabbar, and Magic Johnson, which lent a special brilliance to the career of one of John Wooden's finest showcase stars.

Bill Willoughby

A glance at the *NBA Basketball Encyclopedia* reveals nothing extraordinary about the eight-season pro sojourn of 6'8" forward Bill Willoughby, unless one notices the line at the top of the statistical column devoted to listing a player's college background. Willoughby, like only a small handful of pre-'90s NBA players, doesn't have a collegiate affiliation listed, a fact that makes him one of modern basketball's most special pioneers. Only Moses Malone and Darryl Dawkins share this unique distinction over the four decades of league play stretching between 1950 and 1990.

Willoughby jumped directly to the big time with the Atlanta Hawks as an unlikely 1975 second-round draft choice out of Dwight Morrow High School in Englewood, New Jersey. This was the same year that Dawkins also made a similar unlikely leap as Philadelphia's first-round selection, and only a single campaign after the ABA Utah Stars had inked Virginia prep phenom Moses Malone. The svelte 6'8" Willoughby would enjoy far less pro success (6.0 career scoring average in nearly 500 games) than either the bulky Malone or muscular Dawkins, though he would manage to hang around for eight seasons with six different NBA ball clubs. The most remarkable accomplishment, of course, was merely making the improbable leap of playing levels in the first place.

Phil Woolpert

Over the short haul of a half dozen seasons Phil Woolpert came about as close as anyone in the college ranks to anticipating or matching the relentless winning ways of John Wooden, and he did so with a West Coast powerhouse ball club that preceded Wooden's UCLA dynasty by nearly a full decade. Woolpert inherited a small-school program at San Francisco University that had already known a minor measure of success under legendary mentor Pete Newell and had produced its first All-American (Don Lofgran) the season before Woolpert took charge. Newell (whom Woolpert served as freshman coach in 1949 and 1950) had guided the unheralded Dons into the NIT title game in 1949 and then won the affair, 48–47, over

Phil Woolpert,
University of San Francisco

Loyola-Chicago on the strength of Lofgran's scoring (he had half the team's points) and overall stellar play. The USF Dons' surprise New York victory was at the time one of college basketball's biggest postseason upsets. Under Woolpert the upstart Dons were slow to recapture that previous glory, at least until Bill Russell arrived on the scene as one of the rarest finds in the history of big-time college recruiting. With Russell and a strong supporting cast, however, Woolpert would enjoy one of college basketball's most invincible juggernauts. Over three seasons in the mid-'50s Woolpert would ride Bill Russell and the rest of his stellar recruiting class (which included guards K. C. Jones and Hal Perry and forwards Carl Boldt and Mike Farmer) to two consecutive national titles, direct the first-ever undefeated NCAA championship team, and log the then-longest winning skein (60 games) in collegiate annals.

After the departure of Russell, Jones, and Perry, Woolpert's successes (both at USF where he fell to 6–20 by 1959, and also at San Diego, where his teams played at precisely .500 across seven campaigns) were unfortunately few, though his 1957 USF club (at 22–6, and featuring Farmer and Gene Brown) did climb back into a third successive NCAA Final Four. For several seasons Woolpert had, nonetheless, sat squarely atop the entire college basketball world. And it was Phil Woolpert who deserves a lion's share of the credit for initially appreciating and exploiting the magic of Bill Russell's dominating defense-oriented style of play. Russell himself later was quoted as recalling that coach Woolpert didn't at first think much of his goal-tending defense simply because he had never seen anyone block the opposition's shots before. To Woolpert's undying credit is the fact that he didn't rush headlong into trying to convert his unorthodox recruit into just another oversized jump shooter.

George Yardley

If Dolph Schayes is the single name most often overlooked when it comes to acknowledging prolific past-era scoring stars, George Yardley is perhaps next on any list of players who have, somewhere along the way, lost their hard-earned and much-deserved spot in hoops history. Few today likely recall that Schayes was first to cross the career 15,000-point plateau and that he was also one of only five bygone greats to claim a momentary notoriety as the NBA's all-time scoring leader. Yardley, by turn, has been given equally short shrift when it comes to recognizing his own substantial niche as the first pro to score 2,000 points in a single NBA season.

Arriving in the NBA in 1953 with a much better academic résumé (a master's degree from Stanford) than collegiate cage credentials, Yardley didn't look anything like a typical pro basketball star, even for an era when stationary set shots and plodding offenses were more the rule of the day than soaring one-on-one flights to the hoop. He could launch his unique jumpers with uncanny speed and precision for the era in which he played, swishing his long bombs with remarkable 44 percent accuracy. He was also a skinny 6'5" in stature, built (in one scribe's apt description) like "a human flamingo," and thus appropriately nicknamed "The Bird" (more for his storklike appearance than for any true ability to "fly" or "sky" in the fashion of modern-era players). Neither fans nor opponents were ever very impressed by a lanky skin-and-bones forward who was nearly bald and had unsightly knobby knees and spindly legs. And skeptics were hardly converted when Yardley ran up and down the court with the deceptive loping gait of a short-winded school-yard weekend warrior rather than the powerful glide of a polished pro athlete. Yet while the Pistons' George Yardley (four seasons in Fort Wayne and one and a fraction in Detroit) was hardly a graceful hoopster in his physical appearance, he did own some exceptional workmanlike virtues plus an uncanny ability simply to put the basketball through a hoop with deadly regularity.

George Yardley played for only seven NBA seasons, yet he nonetheless finished with a career 19.2 scoring average and also with a lasting place in the league's formative history. During his most spectacular season—1957–58, when he averaged 27.8 points per game and copped a league scoring title—Detroit's hot-handed "Bird" became the first athlete in pro history to toss in a then-unheard-of total of 2,001 points (Mikan had once reached 1,932) during a single league season. Pro basketball's first 2,000-point man never won many accolades for polished or stylish play; nonetheless, he was one of the most inventive scorers ever to lace up a pair of sneakers and take to the hardwood floor. If early gunners like Yardley and Pettit (who bumped up the NBA record to 2,105 the very next season) have not generated far more attention, this is in large part due, of course, to the mere fact that a true nonpareil named Wilt Chamberlain was soon soaring above the 3,000- and 4,000-point barriers only a handful of seasons later.

"The Original Bird" was not only first to pass one of the NBA's substantial point-making mileposts but also briefly reigned alongside Bob Pettit as one of the sport's most potent offensive weapons during the formative seasons stretched between the early '50s era of Mikan, Joe Fulks, and Paul Arizin, and the early '60s epoch of Wilt Chamberlain, Rick Barry, and Oscar Robertson. Yardley's considerable stature as one of the game's earliest masters of the revolutionary jump shot has only recently received long-overdue recognition with much-deserved selection among the latest class (1997) of inductees into the James Naismith Memorial Basketball Hall of Fame.

Chapter Seven

Biggest Show in Town

"Hoopla" as America's New

National Pastime (1981–98)

The first handful of seasons in the 1980s represented a long-anticipated coming-of-age for the professional version of Naismith's nearly century-old cage game. With the simultaneous arrival of a pair of superstars-in-waiting named Larry Bird and Magic Johnson on the rosters of the sport's two most history-laden franchises, the NBA suddenly and dramatically caught up with, and overhauled, the college sport in terms of runaway fan interest. Before the decade was played out NBA superstars were even almost on a par with major-league baseball diamond favorites and NFL gridiron heroes when it came to lucrative commercial endorsements and household name recognition. When Bird and Magic passed the mantle to an even bigger superstar named Michael Jordan in the latter half of the decade, the transition was altogether complete. In the course of no more than a decade changing tastes had left basketball as the king of all sports. And basketball players were now also the nation's hottest sports commodity.

The arrival of the NBA as kingpin hardly meant a complete collapse of interest in the collegiate sport. The NCAA postseason free-for-all dubbed March Madness had itself become one of our biggest television sporting spectacles by the early '80s, thanks in large part to the record-setting single-game draw for the epic March 1979 championship showdown between the same Larry Bird and Magic Johnson. If the college game was now more than ever perceived as a "farm system" for the popular pro version, nonetheless the college stars themselves maintained their own grip on television and arena audiences around the land.

The NCAA tournament benefited in particular throughout the 1980s from a string of highly dramatic title matchups that served to fuel the annual popularity of "March Madness" as one of America's premier sporting spectacles. And out of those exciting tournament showdowns came a flock of new stars to capture the public fancy. Michael Jordan first titillated public interest with his last-second tournament-clinching 1982 jump shot versus Georgetown in the New Orleans Superdome. Another freshman from that same season—Georgetown's Patrick Ewing—himself became a regular Final Four fixture over the next handful of seasons. Houston University's run-and-gun Cougars with their Phi Slamma Jamma trio of Larry Micheaux, Akeem Olajuwon, and Clyde Drexler generated high-flying excitement even with their late-March defeats. And by the early 1990s Duke—the closest thing to a college dynasty since Wooden had packed it in out in Westwood—was showcasing future pro icons Grant Hill and Christian Laettner, while Michigan's "Fab Five" contingent was writing one of college basketball's great Cinderella stories of the past half-century.

But it was in the 1980s and 1990s, nonetheless, that for the first time in a century of basketball history the professional cage stars far outstripped local college heroes as the game's biggest marquee names. Commercial product advertising and television image-making most assuredly had a great deal to do with the transition. By the 1990s pro sports stars such as Michael Jordan and Shaquille O'Neal were first and foremost media celebrities, and celebrity status was all-too-often only loosely connected to on-court or on-field performances by basketball, baseball, or football headliners. Commercial advertisements (often looking more like movie short subjects or MTV music videos) projected players' images as much as did game action itself. Since basketball sneakers were hotter fashion items than baseball, or football cleats—a teenager can cruise the campus in rubber soled basketball shoes but not in cleated football or baseball footwear—Nike and other companies exploited and reinforced basketball stars as their favorite pitchmen. And music and film moonlighting careers (as rap music icons or celebrity walk-ons in action-adventure films) turned some NBA stars like Shaquille O'Neal and Air Jordan into breathing larger-than-life cartoon characters.

Runaway commercial popularity of pro hoops stars soon predictably impacted on the stability of the college game. More than ever before the sole goal of a collegiate athletic career became the eventual (sooner rather than later) acquisition of a professional contract. College athletic glories themselves were now as secondary for most ballplayers as the outmoded notion of a life-serving academic education. The biggest stars were, by the mid-'90s, leaving college play after two and sometimes only one season. A trend that began in the 1970s had now reached large enough proportions to alter the makeup of the college rosters; major programs like North Carolina, Duke, or Kentucky found themselves rebuilding every two seasons rather than every four. And the celebrity status of both pro and college players seemed to alter and even destroy some of the earlier defining characteristics and appeals of basketball play. Emphasis switched from team strategy to one-on-one offensive displays, and television sports-center highlights rewarded a slam-dunking style over once-cherished fundamentals of long-range shooting, clever ballhandling, and adroit passing. Passing and defensive skills especially seemed to erode, as did middle-range shooting that was once a game staple. And the once-popular controlled team-pattern game taught by legendary coaches from Phog Allen to Adolph Rupp to Bob Knight seemed now to be found almost exclusively in the increasingly popular women's collegiate version of cage play.

If the middle decades of the century had brought black athletes to basketball in droves and revolutionized the sport in the process, it was in the century's final decades that basketball also finally opened fully to talented women athletes. First, the college sport exploded on the scene with Title IX legislation, an NCAA postseason bash, and eventual prime-time television coverage. By the mid-'90s the women's college year-end tournament had its own rapidly increasing tele-vised following. A 1996 women's Olympic Dream Team was almost as popular as its male counterpart (even more so perhaps, since its own quest for a gold medal was not diminished by such one-sided, and thus boring, single-team domi-nation). And in the decade's final years the most recent and most successful effort was also made to launch women's professional leagues. Even the NBA itself jumped into the act with an eight-city league of its own, featuring teams owned by NBA clubs and playing during summer months in showcase NBA arenas. And a rival American Basketball League tried boldly to compete with wintertime col-lege and pro men's action for audience interest before folding near the end of 1998. If, in the late 1950s, college and NBA cage stars were no longer exclu-sively white, so too by the late 1990s were they no longer so exclusively male.

Mahmoud Abdul-Rauf (Chris Jackson)

Two images will always surround Mahmoud Abdul-Rauf (née Chris Jackson) and, unfortunately, neither had much to do with his superlative basketball talents. The first involved Chris Jackson's inherited physical condition (a neurological disorder known as Tourette's Syndrome), which has made him a sterling role model for physically handicapped athletes everywhere. The second—less positive—involves Mahmoud Abdul-Rauf's sincere beliefs in his adopted Muslim faith and the outward results were anything (at least in the minds of a wide majority of fans) but those associated with exemplary behavior. Abdul-Rauf caused a minor storm when he refused to stand with teammates for the pregame playing of the United States national anthem a couple of seasons back, and the negative publicity surrounding the event was certainly not the kind of headline-grabbing the Denver franchise had hoped for when drafting Chris Jackson (his given Christian name) as a college undergrad phenom out of LSU. A near-30-point scorer in two short seasons in Baton Rouge, Jackson's frequent colle-giate high-scoring outbursts have rarely been matched in the pro circuit (though he did become only the fifth player in Denver history to log a 50-point game), which also led to management disillusionment. Traded to Sacramento for Lithuanian import Sarunas Marciulionis in the 1996 off-season, the offensive-minded Abdul-Rauf (his name was legally changed in July 1993) spent the past two seasons trying to elevate his game and his sagging image with a second straight trailender franchise and in a second anything-but-prime-time NBA marketplace. The most remarkable phase of this quick point guard's game remains his accurate free-throw shooting: His streak of 81 in a row is the second-longest in league history, he joined Bill Sharman as the only player with three free-throw streaks of 50 or better, and his career percentage (.909 following the 1997–98 season) at that time was the highest in league history.

Danny Ainge

The baby-faced Ainge sported a youthful expression of innocence that worked to belie his fiery competitive spirit and near-violent intensity as one of the sport's most combative warriors. And the versatile athlete, who was also talented enough to play major-league baseball for three seasons with the Toronto Blue Jays, displayed throughout his career a savvy knowledge of the game that also earmarked him for potential coaching successes at the end of his whirlwind playing career. Ainge played baseball for three years with the big-league Blue Jays while still starring on the hardwood as an All-American at BYU (where he averaged above 20 across four seasons and was the Wooden Award winner for 1981). Ainge's inability to hit consistently in the baseball big time (.220 career batting average in 220 games) soon caused a reassessment of his professional career goals. Struggles on the diamond were weighed against excellent odds for successes on the hardwood court, where Auerbach's Celtics had demonstrated their faith in him with a 31st overall draft selection. Joining the Boston Celtics in time for the 1981–82 season (Larry Bird's third year) proved quickly to be a solid career-advancing decision. Overnight, a baseball bust (relatively speaking) became a basketball bright spot as Ainge became a valuable role player and provided backcourt bench strength. With the strong Boston teams of the mid-'80s Ainge remained a key element in the always-balanced Celtics team mix and rode behind Bird's leadership to a pair of NBA titles (1984, 1986). And a half dozen post-Boston NBA years hardly spelled obscurity, either. There was modest success in Portland (on teams that reached the Conference Finals in 1991 and the NBA Finals versus the Bulls in '92) followed by a late-career peak in Phoenix (where Ainge again played in the championship round versus Chicago in 1993). And finally, as a coach with the Phoenix Suns in the late 1990s, Ainge was a most pleasant surprise right from the start by directing winning and contending teams in his first two winters on the bench.

Kenny Anderson

Anderson is one of the showcase examples of that new breed of athlete who shines brilliantly on the college court for only a season or two before cashing in his immense talents for an early NBA paycheck. And like the majority of the new breed, Kenny Anderson's NBA career has never managed to reach anticipated heights or even imitate the heady achievements of short-lived college days. The lefty-shooting point guard peaked early as a freshman member of the 1990 Georgia Tech "Lethal Weapons III" offense, where he was perhaps the finest of a long line of Yellow Jackets backcourt aces (a list that includes Mark Price in the '80s, Rick Yunkus in the '70s, and Roger Kaiser in the '60s). The triple-threat offense of Dennis Scott (27.7), Brian Oliver (21.3), and National Freshman of the Year Anderson (20.6) rewrote record books as the first trio of teammates ever to each average above 20 for a full year's ACC league play. That winter Anderson also became the school's sixth top ACC rookie in only eight winters. And the playground legend from New York City's Archbishop Malloy High School also paced the ACC in assists, for all his own scoring efforts. A season later the 6'1" speedster upped his scoring output to 25.9, repeated second-team honors on the *Sporting News* All-American squad, and carried the Yellow Jackets on his back almost single-handedly after Scott and Oliver departed for the NBA.

But as a highly touted pro (second overall NBA pick after his sophomore season), Anderson has remained little more than a high-priced journeyman, putting

Kenny Anderson, Georgia Tech

© Georgia Tech University

in stints with New Jersey, Charlotte, Portland, and finally Boston, and never matching the offensive production that made him a phenomenal 23 points per game career scorer in the nation's best collegiate circuit. A contract holdout and feud with New Jersey coach Bill Fitch largely scuttled his promising rookie season; bouncing back under coach Chuck Daly as a second-year mainstay with the Nets, he was again waylaid with a season-shortening injury when flagrantly fouled by New York's John Starks. Anderson's best year was his third, when he played a full schedule, scored almost 19 per game, and dished out nearly 10 assists nightly. Over recent seasons, however, his apparent weaknesses (playing out of control, a scrawny build, and inconsistent perimeter shooting) have always overshadowed his many strengths (classic point guard makeup with an eye toward scoring; excellent ballhandling, passing, and penetrating skills). Anderson was, only a half dozen seasons in the past, the most naturally gifted young point guard in the pro game; by the start of his seventh NBA campaign he was already one of basketball's most overpaid normal achievers.

Jennifer Azzi

With a roster spot in the successful women's American Basketball League, a lucrative endorsement contract to promote women's hair-care products, and an Olympic gold medal tucked in her back pocket, former Naismith and Wade Trophy winner (1990 Player of the Year) Jennifer Azzi is living a dream that few women athletes could even imagine a mere half dozen years back. But the former Stanford University star earlier had to pay her dues with several unglamorous years in the European professional leagues before the women's U.S. basketball "Dream Team" made the female version of Naismith's game prime-time fare in the months leading up to, and culminating with, the 1996 Atlanta Olympics. Azzi's collegiate career had peaked with her multiple Player of the Year selections in 1990. That same year the speedy 5'8" guard out of Oak Ridge, Tennessee, was also the NCAA Final Four MVP while leading Stanford's Lady Cardinal to a first-ever national title and a sterling 32–1 overall season. As a member of the ABL's San Jose Lasers, the pert backcourt dynamo was also expected to be an instant pro league star. However Azzi suffered an unexpected career setback on the eve of ABL play when she was forced to sit out much of the league's debut season with a severe shoulder injury. Further career disappointment came later with the ABL shutdown in fall 1998.

Charles Barkley (NBA "Top 50" Selection)

Barkley earned one reputation as pro basketball's original "bad boy" of the 1990s during his productive decade-and-a-half stay with three NBA teams. On the court in Philadelphia, Phoenix, and Houston, he also earned a second reputation as one of the most intimidating small forwards ever to play the professional game. Tabbed "The Round Mound of Rebound," Barkley was both an imposing physical specimen and an outspoken colorful personality from the first season with Philadelphia in 1984. For nearly a decade he labored to win a championship with a mediocre 76ers team that repeatedly undid his noblest efforts. And along the way he became noted for far more than his ferocious rebounding and unstoppable scoring. Barkley attracted controversy like a lightning rod. His manner of speaking whatever was on his mind (in what were sometimes the most outlandish of terms) made him a favorite among fans and sportswriters alike. Ownership and league officials, however, were often less than thrilled with off-the-cuff interview remarks from their loose-cannon superstar.

Barkley never made serious runs at a championship while with the Philadelphia franchise. A midcareer trade to Phoenix, however, gave a new lease to Barkley's

*Charles Barkley,
Phoenix Suns*

© Frank P. McGrath Jr.

career. Surrounded with a more talented team, the league's best inside power force came tantalizingly close to a league crown against Chicago in the 1993 Finals. Barkley was not only surrounded by a better team in Phoenix but also lifted his own game to a new level by edging Michael Jordan as league MVP. Jordan and the Bulls would prevail in the final series of the season, but not without some gripping action and one game in particular that was a postseason classic. Barkley would make one final career move in 1996–97, when he took his act to Houston for one last shot at a league crown. But by the time Sir Charles had joined forces with Drexler and Olajuwon, his career was already on the downslide. He would play a career-low 53 games (slowed by injuries and suspensions that cost 29 games) in 1997, and without more of an impact from Barkley up front, the aging Rockets were no match for Utah in Western Conference postseason confrontations. The club was only 16–13 in the games he didn't play. But in his 13th season it was still clear that Charles Barkley was still one of the game's top rebounders. He would post the same number of rebounds as Olajuwon while playing 25 less games and would even outrebound the seven-foot center by 39 boards on the offensive end.

Controversy and color followed Barkley to both Phoenix and Houston, and so did an unfortunate spate of injuries that somewhat slowed the second half of his career. But if there were personal roadblocks to a coveted championship ring and also more than a fair share of lawsuits (several for grappling with intrusive fans outside of arenas and inside of his favorite watering holes) and other personal distractions, Charles Barkley, nonetheless, continued to pile up individual performances that eventually made him an undeniable candidate for distinction as one of the best ever among muscular power forwards. Career numbers were lofty enough by 1996 to assure a spot on the NBA Golden Anniversary All-Time Roster: 22,000 career points (23.1 average), a rebound average close to a dozen (11.7); and NBA records for most offensive rebounds in a single quarter and single half. Further distinction has come in the form of a 1993 NBA MVP, five-time all-league first-team honors, and two Olympic gold medals (as a member of Dream Teams I and III). And if Charles Barkley often flashed the familiar self-indulgent personality of the modern-era pro, his work ethic in playing the game was always strictly from the old school.

Len Bias

One of the most talented natural athletes ever to grace the Atlantic Coast Conference, Len Bias would also, in the most perverse fashion imaginable, turn out to be the only major draft-day mistake of Red Auerbach's brilliant Boston front-office career. Auerbach would build a career-long reputation upon remarkable draft-day decisions. There was the maneuver to obtain Bill Russell from the St. Louis Hawks in 1957. There was the prescient selection of Dave Cowens in 1970. There were the related maneuvers in 1980 that brought McHale and Parish on board and left the Warriors holding Joe Barry Carroll as consolation. Two seasons before that there was the cogent selection of Larry Bird, which rivals the Russell pickup as Auerbach's greatest ever. The drafts and trades that united Bird, McHale, and Parish in Boston created the best front line of all time and renewed Boston dominance in the 1980s. The Russell deal was enough to underpin the greatest dynasty in the sport's history. And even a foolish Auerbach move in rejecting Cousy his first year on the job turned golden when fate dealt Cousy to Boston anyway, despite Auerbach's cold shoulder. But in the case of Len Bias, fate was perhaps for the only time entirely uncooperative with the best-laid plans of Boston's front-office genius.

The sensational front-page reports of the final scandalous hours of Len Bias's all-too-short life have forever blurred the great Maryland star's collegiate basketball achievements. Death from a mysterious cocaine overdose not only robbed Bias of his promised future in the fast lane of professional sports celebrity; it also ultimately wiped out a legacy as one of the most brilliant of all ACC performers. Here was a near superhuman player who was often compared with some of the game's best all-time performers, frequently drawing parallels with Jordan for untapped college brilliance and unlimited pro potential. Today the public vividly recalls how

Bias died and what may have been lost in the process; few but the most avid fans of the sport and the league still recall the back-to-back ACC Player of the Year accolades, remember the pure athletic brilliance of Bias's game, or recount the remarkable ACC Tournament performance in 1984 that won MVP honors and clinched his reputation as the most promising sophomore in decades. The 1984 postseason ACC affair found Maryland caught in three tense shoot-outs with longtime rivals NC State, Wake Forest, and Duke. Never was the awesome potential of Len Bias more evident than during that hectic final weekend of frenetic ACC title play when a late-game 14-point scoring spree by the sensational sophomore propelled Lefty Driesell's team over Duke in the championship game. It was a joyous sign of things to come, and also a sad foreshadowing of some things that would regrettably never be.

Rolando Blackman

A Kansas State All-American (*Sporting News*, First Team, 1981), 1980 U.S. Olympian, first-round (ninth overall) NBA draft selection, and four-time NBA All-Star (1985–87, 1990), Blackman enjoyed his most memorable single night during the 1987 NBA All-Star Game in Seattle, where he was one of the leading scorers for a victorious West squad in the highest-scoring midseason classic ever staged. The Dallas guard's 29 tallies in 22 minutes (Tom Chambers had 34) contributed heavily to the West Stars' 154–149 overtime victory in which Chambers edged Blackman for MVP honors. Blackman's career-long scoring was always prolific enough to keep him near the 20-point mark (three times topping that standard) in all but his first and last 2 of 13 seasons and left him (with 16,643 Dallas points) as the Mavericks' all-time franchise leader. The 6'6" guard logged 11 seasons in Dallas before finishing out his career with a brief stint in New York (1993 and 1994), consistently averaging higher as a scorer in postseason action (above 20 in five of his six playoff appearances with Dallas), and proving the most consistent year-in and year-out star over the first dozen seasons of Dallas Mavericks franchise history. An odd career footnote is that the Panama-born (but Brooklyn-raised) Blackman was one of the first Latin American natives to set foot inside of the NBA.

Marty Blake

Marty Blake has become a pro basketball legend without ever bouncing a round ball, launching a jump shot, or even setting foot out of an arena grandstand. While earning his impeccable reputation over the years, in a number of behind-the-scenes pro basketball front-office assignments, it has been foremost as a bush-league bird dog (a talent scout who roams backwater campuses and summer coaches' clinics in search of latent superstars) that Marty Blake has most thoroughly earned his legendary reputation. He has now been on the NBA circuit for 44 seasons and counting, made an early mark on the league as a front-office executive with the Ben Kerner–owned St. Louis Hawks (the only team ever to beat a Red Auerbach–coached team in the NBA Finals in 10 tries), and has for two decades (since the late '70s) also been the NBA's all-knowledgeable director of scouting.

While Blake once rode buses to backwoods towns all over America in search of undiscovered phenoms no one else knew about, he more than anyone over the past half-century has made that bygone approach to scouting entirely obsolete: to-day pro and college talent hounds know of virtually every skilled schoolboy player on the planet thanks to a worldwide scouting networking system that Marty Blake himself all but invented. Hired originally by the Milwaukee Hawks and coach Red Holzman back in 1954 (a season before Bob Pettit, who was one of Marty's earliest and most spectacular signings), Blake originally fine-tuned his international scouting network in the early '70s as general manager of the same franchise, by then located in Atlanta (after its dozen-season layover in St. Louis). Besides Hall of Famer Pettit, Blake's most famous signee was perhaps Pete Maravich (a draft choice which he now regrets, since Dave Cowens was also available to the Hawks at the time). But of all the NBA deals that involved Marty Blake's talented hand over the years, none was more significant than the questionable one he once engineered in 1956 as Ben Kerner's general manager, the league-shaping deal that shipped the Hawks' draft rights to University of San Francisco star Bill Russell to Auerbach's up-and-coming Celtics in exchange for league All-Star Ed Macauley and promising prospect Cliff Hagan. As a final footnote underscoring Marty Blake's well-earned stature as one of basketball's most gifted talent sleuths, it was none other than Blake who headed up the 1996 panel (during his own 42nd winter with the league) that hand-picked the NBA's 50 greatest players as a show-piece promotion for the league's elaborate Golden Anniversary festivities.

Mookie Blaylock

Selected by the New Jersey Nets as the No. 12 overall pick in the 1989 NBA college draft, Blaylock (whose real first name is Daron) would languish several seasons with one of the league's worst teams before a 1992 trade to Atlanta opened new windows on a bright pro career. Noted primarily as a defender but also a proven scorer, Blaylock (a defensive stalwart who still scores nearly 15 per game) has teamed with Steve Smith (one of the best pure shooters and also one of the best post-up guards) in recent seasons in what has developed into perhaps the NBA's best all-around backcourt combo. During a stellar two-season career with a power-house University of Oklahoma team (after transferring from Midland Junior College), the chunky 6'1" guard became the first NCAA player to collect 200 assists and 100 steals in back-to-back seasons. It was an early indication of the athletic skills and tough mind-set that would later make Blaylock one of the very best defensive point guards anywhere in the game. This status as premier defender has been rubber-stamped with five straight selections (1994–98) to the NBA's first or second All-Defensive Team; it has also been further enhanced by Blaylock's stature as league leader in steals during the recent 1996–97 NBA campaign.

Tyrone "Muggsy" Bogues

Pro basketball has been a game strictly for giants since the birth of the NBA at the century's midpoint, and few sub-six-footers have performed in the league as anything more than idle curiosities or specialized role players. In pre-Mikan days this had not been the case, and little men with long-range set shots (of a two-handed variety) did indeed rule the game. Superscout Marty Blake recently looked back

Tyrone "Muggsy" Bogues,
Wake Forest

© Wake Forest University

over his half-century in the sport and singled out Fort Wayne Pistons set-shooting ace Bobby McDermott (see Chapter Five) as a sure bet for his own all-time team. But after a first generation of mobile giants in the late '40s and early '50s the game became one of treetop "goons" and talented leapers. Perhaps the starkest exception was 5'9" scoring machine Calvin Murphy of the Houston Rockets who rattled NBA rims throughout the '70s and into the '80s. Another has been Tyrone "Muggsy" Bogues, whose performances in the current decade with the Charlotte Hornets have proven that there is still space for the talented little man, even if that space earns little recognition on sports-news video highlight reels.

Bogues worked his magic first in the ACC with Wake Forest in the middle seasons of the 1980s, impressing with his floor leadership rather than his stat columns (he did average double figures in scoring as a junior and senior) and twice capturing the Murray Greason Award as team MVP. He was also an All-ACC selection (the smallest one ever) in 1987 before earning distinction as only the fifth Wake Forest player ever drafted in the first round by an NBA club (the Washington Bullets, who made him the 12th overall selection in 1987). On the NBA scene

Bogues experienced an early career upgrade after his rookie campaign when selected in the third round of the expansion draft by the Charlotte Hornets. In Charlotte Bogues emerged rather surprisingly as not only one of the league's top playmakers but also one of the most popular and marketable figures in the entire NBA. Now the all-time franchise leader for Charlotte in both assists and steals, Bogues emerged as a frontline star by leading the Hornets in assists for seven straight seasons (before a 1995 injury brought an end to the string) and ranking as one of only two league players to top 600 in that category every year during the stretch. The diminutive and pesky backcourt ace has, however, earned his most impressive credentials by annually leading the NBA throughout most of the 1990s in the little-noted but highly valued offensive category of assists-to-turnover ratio.

Manute Bol

Manute Bol was the strangest looking pro basketballer of all time and also the most specialized in his ballplaying talents. His pro career scoring average for nine seasons was less than 3 points per contest, and his total number of shot blocks (2,077) as well as his rebounds (2,635) outstripped his point scoring (1,584) by a wide margin. No other NBA player with more than a token appearance ever had more blocks than points, and none logged nearly 12,000 minutes in the league with almost the exclusive role of a goaltender. The 7'6" African Dinka tribesman and native of Sudan was the tallest NBA player ever at the time when he was drafted off the campus of the University of Bridgeport (Connecticut) as a long-term project by the Washington Bullets. Bol had originally been brought to Bridgeport on a basketball scholarship more as an entertainment novelty than anything else, yet his athletic talents developed rapidly enough and his stick-thin body also filled out enough (though never very much) to first earn and then maintain NBA roster spots in Washington, Golden State, Miami, and Philadelphia. Bol twice led the NBA in shot-blocking (1986 and 1989) even though he registered only 2,090 minutes of playing time in one of those seasons and 1,769 the other. The man-child playfully known as "The Dinka Destroyer" was most widely revered in NBA circles for the legend surrounding his once having killed a lion with a spear during a tribal ritual back home in Africa. As a basketball player he left much to be desired and one early '90s preseason magazine scouting report on Bol read as follows:

> Bol can't shoot at all and he hasn't developed any kind of post move. He can't handle the ball and the only thing he can do on offense is grab the garbage and stuff it back in the hoop.

Perhaps no other player with such limited skills has ever logged even a minute of NBA playing time, let alone the nearly 12,000 minutes and nine seasons of court action, which Manute Bol somehow survived.

Sam Bowie

Ralph Sampson (Harrisonburg, Virginia) and Sam Bowie (Lebanon, Pennsylvania) came out of high school in the same year (1979) as perhaps the most talented tandem of giants ever to simultaneously whet the appetite of college recruiters all across the nation. The hype in both cases was something of a mark of certain doom. Both agile seven-footers were already disappointments, to a small degree at least, even before reaching the professional ranks. But while Sampson won three NCAA National Player of the Year accolades at Virginia and disappointed only because he was not quite another Lew Alcindor or Wilt Chamberlain, Bowie proved at Kentucky under coach Joe B. Hall to be less than adequate rather than merely less than unparalleled. Bowie did average nearly 13 points per game as a Wildcat freshman and 17.4 as a sophomore before serious leg injuries forced him to the sidelines for nearly two entire seasons. A remarkable comeback in time for his senior campaign included another double-figure scoring average (10.5) and just enough promise to entice the ever-optimistic pro scouts to take a chance on a high-profile player with towering physique but gimpy extremities.

Fans will always remember Sam Bowie, however, as long as balls are bounced and dunks are slammed, as the seemingly useless giant that Portland Trail Blazers management apparently once deemed more likely as a franchise player than the North Carolina prodigy named Michael Jordan. This is, perhaps, something of an unfair rap for the naturally talented cager whose promising college and pro careers were both sabotaged only by the debilitating leg injuries which kept him at less than 50 percent even in his better seasons. Bowie did recover enough a second time as a pro to log a few campaigns that some lesser player might have been reasonably proud of. Six of his first seven NBA years in Portland and New Jersey would witness double-figure scoring, and he peaked at 15 points per game (1992) and 10.1 rebounds per game (1990) with the Nets just before his career swan song in Los Angeles. The ultimate problem from the standpoint of unforgiving fans and media was that, in three and a fraction NBA seasons in Portland, Bowie produced only half the amount of offense (1,457 points) that Michael Jordan delivered during any single season of his own unparalleled decade-and-a-half Hall of Fame career.

Shawn Bradley

Shawn Bradley was almost as big a reclamation project as Manute Bol when he first entered the NBA as a largely untested collegian with plenty of potential and a seductive physical stature. He stands a towering 7'6" to match Bol's stature, and he was also from the start a phenomenal shot blocker (leading the NCAA as a freshman with a 5.2 average and posting the second-highest rejection total in collegiate history). He even held a share of the college record for rejections in a single game with 14 versus Eastern Kentucky. Yet also like Bol, Bradley has never completely panned out in his journeyman stint with three NBA clubs (Philadelphia, New Jersey, Dallas) across five seasons. His on-court talents have been substantially more diverse than were Bol's: for one thing, he can shoot (both a soft jumper and an arching hook) and for another, he can run the court with remarkable agility. Bradley was therefore a No. 2 overall draft selection (after playing only a single season at Brigham Young, where he averaged a shade under 15 points and eight rebounds nightly), he has so far maintained a double-figure scoring average in the pros, and he has even matched Bol's proven shot-blocking skills as the NBA pacesetter in that department during the 1997 season (his fourth). The big question with Shawn Bradley is not at all whether or not he has the instincts for basketball (which was always a relevant question with the African-born Bol), but rather, whether or not without at least another 50 or more pounds on his lithe frame, he can ever stand up to the nightly pounding that is a hallmark of rugged NBA-style play.

Kevin Bradshaw

Kevin Bradshaw's name has rarely been seen in sports-page headlines, and it has never made waves in the glamorous NBA. But it is featured rather prominently in several places in the NCAA basketball record books. Finishing his career at unheralded U.S. International University (San Diego) after debuting at equally obscure Bethune-Cookman (Daytona Beach, Florida), the 6'6" Bradshaw established a new single-game record for points scored against a major-college opponent when he pumped in 72 versus Loyola-Marymount during the 1991 NCAA campaign. Perhaps the most remarkable feature of Bradshaw's performance was the fact that it occurred in a losing effort, as victorious Loyola-Marymount established the team single-game record with a 186–140 racehorse shootout win. Scoring more than 50 on three other occasions that season, Bradshaw paced the nation in scoring (37.6 points per game); a year earlier he had trailed only Bo Kimble of the same Loyola-Marymount team in the nation's individual scoring derby. With 2,804 career points (12th all time) Bradshaw would earn yet another spot in the record books as the only college player with more than 2,750 career points also to have played for two different schools.

Junior Bridgeman

An eighth overall pick in the 1975 pro draft, Bridgeman quietly posted numbers for scoring (11,517 points and nine straight double-figure seasons) and shooting percentage (both from the field and the free-throw line) that would be a proud accomplishment for any larger-scale NBA superstar. Lost in the lengthy shadows of some more illustrious Milwaukee Bucks teammates (Marques Johnson, Bob Lanier, Sidney Moncrief, Alex English, Bob Dandridge) on some of the league's most solid teams of the late '70s and early '80s, the versatile forward contributed heavily to a pair of Milwaukee ball clubs that twice reached the Eastern Conference finals. As a collegian he also was a consistent winner on powerhouse University of Louisville teams under head coach Denny Crum, all three of which won more than 20 games, and one of which (during his 1975 senior season) reached the elite NCAA Final Four. Although he was a career 1,300-point scorer, Bridgeman's relatively quiet collegiate sojourn at storied Louisville gave little hint of the solid NBA career he was about to log (between 1976 and 1987) after graduating to the professional ranks.

Cindy Brown

A Long Beach State star of the late '80s, Brown entered the record books on February 16, 1987, with an NCAA single-game record 60 points. The mark (achieved with 20 field goals and 20 free throws) came in a 149–69 victory over San Jose State, which saw Long Beach also notch the NCAA one-game team standard for offensive production. Brown's scoring outbursts were not limited to a single game, however, as she also compiled the one-season NCAA points record (974) during the same 1987 campaign. Brown's four-year scoring total (2,696) would also eventually leave her ninth on the all-time career list (fifth at the time of her graduation), while her combined points-rebounds career totals (3,880) remain the sixth highest ever amassed. These were high-water offensive marks sufficient to merit first-team All-American selection in both 1986 and 1987. And Brown's super scoring looks all the more impressive when one remembers that it came a single season before the advent of today's ever-popular three-point shot.

Kobe Bryant

The next beneficiary of the ongoing NBA obsession with marketing its product through glorifying another heir (if not "Air") to the vacated Jordan throne will likely be Los Angeles Lakers prodigy Kobe Bryant. In this sense the gifted son of a former NBA journeyman (Joe "Jelly Bean" Bryant, 1976–83) has already inherited the curse first laid upon Shaquille O'Neal on the eve of Jordan's first retirement and then attached to the rising stars of both Penny Hardaway and Grant Hill in the wake of MJ's return for a several-season extended encore. The hype and hoopla (Kobemania) had indeed already begun with the 1998 NBA All-Star Game telecast, when former NBA stars–turned broadcasters (Isiah Thomas, Bill Walton, and Magic Johnson) sent a barrage of raves over the airwaves almost every time the talented youngster touched the ball. The original script for greatness was written when the 6'6" phenom was drafted directly out of high school (Pennsylvania) by the Charlotte Hornets and then traded immediately to the big-market team in Los Angeles for veteran Vlade Divac. Bryant is, of course, a considerable talent (he can already shoot, drive, dribble, and pass like a top-flight pro), and his lack of any college experience makes his early achievements as a Lakers starter all the more amazing. Early numbers do not exactly shout out true greatness: his rookie scoring average of 7.6 points per game and his accompanying assists (1.3) and rebounds (1.9) marks are almost laughable when compared to another Lakers rookie sensation of the past named Magic Johnson. Yet by being so early anointed as perhaps the next coming of the most celebrated star in league history, it is highly likely that whatever Kobe Bryant achieves throughout his quite-promising NBA career, it will never be quite enough to measure up to runaway expectations.

Jerry Buss and Jack Kent Cooke

Flamboyant real estate mogul Jerry Buss resurrected the fortunes of the Los Angeles Lakers in the late 1970s after that proud franchise had fallen on somewhat hard times for much of the decade between Wilt Chamberlain (L.A.'s first NBA championship in 1972, after seven failures in the final round) and Magic Johnson (the club's second league banner in 1980). More significantly, Buss made a player personnel move after acquiring the Lakers franchise that did much to salvage the entire league and launch it into its era of greatest popularity at the outset of the '80s. That move came in the off-season between the 1981 and 1982 campaigns when the magnate owner inked franchise star Earvin Johnson to a ground-breaking 25-year $25 million contract, which paved the way for future long-term megastar deals which soon reshaped the NBA landscape. With the Magic Johnson deal in his hip pocket the former aerospace scientist (with a USC Ph.D. in chemistry) settled into a two-decade ownership of the Lakers franchise (1979–98), which has witnessed one of the more successful overall runs (five NBA championships and four other title-round appearances) anywhere in professional sports.

Buss is a self-made entrepreneur who started out as a Wyoming ditchdigger in his youth and by middle age had built one of the largest real estate empires along California's Gold Coast. It was, in fact, a pair of real estate empires that actually changed hands back in 1979 with the sale of the Lakers' NBA franchise to Buss. Buss swapped several of his prime holdings—including the Chrysler Building in New York City—for the Los Angeles pro basketball and hockey franchises owned by Canadian multimillionaire Jack Kent Cooke. Cooke sweetened the deal by throwing in the L.A. Fabulous Forum (home arena to the city's NBA and NHL teams) as part of the total package. But in handing over his lucrative sports empire, Cooke also left Buss with another piece of prime property in the form of the playing talents of soon-to-be rookie sensation Earvin "Magic" Johnson.

The Buss-Cooke transaction of 1979 (with a price tag of $67.5 million) had closed the book on a decade that witnessed three drastic overhauls under Cooke of the team's on-court and front-office profiles. Ten years earlier Cooke had trans-formed his ball club (which he had purchased from original Minneapolis owner Bob Short) from yearly bridesmaids into serious title contenders with a deal that had inked oft-traveled Wilt Chamberlain (and paid off with a 1972 championship banner). Five years before relinquishing the team, Cooke had worked yet another blockbuster transaction to again resuscitate his club's sagging fortunes, this time a seven-player swap with Milwaukee's Bucks that landed Kareem Abdul-Jabbar as Chamberlain's adequate successor. And as he prepared to hand over the ball club to Buss, talent-savvy Cooke engineered one final spectacular front-office maneuver that would anchor Lakers fortunes for a full decade to come. Using the first overall pick of the 1979 draft (acquired from New Orleans as compensation for the fateful 1976 free-agent signing of L.A.'s Gail Goodrich), Cooke selected Michigan State sophomore guard Magic Johnson. With that single choice (placed alongside Auerbach's earlier 1978 pick of Indiana State's Larry Bird) a new era was about to dawn, both for the showcase ball club out in Los Angeles and the struggling league as a whole.

John Calipari

John Calipari made headlines when he plucked one of the most lucrative con-tracts ever offered to entice a hot coaching commodity to flee the college ranks for an NBA post. One of the bright young stars in college coaching circles during the early 1990s, Calipari authored a remarkable resurgence for University of Mas-sachusetts basketball, then parlayed his personal successes into a big-bucks deal to coach the long-inept New Jersey Nets franchise in the professional ranks. Eight years on the collegiate circuit (all with Massachusetts) brought almost overnight success that included a half dozen 20-win seasons (two above 30, one at 29, and another at 28), five straight Atlantic Ten championships and corresponding NCAA tourney trips, a .731 winning percentage (193–71), and both a Final Four visit and Coach of the Year plaudits (*Sporting News*) during his final season. Coaching a lackluster NBA roster flooded with overpriced and undermotivated superstars (Kendall Gill, Kerry Kittles, Michael Cage, and Jayson Williams, among others) proved a far stiffer challenge, however, and the perhaps equally overpaid coach struggled his NBA rookie season to a near mirror-image won-lost performance (26–56, .371, fifth place in the Atlantic Division). Using strategies that had worked on intimidated UMass undergraduates—demeaning his players by screaming at them in practice and berating them on the bench—Calipari quickly found that (in one sportswriter's words) the arrogance and massive coach's ego that had often made him a campus success worked against him (and largely sabotaged him) in the talent-rich NBA. John Calipari (who was fired early in the 1999 season) overnight became one NBA big-bucks recruit who had trouble learning the sport's prime lesson—if big-personality coaches rule on the college scene, the NBA is always about the players and almost never about the coach.

Marcus Camby

Calipari's successes at Massachusetts were due as much to the All-American play of center Marcus Camby as to almost any other factor. And the hints of financial impropriety (suggestions he had received gifts from an illegal agent) swirling around Camby when he left campus for the pros may also have had as much influence on Calipari's own flight to New Jersey as did the hefty coaching contract offered by the Nets. Camby, for his own part, was the most lustrous star to perform in a UMass uniform since the school's most famous alumnus, Julius Erving. He was named National Player of the Year for 1996 by several organizations (AP, the National Coaches' Association, and the nation's basketball writers) and also picked up the coveted Naismith and Wooden Awards that same winter. As a unanimous first-team All-American during his junior (final) season, the 6'11" center ranked among the nation's leaders in blocked shots for three seasons and was top scorer and rebounder on the 1996 UMass Final Four team. His first several NBA seasons in Toronto were, in stark contrast, largely a case of unreachable expectations. Despite All-Rookie Team honors his maiden season (14.8 points per game and 6.3 rebounds per game), he hardly stood out as more than run-of-the-mill for such a touted prospect (second overall 1996 draft pick), and a sophomore NBA campaign brought little dramatic improvement on a still-struggling expansion roster. A trade to New York in time for the strike-delayed 1998–99 season, however, held promise of a desperately needed jump start to Camby's short-circuited if still-promising NBA career.

Lou Carnesecca

Twice a National Coach of the Year and also mentor of three NIT semifinalists and one NCAA Final Four entrant, Lou Carnesecca was one of the most storied collegiate mentors in the fabled history of basketball's recognized mecca—New York City. Trained under Joe Lapchick as a nine-year assistant (1957–65), the 1946 St. John's graduate first took over the Redmen (now Red Storm) upon Lapchick's 1965 retirement. He wasted little time in building a legend of his own, which consisted of an eventual 18 20-win seasons in 24 years on the job, NIT or NCAA tournament appearances in every single campaign of his quarter-century career, an uninterrupted string of 24 winning seasons (he never had a losing one), and a sterling .725 career winning percentage (526–200) which is one of the loftiest in NCAA history. The winning percentage was, in the end, even a hair better than the one his mentor Joe Lapchick had compiled throughout his own Hall of Fame tenure. And only eight of the St. John's clubs under his direction ever lost as many as 10 games in a single campaign. A brilliant career was fittingly capped, however, only when Carnesecca was elected to the Naismith Memorial Basketball Hall of Fame in 1991, on the eve of his St. John's retirement.

Pete Carril

If he had coached at Kentucky, Kansas, Indiana, or perhaps North Carolina, Pete Carril would assuredly have been a household name and a living legend within the collegiate coaching fraternity. As it was he built a fairly substantial, if much less advertised, legacy that consisted more of noteworthy underdog achievements than of national championship glories. In 29 seasons as headman at Princeton Pete Carril established a quiet behind-the-scenes record for excellence that left him as the only Division I coach ever to win more than 500 games without benefit of athletic scholarships with which to corral crack athletes. Few ever achieved more with any less: relying year after year on players who were usually physically outmatched by both Ivy League and intersectional opponents, Carril developed a pressing-style defense and methodically patient offense that frequently frustrated and occasionally upset some of the nation's big-reputation powerhouse teams. His 30 seasons brought an overall 525–273 won-lost record, 13 Ivy League crowns, 10 20-win campaigns, and 13 postseason tournament bids.

Carril arrived a handful of seasons too late to enjoy Princeton's biggest star, Bill Bradley, and also the school's best teams that were built around the great All-American and future NBA legend and U.S. senator. But the puckish Carril was never slowed much by a lack of such superstars. His teams suffered only one losing campaign (11–15 in 1985), and he achieved the Ivy League's only NIT championship way back in 1975 (his own eighth season on the job). Election to the Naismith Hall of Fame upon retirement from Princeton hardly marked an end to Carril's inspirational success story. His next stop would be as an assistant coach with the NBA Sacramento Kings, a bench job he accepted in 1996 at the ripe age of 67. It was indeed a ripe age to begin what may prove Carril's biggest career challenge—dealing for the first time with pampered prima donna athletes in a league where ballplayers and not coaches are the entire spectacle.

Joe Barry Carroll

Joe Barry Carroll was built in the mode of an unfortunately all-too-familiar basketball type. He followed in the footsteps of such towering disappointments as Walter Dukes, Darrall Imhoff, Ralph Sampson, Stanley Roberts, and the all-time prototype of the species, Benoit Benjamin. Here was yet another gifted seven-foot center whose bark truly was far worse than his bite—a can't-miss franchise player built on the model of a five-story building, but a good deal softer and less imposing. As a collegian Carroll was a unanimous first-team All-American (1980) and leading scorer (22.3) and rebounder (9.2) for a national third-place team from Purdue. As a pro he was a first overall draft pick by the Golden State Warriors and four times a 20-points-per-game season-long scorer. Yet the team that traded one Hall of Famer (Robert Parish) and the rights to draft another (Kevin McHale) to Red Auerbach in order to pluck Carroll from the draft (one that also featured Darrell Griffith but little else) never got a full return on its investment. Nor—despite 12,000 career points—did the other four NBA franchises (Houston, New Jersey, Denver, and Phoenix) for which the towering Denver native also briefly and inconsistently performed.

Tom Chambers

Chambers, who ranks 24th all time with 20,043 points compiled during 15-plus seasons in the NBA (through 1997), also claimed distinction as the first unrestricted free agent in league history when he left Seattle for the Phoenix Suns in July 1988. The agile 6'10" forward logged five years with Phoenix before moving on to Utah, then a season in Israel, and finally NBA stops in Charlotte and Philadelphia. He boasts a franchise single-game scoring record in Phoenix with 60 points, and for more than a decade he combined outside shooting accuracy with power moves to the hoop (performed with either hand) to rank as one of the league's most productive and inventive all-around scorers. Career highlights came for Chambers in 1987, when he turned in a stellar All-Star Game performance with 34 points on his home floor in Seattle (thus taking MVP honors in the highest-scoring midseason classic ever) and also finished among the league's top dozen scorers for the season (23.3 points per game). With his career virtually at an end early in the 1997–98 season, the former first-round draft pick (eighth overall by San Diego in 1981) was hurriedly dispatched by the Charlotte Hornets to the Philadelphia 76ers in late November after he punched strength and conditioning coach Robin Pound during a heated practice-session altercation. A month later the aging veteran regretfully announced his retirement, thus fading out as far less than the classy team leader he had otherwise been for most of his stellar career.

Calbert Cheaney

Calbert Cheaney owns the distinction of being the top point-scorer (2,613) in Big Ten Conference history. But the Indiana University two-time All-American was far more than just a freewheeling shooter or a freelancing one-on-one school-yard player, a fact not surprising given that his four-year career was spent under hard-nosed coach Bob Knight. His point totals at Indiana were a matter of longevity and not of stratospheric per-game averages, and he received an added boost in the point-making arena from the lengthened schedules of the early 1990s. The Associated Press, *Sporting News*, Wooden, and Naismith Player of the Year in 1993 was, however, as versatile an offensive machine as has ever been seen in Bloomington, specializing in three-pointers (all-time Indiana leader), maintaining an uncanny eye for the basket despite his long-range bombing (second at IU in career field-goal percentage), and proving a paragon of scoring consistency (65 collegiate games with 20-plus points). The rare consistency of Cheaney's offensive production was best demonstrated by his string of 41 straight games in double figures and 58 double-figure outings in his final 59 games at IU. In the end it was perhaps the most telling hallmark of Calbert Cheaney's brilliant Indiana University sojourn, however, that the highest point producer in league history would never win a conference scoring crown, would average less than 20 points per game (19.8) for his four-year stay on the Bloomington campus, and would never post even a single 40-point game. As a collegian Calbert Cheaney always did it in relentless waves and not in bulky bunches. And during the first four campaigns of his relatively quiet NBA career (Washington Wizards), that same low-key consistency has worked to make Cheaney one of the most underrated performers on the professional circuit as well.

Maurice Cheeks

By the end of his 11-year stint with the Philadelphia 76ers in 1989, Mo Cheeks had climbed into the career top 10 list for assists and had, in the process, established a reputation that left him (at the time) only a mere notch below Magic Johnson and Isiah Thomas as the best playmaking guard in the NBA. During the first half of the '80s Cheeks was a key cog on one 76ers team starring Julius Erving and Moses Malone that pulled off only the fourth-ever sweep in NBA Finals history; he was also a vital element on two other Philadelphia squads (1980, 1982) that also reached the postseason championship round. The 6'1" guard out of West Texas State would finish out his pro career in the early 1990s by logging four additional less productive seasons split among San Antonio, New York, Atlanta, and New Jersey. Cheeks completed his NBA sojourn with 12,195 points (11.1 points per game), 7,392 assists, and 2,310 career steals. The latter tally left him as the all-time NBA career steals leader when he retired in 1993, a position of distinction from which he has since been unseated by only John Stockton.

Doug Collins

The pro, college, and coaching careers of Doug Collins have been a roller-coaster ride of some exquisite highs followed by some extreme and even bone-numbing dips. The 1972 Olympian canned a clutch free throw in the waning seconds of the most memorable and controversial gold-medal game on record, then watched in horror with his teammates as a bizarre turn of events and circumstances handed victory to the rival Soviets and thus ended the longtime U.S. domination of the international cage sport. (This was the game in which three seconds were put back on the clock not once, but twice, before the USSR's Aleksander Belov converted a court-length pass into the winning bucket.) Collins's promising NBA career showed brilliant flashes, but in the end, was also short-circuited by repeated nagging injuries. The first overall pick of the 1973 NBA draft, Collins would play in only 415 pro games, enough to establish modest stardom but not enough to post the Hall of Fame numbers and achievements that might have been expected from so gifted an athlete. While healthy, the crack 6'6" sharpshooting guard teamed with Julius Erving,

World Free, George McGinnis, and Darryl Dawkins as a key member of exciting, if not always dominating, Philadelphia 76ers teams in the mid-'70s. His NBA coaching career also consisted of spectacular starts and disastrous terminations. As headman with the Chicago Bulls (1987–89) he stood on the doorstep of a potential dynasty in the late '80s and guided a team featuring Michael Jordan into serious title contention. A strained relationship with the team's superstar led, however, to dismissal after only three roller-coaster seasons. Nearly a decade later he would guide another upcoming team at Detroit graced with another up-and-coming megastar, Grant Hill. But the scenario was soon repeated: after a couple seasons of dramatic progress in the league standings, Collins again wore out his welcome with both his star and his role players and once more quickly found himself on the sidelines. Only in the college ranks did Doug Collins ever seem equipped to ride out the string on top. At Illinois State in the early '70s he was considered one of the purest shooters anywhere in NCAA annals. His senior-season scoring average was above 30 (32.6) and his career mark (29.1) only a fraction under, giving him a pair of the loftiest point-making averages in Division I history.

Jody Conradt

The all-time winningest coach in women's college basketball history and also the first mentor with more than 600 career victories, Jody Conradt has now climbed over the 700-victory plateau and is even within easy striking distance of the 800-win barrier, a rarefied level that would link her with men's legends Adolph Rupp and Dean Smith. She also directed the most successful women's outfit of the 1980s, a Texas Lady Longhorns team that captured nearly 92 percent of its contests during the first eight seasons of women's NCAA tournament competitions (which began in 1982). It was during that mid-career span that Conradt's teams drew the top crowds for women's games anywhere in the land and virtually owned Southwest Conference rivals, at one point winning 188 straight league games without defeat. The peak of this glorious stretch came in 1986 when the Conradt-coached and Clarissa Davis–led Longhorns posted a season's 34–0 mark, and thus became the first women's NCAA champions to boast an unblemished record (a feat matched a decade later by Connecticut and its lanky star Rebecca Lobo). Four of Conradt's players on that team (Kamie Ethridge, Andrea Lloyd, Beverly Williams, and Davis) would eventually be All-Americans, and three would make the next U.S. Olympic team. Personal recognition for Conradt has included National Coach of the Year honors twice (1980, 1986), Southwest Conference Coach of the Year plaudits four times, and a head coaching assignment with the 1987 U.S. Pan American Games squad that brought home a widely expected, but nonetheless cherished, gold-medal victory.

Michael Cooper

For a brief period in the early and mid-1980s Michael Cooper of the Los Angeles Lakers provided NBA fans with high-flying feats and thrills that were almost on a par with those of the young Michael "Air" Jordan, the aging Julius "Dr. J" Erving, or the popular Dominique "Human Highlight Film" Wilkins. He also played a not insignificant role on numerous Lakers teams that were among the strongest in league history. A lowly third-round draft choice out of New Mexico, the 6'6" guard provided valuable sixth-man support on five Lakers world championship teams in the '80s (1980, 1982, 1985, 1987, 1988), also starting 38 games in place of an injured Magic Johnson during a 1981 campaign in which L.A. slipped from contention, yet still won 54 games. A spectacular leaper and scintillating scorer with his highlight-reel slam dunks off of alley-oop passes (his "Coop-a-Loop" shot), Cooper's special forte was, nonetheless, always his defense. Despite the fact that he never scored as many as 20 points in a single NBA game (nor ever averaged more than a dozen), Cooper remained an important cog on L.A. teams that looked to Johnson, Abdul-Jabbar, and Worthy for scoring and to Cooper and Norm Nixon for backcourt pressure defense. Lakers coach Paul Westhead credited Cooper's defensive magic with single-handedly winning as many as a dozen games for the Lakers during his best all-around season in 1981, and he was a regular for a half dozen seasons on NBA first or second All-Defensive Teams. Beat writers and broadcasters tabbed Cooper as the league's top defender in 1987, and he earned first-team defensive honors five times (1982, 1984, 1985, 1987, 1988). Many veteran NBA watchers, in fact, considered Michael Cooper to be the best defensive player on the circuit in the early and mid-'80s, at least until Michael Jordan arrived on the scene.

Bobby Cremins

If Dean Smith was "dean" of ACC coaches in more ways than just his given name, Bobby Cremins is the rising star of the league's coaching fraternity. Having been raised upon Tobacco Road mania as a starter for the potent 1969 and 1970 South Carolina ball clubs coached by Frank McGuire, the Bronx native would return to the league in 1982 when he took over a floundering Georgia Tech program that was struggling for some measure of respectability just two seasons after entering the minefield of ACC competition. If Cremins did not inherit a wealth of talent when he came to Tech from his first post at Appalachian State, he did inherit 1983 ACC Rookie of the Year Mark Price and a second talented freshman named John Salley. With those building blocks the energetic Cremins produced a winning team (18–11) that almost broke even in league play (6–8) in only his third season. By his fourth campaign (with Price and Salley now juniors) he would claim the school's first regular-season and postseason ACC crowns; a year later he would author a second straight 27-win campaign and a second consecutive NCAA appearance. The Bobby Cremins era was, almost overnight, well on its way to becoming the most glorious epoch of the entire Georgia Tech basketball saga.

In his decade and a half as an ACC mentor the former South Carolina star has already climbed straight to the top of the heap at Georgia Tech, overhauling Whack Hyder in 1996 as the school's winningest-ever basketball mentor. And almost as quickly, he has also climbed the success ladder in the ACC, where he now stands in the top five in career league victories (he moved into fourth slot ahead of Lefty Driesell during the recent 1999 season) and where his three ACC tournament trophies are second only to Dean Smith among all active coaches. The success has been almost nonstop for Cremins and his Tech teams since the sudden turnaround of his third season. There have been 13 straight years of postseason tournament

*Bobby Cremins,
Georgia Tech*

© Georgia Tech University

action (1984 and 1994 in the NIT and the remainder in the NCAAs). More than half of these campaigns (7) have featured 20-win seasons; there have been only three losing ACC ledgers (1991, 1994, 1999) during the entire span; top-flight recruiting has brought seven league Rookies of the Year to the Atlanta campus in only 12 seasons; Tech's brilliant 1990 ball club rode its "Lethal Weapons III" offense all the way to a Final Four berth as NCAA Southeast Regional champions.

Such success breeds itchy feet, and Tech and the league nearly lost their whiz-kid coach in the early '90s when Cremins flirted briefly with an opportunity to return to his alma mater as the head coach at South Carolina. But having ultimately renewed his commitment at the ACC school, Cremins has already launched a second phase of heroics highlighted by a trip to the NCAA Midwest Regional semifinals in 1992, a third league tournament title in 1993, and a second regular-season championship during the 1996 campaign. And with the continued winning has come the continued displays of high-potency offense that have always made Cremins-coached teams among the most exciting anywhere in the land. Sharpshooting guards have been a special staple for Cremins and his program down through the years, stretching from stellar rookie Mark Price in 1983 (the league's first rookie scoring champion) all the way to another remarkable freshman named Stephon Marbury in 1996. In between have come Dennis Scott, who alternated at the guard and forward slots while he paced the "Lethal Weapons III" unit as well as the entire league in marksmanship (27.7 points per game) in 1990; repeat All-American Kenny Anderson, who burned the nets at better than 25 a game in 1991; first-round NBA draft choice Travis Best, a 20-point scorer as a senior and also the school's career assists leader; and Stephon Marbury, who flashed the highest level of rookie brilliance the league had seen since Mark Price before departing after a single season for the lure of instant NBA dollars. Under Cremins the stars keep coming in seemingly endless supply. And so do the victories and the thrills.

Charlie Criss

Alongside Calvin Murphy, Spud Webb, and Muggsy Bogues in the imaginary pantheon of basketball's notable oversized "little men" stands 5'8" Charlie Criss, once owner of a 72-point game in the Eastern Basketball League and also author of some especially memorable NBA moments that might well have distinguished the career of any player a full foot or more taller. The pint-sized point guard out of New Mexico State, who played 418 games in the NBA with Atlanta, San Diego, and Milwaukee between 1977 and 1985, twice logged enough playing time and launched enough shots (1978 as a rookie and again four seasons later) to average in double figures as a scorer. But it was the final dozen and a half games of his career and their special circumstances that were attention-grabbing. Criss had hung up his sneakers at Milwaukee shortly after the opening of the 1983–84 season when it became clear he no longer had the speed or fire to play in the league at his reduced size. He did return briefly later in that same season for nine games of emergency duty with his original team in Atlanta. The popular athlete then settled into a comfortable role for 1984–85 as an analyst for Hawks television broadcasts. But the on-court career of Charlie Criss would not die quietly. When a trio of Atlanta guards (Eddie Johnson, Mike Glenn, and Doc Rivers) all went down with injuries, coach Mike Fratello turned to a familiar source for help. Pressed again into unexpected duty Charlie Criss played 29 minutes in one game with Dallas, dealing 11 assists, and started another in which he logged 45 of the overtime game's 53 minutes. In all, he logged four contests and, in the process, became the only man in NBA history to work in the TV booth one night and suit up on the playing floor the next.

Denny Crum

Denny Crum's accomplished coaching career started in the shadows of the game's greatest bench legend—John Wooden—but didn't remain out of the main spotlight very long. For six seasons Crum was Wooden's able assistant and the two often clashed over matters of substitutions and strategy, most notably during the 1971 Final Four in the Houston Astrodome just before Crum's departure for his own head coaching post in Louisville. Crum quickly managed to climb at least partway out from under the long shadows cast by his giant mentor, winning a pair of NCAA championships himself (1980, with Darrell Griffith as his star, and 1986, with freshman sensation Pervis Ellison) as headman for the University of Louisville Cardinals. If he never quite lived up to the standards of John Wooden, however, it would have to be said that he came just about as close as any other NCAA coaching legend of the past quarter-century. In addition to the two NCAA crowns his teams would reach the Final Four on four other occasions: the first time came in his rookie season at the helm and thus allowed a semifinals shoot-out with his former boss (who now had sophomore Bill Walton to squash all challengers). One huge disappointment in Crum's career came with the shocking loss of the gold-medal shoot-out by the Pan American Games squad he coached in 1987 in Indianapolis. It was the defeat by Brazil of that pre-Olympic team with All-American David Robinson in the lineup that marked one of the lowest points of U.S. national team play and set thoughts drifting toward the idea of an NBA Dream Team to carry the national banner. But if there was disappointment a decade ago in Indianapolis, there were plenty of heady achievements before and after to balance the ledger. With 625 career wins and counting, the 27-year head-coaching veteran now stands within perhaps only two seasons of overhauling even the legendary John Wooden in the all-time victories column.

Terry Cummings

It was 13 full seasons after Lew Alcindor turned the trick in 1969–70 before another rookie stood in the NBA top 10 in both rebounding and scoring. That was the considerable feat Terry Cummings accomplished with the San Diego Clippers in 1982–83 by logging 23.7 points per game (10th) and 10.6 rebounds per game while garnering Freshman of the Year accolades in a tight race with Indiana's Clark Kellogg. Unfortunately for the small handful of existing Clippers boosters, it was a season that represented a career high point rather than a mere foreshadow of future expanded greatness, and two seasons down the road the second overall draft pick was traded away to Milwaukee. Not that Cummings entirely faded from the scene or dipped horribly in productivity. He maintained a scoring average above or near 20 over his first eight seasons, eventually climbed close to the 20,000 (18,355 after 1998) career scoring plateau, logged five moderately successful seasons in both Milwaukee and San Antonio, and was several times an All-Star (1985, 1989) and All-NBA selection (1985 second team, 1989 third team). With a lethal combination of quickness, strength, and inside scoring ability, Cummings remained a league force on middle-of-the-pack teams for well over a decade. But his game always disappointed at the defensive end of the floor, and after a bang-up award-winning rookie season, Terry Cummings never again was a pacesetter in any of the NBA's numerous categories for individual or team honors.

Denise Curry

The single UCLA court star to log 3,000-plus points in a brilliant NCAA career was neither Lew Alcindor nor Bill Walton (nor Gail Goodrich, Henry Bibby, or Richard Washington). The rare feat falls instead to Denise Curry, a 6'1" forward who starred for the Bruins' 1978 AIAW national championship team as a freshman, then reached personal milestones across the next three seasons, which included a collegiate record feat of scoring in double figures for all 130 of her college games. Curry's 1,310 career rebounds (allowing for weaker competition under the boards and an extra year of varsity competition) nearly match the three-year career totals of both Alcindor (1,367) and Walton (1,370). If Curry is in a class by herself when it comes to UCLA milestones, she stands in rare company as well when it comes to the national women's arena. For starters, her career scoring total tops that of the current NCAA record holder Patricia Hoskins of Mississippi Valley (unfortunately, NCAA individual records only date from 1982, the season after Curry's career closed out in Westwood); she was a three-time Kodak All-American and twice carried her team to the AIAW national tournament; and she still holds 14 UCLA individual basketball records. All this came in an era that also featured such legends of the women's game as Anne Donovan (Old Dominion), Carol Blazejowski (Montclair State), Cheryl Miller (USC), and fellow UCLA standout Ann Meyers.

Adrian Dantley

Among the NBA's most prolific scorers, only a trio has matched or surpassed Adrian Dantley's rare feat of averaging 30-plus in scoring for four or more consecutive seasons. Jordan and Chamberlain each turned the trick seven years running, while Oscar Robertson checks in with four such high-number seasons to exactly match Dantley's total. Such Hall of Famers as Kareem, Jerry West, Baylor, Pettit, and Dr. J were never able to match such high-scoring consistency, nor were such modern-epoch or past-era renowned gunners as Bob McAdoo (who had only 3), Alex English (never topped 30), George Gervin (none consecutively), or Dominique Wilkins (3 straight over 29). Although Dantley's massive career scoring was able to lift him into the league's all-time top 10 with more than 23,000 points by the end of his 15-season, seven-team career, few would wish to rank Dantley as an offensive force or all-around league star of the same order as Wilt, MJ, or the Big O. But a steady average of a frac-

Adrian Dantley, Buffalo Braves

From the author's collection

tion over 30 between 1981 and 1984 while playing for the Utah Jazz nonetheless provided the shifty 6'5" forward with an indelible place among the game's most memorable point-making machines.

Dantley's individual trophies were certainly numerous enough: two All-American seasons at Notre Dame, NBA Rookie of the Year accolades (1977 with Buffalo), two NBA scoring titles (1981 and 1984), plus six All-Star and two All-NBA selections. But so were his liabilities, which remained obvious for all his basket-making: his slowness of foot made him worthless to teams with legitimate running games, he never contributed to championship teams (he came closest when Detroit reached the NBA Finals his last season with the Pistons), and his reported sour attitude and lack of team play seemingly played a role in his eventually being dumped by three different teams (Utah, Dallas, Detroit) that had originally acquired him at considerable cost for his potent offensive game. On the whole it has to be admitted that no other 6'5" player was ever more artful at manufacturing baskets from a low-post position. But it was an art that brought Adrian Dantley less stature than perhaps any other NBA mainstay who ever climbed over the career 20,000-point plateau.

Clarissa Davis

The University of Texas Longhorns coached by Jody Conradt were a dominant team in women's NCAA play throughout the decade of the '80s. During the first eight seasons of women's NCAA competition, beginning in 1982, Texas was the winningest team in Division I, capturing nearly 92 percent of its regular-season and postseason games. A large part of the reason for such invulnerability was 6'1" forward Clarissa Davis, a talented gunner who paced Conradt's team to a 124–10 overall record during the four seasons between 1985 and 1989. The Davis era at Texas included an unbeaten 1986 season (34–0) and featured the school's only national championship that same winter, when Davis, as a freshman, captured Final Four MVP honors. In one celebrated game Davis popped in 45 points as a sophomore in an upset of top-ranked Tennessee before 24,563 fans in Knoxville (a worldwide attendance record for women's basketball). For both her sophomore and senior seasons the Longhorns ace also earned Naismith Player of the Year accolades to join Cheryl Miller, Dawn Staley, and Chamique Holdsclaw as the only multiple winners of that prestigious honor. And she also averaged 19.9 points and 8.7 rebounds across four stellar seasons, despite the fact that a severe knee injury dramatically slowed her junior-year performance and restricted her to only nine games that season. Even with one campaign largely relegated to injury rehab, the third-best scorer in UT history was also able to amass more career points than anyone else in Southwest Conference women's action.

Darryl Dawkins

Darryl Dawkins is destined to live on in basketball legend as the powerful slammer who once provided one of the most destructive single dunk shots in all of basketball history. In the process Dawkins brought the collapsible rim into the pro and college game and also glamorized the now-popular "TV Sports Center" highlight moment featuring glass-shattering backboard destruction. But the muscular, fun-loving Dawkins was also a most special pro basketball pioneer in still another important sense. Dawkins was one of the earliest to step directly from the high school court

*Darryl Dawkins,
Philadelphia 76ers*

© Frank P. McGrath Jr.

straight into the talent-rich NBA. Although literally hundreds of colleges descended on Orlando's Maynard Evans High School back in 1975 with unlimited scholarship offers for the 6'11" teenage star, Dawkins boldly decided that his game was already too advanced to belong anywhere except with the super-talented and super-physical professionals. The Philadelphia 76ers agreed by making the young Dawkins the first high school player ever chosen in the first round of the NBA talent draft.

Virginia high-schooler Moses Malone had also signed on directly with the pros by inking a contract with the rival ABA only a season earlier. Lesser-known Bill Willoughby would also graduate directly from scholastic play in New Jersey to the Atlanta Hawks the same winter as Dawkins. In subsequent seasons Malone would earn his stripes as an NBA Hall of Famer while Willoughby would never rise above obscurity, despite eight NBA seasons with six different teams. Dawkins would fall somewhere in between, averaging double figures as a scorer for nine straight years with Philadelphia and New Jersey, and pulling down more than 500 rebounds on five different occasions. But there were no All-Star selections or other individual honors to distinguish a journeyman's career. There was, nonetheless, a single moment in the video spotlight that forever set Darryl Dawkins apart from the ordinary and the nondescript.

One night at the beginning of his fifth pro season the giant 76ers center surprisingly earned a unique spot in basketball's lore and legend. The first to smash a backboard or rip down a rim during NBA action had actually been a muscular forward in the 1960s named Gus Johnson. Honeycomb Johnson's rare feat of destruction came with a preseason exhibition slam during his 1963 rookie year in Baltimore. But in an era when the NBA (despite Wilt and Oscar) was still back-page news, the feat went virtually unnoticed. Such was not the case in November 1979 when Dawkins provided backboard bending with its first prime-time exposure. It happened less than a minute into the third quarter of a game at Kansas City. And it happened so fast that anyone in the grandstands who might have blinked missed the entire spectacle. Dawkins swept at the hoop from the right side and slammed home one of his bone-jarring dunks. But this time the backboard simply exploded under the force of the awesome attack and glass splinters rained down on Dawkins and the playing floor around him. A stunned defender, veteran forward Bill Robinzine of the Kings, along with a collection of courtside spectators, all scurried to escape the sudden shower of glittering shards.

Dawkins was as famous around the NBA circuit for his witty and glib boasts as he was for his power moves to the hoop. On this occasion he would explain to the press that an uncontrollable force of "Chocolate Thunder" had somehow escaped from his body. A week later the poetic basketballer came up with another fitting description of his memorable slam, dubbing it a "Chocolate-Thunder-Flying, Robinzine-Crying, Teeth-Shaking, Glass-Breaking, Rump-Roasting, Bun-Toasting, Wham-Bam, Glass-Breaker-I-Am Jam."

Johnny Dawkins

Johnny Dawkins seems the odd man out in the pantheon of immortal Duke cage stars. Here, after all, is the school's all-time leading scorer (total points) and the No. 2 point-maker in ACC history. Here also is one of six Blue Devils down through the years to cop National Player of the Year honors, the fourth of the post-ACC era. But it is Christian Laettner, Danny Ferry, Grant Hill, and Art Heyman who draw the bulk of the nostalgic reminiscences among Duke supporters. Laettner's postseason heroics will perhaps account for one of these shifts in emphasis away from a player of Dawkins's caliber. The others remain a bit more mysterious. The teams on which Dawkins played—at least until his senior season—may not have earned as many headlines. But his senior ball club was the second-winningest in school history (37–3) and did make it to the national title game. And no one on that 1986 team was more often at center stage than backcourt wizard Johnny Dawkins. It was that year when he ran his NCAA-record string for double-figure scoring to 127 games. It was also that senior season when Dawkins became the first two-time consensus All-American in school history.

If the perch Dawkins owns atop the school scoring list was in part earned mainly through longevity (few early stars played as many as four varsity seasons), nonetheless there is something to be said for night-in and night-out game-long and yearlong consistency. While the point totals posted by Dawkins were never sensational like those of Virginia's Buzz Wilkinson or South Carolina's Grady Wallace or Clemson's Butch Zatezalo, they were, nevertheless, relentless. The District of Columbia native would become the first player since accurate records were launched at the end of the '40s to pace Duke in scoring during four different varsity seasons. Across that long stretch his average rarely varied from the range of 18 to 20 points per contest. And Johnny Dawkins was more than just another wild shooter. He was also a talented floor general who intelligently ran Coach K's patterned offense to a perfect tee. With a hunger for the pressure-filled heroics of late-game situations, this clutch player made the deciding play in all four Duke contests decided by less than two points during the charmed 1986 season. John Dawkins was perhaps the closest thing Duke has ever had to Carolina's incomparable Phil Ford.

Anne Donovan

Overlapping for one season in 1980, All-Americans Nancy Lieberman and Anne Donovan led their team at Old Dominion (which also included a third All-American, Inge Nissen) to a repeat AIAW national championship and at the same time provided perhaps the best one-two punch ever to grace the court for women's collegiate play. Donovan, for her part, was a huge (especially for her era) 6'8" center who averaged 20 points and 14.5 rebounds over her entire career, which began with the 1980 title season and ended in 1984 as the school's all-time leading scorer and rebounder. She was the first effective "truly big player" on the women's scene and thus a female counterpart to DePaul's George Mikan or Oklahoma A&M's Bob Kurland 35 years earlier on the men's scene. The 1983 National Player of the Year would cap her career with an Olympic gold medal earned at the 1984 summer games in Los Angeles.

Clyde Drexler (NBA "Top 50" Selection)

The most sensational one-on-one player in Portland NBA history, the high-flying Clyde Drexler first gained wide notoriety as a sensational slam dunker with an early '80s Houston University team that also featured Akeem (later Hakeem) Olajuwon and twice reached the NCAA Final Four. Known mainly for his artistic and often breathtaking dunks, the 6'7" guard was long considered the league's closest parallel to Michael Jordan. If he never did catch Air Jordan's soaring star, he did, nonetheless, evolve quickly into one of the league's most consistent and productive offensive performers. After a decade of sensational and entertaining seasons he topped the franchise record books in numerous offensive categories: games, minutes, points (18,040), offensive rebounds (5,339), and even steals (1,795). Twice in three seasons of the early '90s Drexler paced his team to the championship finals only to be disappointed on both occasions—in 1990 versus the Detroit Pistons and 1992 against the Chicago Bulls. A career highlight moment seemed to come with the head-to-head showdown with Jordan at the end of the 1992 playoff derby. It was, in the end, a disastrous confrontation for Drexler, who was beaten individually

*Clyde Drexler,
Portland Trail Blazers*

© Frank P. McGrath Jr.

(Jordan outpointed Drexler 46–30 in Game 5 after blitzing him 39–16 in the opening contest) while his team was also being rudely manhandled (4–2) by Jordan's juggernaut. Throughout his career Drexler has never shrunk from such challenges, however, nor from bouncing back from their aftermath. Clyde enjoyed three remarkable late-career seasons (maintaining his lofty scoring when reunited with Olajuwon) after a trade sent him to Houston just in time to enjoy an NBA championship, while the temporarily unretired Jordan sat home on the sidelines in Chicago. But perhaps the biggest challenge still lies around the corner in the form of a postretirement assignment as the new head coach of his old college team, the Houston Cougars, a program which of late has fallen on the hardest of times.

Charles "Lefty" Driesell

Maryland's Lefty Driesell always seemed something of an outsider within ACC circles. He has appeared to his sternest critics as a stark contradiction to the league's announced public image (one often belying its true identity) for squeaky cleanness and unquestioned integrity. If his teams won more than they lost, they were always, nonetheless, seemingly plagued by scandal or unsavory rumor and dogged by bouts of ill luck. When he announced on the occasion of getting the Maryland job in 1969 that his goal was to build the ACC also-ran into "the UCLA of the East," the boast was received in most quarters as naive braggadocio likely to inflame all future opponents. If he soon built powerhouse teams they were seemingly always ones that were certain to quickly self-destruct. He always stood near the top of the pack, but he was never a sentimental favorite anywhere outside of College Park. And even if ecstatic fans paraded him around Cole Fieldhouse when his club upset league power South Carolina in 1971, he wasn't necessarily always a wildly popular figure, even on his own home turf.

In the end Driesell's Maryland career would go up in smoke just as many had long predicted it would. It was the same fate that had awaited Ohio State's legendary football mentor, Woody Hayes, and the one that many still believe lies at the end of the road for Indiana's equally flammable Bob Knight. Constant brushes with disaster seemed to have an inevitable cumulative effect. When Len Bias died suddenly of a lethal cocaine overdose in June 1986 (immediately after being picked No. 2 by Boston in the NBA draft), and the tragic events on the Maryland campus were front-page news everywhere around the country, there was sudden and intense scrutiny of every corner of the beleaguered athletic program at College Park. A win-at-all-costs mentality had apparently led to numerous irregularities that ran the gamut from questionable recruitment tactics to shady academic standards to lax supervision for pampered star athletes. Driesell couldn't survive the heat of the scandal, whatever his direct involvements might have been, and he was forced out the door along with athletic director Dick Dull. It was not the end of the road on the collegiate scene for the resilient Driesell; only an end to the limelight cast by super-conference status. Three seasons later the indefatigable coach was back on the job at James Madison University building still another consistent winner.

But there was still much to brag about in Driesell's tenure at Maryland, despite the spate of innuendo, criticism, and 11th-hour failures. There had been overall career winning percentages at Maryland (.686) and at earlier and later posts with Davidson (.730) and James Madison (.643 through 1995) that left the one-time Duke player (he had suited up for Hal Bradley during the first-ever ACC season) among the career winning-percentage leaders in both the league and the nation as a whole. Only Smith and McGuire at Carolina and Krzyzewski at Duke have ever won more regular-season ACC games, although Bobby Cremins will soon occupy Driesell's fourth-place slot on the all-time conference winners list. There were 10 20-victory seasons at Maryland (4 straight in one stretch and 3 straight in another) and 2 more that fell only a single victory shy of that yardstick standard. There were also a pair of league championships, a dozen or so great players produced (Bias, John Lucas, and Tom McMillen head the list), and numerous NCAA postseason visits. There was also an NIT championship in only his third season on the job at Maryland. That win made Lefty the first ACC coach ever to capture a title in the fabled National Invitation Tournament, a fact of some import, even if the Madison Square Garden event had already lost much of its luster from earlier decades. Driesell may have failed at the highest levels almost as much as he triumphed. But the victories were frequent enough and impressive enough, nevertheless, to leave one of the league's most colorful and controversial figures high on the list of the ACC's biggest overall achievers.

Joe Dumars

The late-'80s Detroit Pistons "Bad Boys" drew most of their headlines based on the images of high-profile stars like Isiah Thomas, Dennis Rodman, Mark Aguirre, Vinnie Johnson, and John Salley, along with reputed cage thugs like Bill Laimbeer and Rick Mahorn. But there is little doubt that the 1989 and 1990 Detroit championship teams would not have rested on top of the heap without the steady leadership and stellar all-around guard play provided by backcourt ace Joe Dumars. Through much of his early career Dumars played in the shadow of Isiah Thomas; in the twilight of his brilliant pro sojourn he is again overshadowed by new franchise star Grant Hill. But it is an unavoidable observation that Detroit's late-'80s NBA resurgence coincided precisely with the arrival of Joe Dumars as the No. 18 overall pick (out of McNeese State) in the 1985 NBA player lottery. The ball club's 46 wins and second-place Central Division finish of his rookie outing would mark the second season of a nine-year glory run under coach Chuck Daly with Dumars and Thomas as the main fixtures. Starting with Dumars's second campaign the club went five straight seasons with better than 50 victories and reached the NBA Finals three times during that span. The highlight year for both the Pistons and Joe Dumars came in 1988–89 when the veteran guard's stellar floor generalship and heavy scoring (17.6 points per game in the playoffs) earned individual NBA Finals MVP honors and also the first league title in franchise history.

Tim Duncan

The ACC has produced more than its share of pro superstars, and Tim Duncan boasts excellent credentials for eventually joining the NBA roster of stellar Tobacco Road alumni. A native of the Virgin Islands, the 6'10" Wake Forest center proved a modern-day rarity among undergraduate phenoms by opting to play out his full four years of college eligibility in the ACC, despite a golden opportunity to declare early in 1996 for a dollar-rich NBA draft in which he almost certainly would have been the No. 1 overall choice as a junior. The decision to remain at Wake Forest never resulted in a coveted NCAA title or even a hoped-for Final Four visit, but neither did it diminish by much, if anything, the stock of the 1997 Collegiate Player of the Year. Duncan, who became the draft plumb of the rebuilding San Antonio Spurs in June 1997 (top overall lottery pick as expected), teamed as a rookie with David Robinson in what was easily the most imposing NBA front wall in years. Rookie of the Year honors were a foregone conclusion, but Duncan's surprise nomination to the All-NBA first team made him the first novice to capture that honor since Larry Bird. The sensational rookie-season results now have the Spurs' top prospect perfectly positioned to demonstrate that the earlier decision to defer his NBA debut was a well-considered gamble indeed.

Mark Eaton

Mark Eaton was something of a modern-era NBA version of 1940s Oklahoma A&M star Bob Kurland. He plugged driving lanes with his bulk, intimidated offensive rebounders as much as he intimidated shooters, and earned his keep by swatting away or deflecting numerous enemy shots at the basket. And also like Kurland, Eaton did surprisingly less scoring (he never reached an average of double figures) than might have been expected from a 7'4" behemoth with considerable range and mobility. In two brief seasons at UCLA he recorded less than 200 minutes of playing time and averaged less than a bucket per game. As a dozen-year pro, however, he developed rapidly into one of the most devastating shot blockers in basketball history. In his first 10 NBA seasons (all with Utah) Eaton never finished lower than seventh in shot-blocking numbers. He set a league record with 456 rejections in 1985 and was the league's Defense Player of the Year in 1985 and again four seasons later. Only in his 11th campaign did he fail to record 100 blocks for the first time. Few teams have ever gotten quite such mileage or production as Utah once did out of an unheralded collegian snagged late in the fourth round (72nd player taken overall) of the annual talent lottery.

Sean Elliott

Few of the top collegiate honors escaped the brilliant University of Arizona career enjoyed by 1989 National Player of the Year Sean Elliott. As a senior the 6'8" forward captured the Wooden Award as well as additional prestigious Player of the Year designations from the Associated Press and National Association of Basketball Coaches. In both that final season and the preceding one he was named a unanimous first-team All-American. His performance as leading scorer and rebounder for the 1988 Arizona Final Four squad (35–3, second in the AP and UPI polls, and loser to Oklahoma in the semis) also earned selection to the NCAA All-Tournament team. And for icing on the cake, in his final year with Arizona he also broke Lew Alcindor's Pac-10 record with 2,555 career points. As reward for such stellar campus performances, Elliott was selected as a third overall draft choice by San Antonio, despite questions about an injured knee and consequent pro durability. Once with the pros, this versatile small forward—built after the model of Scottie Pippen—would again prove a solid scorer with an unlimited arsenal, a better-than-expected rebounder, and a standout defender. But his nine seasons with San Antonio and Detroit have, nonetheless, so far failed to produce even a single All-League selection and have only led to two All-Star Game token appearances.

Dale Ellis

Three-point shooting has never had a more proficient practitioner than much-traveled NBA veteran Dale Ellis. The league's all-time leader in career "treys" has now extended his pro career to 15 seasons and counting with his uncanny long-range accuracy and his ability to provide instant firepower off the bench. The ninth overall choice in the 1983 collegiate draft was a two-time All-American and proficient 20-plus scorer in his final pair of SEC seasons at Tennessee.

With first Dallas and then Seattle, the 6'7" forward continued to display a deft shooting touch that made him a 20-point scorer for four straight years after joining the Sonics in his fourth season. His present-day reputation as a three-point specialist first gained widespread dissemination with a victory in the AT&T Long Distance Shootout competition on All-Star Weekend of 1989; by winning the fourth annual competition Ellis broke Larry Bird's secure grip on the first three years of the popular All-Star Saturday three-point event. Pro honors along the way have also included NBA Most Improved Player (1987) and an All-NBA third team selection (1989). One vital footnote to Dale Ellis's tireless career is that he also holds a league single-game record for most minutes played, with an exhausting 69 logged during a marathon extra-session contest in November 1989 between Seattle and Milwaukee.

Pervis Ellison

A tiny handful of freshmen have made major impacts on the NCAA Final Four weekend, which is still college basketball's biggest showcase event, and "Never-Nervous Pervis" Ellison of Louisville's 1986 national champions stands among the most successful of the lot. Arnie Ferrin had paced Utah's all-freshman lineup of NCAA champions way back in 1944; later, Michael Jordan launched a career of seemingly endless heroics with a championship-winning last-second heave in 1982; and Patrick Ewing had almost as large an impact on the 1982 title shoot-out contest as did North Carolina's Jordan. MJ's jump shot with 16 ticks remaining decided the affair, but Ewing, with 23 points (and a game-best 11 rebounds), battled Carolina scoring star James Worthy to a draw and kept the game close to the wire. Ellison would shine every bit as brightly during his own freshman moment in the NCAA limelight. His 25 points (after averaging only 13 for the season) and 11 boards overwhelmed the more balanced Duke attack and authored a tight 72–69 win over the favored Blue Devils. The ice-water-veined frosh sank the crucial free throws with 27 seconds remaining and the national championship squarely on the line. As his reward he was named the first freshman Final Four MVP since Ferrin. But unfortunately for Ellison, for Louisville, and for the NBA teams (Sacramento, Washington, Boston) that would later employ him, the freshman heroics of more than a decade ago provided the apex of an otherwise disappointing career. A season's average of 20 for Washington in his third campaign earned NBA Most Improved Player accolades. But his scoring, rebounding, and playing time numbers have all dipped radically since then, and in recent campaigns the journeyman role player has known only a handful of individual nights when he has been able to crack double figures as a scorer or attract even passing notice with his brief trips off the Boston bench.

Alex English

Denver's top franchise star was one of the quietest (almost unnoticed) all-time greats in the five decades of NBA action. A relentless shooter, Alex English climbed up the list of the league's most productive scorers without ever leading his team very far toward the playoff Promised Land, or without ever turning heads among the league's fans anywhere that was more than a stone's throw from Denver, Colorado. But if he was never flashy, he was always deadly as a point-maker and durable as a night-in and night-out fixture in the Denver lineup during every season of the 1980s, winding up among the NBA's top 10 in games played (seventh at the time of his retirement), field-goal attempts (fifth), and total points (seventh with 25,613). In his entire decade-long stretch with Denver he never missed more than two games in a season; only once did he dip below 25 points per game (23.8 in 1981); he, not surprisingly, became the all-time franchise leader in scoring, and also set the club career record for assists. For nine full seasons (the entire span of the '80s) he averaged more than 25 points per game for the Nuggets and eight times he was a league All-Star selection. It was all enough to earn a deserved slot in the Naismith Memorial Hall of Fame six years after his retirement (1997). But it was also all done inconspicuously enough that he would be left off the league's Golden Anniversary all-time top 50 list, being bypassed for such flamboyant current-era stars (with far fewer statistical credentials) as Scottie Pippen, Shaquille O'Neal, and Clyde Drexler.

Patrick Ewing (NBA "Top 50" Selection)

Patrick Ewing was the prize of the NBA's first-ever draft lottery in 1985, and while he has never led the New York Knicks to an NBA championship, nonetheless the prize pick of a dozen-plus years ago has proven his incalculable worth as one of the most productive and hardest-working centers of the modern era. Indeed, Ewing is undoubtedly the best-ever New York draft choice, and this with a franchise that for years was plagued by its laughingstock failures at the draft-day table (recall, for example, Irwin Dambrot in 1950, Walter Dukes in 1953, Brendon McCann in 1957, Darrall Imhoff in 1960, Paul Hogue in 1962, Jim Barnes in 1964, and Tom Riker in 1972).

There are only a few true "franchise" players left in today's NBA, especially since Jordan decided not to answer the bell for yet another season in Chicago once the labor-strife-delayed 1998–99 season opened for business. There is Olajuwon in Houston and David Robinson in San Antonio and perhaps the two-headed monster of Malone and Stockton in Utah; after that, Ewing alone answers the billing. New York has built its still-

Patrick Ewing, New York Knicks

© Frank P. McGrath Jr.

unfulfilled championship dreams around a single towering figure who perhaps comes closer than anyone to being a true "complete package" when it comes to pivot play. Patrick Ewing swats away shots from enemy bombers, he sweeps the boards clean at both ends of the floor (he paced the league at the defensive end in 1993, his only individual championship), he intimidates enemy forwards and guards who try to drive through the lanes, he inittates fast breaks with pinpoint outlet passes that remind old-timers of Bill Russell, and he is nearly unstoppable when he goes one-on-one against rival centers within dunking range of the bucket. Along-side all these considerable positives is the realization for Knicks fans and man-agement that Ewing is now in the twilight of his career (he turned 35 on the eve of the 1998–99 season); he has, time and again, been unable, without better rein-forcements, to carry the Knicks beyond the Bulls or Pacers in the Eastern Confer-ence postseason chase, and his one NBA Finals shootout with Olajuwon back in 1994 may well have been his last. A wrist injury that kept him on the bench for most of the 1998 season didn't add any optimism.

Ewing has, nonetheless, won many accolades and honors during a brilliant collegiate career at Georgetown and his 13-season sojourn with the Knicks. In the NBA he has been the league's Rookie of the Year, All-NBA First (once) and Sec-ond Team (six times), and All-Defensive Second Team. He pocketed an NCAA championship and carried his John Thompson–coached college team to the national title game in three of his four undergraduate years. He has averaged above 20 as a scorer in each and every NBA campaign and has now climbed above 22,000 career points (cracking the all-time top 20). He owns two Olympic gold medals and anchored the original 1992 U.S. Dream Team. All that seems to remain is the coveted NBA championship ring, and that is one elusive prize that Ewing (like Bob Lanier, the great unrewarded center of two decades back) will now likely have to settle for living without.

Steve Fisher

Michigan's coaching hero of the late 1980s arrived on the scene in a flash of bril-liant (and even more surprising) success, then slowly wore out his welcome with increasing charges of recruiting improprieties and also a questionable ability to properly coddle his several recruiting classes of unproductive underachievers. No other coach, however, ever broke onto the scene with more pressure-packed atten-tion or enjoyed more immediate championship success. At the end of his first six games as a head coach Steve Fisher earned a national championship—a quirk of fate and fortune that will more than likely never again be duplicated.

Fisher's career as a head coach began with the rarest piece of good luck (for him as well as for a crisis-plagued Michigan program) when he was handed the reins of a talented squad in March 1989, which was already holding on to an announced NCAA berth. When Michigan officials dismissed head coach Bill Frieder—who had prematurely announced on the eve of the postseason tournament that he was heading to Arizona State for the upcoming season—and installed his longtime assistant in his slot, it was Fisher who stoically got the job done under unprecedented circumstances. What might have been an altogether demoralized Michigan outfit was overnight inspired by its new leader and immediately pulled off a postseason miracle run (culminating with a dramatic overtime win against Seton Hall) that brought the Wolverines their only national title. Fisher, at dizzying speed, thus became the only coach to capture an NCAA postseason crown before ever losing his first game.

A mere three seasons later Steve Fisher was back with a vengeance on the wings of his "Fab Five" ball club of talented freshman newcomers. Under Fisher the much-heralded unit of Chris Webber, Jalen Rose, Juwan Howard, Ray Jackson, and Jimmy King twice survived Big Ten regular-season disappointments and inconsistent midseason play to storm into NCAA title games once March tournament madness heated up. Twice Fisher and his five phenoms also fell flat against ACC juggernauts (first Duke and then North Carolina) with the national title squarely on the line—proving once more in Steve Fisher's case that old adage that it is always much harder the second (and third) times around. Yet, if the Michigan Fab Five (which broke up after two seasons with Webber's escape to the NBA) failed grandly in their bid to cop a national title, they nonetheless seemed to confirm the coaching and recruiting genius of the Michigan coaching newcomer who, after five trips to the "Big Dance," owned the best lifetime won-lost mark (20–4, .833) of NCAA postseason history.

Things didn't remain so rosy in Ann Arbor during the second half of the 1990s, and Steve Fisher's early momentum was not enough to carry him beyond decade's end, even with (and perhaps largely due to) a string of blue-chip recruits like huge center Robert "Tractor" Traylor and unmotivated forward Maurice Taylor (a first-round draft pick of the Los Angeles Clippers before his senior season). Despite all the talent Michigan did not win a conference title in the '90s, and most of Fisher's best recruits eventually ended up transferring to other schools, bailing out early to the NBA, or falling onto the academic scrap heap (like flashy 1997 point guard Brandon Hughes). There was a 1997 NIT crown (Fisher's last hurrah) as small consolation to the Wolverines' faithful, but in the end Steve Fisher could keep neither the snarling alumni nor the NCAA enforcement staff at bay forever and finally stepped down on the eve of the 1997–98 campaign, leaving his showcase program in a turmoil of transitional crisis exactly one full decade after he himself had benefited so richly from the exact same sad state of affairs.

Bill Fitch

Bill Fitch sits alongside Dick Motta and Gene Shue in the triumvirate of three-decade also-ran NBA coaches who have steadily padded their résumés with mountainous victory totals simply by clinging to miraculous runs of longevity. Thus while Fitch has steadily climbed the ladder among the all-time winningest NBA mentors, he has at the same time proven to be the game's unrivaled relentless loser. The "up" side of the Bill Fitch story is the fact that only Lenny Wilkens has won more games (1,120 to 944 at the end of 1998); the more eye-catching "down" side is that no one has come close to losing as many (1,106). Admittedly, coaching with the Cleveland Cavaliers throughout the 1970s, and then the sad-sack New Jersey Nets and Los Angeles Clippers throughout the '90s has not lent itself to stashing large numbers in the win column. During the intervening decade the former Coe College (Iowa) player and coach enjoyed what must, at the time, have seemed like paradise assignments in both Boston and Houston and took enough advantage to post three Atlantic Division championships and an NBA crown (during Larry Bird's third season) at the first post, and then a runaway Midwest Division banner and second trip to the NBA Finals (versus his old Boston team) when blessed with the Twin Towers (Olajuwon and Sampson) in Houston. Ironically, neither of his two NBA Coach of the Year trophies came in those two heady seasons. The first was garnered with a surprising Cleveland outfit that captured the 1976 Central Division race and featured stellar guards Jim Chones and Campy Russell. The second came in his debut Boston season (1980), where a miraculous 32-game turnaround in the ball club's record had seemingly far more to do with a rookie sensation named Larry Bird than it did with the arrival of a replacement veteran head coach.

Cotton Fitzsimmons

Cotton Fitzsimmons was nearly 40 years old before he landed his first NBA coaching job (for the 1971 season in Phoenix). By the time his career ended in the third week of the 1997 season (when he stepped aside with a Phoenix Suns squad that had begun the campaign winless in eight games), he had climbed into ninth place (832) on the all-time winning list: only Wilkins (1,120), Fitch (944), Auerbach (938), Motta (935), Riley (914 and rising fast), Larry Brown (884), Don Nelson (867), and Jack Ramsay (864) have won more. And unlike Fitch and Motta (who have far more losses than wins), he got there with a credible three-decade winning record and not merely by an instinct for survival alone. Fitzsimmons's two-decade career record culminated at 832–775 (.578), and his service was spread over five franchises (Phoenix twice, Atlanta, Buffalo, Kansas City, San Antonio) and included a pair of NBA Coach of the Year accolades. The honors were pocketed in 1979 when his first season with Kansas City saw that club jump from fifth (last) to first in the Midwest Division, and then a decade later (1989) when he returned to Phoenix, where the signing of free-agent Tom Chambers spurred a 27-game upswing in the Pacific Division standings, which kept the revamped Suns in hot season-long pursuit of the Magic Johnson–led Los Angeles Lakers.

Mike Fratello

Over the course of Mike Fratello's highly successful NBA coaching career, his teams (in Atlanta and Cleveland) have qualified for playoff action in 14 of 17 seasons. Only his first two teams in Atlanta finished below the break-even point, and in his ninth campaign (1995) he became the 24th coach in league history (seventh among active coaches) to cross the 400-victory plateau. He also coached Atlanta Hawks teams in the late '80s that featured high-scoring Dominique Wilkins and posted four seasons in a row of 50-plus victories. His 1987 team in Atlanta was the finest in franchise history, and he was rewarded that year with five different designations as NBA Coach of the Year. Fratello completed his Atlanta employment only three wins behind the franchise career mark held by Richie Guerin. He does, however, hold the Atlanta club high-water mark for winning percentage.

But it is defense that is Fratello's passion, and his genius for designing ball-control schemes and hard-nosed defending designed to hold high-scoring opponents in check has blossomed in recent seasons as headman of the Cleveland Cavaliers. After four years in the broadcast booth following his Atlanta firing, Fratello assumed control in Cleveland for the 1994 season and immediately began setting team and league records, and milestones for stingy defensive play. The 1995 Cavaliers edition, for example, posted the second-best defensive season in NBA history, holding opponents to a season-long 89.8 scoring average. That team held opponents under the century mark on 62 occasions (a franchise record) and under 80 another 17 times (also a club record). It was a familiar tradition for Fratello, whose best Atlanta outfit eight seasons earlier had also featured the NBA's No. 1–ranked defense (which allowed 102.8 points per game and held opponents to a .451 field-goal percentage). The defensive intensity of Fratello's teams is not always popular with today's offensive-oriented players and has not proven very effective in winning postseason games. But it has allowed one of the league's most energetic and dedicated coaches to produce competitive teams even when he doesn't possess the high-profile talent of many of the opponents.

Lloyd "World B." Free

The most colorful name and one of the most flamboyant offensive styles in NBA annals belonged to a free-spirited and well-traveled gunner who piled up numerous personal milestones in his portfolio but was rarely, if ever, mentioned among the league's finest players. Eight seasons of lofty scoring in the late '70s and early '80s peaked with a 30.2 average with the San Diego Clippers in 1980, which left Free as the league's runner-up scorer for the second straight season. Both years he trailed San Antonio's equally freewheeling George Gervin in the race for individual honors. But at Philadelphia, San Diego, Golden State, Cleveland, and Houston, he rarely played for anything that resembled a winner. The exceptions were 1977 and 1978 when Dr. J–led Philadelphia teams of those years dominated the Eastern Division and climbed first to the NBA Finals (losing to Bill Walton and Portland) and a year later to the Eastern Division championship round (falling to eventual playoff winner Washington with Elvin Hayes). A Brooklyn native, who was a hardship draft pick out of tiny Guilford College as a junior, Free hand-picked and self-promoted such colorful monikers as "All-World" and "Prince of Midair" to underscore his elevated freelancing game and even went so far down the road of self-promotion as to have his name legally changed to World B. Free in the mid-'80s. But his showtime game itself never elevated in overall impact above a second-team all-league selection during his first season (fourth overall) with San Diego.

Bill Frieder

The second-winningest coach in the Michigan record book (191–87 over nine seasons), Bill Frieder seemed to have a special affinity for embarrassing moments and disastrous decisions in running both his own career and the high-profile college programs at Michigan and Arizona State he has been entrusted with. During the 1989 season he joined the short list of outstanding coaches who had to witness their teams lose to an unheralded Division I opponent; Frieder suffered this fate at the hands of Alaska-Anchorage, which popped his previously unbeaten and obviously unprepared Wolverines in the Christmastime Utah Classic. But this was a fate that left Frieder in some good company, since a similar red-faced event had also, at one time or another, befallen such bench stalwarts as Lefty Driesell, Bobby Cremins, and Denny Crum, among others. Such was not at all the case, however, with the display of outrageous bad timing that Bill Frieder unleashed upon himself at the end of that same 1989 season, which would surprisingly turn out in the end to be the best in school history. Unfortunately for Frieder, he wouldn't be around for the celebrations when his Michigan team (in the emergency hands of his former assistant Steve Fisher) wrapped up the school's only NCAA championship with a dramatic overtime defeat of Seton Hall out of the Big East Conference, and it was all of his own doing. On the eve of tournament play the veteran coach announced that he had accepted a coaching slot at Arizona State, a move that left exasperated Michigan officials with little choice but to terminate the contract of their "lame duck" before the tip-off of NCAA festivities.

Frieder wasn't apparently done throwing away golden opportunities after his embarrassing departure from Ann Arbor. In seven subsequent years he painstakingly built an emerging powerhouse at Arizona State, which peaked in 1995 at 24–9 and with a third-place Pac-10 finish. Little more than two years later, however, Bill Frieder was again hastily shown the door, this time after suspected recruiting improprieties, campus thefts committed by some of his players, and even allegations of point-shaving and game-rigging (the first serious threats to the game's integrity in almost three decades) left the emerging Arizona State program tainted with the foulest smell in the land.

Kevin Garnett

If there is a single player who seems to symbolize everything that is potentially wrong with today's NBA, it would have to be Minnesota Timberwolves prize project Kevin Garnett. Garnett held the Minnesota franchise hostage for a mind-boggling contract even though his value lies entirely in future promise and his three-season league performance has displayed little that has been so far earth-shattering. While Garnett made a considerable splash in 1995 as the first player in more than 20 years drafted directly out of high school, he grabbed even bolder headlines in summer 1997 when he surpassed Shaquille O'Neal as owner of the richest contract in professional sports history. The $125 million multiyear deal was shattering, not only because it was paid to a novice player, who in two NBA seasons has not yet averaged 20 points per game and has led his also-ran team only in blocked shots, but even more because it outstripped the more than $37 million that owner Glen Taylor had paid for the entire franchise three years earlier. It also left Garnett in the same salary league with Michael Jordan, whose reported $36 million was still the top annual salary. Garnett himself didn't do much to help fans swallow such an exorbitant deal when he first rejected a $105 million package and then testily commented to the press that "it's not about the loot . . . I want the sky, and I'm not going to stop until I reach the top." (Translation: this is not about money or playing talent, it is only about ego.) An intriguing question for NBA watchers over the next half-dozen seasons will be whether 6'11" Kevin Garnett will be best remembered by future generations for his championship rings (like Russell and Magic), his awesome statistics (like Jordan and Chamberlain), his unrivaled court artistry (like Oscar or Dr. J), or merely for the fatness of his bank accounts, the chutzpah of his contract demands, and the size of his unchecked ego.

Hank Gathers

Only the tragedy surrounding the drug-overdose death of Maryland superstar Len Bias has received more press than that involving Hank Gathers. The second player ever to lead the nation in both scoring and rebounding in the same season (his junior year, 1989), Gathers was a 30-points-per-game scorer (over his final two seasons) and second-team All-American for high-scoring Loyola-Marymount when he collapsed and died of a heart ailment on his home floor during the 1990 semifinals game of the West Coast Conference tournament. The powerfully built 6'7" forward-center out of Philadelphia was the league's all-time scoring leader, a two-time WCC tournament MVP, and a certain top pick in the upcoming NBA draft. It was perhaps the most tragic moment in the history of any league tournament (WCC play was suspended and Marymount was handed an automatic NCAA bid based on its regular-season league title); it was also a startling case (which ranks alongside of Wayne Estes in 1965 and Len Bias in 1986) of a great pro career being cut off before it ever had the chance to take flight.

George "Ice Man" Gervin (NBA "Top 50" Selection)

The NBA's legendary "Ice Man" was something of a modern-day version of the unique '50s-era superstar George Yardley—skinny, storklike, obsessively offense-minded, and a nearly unstoppable scorer when he was at the top of his game. Gervin's combined ABA-NBA scoring totals (mostly compiled with San Antonio) place him 10th all time on the points-per-game register (25.1, a fraction behind Dominique Wilkins), and ninth in total career points scored (26,595, a shade ahead of Wilkins). He is also one of only six NBA gunners to win scoring titles in three consecutive seasons (joining Mikan, Neil Johnston, Chamberlain, Bob McAdoo, and Jordan for that final rarefied honor). Gervin captured a fourth individual crown in 1982 to step into select company with Jordan and Chamberlain (Mikan had only two under the NBA banner) as the NBA's only four-time leaders. To add icing to the cake, George Gervin possessed a range of different shots—inside stuffs, outside jumpers, a famed finger-roll, scooping layups, hooks with either hand—as varied as any of the pro game's most memorable offensive machines. Only Jordan and Chamberlain were as proficient at outscoring all their league rivals as was Gervin. And perhaps only Jordan, Chamberlain, and Oscar Robertson can be counted in the tiny number of players who made scoring look quite so easy.

Artis Gilmore

Few heroes of the hardwood (only Dr. J and perhaps George Gervin come to mind) combined loftier achievements in the rebel American Basketball Association with a more sterling résumé in the better established NBA. Gilmore first grabbed headlines by leading unheralded Jacksonville University to a 27–2 record and an NCAA title game showdown with UCLA in 1970. An ABA MVP, Rookie of the Year, and league All-Star at only 23, this quiet but all-powerful giant was also an NBA All-Star 14 seasons later at the then-basketball-ancient age of 36. Yet few cage All-Stars have been, at the same time, more often judged as overall disappointments in the face of such lofty achievements at the game's highest levels. The later (and most unjust) assessment had mostly to do with overblown expectations and with the rugged Gilmore's reserved—almost passive—on-court nature. He rarely spoke out on the floor, in the locker room, or when facing the press, and he seemed at times to hold back even more than Chamberlain. Seven-footer Artis Gilmore was a dominating rebounder and imposing shot-blocking terror who always posted impressive numbers across two decades of consistent pro stardom. And yet the passive and even sometimes sullen-appearing Gilmore was never quiet the top-dollar league star in either pro circuit (his scoring was sometimes modest and he didn't win championships) that many fans and pundits long expected him to be.

But the career achievements of one of basketball's strongest and hardest-working behemoths spell out a Hall of Fame profile no matter what the naysayers and discounters might claim. As a collegian he earned membership (along with Walter Dukes, Bill Russell, Elgin Baylor, Paul Silas, Julius Erving, and Kermit Washington) in the highly exclusive seven-man club of 20-point career scorers who also topped 20 per game as career rebounders. In the ABA he was for five years the dominant center in a league stuffed with power forwards. Gilmore was also an iron man who played 670 straight games at the outset of his pro career, and he never missed a single game in his five campaigns with the ABA Kentucky Colonels. And in the end he owned the highest career field-goal percentage (.599) in NBA history. Artis Gilmore perhaps didn't have much to say when he stepped off a basketball court; yet his game itself always spoke volumes whenever he was on the floor.

Mike Gminski

Throughout the '80s Gminski was an NBA mainstay after leaving Duke as that storied program's all-time leading rebounder and second-leading career scorer. At Durham the 6'11" Connecticut native had been an ACC Player of the Year while a junior (1979) and a consensus All-American as a senior. He twice averaged above 20 in scoring and remained near that level for his career. During his stellar senior season he trailed only Maryland's Albert King in scoring and Virginia's Ralph Sampson in rebounding on the ACC circuit. He was also the league's rebounding runner-up as a freshman (behind Clemson's Tree Rollins), sophomore (trailing Rod Griffith of Wake Forest), and junior (edged out by Maryland's future NBA stalwart, Buck Williams). In the pros with New Jersey and Philadelphia he was a workhorse blue-collar type known for his exceptional long-range shooting (an exception certainly for a rangy 6'11" post player), his tenacious defense, crack foul shooting (he topped 90 percent for the season in 1988 and finished out his career near 85 percent), and always spirited and unselfish team play. In brief, he was every NBA coach's true dream player.

A. C. Green

NBA basketball's new "iron-man" star will likely never get very much attention for his workmanlike playing ethic and probably with good reason. For one thing, the record belonging to Randy Smith (906 straight games), which Green broke with much hoopla early in the 1997–98 season, was only the one being trumpeted by the league and not the real iron-man standard of pro basketball's past. The true milestone is the one held by Ron Boone, which is still a couple of long seasons away. Boone played in 1,041 ABA and NBA contests without interruption, stretching his streak throughout the entire decade of the '70s and into the '80s. But NBA figure filberts for some reason still don't acknowledge ABA numbers as part of their historical legacy. And another factor sapping the importance of Green's celebrated milestone is that the current Dallas Mavericks forward boasts very few apparent star qualities—unlike baseball's iron men Gehrig and Ripken, or even his own NBA predecessors like Red Kerr (the original record holder), Randy Smith, and Boone. He is indeed (and has been throughout his career in L.A., Phoenix, and Dallas) a hard-working rebounder and aggressive defender. But he is only average in skills on offense and does most of his scoring more because he can run and leap than because he owns an elegant or artistic shot. Basketball iron-man distinctions are also of themselves a bit less impressive than those of baseball, since even the workhorse pros answer the bell only several times a week and don't—like baseball's Ripken—have to ignore their aching muscles and bones, literally day in and day out, for a full six-month stretch.

Rickey Green

Rickey Green was the almost-prototype model of the perfect two-way backcourt ace—at least 1960s style. His brief Michigan career was filled with a truckload of honors and a carload of stellar performances. Arriving in 1975 after two productive junior college All-American seasons at Vincennes (Indiana), Green posted consistent scoring averages of 19.9 and 19.5 over his two varsity campaigns, was the leading scorer on the 1976 NCAA runner-up team, earned first-team All-American honors with the 1977 Big Ten champions, and scored more points than any other Michigan player who performed for only two seasons. Green was also runner-up to UCLA's Marques Johnson for selection as the 1977 Collegiate National Player of the Year.

But it was not as a scorer that Rickey Green was most effective and most valuable. As a relentless pressing defender, Green literally terrorized opponents (especially opposing point guards), time and again making crucial steals and launching the famed Michigan fast-breaking offense that usually found long-legged center Phil Hubbard on the receiving end. Green's collegiate act was also just a preview of much loftier things to come. One of the quickest athletes ever to set foot on the hardwood, Green enjoyed an outstanding 14-year NBA career (mostly with the Utah Jazz) that included such milestones as 90 percent free-throw shooting in 1988, more than 4,000 career assists, 1,350 career steals, 45 points in one game, 20 assists in another, and the 1984 NBA steals championship. The most memorable milestone, however—the one Rickey Green will forever be linked with—involved a league achievement and not a team or personal milestone. Rickey Green was the right person in the right place at precisely the right time, when on January 25, 1988, the veteran Jazz guard canned a desperation period-ending three-point shot in Salt Lake City against the Cleveland Cavaliers that was far from an ordinary buzzer-beating heave. That basket turned out to be the celebrated five millionth point in NBA league history. It was a fitting, if ironic, career monument to the 14-season pro veteran who served with eight different teams and was always better known for his ball-pilfering defense than for his adequate but inconsistent performances as a long-range shooter.

Darrell "Doctor Dunkenstein" Griffith

Many may claim the title of basketball's most colorful slam dunker. Julius Erving virtually invented the hang time approach to playing above the rim. Dominique Wilkins earned the legitimate title of "Human Highlight Film" and the bulk of style points in the decade of the '80s. Michael Jordan captured the imagination of an entire generation of hoops fans with his soaring moves to the bucket. Shaquille

O'Neal and Charles Barkley can perhaps lay claim to the most bone-jarring and rim-rattling power moves of the ages. But when it comes to legendary nicknames based on high-flying feats, none can surpass the man they once called simply "Doctor Dunkenstein"—the crown prince of dunk.

Darrell Griffith earned his reputation as a high-flying basket stuffer several years before he became a household-name professional. His reputation for breathtaking aerial moves had spread nationwide even before he was selected as second overall choice in the 1980 NBA draft by the Utah Jazz. The 6'4" guard was already largely unstoppable in only his second college season. Three times he was showcase All-American, and in his senior season, he had also earned College Player of the Year accolades. And Griffith proved to be a team leader and tough-as-nails winner as well as a relentless crowd pleaser when he carried Denny Crum's Louisville Cardinals to a national championship with a 59–54 pasting of once-mighty UCLA in the NCAA tournament finals. Griffith was at his spectacular best in that 1980 NCAA Final Four face-off featuring Louisville, UCLA, Iowa, and Purdue. Rarely, before

Darrell Griffth, Utah Jazz

© Frank P. McGrath Jr.

or since, has a single player so dominated college basketball's final weekend shoot-out. He single-handedly dismantled Iowa in the semifinals to the tune of 34 points, six assists, three crucial steals, and even a pair of demoralizing blocked shots from his outside guard post. In a less-than-well-played championship game it was Griffith's dramatic jumper that broke a 54–54 deadlock and provided the winning margin. Doctor Dunkenstein was again the title game's leading point-maker with 23 and a not-surprising runaway MVP selection. It was a fitting conclusion to a spectacular four-year college career by a player who had become an in-state legend even before he had left Louisville's Male High School. He had, in fact, been so spectacular as a high schooler that many believed the prized recruit would bypass college and sign on directly with the city's popular ABA franchise.

As a novice pro Darrell Griffith proved, even before his rookie season ran its course, that he could outjump and outmaneuver opponents just as easily in talent-filled NBA arenas, while at the same time continuing to entertain with his popular high-wire act of soaring above the rim and slamming home surefire thundering dunks. He surprised numerous NBA skeptics with a brilliant first season that earned top rookie honors and even a bevy of all-league supporters. He hammered home better than 20 points per contest, played the second-most minutes on the Utah team, and also owned the team's second-best totals for points, scoring average, field goals, and defensive steals. In subsequent seasons the spunky Griffith would continue to surprise in even more noteworthy fashion. Unlike many another dunker, who narrowly focused his playground game on inside action near the bucket, the versatile Griffith was soon firing aerial bombs from long range once three-point shooting became the new league rage. In 1984—his fourth pro season—he again opened eyes by pacing all league long-range shooters in three-point field-goal accuracy. It was a rare and surprising feat for a player whose reputation was first made primarily for soaring high above the rim.

Anfernee "Penny" Hardaway

Penny Hardaway is sandwiched somewhere between Shaquille O'Neal and Kobe Bryant as an anointed and largely overpromoted second coming of Michael Jordan. Of the top trio of heavily hyped Jordan clones—Grant Hill, Kobe Bryant, and Hardaway—Penny possesses perhaps the largest dose of raw athletic talent, and his achievements across his first five NBA seasons also outstrip Hill's and Bryant's on paper to date. He was instrumental along with Shaquille O'Neal in lifting his team into one NBA Finals (where it was swept four straight by Houston), and he has proven a potent offensive force since his rookie season (averaging above 20 in his three middle seasons). But he has also, unfortunately, earned something of a reputation for sourness and clubhouse lawyering that has never been for a moment associated with Air Jordan. Hardaway was given the bulk of the credit for running coach Brian Hill out of Orlando, and he also drew charges of malingering while sitting out much of the 1998 season with a nagging injury. He has followed Jordan's mighty footsteps in constructing (with considerable boost from agents and image handlers) worldwide fame as a Nike athletic shoes endorser. Today—less than a half-dozen seasons into his career—Hardaway's familiar commercial image (like that of former teammate O'Neal) sadly far outstrips his once considerable playing stature. When

Hardaway was voted by NBA fans onto the 1998 All-Star Game roster while sitting injured on the sidelines, more than one wag observed that if "Little Penny" (the puppet version of the popular ballplayer used in Nike television commercials) had been on the All-Star ballot he, too, would likely have earned a starting spot for the midseason classic.

Tim Hardaway

A famed rationale for media advertising is the eye-opening observation that there are two dozen mountain slopes in Colorado all loftier than Pikes Peak, yet no one can name a single one. A second such illustration involves the pair of current NBA stalwarts named Hardaway. Anfernee ("Penny") in Orlando has Nike and a cute commercial puppet named "Little Penny" to thank for much of his megastardom. Tim in Miami boasts exactly the same offensive production (they each held a 19.7 scoring average entering the 1998 campaign) but lacks only the slam-dunking flair and the flood of promotional airtime. Few playmakers (including the Orlando namesake) can handle Miami's Hardaway, and his patented between-the-legs crossover dribble known as "the UTEP two-set" (Hardaway played college ball for the University of Texas at El Paso) hypnotizes defenders and clears lines to the bucket. He also features an unorthodox "behind-the-ear" long-range push shot, which is deadly even from three-point range. If there is a negative to the smaller Hardaway's game, it is indeed his size (six feet), which has made defending him easier than it should be and also has caused him to become a gambler (often an unsuccessful one) on defense. But size aside, Tim Hardaway is one of the most explosive point guards found anywhere in today's NBA.

Hersey Hawkins

Few star cagers have made bigger career transitions than Hersey Hawkins. As a schoolboy ace in Chicago he was a 6'3" All-City center for Westinghouse High, renowned in playground circles for unstoppable moves and relentless leaping within 10 feet of the hoop. At Bradley University, miraculously transformed into an unashamed gunner from long range, whose outside firepower was so potent that he led the nation in scoring, he was a National College Player of the Year, posted one of the highest senior-season averages ever tallied (36.3), and finished up his career in fourth place for all-time NCAA point-making. Finally, as a pro in Philadelphia, Charlotte, and Seattle, the same 6'3" leaper has emerged as an all-around floor leader and unselfish team player whose still-potent three-point shooting is more than supplemented by hard-pressing defense and relentless intensity from one end of the court to the other. Such versatility is no small key to Hawkins's career longevity as he launches his second pro decade with a 17.0 scoring average, a solid floor game, and a reputation as the kind of player to build any winning team around.

Chick Hearn

In baseball the "voices of the game" who have transferred diamond action into living room fare by radio magic seem to be a near endless group—Mel Allen, Red

Barber, Vin Scully, Bob Prince, Harry Caray, Bob Elson, Curt Gowdy, Russ Hodges, Ernie Harwell, and a dozen lesser lights in local big-league broadcast markets. Every city seems to have one, and every decade or epoch seems loaded with the entertaining breed. Baseball is, after all, the ultimate radio game. When it comes to basketball, however, there are only two broadcast legends of anywhere near similar stature—the late John Most in Boston and the still-active Chick Hearn in Los Angeles. Johnny Most is best remembered for his single 1965 playoff call ("Havlicek stole the ball! Havlicek stole the ball!"), which is basketball's equivalent of the Russ Hodges rendition of Bobby Thomson's "Shot Heard 'Round the World" home run that clinched the 1951 National League pennant. Hearn, by contrast, is known largely for his considerable longevity, which puts him in the same circles with baseball counterparts like Scully, Caray, and the New York Mets' Bob Murphy. In March 1992 at Cleveland Hearn broadcast his 2,500th consecutive Lakers game; even more remarkable at the time was the fact that the Naismith Hall of Famer had, to that point, missed only two contests during his 32 years on the circuit. Chick Hearn has slowed some in recent seasons, but he remains on the job, is almost as large a celebrity in Lakers circles as Magic or Kareem (he has a star on Hollywood Boulevard's "Walk of Fame" while they don't), and sports a reputation for NBA longevity that is equally as safe for the ages as Abdul-Jabbar's.

Lou Henson

Lou Henson retired at Illinois in 1996 only 3 victories shy (with 661) of catching John Wooden (664) for the final slot among the top dozen winningest NCAA coaches. Two years later he returned to restart his 34-season career with a second tour of duty at his alma mater, New Mexico State, and thus also to inevitably bump one of the sport's largest icons from the prestigious career victory list. Henson (now 681–343 after 35 seasons) built a memorable legacy at Illinois across 21 campaigns that lifted him and his team above some of the league's and the NCAA's most prestigious milestones—200 Big Ten victories, 400 career wins at Illinois, and eventually, 650 career victories before his first and short-lived retirement. But for all his triumphs, the longtime Illini mentor remains one of those clearly successful coaches (he owns a .665 winning percentage) who can never quite satisfy the victory-starved alumni nor squelch ever-present legions of second-guessers. Henson's inescapable career black mark, like former Big Ten rival Gene Keady's at Purdue, is that he carries around a less-than-stellar record (19–19) in NCAA tournament play.

Grant Hill

Like Michael Jordan, with whom he is constantly compared, Grant Hill was a paragon college player whose pro prospects now appear so bright that even stellar collegiate performances may be doomed to fade in the glare of NBA achievement. It is hard to remember how good Jordan really was at North Carolina. And the same might now be said of Grant Hill at Duke. As an NBA newcomer Hill would earn instant attention and credibility as the first rookie ever to top the league's All-Star Game balloting. (Much of the ballot stuffing admittedly had to do partially with a blitz of shoe company promotional campaigns.) Fame almost the equal of Jordan's was also brought on by a perfectly drawn image of clean-cut American wholesomeness and a clever marketing campaign aimed to sell Grant Hill of the Detroit Pistons as the sport's next larger-than-life role model and marquee celebrity.

Operating under slightly less (if only slightly less) intense national media glare, Hill would also prove to be the heart and soul of a several-season Duke juggernaut that was one of the most potent in collegiate cage history. As a freshman and sophomore he would play alongside Hurley and Laettner on a repeat national champion; as a senior he would return to Final Four action and to the national title game. Only the presence of Purdue's Glenn Robinson with his 30-point scoring average may have kept Hill from at least one National Player of the Year trophy. And when the two met head-to-head in mid-March with a trip to the Final Four squarely on the line, it was Grant Hill's turn to demonstrate that he, and not Robinson, was already perhaps the finest all-around young performer to be found anywhere in the land. Facing Robinson nose-to-nose Hill held the nation's top scorer to 13 points, the Purdue star's lowest point total of the entire 1994 campaign.

Chamique Holdsclaw

Chamique Holdsclaw (whose catchy first name is pronounced "Shuh-MEEK-Wuh)— not Grant Hill or Kobe Bryant—may arguably be the closest thing to Michael Jordan now going. Make allowance for the slightly slower, slightly less athletic, much more fundamentally sound women's version of the game, and Chamique Holdsclaw is the most splendid athlete (outside of MJ, of course) found on today's hoops scene. Holdsclaw recently dominated the women's game (collegiate version) every bit as much as MJ did the men's (NBA) version. She is a remarkable shake-and-bake player who seems to soar up and down the court almost on a plane of her own. And like Michael, she wins almost without interruption. For three straight seasons she carried Tennessee to the NCAA women's title and barely missed (when Tennessee fell in the 1999 Regional Finals) surpassing Lew Alcindor as the only athlete ever to win four straight national titles. Before that, her high school team in New York captured four state banners without a postseason defeat. Like Jordan also, Holdsclaw is about to revolutionize the pro game when she inevitably brings her unmatched athleticism to the WNBA for the 2000 season. As one recent article in a major sports periodical aptly phrased it, the best-ever player on the women's college circuit has a whole nation of young female hoopsters dreaming of nothing more than wanting to "Be Like Mique!"

Juwan Howard

Ranking a distinct No. 2 behind Chris Webber on the college quintet that made up Michigan's prized "Fab Five" lineup, Juwan Howard has rapidly been closing the gap in the pro ranks, where he again teamed with Webber as part of one of the NBA's best young front lines at Washington until Webber was traded to Sacramento. Together with the Wizards (nee Bullets) since the 1994–95 season, the pair posted nearly identical scoring marks (19.6 for Howard and 19.4 for Webber). Both have appeared on a single NBA All-Star Game roster (Howard in 1996 and Webber in 1997, both ironically scoring two points in token appearances). In the 1997–98 NBA campaign it was 6'9" Howard at the small forward slot who paced the Wizards in points and field goals, while it was 6'10" Webber at power forward who posted the team lead in scoring average, rebounding, and shot blocking. But like many of today's biggest NBA stars, Juwan Howard is already a victim of his own notoriety and financial successes. The 19 points and eight rebounds he puts up nightly might represent stardom for many top pros in this or any earlier era, but it is likely that one of the league's smoothest-shooting forwards will spend most of his career trying haplessly to match the unreachable expectations generated by a $105 million contract signed in summer 1996. Impossible expectations seem, of course, to be the ongoing legacy of both Howard and Webber, since their two trips to the NCAA Final Four (as freshmen and sophomores) were not nearly sufficient to match the runaway expectations immediately attached to the Fab Five unit by Wolverines faithful when it debuted in Ann Arbor nearly a decade ago.

Bobby Hurley

Duke's Bobby Hurley never posted big numbers anywhere but in the box-score assists columns—and, of course, also in the team victories column. Hurley was never a headline-grabbing scorer (12.4), and his value did not easily translate into individual record-breaking performances. Nonetheless, he may well have been the most talented and effective floor general in ACC league history. This is especially true if the yardstick is reduced to overall championship team performance. Basketball is, after all, very much a team game for all its one-on-one showmanship. And Hurley was very much a prototypical team player. Over the course of his four seasons in Durham, Hurley, along with teammate Christian Laettner, also became very much a staple of year-end Final Four action. Like Yogi Berra and Mickey Mantle with the baseball Yankees, Hurley (1992 Final Four MVP) and Laettner (1991 Final Four MVP) set a multitude of NCAA postseason records simply because they were so frequently on the scene when the bell sounded for the year's closing championship weekend. But Hurley's statistical legacy also reaches a bit beyond the showcase tournament. For when his Duke tenure was finally over, he also found himself standing alone above the pack as the NCAA career assists leader.

Allen Iverson

The late-'90s controversy surrounding the impact of early departures from college ranks by promising superstars who cannot resist the lure of NBA dollars found a focal point in 1997 NBA Rookie of the Year Allen Iverson. Coming off two sensational college seasons at Georgetown under John Thompson, the super-talented six-foot guard declared himself ready for the big time at the end of his sophomore year, then received plenty of external confirmation of his assessment with a No. 1 overall draft selection (Philadelphia 76ers), an NBA Rookie of the Year performance (23.5 points per game), and team leadership in Philly in scoring, three-point shooting, assists, and steals. But off-court immaturity (several minor scrapes with the law) and occasional on-court raggedness (4.4 turnovers per game) led many to question whether Iverson might have been a far bigger impact player as a rookie had he matured two additional seasons under the firm hand of John Thompson.

Jim Jackson

Ohio State's Jim Jackson, like Magic Johnson a decade earlier, was on the verge of NCAA superstardom when he folded up his college career prematurely in 1992 and headed for the NBA. A three-year starter who led the Buckeyes to three NCAA tournament appearances and two Big Ten titles, Jackson did much to restore a brief period of glory to a recently troubled OSU cage program. Before departing as fourth overall draft choice of the Dallas Mavericks, the 6'6" guard-forward strung together a list of personal triumphs that would stamp greatness on any career: Big Ten Freshman of the Year (1990), two-time Big Ten Player of the Year (1991, 1992), UPI College Player of the Year as a junior (1992), 1,785 career points (fifth in Buckeyes history), three-time team leader in scoring, rebounding leader his final season, and a ranking in the school's all-time top 10 in several other important offensive and defensive categories (assists, steals, three-point field goals). The luster has dimmed a bit in the NBA, however. As a gifted player with awesome individual talents and also the rare ability to make those on the floor around him look better (he is a fabulous passer), the one-time college superstar has surprisingly slipped into the role of a much-traveled journeyman (Dallas, New Jersey, Philadelphia, Golden State) who has yet to make an NBA All-Star Team or earn a significant league honor. The considerable luster has not faded, however, from what remains one of the heftiest set of individual accomplishments in the history of the storied Big Ten Conference.

Phil Jackson

If the dynasty Chicago Bulls of the mid- and late 1990s were not Michael Jordan's team, they would certainly have to be Phil Jackson's team. The super-intense coach with a penchant for Zen philosophy and a fanatical dedication to his disciplined team-concept approach to winning may well have enjoyed his miraculous successes and near domination of the league (six titles and a .738 winning percentage) across the entire decade of the '90s simply because he has had Jordan in his lineup (along with Scottie Pippen, Horace Grant, John Paxson, and Steve Kerr). The '90s-era Bulls of Phil Jackson rode Jordan and Pippen (especially Jordan) the same way the '60s Celtics of Red Auerbach rode Russell and Cousy (especially Russell). Yet the greatest tribute to the coach's own role in the mix has repeatedly been voiced by Jordan himself, who continued to insist, and then made good on his promise, that he would once more retire as soon as Jackson's tenure was up in Chicago and that he will never in the future play for any other NBA coach.

Phil Jackson's winning numbers have been equally as phenomenal as those that Auerbach accumulated during his own career heights—perhaps even more so when one considers the back-to-back 72- and 69-win seasons. He trails Auerbach when it comes to consecutive league titles, though it might be argued the gap would be narrower had Jordan not stayed away for nearly two seasons of midcareer retirement. But Jackson was, nonetheless, the fastest coach ever to reach the 500-win plateau. And both his regular-season and postseason winning percentages are higher than Auerbach's (leaving aside the question of a tougher league schedule in Auerbach's era). Jackson's own retirement from the Bulls at the end of his second three-peat in 1998 smells strangely like Jordan's own temporary hiatus. Jackson will likely soon be back—perhaps with his old playing-days team in New York— and the assault on career coaching milestones will once again be renewed.

Phil Jackson, while still a novice coach with the New Jersey Nets

© Frank P. McGrath Jr.

Dennis Johnson

One of the finest defensive players in league history (a nine-time member of the NBA All-Defensive squad) was also a talented playmaker and a dependable clutch scorer for a trio of the most memorable NBA championship teams of the modern era. Dennis Johnson (popularly known as simply DJ) was the second-leading scorer and third-leading assists man with the 1979 Seattle SuperSonics, which captured their only franchise title by blitzing Washington in five games. A backcourt mainstay on both the 1984 and 1986 Boston playoff winners, DJ trailed only Bird as the assists leader on teams that boasted perhaps the finest front wall—Bird, Parish, and McHale— of the modern era or any era. Dennis Johnson also topped 15,000 career points and 5,000 career assists, was NBA Finals MVP with Seattle (1979), and shares an NBA Finals record for free-throw shooting (most made in one half). But it was as a relentless defender that he made his lasting reputation. Long arms, quick hands and feet, and an aggressive ball-pressuring style made him as tough and relentless a straight-up man-to-man defender as found anywhere. An when it comes to endorsements that carry the weight of unquestioned authority, none other than Larry Bird once labeled Dennis Johnson as simply the best he ever played with.

Larry Johnson

Early heroes of the NBA played in relative obscurity when compared with today's high-profile basketball superstars. In the days of Oscar Robertson, Bill Russell, and Wilt Chamberlain, televised basketball was reserved in most of the country for the playoffs alone, only a handful of cities had pro teams, and celebrity product endorsements were reserved for baseball heroes like Mickey Mantle or Willie Mays (more often white stars like Mantle). Today's hoop stars—in stark contrast to their forgotten forerunners—seem to be more often seen in magazine and television advertising spreads then on actual basketball courts. They are huge media celebrities first and foremost, and accomplished athletes almost as an afterthought. One prototypical example is power forward Larry Johnson, lately of the New York Knicks and originally of the expansion Charlotte Hornets. Fans in smaller television markets around the country may see Johnson slamming home monster dunks only two or three times a season. But they have almost certainly seen his gold-tooth punctuated smiles and delightful performance as videoland's "slammin'-est and jammin'-est Grandmama ever"—perhaps even dozens upon dozens of times.

Johnson is the starkest example that in today's world it is endorsement appearances and not artistic performances or career statistics that truly make the NBA ballplayer. Johnson is one of many NBA icons among today's young fans, despite the fact (quick career start to the contrary) that he is also one of the league's biggest on-court busts in recent campaigns. Several seasons back, on the heels of a pair of power-packed inaugural seasons in Charlotte (where he earned Rookie of the Year honors and All-League Second Team), Johnson was considered one of the most electrifying "finishers" in the game. The combination of advanced post-up skills, superb passing, tenacious defense, and hellacious rebounding made the wide-body 6'7" forward one of the game's most remarkable multiple-threat performers. He quickly became the Hornets' all-time leading rebounder in his five seasons there. A transfer via the trade route to New York and a chance to team on the front line with Patrick Ewing has not, however, brought the big dividends expected everywhere in Gotham. For one thing, there was an immediate drop-off in scoring from 20 to 12 per game. But if the offensive thrusts have slowed down in New York, the commercial gimmicks certainly haven't. And the resulting discrepancy is perhaps one of the most visible exclamation points on the misplaced values of today's NBA.

Marques Johnson

Marques Johnson may have been the third-best all-around performer among the outstanding stable of hardwood products turned out relentlessly by John Wooden during the UCLA glory years—at least if one judges by a player's eventual accomplishments in the professional ranks. Not that Johnson's collegiate credentials were anything to blithely dismiss, including as they did a National Player of the Year recognition (1977, when he also captured the Wooden and Naismith trophies), a first-team All-American selection, a single national championship, a pair of visits to the Final Four, and a first-round NBA draft selection (third overall). As a pro Johnson experienced career success primarily with Milwaukee (he also played with San Diego and Golden State), where he normally scored at 20 and better for the potent Don Nelson–coached Bucks teams that captured five consecutive divisional titles during his stay. Career numbers included 13,892 points (better than Wicks, Rowe, Bibby, Walt Hazzard, and even Hall of Famer Walton). Only Alcindor and Gail Goodrich among the Wooden alumni posted better career offensive numbers with the run-and-gun pros. And when it comes to artistic style points, Marques Johnson was indisputably the classiest ex-Bruin of the lot.

Steve Johnson

There are even many professed die-hard pro hoops fans (especially among those who have come to the game since Michael Jordan had already been established as a national icon) who have never heard of Steve Johnson. There are likely also those in the same category of fan who at best have a foggy notion of who Wilt Chamberlain was—or Oscar Robertson, Jerry West, and Elgin Baylor. But the first hypothesis is not nearly as astounding as the latter. Clarence "Steve" Johnson, even during his playing days (1982–91, with Kansas City, Chicago, San Antonio, Portland, Minnesota, Seattle, Golden State), could never claim to be a household NBA name, even during those seasons when he was far and away the most proficient goal scorer the NBA had to offer. But there are some rather noteworthy features of Johnson's decade-long pro career, beyond his penchant for wearing a different uniform just about every season. As a consensus first-team All-American at Oregon State in 1981, the 6'10" mobile center led the nation in field-goal percentage for the second season running. It was a talent he would develop into a high art over the next decade of professional play. As adept as anyone in history at only taking those close-range lay-ins that he was likely to make (and making most of the ones he dared take), Johnson amassed the third-highest field-goal percentage in NBA history (.572), trailing only the more name-worthy Artis Gilmore (.599) and the equally anonymous Mark West (.592) in this often overlooked statistical category.

George Karl

The most frequently asked question around NBA circles over the past half-dozen seasons has always been seemingly the same—and it never has to do with whether Michael Jordan and the Bulls were primed for another championship, whether Patrick Ewing and the New York Knicks would again disappointment the nation's largest contingent of pro hoops fans, or whether or not the latest collegiate freshman sensation (whether named Iverson, Marbury, or Bibby) was about to become the NBA's latest multimillionaire. Rather, the question always seemed to be whether or not the Seattle SuperSonics would finally pull the plug on super-successful coach George Karl (442–305 entering his final Seattle season of 1997–98) in light of still another postseason Seattle collapse during the May and June annual run at the league championship. Seattle teams coached by Karl owned the Pacific Division between 1993 and 1998, finishing on top four times and runner-up twice and always winning 55 games or more. But there were constant postseason collapses (or what were popularly seen as collapses): a 1993 division finals seventh-game loss to Phoenix; 1994's shocking first-round upset at the hands of lowly Denver; 1995's similar first-round scuttling by the Lakers; a 1996 near miss in the Finals against the potent Bulls; subsequent failures to overhaul the Utah Jazz and earn a rematch with Chicago. Karl probably never deserved as much of the blame for Seattle's inabilities to win a championship as did the often inconsistent play of Shawn Kemp, Gary Payton, Detlef Schrempf, Hersey Hawkins, Sam Perkins, and others who missed the crucial shoots and committed the vital turnovers. But pro coaches are hired to eventually be fired, and Karl finally met his long-expected fate after a fourth straight postseason disappointment in 1998, another intolerable loss to Utah on the way to a return championship face-off with the Chicago Bulls. He signed with the Milwaukee Bucks the following season.

Gene Keady

Gene Keady has finally overhauled Ward Lambert as the winningest coach in Purdue University history (he won his 400th game at Purdue early in the 1998–99 campaign) and thus emerged from the shadows of at least one Hoosier coaching legend. Yet Keady is, nonetheless, no closer to crawling out from under the huge shadows cast by state rival Bob Knight down the road in Bloomington. Keady is a tenacious battler (he once played football with the Pittsburgh Steelers in the NFL), and his coaching philosophy has always (like Knight's) demanded mental toughness from his usually overachieving players. Mental toughness has been the necessary byword in West Lafayette (Indiana) because Keady has had a tough row to hoe and a series of tough acts to follow.

First there has been the matter of the huge shadow cast by Bob Knight throughout the Hoosier state and throughout the entire present-day Big Ten Conference. Even when Keady wins (he has seven Big Ten titles in his 18 seasons and three straight in the recent past), Knight seems more likely than not to be the biggest story around Midwest college hoops circles. Over the past decade Keady has constructed some of the best teams (like the 29–5 1994 outfit that lost the NCAA Regionals to Duke), recruited some of the best athletes (Troy Lewis, Everette Stephens, Steve Scheffler, Glenn Robinson, Brian Cardinal), and enjoyed some of the best seasons (25–5, 29–4, 29–5, and most recently 28–8) in league play. But while Keady has kept the Boilermakers at the top of one of the nation's premier conferences, he has never quite been "No. 1" in the hearts of a vast majority of Hoosier cage fanatics. Keady admittedly wins his fair share (and then some) of prestigious league titles. But it is Knight and his Hoosiers who live for the Final Four (they have been there three times since Keady came to Purdue) and grab the truly big prizes in the form of NCAA national titles.

Keady has had another long shadow to escape closer to home as well. This is the still-looming legend of the greatest of all Boilermakers coaches, Ward Lambert. Lambert, with his tradition of All-American players and conference banners, still hovers over Purdue basketball, and his own 29-year reign was truly the stuff of magic. It brought the storied basketball-crazy school its biggest batch of Big Ten titles banners (11), its only pretense to a national championship (back in 1932, before a national tournament decided such issues), and also, arguably, its finest player (John Wooden in 1930–32). And there are also a couple of other Purdue coaching giants whose short tenures brought postseason accomplishments that Keady has never been able to reach. George King took a Rick Mount–led team to the national title game against Lew Alcindor and Wooden-coached UCLA in 1969, and Lee Rose barely missed doing the same exactly a decade later (in the final season before Keady's debut with Purdue). Keady's greatest teams, by contrast, never seem to quite get over the hump in postseason play, reaching the Regional championship level on only one occasion (1994) and getting bumped in the opening round an embarrassing five times.

Nonetheless, Gene Keady has already built a record for the ages in West Lafayette. His 432–187 20-season career ledger (that includes two opening years at Western Kentucky) is among the country's best, even if his lackluster NCAA 13–15 tally remains the bane of his career. It is a record that today places him third on the all-time Big Ten winning list (behind only Knight and Lambert, counting conference games only) and third as well in overall winning percentage (trailing the same pair). Entering the final season of his second decade, that record is still far from complete.

Shawn Kemp

Shawn Kemp's name will forever be linked with those of Moses Malone, Darryl Dawkins, Bill Willoughby, Joe Graboski, Kevin Garnett, and Kobe Bryant—among the handful of NBA players who leaped into the league directly from the high school campus. For a while it looked like Kemp might well give Malone a run for his money as the best of this select circle of underage overachievers. But in recent seasons the giant-sized Indiana native (who attended Trinity Valley Community College and Eddie Sutton–coached Kentucky but was never academically eligible for basketball) has seen his career spiral downward from that of a skinny megastar-in-waiting to that of just another overpriced and undermotivated NBA malingerer. There have been some most impressive individual numbers (five straight seasons of above 50 percent field-goal accuracy) and impressive achievements (six All-Star Game appearances) along the way, though these have often been dulled considerably by postseason failures by a talented Seattle SuperSonics team for which Kemp

Shawn Kemp,
Seattle SuperSonics

© Frank P. McGrath Jr.

was the big gun throughout most of the 1990s. He became, in short order, the franchise's career blocked-shots leader on the defensive end of the floor while consistently scoring near 20 at the other end and also earning All-NBA second-team honors three straight years (1994–96). But if Kemp has often dominated individual games, the only place he has dominated NBA stats has been in the negative area of excessive and team-harming fouling: he paced the NBA in disqualifications in 1992 and 1994 and tied for that distinction in 1997, and he has overhauled every other league player in total fouls committed on two different occasions. When Kemp opted to abandon a Seattle team poised for a second run in three years at the NBA Finals in order to ink a slightly more lucrative 1997 free-agent deal with the lackluster Cleveland Cavaliers franchise, fans were handed perhaps the clearest insight into the mentality of Shawn Kemp. Winning championships in today's NBA (at least for those cut in the Shawn Kemp mold) is not nearly as important as padding personal lifestyles.

Jason Kidd

Only twice has the NBA's Rookie of the Year plaque (once called the Eddie Gottlieb Trophy and now sold to corporate sponsorship as the Coca-Cola Classic Award) been a shared affair. It first happened back in 1971 when Boston's Dave Cowens (a future Hall of Famer) had to divide the honor with Portland's Geoff Petrie (a forgotten career journeyman). The repeat came in 1995 when Jason Kidd (second overall draft pick by Dallas) split the recognition with Grant Hill, leaving $70-million-a-year man Glenn Robinson (the top draft selection) sitting on the sidelines. It is not unreasonable to speculate that Grant Hill's subsequent performances have been rapidly moving the young Detroit star in Cowen's career direction, while those of Kidd threaten to put him in the same class with Petrie. One of the league's more flashy playmakers when his game is at its peak, Kidd has nonetheless captured only one notation in the NBA record books during his first four campaigns split equally between Dallas and Phoenix. He managed to lead the entire circuit in turnovers as a second-year man, which is not exactly a fast-track performance pointing toward the Naismith shrine in Springfield.

Bernard King

King's comeback from a serious knee injury was one of the most compelling NBA stories of the late '80s and early '90s. His big-time scoring outburst throughout those years and the half dozen that preceded was also highly noteworthy. But on the whole, both the college (Tennessee) and pro careers of this remarkable scoring machine had as many deep valleys as unmatched mountain peaks. His three solid years of 25-plus scoring earned first-team All-American status in 1977, the best field-goal percentage in the country as a freshman, and seventh overall pick in the NBA draft (New Jersey Nets) while still an undergraduate. Those seasons in Knoxville also were marred by several scrapes with the law and by constant rumors of drug and alcohol abuses. As an NBA star the roller coaster continued: there were four All-League selections and four All-Star Game invitations sandwiched between struggles with self-discipline and several bouts with alcohol that kept him moving from franchise to franchise; King played with New Jersey (two seasons), Utah (one year), and Golden State (two seasons) before settling in for longer hauls with the Knicks and Washington Bullets. Throughout both troubled times and good times King continued to score as few players ever could, and his remarkable moves around the hoop and unmatched quick shooting release finally brought an individual scoring crown in 1985 (with the Knicks) and even a rare back-to-back pair of 50-point games. It was at the tail end of his best-ever season of 1985 (32.9 points per game) that King suffered the deepest valley of his NBA years—a severe knee injury that ended his year, cost him all of the following season, and convinced most NBA watchers that his career was suddenly over. It was in the face of this debilitating injury that King launched his second miraculous comeback (the first had been the return from substance-abuse treatment that had robbed him of almost the entire 1980 campaign) by bouncing back for a trio of late-career 20-plus scoring seasons in Washington, before a second knee operation finally closed the door on a brilliant offensive career.

Bobby Knight

Bob Knight never played a moment of professional basketball, nor has he ever coached at the play-for-pay level. Nonetheless, Knight holds an intimate connection with the only two teams—both from the Big Ten—ever to send an entire starting five directly into the NBA-ABA ranks. First there was the national champion Ohio State team of 1960 (Lucas, Havlicek, Siegfried, Mel Nowell, and Joe Roberts) on which Knight was the unheralded "sixth man" role player. And a decade and a half later there was, of course, the undefeated Indiana University NCAA championship outfit (Scott May, Kent Benson, Tom Abernethy, Quinn Buckner, and Bobby Wilkerson) that Knight coached to the only perfect season in modern Big Ten history. And both wear the clear stamp of Bob Knight's presence.

Knight was not a star on the 1960 OSU national championship club. His playing career was limited to a narrowly defined role; but in that role, Knight already was able to display the telltale marks of a born winner. His one moment of glory was a moment that he seized and converted into near-victory of the most dramatic sort. As a junior reserve with only a four-point scoring average, Knight came off the bench to sink a key driving bucket with 1 minute 41 seconds remaining in the NCAA title game against downstate rival Cincinnati, temporarily rescuing the defending champions and sending the limelight game into tense overtime. In the end Knight's heroics were wasted, as the Buckeyes wilted during the final stanza and lost the first of two disappointing title shoot-outs with the Bearcats. Knight's only two points of NCAA championship play were nonetheless the biggest points of his undistinguished playing career and an early sign of his penchant for NCAA postseason heroics.

But it was obviously as a coach that Bob Knight has made his lasting mark (few even remember that he once suited up as a major-college player). Since The General's arrival in Bloomington a quarter-century back, the Indiana basketball program has been a national symbol for winning excellence. The top boasting points of Knight's career are, of course, the overall winning percentage (now at .727 with Indiana), the 11 Big Ten titles (last one in 1993), three national championships (1976, 1981, 1987), and the rapid climb up the ladder toward the highest victory total in collegiate basketball history (a reasonable goal for the legendary mentor before the end of another decade). Knight has climbed the career-victory ladder with amazing speed, being among the youngest coaches to obtain the 200-, 300-, 400-, 500-, 600-, and 700-victory plateaus. Victory 200 (93–56, Georgia, 1976) would come at age 35; his 300th win (83–69, Northwestern, 1980) would be owned by age 40; four years later the 400th victory would also be pocketed (81–68, Kentucky, 1984); by 48, Knight garnered 500 wins (92–76, Northwestern, 1989); and by 52, he had reached 600 (75–67, Iowa, 1993). Number 700 rolled off the assembly line late in the 1996–97 season (70–66, Wisconsin). At his still-young age (he is the youngest ever to win both 600 and 700), Knight seems certain to crack 800 and challenge both Rupp and Dean Smith before his career closes in Bloomington.

Knight's legacy within the tradition-laced Big Ten is eternally assured. Ironically, it was in a game against arch-rival Purdue (74–73, 1989) that Knight became the winningest coach in conference annals, surpassing the mark held by the Boilermakers' Ward "Piggy" Lambert. And in terms of winning percentage, Bob Knight is in a league of his own; his current .727 mark (720–270) makes him the only coach in league history to stand above a 70 percent winning level. Knight's current marks for winning efficiency have no challengers from the past epochs of Big Ten play; it's hardly likely they will face any serious challenges in the foreseeable future.

With Knight's coaching successes also have come controversy. Mild storms have surrounded an enigmatic coach, who has been labeled, variously and contrastingly, as an out-of-control egomaniac, tunnel-visioned and self-centered, a model disciplinarian, an unparalleled leader and teacher of young men, and perhaps even the greatest college coach in history. Knight has always insisted on total dedication to a team concept from his players (something that was commonplace decades in the past), a demand to which many pampered athletes of the modern era have not been able to adjust. His behavior on the sidelines has often been somewhat outrageous. Well-publicized incidents include his making an analogy between stress and rape during an NBC Television interview in May 1988, taking Indiana players off the court after he had drawn a third technical foul and automatic ejection during an exhibition game with the Soviet Union National Team in 1987, throwing of a chair onto the playing floor during a 1985 contest versus Purdue, pulling Hoosier player Jim Wisman off the court by his jersey before a full house in Assembly Hall (IU's home court) in 1976, and allegedly striking a Puerto Rican security guard during a 1979 Pan American Games team practice. Yet amid this ceaseless controversy, Knight has continued to produce winning teams like clockwork; when he achieved his 300th victory at age 39 he became the youngest college coach ever to accomplish the feat.

But there is far more to the Bob Knight story than league and NCAA title banners and the endless strings of games and honors won. There is also the side of Knight and his program often buried by the enthusiasm of alumni and fans over on-court victory, or by the barrage of criticisms from detractors who harp on Knight's many outbursts with the press and his stern discipline with his own players. This is the side of a man and coach who represents lofty principles of excellence in education as well as in athletics, and who teaches lessons of loyalty and honor alongside those of skilled basketball play. This side of Knight is seen in the exemplary graduation rates of his players; it is also measured by the personal and business successes of so many of his ex-players after graduation (as well as his assistant coaches after assuming their own head-coaching slots). And there is also the deep bond between former and current Knight athletes, which makes IU basketball one of the nation's most special sports-world stories. In every way, basketball tradition at Indiana has become the stuff of legend under Bob Knight. And this has miraculously transpired in spite of the fact that coach Knight himself has always remained the largest Hoosier legend of all.

Mike "Coach K" Krzyzewski

The coach with a hopelessly unspellable (Krzyzewski) and largely unpronounceable (Sha-shef-ski) name has now resided on Duke's Durham campus for 17 full seasons. That stretch, the longest tenure in Duke history, has been quite enough to send Krzyzewski to the head of the list in career and league victories at a school that boasts perhaps the second-richest ACC cage tradition of all. Included in the remarkable tenure has been an overall winning percentage above 70 percent (one of the five best in league annals), the second-highest career victory total among all-time league coaches (barely edging out Everett Case), the runner-up total of NCAA tournament individual game victories, five national Coach of the Year honors (a pair of these in consecutive seasons), four ACC regular-season crowns, four ACC tournament trophies, two selections as ACC Coach of the Year, five 5 consecutive NCAA Final Four visits (eight overall in a span of 10 seasons), and a pair of national championships alongside 3 additional visits to the national championship game. It has all been enough to earn equal billing with Dean Smith as the Southland's most celebrated active head coach. And also enough to build a modern-day coaching legend of such proportions that the Duke mentor is now universally known to hoops fans nationwide simply as the irrepressible and often invincible Coach K.

Mike Krzyzewski interned at Army under Bob Knight, first as player and then as assistant coach, before launching his own career as the Cadets' headman back in 1976. Five seasons at the U.S. Military Academy did produce one 20-victory campaign and a second 19-win season—a neat trick with such limited resources—and also featured a single invitation to NIT postseason play. Yet these apprenticeship seasons hardly displayed the kind of brilliance that lay in store for Duke followers during the next two decades. Coach K arrived at Durham in 1980 just in time to inherit a program clearly in rebuilding mode and a talent base featuring limited potency in the form of holdovers Gene Banks, Vince Taylor, and Kenny Dennard. A spring 1982 recruiting class headed by Johnny Dawkins and Mark Alarie was an early signal, however, that the new Duke mentor had the wherewithal to rapidly restore the decimated team in Durham to its earlier levels of expected brilliance. Coach K crossed the 20-victory plateau during his fourth season at Durham and never fell below it again for the run of the entire next decade.

Despite 11 straight 20-win seasons and other such standard measures of achievement, Coach K's legacy will likely always be the 5-season stretch of NCAA mastery that included his two national titles, a third runner-up finish, and two defeats in the national semifinal games. Over the 57-year history of the nation's premier postseason event, only John Wooden has made it to the season's final weekend as many times without interruption (Wooden's string, of course, stretches all the way to 10). Clearly, the prime postseason event has been Mike Krzyzewski's grandest stage. He would take his various teams into 11 consecutive editions of March Madness between 1984 and 1994; overall, he has been able to guide his constantly changing charges to postseason play in 14 of 17 years on the job at Durham. He remains the second-winningest active coach in NCAA competition with a stunning 44–11 record for a winning standard of exactly 80 percent. Forty-four individual game victories also rank him third all time in tournament history. It is a coaching legacy that stands outside the shadow of all save the venerable Dean Smith. And like Smith, Coach K is a man equally venerable for his teaching skills, renowned for his successes in recruiting and training future pro cage stars, and admirable for his consummate professional behavior both during the frequent thrill of victory and the much rarer agony of defeat.

Christian Laettner

Duke's fifth National Player of the Year (1992) was also the first man ever to appear in four straight NCAA Final Fours. Laettner's legacy was, of course, the NCAA championship tournament for which he is the all-time scoring leader (407 points in 23 total games). In this sense he was the combined Yogi Berra, Bobby Richardson, and Mickey Mantle of college basketball. Here also was a player whose on-court grace and style was every bit the equal to his championship achievements. Christian Laettner clearly had a nose for the big play in the big game, especially once the month of March rolled around. He will perhaps always be best remembered for his game-winning 1992 miracle heave against Kentucky, when he launched a buzzer-beater from the free-throw arc in the waning seconds of overtime. It was a near instant replay of the 1991 Eastern Regional long-range shot that had similarly closed out Connecticut, again in overtime and again with no more than a few clock-ticks remaining. But with Laettner, there were many such big games and many tastes of championship victory: his 1991 and 1992 squads captured national titles, his sophomore squad reached the Finals where it was blown off the floor by UNLV, and his freshman outfit lost an NCAA semifinal matchup with Seton Hall but was, nonetheless, an ACC runner-up.

If there was ever a "go-to" guy of the modern era of college basketball, Laettner seemed to own the label as Tom Gola, Lew Alcindor, and Bill Walton had owned it in earlier decades. Laettner's rather average NBA career has seemed like an afterthought in the face of so much winning as a collegian, and what would have ordinarily been the achievement of a lifetime as the only collegian selected for a roster spot on the original 1992 U.S. Olympic Dream Team seemed, in Laettner's case, to have been no more than a career footnote. Christian Laettner (while at Duke at least) thus performed in the classic tradition of Oscar Robertson, Bill Bradley, and Tom Gola and numerous other NCAA headliners of the past. But thanks to the modern miracle of televised sports, he also did so in an era when many more fans could be counted on to be watching.

Bob Lanier, Detroit Pistons

© Detroit Pistons

Bob Lanier

One cage historian of note—Alex Sachare—has called Bob Lanier basketball's Ernie Banks. The reference, of course, is to the baseball Hall of Famer's lengthy and distinguished career pulling on the uniform for annual losers and his ill-deserved fate of always looking in from the outside during postseason playoffs. Unlike Banks, Lanier knew the taste of playoff action—it is almost an impossibility to spend much time in the NBA without some playoff experience, since the league's seemingly meaningless yearlong marathon schedule is destined only to eliminate a small handful of teams from the "second season." Lanier actually logged 67 postseason games during his 14 campaigns, but his Detroit (1971–80) and Milwaukee (1980–84) teams never made it to the championship round, and the 6'11" eight-time All-Star center thus never came close to earning a championship ring. Lanier was, nonetheless, a dominating player, in college with St. Bonaventure where he was the leading scorer (29.1) and rebounder for the 1970 NCAA fourth-place team, and in the NBA where his stature as Detroit's all-time scoring and rebounding pacesetter and as one of the league's top players of the 1970s earned a much-deserved spot in the Naismith Hall of Fame (1991).

Lisa Leslie

If there is one basketball scoring mark that would seem safe for the ages (along with Wilt's 100-point NBA game and Frank Selvy's 1954 trip over the century mark in NCAA competition), it would likely be Cheryl Miller's California high school state-record 105 points back in 1982. But that mind-boggling mark is only still on the record books today thanks to a high-minded schoolgirls coach who pulled his embarrassed club off the court at intermission in 1990 when Lisa Leslie's Inglewood High teammates fed her shamelessly in a somewhat unsportsmanlike all-out effort to shatter Miller's landmark. Leslie had to settle for 101 points (her team's entire output) earned in a single half. If the gangly 6'5" Leslie didn't over-haul Cheryl Miller in the record books, however, she came close to matching Miller's collegiate reputation in subsequent years. At USC (Cheryl's alma mater) Leslie was the first four-time All–Pac-10 selection since Miller and climbed to third (2,414, 20.1 points per game) on the school's scoring charts and fourth in rebounds (Miller is the record holder for both). She again fell slightly short of her famous predecessor as a three-time All-American (Miller was a four-time selection) and a 1994 National Player of the Year (Miller won a trio of such awards), but she did match Miller's 1984 Olympic gold medal. In recent seasons Leslie has continued her assault on the record books as a showcase player (Los Angeles Sparks) in the popular NBA-sponsored summer-season WNBA.

Guy Lewis

Here was one coach who seemed to make a career out of near misses. In the won-lost department Lewis missed by an eyelash (a mere eight games) of cracking the charmed circle represented by 600 career coaching victories. Five times he reached the prestigious NCAA Final Four with his University of Houston Cougars teams, and yet he never brought away a championship (a record for such futility), reaching the title game in consecutive years (1983 and 1984) only to be upset with his famed Phi Jamma Slamma squad of Olajuwon, Drexler, and Micheaux first by Jim Valvano–coached North Carolina State and next by John Thompson–coached Georgetown. Between his many disappointments Guy Lewis did have his moments. He was National Coach of the Year in 1968 (when his 31–2 squad was ranked No. 1 in the polls but torpedoed in the national semifinals by Wooden and UCLA) and again in 1983 (when his 31–3 team was again consensus No. 1 but unaccountably lost a seemingly safe lead down the stretch of the title game after the coach's question-able decision to adopt a conservative clock-killing spread offense). To clinch his near-miss reputation, Lewis twice owned the second-best player in the country— in 1968 when Elvin Hayes played in the shadows of Alcindor and again in 1983 when Akeem (not yet Hakeem) Olajuwon chased first Ralph Sampson and then Michael Jordan.

Nancy Lieberman-Cline

Induction into the Naismith Basketball Hall of Fame with the Class of 1997 finally brings fitting recognition to the glorious career of the former All-American and professional pioneer who early on did more to advance and popularize modern women's basketball than perhaps any other single figure. Nancy Lieberman-Cline has now joined Anne Donovan as the second Naismith inductee from Old Domin-ion University, but many knowledgeable followers of the women's game would probably argue that it should have been the other way around. After a spectacular collegiate career (1980 National Player of the Year, two 20-plus scoring seasons,

2,430 career points), the first flash-and-dash player of the modern women's era starred for two short-lived women's pro circuits (averaging 32 points per game with the Dallas Diamonds of the WBL) in the early 1980s before both quickly folded. Lieberman-Cline also blazed new trails in 1987 and 1988 when she became the first woman to compete in a men's league, playing for two different USBL summer-league franchises. She also wrote a best-selling autobiography entitled *Lady Magic* in reference to the nickname earned at Old Dominion with her fancy passing and ballhandling skills.

After a decade of endless campaigning for a legitimate women's pro circuit, Lieberman-Cline saw her dream realized with the June 1996 debut of the summer-season WNBA, a second post-Olympic women's circuit showcasing dozens of talented ex-collegians plus a representative sample of the 1996 women's gold-medal–winning Olympic stars (including Sheryl Swoopes, Rebecca Lobo, and Lisa Leslie). Despite her now rather advanced age of 39 years, Lieberman-Cline herself suited up for the new league as a still-agile guard with the Phoenix Mercury franchise and also spent several preseason months constantly on the road as a high-profile spokesperson for the new NBA-sponsored venture.

Rebecca Lobo

A few seasons back she was the most celebrated player in women's college basketball, and today she remains the most decorated performer (male or female) in Big East Conference history. But since joining the WNBA (New York Liberty), Rebecca Lobo's star has fallen considerably from the pre-Olympic period in which she starred on one of the most successful women's NCAA outfits ever and garnered most of the available collegiate roundball awards. The 6'4" forward was the ace scorer and rebounder on a 1995 35–0 Connecticut team that raced to the national championship with the most victories ever posted by an undefeated NCAA team (men's or women's). That same honor-laced year she appeared on David Letterman's popular late-night network television show, was featured as a magazine cover girl, and even found time to earn academic Phi Beta Kappa honors and co-author a best-selling book with her mother, detailing the latter's courageous bout with cancer during Rebecca's junior and senior seasons. Lobo was also the 1995 National Player of the Year, the Big East's career rebounding leader (1,268), second all-time scorer at UConn (2,133), a two-time All-American, and four-season All-Big East pick. Lobo's game was more raw power than flash, however, and during 1996 Atlanta Olympic performances and subsequent pro-league play, her image has slipped steadily behind those of more colorful and dramatic players such as Nikki McCray, Dawn Staley, Sheryl Swoopes, Natalie Williams, and Teresa Edwards among others.

Karl Malone (NBA "Top 50" Selection)

He carries one of basketball's most catchy and appropriate nicknames ("The Mailman") and one of the game's most relentless work ethics as part of his considerable star-quality package. And Utah's Karl Malone is all business when it comes to doing what he does best—moving the basketball from the defensive backboard directly into the enemy hoop for yet another valuable score. Here is a player who, for almost a decade, has had no true peer at the power forward position and few rivals as a total-package offensive force. It might even be claimed that Malone is now the perfect prototype for pro basketball's least glamorous bulk and brawn position. If he has routinely known the frustration of missing out on the ultimate prize of a championship ring—losing to Michael Jordan's Bulls in the final play-off series two seasons running—his individual honors have been, nonetheless, numerous. He owns two Olympic Dream Team gold medals, is the all-time Utah Jazz scoring leader, stands a shoo-in to finish his Hall of Fame–bound career in the league's all-time top five in scoring, already holds the NBA mark for most consecutive seasons with 2,000-plus points (11, outstripping both Jordan and Chamberlain), was league MVP once (1997) and All-Star Game MVP twice (1989, 1993), and has won All-NBA first-team honors a remarkable 10 times.

Karl Malone is also a marvelously conditioned athlete who works ceaselessly in the off-season weight room to keep his showcase body finely tuned for the up-coming season's NBA wars. And over a dozen seasons the league's heftiest inside defenders have paid the price for that relentless work regimen. "The Mailman" delivers the ball with authority into the waiting net almost any way imaginable (slams, lay-ins, soft jumpers, spin hooks), but most often with a jarring power move or a ruthless slam that is nearly impossible to defend. In 12 seasons Utah's durable tower of strength has averaged better than 26 points per game, one of the highest scoring ratios on record for a player who has never won an individual league scoring crown. The lack of scoring titles is similar, of course, to the experience of Oscar Robertson (playing in the era of Wilt Chamberlain); four straight seasons (1989–92) he was runner-up to Jordan, a fifth year (1993) he was third, and a sixth (1997) he again trailed Jordan only. He has also proven amazingly durable—a credit to his off-season workout program—missing only four games over his first 12 seasons as a pro. The last time Karl Malone missed a regular-season contest is now more than a half-dozen seasons in the past.

What is most often overlooked about Malone's complete inside game is the versatility of his talents. A power move to the hoop by "The Mailman" rarely misses, but when it does a foul shot is often the result. For five straight seasons at midcareer (1989–93) Karl Malone traveled to the free-throw stripe (and also converted) more than any other league player. This is a distinction he has again claimed over the past two NBA seasons. And the muscular physique of this marvelous athlete is capable of deflecting enemy offenses as well. Malone runs the floor with grace, plays hard-nosed defense with incredible tenacity, and simply owns the backboards (twice pacing the league at the defensive end) night after night at both ends of the floor.

Moses Malone (NBA "Top 50" Selection)

There isn't a longtime pro basketball watcher anywhere on the planet who doesn't select Chamberlain, Russell, and Abdul-Jabbar as his three greatest centers ever. After that the debate rarely, if ever, today departs from Moses Malone versus Hakeem Olajuwon for the No. 4 slot. Malone finished his career with 29,580 tallies, barely missing out on joining Abdul-Jabbar, Wilt, and Dr. J as the game's only 30,000-

point men. Basketball's most durable big man, behind Kareem Abdul-Jabbar and Robert Parish, Malone passed Elvin Hayes in 1994 to move into fifth place on the all-time combined ABA-NBA career scoring list. He is now also the NBA's career record holder for offensive rebounds (6,731), and also overtook Hayes and Havlicek for third on the all-time games-played listing (1,312) before finally retiring in 1995 at the end of 21 campaigns. But what makes Moses Malone quite so distinctive in NBA history has more to do with the odd beginning of his career two decades ago than it does with his milestone-strewn final few seasons that closed out in the middle portion of the 1990s. When he jumped directly from Petersburg (Virginia) High School to the ABA Utah Stars in 1974, the giant basketball prodigy became the first athlete to reach the pro circuit without playing any college ball since the late 1940s. Others (from Bill Willoughby and Darryl Dawkins in the '70s to Kobe Bryant and Kevin Garnett in the '90s) would later make similar spectacular leaps, but no other player has ever done so as the first giant step of what would turn out to be a Hall of Fame–level career.

Danny Manning

Danny Manning is one celebrated and unanimous Collegiate Player of the Year (Naismith and Wooden Award winner with Kansas in 1988) who has never quite sustained that same kind of magic in the professional ranks, despite a decade of double-figure scoring (mostly with the Los Angeles Clippers and Phoenix Suns) and a pair (1993, 1994) of NBA All-Star Game appearances. Injuries have been one factor in the decline, limiting the lanky forward-center to but 26 games as a rookie (after arriving as the overall top draft pick) and less than 80 games in his first two full seasons (1995, 1996) in Phoenix. The son of NBA and ABA journeyman Ed Manning, the three-time All-American ironically gained his prime notoriety in the NBA as the player traded (from the L.A. Clippers to Atlanta) straight up for megastar Dominique Wilkins in February 1994, one of the biggest celebrity trades of the current decade. It was a transaction that did little to benefit either club involved, as both the principles played only several months with their new franchises before opting for free agency at season's end (Manning with Phoenix and Wilkins with Boston). Although he has now logged more than 10,000 NBA career points (17.7 career average through his first nine seasons), Manning's career highlights, none-theless, all harken back to college days at Kansas, including a 1988 NCAA championship ring (when he was also NCAA Final Four MVP) and a bronze medal earned on the 1988 U.S. Olympic team.

Bob McAdoo

Bob McAdoo is a monument to the individual star who piled up reams of impressive statistics but never seemed to make any of the teams he occasionally carried on his shoulders any better or more competitive for all his heavy-scoring presence. If there is a unique niche for the 6'9" pivotman out of North Carolina (where he played a single 1972 All-American season as leading scorer on the NCAA third-place team), it is the fact that probably no one ever playing the post position shot the ball any better than this second overall NBA draft pick of the Buffalo Braves. His pro career

(Buffalo, New York, Boston, Detroit, New Jersey, Los Angeles Lakers, Philadelphia) spread over 14 seasons, and it boasted three consecutive scoring crowns early on (in his first 3 seasons, all with Buffalo) and two NBA team titles in his twilight years (with Los Angeles in 1982 and 1985). While he logged the bulk of his playing time in the pivot, McAdoo launched most of his frequent missiles as medium-range jumpers, a fact that underscores the brilliance of his career-long .503 shooting percentage. Most memorable about Bob McAdoo in the NBA was his inside quickness and deft shooting touch, which allowed him to constantly outmaneuver and outscore the much rangier inside players he matched up against. Most overlooked about his stellar career was his "second life" in Europe where, between the ages of 35 and 41, he logged seven remarkable seasons as a scoring star in the high-quality Italian professional league.

Nikki McCray

Arguments about the most complete or most talented women's hoopster—an honor once ceded to Nancy Lieberman-Cline and later usurped by Cheryl Miller—today usually comes down to debate between the flashy athleticism of collegian Chamique Holdsclaw versus endless on-court accomplishments of professional Nikki McCray. Holdsclaw has already, perhaps, moved into first place in the hearts and minds of Tennessee Lady Volunteers fanatics, but McCray supporters still have a legitimate case for their favorite when it comes to overall impact. As a collegian the 5'11" guard-forward was the emotional leader and defensive stalwart for a Tennessee outfit (at 122–11) that enjoyed the best stretch in school history until Holdsclaw's recent three-peat national champions. As an Olympian she was a Dream Team spark plug who did heavy-duty scoring in Atlanta alongside Lisa Leslie, Sheryl Swoopes, Katrina McClain, and Ruthie Bolton. As a professional McCray quickly became the featured showpiece of the ABL, which jumped into action a season ahead of the higher profile WNBA. (Before folding in 1998 the ABL seemed to be like the old '40s-era NBL—it had the better players and more competitive game; the WNBA parallels the old BAA with its plush NBA arenas and big-city markets.) In the inaugural ABL campaign McCray was MVP and linchpin of the league-champion Columbus Quest. She made her biggest splash, however, in the fall of 1998 by defecting to the rival WNBA, claiming the rival league could offer better career exposure and thus better commercial endorsement possibilities. The ABL's loss of its best player to the NBA-sponsored circuit was significant because it seemingly signaled perhaps the first movement toward what many already saw as an inevitable merger of the competing women's pro circuits.

Xavier "X-Man" McDaniel

Some super talents have to be content in the end with lesser status in the sports history books as answers to trivia teasers or as owners of obscure (if nonetheless considerable) achievements. One is Wichita State 1985 All-American Xavier McDaniel who earned his lasting niche as one of only three players in NCAA history (the others were ill-fated Hank Gathers of Loyola-Marymount in 1989 and Kurt Thomas of TCU a decade later in 1995) to simultaneously lead the nation in scoring and rebounding. McDaniel was first to turn the trick, when as a senior, he rattled home 27.2 points per game while averaging 14.8 in board clearing. Gathers scored more (32.7) but rebounded less (13.7) in his "double" season, while Thomas fell a fraction short of McDaniel in both categories (28.9 and 14.6). Once joining the pro ranks (fourth overall pick by the Seattle SuperSonics), the "X-Man" proved far less imposing: he did score above 20 for the season on four separate occasions (yet never better than 23) and topped out with an 8.6 rebounding average in his second of nine NBA seasons.

Kevin McHale (NBA "Top 50" Selection)

My own vote would probably still fall to Mikan, Mikkelsen, and Pollard when it comes to selecting the best-ever NBA front line. The "Tall Timbers" outfit in Minneapolis at the dawn of league history did, after all, win six championships in their seven seasons together and also revolutionized the way the game was played (by forcing legislations that changed the foul lanes, introduced the 24-second shot clock, and barred defensive goaltending—all aimed at neutralizing Mikan and his sidekicks). Pundits like *Boston Globe* beat writer Peter May, who has

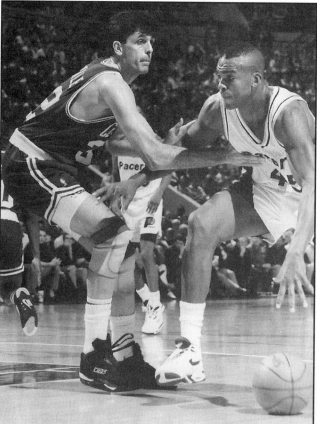

Kevin McHale (left), Boston Celtics

© Frank P. McGrath Jr.

more tunnelized vision when its comes to anything involving Red Auerbach and the Boston Celtics, would dismiss the old-timers in Minneapolis in favor of the Boston crew of the 1980s epoch—Larry Bird, Robert Parish, and Kevin McHale. And it must be admitted that May (in his book entitled *The Big Three*) states an awfully convincing case.

McHale's part of the argument (whether he is compared to Mikkelsen or Pollard—Hall of Famers both) is difficult to discount. As a 6'10" tower of strength with one of the longest pair of arms in the NBA since Walter Dukes of the Mikan era, McHale is, without doubt, one of the premier low-post scorers (20,517 regular-season and postseason career points) in NBA annals. He possessed a turnaround jumper that was impossible to block; his long legs and arms allowed pivot moves that left any defender confused and overmatched; and his work ethic was so strong that he even eventually turned himself into one of the league's lankiest adequate three-point shooters on record. While he was slow of foot and often prone to nagging injury, he always made up for any such deficiencies with a will and intelligence that were matched nowhere in the league except by the two giants (Bird and Parish) playing alongside him. With the most durable center of all time (Parish), the best all-around "point-forward" ever invented (Bird), and the last of the Boston line of great sixth-man subs turned into frontline superstars (Ramsey, Havlicek, and finally McHale), it is not surprising that Boston fought Magic Johnson's Lakers tooth and nail across the 1980s for domination of perhaps the NBA's strongest decade ever.

Cheryl Miller

The brightest star of the 1980s and also arguably of the entire history of women's collegiate hoops action (at least until Chamique Holdsclaw came on the scene) was

Cheryl Miller, USC

© University of Southern California

indisputably Southern Cal's electric and personable Cheryl Miller. Like Ann Meyers (sister of NBAer Dave Meyers) at UCLA a decade earlier, Cheryl Miller too came from a basketball-playing family that also featured a brother—Reggie—destined for his own college (UCLA) and pro (Indiana Pacers) stardom as one of the game's most deadly three-point shooters. But for all his own net-burning skills, NBA star Reggie Miller was never the biggest offensive threat in his own family; that honor clearly belonged to Cheryl from the day she knocked home a single-game record 105 points for a national high school scoring mark that has yet to be bested.

Cheryl Miller's 3,405 high school career points and 3,018 college tallies would make her one of the most productive offensive weapons in all of cage history—on either side of the locker room. The only three-time Naismith Award winner and later Naismith Hall of Famer

475

was also the only Southern Cal player, male or female, ever to have her uniform number permanently retired. But this first four-time Kodak All-American (1983–86) was far more than just the game's most talented athlete, as great as that accomplishment might be in and of itself. For it was Cheryl Miller's flamboyant personal style and special flair for on-court dramatics (another trait shared with her NBA brother) that as much as anything else heaped national attention on women's basketball when the sport finally boomed during the mid-'80s. It was Cheryl Miller, almost single-handedly, who first personified the grace of women's basketball as a prime-time sporting entertainment.

Reggie Miller

Reggie Miller is the most popular player in the history of the Indiana Pacers NBA franchise (also the club's all-time leading scorer); it is arguable that the 6'5" guard is the best pure shooting guard in the league sans the incomparable Michael Jordan; and few NBA stars have a bigger reputation for trash-talking flair. Miller has arrived during the '90s as one of the sport's largest icons. Nonetheless, the two-time "Dream Team" selection has never been able to push his keenest competitors out of the limelight.

Reggie Miller always seemed to be playing in someone else's shadow. Reggie's career has always, in fact, been dimmed by the predominating surrounding shadows. First there was the ongoing struggle to outdo the reputation of his famous sister, the best women's player of all time. Later, as a star at UCLA, Reggie led his team to a postseason NIT title while only a sophomore; still, he could never quite rise to the same brilliant level as so many earlier UCLA Bruins heroes like Lew Alcindor (later known as Kareem Abdul-Jabbar), Bill Walton, Gail Goodrich, or his own college coach, Walt Hazzard. And in the NBA Reggie has also always been known as merely the league's "second-best" overall shooting guard, forced to take his spot behind the remarkable Michael Jordan. Even in his adopted hometown of Indianapolis there was always the impossible legend of favorite native son Larry Bird to deal with. It was against all these numerous ghosts that Reggie Miller doggedly constructed his own lasting legend—as basketball's premier "trash-talking" showboat, as one of the NBA's most irrepressible personalities, and above all, as the most entertaining dead-eye long-range shooter in all of pro basketball history.

But if he has never entirely escaped these shadows, Miller has posted a remarkable effort in building his own looming image in the world of professional sports, despite all the heavy competition. Outside of the incomparable Michael Jordan in Chicago, it is arguable indeed that no player is more revered in his NBA hometown than is Reggie Miller in Indianapolis. This in spite of a personality that has often left Miller mentioned prominently among the league's "bad boys" and colorful flakes. No current player has a larger reputation for trash talk. But few, if any, have an equal reputation for also shooting the basketball. Because of Jordan's brief retirement, no other player but Miller has paced his team (the same team) in scoring every season of the past decade. And only Jordan ranks higher in most expert eyes as the best pure shooting guard found anywhere in the league.

The NBA career of the Indiana Pacers' all-time career scoring leader seems distilled in three marvelous postseason moments at the tail ends of the 1994, 1995,

Reggie Miller, Indiana Pacers

© Frank P. McGrath Jr.

and 1996 NBA campaigns. First came a record-breaking fourth-quarter scoring binge in Game 5 of the 1994 conference finals shoot-out with the New York Knicks. It was a center-stage moment in front of a national television audience punctuated by a verbal duel with Knicks super fan Spike Lee and underscoring Miller's potential for turning any near-defeat into victory with his hot shooting touch. A year later came another sensational game-ending shooting barrage against the same Knicks on the same court, which again stole a crucial playoff victory. This time the dead-eye Miller concentrated his comeback efforts not on the final full quarter, but rather the final minute of game action. And finally, there was a dramatic return to action after a serious eye injury during the final first-round game of 1996 that saw the Pacers eliminated by the Atlanta Hawks. Reggie's efforts were again not enough to prolong the Pacers' postseason, but they again demonstrated his immense skills and underscored his love affair with the basketball-savvy Indiana fans.

Doug Moe

Doug Moe might well have been among the biggest ABA stars had not injuries cut short his career after only a handful of high-scoring seasons. And the same Doug Moe might have stood among the winningest NBA coaches had not the bulk of his colorful bench career been spent with one of the league's most talent-thin, if nonetheless entertaining, franchises. As a star player at North Carolina under Frank McGuire (and a teammate there of Larry Brown) Moe twice earned second-team All-American honors but subsequently sat on the NBA sidelines after shadowy implications of impropriety in the 1961 collegiate point-shaving scandals. He had teamed with York Larese for the Tar Heels as a renowned one-two punch that led UNC to a top 10 ranking in 1961 and an ACC title that same year; the pair both averaged above 20 in scoring, and Moe was also second in the conference in rebounding. Given a shot with the ABA late in the decade, he enjoyed two big-scoring seasons (24.2 and 19.0) with the New Orleans and Oakland franchises before gimpy knees took their toll. As an NBA head coach he would compile 628 career wins and a positive ledger that was, at career's end, 100-plus games over the break-even mark; the bulk of the wins would come with Denver during a career that opened (1976) in San Antonio and closed (1993) with one partial season in Philadelphia. Despite staying above water with often mediocre teams Moe was most renowned in his heyday (throughout the '80s in Denver) for fiery sideline displays, open-collar sport shirts that were always garish low-fashion statements, a dogged belief in the up-tempo style of game, and a reckless run-and-gun style of play that kept scoreboards humming around the circuit but never won enough games to make any serious championship challenges during the all-important postseason playoffs.

Alonzo Mourning

A headline-grabbing NBA Rookie of the Year season is sometimes more a matter of good timing than it is of mere talent. Jerry West had the clear misfortune of debuting the same year as Oscar Robertson. Magic Johnson's rookie campaign unfortunately had to compete head-to-head with Larry Bird's curtain raiser. And talented Alonzo Mourning had the tainted luck to compete for rookie honors with a megastar named Shaquille O'Neal. The only apparent flaw in Mourning's rookie performance with expansion Charlotte was the simultaneous presence of the huge rival center playing for another league newcomer, the Orlando Magic. Another impediment to a breakout first NBA season was hostile contract negotiations with Charlotte's front office, which cost the second overall draft pick valuable preseason preparation.

Mourning was a much-heralded schoolboy recruit out of Chesapeake, Virginia, who rated at the top of an outstanding 1988 class of college recruits—ahead of Chris Jackson (Mahmoud Abdul-Rauf), Shawn Kemp, and Billy Owens. In his freshman season at Georgetown he led the nation in blocked shots; during his second campaign he became the first player ever named both Big East Player of the Year and conference Defensive Player of the Year during the same season. Graduating to the pro circuit on the heals of teammate Dikembe Mutombo, Mourning was an immediate impact player as a rookie (21 points per game, 10.3 rebounds per game), despite his holdout and missed training camp. While the expected breakout into full superstar status has not yet come in three seasons with Charlotte and four with Miami (where he was traded in a blockbuster seven-player deal in November 1995), Mourning's pro résumé has remained an impressive one. If he lost out to O'Neal in top-rookie balloting, most NBA insiders from the beginning had him pegged as a far more polished and dedicated athlete than Shaq. Potential superstar status still seems almost a foregone conclusion for a workhorse, if sometimes temperamental, player, whose arsenal includes both a vast array of low-post moves and a soft-shooting touch from the perimeter that is the envy of most of the league's competing centers.

Chris Mullin

The list is quite lengthy when it comes to celebrated college stars who have transformed themselves (sometimes by bad behavior, sometimes by smallness of heart, and sometimes simply by shortfalls in God-given talent) into altogether run-of-the-mill journeymen pros. Chris Mullin fits the profile, though at times he has threatened to bust out into at least moderate NBA stardom. As a collegian at St. John's in the mid-'80s, the 6'6" lefty-shooting guard-forward earned just about every recognition and turned just about every head possible. He made all the All-American squads as a high-scoring junior and senior, earned National Player of the Year recognition, finished up as the all-time scorer in the Big East Conference, and surprised no one as the No. 7 pick (Golden State Warriors) in the 1985 NBA draft. As a collegian he also enjoyed the first of two Olympic team spots (the second coming as a privileged member of Dream Team I in 1992). Mullin's high-octane offensive game also grabbed headlines with two solid debut seasons, yet was briefly sidetracked by entry into alcohol rehab in 1987–88. After a successful effort to turn around his drinking problems, the six-time All-Star only seemed to get that much better, averaging above 20 six straight seasons (five above 25) in one stretch and maintaining a career average above the magic 20 mark over a dozen seasons before a trade brought him to the Indiana Pacers. Under rookie coach Larry Bird and playing alongside fellow veteran Reggie Miller, Mullin underwent another career revival with an Indiana team that nearly upended the defending champion Chicago Bulls in the 1998 conference finals. But for all his solid play, Chris Mullin has rarely ever been ranked among the showcase guards or forwards in the league, and his role has always been that of a valuable and solid team player who contributes in the shadows of franchise superstars like Mitch Richmond or Tim Hardaway (at Golden State) or Reggie Miller and Rik Smits (with Indiana).

Dikembe Mutombo

Dikembe Mutombo wears a most distinctive and burdensome basketball pedigree. He is one of what, for a brief time, seemed a semiregular pipeline of towering John

Thompson–trained centers who stepped directly from the Georgetown University campus into the role of an NBA franchise player. First came Patrick Ewing, who almost single-handedly (if a bit belatedly) resurrected the New York Knicks as a serious NBA postseason force. Then came Mutombo with his mixed-bag reputation—he was an awesome shot blocker but an unpolished gem on offense who parlayed a third-team All-American selection into a slot as the fourth overall NBA pick. And lastly there was Alonzo Mourning, the sure-fire 1993 NBA prize rookie had it not been for Shaquille O'Neal.

Sandwiched between Ewing and Mourning, the personable and understated (as a person and player) Mutombo has inevitably suffered endless unfavorable comparisons. He does not, for starters, have the shooting range of either Ewing or Mourning. An African native like Olajuwon—who like Hakeem took to the game rather late—Mutombo has yet to fine-tune his passing game or to the subtleties of evading (or exploiting) double-teaming defenses. But there has always been a side to Mutombo's still-evolving game for which his exceptional strength and natural reflexes have left him most ideally suited—defense. He holds the NBA career record for most blocked shots per game (with a minimum of 400 games played) and the most consecutive seasons leading the league in per-game blocks (four). He has twice been NBA Defensive Player of the Year (1995, 1997) and has paced the NBA in total blocks five years running. Mutombo doesn't score much for a seven-footer (his career average is 13 points per game), but his additional talents as a rebounder (11.6, second in the league in 1997) and his lofty field-goal percentages (especially since joining Atlanta in 1997) make him one of the major inside threats even at the offensive end of the floor. Cut in the image of Bill Russell, Dikembe Mutombo is one of the most dominating defensive centers of this or any other NBA epoch. And also like Russell, the 7'2" agile import from Zaire provides just enough unexpected offensive zing to increase opponents' worst nightmares.

Don Nelson

Don Nelson was Red Auerbach's biggest bargain, picked up off the waiver wires for a few bucks in 1965 (after a mediocre debut with the Chicago Zephyrs and Los Angeles Lakers) and hanging around for 11 productive seasons as one of the most reliable clutch performers on the league's yearly best all-around team. Nelson might have never coached an NBA game (he ranks seventh in all-time victories, sandwiched between Larry Brown and Jack Ramsay) and he would still stand among the pro game's most memorable figures. As a player with Auerbach's Boston Celtics the Iowa All-American never won many individual distinctions. He was never among the league's leaders in scoring or rebounding or shot blocking, he only averaged double figures as a scorer once in his first five seasons, he was only occasionally a starter, and he never made a league All-Star team or All-NBA selection list. His one record-book distinction is that of leading the circuit in field-goal percentage in his 13th and penultimate season. But there have not been many in league annals who were better role players and who contributed in one fashion or another to the winning of more championship banners. Nelson boasts five NBA championship rings as a player (1966, 1968, 1969, 1974, 1976), and he contributed heavily to every one of those Boston glory seasons. He was a deadly jump-shooter and one of the most unflappable performers under the pressures of postseason play. Of the few individual distinctions Nelson did earn, one has overbearing significance—his number "19" is one of the 13 retired jerseys that long graced the rafters of legendary Boston Garden.

Akeem (Hakeem) "The Dream" Olajuwon
(NBA "Top 50" Selection)

An early measure of Hakeem Olajuwon's awesome basketball potential was signaled by his choice (over Michael Jordan and Charles Barkley) as the top pick of the hometown Rockets in the deep 1984 NBA college draft. At career's end (for all three) it is a full vindication of that selection that no other player of the era (with the clear exception of Jordan) has earned more likely deification among the sport's dozen or so all-time best than the African native who never touched a basketball until near the end of his high school years. Hakeem (then called Akeem) launched his unlikely pro basketball sojourn as a mere half of one the NBA's most celebrated duos of all time. Olajuwon—when teamed with prized 1983 rookie seven-footer Ralph Sampson—made up 50 percent of the famed "Twin Towers" front line that first did battle in 1984 for a newly revived Houston Rockets team. The experiment with two towering inside post men was destined to early failure, since Sampson quickly proved to be one of the most dramatic busts in the half-century of NBA play. But while Sampson's star crashed and burned, Olajuwon's only soared to new and unexpected heights. And a decade and a half later the super-talented Nigerian had evolved into one of the supreme solo acts in league annals. Hakeem has wasted little time over the past 15 seasons establishing himself as one of the game's most dominating big men of any NBA era.

Few could have predicted during Hakeem's rookie season that Olajuwon and not Sampson would one day soon become perhaps basketball's most versatile pivotman ever. Sampson, after all, had once earned raves with several All-American seasons in the prestigious Atlantic Coast Conference. Despite leading Houston's Cougars to three straight NCAA Final Four appearances, Olajuwon, on the other hand, was a mere basketball novice during his own All-American collegiate years. The former soccer goalie had taken up basketball only three years before enrolling at Houston. He was still in the process of learning roundball fundamentals at the same time he was earning his first NBA paychecks. But Olajuwon seems to learn faster than almost anyone who ever dribbled or shot a basketball.

The NBA career of Hakeem Olajuwon began with a bang, then elevated still further to a virtual explosion of rebounding, slam dunking, and shot-blocking firepower. As a 1984–85 novice he averaged 20.6 points per game and claimed the runner-up spot behind Michael Jordan in top-rookie balloting. He soon proved the quickest pivotman since Bill Russell, leading his team in steals in seven of his first eight NBA campaigns. In 1989 he established an NBA first with over 200 steals and 200 blocked shots in a single season. In 1990 he became the second player ever to grab 1,000 rebounds and block 300 shots for the year. And he would soon be only the third player in NBA annals to record 10,000 points, pull down 5,000 rebounds,

Hakeem Olajuwon,
Houston Rockets

© Frank P. McGrath Jr.

and cross the 1,000 threshold in steals, assists, and blocked shots. Only Kareem and Dr. J had reached such a plateau before Hakeem Olajuwon.

Many a rim has been rattled over the years by a jarring Olajuwon dunk, sending defenders back on their heels and inspiring pure crowd frenzy. In 1994 (with Jordan temporarily on the shelf) Olajuwon and his Houston Rockets finally arrived at the top of their game, winning the first of two consecutive NBA titles as the league's best contemporary center took regular-season and postseason MVP honors. Few NBA rivals of any size can match the Nigerian's quickness or raw leaping ability, and fewer still have ever played with Olajuwon's nightly intensity at both ends of the floor. No center since Wilt Chamberlain has owned the same soft touch on jump shots taken a dozen or more feet from the basket. Discussions of best-ever NBA centers always begin and end with only three candidates—Wilt, Russell, and Kareem. By the time the 1990s have finally closed there will, at last, also be a legitimate fourth contender intruding on those discussions.

Lute Olsen

Lute Olsen had a rather checkered reputation in the coaching ranks before 1997, despite some spectacular individual achievements and a solid quarter-century reputation for consistent winning. His nine Big Ten seasons in Iowa brought six 20-victory campaigns, one league championship, and one trip (1980) to the NCAA Final Four (an eight-point semifinals loss to eventual champion Louisville). At Arizona the record has been close to phenomenal with 11-straight 20-win campaigns and only 3 early seasons of double-figure losing. But despite a slew of Pac-10 titles (six) and a regular annual seat in the NCAA March shoot-out, there were constant complaints back home about underachieving Arizona teams that either lost in the opening rounds or, on a couple of occasions, failed to sustain momentum in the tournament's final sessions. In 1988 a 35–3 Arizona team starring Sean Elliott and boasting future baseball notable Kenny Lofton climbed to the final weekend and then slipped against Oklahoma in the semifinals. The 1994 edition with Damon Stoudamire was a Final Four victim of title-bound Arkansas. But if Lute Olsen seemed never to win the big ones when expected, he finally cashed in all his chips (and also ended much of the griping) with a Cinderella team that shocked favored Kentucky for the 1997 national title and made history by upsetting three No. 1 seeds (Kansas, North Carolina, and Kentucky) along the way. A pair of stellar young guards—junior Miles Simon and sophomore Mike Bibby (both sons of former pros)—carried the load in the overtime championship victory in Indianapolis. But the biggest news of the 59th annual NCAA March Madness gathering was that Lute Olsen—owner of 565 career victories—had finally taken college basketball's biggest monkey off his back.

Shaquille "Shaq" O'Neal (NBA "Top 50" Selection)

He is one of today's most popular celebrity athletes, and his "Shaq Attack" style of slam-dunking inside play now terrorizes helpless NBA defenders from New York to Chicago to San Antonio. O'Neal may not be quite ready (as NBA marketers once hoped) to supplant Jordan as the sport's top icon, but he certainly is a strong rival to Olajuwon and Ewing and David Robinson as the best NBA center of the current decade. In only a half-dozen seasons he has not only become perhaps the sport's most glamorous new superstar—poised to inherit the mantle now that Jordan has finally retired after his second three-peat in Chicago—but has also emerged as one of the nation's premier celebrity marketing fixtures in the process. Shaq is today every bit as omnipresent in television and magazine commercials, on video (as star of the popular movie *Blue Chips*) and over the radio airwaves (with his own rap music recordings) as he is on the hardwood floors around the NBA. And this is a large part of the problem with an athletic career whose hype and promise has to date far outstripped its on-court achievements.

O'Neal's NBA honors and milestones have not been inconsiderable over the past several seasons. He captured one of the two scoring titles available during Jordan's brief first retirement and was runner-up for the second. He carried the Orlando Magic into the NBA Finals against Houston and Hakeem Olajuwon, but was then outplayed by his post-position rival and failed to deliver the title that

*Shaquille O'Neal,
Orlando Magic*

© Frank P. McGrath Jr.

would mark his arrival as a superstar. His big numbers on offense have only been surpassed by the size of his contracts in Orlando and now Los Angeles. He was a featured player on the gold-medal Olympic team of 1996 and ran away with Rookie of the Year honors in his maiden campaign.

But there are, nevertheless, huge downsides to the Shaquille O'Neal image as one of the league's top players. His teams' failures during postseason in both Orlando and Los Angeles have been largely attributable to his unbalanced talents, especially his atrocious free-throw shooting, which becomes his teams' Achilles' heel late in crucial games. For all his pretenses as the league's top big man, he has few claims to the title when compared to Olajuwon and David Robinson, and perhaps even Patrick Ewing and the emerging Rik Smits. A selectee on the NBA Golden Anniversary list of the league's all-time 50 greatest players, O'Neal has, nonetheless, never been a first-team All-NBA selection, always losing out to Olajuwon or Robinson for the honor. Michael Jordan may have been, for years now, a fortunate beneficiary of the greatest public relations campaign (read here marketing campaign) in NBA history—also in American entertainment history—but at least MJ delivered enough year-in and year-out shattering performances to almost justify the runaway hype. To date, the league's similar attempt to sell O'Neal as an unparalleled icon for today's young fans seems to fall almost as far off target as one of Shaq's own misguided missiles from the free-throw line.

Robert Parish (NBA "Top 50" Selection)

Iron man is a label usually attached to Ron Boone, Randy Smith, Kareem Abdul-Jabbar, or more recently, A. C. Green. But perhaps it best fits longtime Boston Celtics tower of strength Robert Parish. The Parish career résumé features records for most NBA seasons played (21) and most games played (1,611), a pair of milestones recently captured from Kareem. That kind of rugged longevity has also allowed "The Chief" to garner an additional NBA standard for defensive rebounds (10,117), to log 23,334 points and 14,715 rebounds, to play in nine NBA All-Star Games, to garner the NBA playoff record for career offensive rebounds (571), and to collect three NBA championship rings in Boston (in the lineup with Bird and McHale) and one in Chicago (alongside Michael Jordan). When it comes to aesthetic assessment rather than raw numbers, many have also concluded that the decade-long Boston front line of Parish, Bird, and McHale was simply the best front-wall combo ever to play the game. There was only one drawback to Parish's hanging around the NBA until he was nearly 44 years old: his feats of stubborn longevity moved back by a few seasons his inevitable first-ballot election into basketball's top shrine at the Naismith Memorial Hall of Fame.

Gary Payton

If Michael Jordan in Chicago and Dennis Johnson in Boston were the best defensive guards ever (or at least of the modern slam-and-jam era), Gary Payton in Seattle doesn't fall very far behind. His impact is felt on the floor far more than in the stat books: he hounds the ball and gives constant fits to opposing point guards trying to advance play into the forecourt or trying to run an unimpeded offense. But Payton (like Johnson and certainly Jordan) takes equal care of business at the offensive end of the floor. He handles the ball with expertise in the open court, he penetrates and finishes, and above all he loves to run and create as hub of the explosive Seattle fast break. To add to his overall nuisance value in harassing opponents, Gary Payton also carries one of the game's biggest reputations as a noted "trash talker" and verbal intimidator.

Sam Perkins

From a strictly historical perspective, North Carolina's Sam Perkins may well be one of the ACC's most underappreciated legends. Certainly Perkins is rarely first (or even second, third, or likely fourth) on the lips of any Tar Heels fan reliving past glories. Yet he is the all-time rebounding champion and second-leading scorer for a school that has rung up basketball legends the same way that the New York Yankees have long run up Cooperstown Hall of Famers. Perkins may well take a backseat to Jordan, Ford, and Worthy in collective Tobacco Road memories, but he doesn't have to do so in the Carolina record book. It is there that he stands second only to Phil Ford as all-time scoring leader, alone at the top of the heap among all-time Carolina rebounders and shot blockers, and also in the top dozen for career field-goal percentage and free-throw shooting accuracy. This is saying quite a bit at a school that has produced the likes of Lennie Rosenbluth, Michael Jordan, Billy Cunningham, James Worthy, Jerry Stackhouse, Brad Daugherty, Charlie Scott, Walter Davis, Kenny Smith, and a seemingly endless host of other remarkable cage prodigies.

Scottie Pippen (NBA "Top 50" Selection)

There may have never been a better No. 2 star in an NBA lineup than Scottie Pippen, unless it was Jerry West behind Elgin Baylor or Kareem Abdul-Jabbar behind Magic Johnson in Los Angeles, or any of a number of Hall of Fame Auerbach-era Boston Celtics (Cousy or Heinsohn or Havlicek come readily to mind) who shared the Bos-

Scottie Pippen, Chicago Bulls

© Frank P. McGrath Jr.

ton lineups for 12-plus years with Bill Russell. Pippen is so athletic that he is even best described as acrobatic, his moves to the hoop are more polished and varied (and also more creative) than anyone's but Jordan's, and he is an electrifying "finisher" who also stands almost on par with MJ himself. More remarkable still is the fact that Pippen's greatest value is his presence on the floor as a defender. While averaging close to 20 points per game for his 11-year career (above the 20 plateau the past half-dozen winters), he has once led the circuit in steals per game (1995) and boasts seven nods on the NBA All-Defensive first team. The potent combination of offense and defense has also made the fifth overall draft pick (by Seattle) a four-time first-team All-NBA choice, a two-time second-teamer, and a one-time third-team choice. When Jordan took his brief sabbatical of 1993 and 1994, Pippen could not carry the Bulls back to the championship circle as a solo act, but he did assert his personal presence as MVP choice in the league's 1994 midwinter classic All-Star Game. NBA old-timers in New York, Philadelphia, Detroit, or Boston might have been a bit surprised (even stunned) by selection of the Chicago star over some of the league's more reputable pioneers (like George Yardley) or lofty point-makers (like Dominique Wilkins) when the Golden Anniversary 50 all-time best were anointed. But in Chicago most current-era Bulls fans would likely put Scottie Pippen on the all-time starting five.

Rick Pitino

The most thankless assignment in basketball coaching history has long been that of living up to the legend of Adolph Rupp in Kentucky, and Rick Pitino a few years back nearly pulled it off. Had he stayed around in the Bluegrass state a few more seasons, he might even have done so eventually. As it was he twice took the Wildcats to the NCAA title game in his final two seasons, won five SEC crowns in eight campaigns, put Kentucky back in the NCAA winner's circle with a 1996 national title, won 28 games four seasons in a row, and had UK consistently near the top of the national polls throughout most of his tenure. After a single losing campaign in 1990 his next half-dozen Wildcats juggernauts averaged a seasonal record of 27–8 and finished as low as second in the Southeastern Conference only once. Even his final Kentucky team, which posted a mediocre 17–13 yearlong mark, clawed its way into an NCAA title match with Cinderella Arizona and nearly pulled off one of the most surprising postseason finishes in decades. He was *The Sporting News* selection as College Coach of the Year in both 1987 at Providence and also 1991 in Lexington, and managed to fulfill his grossly inflated charge by adding to the impressive collection of UK national championship trophies. Maddening consistency was thus the final measure of Kentucky's biggest coaching idol outside of Rupp—just as it had been with the Baron himself—and for four straight years between 1993 and 1996, the Pitino-led Wildcats posted absolutely identical 28–7 ledgers.

Lataunya Pollard

There are only 13 women collegians who can boast 3,000 career points and Lataunya Pollard is one among that select number. The 5'10" guard out of East

Chicago (Indiana) was also almost single-handedly responsible for turning Long Beach State College into a women's cage powerhouse in the early '80s, when she won three All-American honors, picked up the coveted Wade Trophy as outstanding women's player of the 1983 season, and was twice acknowledged as West Coast Athletic Association Women's Player of the Year. More importantly, however, was Pollard's pioneering role as a "full-court player" who was instrumental in speeding up the transition style of play in women's college basketball. Pollard carried Long Beach to four straight postseason tournament appearances (three AIAW and one NCAA) while also setting four career and three single-season offensive marks (including those for points scored, scoring average, and field-goal accuracy). She was so popular among Long Beach fans in the early '80s—despite the still low-profile status of women's hoops during that era—that she even once rode atop the city's float in the annual Pasadena New Year's Tournament of Roses Parade.

Mark Price

Mark Price was a true trailblazer at Georgia Tech, especially when it comes to that chapter of the school's cage history devoted to membership in the Atlantic Coast Conference. As the first freshman in ACC history to top the circuit in scoring, the sharpshooting guard from Enid, Oklahoma, would launch a remarkable string of Tech ACC first-year performers who brought the new league school a unique distinction of owning four consecutive top-rookie selections. He would also play the leadership role on the first Yellow Jackets contingent to capture a league regular-season title as well as an ACC tourney championship. He would reign, as well, as the school's first-ever ACC Tournament MVP and its first league scoring champion, and he would also be Georgia Tech's initial four-

Mark Price, Georgia Tech

© Georgia Tech University

time all-league selection. Yet it was as a phenomenal shooter that Mark Price is best remembered around the Georgia Tech campus. He remains the only man in school annals to lead the squad in scoring in four different seasons. By the time he left campus, this polished competitor that many considered too slow for top-level backcourt play had made a serious dent in just about every existing school offensive record. He still ranks high in a number of school all-time offensive categories: points (second), scoring average (seventh), field goals made (third) and attempted (first), three-point field goals (seventh), three-point field-goal percentage (first), free throws made (third) and attempted (ninth), and free-throw percentage (third). But if Price was an offensive show in his years in Atlanta, he was also a proven winner. Before his arrival Tech could boast only a 22–57 overall ACC ledger and a 4–28 ACC league mark. By the time he moved on to a stellar NBA career, the Jackets had succeeded in capturing a league title, visited the postseason NIT, and twice been included in the year-end NCAA shoot-out, which is the grandest stage for collegiate basketball action.

Glen Rice

Michigan All-American Glen Rice has quietly emerged during the late '90s as one of the NBA's most talented and productive offensive performers. As a collegian he is also in the record books with the highest individual point total (184 in 1989) in any single NCAA tournament. Of all the huge stars in Michigan cage history, few have performed consistently better than 1989 NCAA tournament MVP Rice. A part-time player as a freshman (7.0 points per game), the future NBA All-Star Game MVP slowly matured into an offensive machine who captured league scoring titles his junior (22.9) and senior (24.8) seasons, climbed to first (now second behind Indiana's Calbert Cheaney) on the Big Ten's all-time scoring list, surpassed Mike McGee as Michigan's leading career scorer (2,422), and finished his career as leading scorer and rebounder on a crack 1989 Michigan NCAA champion. A mobile 6'7" guard-forward capable of playing inside or out, Rice still reigns as the Big Ten's single-season three-point field-goal pacesetter (55 in 1989) and also holds records at Michigan for career games played (134), career three-pointers (135), single-season points (949), and single-season field goals (363). In the summer of 1989 Rice became the NBA's fourth overall draft pick when selected by the expansion Miami Heat. Five seasons later he would rank as that team's all-time scoring leader before a multiplayer deal sent him to the Charlotte Hornets.

But it was in the dramatic 1989 charge to the national championship under replacement coach Steve Fisher where Rice enjoyed his finest hour. In the two decades from 1975 to 1994 only one player was able to score more than 25 points in each of the two games at a single Final Four (it had last been done by UCLA's Richard Washington). Rice was that player, and his championship point production included a record 27 three-point buckets and a record 184 total points in six tournament games. The steady hand of Steve Fisher may well have contributed a much-needed emotional lift for the disoriented Wolverines in the wake of Bill Frieder's sudden departure on the eve of 1989 March Madness action. But it was Rice who provided the bulk of the firepower that was the true key to Michigan's first-ever national title.

Mitch Richmond

While Richmond may not fall into the same category with superstars like Jordan, George Gervin, Alex English, or especially Oscar Robertson, nowhere can be found a more perfect prototype of the classic designation known as "pure scorer." The 10-season Sacramento Kings veteran year in and year out has maintained a scoring pace (15,748 points, 23.1 points per game) that always makes him a thorn in the side of any defense, even if his numbers have never seriously challenged for a league scoring title. Yet the 1989 Rookie of the Year out of Kansas State collects those points in a manner that provides an image of one of the NBA's most perfectly constructed offensive machines. His jump shot is deadly even with a gang of defenders hanging all over him, he drives the lane with fearless abandon and finishes consistently when he reaches the hoop, and he uses his muscular frame inside to overmatch defenders who are his own size (6'5"). His career highlight moment (a rare one for a player buried in Sacramento) came with an MVP performance (and 23 points) in the 1995 NBA All-Star Game.

Pat Riley

As a collegian Pat Riley played for one of the most memorable losers in NCAA Finals history—the all-white 1966 Rupp-coached Kentucky team defeated by all-black Texas Western. He was high scorer for Rupp's Runts at 22 points per game and teamed there with future ABA great Louie Dampier. As an NBA player he logged three seasons in San Diego and three in L.A., one as a bench player with the potent 1972 Lakers championship outfit coached by Bill Sharman. But all the best was yet to come. For as a pro mentor in Los Angeles, New York, and Miami, the same Pat Riley has been nothing short of one of pro basketball's largest winners of the modern era or any other era. Riley inherited (from Paul Westhead early in 1981–82) and then successfully directed the Kareem-inspired "Showtime" Lakers outfit that was a championship fixture of the mid-'80s. He next took his high-profile act to New York, where in a single 1991–92 campaign, he fully resurrected long-dormant Knicks fortunes, then kept the Ewing-led Knicks at the championship doorstep for three additional 55-plus-win seasons. It is an act he has recently also been replaying as coach and GM in Miami over the past several winters. The sum of Riley's NBA coaching impact has been a position as fifth-winningest NBA-ABA coach ever at the start of the 1998 campaign (he was then only 21 victories short of Dick Motta for fourth slot), the highest winning percentage (by a wide margin at .700-plus) of any of the dozen coaches at the top of the all-time victory list, and the first repeat title winners (back in 1987 and 1988) after two full decades of constant post-Auerbach NBA championship flux.

David Robinson (NBA "Top 50" Selection)

If San Antonio's David Robinson ranks a few notches behind Houston's Hakeem Olajuwon and New York's Patrick Ewing as the top all-around contemporary NBA center, it is probably only because of a subtle difference in playing style. Olajuwon and Ewing are more traditional post men who employ bulk and brawn to intimidate and to totally control a zone that extends 5 to 10 feet from the basket. Robinson is a much more mobile giant, one who will entice his counterpart into a no-man's land near the top of the paint and then bury him with a series of deadly jumpers, hooks, and fadeaways. It is a technique that was sound enough to allow "The Admiral" to emerge as the NBA's first individual scoring leader during what appeared at the time (in 1994, with MJ's first and only temporary retirement) to be the dawn of basketball's post-Jordan era. By edging Shaquille O'Neal and Olajuwon for the 1994

David Robinson,
San Antonio Spurs

© Frank P. McGrath Jr.

individual scoring crown, the Spurs ace also became the first true center to pace the NBA in point-making since Kareem Abdul-Jabbar way back in 1972.

But a description of Robinson's unorthodox post-play style should not suggest that his game is "soft" or even nonphysical by nature. When play shifts to the opposite end of the court, Robinson emerges as one of the most intimidating defensive bruisers the league has seen in years. The towering former Naval Academy All-American is already the Spurs' all-time leader in blocked shots, a category in which he now ranks 23rd in NBA history and 12th among active players (at the end of the 1997 season). In 1992 he was also the only post-position player in the entire league to rank in the top five in steals. And his trophy case displays an award for NBA 1992 Defensive Player of the Year.

The reason that Robinson prefers to clear out of the clogged traffic lanes and face the hoop actually has everything to do with his special brand of offensive talent. This mobile big man's perimeter game is best suited to exploit most fully his major asset—his lightning-like quickness operating from the low-post position.

Given room to maneuver, he will unleash catlike spin moves to the hoop that no seven-foot defender can likely hope to block. When he doesn't sink such a shot, he at least winds up on the foul line in most cases, spending more time at the charity stripe in recent seasons than anyone except Utah's Karl Malone.

Glenn Robinson

If there is a prototype for the grossly overpaid and ultimately disappointing professional cage star of the current decade, that prototype is found with Glenn Robinson of the Milwaukee Bucks. A clear choice as No. 1 draft pick after a stellar season as a Purdue junior (basketball eligibility sophomore) in 1994, Robinson and his agent demanded a contract worth $100 million from the Milwaukee franchise that held rights to his selection. It was an amount that most observers (not only fans but also veteran NBA stars making a mere fraction of that amount) found incredulous in the case of an athlete with no proven performance on an NBA court. Robinson's haul for signing would eventually be closer to $70 million, but this did not soften the blow when the league's supposed top new attraction reported late to preseason camp as a result of his contract holdout, scored profusely (20-plus per game) but gave away nearly as many points as he made with shoddy defensive skills, trailed Detroit's Grant Hill and Dallas's Jason Kidd for Rookie of the Year honors, and (most importantly) failed in his first and subsequent seasons to lift the Milwaukee ball club from its lackluster season-long performances at the bottom or near-bottom of the Central Division heap.

If Robinson has been both overrated and overpaid as a pro and overhyped as a collegian as well, this is not to indicate that he was not indeed, at moments, one of the most glamorous collegiate stars of the present decade. For one marvelous season the Purdue star dominated the NCAA scoring stats, established Big Ten and school records for point production, and found near-unanimous support for selection as the 1994 stellar performer in the collegiate ranks. With a scoring standard of 30.3 Robinson was an easy winner of both the annual Naismith and Wooden Awards as top collegian and also a consensus first-team All-American. He was the first Purdue player and first Big Ten performer to lead the nation in point-making in three decades, and the first in school and league history to amass 1,000 points in a single season. But for all that he gave Purdue fans to cheer about in terms of individual accomplishment, there was to be no long-awaited national championship attached to Robinson's dominant offensive play—not even a trip into the tournament's Final Four as most Purdue watchers had casually assumed. Purdue came close, but Robinson was outplayed by future NBA superstar Grant Hill, and the Boilermakers tumbled to Duke in the NCAA regional finals. And then, after two seasons, Robinson was suddenly gone, taking his unlimited promise with him to the NBA.

Dennis Rodman

A distressingly large number of recent NBA talents have dissipated their promising careers with immature off-court indulgences and ego-driven on-court displays of rank selfishness. Players like Isaiah Rider, Derrick Coleman, and Allen

Dennis Rodman, Detroit Pistons

© Frank P. McGrath Jr.

Iverson come quickest to mind. Yet with contemporary basketball's most outrageous self-promoter and notorious "bad boy" Dennis Rodman, behavior seemingly in the worst interests of the game has somehow miraculously been merged with a continuing legacy as the sport's premier rebounder and defensive star of the modern era. As Rodman's personal appearance (ever-changing hair colors, a muscular body covered with tattoos and a penchant for cross-dressing in public), reputation for on-court pouting, referee baiting, and loose personal lifestyle have all seemingly spun out of control, nonetheless the league's rebounding paragon has continually entrenched himself among the handful of legendary talents who have been able to control a basketball game without ever taking a single shot. In this category he stands alongside Bill Russell, Nate Thurmond, and Paul Silas as one of the sport's most devastating all-time rebounding and shot-rejecting one-man forces.

Rodman originally blossomed in Detroit under coach Chuck Daly, where the second-round draft selection from Southeastern Oklahoma State was groomed as a defensive stopper and frontcourt sparkling reserve on the two-time Detroit championship teams featuring Isiah Thomas and Joe Dumars and known as "The Bad Boys." It was at the NAIA school that Rodman first demonstrated his special talent by averaging 25.7 points per game and twice winning the NAIA rebounding crown. He first made his mark on the pro league by leading the NBA in field-goal percentage during the Pistons' first championship season. When the team repeated its title Rodman had moved into the starting lineup and was not only a league All-Star but also NBA Defensive Player of the Year. A season later the Pistons' reign was ended, but Rodman again was the NBA's top defender. And in his final two seasons with Detroit Rodman captured the first of his string of league rebounding titles which would eventually stretch to seven in the 1998 season.

Rodman's first NBA rebounding crown came with a career-high 18.7 average, which was the highest since Chamberlain's 19.2 20 seasons earlier. While Rodman's overall numbers do not match those of board-sweepers from the '50s and '60s, when the art was more practiced and when board-sweepers received a considerable assist from lower shooting percentages, his relentless and single-minded pursuit of caroms has, nonetheless, carved out a special place in league history. A sixth league title tied him for second place on the NCAA career list with Moses Malone. A seventh title in 1998 left Rodman alone in the career standings behind Chamberlain with the likely insurmountable total of 11 individual rebounding championships. The comparisons tilt in Rodman's direction when it is observed that almost all the other great NBA board-sweepers have been centers, not forwards like Rodman. No other forward in league annals has come close to Rodman's rebounding proclivities. And adjusting for variations in shooting percentages (and thus rebounding opportunities), Rodman's numbers rank favorably alongside the higher career averages of players like Chamberlain, Russell, Thurmond, and Silas.

Disciplinary problems in San Antonio (where Rodman was traded in 1993) detracted from his rebounding greatness in the mid-'80s. His signing by the powerhouse Chicago Bulls for the 1996 campaign had naysayers claiming that the franchise featuring Jordan and Pippen had made a colossal mistake in taking on a player likely to disrupt team harmony. Yet Rodman (while still featuring changing hair colors and even signing on in the off-season as a professional wrestler) contributed heavily to two Chicago NBA world titles and the two best single-season won-lost records in league record books. Dennis Rodman may long be remembered after his playing days as basketball's most outrageous self-promoter, but he unarguably deserves an equal niche in the sport's collective memory as the greatest rebounding forward and big-impact defensive player of pro basketball's first half-century.

Nykesha Sales

What might have been the glorious finale of one of the showcase performers of late-'90s women's college basketball was suddenly and tragically turned into a nightmare of cheap showmanship that left Nykesha Sales and her University of Connecticut career as an object of controversy rather than adoration. The unfortunate events came in the final weeks of the 1998 season as Sales—the most recent star for one of the nation's premier programs—closed out an All-American career and closed in on a school scoring record that had escaped the clutches of two other major UConn stars who had immediately preceded her—Rebecca Lobo and Karen Wolters, both National Players of the Year. Lobo had fallen only a stone's throw from the record of 2,177 points held by Kerry Bascom when she wrapped up her own career with 2,133. Sales had moved within a single point of the mark when she ruptured her Achilles tendon in the penultimate game of her senior season while driving for a hoop that would have clinched the new record. Circus soon replaced legitimate athletic competition when Huskies coach Geno Auriemma allowed his injured star to enter the lineup for an opening tip in the season's finale; Sales hobbled on crutches for a record-breaking layup (later stricken from the books) while cooperative teammates and opponents stood by as noninterfering specatators.

Ralph Sampson

Numerous are the athletes who have enjoyed stellar college careers and yet proven highly ordinary or even remarkably unproductive as professionals. The list would have to include Art Heyman, whose incomparable Duke All-American career was never matched by equal NBA prowess. Bill Bradley was hardly a bust in the pros, but then again he was never the once-in-a-lifetime superstar that had graced the campus at Princeton. Philly's Tom Gola somehow transformed one of the greatest college careers ever into one of the least memorable NBA sojourns. And David Thompson saw his ABA and NBA careers, in the end, sabotaged by drug problems. Of course, in the case of Gola and Heyman, it may have been limited physical skills that let down gritty college performers once they reached the more demanding pros. Nowhere, however, is there to be found a greater slide from collegiate stardom to NBA mediocrity than with the roller-coaster career of seven-footer and ACC legend Ralph Sampson.

Sampson entered the NBA's 1983 college player draft with press clippings as lengthy and prospects as lofty as any All-American could ever boast. When Houston grabbed Sampson with the luck of a coin flip in 1983 and then elected hometown college star Hakeem Olajuwon a year later (ahead of Michael Jordan and Charles Barkley), the Rockets seemed to have clinched their championship future for the next decade. Headline stories everywhere billed the new "Twin Towers" as the can't-miss unstoppable force that would rule the remainder of the decade. By tabbing Olajuwon, the Houston team would indeed get the franchise player on whom later championships would hinge. But the selection of Sampson quickly proved one of the biggest boondoggles in NBA drafting history. The three-time Collegiate Player of the Year never proved to be much of a scorer in the pros, just as he had never dominated the scoring categories in college. But neither was he a dominating force in any other aspect of the game. There was one memorable shot that won a single playoff series. But this was hardly the stuff of a future dynasty, destined to conjure memories of Lew Alcindor or Bill Russell or Wilt Chamberlain or even Nate Thurmond and Willis Reed.

Sampson's college career, when looked at in retrospect, may have also been something of a disappointment. He did bring Virginia an NIT title as a freshman and a trip to the NCAA Final Four as a sophomore. But the final two seasons in Charlottesville never brought the coveted national title that was expected with potentially so dominant a player. Sampson never seemed motivated to pile up points or individual records for scoring or rebounding; but unlike Alcindor at UCLA, he did not make his team unbeatable, either. There were many solid performances perhaps only soured by unrealistic expectations for an athlete so big and apparently gifted. And for three straight years there were selections as National College Player of the Year. But with Sampson, one was always left with the feeling that there should have been so much more. The doubts that shadowed the giant in Charlottesville were clearly and loudly affirmed once he took his act—with seemingly little enthusiasm—into the unforgiving proving grounds that made up the NBA.

Jack Sikma

There are many impressive numbers that comprise the 14-year NBA stats of Jack Sikma. More than 17,000 points, a career 15.6 scoring average and no season without double figures, nearly a steal-per-game average as a pivotman (one season with triple figures in that category), more than 1,000 blocked shots, and 10,000-plus rebounds. Prize-winning achievements are also numerous for the 6'11" stalwart who split his career between Seattle (nine seasons) and Milwaukee (five). These include seven league All-Star Game selections, membership on the 1982 NBA All-Defensive Team, one NBA championship ring (Seattle, 1979), and two appearances (in his first two pro seasons) in the NBA championship finals. But what was most memorable about Jack Sikma was his relentless workmanlike dedication to his game and a surprising shooting touch away from the basket that made him nearly impossible to defend and also left him as one of the league's finest free-throw shooters (a rarity among near seven-footers). Two seasons his accuracy from the charity stripe climbed above 90 percent, and his career mark was a most impressive .849 (one of the loftiest ever for a center or power forward). With a scoring average in the upper teens, aggressive rebounding talents (he was second in the league in 1982), more than a thousand blocked shots, and a free-throw style and medium-range jumper that were both uncanny for a big man, Jack Sikma was one of the most versatile of all modern-era NBA centers.

Lionel Simmons

The primary offensive skills are those of scoring and rebounding, and among college greats almost no one combined these basic talents more prolifically than La Salle University '80s-era standout Lionel Simmons. The point-making and board-clearing numbers posted by Simmons across his four-year college career (1987–90) are truly staggering. Only one player in a full century of college action has amassed a larger combined total of points and rebounds, and that player ironically also starred at La Salle—Tom Gola, whose scoring-rebounding combined totals (4,663) edge

Lionel Simmons,
La Salle University

those of Simmons (4,646) by only a mere handful. Gola (1952–55) was more the rebounder (one of only two—along with Joe Holup at George Washington University in the same seasons—ever to collect more than 2,000) and Simmons more the scorer (finishing third after Pete Maravich and Freeman Williams on the all-time list). Simmons stands alone, however, as the only collegian ever to amass more than 3,000 points (3,217) while at the same time collecting more than 1,100 rebounds (1,429). His heady college career was capped in 1990 with the Naismith Player of the Year Award and a seventh overall selection (Sacramento) in the NBA draft. Yet as a pro, success has been far more limited, though the muscular 6'7" forward did finish second to Derrick Coleman in 1991 Rookie of the Year balloting and did enjoy three productive seasons at the very outset of his NBA career. In recent seasons, however, Simmons has slipped drastically as an offensive force, and a half-dozen years into his mediocre career in Sacramento, he was only a part-time player who averaged less than double figures (after 1995) and saw drastically decreased playing time (less than 1,000 minutes in 1996 and barely 500 in 1997) on one of the league's most truly inept teams.

Randy Smith

Randy Smith's name emerged from obscurity early in the 1997–98 NBA season when A. C. Green overhauled Smith's long-standing NBA mark for consecutive games played. The record, which had stood since March 1983, was set by Smith across 11 seasons with Buffalo, San Diego, Cleveland, New York, and Atlanta. Playing mostly for backwater league teams and also in a 1970s-era of near dormancy for the NBA, Smith's iron-man feats drew little notice at the time they were carried out and drew little subsequent attention in available tomes on NBA history. But his regularity in the lineup for more than a full decade did allow the fleet 6'3" guard (who had been more of a soccer standout in college at Buffalo State) to post some rather surprising career numbers. His 16,262 career points are more than Pete Maravich or Walt Frazier could muster, his 976 games played top Jordan's total and more than double Mikan's, and his 1,403 steals rank in the career top 15.

Steve Smith

Steve Smith is currently one of the NBA's most effective shooting guards and combines with playmaker Mookie Blaylock to give the Atlanta Hawks one of the most talented backcourt duos found anywhere on the pro hoops circuit. Smith, like Blaylock, languished for several seasons on another league team (in this case the

Miami Heat, where he was the club's MVP in 1993 and a league first-team All-Rookie selection in 1992) before a trade to Atlanta (along with Grant Long for seven-footer Kevin Willis) placed him under the guidance of Naismith Hall of Fame player and coach Lenny Wilkens. With Atlanta the Michigan State all-time leading scorer lifted his offensive performance to more than 18 points per game during his first full season under Wilkens and alongside Blaylock (1996) and then above 20 points per game a year later. The 6'8" speedster with his wealth of talented driving moves to the bucket paced Atlanta in scoring (18.9) during a 1997 postseason that featured a surprise first-round success against Detroit (3–2) and a second-round loss in five games to the champion Chicago Bulls. One of the top half-dozen career scorers in Big Ten Conference history, Smith has yet to live up entirely to impressive collegiate credentials, which included regular All-Conference and All-American honors and two seasons of 20-plus scoring. Yet despite the reams of unfulfilled potential, one popular 1997–98 preseason pro basketball annual publication nonetheless rated the Hawks' top offensive weapon as the NBA's fifth-best overall shooting guard, ranking Smith in this category behind only the high-profile quartet of all-everything Michael Jordan, sweet-shooting Mitch Richmond, long-range bomber Reggie Miller, and prodigal superstar Latrell Sprewell.

Rik Smits

Rik Smits was in the league 10 years before he earned his first NBA All-Star Game berth, an unprecedented, if somewhat dubious, boasting point. Yet this was only one sign that the 7'4" Indiana Pacers center was one of the most underrated NBA performers of the '90s, and perhaps even one of the least appreciated agile big men of all time. A two-time East Coast Athletic Conference Player of the Year, the native of the Netherlands was the second overall choice of the 1988 draft (after Danny Manning of Kansas), a selection based more on his awesome size and considerable promise than on his 18.2-points-per-game scoring average at unheralded Marist College. Yet as an all-rookie-team performer for the Pacers in his first season the "Flying Dutchman" was far from a project in

Rik Smits, Indiana Pacers

© Frank P. McGrath Jr.

the traditional sense: he was coordinated, mobile, and had the shooting touch of a small forward. Smits's weaknesses early on were a lack of upper body strength and an apparent unwillingness to be aggressive on both offense and defense, factors that kept him from being a truly dominant inside force and also resulted in excessive fouling (he twice led the league) during his earliest seasons. While Larry Brown built solid Indiana teams around Smits's developing inside power and Reggie Miller's long-range shooting in the mid-'90s, chronic foot pain, nonetheless, slowed the seven-footer and even threatened his NBA career in 1997. Corrective surgery on the eve of the 1997 season cost the Pacers their star center for nearly half a campaign, but also alleviated the problem and seemingly provided a new career lease for the huge Dutchman. Smits's quick start at the outset of the 1998 season, along with a simultaneous upswing in performance by his Pacers team under new head coach Larry Bird, finally resulted in All-Star Game recognition for one of the finest shooting post players of the past decade.

Latrell Sprewell

If there is a classic bonehead play in basketball's 10-plus decades, it has to be the outrageous moment of "gangster" violence perpetrated by Golden State Warriors guard Latrell Sprewell early in the 1997–98 season. The forgettable moment involved a physical assault on coach P. J. Carlesimo during a Warriors practice session and led to league suspension of the wayward ballplayer, followed by expected legal action for reinstatement by the athlete and his battery of attorneys. A subsequent arbitrator's ruling against the league's yearlong ban and heavy fine levied on Sprewell proved to be one of the NBA's darkest and most embarrassing hours of recent decades. All in all, there were obviously no winners in this infamous case. In his uncontrolled moment of physical violence directed at his helpless coach, Sprewell threw away both a multimillon-dollar playing contract and an additional source of hefty endorsement income, which, taken together, were perhaps the size of the gross national product of the island nation of Haiti. Basketball's most infamous 'bonehead" thus became the first professional athlete in the modern era of megabucks salaries to be fired from his job for his inability to exert even a modicum of personal self-discipline. Before the incident Sprewell's talents (which were certainly considerable) barely stayed a step ahead of his reputation for sullenness (which was nearly as lofty). In his first five NBA seasons basketball's most infamous "gangster" averaged above 20 points on three occasions and barely missed that mark on a fourth. He was an All-League first-team choice in his second campaign and has appeared on three All-Star Game rosters (knocking down 19 points in the 1997 classic). But even hefty scoring was not enough to cancel out Sprewell's demonstrated disdain for playing defense, and his team value was further diminished by an inability over his first several seasons to play harmoniously alongside fellow All-Star guard Tim Hardaway. Even before the violent incident, which marred the 1997 Warriors season, and in turn jacked up Sprewell's reputation as an overpriced malcontent, it seemed difficult to think of another single player in the present-day NBA who got less positive mileage (such as contributions to team performance) out of his quite awesome natural talents.

Jerry Stackhouse

One of the most highly touted of Dean Smith's many fine North Carolina All-Americans, Jerry Stackhouse is also one of pro basketball's biggest disappointments of the current decade. Abandoning the ACC at the end of his sophomore season as the third overall NBA pick, Stackhouse did manage to lead the lowly Philadelphia 76ers in scoring (19.2 points per game) as an explosive rookie, yet failed to match preseason hype and lost out in the top-freshman balloting to Toronto's flashy Damon Stoudamire. As an NBA sophomore he was soon overshadowed by still another NCAA early-departure case who emerged as the new rookie backcourt ace for Philadelphia. Allen Iverson, out of Georgetown, was the league's next freshman sensation, whose even more lofty scoring and spectacular ballhandling buried Stackhouse's game in the local press. While his own scoring (20.7) held to his rookie pace, Stackhouse's stock seemed to dip precipitously in the Liberty City once Iverson was on the scene. And so did his attitude once there didn't seem to be enough basketballs on the floor to satisfy the two young backcourt hotshots. Acquisition of Jim Jackson from New Jersey bumped Stackhouse from a guard post to the small forward slot, a role he was more familiar with in college, but it was altogether apparent after only one NBA season that the former Tar Heels All-American needed serious work on his ballhandling and long-range shooting skills. It was not surprising that, before the middle of his third season, Stackhouse had already been dealt to Detroit, and at the same time, found his once promising career already in need of some serious reconstruction. Jerry Stackhouse may be the best illustration yet of the obvious pitfalls of early departure to the NBA by young players whose physical talents are abundant but whose overall games have not yet undergone necessary maturation and whose psychological maturity levels are also not yet ready for the rigors of a seemingly endless NBA season.

Dawn Staley

Who is the only player in storied ACC history to register more than 2,000 points, 700 rebounds, 700 assists, and 400 steals? Ralph Sampson, James Worthy, Sam Perkins, David Thompson, John Lucas, or Michael Jordan might all be good guesses. The answer—surprisingly, perhaps, for those who focus only on the men's hoops game—is University of Virginia women's Player of the Year (in both 1991 and 1992) Dawn Staley, and the rare distinction is not the only one that this fireplug 5'6" guard owns. Staley is also one of but two multiple-year winners of the prestigious women's Naismith Award (for College Player of the Year)—an honor shared with USC Hall of Famer Cheryl Miller. And she also shares with Miller (and now also with Chamique Holdsclaw) the rare distinction of leading her team to three NCAA title games (a feat that Tennessee's Holdsclaw failed to surpass during the recent 1999 campaign). Once college days ended for the Philadelphia native in 1992, further glories would come for Staley as a member of the gold medal 1996 women's Olympic squad and as a star with the Richmond Rage in the short-lived women's American Basketball League. In the latter capacity Staley set inaugural season highs in the new circuit for single-game steals and minutes played as well as earning first-team All-League honors at guard. An irony surrounding the remarkable college and pro cage career of the diminutive Dawn Staley is the fact that she once honed her court skills on the same neighborhood playground in Philadelphia that also produced former Loyola-Marymount All-Americans Hank Gathers and Bo Kimble.

John Starks

Three-point field goals and John Starks are almost synonymous. This does not mean that Starks owns the bulk of NBA records in this statistical department, although he does claim a small collection of long-range shooting marks. It does mean, however, that he has unleashed some of the league's most memorable prime-time bombs, and has done so in front of some of the sport's largest postseason television audiences. In other words, like so much in today's world of professional or big-time college sports, Starks's overall "rep" is largely a matter of "image" and based only tenuously on actual substantive achievement. As a collegian he played on three different junior college campuses before a single productive campaign with Oklahoma State. Once moving to the NBA (where he was undrafted but signed originally as a free agent with Golden State), Starks became noted for gritty playoff performances in the mid-'90s, especially against Michael Jordan and the Chicago Bulls and Reggie Miller and the Indiana Pacers. He was one of the few bright spots for New York in the 1994 NBA Finals loss to Houston, firing his long-range missiles with special effectiveness and even setting a record with 50 three-point attempts for the seven-game series. Among league three-point bombers he has never been at the top of the single-season or career lists, but has nevertheless turned in some noteworthy record-breaking performances. He shares the regular-season single-game mark for treys connected in a half, and also the playoff record for most in a single half. The ultimate career highlight came in the 1997 season, however, with the league's prized Sixth-Man Award for yearlong outstanding play off the New York bench.

Norm Stewart

Missouri's 30-year headman cracked a new milestone when he reached 700 career wins early in the 1997–98 campaign, today sits on the heels of Bob Knight in eighth place among Division I leaders in career victories (711–366), and has even overtaken legendary Phog Allen as the winningest coach in Big Eight (now Big Twelve) Conference history. None of that has likely earned the colorful Norm Stewart a nod on anyone's top 10 list of all-time coaching greats, since if he has won relentlessly over the years during the months of December, January, and February, he has enjoyed only mediocre results when it comes down to playing for the marbles during March tournament time. Stewart's lifetime NCAA mark stands at only 12–16, he has only ever advanced (twice) as far as a regional runner-up slot in the NCAAs, and he has lost his only two outings in NIT action. There have been many 20-win seasons (16 altogether) for Stewart since coming back to his alma mater in 1967, as well as eight conference regular-season crowns, a half-dozen league tournament titles, and two National Coach of the Year selections (1982 and 1994). But the sum total seems, nonetheless, to be the quietest career impact among any of the long-lived bench bosses who have managed to earn a spot in history with their membership in the exclusive 700-wins club.

John Stockton (NBA "Top 50" Selection)

Throughout the late '80s and all of the '90s, the No. 16 pick from the 1984 NBA draft (the draft that also produced Jordan, Olajuwon, Barkley, and Sam Perkins) has steadily and quietly constructed a reputation as the best playmaker in modern-era basketball. Such reputation is built on the loftiest assists total in NBA history as well as numerous additional claims as the best set-up man (perhaps outside of Magic Johnson) that the game has so far produced. Stockton came out of unheralded Gonzaga College (where he paced the West Coast Athletic Conference in points scored as a senior and in assists and steals all three seasons) and began his full-scale assault on NBA playmaking marks as soon as he cracked the Utah Jazz starting lineup in 1986–87 as a third-year player. He first overhauled the single-season NBA assists record in 1988 with 1,128; has twice subsequently bettered that standard; was the first player to top 1,000 assists for five straight seasons; paced the league a record nine straight times; has played in 10 All-Star Games (MVP in 1993) and two NBA Finals; and has long teamed with Karl Malone as the best inside-outside offensive combination of the current decade and perhaps of the entire modern-NBA era. A less-noticed and less-publicized aspect of Stockton's record-setting career is the fact he also now stands first on the all-time steals list (2,531) after recently overhauling Mo Cheeks (2,310) for the top slot in one of the sport's most underrated defensive categories. Only Stockton and Cheeks boast as many as 2,000 career thefts in the full half-century of NBA action.

© Frank P. McGrath Jr.

John Stockton, Utah Jazz

Damon Stoudamire

Few NBA rookie seasons have been more stellar or more storybook than the one enjoyed by Damon Stoudamire in 1996 with the expansion Toronto Raptors. With little first-year roster talent to boast beyond their top draft pick, Raptors coach Brendan Malone turned the ball and the game plan over to his showcase rookie out of Arizona, and Stoudamire led the team in both scoring (19.0, 1,331) and assists (9.3) as well as giving Toronto fans almost their only reason for packing into the oversized SkyDome for a bird's-eye view of showcase NBA action. A season later, under a new coach (Darrell Walker), Stoudamire avoided any sophomore jinx by pacing the second-year franchise in every major individual category except rebounds, steals, and blocks. By year three, however, the NBA honeymoon had already ended for the lowly Raptors. Coach Walker and GM Isiah Thomas were on their way out the door, and the talented Stoudamire was being dangled as trade bait by a newly minted ball club already scrambling to rebuild its image and its less-than-potent one-player-oriented on-court attack. By midseason one of the league's best young point guards had been dealt away to Portland in a multiplayer deal that overnight reshaped the look of Toronto NBA basketball.

Pat Head Summitt

Only Judy Conradt has climbed higher in the women's coaching ranks than Pat Head Summitt. The 25-year University of Tennessee veteran trails only the Texas-Austin legend in Division I career victories, climbing over the 500-win plateau in 1996 and achieving the 600-level early in the 1998 campaign. And when it comes to national championships, Summitt is in a class by herself with six (1987, 1989, 1991, 1996, 1997, 1998), owns the only consecutive women's NCAA championships since Southern Cal's double triumphs of 1983 and 1984, and stood poised for a possible four-peat in 1999 before her team's surprise ouster in the 1999 regional finals. Pat Summitt's 1998 squad featuring All-American junior sensation Chamique Holdsclaw (choice of many as the most talented women's player yet seen) and 6'4" center Tiffani Johnson may indeed have been the most powerful and balanced undergraduate women's team ever assembled. And in racking up the first back-to-back-to-back titles (1996–97–98) since Immaculata (1972–73–74) and Delta State (1975–76–77) at the dawn of women's national championship play, Pat Summitt has already earned her lasting piece of collegiate coaching immortality.

Sheryl Swoopes

The NCAA Final Four single-game scoring record actually resides on the Lubbock campus of Texas Tech University with women's ace Sheryl Swoopes and not at UCLA with more-celebrated men's star Bill Walton. The six-foot dynamo women's "Dream Team" Olympian (1996) logged her own dream game with a 47-point scoring outburst during the 1993 NCAA championship finale versus Ohio State. It was the perfect cap to a brief two-season career, which also witnessed a solid 25-point career scoring average, a pair of Kodak All-American recognitions, and unanimous selection as 1993 National Player of the Year. Also featured on Swoopes's remarkable basketball résumé is 1991 National JUCO Player of the Year recognition, earned while setting 28 school records while performing for South Plains Junior College (Texas). On the heels of her Olympic triumphs Swoopes joined gold medal teammates Rebecca Lobo and Lisa Leslie as the prime attractions of the newly formed WNBA summer pro circuit, although she was required to take a brief leave of absence from game action (due to the birth of her first child) shortly before joining the roster of the new league's Houston Comets franchise.

Jerry Tarkanian

Two features have attached themselves to the coaching career of the colorful figure known universally as "Tark"—his magnet-like attraction for scandal and controversy, and his ability to pile up victories at a record pace. For starters, Tarkanian's winning percentage (.828) after 25 seasons at Long Beach State, Nevada–Las Vegas, and most recently, Fresno State was the loftiest in Division I history. His team's 14 wins in 1997 caused a slip behind both Clair Bee (.826) and Adolph Rupp (.822) in that category. His 667 career wins, however, have now bumped him ahead of John Wooden into 12th place on the all-time list. He has been a National Coach of the Year once (1983 at UNLV), captured one NCAA championship (1990 with UNLV), reached the Final Four 4 times with his Running Rebels Vegas teams, and won 10 consecutive conference championships with the UNLV program. The downside was that his program at UNLV was constantly plagued in the late '80s and early '90s by rumors of recruiting improprieties, his teams often included players unable to meet admissions requirements elsewhere, and his final Rebels outfit (26–2) sat out the postseason on probation. That probation had actually been scheduled for a season earlier but had been postponed in order to allow the reigning national champions to defend their NCAA crown. After leaving UNLV for a pro job with San Antonio, Tark suffered further damage to his Jekyll-and-Hyde image when he failed to adjust to the egos of NBA stars and lasted only 20 games into his first NBA campaign.

For all the questions that surrounded academic standing of members of his 1990 and 1991 teams, there can be little doubt that those two squads were among the best ever assembled in the college ranks. The 1990 national champions became the only team to score 100 points in a title game when they manhandled Duke 103–73 and established a new record for widest victory margin in the process. A season later the defending champs were the first team since Larry Bird's Indiana State outfit (1979) to enter the NCAA postseason undefeated, yet they slipped to revenge-minded Duke 79–77 in a surprising national semifinal. Nonetheless, that final great Tarkanian-coached team earned a special place in history as the only college squad ever to boast four teammates (all future NBAers) who all scored above 1,500 career points: Stacey Augmon (2,011), Greg Anthony (1,738), Anderson Hunt (1,632), and Larry Johnson (1,617).

Roy Tarpley

One of the great cases of abandoned promise and unfulfilled potential attaches itself to the tragic career of 1986 Michigan All-American and subsequent NBA bust Roy Tarpley. Few players have come out of the college ranks with more skills or larger promise than the seven-foot center-forward who was a unanimous Big Ten Player of the Year as a junior; almost none has proven more painfully successful at practicing the art of self-destruction and career sabotage. At Michigan Tarpley seemed a can't-miss pro prospect while leading the Wolverines to a 54–9 overall record and back-to-back league titles during his final two seasons. The seventh overall pick in the 1986 NBA draft, Tarpley made modest progress his first five pro seasons with the Dallas Mavericks (averaging 12.6 points per game overall, above 20 at the start of an aborted final 1991 campaign) before first injuries and then a series of run-ins with law enforcement agencies and the league's substance abuse policies scuttled his awesome promise. Highlights of Tarpley's misbegotten off-court career included an arrest for speeding and drunken driving in Dallas (March

1991), initial NBA suspension of 49 games for noncompliance with a drug treatment rehabilitation program (1988–89 season), new suspensions for repeat violations of his drug aftercare program (November 1989 and April 1991), and final dismissal from the NBA (October 1991) for a "third strike" violation under the league's anti-drug agreement. The wayward hoopster would later spend several years after his original NBA ban playing in such second-level venues as the CBA (Wichita Falls), USBL (Miami Tropics), and Greek Professional League (Aris Thessaloniki and Olympiakos) in a futile attempt to gain NBA reinstatement. Lost in all the negative publicity and buried by the shipwreck that was his brief pro career is the fact that Tarpley was a legitimate enough talent to set a Dallas franchise record for single-game rebounds (25), become the first reserve in NBA history (1988) to finish in the season's top 10 in rebounding, and post 7 of the 10 games of both 20 points and 20 rebounds recorded in Dallas franchise history.

Deborah Temple

There are a few women basketballers—like a similar handful of their male counterparts—who have become footnotes to basketball history due to a single fortuitous moment of achievement or accident, or perhaps one overpowering performance never again to be duplicated by themselves or anyone else. Annette Kennedy is one name etched on such a list, as a result of a single night's offensive explosion (on January 23, 1981) in which the SUNY-Purchase standout gunned in 70 points in a game against Pratt Institute to establish a new women's small-school record. West Virginia's Georgeann Wells enjoyed a brief instant of headline status (December 21, 1984) as the first woman to dunk a basketball in game competition. And Jody Beerman of Central Michigan authored a more consistent achievement when she logged an NCAA record 57 consecutive free throws during the 1986–87 season. Deborah Temple is also a mainstay of any such listing of short-lived wonders on the strength of her own record-smashing 40-rebound game for Delta State against Alabama-Birmingham in 1983. The magnitude of Temple's performance—easily the most impressive among this short list of historical footnotes—is clinched by the fact that only four players in the century-long history of men's large-school play have ever topped the one-game total of the Delta State standout. That short list includes Bill Chambers of William & Mary (51), Charlie Slack of Marshall (43), Tom Heinsohn of Holy Cross (42), and Art Quimby of Connecticut (40)—and all turned the trick in the early '50s, during a men's era of lower shooting percentages and more aggressive rebounding strategies.

Isiah Thomas (NBA "Top 50" Selection)

At the collegiate level Isiah Thomas was Bob Knight's problem child; but what a marvelous problem child to have on board. Behind Thomas's brilliant display in the NCAA title game of 1981 (23 points and several clutch second-half steals), the Hoosiers claimed the most dramatic and unexpected of their three national titles earned under Knight. Two brilliant seasons at Indiana University were not, however, exceptionally happy times for the Chicago product, who earned All–Big Ten plaudits as a freshman and consensus All-American honors for his sophomore (and

*Isiah Thomas,
Detroit Pistons*

© Frank P. McGrath Jr.

final) season. Thomas and Knight clashed repeatedly, and the flashy point guard never could adjust to what he considered impolite and dehumanizing behavior toward players by his fiery mentor. Knight once grabbed Thomas by the jersey to administer admonishment before national TV cameras during a 1979 Pan American games contest.

Despite such flammable moments with Knight and poor early-season play by the 1980–81 title-bound Hoosiers, the sophomore team captain rallied his IU squad all the way to the memorable national championship triumph over North Carolina in Philadelphia's famed Spectrum arena. That upset title victory with its NCAA tournament MVP performance marked the swan song of Thomas's brief collegiate career. As a first-round and second overall hardship draft choice (after fellow Chicagoan Mark Aguirre) plucked by the Detroit Pistons in the 1981 NBA player lottery, Thomas entered the pros as a much-heralded but slightly undersized 20-year-old rookie in the fall of 1981. But any and all skeptics were quickly answered as Thomas's impact on the NBA was both immediate and lasting. A decade and a half later, the short-term IU great would stand behind only John Havlicek and Magic Johnson as the most distinguished among NBA Big Ten alumni.

As an NBA player the talents that were never fully unleashed under Knight's tight control at Indiana became quickly apparent in the more wide-open freelancing NBA game, and such breakout skills were also sustained long enough to build one of the most impressive pro careers of the 1980s. That career included two NBA All-

Star Game MVP awards, a nod as NBA Finals MVP (1990), two championship rings, and three All-League first team selections. It also featured such remarkable one-night performances as the 25 single-quarter points scored on a badly swollen ankle against the Lakers in the 1988 championship finals, and also a 16-point outburst in the final minute and a half of a playoff contest with the Knicks. Isiah Thomas was never as overwhelming an NBA icon as Bird, Magic, or Jordan. But he was perhaps the league's toughest inch-for-inch competitor since the retirements of Jerry West and Oscar Robertson.

Kurt Thomas

A severe leg injury at the end of a marginal player's sophomore season is likely to spell the end of any lingering dreams for a major impact on the college basketball world. In the case of 6'9" Texas Christian forward Kurt Thomas such misfortune would prove a springboard to one of the most miraculous individual turnarounds found anywhere in collegiate basketball annals. As a freshman and sophomore Thomas logged 49 games with limited contribution, averaging a minuscule 0.8 points per game as a little-used freshman and 7.1 as a sophomore starter before sustaining a fractured left tibia just before his team's appearance in the 1992 postseason NIT. After extensive rehabilitation the game athlete was able to return two seasons later for a junior campaign in which he displayed considerable pro promise as a 20-point scorer who also carried a near-double-figure rebounding average. It was as a senior, however, that Thomas suddenly exploded on the national scene, pacing the nation in both rebounding (14.6) and scoring (28.9) and clinching a spot among the top 10 1995 NBA draft picks. The leap from No. 58 to No. 1 among the country's individual scorers was one of the largest in NCAA history. The rare double in individual national titles was only the third ever recorded (the others credited to Xavier McDaniel in 1985 and Hank Gathers in 1989).

John Thompson

A one-time NBA backup center for the mid-'60s Boston Celtics lost in the shadows of Bill Russell, John Thompson has emerged from those shadows in recent decades to build one of the country's most successful college cage programs and also to construct one of its largest individual collegiate coaching legends. It is a legend and a ledger that includes 600-plus victories, 18 seasons of 20-plus victories, three National Coach of the Year selections, one NCAA championship and two additional heartbreaking near misses, a half-dozen Big East Conference tourney championships, and an Olympic head-coaching assignment. In the process Thompson has followed in Russell's footsteps, always tainting basketball achievement with outspoken racial crusading, which has impressed a majority of fans (as did Russell's) as being unnecessarily divisive and unwisely confrontational. Thompson's Georgetown University teams (especially those featuring superstar centers Patrick Ewing, Dikembe Mutombo, and Alonzo Mourning) have often won games at record levels; have usually stood near the top of one of the nation's powerhouse conferences; have produced a bevy of NBA players, including superstars Ewing, Mutombo, and Mourning; and have featured four Final Four appearances and one thrilling national championship. Yet Thompson's most notorious moments—the one's burned in the public eye—involve either boycotts or protests or tirades in the name of battling perceived racism. And there are also the inconsistencies of a coach who often rails at others for exploiting black athletes while at the same time accepting a hefty $200,000 fee from Nike in exchange for the company's logo on Georgetown uniforms, or who boasts of the graduation rate (98 percent) of his ballplayers, while at the same time admitting academically unprepared athletes (like Michael Graham or John Turner in recent seasons) and then bouncing them from his program at the first hint of classroom difficulties. If there is any difference in the often brusque behavior of John Thompson and the parallel performances of Indiana's legendary Bobby Knight, it has seemingly been only that the self-serving actions of the former are usually mollified by a better (or at least more identifiable) external social or political cause.

Mychal Thompson

Nothing in the history of Minnesota basketball comes close to the four-year act staged by Bahamas-born Mychal Thompson. Not even Kevin McHale, Lou Hudson, Trent Tucker, Archie Clark, or a boatload of other Golden Gophers who also followed up with highly successful NBA careers. Open the Minnesota basketball media guide or record book and it reads like a Mychal Thompson curriculum vitae. All the following entries are joined with the name of the greatest big man in Gophers history: career marks for points (1,992), field goals (823), field-goal percentage (.568), and rebounds (956); season records for points (647), scoring average (25.9), and field goals (265); plus the individual single-game record for blocked shots (12). One can add to the numbers a unanimous first-team All-American selection in 1978, a second-team All-American accolade a season earlier, and a No. 1 overall selection (Portland Trail Blazers) in the 1978 NBA college draft.

But while Thompson's star glittered brightly in the basketball heavens of the Minnesota northlands, it remained something of a dimmer orb in much of the rest of the nation, at least until NBA glory (with the Trail Blazers and Lakers) made the Gophers' giant a much more recognizable figure. This was due largely to Thompson's complete absence from the media circus of postseason NCAA play. He should have been there in 1977 when, as a junior, he combined forces with freshman Kevin McHale and senior Ray Williams to trigger a brilliant 24–3 campaign that all went for naught when a series of NCAA rules violations resulted in a forfeited schedule and a seat on the postseason sidelines. It was an unfortunate break, which cost thousands of tournament fans a glimpse of a superb shooting and rebounding post player already on a crash course toward certain NBA stardom.

Rudy Tomjanovich

Rudy Tomjanovich is one of only a handful of head coaches to post back-to-back NBA titles. He is far more widely remembered, however, as innocent victim of perhaps the sport's most outrageous on-court assault. The infamous moment occurred in December 1977 when the hefty-scoring Houston forward innocently raced to the defense of teammate Kevin Kunnert during an on-court brawl and was viciously kayoed by a blind-side punch thrown by Los Angeles Lakers star Kermit Washington. Massive resulting injuries to Rudy T's jaw, eye, and cheek were immediately life-threatening, later career-threatening, and sidelined one of the league's top players for the remainder of the 1977–78 NBA season. Washington was, ironically (and perhaps quite fittingly), marred by the unsavory incident even more than the true victim, though this did not diminish either Rudy T's physical suffering or his inevitable career setbacks. The league reacted swiftly with fines and a 60-day suspension, which translated into $50,000 in lost wages for Washington; the Los Angeles ball club also reacted by admitting embarrassment over Washington's behavior and quickly unloading him to Boston; fans provided their own reactions in kind with merciless booing and catcalls, which followed Washington everywhere throughout the remainder of his league career.

Tomjanovich, for his own part, eventually bounced back a season later, playing at first with a cumbersome plastic mask to project his partially reconstructed face. By career's end in the early 1980s he had posted impressive numbers which included a 10-season 17.4 scoring average and better than 13,000 points and 6,000 rebounds. Such success had always been a part of Rudy T's basketball life. At Michigan he was a memorable All-American who averaged 26 points per game as a junior and above 30 as a senior. And when playing days closed, he would turn next to coaching, where he first put in a decade-long internship (as a Rockets assistant) and then eventually built a successful record (.600-plus winning percentage and back-to-back NBA championships in 1984–85), which today nearly obliterates his NBA on-court achievements. Even the two NBA titles, however, were not sufficient entries in the Rudy Tomjanovich career ledger to quite overshadow a single tragic moment which yet remains one of the league's darkest hours.

Kelly Tripucka

Among second-generation pro athletes following in the footsteps of famous fathers, Kelly Tripucka was one of basketball's most successful examples. His father had been a football great at Notre Dame and also in the early pretelevision days of the NFL. The younger Tripucka would build plenty of legends of his own, first at Notre Dame as one of the school's most memorable offensive weapons (following in the tradition of Austin Carr, John Shumate, and Adrian Dantley), and then later in Detroit as one of the mainstays of formidable Pistons teams starring Isiah Thomas and Bill Laimbeer in the mid-'80s. A surprising first-round (12th overall) pick in the 1981 draft, Tripucka's five-season sojourn with the Pistons would peak with an onslaught on the club's rookie scoring records in 1982 (21.6 points per game) and an even more prolific sophomore campaign, which included a team-record 56 points against Chicago on January 29, 1983, and the league's third-best yearlong scoring mark. Eventually a defensive liability in the emerging Detroit attack, the aggressive 6'6" forward was eventually traded to Utah in 1986 (along with Kent Benson for Adrian Dantley) and finished out his career with the expansion Charlotte Hornets before returning to Detroit in 1993 as a popular Pistons television game analyst.

Jim Valvano

N.C. State's Jimmy "V" was the perfect coaching personality for the modern era of American sport—flamboyant, brash, and outspoken, often more image than substance, more at home postulating to a huge audience in front of a camera than patiently and obscurely teaching basketball's fine points during a closed-door practice session. His own story line was even larger than that of any of his players— after the fashion of Indiana's Bobby Knight, LSU's Dale Brown, and Kentucky's Rick Pitino. This was especially true of the postcoaching years, when he first performed as a popular television analyst of college games and later bravely and very publicly battled the bone cancer affliction that would prematurely end his life in 1993. Valvano's entire career seemed to flash before a decade of fans like a series of the short-attention-span video highlights that are the staples of today's televised sports broadcasts. His most memorable image is, of course, that of the overjoyed and unrestrained victor, running aimlessly across the court in search of someone to hug in the seconds immediately after the breathtaking conclusion of a thrilling 1983 NCAA title-game victory.

It didn't take Jim Valvano long to make an impression once he came to tradition-rich N.C. State from the basketball hinterlands of New York's Iona College, fresh off a pair of 20-win campaigns and a pair of NCAA postseason appearances. When he publicly announced that he didn't much care what his salary would be and that he was willing to take a pay cut for the thrill of an ACC coaching opportunity, he clinched the popular assessment in Raleigh that he was something of a lovable screwball. But if his opinions often seemed wacky, his abilities to coach and inspire were not long open to question. It took the whirlwind coach only a single season of feeling his way through difficult ACC territory with a break-even record before his second Wolfpack squad shot above the 20-win plateau. Over the next nine seasons that closed out his career he missed that charmed circle of 20 wins only twice— once with 19 victories and once with 18. His teams, on the other hand, never missed a postseason tournament trip until a final campaign was closed off with NCAA suspension in the wake of reported recruiting violations. It was those recruiting violations that finally embroiled Valvano's career as both head coach and athletic director and eventually led to his premature resignation. But even the final implication of scandal could hardly dim or tarnish one of the country's brightest coaching careers in the modern era.

Valvano's career at N.C. State was piled high with heady achievement. There were five straight 20-win seasons, a 1987 ACC Tournament championship, and NCAA Final Eight appearances in both 1985 and 1986 (the year the basketball coach also took the reins as athletic director). ACC Coach of the Year honors followed in both 1988 and 1989, and the latter season also saw a second league regular-season crown to complement the one shared with North Carolina and Georgia Tech back in 1985. The 10-year stay at Raleigh ended with a 209–114 ledger; the overall career mark was a sterling 346–212 for a 19-year span.

Just as Norm Sloan's many achievements with the Wolfpack were all shoved to the back burner by his single stellar national championship campaign, so it was also with Valvano, whose crowning and career defining moment would forever be the miracle late-season charge through the NCAA field in March of 1983. A third-place regular-season finish that year was followed by nine postseason wins in a row, the final six in NCAA action and several of these by only one- or two-point margins. Along the way there was, of course, a good deal of raw luck to complement the magic of Jimmy V's sideline coaching skills and inspired emotional leadership. The most gripping contests were perhaps the 69–67 two-overtime first-round conquest of upstart Pepperdine and the tense 63–62 defeat of league rival Virginia and Ralph Sampson in the West Regional finals at Ogden, Utah. The gut-wrenching championship victory over Akeem Olajuwon and the Phi Slamma Jamma Houston Cougars, which capped the dizzying charge, is today still etched in the public imagination by Lorenzo Charles's last-second dunk and by Valvano's wild and joyous sprint across the mayhem-filled court at Albuquerque. That 1983 title game itself—like the wild-man coach who engineered it—was the pure stuff of outrageous fantasy. It was indeed the very best of rewards that college basketball has to offer.

Tara Vanderveer

While a third edition of the NBA-sponsored "Dream Team" demanded the bulk of international media attention during the 1996 Olympic basketball competitions, it was the gold medal U.S. women's team coached by Tara Vanderveer that not only seemed to capture the hearts of American hoops fanatics but also boosted interest in the women's game to record levels. Vanderveer is as big a success story in her own right as the star-studded lineup featuring Sheryl Swoopes, Teresa Edwards, and Jennifer Azzi (among others) that she directed in Atlanta. In the span of a decade the former Idaho and Ohio State mentor was able to resurrect a long-downtrodden Stanford program (1–7 in the Pac-10 her first season) and build it into a two-time national champion. Considered one of the college game's top bench strategists, Vanderveer has had her Stanford Lady Cardinal squad in five Final Fours, walked off with NCAA titles in 1987 and 1991, twice (1988 and 1991) been tabbed National Coach of the Year, won over 400 career games, and constructed a lifetime winning percentage that hovers near the .800 plateau. But it is Vanderveer's intimate knowledge of the nuts and bolts and Xs and Os of basketball strategy that sets her apart from her peers and has stirred enough attention that her name is mentioned not infrequently as a potential coaching candidate for the men's professional ranks. It is a knowledge built on a love for the game so intense that Vanderveer reportedly spent long hours observing and studying Bob Knight's Indiana University practice sessions while herself a player on the Bloomington campus. And in high school the future coach reputedly signed up as a mascot for the boy's varsity squad so she could travel to road games and scrutinize its every strategy.

Dick Vitale

No basketball fan is neutral when it comes to the issue of college basketball color announcer Dick Vitale. In an era when basketball has been built on individual celebrities like Jordan, Shaq, Dennis Rodman, and Grant Hill—as equally renowned for their commercial endorsements and movie star lifestyles—Dick Vitale has become one of the grandest icons of them all. And this has been accomplished by a man who can neither dribble, shoot, jump, or even describe the game from the broadcast both with much eloquence or insight. As college basketball's top ambassador, pitchman, and media guru, Vitale has built his fame on a brash and grating style of loud hype and circus-style silliness. None can question his love for the game, but many have tired of his ceaseless parade of overworked clichés, and more still have questioned the impact of his constant glorification of selfish one-on-one style play ("moves" and "slams" and "showtime solos") and his endless hyping of individual coaching favorites (especially Dean Smith; Coach K; and The General, Bob Knight). In an age of basketball as showmanship and big-dollar entertainment, Vitale has become the most visible circus barker in his roll as color analyst with ESPN. In the process he has become almost as big an institution as the game itself.

Anthony "Spud" Webb

Everything about Spud Webb—NBA basketball player—bordered on the slightly unusual and even the outright bizarre. There was the nickname, which was reportedly given to him as a youngster and had nothing to do with his later NBA fame—though it was indeed a reference to the '50s-era Russian space satellite and thus a perfect moniker for a pioneering high-flyer. There was his size and appearance on an NBA playing floor, and especially his presence alongside such leapers as Michael Jordan and Dominique Wilkins in the showcase slam-dunking contest at the NBA All-Star Weekend. Ultimately there was the fact that 5'7" dervish Webb was in the NBA at all—in an age when the game is played above the rim by giants who dwarf even robust six-footers.

A dozen-year NBA veteran, Anthony Webb today stands alongside Tyrone Bogues (3 inches shorter at 5'4") as the most celebrated "midget" of the modern basketball era. Like Bogues, Webb built his game on incredible quickness, a natural shooting eye, and relentless and tenacious ball-hawking abilities. And like Bogues, he launched his career in the finest college circuit in the land, the ACC, where he performed admirably at North Carolina State. Webb's ability to survive in the league and even play an important offensive role in Atlanta and Sacramento was based on his innate quickness. When opponents jammed the driving lanes he could hit the deadly jumper from outside. And he was such a great leaper that he even blocked shots on occasion. It was the latter ability to sky with players a foot or more taller that set Webb's career apart from and above that of Tyrone Bogues. His first impact came with his surprising showcase performance in the league's All-Star Weekend slam-dunking festival where he became the most surprising winner ever as a 1986 rookie. And it was the same jumping skill that continued to earn him a place in the league when serious competition and not showcase exhibition was the first order of business.

Chris Webber

One unfortunate moment of infamy will perhaps always capsulize the unfulfilled collegiate promise of the most precocious among Michigan's stable of "Fab Five" phenoms. With the final precious seconds ticking away in the 1993 NCAA title game and North Carolina nursing a slim 73–71 lead, Michigan's touted sopho-more center was trapped with the ball along the sideline by two pressing Tar Heels defenders. In a crucial loss of concentration, which will likely haunt Wol-verines faithful for eons, the consensus All-American desperately called for a time-out, which Michigan no longer had. In a single lapse of court presence the game was lost, as was the national title and ultimately the Fab Five dream of championship success. It's an unfortunate image to permanently brand an other-wise stellar collegiate career. But the moment is perhaps made all the bigger by Webber's own subsequent actions—his early departure from Michigan a few months later to join the pro ranks, his contractual disputes with the Golden State Warriors on the heels of his 1994 NBA Rookie of the Year season, and his com-plaints about respected coach Don Nelson, which forced an early-season 1994 trade to the Washington Bullets.

But for all his later misjudgments and tarnished image, Webber was for two seasons a marvelous player for one of the most talented Michigan teams in decades. He was the leading scorer and rebounder on two NCAA runner-up teams during just two seasons of college play, remains but one of a tiny handful of players to end each of his undergraduate campaigns in the season's final tournament game, appeared in a dozen NCAA contests, and led his team to victory in all but the two most important of these showdowns. Finally, he was the first player taken in the NBA draft (by Orlando, which immediately traded him to Golden State for projected superstar Penny Hardaway), thus joining the select club of Walt Bellamy, Kent Benson, Mychal Thompson, Magic Johnson, Joe Barry Carroll, and Glenn Robinson among Big Ten Conference stalwarts who can boast that honor.

Dominique Wilkins

Basketball's "Human Highlight Film" has evolved from the NBA's top-ranking acrobatic slam-dunking sideshow into one of the premier offensive players of the modern epoch. Overcoming a severe late-career Achilles tendon injury, which nearly ended his playing days in 1992, Wilkins has stormed back in spectacular fashion. His scoring totals now place him 10th in career average (25.3) and also in the top 10 for total points (NBA games only), and with one or two more semiproductive seasons remaining, a 30,000-point career still seems within the realm of possibility. Wilkins's ironic legacy, nonetheless, seems to be that of being the last NBA scoring champion (1986) before Michael Jordan took personal charge of the title a decade ago. But as with the case of Oscar Robertson playing behind Wilt Chamberlain, had it not been for the presence of the NBA's most awesome point-maker ever, Wilkins himself might well rank high up on the list for most individual scoring titles.

For the better part of the 1980s Dominique was synonymous with the Atlanta Hawks franchise. In more recent seasons Nique has turned into one of basketball's most high-priced journeymen. His career as franchise player in Atlanta ended in February 1994, with a trade to the Clippers for Danny Manning shortly after he had worked his way back to stardom from the severe Achilles rupture that threatened his career. Brief stops with the L.A. Clippers (where he played less than two months) and Boston Celtics (where he scored the final points ever recorded in historic Bos-

*Dominique Wilkins,
Los Angeles Clippers*

© Frank P. McGrath Jr. and Marie S. McGrath

ton Garden) were followed by a brief stopover in Europe. With Club Panathinaikos in Greece he would win his first championship—the men's European Cup—while capturing tournament MVP honors. And then it was back to the NBA for one final fling in San Antonio, where an 18.2 scoring average at age 37 indicated that neither injury nor biological clock had yet slowed the game's highest flyer. Through all this gypsy existence Wilkins continued his climb to higher and higher levels in the record books, passing 26,000 career points and 1,000 games played, and approaching 10,000 field goals made. Unfortunately, most of these final seasons were played in relative obscurity with basement NBA teams, which only dulled some of the luster of one of the most productive careers in league history. Eighties fans will never forget the image of Wilkins as a slam dunker (he twice won the All-Star Game dunking contest) on equal par with Jordan and Julius Erving. Yet for all this fame, Wilkins was likely the most overlooked superstar of his generation. When the NBA announced its anointed list of 50 greatest all-time players in time for the Golden Anniversary season of 1997, it was arguably the name of Dominique Wilkins that was the most glaring omission from that august mythical roster.

Roy Williams

If Dean Smith, John Thompson, and Bobby Knight are the ranking elder statesmen of college basketball's coaching fraternity, Kansas mentor, and former 10-year Dean Smith assistant Roy Williams is without question the profession's grandest Young Turk. In the decade of the '90s no one else has enjoyed quite the same year-in and year-out success, even if that success has so far always stopped bothersomely short of an NCAA national championship. Williams has had his Jayhawks above the 25-victory mark every one of his 10 seasons but the first, he has kept his teams near the top of the national polls year after year, he has mounted serious postseason challenges (even been the odds-on favorite on two separate occasions), and he has launched a winning pace (282–62, .820) that—if maintained—will put him in the same company as Smith, Knight, Rupp, and Kansas legend Phog Allen before his career is over. At the same time, Roy Williams has experienced a career of bitter disappointments, albeit the kind of disappointments most other coaches might covet. His powerhouse 1997 team (34–2) stood atop the wire service polls virtually all season before suffering a shocking (to Kansas faithful at least) loss to eventual winner Arizona in the NCAA Southeast Regional. With lottery-pick star forwards Raef LaFrentz and Paul Pierce foregoing early NBA departure one season later, Kansas (35–4) was again the odds-on favorite for an NCAA title and again disappointed with an early-round tournament exit. Yet for all the recent disappointment, Kansas entered the 1998–99 season with a 60-victory string intact on the home floor at legendary Allen Fieldhouse and with the winningest Division I coach still on its payroll.

Lynette Woodard

Any ballot for the greatest woman collegiate player includes at least five names without any pause for debate—Cheryl Miller, Nancy Lieberman (Cline), Carol Blazejowski, Ann Meyers, and most certainly, Lynette Woodard. Woodard is probably best known of the quintet among the general public due to her brief and much publicized stint as the first woman ever to play for the Harlem Globetrotters. If it was the 'Trotters' sojourn that gave Woodard the biggest claim on notoriety (along with her reputation for being able to dunk a basketball), it was the scoring numbers compiled over her four-year career at the University of Kansas (1978–81) that earned a lasting spot in basketball history. Although her career predated "official" NCAA women's records, the six-foot Kansas star nonetheless ranks as the all-time leading women's scorer with a massive point total (3,649) that trails Pete Maravich's men's NCAA record by a mere 18 points. A four-time All-American and two-time Olympian (captain of the 1984 gold medal squad), Woodard paced Kansas to a four-year mark of 108–32 and three appearances in the AIAW national tournament. She was also the 1981 Wade Trophy winner as the nation's top female player and a landslide choice as Big Eight Conference Player of the Decade for the 1980s. Post-Globetrotters stints have included professional seasons in Italy and Japan, an assistant coaching post at Kansas, a spot as athletic director for the Kansas City public schools, and a recent roster spot (in her mid-30s) with the Cleveland Rockers of the newly formed WNBA women's pro circuit.

James Worthy (NBA "Top 50" Selection)

Had James Worthy played in any other collegiate league or for any other college team, his reputation (and his place in the record books) might have been far larger. It is indeed difficult to stand out in the power-packed ACC or to earn a true piece of individual immortality in a program as tradition-rich as the one at North Carolina (especially during the Dean Smith era). As it was, however, Worthy would grab for

James Worthy,
Los Angeles Lakers

© Frank P. McGrath Jr.

himself a not inconsiderable piece of ACC and UNC fame and fortune. The 6'9" junior consensus first-team All-American was the season's leading scorer for a 1982 NCAA champion Carolina outfit, and also the leading point-maker with 28 tallies in the NCAA title victory over a Georgetown University team that featured freshman phenom Patrick Ewing. Yet while Worthy was dominating enough throughout the entire stretch of March Madness to earn tournament MVP honors, few fans in subsequent years would remember much about the dramatic championship victory beyond the clutch last-minute winning shot launched by a sensational freshman teammate named Michael Jordan.

If Worthy seemed to thrive on being a big fish in an even bigger pond while traveling the collegiate circuit, the same fate followed him into the NBA in 1983 (as first overall pick in the 1982 draft). With the Lakers teams of the mid-'80s he would again often be forced into the shadows by Magic Johnson, Kareem Abdul-Jabbar, and even sometimes by one-time UNC teammate Sam Perkins. It is, nonetheless, unlikely that the Lakers could have won quite so consistently without James Worthy in the fold. His career numbers were solid (16,320 points and a 17.6 career average), his individual honors were considerable (NBA third team in 1990 and 1991, All-Rookie Team in 1983, and NBA Finals MVP in 1988), especially in so full a stable of competing stars, and as a member of three championship teams (1985, 1987, 1988) his impact in key games often simply could not be overlooked. Worthy's nine-season and 143-game playoff shooting percentage of .544 ranks as one of the best in NBA annals. During the championship season of 1988 it was Worthy, for once, who was indisputably the biggest Lakers "Showtime" weapon of them all. His first-ever career triple-double (36 points, 16 rebounds, 10 assists) came fortuitously in Game 7 of the 1988 NBA Finals and provided firepower for the 108–105 victory over Detroit, which gave Los Angeles its fifth league crown of the Lakers-dominated decade.

Kay Yow

The list of ACC coaching greats over the past quarter-century might well justify its own special wing in Springfield: Dean Smith, Mike Krzyzewski, Lefty Driesell, Bobby Cremins, Terry Holland, Norm Sloan, and Jim Valvano. It is not a stretch to suggest that the name of Kay Yow also merits a prominent billing on that list. Among women's coaching legends, only four—Jody Conradt, Pat Summitt, Vivian Stringer, and Sue Gunter—own more career victories. In the ACC wars only Chris Weller at Maryland stands ahead of Yow in the victory column. Kay Yow posted a 75 percent winning ratio at tiny Elon (North Carolina) College before taking the reins at North Carolina State in fall 1975; over the past 22 seasons with the Wolfpack she has nearly maintained that mark, compiling close to 500 victories and hovering near the 70 percent winning level. Other conference achievements include four ACC titles, 17 visits to postseason tournament play, 11 ACC tournament title games, eight N.C. State All-Americans, and 21 players who have earned all-conference honors during an identical number of seasons at the helm. Breast cancer and a resulting mastectomy slowed Yow in midcareer but were not enough to keep the inspirational coach and teacher from her spot as coach of the 1988 Olympic squad, which captured a gold medal in Seoul. Yow also boasts an accomplished set of coaching siblings: sister Debbie (coach at Kentucky and Florida and athletic director at Maryland) and sister Susan (coach at Drake and Kansas State and player under Kay at N.C. State).

Dave Zinkoff

Although they are an ever-present intrusion in the tapestry of every NBA game, few fans know their names or faces or even have much conscious awareness of their presence. Basketball public address announcers are a crucial ingredient of the basketball arena experience, and yet, by their very nature blend into the background of arena spectacles in the same manner as dancing mascots, cheerleaders, and ingenious staged promotions that flood the playing floor during every television time out. Dave Zinkoff in Philadelphia was a most rare exception. Widely reputed as one of the most colorful courtside voices in the game's history, "Zinky" was an undeniable feature player in the entertainment spectacle during several decades in Philadelphia's Spectrum arena. Among his more famous signature enunciations were "Errrrr-ving" (following each bucket by Dr. J), "By George!" (after any score by George McGinnis), and "Shooting tttttt-oooooo" (when announcing a pair of tosses from the charity stripe). Before the popular "Voice of Philadelphia" became a courtside fixture in the City of Brotherly Love he earned another small niche in basketball lore as traveling secretary and general Man Friday for Abe Saperstein's legendary Harlem Globetrotters. In this later capacity Zinkoff also co-authored (with Edgar Williams, a Philadelphia *Inquirer* features writer) the substantial 1953 book *Around the World with the Harlem Globetrotters*, easily the most readable and informative history of basketball's cherished barnstorming outfit.

Epilogue

The Greatest Player in History

Baseball's "myths" and "fabrications" are the very essence of the diamond sport and thus the glue of its wondrous and sustaining history. Ball fans cling to such cherished fabrications as the Abner Doubleday "invention" myth; the heroics of Babe Ruth's "called" home run shot during the 1932 World Series; the inspired tale of Jackie Robinson's painful pioneering role as the first black American allowed to play big-league baseball; and dozens more such staples of baseball's irrepressible folklore.

Little matter that such quaint historical vignettes are indeed all "myths" in the most pejorative sense of the term, and that all are thus more or less false accounts of the game's verifiable on-field record. Doubleday never fondled a stitched baseball nor set foot upon a diamond-shaped ball field; Ruth was clearly pointing at bench jockeys in the Chicago Cubs' dugout (reminding that he still had one swing remaining) and not at the center-field bleachers (warning of where the next delivery might land); Robinson was the first African-American to cross the 20th-century baseball color line, but he was neither the first nonwhite during the current century (several dark-skinned Cubans got there first) nor the first African-American "black" from the full history of organized baseball. Such cheerful distortions of the historical record are, after all, the ingrained fabric of the game itself. They are the necessary fanciful tales of a sport built upon the muscular shoulders of folklore— tales passed down from generation to generation as a living legacy of a game that is far more the stuff of truth-bending legends, dusty records, and shadowy ephemeral memories than it is of spellbinding game action itself.

Basketball—with its less visible historical overtones—seemingly has only one such sustaining myth to its credit. And this, as it turns out, is a fabrication of rather recent origins. It is the well-endowed "Jordan Supremacy Myth," which boldly claims that Chicago Bulls superstar Michael Jordan was the greatest all-around basketball player ever to lace up a pair of high-top sneakers or shoot at modern versions of Dr. Naismith's primitive peach baskets.

This modern-day Jordan Myth goes so far as to suggest that no one else even approximates Chicago's heralded superstar when it comes to tabbing the most talented cage paragon ever to dribble, feint, or slam-dunk. It is well-worn liturgy in the Chicagoland sporting press and standard staple among fans and writers just about everywhere else to boot. Of course, for crusty old-timers who have paid attention to the game's evolution across several decades or more, the Jordan Supremacy Myth (at least the part that says that no possible rivals exist to the Airness Throne) is just as much fabrication as the Babe Ruth "called shot" or Abner Doubleday's pioneering efforts in Cooperstown.

Despite Jordan's on-court greatness over a decade and a half, the claims for unrivaled superiority across the game's entire history seemingly carry a strong aroma of unsubstantial myth-making. This appears to be the case for at least each and every one of the following reasons. Support for such a claim, first off, has been nurtured from the start by the constant drone of public relations geniuses, product pitchmen, and media "talking heads" (of which there are many), and not by the measured and cautious analyses of legitimate basketball historians (of whom there are shamefully few). Evidence—where hard evidence is ever cited—comes heavily in the form of standards for excellence that are skewed entirely toward the current fan preferences of style (showy individual offensive maneuvers and powerful slam dunking) and ignores highly valued skills that formed the standard for earlier eras (viz., constrained control of individual offensive talents, complete and balanced offensive and defensive skills, rock-solid fundamentals, and team-oriented play). Little or no consideration is given to numerous mitigating factors that contribute mightily to Jordan's dominance over today's game (for starters: a weakened league with few solid teams and little team-oriented play; the abandonment of "traveling" as an offensive violation; a dearth of rival contemporary stars to share Jordan's throne the way Bird and Erving shared Magic Johnson's, and Chamberlain, Russell, West, and Baylor shared Oscar Robertson's). And finally, the "myth" of Air Jordan's unrivaled superiority over all past-era stars may also share the more negative sense of the term as well—that is, it simply isn't altogether true.

The claim for Jordan's unquestioned rank above all previous legends of the game (namely Chamberlain, Robertson, Russell, Baylor, Bird, and Magic Johnson) is also likely one doomed to erode as time lapses and as historical perspective gradually returns to the basketball scene. The problem is, of course, that most basketball fans—and most professional basketball commentators as well—have flocked to the winter sport only during a past decade crowded with the feats of Magic Johnson, Larry Bird, and Air Jordan. Earlier stars of hoopdom, for all their one-time appeal to the smaller coterie of pre-1980s basketball fans, have almost no hold on the modern fan's imagination. Certainly not in a manner that would parallel the legendary giants of baseball or even the past-era stars of the gridiron sport of football. Every diamond fan, to cite the obvious example, is weaned on stories of Ty Cobb, Tris Speaker, and Walter Johnson, or at least on tales of Mantle, DiMaggio, Aaron, and Willie Mays. Basketball fanatics are indeed few who can conjure up even a handful of names of the largest pro or college stars from the '50s, '60s, or '70s.

One downside of current runaway NBA popularity is clearly this near-total loss of historical perspective. Chicago's Jordan-era Bulls with their string

© Frank P. McGrath Jr.

Michael Jordan does not—as Nike ads would have us believe—soar above the fetters of gravity; nor does MJ stand out quite as entirely in a class by himself as supporters contend—at least not when it comes to sanctifying the greatest all-around basketballer of the ages.

of championship victories and record-breaking win-loss ledgers provide one stark example. (Chicago's six championships over eight seasons, in what is arguably a watered-down league, is blithely assumed to outstrip Boston's truer dynastic run of eight straight NBA crowns.) Jordan himself provides another. Memory is indeed quite short in a sport where heavily marketed contemporary court celebrities like Shaq O'Neal, Karl Malone, and Scottie Pippen are enshrined over some of the game's most important pioneers (Bob Davies and George Yardley, for example) on the NBA's own official Golden Anniversary list of "Fifty Greatest" players of all time.

In Jordan's case the issue is not at all whether MJ is one of the true greats ever to play the game. That fact has been well established by the highest career scoring average to date, as well as by runaway fan popularity that knows no parallel in league annals (and perhaps even in the annals of American sports history at large). Jordan may indeed even be the best ever to play the game. Certainly he is without challenge as the lone candidate for enshrinement as basketball's most celebrated all-time megastar. But this does not necessarily mean—as advocates of today's version of the sport endlessly crow—that Jordan does not have legitimate rivals for the title of all-time best. *Most popular* or *most celebrated* does not always neatly equate with *most deeply talented*—in any sporting arena or any walk of life. When it comes to assessing Jordan's legitimate rivals, the field is a bit more crowded than might appear to be the case at first blush.

Basketball's past, as popularly conceived, stretches back perhaps to the debut of Bird and Magic (1979–80) and seemingly no further; pioneering stars of only a few decades back like Jerry West or Hal Greer or Walt Bellamy are as lost to contemporary rooters as are 19th-century baseballers with names like Mike "Slide" Kelly, Ross Youngs, or Wee Willie Keeler. Yet as more clear-minded sports historians flock to basketball in search of fresh subject matter, and as the din of the sports world's greatest marketing and promotional blitz eventually subsides around the remnants of Jordan's career, a fair balance will hopefully and inevitably somehow be struck. For one thing, it will again be realized at some point that the soaring slam dunks, which are almost the sole gratification for today's fans, are indeed not the only standard for judging phenomenal cage play—in reality such hop-skip-and-a-jump dunks unaccompanied by legitimate dribbling reflect an extremely small dimension of basketball-playing skill.

And as more fans scan the statistical records compiled by earlier generations of players, it will remain obvious that Jordan is on a par (no less but no more) in statistically measured performance with a handful of basketball's true lost avatars—legends with names like Robertson, Chamberlain, West, Baylor, and Russell. By career's end Jordan will match, but certainly not bury, most of Chamberlain's scoring legacy, yet will nonetheless fall far short of such mind-blowing achievements as the 100-point game, the 50-point season's average, and the five straight 35-plus scoring averages owned by Wilt. On all-around balance Oscar Robertson's combined scoring, rebounding, and assists will still outshine Jordan's best efforts. (Jordan has never come close to averaging a yearlong triple-double—his *career* total stands at fewer than three dozen—a pace Oscar held for five long seasons.) And in the championship arena it is likely that no one (Jordan included) will ever approach Russell's decade-long penchant for collecting championship rings. With his current streak of titles in Chicago, Jordan is, to date, only halfway down the road to matching Russell's 1960s-era Boston skein.

Since comparing eras in basketball, like in all other sports, is risky business at best, one is left with the recorded numbers alone to debate. Here Air Jordan, despite his 10 scoring titles, simply does not match up as a prolific point-maker to the behemoth Chamberlain, who once scored 100 points in a single game and then averaged 50-plus for a full season's play. Jordan has rarely dominated either a single contest or an entire postseason in quite the same manner as did the imposing Bill Russell, a defensive dervish who controlled the hardwood without any significant scoring at all. And certainly Jordan does not rank any higher in versatility than the incomparable Oscar Robertson, who once came within a narrow margin of averaging today's coveted "triple-double" (double figures in scoring, rebounding, and assists) for an entire decade-and-a-half NBA career—and actually did so across five full NBA seasons.

◆　◆　◆

The greatest injustice resulting from basketball's relative obscurity during the 1950s and 1960s is perhaps the true misfortune that a half dozen or so among the greatest performers of the sport's century-long history have inevitably been largely lost on the shortsighted American sporting public. But the records left behind by these fabulous pioneering superstars remain sufficient—once revived by the persistent historian—to speak most eloquently for their lost progenitors.

Today it is, above all, point scoring and that hallmark of versatility, the "triple-double," that are everywhere touted as truest yardsticks of individual hoop performance. The triple-double seemingly holds special favor with today's media as a measure of all-around skill; whenever a player reaches such totals in a single game, it cannot fail to be mentioned as a rare mark of achievement. Yet Oscar Robertson—phenomenal shooting, passing, and rebounding guard for the 1960s Cincinnati Royals—rang up triple-doubles with such frightening regularity that the real news was made only on those rare nights when opponents somehow happened to hold Oscar to less than 10 rebounds or prevent him from logging at least 10 assists (no one ever corralled Oscar's scoring).

Fans also goggle when Jordan scores 60 in a game (something he has done on a half-dozen occasions). But the fabulous Big Dipper, Wilt Chamberlain, accomplished this same feat no less than 32 times. Jordan's impressive mark of 37 games scoring 50 or more points pales next to Wilt's total of 118 50-plus games. And Bill Russell, for his own part, was the only player in history to pile up championships in record numbers and dominate ball games for more than a decade—night in and night out—without ever needing to score even a single point. When Russell did make baskets (he averaged 15.1 points per game for his career) it was an event almost totally irrelevant to his team's victory-column successes.

And there were other legendary players of the '50s and '60s who set standards that still eclipse modern-era performances. George Mikan, to take the best example, was so dominant under and around the hoop that the league's front-office gurus had to drastically alter the long-standing rules under which the game was being played (introducing widened lanes, shot clocks, and new fouling rules). And Elgin Baylor invented high-flying "moves" that were so marvelous that veteran writer Alexander Wolff would describe him as "a pioneer of the game's third dimension, that uncharted fastness that makes wannabes of fans everywhere."

Jerry West—L.A. Lakers scoring machine of the '60s and early '70s—was such a frequent and deadly outside shooter that, had a three-point goal existed during his era, the Lakers guard would likely have outstripped Jordan by a wide margin in annual scoring titles. As it is, West scored 25,192 points in 14 seasons to Jordan's 29,277 in a dozen-plus campaigns.

In its modern-day era the game of pro basketball was redefined by high-flying Julius Erving with his invention of hang time moves and his acrobatic above-the-rim style of play. It was Julius Erving, after all, who made Michael Jordan possible. Yet Dr. J enjoyed his own halcyon days in the now forgotten and, even back then, largely ignored American Basketball Association. When Erving transferred his game into the NBA arenas in the late '70s, he did so at a time when the sport was withering away under lack of national television exposure and the absence of any broad-based fan enthusiasm.

Pro basketball in the wake of Dr. J was soon rescued from growing obscurity by the twin arrivals of Magic Johnson (urban-born exemplar of black playground style) and Larry Bird ("Great White Hope" from small-town Indiana)—a pair of glamorous heroes for the 1980s. Bird was indisputably the greatest all-around forward since Bob Pettit, and Magic emerged overnight as the most talented and athletic playmaker the game had ever known. And most fortuitous as well for the Bird-Magic head-to-head duels, the major television networks also found the game at exactly the same moment.

Finally, in the afterglow of Bird and Magic and on the crest of the game's new televised popularity, rode Michael Jordan, the most celebrated ballplayer ever, and one who was (for the first time in the NBA, at least) as much a product of Madison Avenue mega-hype and clever pop culture promotion as he was an author of spectacular on-floor basketball feats. To be sure, Jordan's game-time achievements were themselves quite memorable. So much so that Air Jordan and the NBA have ridden hand in glove into a rosy present that today stands as the zenith of the sport's evolving history.

Basketball's ongoing evolution has been remarkably steady, yet always dramatic. The pro game dawned with Mikan, Cousy, and Pettit, the forgotten heroes of the '50s; it matured with Wilt Chamberlain, who was perhaps too awesome a phenomenon to be fully appreciated in his own era or even to be adequately assessed from the vantage point of later eras. Finally, there emerged those much undervalued superstars from basketball's lost "Golden Age" in the 1960s—Oscar Robertson, Elgin Baylor, and Jerry West. The evolution continued with the "savior" roles filled by Julius Erving in the '70s and Bird and Magic in the '80s, and has finally arrived at center stage on the American sporting scene with Air Jordan.

If Jordan has been somewhat overrated and most certainly overhyped, he was, nonetheless, just the spectacular showpiece needed by the masses of new fans who tuned in and turned on to basketball's television era of the celebrity-drenched 1990s. Across a full half-century the National Basketball Association has provided a full pantheon of heroes equal to those in any other American sport. Until recently basketball's prime showpieces have not always been as visible and were surely never as fashionable as their baseball and football counterparts. But now, seemingly, their long-overdue moment in the national spotlight has finally come.

Who, then, was the greatest among the greatest? Has any player, ancient or modern, ever matched Michael Jordan for spectacular individual play or as a one-man winning force? What follows is one basketball historian's comparison of that small handful of superstars who might merit classification as the best ever to play the game. Discussion begins and ends with the two most superior all-around players ever to lace up sneakers—Oscar Robertson and Michael Jordan—as well as with the most outstanding offensive and defensive immortals—those titanic rivals of the '60s, Chamberlain and Russell. Wilt Chamberlain would often score 50 or 60 points in a losing effort. Bill Russell could fail to score even in double figures—or even fail to score at all—and yet still pace his team to seemingly endless strings of championship victories.

There doesn't seem to be anyone else who can truly compete for the all-time-best label. Bird was incredible as an uncanny long-range shooter and proficient passer, yet still doesn't measure up to either Jordan or Chamberlain on the offensive end of the court, and certainly not to Russell at the defensive end. And it is undeniable that the lead-footed and earthbound Bird falls far short of Oscar as an all-around basketball talent. Magic Johnson is the single remaining true behemoth from the modern age, yet Magic, for all his razzle-dazzle "showtime," was never quite enough an all-around basketball paragon (especially when it came to scoring or rebounding) to rival "The Big O" from Cincinnati.

Let us look a bit closer, then, at four titans who loom above all challengers. The case for Jordan can be quickly put aside: Jordan is indeed a nonpareil of the modern era. Yet when compared to Russell, Chamberlain, and especially Oscar, Air Jordan falls short on several counts. Russell and Wilt have their backers for "No. 1" as well, but each falls victim to a largely one-dimensional career. Oscar is left then, almost by default, as the prime candidate for deification. It is "The Big O" alone who still most merits sanctification as the best "total package" ever to take flight on the hardwood floor.

Michael "Air" Jordan—Most Popular Player on Madison Avenue

Let's put the issue to rest immediately—Michael Jordan is *not* a lock as the greatest player of all time. At least not in the hands-down manner usually claimed. Jordan is, undoubtedly, the most celebrated athlete ever to walk the face of the earth. None has earned more television time, pitched more products, banked more dollars, or enjoyed more instant name and face recognition worldwide. The man known simply as "Michael" or "MJ" from Tokyo to Topeka is also arguably the most flashy showman ever to grace the NBA (though some may contend that Erving is still the reigning champion in this quarter). In an age that worships style and showmanship and confuses celebrity and fame with raw talent or polished performance, it is little wonder that Jordan has been so widely

Michael Jordan's Milestone Achievements

Highest career NBA scoring average (31.4)

Most NBA season scoring titles (10)

Most consecutive NBA season scoring titles (7, tied with Wilt Chamberlain)

Only six-time NBA Finals MVP

NBA All-Star Game career scoring average leader (21.1)

Only NBA scoring leader also named "Defensive Player of the Year" (1988)

Highest career NBA playoff scoring average (33.4)

Most points scored in an NBA playoff game (63)

Highest NBA single-series playoff scoring average (41.0)

Most NBA career points for a guard (29,277)

Most NBA single-season points for a guard (3,041, 1987)

One of two NBA players to log 3,000 single-season points (with Wilt Chamberlain)

First NBA All-Star Game Triple-Double (1997)

Second-highest NBA total of 50-plus-point games (37, after Wilt Chamberlain)

Five-time NBA MVP

hyped as "the greatest" in the game's history. But the greatest showman is not automatically the greatest all-around ballplayer. And the game's flashiest or most charismatic star is not simply by fiat its most fundamentally talented or richly endowed practitioner.

The case for rivals to the throne can be put succinctly. Julius Erving was a more powerful and even a more dramatic dunker than Michael is—or even than MJ was in his prime. Bill Russell remains the more dominant individual force since he was able to lead his club single-handedly to championship after championship, and do so by playing at only one end of the court—the end where the Celtics didn't even have the ball. Wilt Chamberlain was a more intimidating athlete and also the greatest offensive machine the sport has ever witnessed at any level of play. Michael never scored 100 in a game or even came close, never averaged 50 points (or even 40 points) for a full season, never averaged nearly 30 rebounds nightly for a season, or scored 50 points in a playoff game *as a rookie* (Wilt did it twice); or scored better than 40 points more than 270 times (Jordan has reached the mark slightly more than 100 times), or tallied 50 points in a game 45 times *within a single season*. Jordan's offensive numbers simply don't challenge Wilt's from any angle of comparison. And for overall offensive and defensive play, Jordan's exceptional versatility still does not match that of Oscar Robertson, the efficient and workmanlike guard who averaged a triple-double for an entire NBA campaign.

Why then do so many still believe Jordan to be the greatest? Three elements contribute most strongly to Jordan's recent deification by press and public alike. For one thing, the multitudes among today's hoops fans have, for the most part, only discovered the game a decade or so back and have no collective memory whatsoever of past-generation stars like Oscar or Wilt or Russell. Quite lamentably there has been no emphasis on tradition in basketball such that a previous generation of fans has handed down the legends of Robertson and Chamberlain and Baylor and West the way that baseball fans for decades have kept alive the sparkling legends of Ruth, Cobb, Mantle, Mays, and Jackie Robinson (or even the less substantial legends of second-tier stars like Carl Hubbell, Tony Lazzeri, Pete Reiser, and Dizzy

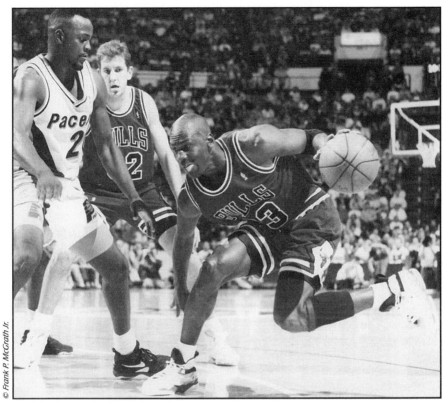

© Frank P. McGrath Jr.

If Air Jordan has been perhaps overrated and most certainly overhyped, he was nonetheless just the spectacular showpiece needed by the masses of new fans tuning in and turning on to basketball's television era during the celebrity-drenched 1990s.

Dean). Journeymen baseballers of the '50s and '60s (Bobby Richardson, Camilo Pascual, Harvey Haddix) have far more present currency than do major talents from the pro basketball circuit of the same decades (say Dolph Schayes, Earl Monroe, or Bob Pettit). Secondly, today's standards now elevate "showtime moves" above all-around basketball skills like clean passing, team defense, and foul shooting. It is the 10-second video highlight film that gets universally employed as the main measure of professional skill. Dazzling dunks and end-to-end solo dribbling exhibitions outstrip far more subtle displays of efficient ballhandling and the engineering of synchronized team offense.

And then there is the issue of a print and video media that has constructed a full-fledged industry around the hyping of Michael Jordan. The league itself has largely done the same, basing its recent popularity on the image of Jordan as the greatest sports-world showman in recorded history. Michael has sold countless books, floods of newspapers, and hours of television time, a tidal wave of videotapes, and also (most importantly) millions of NBA game tickets.

But even more telling in this final regard is the seemingly ceaseless propaganda blitz mounted by a Nike sporting goods company campaign designed to generate billions of dollars in corporate sales. Michael's rank as the greatest basketball player, the greatest pure athlete, the greatest everything imaginable, has all been a necessary element in the corporate success of Nike and of the several dozen other high-profile companies that ride precariously on the coattails of Air Jordan's legend. In short, Michael Jordan has, for the past decade, been a pure marketing sensation. Michael's 1998 $32 million NBA single-season contract represents only a hefty portion of his own annual earnings and only a small fraction of the revenue he generated for the league and the numerous corporate giants who employed him.

In large part the enhancement of Jordan and diminution of Robertson as the game's greatest performer is a reflection of precisely how far basketball has actually moved in recent decades toward becoming an individualistic "one-on-one" game. It is the solo player—especially the solo offensive player with the most spectacular playground moves—who is most readily identified in the public view as the sport's true model of perfection. Of course, Robertson was a brilliant one-on-one player in his own right. Oscar, however, performed in a basketball era that held to far different standards of on-court perfection, shunning dunking and elevating "playground cool" over playground pizzazz. Today's standards are much more attuned to an elevated and razzle-dazzle game in which Jordan is supreme practitioner—the game, in fact, which has made Air Jordan possible.

This is not to say that Jordan was not always a spectacular basketball player performing on a level that seemed almost to be his alone. If only as the highest-scoring pro basketballer in history on a per-game basis, he demands legendary status. MJ has played the major (if not single-handed) role in twice winning three consecutive NBA championships, although it can be argued astutely that these titles came in years when the league was at its competitive weakest in perhaps two decades. He did post seven straight scoring titles, although again, these came in an era when for much of the time there was a true paucity of other great point-makers (Bernard King, Dominique Wilkins, and Karl Malone are not Jerry West, Elgin Baylor, and Oscar Robertson). And Michael can never be denied as an unparalleled offensive showman who ranks right alongside Erving, Elgin Baylor, and perhaps Connie Hawkins as the leading sure-fire generators of instant crowd thrills.

And then there was the 1988 season in which Jordan was MVP, All-Star Game MVP, and league scoring champ, racked up 40 points in the All-Star Game, registered 10 steals in one game and 59 points in another, and was even the league's Defensive Player of the Year. Only Wilt in 1961–62 had a better year, yet while Wilt in his third season far outdistanced MJ's best campaign at the offensive end, it is also true that the Big Dipper paid almost no heed to his defensive role in that or almost any other season. Only Erving had a more flamboyant style; what Julius lacked was the same size stage. Only "The Big O" possessed a fuller and more balanced arsenal of talents. But neither Wilt nor Dr. J nor Oscar had Nike or the age of the ubiquitous television image to bolster their individual or collective cases.

Bill Russell—Greatest Defensive Player Ever Invented

All Michael Jordan now has to accomplish is to win five more NBA crowns without interruption and he will stand in the same league with Bill Russell. Except, of course, for the reasonable argument that Russell played during an era when winning league titles was a far more challenging accomplishment. One has to remember that year after year Russell and his Boston teammates had to climb the postseason hurdle of Warriors and 76ers teams built around Chamberlain and Lakers outfits anchored by West and Baylor—rival teams that boasted rosters that looked something like modern-era NBA All-Star squads. In the 1960s there were no NBA lineups fleshed out with a string of CBA refugees or with collegiate hardship cases (sometimes even fresh high school grads) still learning how to play the pro-style game. And there is also the issue of individual statistics to be debated; if Russell seems to be overwhelmed by Jordan in the area of career numbers, there are numerous extenuating circumstances to be considered.

When Bill Russell played in the NBA, blocked shots were neither counted as an "official statistic" nor kept in the record books. This is about the same as not counting home runs when Babe Ruth played or not tracking batting averages for Ted Williams, Stan Musial, and Tony Gwynn. Or perhaps ignoring stolen bases as an official category in the dead-ball age of Ty Cobb or the astroturf era of Rickey Henderson.

But while there are no official numbers on Bill Russell's blocked shots, there are indeed plenty of eyewitness accounts from fans, writers, and opposing players themselves. And all agree that Russell used the blocked shot to totally dominate games and even to revamp the sport as no one had ever revamped it before him. Cincinnati star Jack Twyman spoke for a decade-worth of Russell opponents: "Russell was the greatest impact player in any sport. He couldn't throw the ball in the ocean, but he allowed his teammates to press and gamble. You knew that if you got by Cousy or Heinsohn, that SOB Russell was back there waiting to block your shot. No one ever dominated a sport the way Russell did with the Celtics."

Of course, it was something of a pure distortion to suggest that Russell couldn't even heave the ball into the ocean. Cousy set the record straight on that matter: "If we needed him to, Russ could have averaged 20 points for us. For God's sake, he got 15 a game and we only had one play for him to shoot the ball. When we were clicking, he'd get a half-dozen slams a game on lob passes off the fast break. Even though he didn't have a shooting touch, he arranged his game so he never had to take a bad shot."

Perhaps much of the credit for creating Bill Russell as a superstar can be laid squarely at the doorstep of Red Auerbach. It is likely that no other coach would have made the gangly shot-blocker a top draft pick, trading away his star player (Ed Macauley) and top rookie (Cliff Hagan) to obtain such a one-dimensional prospect, and then built a complete team around his shot-blocking style. More likely, other NBA coaches inheriting Big Bill's physical talents would have labored to turn him into an effective scorer and, in the process, would have lost most of his unique contribution to the game. Red Auerbach saw from the beginning that here was a special and rare player who didn't have to score points to be remarkably effective at both ends of the floor.

Nor was his defensive prowess the run-of-the-mill sort of stuff. Russell didn't block shots simply to intimidate an opponent or to make personal statements based on ego battles like today's trash-talking rim defenders. His game was controlled and oriented entirely toward fitting into Auerbach's scheme for fashioning an invincible champion. Russell used his defense to launch the Boston constant-motion

Transcendental Graphics

All Michael Jordan has now to accomplish is to win five more NBA crowns without interruption and he will finally stand in the same league as a championship force with Bill Russell of the Boston Celtics.

offense. He would defend the goal in order to open up the inevitable fast break that would be ignited after each missed shot by the enemy. Russell would never knock an opponent's missile into the third row of courtside seats; instead he would guide the ball (either a shot he blocked or a rebound he had corralled) to a fast-breaking guard (usually Cousy) who would propel it ahead to a streaking Heinsohn or Frank Ramsey for an instant score. Russell was thus the ultimate defensive weapon. And as such, he dominated games, entire seasons, even a whole decade, without having to score a single basket himself.

There were other unique facets of Bill Russell, the basketball player. He was quietly efficient on the floor, yet burned with a competitive fire perhaps never matched in any other player—certainly not another post-position player of his size and his awesome talent. Here was the ultimate advantage that Russell always owned over Wilt and any of his other rivals in the trenches. And Russell was also one of the smartest men ever to play the game—a meticulous student of defensive positioning and of shooting and rebounding angles, ball movements, and other nearly invisible elements of the game.

He was also his own man and thus not always popular with a working press or with Boston fans. He shunned signing autographs (maintaining a strong distaste for hero worship), spoke out angrily on civil rights and racial intolerance, openly criticized the city of Boston for its treatment of black athletes, bypassed his own induction ceremony at the Naismith Memorial Hall of Fame, and attended the retirement ceremony for his number "6" at the Boston Garden only on the condition that it be held before the arena gates were opened to the public. Grace and composure on the playing court were an effective mask for inner turmoil and seething hidden anger; Russell usually vomited in the locker room before any important game, a surefire signal to his teammates that Big Bill was more than ready for the heat of battle.

The true legacy of Bill Russell, of course, is not uncovered by perusing his statistical line in the *Basketball Encyclopedia*. But it is found in the record books, nonetheless—over on the page devoted to yearly NBA championship results. No other player in hoopdom's history owns 11 world titles and none likely ever will; no one else even comes close. Teammate Cousy was around for the raising of six of those banners; Tom Heinsohn survived long enough to share eight of those rings. Neither one might have ever tasted the victory champagne even a single time without Russell as a teammate.

Auerbach's Celtics (while the famed Redhead was first coach and then later GM) won 11 titles in but 13 seasons in what still stands without challenge as the greatest winning legacy in all of American professional sports. And they didn't win a single one of those titles without their big man at the post—Bill Russell. In fact, it seems quite evident that they won every one of those titles only because they had Bill Russell standing around the basket providing the most relentless intimidating force basketball has ever known.

Wilt "The Stilt" Chamberlain—Best Offensive Player by a City Mile

It is almost impossible in today's age of heavily hyped flyers like Michael Jordan and Scottie Pippen to come close to appreciating the one-time stature of the giant Wilt Chamberlain. All excuses aside for Chamberlain's occasional lack of hustle, for his failure to win as many team championships as expected, and for the uneven talent of the age he played in, it is axiomatic that Wilt's stature as the game's greatest physical force can never be legitimately challenged.

Here, simply put, was the greatest big man basketball has ever witnessed. And even more simply stated (and equally provable by the numbers alone), here was the greatest scorer who ever lit up the nets of college and pro arenas everywhere he played. Wilt's scoring totals are his ultimate legacy and, like the man himself, they are simply huge.

One season alone is sufficient to elevate Wilt to an unapproachable class by himself. That year was only his third in the league, and it was also the year that launched basketball's individual scoring milestones straight into the stratosphere. It was a season of aberrant performances parallel to Ruth's and Maris's 60-homer seasons in baseball, and yet in the end, there is no true comparison of Chamberlain's prodigious scoring with Ruth's prodigious longball bashing. For Chamberlain outdistanced all his rivals (past and future) like no one has ever done on a baseball diamond. Ruth would have had to hit 75 homers to enjoy the same cushion over his nearest rival, Gehrig with 47. (Chamberlain's 4,029 total points outstripped Bellamy's runner-up 2,495 by 38 percent.) And Wilt posted his ungodly numbers in the very season when Baylor also averaged 38.3 points per game (a total that no one but Chamberlain has ever matched), when a rookie named Walt Bellamy also conquered the 30-point level, and when a guard in Cincinnati named Oscar Robertson quietly *averaged* a triple-double in scoring, rebounding, and playmaking as a capper.

The numbers Wilt posted in 1962 stand beyond the reach of any mere mortal; he played nearly every minute of the season (truly phenomenal in the NBA), netted 100 points in a single game, posted his mind-bending 50.4 scoring average, registered 45 games of 50 points or more, scored 50 or better in seven consecutive games (also in five straight and six straight on two other occasions), topped 4,000 points for the only time in league history, and registered 63 games of 40-plus points. Double the totals of Jordan's very best year, and you have an equal contest!

Transcendental Graphics

It is almost impossible in today's age of heavily hyped flyers like Michael Jordan and Scottie Pippen to come close to appreciating the one-time imposing stature of the giant Wilt Chamberlain.

Forget about the endless claims that "The Big Dipper" could always be counted on to "wilt" in the heat of postseason competitions; that Chamberlain had the soft attitude of a loser and was easily intimidated by a more ferocious Russell; that Wilt could seemingly do everything on a basketball court except what he was paid for—win championships. Such complaints are little more than mean-spirited naysaying. And they are also, in large degree, belied by the fact that Chamberlain anchored two of the biggest winners (1967 Philadelphia 76ers and 1972 L.A. Lakers) in NBA history.

The list of Wilt's statistical accomplishments reads like the pages of a science fiction novel entitled *Giant From Planet Zenon Conquers Basketball*. There are two distinct ages of scoring and rebounding statistics in NBA annals: one is the epoch before and after Wilt, and the other is the "Age of Chamberlain," which stretches from 1960 (his first season of seven consecutive scoring titles) to 1967 (the year his scoring finally slacked and yet he won his first NBA team crown).

For those who think that Chamberlain was nothing more than a one-dimensional dunker who only went out after scoring titles and eschewed team triumphs, it is also instructive to recall the "New Wilt" of the late '60s and early '70s. Chamberlain underwent a remarkable career transformation in midstream that is altogether unparalleled within the history of cage play. Convinced by 76ers coach Alex Hannum that he could prove more effective to a championship unit by rebounding, playing defense à la Russell, and dishing the ball to unguarded teammates, Wilt, overnight, became the consummate team player. Six years after burning up the NBA with his 50.4 scoring average, the same player was leading the circuit in assists with 702 (1968). Teamed with Gail Goodrich and Jerry West in Los Angeles four seasons later (1972), Wilt earned another NBA title by setting up the hot-shooting Lakers' outside game with his total domination of the inside boards.

In the end it was the true test of Wilt Chamberlain's rare basketball skills that, in the latter phases of his career he was so thoroughly able to perform a complete about-face and become another type of player entirely. Here indeed was sufficient evidence in itself that Wilt Chamberlain could do absolutely anything he wanted to on a basketball court.

Oscar "Big O" Robertson—Greatest All-Around Player on the Planet

Few fans who have come to the sport alongside Magic, Bird, and Jordan will be easily convinced, but Oscar Robertson was far and away the greatest basketball player ever to step onto a hardwood floor. The evidence is so convincing as to be almost redundant. Consider Oscar's rookie NBA season alone—the year in which, as a 22-year-old novice, he garnered 30.5 points per game (outclassed by only Chamberlain and Baylor), averaged a league-best 9.7 assists (ending Cousy's long reign in this department), made 47.2 percent of his field-goal tries and 82.2 percent of his free throws, and pulled down better than 10 rebounds a contest to outclass every other guard in the league in the board-sweeping category. NBA historian Leonard Koppett has suggested that, since each rebound during that earlier era was worth about a point (considering 1961 leaguewide shooting percentages), and each assist naturally equates to two points, Robertson's overall rookie contribution (adding in his own scoring) amounted to better than 60 points per game. Since he also provided every imaginable intangible—soft feeds to teammates in scoring position, clutch baskets that bolstered team confidence, relentless stress on opposing team defenses, exceptional defense, fouling out of only three contests all season—many were already referring to Oscar as "the best basketball player the human race had yet produced" (Koppett's phrasing) before the door had even closed on his rookie season.

For further evidence there is again the 1961–62 season in which Oscar's prime statistics (30.8 points per game, 12.5 rebounds, 11.4 assists) stand as the most balanced overall performance in basketball history. No one else has reached double figures for a full NBA season in all three primary hallmarks of performance. While leading the circuit regularly in assists (six times with two second-place finishes) Oscar also reached the top 10 in rebounds (while playing as a guard), and posted two second-place finishes and five third-place finishes in the individual scoring race during his first seven seasons (equivalent to a flock of individual titles in another era, keeping in mind that Chamberlain and Baylor were playing at the same time).

Jordan has scored slightly more (but doesn't match up to Oscar in either assists or rebounds); Magic Johnson is the only player to top Oscar's career assists-per-game average (but Magic can't compare as a scorer); and no guard ever rebounded better. The case is already closed, and the majority of the ballots would have to fall on Robertson's side of the ledger.

The true measure for selecting a "greatest player" or "all-time best" is the degree to which he rates at or near the top in each and every one of the game's major categories of performance. And the three standard statistical measures of such individual greatness have, from the earliest days, been a player's cumulative totals in scoring, rebounding, and feeding the ball (assists) to teammates in scoring position. While triple-doubles in a single game are today's hallmark of greatness, in Oscar's case such milestones were a matter of mere normalcy. "Big O" regularly approached triple-double seasonal numbers in each of his first five NBA campaigns: 1961 (30.5 ppg, 10.1 rpg, 9.7 apg), 1962 (30.8 ppg, 12.5 rpg, 11.4 apg), 1963 (28.3 ppg, 10.4 rpg, 9.5 apg), 1964 (31.4 ppg, 9.9 rpg, 11.0 apg), 1965 (30.4 ppg, 9.0 rpg, 11.5 apg).

The *five-year* cumulative average is mind-boggling: *30.3* points per game, *10.4* rebounds per game, *10.6* assists per game. If occasional triple-doubles are any true standard for superstar sanction, then Oscar Robertson seemingly played on a separate planet and ruled on a separate plane of perfection. Oscar admittedly didn't dominate the league by winning scoring titles, but this was simply because he fell into an age that had too many rivals with names like Chamberlain, Baylor, West, Bellamy, and Barry—immortals not for a moment to be confused with the Dominique Wilkinses, David Robinsons, Karl Malones, and Alex Englishes who Jordan has battled annually for scoring dominance. (In each of the seven straight years that Chamberlain copped scoring titles there was at least one other 30-points-per-game rival, usually Oscar; only twice did this happen during Jordan's seven-year reign.) And Oscar also didn't dominate the highlight films (when there were any) by courting the fancy dunks or dipsy-doodle moves seemingly required for mass fan appeal in today's hyperbole-filled "showtime" market.

What Oscar Robertson *did* do was perform at a higher level (and for a longer period) in more vital areas than any other player of any other epoch. His only weakness—the one area besides pure flashiness, where Jordan was clearly superior—was in the realm of defense. Oscar never ranked among the best defenders in the league. But then he didn't have to (and he also played in an era more jammed with defense stars than is the case in the current decade). While Oscar may not have intercepted passes and stripped dribbles from his rivals with the same frequency as MJ, he may not have been all that far behind (no accurate comparisons are possible

Oscar Robertson boosters need point no further than the 1961–62 NBA season, in which Oscar's prime-time statistics (30.8 ppg, 12.5 rpg, 11.4 apg) stand as the most balanced overall year-long performance in basketball history.

since steals were not an "official" statistical category before Oscar's final season); certainly Robertson far outdistanced Jordan as a defensive rebounder. He was a solid enough defender, nonetheless, to get the job done, and that was all that was ever demanded of him during his own sojourn on an NBA floor.

Oscar's best defensive weapons were, in the end, rebounding and his knack for keeping his opponents so off-balance while he had the ball at their end of the court, that their own stamina—and thus their own offensive performance—always

Oscar Robertson's Milestone Achievements

First three-time national collegiate scoring champion (1958, 1959, 1960)
First college sophomore to lead nation in scoring
Three-time college "National Player of the Year" (UPI, USBWA)
All-time college scoring leader at graduation (surpassed by Pete Maravich)
Held 14 career NCAA scoring records at graduation
One of two players in Top Ten in NCAA and NBA career scoring (with Elvin Hayes)
One of three players to average 30-plus points for three college seasons
One of three players to score 900-plus points in three college seasons
Fifth all-time in NCAA career combined points and rebounds
Fourth-highest percentage of team's points scored in college career
Second-most 40-plus-points college games versus Division I opponents
Six-time NBA assists leader
All-time NBA career assists leader at retirement
Second-highest NBA career points at retirement (after Wilt Chamberlain)
Second-highest NBA career scoring average for guards (after Michael Jordan)
Most NBA career rebounds for a guard (7,804)
Three-time NBA All-Star Game MVP (matched only by Bob Pettit)
NBA All-Star Game career point-scoring leader
Second-highest NBA All-Star Game career scoring average (after Michael Jordan)
Only season-long Triple-Double in NBA history (1962)
Highest career overall points-rebounds-assists average in NBA history
Ranks in NBA career Top Ten in eight statistical categories
Second-highest NBA career free throw total (after Moses Malone)
Third-highest NBA career assists total (after John Stockton and Magic Johnson)
Scored 40-plus points in 77 NBA games (third-most all time)

suffered rather drastically. Robertson may not have blocked countless shots or logged numerous steals, but he did absolutely everything else—and did it all better than anyone else before or since.

In the end, comparing ballplayers from different eras—especially in the constantly self-renewing cage sport, a game which has evolved far more radically since midcentury in playing styles and rule structure than either its baseball or football rivals—is much like comparing apples with oranges or peaches with pears. Or perhaps more like comparing dribblers with dunkers, or high-flying slammers with set-shot artists. The game has recast its appearance radically since it became a prime-time television spectacle, and like baseball, it has seemingly changed largely for the worse.

Today's basketball has become far more one-dimensional in design, transformed into a series of repeated slams and jams at both ends of the court, reduced to an endlessly repeated highlight film featuring spectacular but mind-numbing individual "showtime" moves. Personal showmanship has indeed replaced inspired team play; one-on-one specialization overwhelms all-around ballhandling and shooting skills. Fundamentals of free-throw shooting, pinpoint passing, offensive movement without the ball, tenacious team defense—all these staples of a bygone era—have now flown out the window seemingly everywhere except in the game today being played by the women collegians. For those who still respect versatility, however, there seems to be little to debate. Oscar Robertson indeed remains the greatest pure basketball player ever invented.

Transcendental Graphics

Few fans who have come to Naismith's sport in the epoch of Magic, Bird, and Air Jordan will be easily convinced, but Oscar Roberston may well have been the greatest natural basketball talent ever to take to the hardwood floor.

♦ ♦ ♦

The issue of the greatest basketball player seems, in the end, to come down to Jordan versus any one of two or three other possible rivals from the game's largely forgotten past. Jordan may well hold an indisputable edge in overall numbers now that his career is finally closed for the second time. He failed to overhaul Chamberlain in total points produced, and his championship ring count, although impressive, did not approach that of Bill Russell, and he never posted quite the scoring numbers that Wilt amassed at the very peak of his own Jekyll-and-Hyde career.

Style points, on the other hand, can never be altogether resolved, and the debate will always turn inevitably on less objective matters having to do with aesthetic appeal (something that finds new standards of taste for almost every generation) and overall effectiveness as a multidimensional player. The point to be made here is simply that the debate itself is not nearly as one-sided as '90s-only fans and Jordan-promoters would have us believe.

Two of three true rivals to Jordan's universally acclaimed crown carry a very hefty argument in their own favor for ultimate superiority. And even a third—Russell—was equally dominant or perhaps even more dominant in a much tougher era, one jammed with Hall of Famers like Pettit, Wilt, Baylor, Robertson, West, Schayes, Hagan, and Arizin, and a full complement of lesser paragons like Hal Greer, Nate Thurmond, Jack Twyman, Jerry Lucas, and Wayne Embry. Wilt admittedly fails as a top-notch competitor, which, in one sense, only seems to enhance the argument for his unmatched natural skills. Chamberlain hardly seemed to try much of the time, and yet still ranks near the top of everyone's pantheon. Russell, by contrast, toted his teammates on his shoulders for more than a decade, as none—not even Jordan, who played alongside Pippen—ever has. (At least not for so long and against such ruthless competition.) And as an all-around nonpareil talent, who could do absolutely everything the game demanded without parallel, and seemingly almost without effort as well, Oscar Robertson will perhaps never again be matched. Robertson's unique status seems especially safe if basketball continues its current drift farther and farther away from a game that values balanced and polished fundamentals over showy one-dimensionality.

In an era that maintains an ongoing love affair with the "triple-double" as a standard measure of diverse excellence, it is indeed quite ironic that a player has today been largely forgotten whose whole career comprised a ledger of triple-double performances. The problem, of course, is that few fans saw Oscar play on more than a sporadic basis since the league in which he performed was, for all its talent and skill level, never a prime-time entertainment spectacle. Throughout Robertson's prime seasons the NBA remained a dozen-city league, enjoyed limited television coverage, and ranked as a minor-league sport in the public imagination. Yet those who were blessed with seeing the Big O in his full bloom, almost to a man, maintain the assessment that he was every bit an equal talent to Michael Jordan and perhaps even quite a bit more.

In the end, perhaps the only fair way to measure all-time greatness is to consider the degree to which a player dominates during his own era. Comparisons between eras and between players of different eras are at best only suggestive and at worst always misleading. A judgment based on aesthetic appeal or style points is equally tenuous, since any such measures are highly subjective and turn on the particular standards of excellence in vogue at the moment of judgment. Statistical measures don't seem to do the trick, either, since statistical comparison will only establish, in this case, that Jordan was the true equal of past greats. It will not clearly clinch the case for His Airness over Chamberlain (whose most remarkable scoring feats still dwarf Jordan's) or Robertson (especially when taking college as well as pro careers into consideration) or Russell (who still maintains an uncatchable lead in team titles won), and it certainly won't leave Jordan with the field to himself—as his most zealous supporters would want to claim.

When the measure is the fairer one of domination in a player's own era, then the judgment is perhaps on more substantial grounds. But the trouble here is that, while Jordan soars above his contemporaries, the only area in which he seems to do so by leaps and bounds is in the realms of celebrity status, commercial visibility, and raw airtime (of the television and not the hang time variety). Clearly Jordan does not dominate his own era to anywhere near the degree that a Mikan dominated the pro game's infancy during the late '40s and Chamberlain dominated its "Golden Decade" of the early '60s. Mikan was so far ahead and above his rivals that drastic new playing styles (rough-and-tumble hacking and banging around the basket and slowdown clock-killing offenses) had to be adopted to curtail him, and wholesale rules changes (goal-tending strictures, a shot clock, and expanded free-throw lanes) had to be instituted by the league to stop him. Jordan has never known quite such mastery—the only "rule change" stimulated by MJ appears to be a relaxation on traveling and foul calls in order to enhance (not limit) his showcase performance. And when it comes to comparing Jordan's scoring reign with Chamberlain's, the degree of dominance is equally one-sided. Jordan has won the bulk of his scoring titles by no more than average margins (2.7 points per game ahead of Dominique Wilkins in 1993, 2.1 over Karl Malone in 1992, 2.5 ahead of Bernard King in 1991). Chamberlain outdistanced his nearest rivals by unthinkable margins (6.4 beyond Jack Twyman as a rookie in 1960, 18.8 above Walt Bellamy in 1962, 10.8 over Elgin Baylor in 1963).

In the end then, the argument for Jordan's unmatched ranking indeed always comes down to style points. MJ is admittedly the most aesthetically pleasing and endlessly thrilling player to watch—now or in any epoch of the past. But while such a measure is substantial, it is also shaky in its foundations. It may well last only until a new popular style and a new standard for perfection find their way smartly into vogue. Future generations of fans may well reject Air Jordan's soaring solo flights, just as today's watchers remain cool to memories of Oscar Robertson's nightly clinics in polished yet restrained perfection.

Basketball Time Line

Capsulized below are major events that have marked the first 100-plus years of collegiate and professional basketball competition. Each year has brought something of significance to the historical evolution of our most popular team spectator sport. Here are all of basketball's defining moments in brief capsule form. Highlights of professional basketball history are distinguished by italics. Individual players, coaches, and peripheral figures who have separate entries in *The Biographical History of Basketball* are designated by boldface.

1894–95—(February 9) The first formal intercollegiate game is played between Hamline College (St. Paul, Minnesota) and the Minnesota State School of Agriculture, with the Hamline team falling, nine goals to three. Nine contestants play for each side. One month later Haverford College defeats Temple University 6–4 in another nine-to-a-side contest. California and Stanford are believed to have played the first women's intercollegiate game (in April) but no score is recorded. The original free-throw line at 20 feet from the basket is now experimentally placed at 15 feet.

The Buffalo Germans pro team, organized at the Buffalo YMCA with stars Al Heerdt and Eddie Miller, soon dominates amateur tournaments, while also touring against other professional clubs. The Germans compile an overall 792–86 record across three decades (before disbanding in 1929) and once amass 111 consecutive victories before losing to Herkimer (New York) managed by **Frank Basloe***.*

1895–96—(January 16) Football pioneer **Amos Alonzo Stagg** (an associate of **Dr. James Naismith** at Springfield College in 1891) coaches the University of Chicago club team to a 15–12 victory over the YMCA team representing the University of Iowa. This is the first five-on-a-side college game on record. Backboards (10 feet above the floor) are used for first time, with open nets allowed on baskets.

1896–97—(March 20) Yale University defeats University of Pennsylvania 32–10 in the first official "conference" game between Ivy League schools. Yale is first team to employ the "dribble" as an offensive strategy. Beginning with this season a field goal is changed from one to two points and a free throw is changed from three points to one point. Five-man teams become standard.

(November 7) The first documented professional game is held in Trenton, New Jersey, as the Trenton Basketball Team (formerly the Trenton YMCA Team) defeats Brooklyn's YMCA club 16–1 at the city's Masonic Temple Hall. The Trenton "Y" team became a ticket-selling

independent club after being expelled by local YMCA officials. The game is played within a chicken-wire cage built by **Fred Padderatz***, the team's part-time manager.*

1897–98—Rules are adopted banning "overhead" dribbles (tapping the ball in the air volleyball style), and also outlawing the "double dribbles" (discontinued dribbles) or two-handed dribbles. The free-throw line is now standardized at 15 feet from the hoop.

The first known professional league is formed in the Philadelphia area and ambitiously called the National Basketball League. Six teams compete, and the championship is won by a Trenton club coached by Fred Cooper. The league lasts five seasons before folding. Other short-lived leagues follow, including the Eastern League, Central League, Hudson River League, and New York State League.

1898–99—**James Naismith**, fresh from earning a medical degree in Colorado, is appointed head of the physical education department and coach of the basketball team at the University of Kansas. The Jayhawks play their first official game February 3 against the Kansas City YMCA.

1899–1900—The Yale team barnstorms across the country during the Christmas holidays in what is advertised as the "longest trip ever taken by a United States college team." Nebraska's Cornhuskers become college basketball's first recognized unbeaten team, remaining undefeated over 19 games and three full seasons (1898–1900). Dartmouth embarrasses Boston College 44–0 in an exhibition match at the annual New England Sportsman's Show in Boston's Mechanics Hall. This is the largest recorded shutout during the sport's first decade.

1900–01—Yale University, Trinity College (Hartford, Connecticut), and Wesleyan College (Middletown, Connecticut) form the first formal collegiate basketball conference, called the Triangle League. This same winter a second confederation, the New England League, is formed by Dartmouth, Holy Cross, Amherst College, Williams College, and Trinity College. Also, Columbia, Cornell, Harvard, Princeton, and Yale band together to form a confederation called the Eastern League, and Yale claims the first league title.

1901–02—The University of Minnesota team compiles a 15–0 record in Western Conference (Big Ten) play and will eventually extend its winning streak to 34 games, not losing again until 1904. The University of Pennsylvania, which dropped the sport four years earlier due to inadequate facilities, returns to competition.

1902–03—A new rule is adopted (it will remain in effect through 1908) that prohibits the dribbler from shooting the basketball. Cadet "Vinegar Joe" Stilwell (who later earned World War II fame as a military general) organizes the first basketball team for the United States Military Academy at West Point. Bucknell University defeats the Philadelphia College of Pharmacy 159–5 with Bucknell player John Anderson scoring 80 points.

1903–04—(July 13–14) The Olympic Games in St. Louis are host to a national college basketball tournament billed as the Olympic World's College Basketball Championship. This is an outdoor event featuring only three schools (Hiram College, Wheaton College, and Latter Day Saints College, which is today Brigham Young University). Hiram defeats Wheaton 25–20 and Latter Day Saints 25–18 to win tournament title. The first "suction-sole" shoes are advertised by Spalding, marking the birth of basketball sneakers.

1904–05—Potsdam Normal College (New York) humiliates Plattsburgh Normal by a 123–0 score, the most lopsided game recorded during the first decade of college play. In April representatives of 15 colleges meet in Philadelphia (and later New York) to standardize rules, gain control of the collegiate game from the AAU, and form their own governing body that would eventually become known as the National Collegiate Athletic Association (NCAA). **Christian Steinmetz** of Wisconsin becomes the first collegian to surpass 1,000 career points.

1905–06—The Western Athletic Conference (later called Big Ten Conference) launches its first formal winter of league championship competition, with Minnesota (6–1) edging Wisconsin (6–2) for the league title. Spalding publishes its first *Official Collegiate Basketball Guide*, focusing on six Eastern (Ivy) League teams (Yale, Harvard, Princeton, Columbia, Cornell, Pennsylvania) and a single Western Athletic Conference school (Minnesota).

1906–07—**Dr. James Naismith** gives up his job as basketball coach at Kansas (turning the reins over to **Forrest "Phog" Allen**) yet remains on the school's faculty as a physical education instructor until 1937. The University of Chicago, coached by **Joseph Raycroft**, launches a four-year period of dominance in the Western Athletic Conference with a 22–2 overall record and 6–2 conference mark.

1907–08—Western Athletic Conference power Chicago (after besting Wisconsin on a "miracle" last-second shot by **Pat Page**) defeats Eastern champion Pennsylvania in a home-and-home playoff series and is declared the winner of the "unofficial" national championship. A player committing five fouls (including traveling or other such violations) is now disqualified from a game.

1908–09—A rule is adopted that disqualifies a player once he commits five *personal* fouls. National concern about roughness in college sports reaches its height when President Theodore Roosevelt expresses his own concern about increasing serious injuries in college football competition. Harvard president Charles Eliot recommends colleges ban basketball, since it is even more brutal than football. The Missouri Valley Conference is formed with two divisions.

1909–10—Glass backboards (invented by Chicago's 1909 Player of the Year **John Schommer**) are employed for the first time in a bold experiment designed to make it easier for spectators to view games. The University of Chicago, with National Player of the Year **Harlan "Pat" Page**, establishes itself as one of the early dynasty teams by winning its fourth straight Western Athletic Conference (Big Ten) title. Schommer and Page combine to lead Chicago to a 78–12 decade-long record.

1910–11—A second referee is optionally added to college games to cut down on violent play, and players are now disqualified after four personal fouls. Future barnstorming pro star and Hall of Famer **Barney Sedran**, at 5'4", leads CCNY in scoring from 1909 to 1911 and becomes the sport's first noteworthy long-range-shooting little man.

1911–12—Wisconsin (12–0) and Purdue (10–0) both complete undefeated seasons in the Western Athletic Conference (Big Ten) and share the title on the basis of winning percentage. The shared trophy is the second of Purdue's eventual league-leading 20 Big Ten championships.

1912–13—Open-bottom nets, already in use for several years, are officially sanctioned for use in all amateur championship contests. (Cylindrical wire baskets were first produced in 1893 by Lew Allen in Hartford, Connecticut, and braided cord nets appeared the following year. Before 1912 referees pulled a chain attached to bottom of the net to release the ball from the basket.)

1913–14—A new rule awards out-of-bounds balls to the team not touching the ball inbounds last. Before this rule players were allowed to "scramble" over the line for out-of-bounds balls with the first player over the line to touch ball gaining possession.

1914–15—AAU officials agree to meet with representatives of both the YMCA and International Athletic Association (early name for NCAA) to standardize rules for amateur play everywhere across the country. Standing zone defenses are introduced to combat a patterned offensive style introduced by **Doc Meanwell** at Wisconsin and remain a popular defensive style for the next full decade.

*Ex-CCNY star **Barney Sedran** leads the Carbondale (Pennsylvania) pro team to 35 consecutive wins and the championship of the Tri-County League, while also playing for Utica in the New York State League. Sedran once scores 17 baskets in a game without the benefit of backboards.*

1915–16—The University of Texas team finishes its third straight undefeated season with a 12–0 record to extend its unbeaten string to 40 games. Rules governing the act of "dribbling" are standardized.

*The Troy Trojans club undertakes a barnstorming tour through Midwest states and wins all 38 games. The famed team, organized by Lew Wachter and formed around 6'6" star **Ed Wachter**, dominates several early pro leagues and is also known as the "Wachter Wonders." The team pioneers the use of the bounce pass and court-long outlet pass.*

1916–17—Texas runs its record unbeaten streak to 44 before finally losing to Rice University 24–18. The national rules committee governing amateur play outlaws glass backboards by legislating that all backboards must be painted white. This attempt at uniformity will be dropped after several seasons.

1917–18—(February 9) The first tie in college basketball history occurs when an official scorer's error leaves Kentucky and Kentucky Wesleyan knotted at 21 apiece. Baskets are moved two feet inside the playing court, thus allowing shots to be taken from anywhere within the playing area. Michigan becomes the 10th team in the Western Athletic Conference, and sportswriters begin referring to the league as the Big Ten.

***Eddie Gottlieb** forms the Philadelphia barnstorming professional team known as the SPHAs, named after the South Philadelphia Hebrew Association, which provides sponsorship. The team competes for Eastern barnstorming supremacy in the '20s and '30s with the Original Celtics and the Rens (both of New York) and also later dominates the American Basketball League under the name of Philadelphia Hebrews.*

1918–19—Newspaper reports on college games begin referring regularly to the cage sport as "basketball" (one word) rather than "basket ball" (two words) as in previous years. **Nat Holman**, star professional player with the famous New York Original Celtics, takes over as the paid head coach at New York University.

1919–20—(March) NYU defeats CCNY 39–21 in a game staged at the 168th Street Regiment Armory before an overflow crowd of more than 10,000. This landmark contest reveals the enormous financial potential of college basketball games.

1920–21—A new college rule allows a player removed from the game to reenter play one time only. Michigan, Wisconsin, and Purdue share the Big Ten title with identical 8–4 records.

1921–22—Backboards are moved two feet from end walls, thus preventing the popular practice of players jumping up on walls to shoot layups. The University of Kansas begins back-to-back seasons atop the college basketball world with 16–2 (1922) and 17–1 (1923) records. This Jayhawks team is later remembered for its cast of coaching celebrities: head coach **Forrest ("Phog") Allen**, assistant **James Naismith**, and little-used reserve player **Adolph Rupp**.

*The Original Celtics of New York emerge as the dominant barnstorming team with the addition of stars like **Henry "Dutch" Dehnert**, Swede Grimstead, and **Johnny Beckman** to a potent contingent including **Pete Barry** and Johnny Witte organized after World War I by promoter **Jim Furey**. Adding feature players like **Nat Holman**, Chris Leonard, **Joe Lapchick**, and Davey Banks sustain the team's reputation throughout 1920s. Furey signs players to the first individual contracts in basketball history (the first time players are paid by the season and not by the game). The team's constant experimenting leads to such innovations as zone defense and offensive pivot play.*

1922–23—Ott Romney begins a highly successful coaching stint at Montana State, which will see him post a 144–31 record over the next five seasons. The United States Military Academy decides to improve its basketball program after several embarrassing defeats by Navy and hires successful coach Harry Fisher away from Columbia College.

1923–24—A new rule ends the practice of awarding free-throw shots for violations such as traveling and double-dribbling. A rejuvenated U.S. Military Academy team under coach Harry Fisher compiles a two-year winning streak that finally ends at 31 games.

1924–25—A new rule specifies that the player fouled must take the free throws that are awarded. Previously, "designated free-throwers" were regularly used. The practice of each player shooting his own free throws is pioneered in 1910s by the famed pro barnstorming team (also the inventors of bounce passes), the Troy (New York) Trojans.

1925–26—The Kansas Jayhawks under coach **Phog Allen** win their fourth of six consecutive Missouri Valley crowns, posting a 16–2 record. Purdue, Michigan, Indiana, and Iowa finish in a rare four-way tie in Big Ten Conference. Player of the Year **Victor Hanson**, a three-time All-American, leads Syracuse to the mythical national championship as well as a 48–7 record over a three-year career.

The American Basketball League (organized by Washington laundry tycoon George Preston Marshall, Chicago pro football owner George Halas, and Cleveland department store magnate Max Rosenblum) opens its first season in a pioneering attempt to make professional basketball a legitimate major-league sport.

1926–27—Dartmouth wins its first Eastern (Ivy) League title in 15 seasons with a 26–24 thriller over Princeton as the Tigers miss a tying basket with only 10 seconds left. Michigan wins its first-ever Big Ten Conference championship. **Phog Allen** and **James Naismith** at Kansas lead a successful fight to overturn a new proposal outlawing dribbling by restricting players to a single bounce of the ball (this anti-dribble legislation being introduced by Wisconsin's **Doc Meanwell**).

*The famed Original Celtics join the ABL during its second season of operation (after the league bans members from playing exhibitions with the Celtics) and capture the league championship. The Philadelphia Warriors, operated and coached by **Eddie Gottlieb**, also join the ABL. The Harlem Globetrotters are formed in Chicago by **Abe Saperstein** and play their first road game on January 7 in Hinckley, Illinois. The Globetrotters win 101 of 117 games during their first barnstorming winter with a roster featuring "Toots" Wright, "Fats" Long, "Kid" Oliver, Andy Washington, and "Runt" Pullins.*

1927–28—A record crowd of 10,000 in Pennsylvania's new Palestra Gym (opened January 1, 1927) watches Penn defeat Princeton 24–22 for the Ivy League title. Victory comes on a 30-foot basket with two minutes remaining by reserve forward Donald Noble. Oklahoma posts an 18–0 record to win the Missouri Valley title and end the University of Kansas's reign of six straight conference crowns.

The Original Celtics dominate the ABL's third season of operation, finishing 40–9 with an 11-game lead over Gottlieb's Philadelphia entry. **Joe Lapchick, Nat Holman, Dutch Dehnert, Pete Barry,** *and Davey Banks are the nucleus of a team that wins 15 straight in midseason. Ex-Syracuse University All-American and Cleveland Rosenblums star Vic Hanson quits the ABL in protest over rough playing style.*

1928–29—George Gregory, All-Eastern Conference center for Columbia, earns notoriety as the first noteworthy black player at an East Coast college. Sporting goods manufacturers first introduce concealed-lace basketballs, an innovation that eliminates irregular bounces plaguing dribblers and passers during earlier games. Oklahoma enjoys a second straight undefeated season (10–0) in the Missouri Valley Conference, and the St. John's "Wonder Five" team posts an 18-game win streak and 23–2 record. A new rule defines "charging fouls" as a new type of violation.

The eight-team ABL enjoys its most competitive season in the fourth year of operation, with the Cleveland Rosenblums gaining the championship in a four-game sweep of Fort Wayne. The Original Celtics club is disbanded, with Lapchick, Dehnert, and Barry joining Cleveland, and Holman and Banks (the league's top scorer) now playing for the all-Jewish New York Hakoahs. Saperstein's Globetrotters add colorful Inman Jackson to lineup and first experiment with clowning routines that would become their trademark.

1929–30—All uses of rope or chicken wire around the edges of the court are eliminated. Nonetheless, players will continue to be known as "cagers" as a result of the earlier practice. With two All-Americans in **Charles "Stretch" Murphy** and **John Wooden**, Purdue finishes an unbeaten Big Ten season at 10–0. Two officials, rather than one, become the standard for college games.

1930–31—(January 21) First Madison Square Garden tripleheader is staged by sportswriter Dan Daniel and draws more than 16,000 fans. The three games involve Columbia, Fordham, Manhattan, NYU, St. John's, and CCNY, and launch a lasting popularity of MSG college basketball events. The St. John's "Wonder Five" team builds a 27-game winning streak and a four-year 86–8 record as the best collegiate team of the era.

The short-lived American Basketball League plays its final season under the cloud of the Great Depression, decreased player salaries, and the loss of stars like **Nat Holman** *and* **Johnny Beckman.** *The final championship is won by the Brooklyn Visitations over a Fort Wayne team led by rookie player-coach* **Branch McCracken** *of Indiana University.*

1931–32—Three-time All-American guard **John Wooden** leads Purdue to its second Big Ten title in three seasons and paces **Piggy Lambert's** fast-breaking team in scoring with 154 points. Legendary **Clair Bee** begins a two-decade tenure as head coach at Long Island University during which his teams will win 95 percent of their games.

The New York Renaissance Five pro club begins a four-year peak barnstorming period, posting a 473–49 record between 1932 and 1936, capturing 88 straight in 1933, and staging memorable games with the still-operating Original Celtics. Top Rens stars include 6'4" **Charles "Tarzan" Cooper,** *6'5" Wee Willie Smith, and 5'7"* **Clarence "Fats" Jenkins.**

1932–33—A rule is introduced requiring teams to advance the ball over the halfcourt line in 10 seconds. This rule results from 1932 games between USC-UCLA and Kansas-Missouri in which stalling teams attempted to hold the ball under their own basket. Also, no player *with the ball* is allowed to stand in the free-throw lane for more than three seconds.

1933–34—**Ned Irish** plans to promote a showcase game between NYU and CCNY in Madison Square Garden, but the plot falls through when a conflict with a scheduled boxing match kills the proposed deal. In his third year at Long Island University (LIU), coach **Clair Bee** leads his team to a 27–1 mark, losing only to St. John's. The first basketball stamp is issued in the Philippines.

1934–35—(December 29) The first intersectional college basketball doubleheader at Madison Square Garden is staged by sportswriter **Ned Irish** and draws a throng of 16,180 to witness NYU beat Notre Dame, and Westminster (Pennsylvania) defeat St. John's. Circumference of the ball is officially reduced from 32 inches to between 29½ and 30¼ inches.

1935–36—The United States team (comprised largely of college players) wins the first basketball gold medal in the Olympics by defeating Canada on an outdoor dirt court during a driving rainstorm in Berlin, Germany. **James Naismith** tosses up the first ball of the Olympic tournament. **Hank Luisetti** of Stanford revolutionizes offensive play by shooting balls one-handed and averaging 20 points per game for the season.

1936–37—(December 30) A memorable intersectional battle in Madison Square Garden sees Stanford, with **Hank Luisetti**, overcome **Clair Bee's** undefeated LIU team by a 45–31 score. This landmark game ends LIU's 43-game victory string and establishes legitimacy of Luisetti's one-hand shooting style and also of West Coast–style wide-open play. NAIA (small college confederation) launches its first postseason tournament in which Central Missouri earns the championship by besting Morningside (Iowa) 35–24.

1937–38—Temple University captures the first National Invitation Tournament title at Madison Square Garden with a 60–36 victory over Colorado. On New Year's Day Stanford's **Hank Luisetti** scores a then-phenomenal 50 points versus Duquesne, thus becoming the first modern-era college player to top the half-century point total. The rule requiring a center jump after each field goal is eliminated.

*The NBL forms in the Midwest as a fledgling pro league with plans to sign popular college stars after graduation. Goodyear (Akron), Firestone (Akron), and General Electric (Fort Wayne) industrial league teams join forces with 10 barnstorming pro clubs to form the circuit, but teams play uneven schedules varying from 3 to 18 games. Purdue's **John Wooden** stars for the Whiting (Indiana) All-Americans team.*

1938–39—Oregon's "Tall Firs" (with 6'8" star **Slim Wintermute** and coached by **Howard Hobson**) win the first postseason NCAA tournament with a 46–33 victory over Ohio State in Evanston, Illinois. The championship game is played in Northwestern University's Patten Gym before only 5,500 fans.

*The barnstorming New York Rens post a 112–7 record and capture the winner's trophy in the first World Professional Tournament in Chicago by defeating the NBL's Oshkosh All-Stars with ex-Kentucky star **Leroy "Cowboy" Edwards**. **Pop Gates** scores 12 of his team's 34 points in the championship game. The Rens will finally disband after World War II with a 2,588–529 all-time record.*

1939–40—(February 28) Basketball appears on television for the first time as station W2XBS in New York airs college doubleheader action from Madison Square Garden for an estimated viewership of not more than several hundred. The sparse electronic audience witnesses Pittsburgh defeat Fordham 57–37 and NYU best Georgetown 50–37. Backboards are moved from two feet to four feet away from the end line. **James Naismith** dies (November 28) at the age of 78 in Lawrence, Kansas.

The Harlem Globetrotters establish serious basketball credentials with a championship victory in Chicago's World Professional Tournament, edging the George Halas–owned Chicago Bruins 31–29 in overtime in the final game. The 'Trotters also begin a long-standing exhibition series against a collection of college all-star teams.

1940–41—Basketball celebrates its first half-century as the Wisconsin Badgers defeat Washington State 39–34 to capture the third NCAA postseason tournament. Wisconsin becomes one of biggest surprises in NCAA history since the school had finished ninth in the Big Ten race a season earlier. Naismith's posthumous book is published under the title of *Basketball, Its Origins and Development*. Fan-shaped backboards are legalized.

*An NBL team for the first time wins the World Pro Tournament in Chicago when the league-champion Oshkosh All-Stars fall to the surprising Detroit Eagles (coached by former Original Celtics star **Dutch Dehnert**) in an all-NBL final. The same two teams will meet for the World Tournament title a year later with the results reversed when Oshkosh rallies to 43–41 victory behind ex-Wisconsin All-American Gene Englund.*

1941–42—**Stan "Stutz" Modzelewski** of Rhode Island State College breaks **Hank Luisetti's** career national scoring record with 1,730 points. Luisetti's alma mater, Stanford, captures the NCAA title, however, besting Dartmouth 53–38 despite the absence of star **Jim Pollard**, who is bedridden with the flu.

1942–43—Wyoming's **Kenny Sailors** is credited with popularizing the jump shot. Wartime player shortages cause numerous schools to allow freshmen in varsity competition and lead others to cancel their season's schedules. Illinois's "Whiz Kids" team is undefeated in Big Ten play and acknowledged as the best team in the country, but the Illini decline to compete in either postseason tourney so that players can enlist in the military. The first Red Cross Benefit Game is staged by **Ned Irish** in Madison Square Garden, matching NCAA champion Wyoming and NIT winner St. John's.

1943–44—New rules include a five-foul limit on individual players regardless of the number of overtimes. In addition, defensive players are banned from touching the ball on its downward flight toward the basket (goaltending), a restriction aimed at giants **George Mikan** (DePaul) and **Bob Kurland** (Oklahoma A&M). St. John's becomes the first back-to-back winner in the NIT by nipping DePaul 47–39 behind coach **Joe Lapchick**.

1944–45—**Bob Kurland** leads Oklahoma A&M (with coach **Hank Iba**) to the first of two NCAA tourney titles, a 49–45 triumph over NYU. **George Mikan** enjoys his finest hour in college while leading DePaul to the NIT championship with a 71–54 victory over Bowling Green. The two giants then meet in a much-heralded Red Cross War Relief Benefit game at Madison Square Garden, but the match fizzles when Mikan fouls out after 14 minutes and Oklahoma A&M wins easily. The number of time-outs allowed is increased from four to five, and unlimited substitution is permitted for the first time.

1945–46—Oklahoma A&M, behind giant **Bob Kurland**, becomes the first school to win back-to-back NCAA tourney titles, nipping North Carolina 43–40. Kurland is also the first NCAA tourney repeat MVP. One of the year's highlights is a spectacular 55-foot shot by Rhode Island State's **Ernie Calverley** during the NIT semifinals. Ohio State and Northwestern set a Big Ten single-game attendance record (22,822) in Chicago Stadium.

Iowa's Murray Wier captured the first NCAA individual scoring title in 1948 ("official" statistics were not kept before that season) and remains to date the shortest player, at 5'9", ever to rank as the country's top major college scorer.

© University of Iowa

1946–47—Holy Cross College, with freshman **Bob Cousy** and senior George Kaftan, becomes the first New England team to win a national championship, edging Oklahoma 58–47 in a spirited NCAA title game. **Bob Davies** pulls an amazing double by coaching alma mater Seton Hall to a 24–3 record while also earning NBL MVP honors while playing for the Rochester Royals in the established Midwest professional league.

*Pro basketball debuts its modern era when the BAA forms in Eastern cities to rival the existing NBL. The New York Knicks defeat the Toronto Huskies in the first BAA game, played in Toronto's Maple Leaf Gardens. The Washington Capitols, coached by **Red Auerbach**, dominate the regular season, but **Eddie Gottlieb's** Philadelphia Warriors capture the first BAA crown. The Chicago American Gears, with **George Mikan**, cruise to the NBL championship.*

1947–48—Murray Wier of Iowa wins the first "official" NCAA scoring title with an average of 21 points per game. Kentucky's "Fabulous Five" outfit featuring All-Americans **Alex Groza** and **Ralph Beard** paces the United States Olympic team to a 65–21 gold-medal victory over France during the 1948 Summer Games in London.

*Four of the original 11 BAA franchises fold before the second season, and the Baltimore Bullets are brought into the league to balance the divisions at four teams apiece. Baltimore, behind player-coach **Buddy Jeannette** and top rookie Paul Hoffman, edges Phila-*

Duquesne's Chuck Cooper made cage history in June 1950 as the first black collegian drafted by the NBA when he was selected by the Boston Celtics. Cooper was not, however, the first black to play in an NBA game as is often erroneously credited.

Transcendental Graphics

delphia for the league championship. **Carl Braun** *of New York posts a new scoring record with a 47-point game, while* **Joe Fulks** *of Philadelphia logs the highest per-game average for the second consecutive year.* **George Mikan** *joins the new Minneapolis Lakers team in the struggling NBL and paces the first-year club to a postseason title.*

1948–49—(January 18) The Associated Press announces results of its first-ever weekly basketball poll: Saint Louis University is ranked first. Behind **Alex Groza** and **Ralph Beard**, Kentucky equals Oklahoma A&M's earlier accomplishment of repeat NCAA tournament victories. A second straight NCAA title for **Adolph Rupp** is, ironically, a 46–36 victory over none other than Oklahoma A&M. A new rule allows coaches to speak with players during time-outs. Rectangular glass backboards become official for all college games.

Fort Wayne, Minneapolis, Rochester, and Indianapolis abandon the NBL for the BAA, which now has the most glamorous pro star in **George Mikan** *and the best teams in the Minneapolis Lakers and the Rochester Royals. Minneapolis wins a second crown (in two different leagues over two seasons) while Mikan edges* **Joe Fulks** *for individual scoring honors. Fulks pours in a remarkable 63 points in a February outing versus Indianapolis for a new single-game scoring mark.*

1949–50—For the only time in history one school wins both the NCAA and NIT tourneys in the same postseason. CCNY, loser of five regular-season games, closes fast and defeats Bradley twice for twin trophies. The first two black players (**Chuck Cooper** of Duquesne and **Earl Lloyd** of West Virginia State) are drafted out of the collegiate ranks by NBA teams (Boston and Washington).

Six surviving NBL teams join the BAA, and the combined league is renamed the National Basketball Association. The Syracuse Nats win the Eastern Division by a runaway mar-

*gin, but play a weak schedule mainly filled with Western Division opponents. The new Indianapolis team features the entire starting lineup from two-time NCAA champion Kentucky, including **Alex Groza**, who challenges **George Mikan** as the NBA's top player. Central Division champion Minneapolis, with unstoppable Mikan, captures the first NBA title in a six-game series versus Syracuse.*

1950–51—(January) A shocking college basketball game-fixing scandal begins to unravel when Manhattan College star **Junius Kellogg** reports to his coach that he has been offered a $1,000 bribe. Teams most damaged are CCNY, LIU, Manhattan, Bradley, Toledo, and Kentucky; former Kentucky stars **Alex Groza** and **Ralph Beard** are banned for life from NBA play as a direct result of their involvement in point shaving. **Ernie Beck** of Pennsylvania becomes the first "official" NCAA rebounding champion.

*The NBA integrates with **Earl Lloyd** in Washington (first black to appear in an NBA game), **Chuck Cooper** in Boston (first black taken in the college draft), and **Sweetwater Clifton** in New York (first black signed by the NBA). An unwieldy 17-team circuit is reduced to 11 teams and two divisions. **Bob Cousy** and **Ed Macauley** are awarded to Boston in special dispersal drafts after the St. Louis and Chicago franchises disband. Despite the best regular-season record, Minneapolis and **George Mikan** stumble in postseason play and Rochester captures the NBA title by defeating New York in seven games.*

1951–52—Former Oklahoma A&M star **Bob Kurland**, who bypassed a pro career, paces the 1952 U.S. Olympic squad to another gold-medal triumph with a 36–25 victory over the Soviet Union in Helsinki. Seattle University's pint-sized guard **Johnny O'Brien** becomes the first-ever college player to reach 1,000 points in a single season, then finishes up with a career-record 2,537 points the following year.

*The first stability arrives in the NBA as the 10-team league completes the season without further franchise casualties, although the Tri-Cities Hawks relocate to Milwaukee. Indianapolis Olympians stars **Alex Groza** and **Ralph Beard** are implicated in college betting scandals on the eve of the season and banned from the NBA. The New York Knicks return to the Finals versus **George Mikan's** Lakers and lose another seven-game series. Mikan's string of five consecutive scoring titles (two in NBL, one in BAA, two in NBA) is snapped by Philadelphia's **Paul Arizin**.*

1952–53—**Clarence "Bevo" Francis** becomes a national celebrity when he scores 116 points in a small-college game for tiny Rio Grande of Ohio. Francis also averages 50.1 points per game, but his marks are thrown out by the NCAA records committee since many of his team's 39 games were against opponents that were not four-year colleges.

Bob Cousy *sinks a record 30 of 32 free throws and logs 50 points, as Boston tops Syracuse in the longest-ever postseason game lasting four overtimes. Cousy's performance of dribbling out the game clock and drawing numerous fouls is later credited as a major inspiration behind Syracuse owner **Danny Biasone's** proposal for NBA shot clock legislation two seasons later. Both NBA regular-season division leaders make it to the Finals for the first time, and Minneapolis has little trouble besting New York in five games. Philadelphia center **Neil Johnston** edges **George Mikan** for the first of three consecutive individual scoring titles.*

1953–54—**Bevo Francis** repeats his 100-point performance with 113 against Hillsdale (Michigan), but Francis is overshadowed by **Frank Selvy** (Furman), who also cracks the century mark in a major-college game against Newberry. Selvy, in the process, also becomes the first major-college player ever to post a 40-point scoring average. But the big story is tiny La Salle College, which earns an NCAA title behind junior rebounding and scoring phenomenon, **Tom Gola**.

Frank Selvy, the only Division I player ever to score 100 points in a game, averaged more than 40 per game in 1953–54.

Transcendental Graphics

Tom Gola was the first official national player of the year in 1955 and still holds NCAA records for combined points and rebounds.

© La Salle University

The era of Mikan and his Minneapolis dynasty closes with a third consecutive Lakers championship, the team's sixth in seven seasons (including one in the NBL). The failure of the Indianapolis franchise leaves the NBA with only nine teams. A one-year experiment with an opening-round playoff round-robin (three teams, with two surviving) proves unsuccessful and unpopular. Minneapolis survives a rugged, foul-plagued seven-game Finals with Syracuse for its swan-song title.

1954–55—Unheralded San Francisco University becomes king of the basketball world behind its defensive enforcer **Bill Russell**. Although his team loses to Russell's 77–63 in the NCAA Finals, La Salle's **Tom Gola** ends his own career with a record lifetime rebounding total that has still never been topped. In *Sport* magazine's poll of 123 coaches, **George Mikan** of DePaul University and the Minneapolis Lakers is named the greatest basketball player of the half-century.

*It is a landmark season for the NBA with new shot-clock legislation introduced and **George Mikan** retiring on the eve of the campaign. Average team scoring across the league jumps from 79.5 to 93.1, and Boston averages better than 100 for its 72 games. The Baltimore franchise folds at the outset of the season leaving the NBA with two four-team divisions, a format that will last for only seven seasons. Veteran NBA referee Charley Eckman is named coach in Fort Wayne and surprisingly guides the Pistons to the NBA Finals versus eventual champion Syracuse. **Bob Pettit** launches a Hall of Fame career with a Rookie of the Year season in Milwaukee, edging teammate **Frank Selvy** for the honor.*

1955–56—Yale coach **Howard Hobson** leads a successful drive to have foul lanes for college and high school play expanded from 6 feet to 12 feet. San Francisco, under coach

Phil Woolpert, runs its winning streak to a remarkable 55 games and defends its national title in **Bill Russell**'s final game with an easy 83–71 victory over Iowa.

*The NBA's first 20,000-point man, **Bob Pettit**, earns the first of his two scoring crowns playing for a Hawks team relocated from Milwaukee to St. Louis. Philadelphia and Fort Wayne are the year-end divisional leaders and meet in the NBA Finals, Philadelphia coasting to the title behind the potent offensive tandem of **Paul Arizin** and **Neil Johnston**, two of the league's top three point-makers. Promising rebounding star **Maurice Stokes** launches a tragically short career in Rochester as the league's top rookie.*

1956–57—The most thrilling NCAA final game ever finds North Carolina upsetting Kansas and **Wilt Chamberlain** in a dramatic three-overtime nail-biter. Early in the season the record University of San Francisco winning streak finally ends at 60 games. Another ending also comes when Kansas coach **Forrest "Phog" Allen** retires after 46 seasons and 746 victories.

*The Boston Celtics alter the league's future by landing **Bill Russell** in the preseason draft after a trade for Russell's rights sends **Ed Macauley** and **Cliff Hagan** to St. Louis. **Tom Heinsohn** is the Rookie of the Year, since Russell misses early-season games to play for the gold-medal U.S. team in the Olympics. With Russell in the lineup during the postseason, Boston wins its first-ever championship in an exciting seven-game NBA Finals shoot-out with **Bob Pettit** and the St. Louis Hawks.*

1957–58—Offensive goaltending is banned. Cincinnati sophomore **Oscar "Big O" Robertson** becomes the first rookie ever to win the national scoring title (35.1 points per game) and is also the first athlete ever named National Player of the Year in his debut campaign. A new rule allows teams to shoot a bonus free throw once the opponent commits seven fouls during a half.

*The Fort Wayne Pistons relocate to Detroit and the Rochester Royals move to Cincinnati as the NBA abandons smaller markets. The St. Louis Hawks, with **Bob Pettit**, enjoy a dream season and unseat Boston as league champion. Pettit pours in 50 points in the final title-clinching game. **George Yardley** of Detroit is the first to record 2,000 points in a single NBA season.*

1958–59—Brilliant shooter **Jerry West** narrowly misses out on an NCAA title when his West Virginia University team is nipped 71–70 by a California club coached by defensive wizard **Pete Newell**. Cincinnati's **Oscar Robertson** wins a second straight national scoring title and Player of the Year honors.

*Sensational **Elgin Baylor** debuts with Minneapolis and adds background excitement to a season dominated by **Bill Russell**, **Bob Cousy**, and **Red Auerbach**'s Boston Celtics. Baylor is potent enough in the postseason to carry the sub-.500 Lakers into the NBA Finals, where Boston completes NBA's first four-game sweep of championship round. The Celtics' championship victory is the first in a record string of eight straight league titles.*

1959–60—Ohio State wins the national title with one of the strongest teams in NCAA history, a mostly sophomore club featuring **Jerry Lucas**, **John Havlicek**, and **Larry Siegfried**. **Oscar Robertson** closes his brilliant career with a three-year NCAA scoring record, but still no trip to the NCAA championship game. Robertson and West Virginia's **Jerry West** pace the strongest U.S. Olympic team ever assembled to yet another gold medal during the Rome Summer Olympics.

*Wilt Chamberlain enters the NBA after a season with the Harlem Globetrotters and changes the face of offensive play forever. Wilt averages 37.6 points per game, scores 50-plus seven times, outrebounds all rivals (27 rebounds per game), plays nearly 48 minutes of every game, and draws a salary twice that of Boston's highest-paid player, **Bob Cousy**. Wilt is no real challenge to Boston and Cousy, however, with the Celtics posting their fourth straight*

Wilt Chamberlain of Kansas never had the incomparable impact upon the collegiate game that was expected and that he would later enjoy with the pros. Yet basketball's most memorable giant did carry the Jayhawks to the very brink of the 1957 national championship in perhaps the most thrilling NCAA title contest ever staged.

Transcendental Graphics

*regular-season-best record and capturing a second straight NBA title, again outlasting St. Louis and **Bob Pettit** in seven games.*

1960–61—Ohio State fails to defend its national title when the Buckeyes are upset in the NCAA Finals by in-state rival Cincinnati. Bearcats ironically become the champs one year after losing star **Oscar Robertson**, and this overtime championship victory makes new coach **Ed Jucker** the first mentor ever to win a national title in his rookie season as the head coach at a Division I school.

*Oscar Robertson and Jerry West arrive on the scene as sensational NBA newcomers, and the Minneapolis Lakers transfer to a new West Coast home in Los Angeles. Robertson posts one of the best rookie seasons ever (third in scoring, tops in assists, best rebounding guard in the league), but Boston is still the class of league play and loafs to still another title, this time routing St. Louis in the NBA Finals. **Wilt Chamberlain** is the first to top 3,000 points in a single season.*

1961–62—Cincinnati's Bearcats make it two in a row by repeating their NCAA Finals triumph over **Jerry Lucas**, **John Havlicek**, **Gary Bradds**, and company. Lucas's injury in semifinal play against Wake Forest prevents the Buckeyes' three-time NCAA final-ists from bowing out as champs, but Lucas does end his career as the first player ever to win five national statistical titles (two for rebounding and three for field-goal percent-age). St. Bonaventure loses a 99-game home winning streak, and Ohio State sees its regular-season winning skein stopped at 47 games. Duke is the first college team to feature uniforms with players' names on the back.

The NBA's greatest offensive season features never-to-be-equaled records by **Wilt Cham-berlain**, *who averages 50.4 points per game, pours in 100 in a single game (February 2), and logs 48.5 minutes per contest.* **Oscar Robertson** *also averages a triple-double for the entire campaign, while Chamberlain (56) and* **Elgin Baylor** *(61) set playoff single-game scoring records.* **Walt Bellamy** *averages 31.6 points per game as a rookie, and Baylor records the highest non-Chamberlain season's average (38.8), although Baylor's playing time is reduced to only weekends by military service. A memorable last-second missed shot by* **Frank Selvy** *allows Boston to gain an overtime victory in Game 7 for its fourth straight title, making the Russell-Auerbach team first to boast more than three NBA titles in a row.*

1962–63—Loyola (Chicago) pulls off one of the biggest upsets in NCAA history by defeating two-time champion Cincinnati in an overtime title game matching the nation's top offensive team (91.8 points per game) versus the top defensive club (52.9 points allowed per game). One-eyed guard Tom Boyer of Arkansas becomes the first player to win back-to-back national free-throw shooting titles. SEC champion Mississippi State ends the school's racially motivated three-season boycott of NCAA tourney competi-tion and loses to eventual champion Loyola (with four black starters) in a Mideast Regional semifinal game.

The Philadelphia Warriors and **Wilt Chamberlain** *relocate to San Francisco, breaking up the marquee Boston-Philadelphia Eastern Division rivalry. The Celtics capture their fifth straight title over Los Angeles after* **Oscar Robertson** *and Cincinnati push Boston to the full limit in the Eastern Division Finals.* **Bob Cousy** *retires, ending the first phase of Boston's decade-long dynasty.*

1963–64—UCLA, under **John Wooden**, wins its first national title and posts its first unbeaten season while fielding a small but defensively solid team of **Walt Hazzard**, **Gail Goodrich**, Fred Slaughter, and Kenny Washington. Cincinnati's 86-game home-court winning streak, which began in 1957, is snapped by Kansas. Bowling Green's **Howie Komives** hits 50 consecutive free throws in the season's last five games to edge defend-ing champ **Nick Werkman** of Seton Hall for the national scoring title.

Maurice Podoloff *retires and is replaced by* **J. Walter Kennedy** *as NBA commissioner. Two franchise moves involve the Chicago Zephyrs becoming the Baltimore Bullets and the Syra-cuse Nationals becoming the Philadelphia 76ers.* **Oscar Robertson** *interrupts* **Bill Russell's** *string of three consecutive MVP awards, but the invincible Boston Celtics run their cham-pionship string to six, longest ever by any major-league sports franchise.*

1964–65—UCLA wins its second straight national title on the strength of balanced offense and defense from **Gail Goodrich** and Kenny Washington. Princeton's **Bill Bradley** steals the NCAA tournament spotlight with a record 58-point performance in the Final Four con-solation game. At season's end New York City schoolboy standout **Lew Alcindor** decides he will attend UCLA in the fall and play for coach **John Wooden**. The now almost-ignored NIT postseason event expands its field from 12 to 14 teams.

Wilt Chamberlain *is traded from the Warriors to the Philadelphia 76ers for three players and $150,000 in the aftermath of the midseason All-Star Game. Philadelphia, with Cham-berlain, pushes Boston to a seventh game in the Eastern Division Finals, but the Celtics*

Lucius Allen teamed with Lew Alcindor on UCLA's sensational 1965–66 freshman team, which manhandled the Bruins' varsity, defending national champions.

Spencer Haywood defected from Denver in the ABA to Seattle in the NBA in 1970, which led to the older NBA instituting its hardship draft for underclassmen.

again escape on a memorable last-second steal of an inbounds pass by **John Havlicek.** *Boston routs Los Angeles in an anticlimactic NBA Finals after the Lakers are weakened by an injury to* **Elgin Baylor.**

1965–66—UCLA falters after a preseason loss to its own freshman team led by newcomers **Lew Alcindor** and **Lucius Allen.** Purdue's **Dave Schellhase** edges Idaho State's Dave Wagnon by .04 point to become the final Big Ten national scoring champ until the 1990s. In NCAA tourney action surprising Texas Western squares off with Kentucky and beats Rupp's team 72–65 in a classic confrontation between black-style playground ball and white-style disciplined pattern offense.

Boston wins its eighth title in row, spurred on in the NBA Finals versus Los Angeles by **Red Auerbach's** *retirement announcement. For the first time in 10 years, however, Boston is not the Eastern Division regular-season leader, finishing one victory short of Philadelphia. Auerbach closes the most successful coaching career in NBA history with 938 wins (1,037 counting postseason games).* **Bill Russell** *is named Auerbach's replacement and the league's first black coach.* **Rick Barry** *debuts as a hot-shooting rookie, trailing only Wilt, Oscar, and* **Jerry West** *in season's scoring average.*

1966–67—UCLA sophomore sensation **Lew Alcindor** records the highest field-goal percentage to date in the college record books and leads the Bruins to both an NCAA title and an undefeated (30–0) season. Texas Christian University center James Cash is the first African-American to play varsity basketball in the Southwest Conference. Kentucky (13–13) suffers its only nonwinning season during **Adolph Rupp's** 41-year coaching tenure.

NBA enters its 21st season, its last as a 10-team circuit. Philadelphia (68–13 for a new league victory record) boasts one of best teams ever with Chamberlain finally sacrificing scoring for a total team concept. The predictable result is a long-overdue end to Boston's string of eight straight NBA titles. Another string ends when **Rick Barry** *replaces Chamberlain as the league's individual scoring leader.*

1967–68—(January 20) A crowd of 52,693, the largest ever to see a college basketball game, jams the Houston Astrodome to watch Houston's Cougars and **Elvin Hayes** end UCLA's win streak at 47 games. At season's end UCLA makes it two in a row in postseason play with a 78–55 thrashing of North Carolina that represents the biggest victory margin to date in the NCAA Finals. When Alcindor and other top stars decline tryouts with the U.S. Olympic team, unknown former junior college star **Spencer Haywood** (University of Detroit) paces the United States to yet another gold-medal victory. Dunk shots (primarily as a result of **Lew Alcindor**) are ruled illegal for both NCAA games and pregame warm-up drills.

*Bill Russell and Boston return to the top rung in the NBA. After trailing Philadelphia by eight games over regular season, the Celtics defeat the 76ers and the Lakers during the postseason. Seattle and San Diego (later Houston) join the NBA as expansion franchises. The Knicks, Lakers, and 76ers move into new large-capacity arenas. The ABA debuts as a rival league and demonstrates chaos and color that will mark its nine-year history. New York playground legend **Connie Hawkins** (banned from the NBA) is the first ABA scoring leader and Hawkins's Pittsburgh Pipers are the maiden ABA champions.*

1968–69—**Pete Maravich** (LSU) scores 50 points or better nine different times for the second straight year. UCLA runs its string of NCAA titles to three, the first school ever to accomplish this feat. **Lew Alcindor** also becomes the only player named NCAA tourney MVP for three straight seasons.

*Boston captures the final title of its long championship skein, its 10th in 11 years, and 9th during the decade. Russell retires as player-coach, and the Boston Dynasty era finally closes. Chamberlain is traded to Los Angeles for three players in a blockbuster preseason deal giving L.A. Mr. Inside (Baylor), Mr. Outside (West), and Mr. Giant (Wilt) on the same roster. San Diego's **Elvin Hayes** matches Wilt's unique feat as a rookie scoring champion. UCLA's **Lew Alcindor** rejects the ABA and signs with the NBA's Milwaukee Bucks, severely damaging the new circuit's hopes to land superstar players and thus compete equally with the older league.*

1969–70—UCLA wins its fourth NCAA title in a row, knocking off Jacksonville, with seven-footer **Artis Gilmore,** in the Finals. **Pete Maravich** sets a single-season scoring record (44.5), which still stands and also finishes with a career scoring mark (3,667 points) that is yet to be challenged. Maravich (with 64) and Kentucky's **Dan Issel** (51) each score

© The Topps Company, Inc.

High-scoring Rick Mount

more than 50 points in the same game. Purdue's **Rick Mount** sets the Big Ten single-game mark with 61, but his team loses the game (108–107) against Iowa.

*The New York Knicks set a new league consecutive-wins mark with 18 straight early in the season. **Lew Alcindor** (Kareem Abdul-Jabbar) debuts with Milwaukee and trails only **Jerry West** for NBA scoring honors. The New York Knicks remain the big story at year's end with most regular-season wins (60) and a seven-game hard-fought victory over L.A. and **Wilt Chamberlain** in the NBA Finals, paced by an emotional return from injury by **Willis Reed** in Game 7. Denver Rockets rookie sensation **Spencer Haywood** leads the ABA in scoring and rebounding.*

1970–71—UCLA loses only once, to Notre Dame, when **Austin Carr** scores 46 for the Irish. It will be the final Bruins loss preceding a record 88-game winning streak. UCLA's postseason winning streak also reaches 28 games when the Bruins defeat Villanova 68–62 for their fifth straight national championship banner. **Julius Erving** leaves the University of Massachusetts after his junior season for a pro career in the ABA without ever having played in an NCAA tournament game. Carr averages 38 points per game for the second consecutive year and also finishes second in national scoring race for second straight time, thus becoming the most prolific scorer in NCAA history never to lead the nation in point-making.

*NBA celebrates its 25th season by adding Buffalo, Cleveland, and Portland as expansion cities. Veteran star **Oscar Robertson** joins the Milwaukee Bucks and, with **Lew Alcindor** (league scoring leader), carries the team to the NBA title. Milwaukee's sweep of Baltimore in the NBA Finals is only the second in league history, and their midseason 20-game win streak erases a one-year-old record set by New York. **Spencer Haywood** defects from Denver in the ABA to Seattle in the NBA and (since his college class had not yet graduated) spurs a legal struggle, which results in the NBA instituting its "hardship draft" for underclassmen.*

1971–72—(March 20) Immaculata College defeats West Chester 52–48 to win the first AIAW (Association of Intercollegiate Athletics for Women) tournament. UCLA retools under stellar sophomore center **Bill Walton**, finishes with a perfect 30–0 record and sixth straight NCAA title, and also runs its unbeaten string to 45 games. Walton becomes the only player besides **Oscar Robertson** (1958) ever named National Player of the Year in his first season of competition. **"Baron" Adolph Rupp** retires after 41 full seasons at Kentucky with an unmatched 876–190 career record.

*(November 5–January 7) The Los Angeles Lakers post the longest unbeaten streak in major-league sports history with 33 in a row under coach **Bill Sharman**. The Lakers also record the best-ever full-season record (69–13) and claim their first West Coast NBA crown. **Charlie Scott** of the Virginia Squires posts the highest single-season scoring average in the nine-year history of the American Basketball Association. Under coach **Bob Leonard**, the Indiana Pacers become the ABA's first two-time champion.*

1972–73—UCLA wins its seventh NCAA title and extends its unparalleled unbeaten string to 75 games. **Bill Walton** captures his second tourney MVP honor and puts on perhaps the greatest single-man show in NCAA Finals history, making 21 of 22 field goals for 44 total points in a title-game slaughter of Memphis State. Freshmen are once again allowed to compete at the varsity level.

Nate "Tiny" Archibald establishes the role of the small man and becomes the first and only player to lead the NBA in scoring average and assists during same campaign, also becoming the smallest scoring champ in league annals. Archibald's team, the Cincinnati Royals, relocates as the Kansas City–Omaha Kings. The Philadelphia 76ers post the worst NBA record ever (9–73), breaking the mark set by Providence (6–42) in 1948. The Indiana Pacers capture their second straight ABA crown and third in six years.

1973–74—(January 19) UCLA's win streak is stopped at 88 straight by Notre Dame with a 71–70 upset victory in South Bend. North Carolina State, behind sensational forward **David Thompson**, becomes the year's biggest story, recovering from an early-season loss to UCLA's Bruins to win the national title, upsetting **John Wooden's** Bruins 80–77 in double overtime during the NCAA semifinals. N.C. State's Tim Stoddard is the only player to appear on an NCAA basketball championship team and later play in baseball's World Series.

*Wilt Chamberlain retires on the eve of the season to become coach of the ABA San Diego Conquistadors, closing 14 seasons as the all-time scoring leader (with more than 31,000 points and 23,000 rebounds). Hall of Famers **Oscar Robertson** and **Jerry West** also play their final campaigns. ABA play finally gains some serious media attention as league headliner **Julius Erving** moves from the Virginia Squires to the New York Nets, wins a second league scoring title, and carries his team to league championship honors.*

The American Basketball Association never reached equal footing with the NBA during its nine-year life span, but it did, nonetheless, produce an exciting new generation of pro stars like Charlie Scott of the Virginia Squires, who posted the league's highest-ever scoring average in 1972.

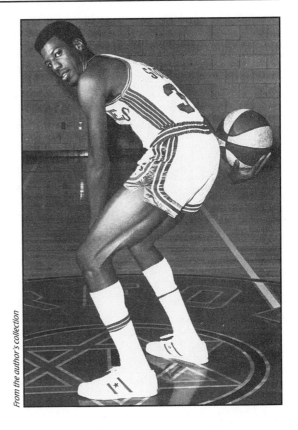

From the author's collection

1974–75—The NCAA tournament field is expanded to 32 teams, and UCLA returns to the top spot and claims one final title before closing out the Wooden Dynasty era. Indiana (31–1) might have ended the Bruins' hopes for a rebound victory, but **Bob Knight's** Hoosiers lose their only game of the season in the NCAA Regionals to runner-up Kentucky when star scorer **Scott May** is forced out of action with a broken arm. Wooden retires after the NCAA Finals with a 664–162 29-year record.

*The New Orleans Jazz are added as the 18th NBA team, and **Bill Walton** enters the league with Portland as a much-coveted rookie but spends most of the season injured. Buffalo's **Bob McAdoo** edges San Francisco's **Rick Barry** for his second of three straight scoring titles, but the Warriors, nonetheless, ride Barry's offense to their first championship in two decades. **Moses Malone** becomes the first modern-era player to bypass college and jump directly to the pros with the ABA's Utah Stars.*

1975–76—Indiana replaces UCLA at the top of the college basketball world with an undefeated 32–0 season and an easy 86–68 NCAA Finals victory over conference rival Michigan. **Bobby Knight's** Hoosiers thus finish their glorious two-year run with only a single defeat alongside 64 victories, and Hoosier forward **Scott May** is the consensus National College Player of the Year.

*The ABA celebrates its final season with its best-ever championship round between New York, featuring **Julius Erving**, and Denver, regular-season pacesetter with 60 wins. Four ABA teams (San Antonio, New York, Indiana, Denver) are accepted into the NBA in*

Tiny Archibald established an NBA milestone in 1973 as the only player ever to lead the pro circuit in both scoring and assists. Archibald's 13-year stellar NBA career included stints with Cincinnati, Kansas City, the New York Nets, Boston, and Milwaukee.

From the author's collection

*preparation for the 1977 season, expanding the NBA to 22 teams. Other NBA changes include replacement of **Walter Kennedy** with **Larry O'Brien** as commissioner and the trade of **Kareem Abdul-Jabbar** from Milwaukee to Los Angeles. Boston, with **Dave Cowens**, **John Havlicek,** and **Paul Silas** as frontline stars, returns to the top of the NBA heap. The Celtics' 13th title is won on the strength of a three-overtime Game 5 victory versus Phoenix in one of most dramatic NBA final-round games in history.*

1976–77—The dunk shot is reinstituted in college basketball after a nine-year absence. Postseason play is filled with plenty of drama and emotion as Marquette captures the NCAA title, 67–59, over often-frustrated **Dean Smith** and his North Carolina Tar Heels. Veteran Marquette coach **Al McGuire**, who had announced his retirement when his team floundered at midseason, watched in tears as his Warriors wrapped up an upset NCAA championship.

*__Julius Erving__ enters the NBA with Philadelphia and ushers in a new era of soaring hang time–style play. **Bill Walton** enjoys his single dominant pro season and carries Portland to the league title over the Erving-led 76ers. Numerous ABA stars are absorbed into the NBA with the most important acquisitions being **Moses Malone** with Houston and **Artis Gilmore** in Chicago.*

Julius Erving brought his soaring slam-dunking style from the ABA to the NBA in 1976 and ushered in a new epoch of hang time basketball, which today captivates 1990s fans. In addition to being one of the most exciting players ever, Dr. J is also one of only three pros (with Chamberlain and Abdul-Jabbar) ever to log 30,000 career points.

© Frank P. McGrath Jr.

1977–78—Gunner **Freeman Williams** of Portland State wins his second straight national scoring title (35.9) and finishes second on the all-time career scoring list behind **Pete Maravich**. But the year's most sensational individual clutch game is turned in by Kentucky's **Jack "Goose" Givens**, who hits 18 baskets for 41 points to lead the Wildcats to a 94–88 victory over Duke in the national title game.

The Washington Bullets and Seattle SuperSonics end the season as Cinderella teams meeting in the NBA title round. Two early-season violent incidents involving Lakers **Kareem Abdul-Jabbar** *and* **Kermit Washington** *mar the NBA campaign. Abdul-Jabbar punches Milwaukee Bucks rookie* **Kent Benson** *and misses two months with a broken hand. Washington throws a blind-side punch at Houston's* **Rudy Tomjanovich**, *severely damaging Tomjanovich's jaw and eye socket, ends his season prematurely, and nearly halts his career.*

1978–79—The most memorable one-on-one shoot-out in NCAA Finals history matches future NBA greats **Larry Bird** of Indiana State and **Earvin "Magic" Johnson** of Michigan State. MSU comes out on top and hands Bird and his Sycamores their only defeat of the season. Bird finishes his brilliant college career fifth on the NCAA's all-time scoring list. UCLA sets an NCAA record with its 13th consecutive conference (Pac-8, Pac-10) championship.

*Buffalo Braves become San Diego Clippers in complex deal that also finds Buffalo and Boston franchises swapping owners. Seattle and Washington enjoy an NBA Finals rematch, which this time falls to the Seattle SuperSonics coached by **Lenny Wilkens**. **George Gervin** of San Antonio wins second of three straight individual scoring titles. Three referees are used on experimental basis but the system is dropped at season's end.*

1979–80—**Ann Meyers**, a four-time All-American at UCLA, is the first woman to sign an NBA contract (with the Indiana Pacers) but Old Dominion University senior **Nancy Lieberman** is named the year's most outstanding women's player. In the season's most sensational moment guard Les Henson of Virginia Tech cans the longest basket (89'3") on record to stun Florida State at the buzzer. The NCAA tourney field is upped to 48 entrants, and Louisville captures its first NCAA title behind the sensational all-around play of slam-dunk wizard **Darrell Griffith**.

*NBA adds the three-point field goal (23'9" at the top of the key) and alters the schedule so teams will be facing their own division rivals more frequently. The New Orleans Jazz franchise is shifted to Salt Lake City, Utah. Sensational rookies **Earvin "Magic" Johnson** and **Larry Bird** debut, with Bird winning Rookie of the Year honors but Johnson pacing the Los Angeles Lakers to a league championship.*

1980–81—(November 29) Ronnie Carr of Western Carolina University scores the first-ever collegiate three-point goal as the new scoring rule goes into effect on an experimental basis in the Southern Conference. **Bob Knight** captures a second national title with the Indiana Hoosiers, defeating **Dean Smith's** North Carolina 63–50. Indiana's star performer is sophomore guard **Isiah Thomas**, who soon departs the college ranks for a promising pro career with the Detroit Pistons.

*Boston pulls off a series of remarkable comebacks in the Eastern Conference Finals with Philadelphia, rallying behind **Larry Bird** from a 3–1 hole by erasing second-half double-digit deficits three games in a row. The Celtics continue their roll in the championship round against Houston, winning their 14th franchise crown and the first of three during 1980s and the Larry Bird Era.*

1981–82—The NCAA conducts the first women's postseason tourney, with Louisiana Tech defeating Cheyney State 76–62 for the tournament title. Veteran ACC coach **Dean Smith** finally wins a national title for North Carolina. Victory comes when freshman **Michael Jordan**—future all-time NBA great—drills a last-second jumper before a record crowd of 61,612 in the New Orleans Superdome. **Harry Kelly** of Texas Southern wins the first of his two straight national scoring titles, and Louisiana Tech sets a new record in women's play with 54 straight victories. Jump balls are now used only to start games and overtime periods, with alternating-possession arrows replacing other jump-ball situations.

*(March 6) The San Antonio Spurs defeat the Milwaukee Bucks 171–166 in three overtimes in the highest scoring game in pro history. The Denver Nuggets, under coach **Doug Moe's** run-and-gun style, become the first team in NBA history to score 100-plus points in all 82 regular-season games, but they are also the first team to allow more than 100 in every game. The Lakers promote **Pat Riley** to head coach early in the season, and Los Angeles rolls to another title behind the brilliant play of **Magic Johnson**, NBA Finals MVP for the second time in three years.*

562

1982–83—Akeem (later Hakeem) Olajuwon, Clyde Drexler, and a Houston team known as "Phi Slamma Jamma" make headlines during most of the regular season with a 31–3 record and the nation's top ranking. But the Cougars are upset in a dramatic NCAA title game by North Carolina State. The **Jim Valvano**–coached Wolfpack is the first team ever to win the national title after losing 10 or more regular-season games.

Milwaukee's Sidney Moncrief is named the NBA's first Defensive Player of the Year and Philadelphia's Bobby Jones captures the league's first-ever Sixth Man Award. Julius Erving earns his only NBA championship ring as Philadelphia takes 12 of 13 postseason games and sweeps Los Angeles in the title series. Houston suffers the league's worst record but is rewarded with the top draft pick and chooses Virginia's seven-foot Ralph Sampson.

1983–84—North Carolina is ranked No. 1 for the second time in three years, and **Michael Jordan** is the Tar Heels' top scorer for the third year in a row. But the big story in postseason play is Houston's second NCAA finals defeat in a row. This comes when **Patrick Ewing** and Georgetown top **Akeem Olajuwon** and his Cougars in a celebrated year-end battle of the nation's two top big men.

Larry O'Brien retires as NBA commissioner and is replaced by David Stern, the league's 41-year-old executive vice president. The playoffs expand from 12 to 16 teams and the first round changes from a best-of-three to a best-of-five. The Celtics and the Lakers clash in the Finals for the first time in 15 years. Boston again comes out on top in a dramatic deciding game, keeping alive Boston's remarkable string for victorious final-round seventh games.

1984–85—(December 21) Georgeann Wells of West Virginia is the first woman to slam-dunk a ball during NCAA game action. Two Big East powerhouses, Villanova and Georgetown, square off in the men's NCAA title game, and the Wildcats surprise the defending champion Hoyas 66–64. The NCAA tournament field has now been expanded to include 64 teams. **Xavier McDaniel** of Wichita State becomes the first player to lead the nation in both scoring (27.2) and rebounding (14.8) simultaneously.

Portland commits an all-time draft-day gaffe by selecting Sam Bowie over Michael Jordan with the No. 2 selection. Bernard King of New York is the league scoring star, but Jordan debuts as Rookie of the Year with a stellar 28.2 average bested only by King and Larry Bird. A bumper rookie crop also includes top pick Hakeem Olajuwon (Houston), Charles Barkley (Philadelphia), and John Stockton (Utah). After eight losses to Boston in the NBA Finals the Lakers finally steal a title from the Celtics, capturing the deciding Game 6 at Boston Garden.

1985–86—A 45-second shot clock is instituted for all men's games. Led by All-American guard **Johnny Dawkins**, Duke (37–3) finishes atop the wire service polls for the first time since national rankings began. The Blue Devils are upset in the NCAA title game, however, by Louisville and its sensational freshman **Pervis Ellison**. UCLA's streak of 32 consecutive winning seasons in conference competition finally ends.

Larry Bird joins Bill Russell and Wilt Chamberlain as the only back-to-back-to-back MVP winners and earns his third and final championship ring. Atlanta's Dominique Wilkins captures his only scoring title, and Michael Jordan (limited to 18 regular-season games by foot injury) sets the first of his many major scoring marks with 63 points in a playoff contest at Boston Garden. The Celtics, aided by the remarkable backup play of veteran Bill Walton, post a franchise-second-best 67–15 record on their way to a 16th NBA crown.

1986–87—A new rule allows three points for any field goal made from beyond a perimeter line 19'9" from the basket. Nevada–Las Vegas (UNLV) dominates regular-season play with but a single loss and a yearlong No. 1 ranking but is tumbled in NCAA tourney play by eventual champion Indiana. **Bob Knight's** Hoosiers are NCAA champs for the fifth time. Maryland's Ben Wade becomes the first-ever African-American coach to serve in the prestigious Atlantic Coast Conference.

The Boston Celtics' quest to repeat their title is scuttled mainly by a dramatic Los Angeles victory in Finals Game 4, memorable for Magic Johnson's game-winning "junior sky hook" shot, which turns around the entire series. **Michael Jordan** *launches a relentless hold on the scoring title with the biggest offensive season since the early '60s, becoming the first individual to surpass the 3,000-point mark since Chamberlain in 1963. The free-wheeling offense of the champion Lakers earns the unforgettable moniker of "Showtime," as* **Magic Johnson** *enjoys his career-best scoring mark, earns first MVP trophy, and takes his fourth assists title.*

1987–88—Hersey Hawkins of Bradley leads the nation in scoring (36.3) and Kansas, paced by All-American center **Danny Manning**, wins the NCAA tournament despite not finishing in the regular-season Top Ten rankings. Center Steve Scheffler completes his career at Purdue with a new NCAA career record (68.5) for field-goal percentage.

Pat Riley's *Los Angeles Lakers post the first repeat NBA championship since Boston's dynasty ended in the late '60s.* **James Worthy** *is the postseason star for L.A. with a brilliant triple-double in Game 7 and Finals MVP honors.* **Michael Jordan** *establishes dominance in only his fourth season, repeating as scoring champion and gaining an NBA first by also being named Defensive Player of the Year.*

1988–89—Michigan pulls a major surprise at the end of the season when **Steve Fisher** takes over the team during the NCAA tournament and guides the Wolverines to their first-ever national title. During regular-season play Loyola-Marymount (California) displays its high-powered fast-breaking offense with a 181–150 victory over U.S. International in which several NCAA records are set, including most total points, most points by one team, and most points by a losing team.

Kareem Abdul-Jabbar *completes his record 20th season and retires as the all-time leading scorer with 38,387 regular-season points (44,149 with postseason included). Abdul-Jabbar does not go out a winner, however, as the Detroit Pistons block L.A.'s attempt at a third straight title with a sweep of the NBA Finals.* **Larry Bird** *misses almost the entire season after bone-spur surgery, but rival* **Magic Johnson** *wins his second NBA MVP and* **Michael Jordan** *captures a third straight scoring title.*

1989–90—The West Coast Conference Tournament finals are marred by tragedy when Loyola-Marymount star **Hank Gathers** collapses on court and dies later that same day of a previously undetected heart ailment. UNLV, under coach **Jerry Tarkanian**, enjoys a phenomenal regular season (35–5) and also rolls to a 30-point trouncing of Duke in the NCAA Finals. La Salle's **Lionel Simmons** ends his career with a record 115 consecutive games scoring in double figures.

NBA opens a season without **Kareem Abdul-Jabbar** *for the first time in two decades, yet the Kareem-less Lakers still post the best record at 63–19. The Detroit Pistons repeat their NBA title with a five-game drubbing of Portland keyed by* **Vinnie Johnson's** *buzzer-beater in Game 5.* **Michael Jordan** *becomes the first player other than* **Wilt Chamberlain** *to log four straight scoring titles, and the NBA grows again with expansion franchises in Minnesota and Orlando.*

1990–91—Defending national champion UNLV loses its title when ousted by eventual champ Duke in the national semifinals. The Runnin' Rebels nonetheless go down in history as one of the most potent teams ever and the only squad ever to have at least four teammates (Stacey Augmon, Greg Anthony, Anderson Hunt, and Larry Johnson) finish with more than 1,500 career points.

Lionel Simmons of La Salle University celebrates scoring career point No. 3,000 in February 1990. One of the most prolific scorers in college history, Simmons would end his career with an NCAA record 115 consecutive games scoring in double figures and would rank second behind only former La Salle star Tom Gola in combined career points (3,217) and rebounds (1,429).

© La Salle University

Magic Johnson passes Oscar Robertson as the career assists leader in what proves to be Magic's final full campaign. Michael Jordan parlays his fifth scoring title into the first NBA crown for the Chicago Bulls, who win four straight against the Lakers after a last-second opening-game loss in the NBA Finals. Jordan's NBA title is the first for a league scoring champion since Kareem Abdul-Jabbar paced Milwaukee and the league in 1971.

1991–92—Duke (35–2) becomes first NCAA back-to-back titlist since UCLA's dynasty closed 18 seasons earlier. A lopsided 71–51 victory in the NCAA Finals comes against Michigan's heralded "Fab Five" all-freshman team. Duke's **Bobby Hurley** becomes the shortest Final Four MVP winner since Temple's **Hal Lear** in 1956, but the true NCAA tourney star is the Blue Devils' **Christian Laettner**, who finishes his career as the all-time postseason scoring leader and also hits a dramatic last-second game-winning shot in the East Regional Finals versus Kentucky.

Magic Johnson unexpectedly announces his retirement after testing HIV-positive, then returns to collect the All-Star Game MVP in a dramatic farewell performance. The NBA announces the "Dream Team" to compete in the 1992 Barcelona Olympics. Michael Jordan nears Chamberlain's long-standing record for consecutive scoring titles and joins Bird and Magic Johnson as a three-time MVP. Larry Bird also bows out of the league due to a career-ending back injury.

1992–93—Michigan's Fab Five again fails in the NCAA final game as **Chris Webber** calls a time-out that Michigan doesn't have in the game's closing seconds to seal a 77–71 victory for North Carolina. Duke's **Bobby Hurley** completes his career with an NCAA-record

1,076 assists, while Mississippi Valley ace shooting guard Alphonso Ford becomes the only Division I player ever to score more than 700 points and average more than 25 points per game in each of his four college seasons.

*Chicago earns its third straight championship, the longest NBA reign since Boston's eight straight throughout the early and mid-'60s. **Michael Jordan** extends his personal string of scoring titles to seven, matching the NBA record of **Wilt Chamberlain**, but loses the MVP crown to **Charles Barkley**. A triple-overtime Finals Game 3 between Chicago and the Phoenix Suns is highlighted by a postseason-record 62-minute star-studded performance from Phoenix Suns guard **Kevin Johnson**.*

1993–94—The collegiate shot clock is reduced from 45 seconds to 35 seconds and trash-talking is banned. Purdue's **Glenn Robinson** is the National Player of the Year after he becomes the first Big Ten player to lead the nation in scoring in more than three decades, as well as the first Big Ten scorer to top 1,000 points in a single season. Ricky Nedd of Appalachian State establishes a new career mark (69.0) for field-goal percentage. The national free-throw shooting average (67.1 percent) is lowest since the 1959 season.

***Michael Jordan** shocks the entire sports world by announcing his retirement at age 30 on the heels of three consecutive NBA titles and seven straight scoring crowns. In Jordan's absence **David Robinson** edges **Shaquille O'Neal** for the NBA scoring title as hulking centers dominate point-making for the first time in more than two decades. Houston's **Hakeem Olajuwon** steps into Jordan's shoes as the league MVP and leads the Rockets to a seven-game championship over New York, the Knicks making their first appearance in an NBA Finals since 1973. Indiana's **Reggie Miller** authors one of the greatest-ever single-game postseason performances with 25 of his 39 points in the fourth quarter of Game 5 during the Eastern Conference Finals.*

1994–95—UCLA, under seventh-year coach Jim Harrick, returns to the winner's circle with an NCAA tournament championship win over Arkansas. North Carolina's brilliant second-year forward **Jerry Stackhouse** is consensus College Player of the Year, while Texas Christian University's **Kurt Thomas** accomplishes a rare feat as the third player ever to pace the nation in both scoring and rebounding simultaneously. The University of Connecticut becomes the first school ever to have both men's and women's teams rated No. 1 in national polls during the same week.

***Kevin Garnett** joins the likes of **Darryl Dawkins**, **Moses Malone**, and **Bill Willoughby** as the first prep star in more than 20 years drafted directly into the NBA. **Michael Jordan** makes major news by returning from a brief trial with minor-league baseball to restart his NBA career in mid-March. Jordan fails to lift the resurgent Chicago Bulls beyond the conference semifinals and Houston captures its second straight crown, defeating the **Shaquille O'Neal**–led Orlando Magic. Big men continue newfound league domination, with **David Robinson** replacing **Hakeem Olajuwon** as MVP and O'Neal unseating Robinson as scoring champ. Storied Boston Garden closes its doors as the BAA-NBA's last original arena. **Dominique Wilkins** scores the final basket at the legendary site.*

1995–96—**Rebecca Lobo** of the University of Connecticut's undefeated 1995 NCAA women's championship team makes history by signing a contract with the men's pro United States Basketball League and landing a contract to promote Nike athletic shoes. Massachusetts dominates most of the collegiate season for the first time ever behind Player of the Year **Marcus Camby**, yet stumbles in national semifinals against Kentucky. The Wildcats, under coach **Rick Pitino**, return to the zenith of the collegiate basketball world with their sixth national title, upending surprised Syracuse University in the season's final game.

***Michael Jordan's** Chicago Bulls also regain championship status with a six-game trouncing of the Seattle SuperSonics in the NBA Finals; Chicago and Jordan thereby earn a fourth* *overall NBA crown. Jordan also regains dominance as the league's top scorer, averaging 30.4 for his eighth scoring crown and also earning his fourth MVP award. Chicago enjoys the greatest single season in league history with a 72–10 record, then finishes 15–3 in postseason for a top overall combined mark of 87–13. The Toronto Raptors and Vancouver Grizzlies debut in Canada as the NBA goes international with its latest expansion.*

1996–97—Arizona pulls a surprise victory in the NCAA tournament in Indianapolis, upsetting top seeds Kansas (in the Regionals), Minnesota, and defending champion Kentucky en route to the title. **Rick Pitino** abandons Kentucky for one of the richest-ever pro coaching contracts with the NBA's Boston Celtics. **Dean Smith** (who will announce retirement on the eve of the 1997–98 season) makes the biggest coaching headlines of decade by overhauling **Adolph Rupp's** once-invincible record for career coaching victories. **Tim Duncan** ends his three-year career of ACC dominance emerging as consensus NCAA Player of the Year and a top pro draft choice.

Michael Jordan reaches new milestones leading the Bulls to a second record-setting campaign of 69 regular-season victories. Karl Malone wrests the MVP crown from Jordan and the pair squares off in the title round when Utah makes its first visit to the NBA Finals. Coaches begin to share megasalary headlines as Larry Bird returns to NBA prominence as Indiana Pacers mentor for 1997–98, Rick Pitino signs a $70-million deal as coach–general manager in Boston, and Larry Brown leaves Indiana to earn a huge contract from Philadelphia. The NBA cashes in on the women's hoop craze by launching its own summer league (WNBA) to rival the year-old women's American Basketball League (ABL). The NBA also celebrates its Golden Anniversary season with a 50 Greatest Players list, including 11 active stars. On the eve of the new 1997–98 season and opening of its second half-century, the NBA makes history with the hiring of the league's first two female referees, Dee Kantner and Violet Palmer.

1997–98—Ancient tradition and groundbreaking change merged for Bluegrass fans as Kentucky again lands atop the heap, winning the seventh NCAA national title. The accomplishment comes under Tubby Smith, rookie mentor in Lexington and Kentucky's first-ever black coach. The collegiate headline story, nonetheless, remains **Dean Smith's** departure at North Carolina, where longtime assistant Bill Guthridge debuts with a 34–4 year that concludes in the NCAA Semifinals.

A final chapter is written in the NBA where Michael Jordan dazzles with a swan-song season that produces a sixth title for the Bulls and closes out the greatest dynasty since Boston's glorious runs of the 1960s. Chicago's juggernaut squad is hastily dismantled at season's end with Jordan and coach Phil Jackson retiring, and Scottie Pippen (Houston) and Dennis Rodman (signed by L.A. but later released) pursuing free agency.

1998–99—Duke (16–0 in the ACC) and Connecticut (with top pro prospect Richard Hamilton) remain only slightly above the crowded pack during regular-season men's play in one of the most balanced college campaigns in decades. Tennessee's **Chamique Holdsclaw** ends a brilliant four-year run as the top all-time women's cager.

In Jordan's wake, the NBA's recent decades of magical growth seem to tumble into a freefal. An acrimonious labor dispute causes the first regular-season play stoppage in the NBA's half-century history, as a lockout-shortened season opens in February. A further blow comes with the financial collapse in early winter of the three-year-old women's American Basketball League.

Recommended Readings

Below are the author's suggestions for further readings on the history, evolution, and important figures of the American national game of basketball. Since I am neither cursed with the bad taste nor blessed with the detached judgment to rank my own dozen basketball titles among the following categories—yet, since I have contributed heavily in the past to ongoing basketball scholarship—I have listed my own contributions under a separate non-evaluative heading.

Top Ten Books on Basketball History

Berkow, Ira. *Oscar Robertson, The Golden Year 1964*. Englewood Cliffs, New Jersey: Prentice-Hall Publishers, 1971.

Devaney, John. *The Story of Basketball—The Stars, The Teams, The Great Moments*. New York: Random House Publishers, 1976.

Dobrow, Marty. *Going Bigtime: The Spectacular Rise of UMass Basketball*. Northampton, Massachusetts: Summerset Press, 1996.

George, Nelson. *Elevating the Game: Black Men and Basketball*. New York: HarperCollins Publishers, 1992.

Hollander, Zander (Editor). *The Modern Encyclopedia of Basketball*. Revised Edition. New York: Four Winds Press, 1973.

Jares, Joe. *Basketball: The American Game*. Chicago: Follett Publishing Company (A Rutledge Book), 1971.

Lazenby, Roland. *Airballs: Notes from the NBA's Far Side*. Indianapolis: Masters Press (Howard W. Sams), 1996.

Packer, Billy and Roland Lazenby. *The Golden Game—The Hot Shots, Great Moments and Classic Stories from Basketball's First 100 Years*. Dallas: Taylor Publishing Company (Jefferson Street Press), 1991.

Pluto, Terry. *Loose Balls: The Short, Wild Life of the American Basketball Association as Told by the Players, Coaches, and Movers and Shakers Who Made It Happen*. New York: Simon & Schuster Publishers (A Fireside Book), 1990.

Salzberg, Charles (Editor). *From Set Shot to Slam Dunk: The Glory Days of Basketball in the Words of Those Who Played It*. New York: E. P. Dutton Publishers, 1987.

Top Five Books on Basketball Culture

Axthelm, Pete. *The City Game: Basketball from the Garden to the Playgrounds*. New York: Harpers Magazine Press, 1970.

Feinstein, John. *A Season on the Brink: A Year with Bob Knight and the Indiana Hoosiers*. New York: Macmillan Publishers, 1986.

Halberstam, David. *The Breaks of the Game*. New York: Alfred A. Knopf Publishers, 1981 (New York: Ballantine Books, 1983).

Higdon, Hal. *Find the Key Man*. New York: G.P. Putnam's Sons, 1974.

Ryan, Bob and Terry Pluto. *Forty-Eight Minutes—A Night in the Life of the NBA*. New York: Collier-Macmillan, 1987.

Top Five Basketball Team Histories

Greenfield, Jeff. *The World's Greatest Team: A Portrait of the Boston Celtics, 1957–69*. New York: Random House Publishers, 1976.

Lazenby, Roland. *The Lakers: A Basketball Journey*. New York: St. Martin's Press, 1993 (Indianapolis: Masters Press, 1996).

Rice, Russell. *Kentucky: Basketball's Big Blue Machine*. Huntsville, Alabama: The Strode Publishers, Inc., 1976.

Thornley, Stew. *Basketball's Original Dynasty: The History of the Lakers*. Minneapolis, Minnesota: Nodin Press, 1989.

Triche, Arthur (Editor). *From Sweet Lou to 'Nique: Twenty-Five Years with the Atlanta Hawks*. Atlanta, Georgia: Longstreet Press, 1992.

Top Five Basketball Biographies and Autobiographies

Kerkhoff, Blair. *Phog Allen—The Father of Basketball Coaching*. Indianapolis: Masters Press (Howard W. Sams), 1996.

Levine, Lee Daniel. *Bird—The Making of an American Sports Legend*. New York: McGraw-Hill Book Company, 1988.

Russell, Bill and Taylor Branch. *Second Wind—The Memoirs of an Opinionated Man*. New York: Random House Publishers, 1979.

Webb, Bernice Larson. *The Basketball Man—James Naismith*. Lawrence, Kansas: University of Kansas Press, 1973.

Wolf, David. *Foul!—The Connie Hawkins Story*. New York and Chicago: Holt, Rinehart and Winston Publishers, 1972.

Top Five Volumes on Basketball Statistical Analysis

Bollig, Laura E. (Editor). *NCAA Basketball: The Official 1995 College Basketball Records Book*. Overland Park, Kansas: National Collegiate Athletic Association, 1994. (Issued in annual editions)

Heeren, Dave. *Basketball Abstract—Basketball Yearbook and Fantasy Guide* (1995 Edition). Indianapolis: Masters Press (Howard W. Sams), 1994.

Manley, Martin. *Martin Manley's Basketball Heaven* (1990 Edition). New York and London: Doubleday and Company, 1989. (Also 1988 and 1989 editions with similar format)

Sachare, Alex (General Editor). *The Official NBA Basketball Encyclopedia*. Second Edition. New York: Villard Books, 1994.

Savage, Jim (Editor). *The Encyclopedia of the NCAA Basketball Tournament*. New York: Dell (Bantam-Doubleday Publishers), 1990.

Top Five Coffee-Table Pictorials

Gutman, Bill. *The Pictorial History of College Basketball*. New York: Gallery Books (Brompton-Bison Books and W.H. Smith Publishers), 1989.

Hoffman, Anne Byrne (Editor). *Echoes from the Schoolyards: Informal Portraits of NBA Greats*. New York: Hawthorne Books, 1977.

Packer, Billy and Roland Lazenby (Editors). *College Basketball's 25 Greatest Teams*. St. Louis, Missouri: The Sporting News Publishing Company, 1989.

Ryan, Bob. *The Boston Celtics—The History, Legends & Images of America's Most Celebrated Team*. Boston: Addison-Wesley Publishers, 1989.

Wolff, Alexander. *100 Years of Hoops—A Fond Look Back at the Sport of Basketball*. New York: Oxmoor House (Sports Illustrated), 1991.

Top Five Basketball Literature Anthologies and Sociological Studies

Cole, Lewis. *A Loose Game: The Sport and Business of Basketball*. Indianapolis: The Bobbs-Merrill Company, 1978.

Ross, John and Q. R. Hand Jr. (Editors). *We Came to Play—Writings on Basketball*. Berkeley, California: North Atlantic Books, 1996.

Rudman, Daniel (Editor). *Take It to the Hoop—A Basketball Anthology*. Richmond, California: North Atlantic Books, 1980.

Telander, Rick. *Heaven Is a Playground*. New York and London: Simon & Schuster (A Fireside Book), 1988 (1976).

Wimmer, Dick (Editor). *The Schoolyard Game: An Anthology of Basketball Writings*. New York: Macmillan Publishers, 1993.

Top Five Histories of College Basketball

Douchant, Mike (Editor). *Encyclopedia of College Basketball*. Detroit and Washington, D.C.: Visible Ink Press (Gale Research, Inc.), 1995. (Subsequent annual editions)

Gergen, Joe. *The Final Four—An Illustrated History of College Basketball's Showcase Event*. St. Louis, Missouri: The Sporting News Publishing Company, 1987.

Gutman, Bill. *The History of NCAA Basketball*. New York and Avenel, New Jersey: Crescent Books (Random House Publishers), 1993.

Isaacs, Neil D. *All the Moves: A History of College Basketball*. Philadelphia and New York: J.B. Lippincott Company, 1975.

Morris, Ron (Editor). *ACC Basketball: An Illustrated History*. Chapel Hill, North Carolina: Four Corners Press, 1988.

Top Five Histories of Professional Basketball

Isaacs, Neil D. *Vintage NBA—The Pioneer Era, 1946–1956*. Indianapolis: Masters Press (Howard W. Sams), 1996.

Koppett, Leonard. *24 Seconds to Shoot: An Informal History of the National Basketball Association*. New York: Collier-Macmillan, 1968.

Lazenby, Roland. *The NBA Finals: The Official Illustrated History*. Dallas: Taylor Publishing Company, 1990.

Peterson, Robert W. *Cages to Jump Shots: Pro Basketball's Early Years*. New York and London: Oxford University Press, 1990.

Pluto, Terry. *Tall Stories: The Glory Years of the NBA, in the Words of the Men Who Played, Coached, and Built Pro Basketball*. New York: Simon & Schuster Publishers (A Fireside Book), 1992.

Author's Previous and Forthcoming Basketball Histories and Basketball Biographies

Bjarkman, Peter C. *Hoopla: A Century of College Basketball, 1896–1996*. Indianapolis: Masters Press (Howard W. Sams), 1996. (1998 paperback edition)

Bjarkman, Peter C. *ACC—Atlantic Coast Conference Basketball*. Indianapolis: Masters Press (Howard W. Sams), 1996.

Bjarkman, Peter C. *Reggie Miller, Star Guard*. Springfield, New Jersey: Enslow Publishers, 1999. Enslow Sports Reports Series (Juvenile).

Bjarkman, Peter C. *Sports Great Scottie Pippen*. Springfield, New Jersey: Enslow Publishers, 1996. Enslow Sports Great Series (Juvenile).

Bjarkman, Peter C. *Sports Great Dominique Wilkins*. Springfield, New Jersey: Enslow Publishers, 1996. Enslow Sports Great Series (Juvenile).

Bjarkman, Peter C. *Top 10 Basketball Slam Dunkers*. Springfield, New Jersey: Enslow Publishers, 1995. Enslow Top 10 Sports Series (Juvenile).

Bjarkman, Peter C. *Big Ten Basketball*. Indianapolis: Masters Press (Howard W. Sams), 1994.

Bjarkman, Peter C. *Slam Dunk Superstars*. New York and Avenel, New Jersey: Crescent Books (Random House Value Publishing), 1994.

Bjarkman, Peter C. *Shaq: The Making of a Legend*. New York: Smithmark Books (Brompton-Bison Books and W.H. Smith Publishers), 1994.

Bjarkman, Peter C. *The Encyclopedia of Pro Basketball Team Histories*. New York and London: Carroll & Graf Publishers, 1994.

Bjarkman, Peter C. *The History of the NBA*. New York and Avenel, New Jersey: Crescent Books (Random House Publishers), 1992.

Bjarkman, Peter C. *The Boston Celtics Encyclopedia*. Champaign-Urbana, Illinois: Sports Publishing, Inc. (Sagamore Publishing), 1999 (forthcoming).

Ten Important Recent Additions to Basketball Literature

Anderson, Dave. *The Story of Basketball*. Revised Edition (with "Foreword" by Grant Hill). New York: William Morrow (Beech Tree Books), 1997.

Condor, Bob. *Michael Jordan's Fifty Greatest Games*. New York: Carol Publishing (Citadel Press), 1998.

Decourcy, Mike. *Inside Basketball: From the Playgrounds to the NBA*. New York: Metro Books (Michael Friedman Publishing Group), 1996.

Gould, Todd. *Pioneers of the Hardwood: Indiana and the Birth of Professional Basketball*. Bloomington and Indianapolis: Indiana University Press, 1998.

Kalinsky, George (with text by Phil Berger). *The New York Knicks: The Official 50th Anniversary Celebration*. New York: Macmillan, 1996.

May, Peter. *The Big Three: The Best Frontcourt in the History of Basketball*. New York: Simon and Schuster, 1994.

Mikan, George, and Joseph Oberle. *Unstoppable: The Story of George Mikan*. Indianapolis: Masters Press (Howard W. Sams), 1997.

Sachare, Alex. *One Hundred Greatest Basketball Players of All Time*. New York: Simon and Schuster (Pocket Books), 1997.

Shouler, Ken. *The Experts Pick Basketball's Best 50 Players in the Last 50 Years*. Lenexa, Kansas: Addax Publishing Group, 1998.

Triptow, Richard F. *The Dynasty That Never Was—Chicago's First Professional Basketball Champions: The American Gears*. Chicago: Self-published, 1997.

Index

Page numbers in italic refer to photos and captions.